Oman & Arabian Peninsula

Kuwait
p78

Bahrain
p46

Qatar
p209

Saudi Arabia
p241

Oman
p116

United Arab Emirates
p284

Oman
p116

Yemen
p362

THIS EDITION WRITTEN AND RESEARCHED BY
Jenny Walker,
Stuart Butler, Anthony Ham, Andrea Schulte-Peevers

Contents

ON THE ROAD

SHARQIYA SANDS, OMAN
P155

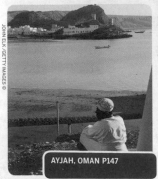
AYJAH, OMAN P147

Contents

GRAND MOSQUE, MUSCAT,
OMAN P128

ON THE ROAD

BURJ KHALIFA, DUBAI
P291

NIKADA /GETTY IMAGES ©

Contents

MUTRAH SOUQ, OMAN
P138

NAKHAL FORT, OMAN
P174

SPECIAL FEATURES

Hajj: the Ultimate
Traveller's Tale

Welcome to Oman, UAE & Arabian Peninsula

The spectacular emptiness of the Arabian landscape provides a blank canvas for a colourful riot of cultural, religious, intellectual and trading wonders.

The Desert

'No man,' wrote Wilfred Thesiger of his travels with the Bedu across the Empty Quarter, 'can live this life and emerge unchanged... He will carry, however faint, the imprint of the desert.' The austere allure of the desert has attracted Western travellers to Arabia for centuries. Marco Polo and TE Lawrence are among many famous travellers beguiled by the beauty of the barren landscapes and the challenge they suggest to body and soul. Thankfully, modern travellers no longer need risk life and limb to encounter the wilderness as roads and camps make encounters with the desert possible for all.

Urban Landscapes

When asked what they most like about their land of sand dunes, the Bedu near Al-Hashman in Oman reply: 'Coming to town'. Town! This is the Arabia of the 21st century, built on oil and banking – sophisticated communities looking to the future with vision and creating empires out of sand, or rather on land reclaimed from the sea. For those looking for a dynamic urban experience, the Gulf cities are the place to find it. With high incomes per capita, elegant towers, opulent hotels and eccentric malls, these cities offer the 'pleasure domes' of the modern world.

Legendary Hospitality

The essence of the Arabian Peninsula lies in its people: good-natured haggling in souqs, cursing on long journeys, sharing of sweet tea on the edge of wild places. Unifying all, there's Islam, a way of life, the call to prayer carried on an inland breeze, a gentle hospitality extended towards strangers. And this is what many travellers most remember of their visit to the region – the ancient tradition of sharing 'bread and salt' and of ensuring safe passage, albeit given a modern context. Visitors can expect friendly exchange as equally in supermarkets as in remote desert villages.

Cultural Riches

It's hard to think of Arabia without conjuring the Queen of Sheba holding court at Ma'rib in Yemen; camel caravans bearing frankincense from Dhofar in Oman; dhows laden with pearls from Dilmun; the ruins of empire in Saudi Arabia's Madain Saleh. The caravans and the dhows may be plying different trades these days, but the lexicon of *The Thousand and One Nights* that brought Sheherazade's exotic, vulnerable world to the West, still helps define the Peninsula today. Visit a fort, barter in a souq or step into labyrinthine alleyways and you'll immediately discover the perennial magic of Arabia.

Why I Love the Arabian Peninsula

By Jenny Walker, Author

Mention the name 'Arabia' and a host of exotic images appear. I've spent half my life studying these images – of deserts, nomads and expressions of religious zeal – in various academic pursuits. But there's so much more to the complex, sophisticated urban culture of modern Arabia than conjured by those stereotypes. I love the Peninsula because each day I encounter that complexity and the gracious, warm-hearted Arab people who lie at the core of the region's enduring appeal. And of course the desert, with its life against the odds, has inevitably crept into my soul!

For more about our authors, see page 527

Above: Sheikh Zayed Grand Mosque (p328), Abu Dhabi, United Arab Emirates

Oman, UAE & Arabian Peninsula

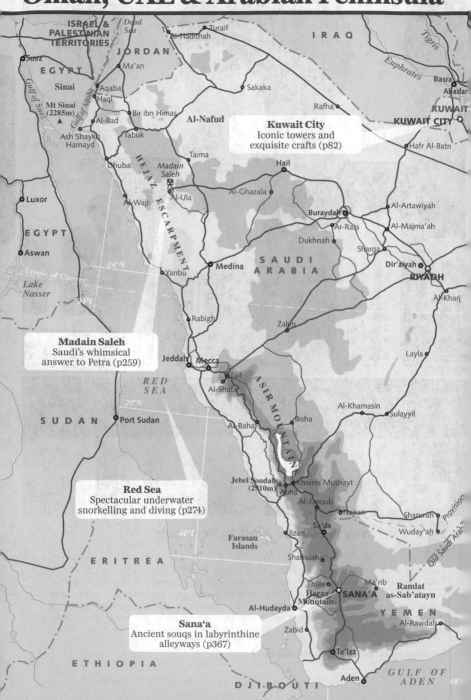

Kuwait City
Iconic towers and exquisite crafts (p82)

Madain Saleh
Saudi's whimsical answer to Petra (p259)

Red Sea
Spectacular underwater snorkelling and diving (p274)

Sana'a
Ancient souqs in labyrinthine alleyways (p367)

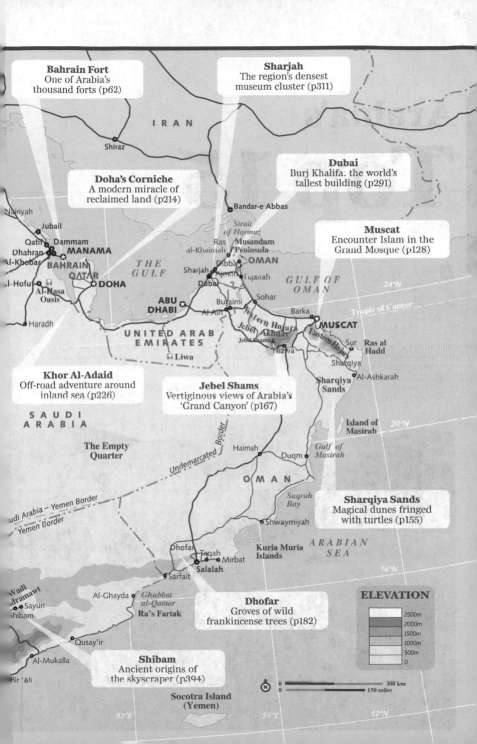

Bahrain Fort
One of Arabia's
thousand forts (p62)

Sharjah
The region's densest
museum cluster (p311)

IRAN

Shiraz

Dubai
Burj Khalifa: the world's
tallest building (p291)

Doha's Corniche
A modern miracle of
reclaimed land (p214)

Bandar-e Abbas

Muscat
Encounter Islam in the
Grand Mosque (p128)

Nairiyah
Jubail
Qatif   Dammam
Dhahran   MANAMA
Al-Khobar   BAHRAIN
Al-Hofuf   QATAR
Al-Nasa   DOHA
Oasis

Strait
of Hormuz
Ras
al-Khaimah   Musandam
Peninsula   OMAN
Dibba
Sharjah   Ajman   Fujairah
Dubai

THE
GULF

GULF OF
OMAN

24°N

ABU
DHABI

Buraimi   Sohar
Al-Ain   Barka

Tropic of Cancer

Haradh

UNITED ARAB
EMIRATES

Western Hajar
Jebel Akhdar
Jebel Shams

Eastern Hajar

MUSCAT

Sur   Ras al
Hadd

Liwa

Nizwa

Shatqiya

Khor Al-Adaid
Off-road adventure around
inland sea (p226)

SAUDI
ARABIA

Jebel Shams
Vertiginous views of Arabia's
'Grand Canyon' (p167)

Sharqiya
Sands   Al-Ashkarah

Island of
Masirah   20°N

The Empty
Quarter

Undemarcated
Border

Haimah   Duqm

Gulf of
Masirah

Saudi Arabia – Yemen Border
Yemen Border

OMAN

Suqrah
Bay

Shwaymiyah

ARABIAN
SEA

Sharqiya Sands
Magical dunes fringed
with turtles (p155)

Wadi
Hadramawt
Sayun
Shibam

Dhofar   Taqah
Salalah   Mirbat

Kuria Muria
Islands

16°N

Al-Ghayda   Ghubbat
al-Qamar
Ra's Fartak

Sarfait

Dhofar
Groves of wild
frankincense trees (p182)

ELEVATION

| | 2500m |
| 2000m |
| 1500m |
| 1000m |
| 500m |
| 0 |

Qusay'ir

Al-Mukalla

Shibam
Ancient origins of
the skyscraper (p394)

Bir 'Ali

N   0   300 km
    0   150 miles

Socotra Island
(Yemen)

52°E   56°E   12°N

Arabia's
Top 15

Arabia's Desert Dunes

1 For centuries, Westerners have been attracted to the great desert wilderness of Arabia, drawn by its limitlessness yet repelled by the void. 'This cruel land', wrote Wilfred Thesiger, after crossing the Empty Quarter on foot with the Bedu, 'can cast a spell which no temperate clime can hope to match.' Feel the desert's allure in Oman's Sharqiya Sands (p155) or in the dunes of Liwa (p336) in the United Arab Emirates, but beware: the summer sands don't take prisoners, and the only stranger you're likely to meet between dunes is yourself.

Sharqiya Sands, Oman

Towering Burj Khalifa

2 Slicing through the slipstream of the sky's superhighways, there is no more potent a symbol of the Arabian Peninsula's aggressive hunger to dominate the future than the audacious tower blocks that rise from the cities of the Gulf. At 828m, Burj Khalifa (p291) in Dubai is the tallest building in the world. Dine on top of this or any of the region's futuristic totems of steel and glass and you can ponder the breaking of glass ceilings while peering from the clouds at the 'business-as-usual' carrying on at ground level.

Souqs – Arabia's Trading Places

3 They may not match the stock exchanges of New York, London or Tokyo in terms of dollars traded, but they claim a far more ancient lineage. Get lost in any of the region's labyrinthine souqs, especially in Doha's Souq Waqif (p216), Muscat's Mutrah Souq (p123) or Souq Al-Milh (p367) in Sana'a and participate in brisk trading in olives, the haggle-to-the-death of cloth merchants, and a collusive wink-and-a-nod over gulled customers.

Mutrah Souq, Oman

Encountering Islam

4 In Arabia, the birthplace of Islam, faith is a living, breathing reality inextricably entwined in the daily lives of Peninsula inhabitants. For a visitor, Islam is encountered in the haunting call to prayer and in the warmth of welcome enshrined in the Muslim code of conduct. Visit the Grand Mosque (p128) in Muscat or the spectacular Museum of Islamic Art (p215) in Doha, and see how faith has also been expressed in masterpieces of ceramic, carpet and furniture design.

Grand Mosque, Oman

Jebel Shams: Mountain of the Sun

5 In contrast to the vast desert plains of Arabia's interior, the Peninsula boasts some of the highest mountains and deepest canyons in the Middle East. Camp at the top of Oman's Jebel Shams (p167) in winter for the exciting spectacle of hail thundering into Wadi Ghul – Arabia's very own Grand Canyon. Rain breaks on the mountains sporadically all year: watch how the precious water is channelled through ancient irrigation systems (known as *aflaj*) to bring life to plantations and a network of high-altitude villages.

Wadi Ghul, Oman

CHRIS MELLOR / GETTY IMAGES ©

Red Sea Diving

6 Flanking the shores of Saudi Arabia, the crystal-clear waters of the Red Sea are home to epic dramas. In some of the world's finest diving sites, clown fish play the comedians in coral gardens fit for a Zefferelli stage set, while sharks wait in the wings for heroic small fry. You don't need to dive for a balcony view: don a mask, snorkel and flippers and swim anywhere off the coast at Jeddah (p250) and you can't help but applaud the spectacle.

Ruins of Empire and Saudi's Petra

7 They rise out of the gravel plains like lost camels, or sit crumbling to dust on mountain ridges. They speak of past greatness, prophets, kings and forgotten dynasties. Some, like the thousands of burial mounds (p63) that bruise and curdle the soil in Bahrain have been accommodated in an urban landscape. Others, like the superb Nabataean ruins at Madain Saleh (p259) in Saudi Arabia stand proud on forgotten plains. Sit among these ruins of empire and it's easy to contemplate human frailty.

Qasr Farid tomb, Madain Saleh, Saudi Arabia

Heaven Scented Frankincense

8 Gifted by wise men to babes (according to the Bible), and queens to kings (Queen Sheba to King Solomon), harvested from the bark of ugly trees in the mist-swirling magic of summertime in Oman and Yemen, frankincense is responsible for the history of Arabian empires. Catch its tantalising aroma in the house of a newborn, buy the curdled beads of amber-coloured sap in the souq, or visit the living trees in Dhofar (p182) in the middle of the region's unique July *khareef* (rainy season).

Perfume bottles, Mutrah Souq, Oman

Yemen's Manhattan of Arabia

9 From the cooling wind towers of Muharraq Island (p66) in Bahrain to Saudi watchtowers and the enigmatic towers of mountain burial in Bat (p170), Oman, the architects of Arabia have for centuries favoured the vertical rather than the horizontal. If the security situation allows, stroll the mud Manhattan of Yemen's fabled Hadramawt (p394), clamber through the old quarter of the capital, Sana'a (p366), or visit just about any village in southern Arabia to see where the trend for high-rise living came from.

Shibam, Yemen

Sharjah – A Cultural Cornucopia

10 It may not generate the headlines of neighbouring Dubai but Sharjah (p311) has quietly grown into the cultural hub of Arabia. In a celebration of local and indigenous heritage, Sharjah boasts the largest cluster of museums in the region, including such gems as the Sharjah Heritage Museum (p311). With the historic old quarter and chaotic alleyways being renovated in the 'Heart of Sharjah' project, the city offers a sense of Arabia in the midst of the modern.

Central Souq (p316), Sharjah

Tareq Rajab Museum

11 Arabia's riches can be counted by more than the latest car or designer handbag. Gold twine in a dress cuff, a bead of carnelian threaded for a loved one, a basket woven with camel leather, words of wisdom entwined in a silver amulet – these are the riches of the region's ancient craft heritage. Find the most precious pieces collected under one roof in the enchanting, underground Tareq Rajab Museum (p84) in Kuwait City.

Brass handle, Tareq Rajab Museum

Walking on Water along Doha's Corniche

12 Modernity in many Peninsula countries can be summed up in two words: reclaimed land. Take part in the promenade of nations along Doha's corniche, (p214) or indeed any of the Gulf corniches, and chances are you'll be walking on water – or at least where water once was. But then again, you can climb any mountain in Arabia and claim the same: most of it was once under the sea and it would appear that modern architects are keen to reverse the tide on prehistory.

Arabia's Formidable Forts

13 Cresting a hilltop, guarding the coastline, walling a village or securing a dried-out river bed, there is barely a town in Arabia without some kind of crumbling battlement. Oman has some of the best-preserved of the Peninsula's forts in Bahla, Nizwa, Nakhal and Rustaq, but for a whole day out, Bahrain's Qala'at al-Bahrain (p62), with its museum, coffeeshop and nighttime illuminations, is hard to beat. Learn your forts (military only) from your castles (fortified residence) before exploring some of these magnificent buildings.

Nizwa Fort (p162), Oman

Off-Road Adventure

14 The ubiquitous 4WD on Arabian roads are the modern 'ships of the desert' and they can transport you into unimagined dimensions – including stuck in sand and mired in mud. However, with careful planning, and sticking to prior tracks, a 4WD off-road trip in Arabia – to Qatar's beautiful Khor Al-Adaid (p226), for example – is an unforgettable experience. Follow the locals over dunes, through floodwater, up mountains and over escarpments to see the best of the Peninsula's varied landscape, and discover the myriad plants and animals that call it home.

The Kuwait Towers

15 Icons are not always what they are cracked up to be – as illustrated by the commissioning of the faintly ridiculous giant coffee pots, incense burners and pearl monuments cast in concrete in Arabian town centres. There are exceptions, however, and the Kuwait Towers (p85) is a case in point. Visit these iconic water towers to understand the strategic significance not just of a monument, but of the country the towers have come to represent in this much-fought-over corner of the Middle East.

Need to Know

For more information see Survival Guide (p475)

Currency
Bahraini dinar (BD); Kuwaiti dinar (KD); Omani rial (OR); Qatari riyal (QR); Saudi riyal (SR); UAE dirham (Dh);Yemeni riyal (YR)

Language
Arabic (English widely spoken)

Visas
Visas, required by all visitors, are available for many nationalities on arrival at international airports and most land borders (except Saudi Arabia and Yemen).

Money
ATMs widely available; credit cards widely used.

Mobile Phones
Local SIM cards available for international calls, topped up with prepaid cards.

Time
Saudi Arabia, Kuwait, Bahrain, Qatar and Yemen are three hours ahead of GMT/UTC. The UAE and Oman are four hours ahead of GMT/UTC.

When to Go

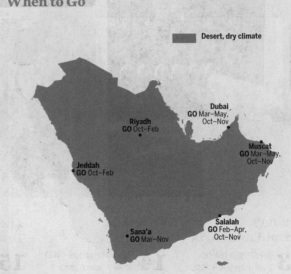

Desert, dry climate

Dubai
GO Mar–May, Oct–Nov

Riyadh
GO Oct–Feb

Muscat
GO Mar–May, Oct–Nov

Jeddah
GO Oct–Feb

Salalah
GO Feb–Apr, Oct–Nov

Sana'a
GO Mar–Nov

High Season
(Nov–Mar)

➡ Perfect weather at sea level with clear, sunny days and cool evenings.

➡ Shopping festivals and sporting events coincide with these cooler months.

➡ Booking accommodation is necessary; expect highest rates in December.

Shoulder
(Aug–Oct)

➡ Good time to visit southern Arabia with light rains turning the desert hills green.

➡ The *khareef* (rainy season) festival in southern Oman attracts many Gulf visitors leading to higher acommodation prices.

Low Season
(Apr–Jul)

➡ Extreme heat and high humidity make this a season to avoid in most parts of Arabia.

➡ Big discounts often available for accommodation.

➡ Best time to visit mountain areas.

Websites

Al-Bab (www.al-bab.com) Meaning 'The Gate', this is a gateway to the Arab world with links to dozens of news services, country profiles, travel sites and maps.

Al-Jazeera (www.aljazeera.com/news/middleeast) The controversial satellite service runs this popular news-and-views-oriented website.

Arabnet (www.arabnet.me) Useful Saudi-run online encyclopaedia of the Arab world, collecting news and articles, and links to further resources, organised by country.

@llo Expat Middle East (www.middleeast.alloexpat.com) An information service with networking opportunities exclusively for expats.

Lonely Planet (www.lonelyplanet.com/middle-east) For succinct summaries on travelling to the Peninsula, combined with travel news and 'postcards' from other travellers. The Thorn Tree forum allows you to ask questions before you go or dispense advice when you get back.

Staying Connected

Staying connected in the Peninsula is easy. All countries have International Direct Dialling (IDD) facilities via satellite links. Mobile phones are easy to buy and local SIM cards are widely available in all cities and most airports across the region. Roaming charges apply for non-local SIM cards and it is worth checking the rates before travelling. Internet access is generally offered free in most midrange hotels and free wi-fi is becoming the norm in many coffeeshops and hotels. Unless you are off-road in the desert or camping in the mountains, use of all connectivity devices (smartphones, tablets and so forth) is virtually guaranteed.

Exchange Rates

	US$1	UK£1	€1
Bahrain (BD)	0.38	0.59	0.48
Kuwait (KD)	0.28	0.44	0.38
Oman (OR)	0.39	0.58	0.49
Qatar (QR)	3.64	5.51	4.68
Saudi Arabia (SR)	3.75	5.68	4.82
UAE (Dh)	3.67	5.56	4.72
Yemen (YR)	214	325	275

For current exchange rates see www.xe.com.

Daily Costs

Budget:
Less than US$200

➡ Shared room in budget guesthouse: US$100

➡ Street fare with self-catering at local markets: US$10

➡ Public transport: US$5

➡ Entry costs: US$5

Midrange:
US$200–US$500

➡ Double room in a midrange hotel: US$200

➡ Car hire: US$100

➡ Entry costs/unguided activities: US$10

Top End:
More than US$500

➡ Double room in five-star hotel or resort: US$300

➡ International-style buffet lunch/dinner: from US$30

➡ 4WD car hire: US$200

➡ Entry costs/guided activities: US$100

Arriving in the Arabian Peninsula

The region is well served with major international transport hubs. The main airports are listed below. Airport taxis are the main method of transport from airport to city centre.

Bahrain International Airport (p62)

Kuwait International Airport (p114)

Muscat International Airport (Oman; p140)

Doha International Airport (Qatar; p238)

King Khaled International Airport (Riyadh, Saudi Arabia; p280)

Abu Dhabi International Airport (UAE: p334)

Dubai International Airport (UAE; p308)

Sana'a International Airport (Yemen; p408)

Safe Travel

Despite residual issues following the Arab Spring in 2011, the region is, by and large, safe to travel in with the exception of Yemen. In Yemen the ongoing insurgence and tribal conflict combines with a threat of terrorism and kidnapping to exclude it from all but the most hardy of travellers. At the time of writing, the situation in Bahrain remained somewhat volatile but all other countries in the region were stable and safe to visit. Check with your embassy website for the latest travel advice.

For much more on **transport**, see p490

If You Like...

Shopping

Peninsula shopping is as much about chatting as buying. Whether purchasing designer-wear in Gulf malls, or haggling over incense in Yemen's labyrinthine souqs, spare time for tea with the vendor.

Souq Waqif Doha's tasteful reinvention of its Bedouin roots includes traditional coffeeshops. (p216)

Mutrah Souq Indian Ocean trade remains unchanged in Muscat's aged souq. (p123)

Dubai Mall This Emirate pleasure dome includes a walk-under aquarium. (p293)

Ibb Market Get lost among the copper coffee pots in this celebrated Yemeni souq. (p384)

Souq Al-Milh Cross-legged vendors sell chickens, guns and roses in Sana'a's capital chaos. (p367)

Nizwa Souq Famed for Omani silver daggers but also brisk trading in goats. (p162)

Jeddah Souqs Saudi's gold souqs sell 22kt eye candy, but the buzzing atmosphere at Souq al-Alawi (p253) is free.

Riyadh Camel Market Fascinating – if not the most obvious place for a souvenir. (p250)

Bab al-Bahrain Pearls are still found in this gritty warren of shops. (p52)

Old Souq, Kuwait City Heaped-high olives and dates, headdresses and perfumes under one roof. (p89)

Forts & Castles

While every country in the Arabian Peninsula has its own set of crenulations, the best forts and castles are found in eastern Arabia, keeping back trouble from the sea.

Jabrin Castle Unique painted ceilings distinguish this perfectly formed Omani castle. (p170)

Qala'at al-Bahrain Spectacular by night, Manama's fort looms over the sea. (p62)

Nakhal Fort Restored Omani forts at Nakhal (p174) and Rustaq (p174) guard the passes between desert plain and mountain interior.

Al-Jahili Fort This fort in Unesco heritage site Al Ain, in the United Arab Emirates (UAE), honours British desert veteran Thesiger. (p340)

Fujairah Fort Part of a village reconstruction that shows the UAE has a history and not just a future. (p344)

Najran Fort This Saudi fort did take prisoners – unlike the Empty Quarter sands on which it stands. (p264)

Al-Zubara Fort, Qatar Interesting mostly for its location at the end of nowhere in the middle of nothing. (p228)

Bahla Fort After two decades of restoration, this magnificent castle and Unesco World Heritage Site dominates Oman's village of magic, potters and ancient walls. (p169)

Husn Thilla Like most architecture in Yemen, this fort blends seamlessly into the rocky outcrop it is built upon. (p376)

Nizwa Fort Castle buffs will like to know that a round tower makes Nizwa Fort unique in Arabia. (p162)

IF YOU LIKE... ANCIENT HISTORY

Visit the supposed haunts of the legendary Queen of Sheba at the Museum of the Frankincense Land in Salalah or the town of Ma'rib (p388) in Yemen.

Museums

Most of the big cities of the Gulf have invested in fine, and often quirky, collections of regional artefacts in an attempt to capture their disappearing heritage.

Museum of Islamic Art Doha's world-class museum is housed in an iconic IM Pei building. (p215)

Tareq Rajab Museum This stunning collection of regional crafts was mercifully saved the Gulf War devastation of Kuwait's National Museum. (p84)

Bahrain National Museum This excellent ethnographical museum in Manama proves that there was indeed life before oil. (p49)

National Museum, Riyadh A full-scale reconstruction of a Nabataean tomb saves the trouble of journeying to Madain Saleh. (p243)

Sharjah Heritage Area A living museum of restored houses, museums and souqs captures the tiny Emirate's heyday. (p311)

Oil Museum, Bahrain Marking the place where black gold was first struck in Arabia. (p66)

Khasab Fort Housed in a typical Omani fort, this is one of the best little ethnographic museums in the region. (p177)

Al-Jahili Fort, Al Ain, UAE This 19th-century royal summer residence houses a fascinating museum showcasing the desert travels of British explorer Wilfred Thesiger. (p340)

National Museum, Sana'a One of the biggest and best collections of pre-Islamic artefacts on the Peninsula. (p370)

Al-Qurain Martyrs' Museum Discover what invasion meant to an ordinary family in a suburban house in Kuwait. (p91)

(Above) Jabrin Castle, Oman

(Below) Dubai Aquarium (p294), Dubai Mall, United Arab Emirates

Desert Landscapes

If you thought 'desert' means sand, think again. The Peninsula (and in particular Oman, Saudi and Yemen) is full of diverse and spectacular landscapes that redefine the term.

Sharqiya Sands, Oman A fraction of the size of the Empty Quarter dunes but just as beautiful and much more accessible. (p155)

Khor Al-Adaid, Qatar An inland sea, netted by high dunes, sparkling with shoals of silver sardines. (p226)

Wadi Dharbat, Oman Camels and cows share abundant herbage in the region's seasonal mists. (p188)

Wadi Ghul, Oman Vertiginous glimpses into the Grand Canyon of Arabia from the top of Jebel Shams. (p167)

Al-Ula, Saudi Arabia Magnificent wind-blown pillars of sandstone turning copper-coloured at sunset. (p257)

Al-Soudah, Saudi Arabia Peregrine-eye views of the coastal plain from the soaring escarpment. (p264)

Liwa, UAE Date plantations punctuate the sand dunes on the edge of the Empty Quarter. (p336)

Shaharah, Yemen Switchback glimpses of livid green, terraced fields. (p379)

Mughsail, Oman Blowholes fling fish, seaweed and unsuspecting crabs into the air beneath Dhofar's dramatic undercliff. (p190)

Musandam Peninsula, Oman Deeply incised fjords of leaping dolphins and hidden villages. (p177)

Architecture

Dubai, Abu Dhabi and Doha are putting the Arabian Peninsula on the map for innovative architecture. A few ancient wonders in Saudi and Yemen show it has ever been thus.

Madain Saleh, Saudi Arabia The Nabataean monuments of this 'petite Petra' lie in a wind-sculpted desert of sandstone. (p259)

Burj Khalifa and Burj Al-Arab, Dubai Both equally cutting edge, and winning the prize for height and flare respectively. (p291) and (p295)

Beit Sheikh Isa bin Ali, Bahrain Best example of the air-conditioning wizardry of 18th- and 19th-century wind-tower architecture. (p66)

Arab Fund Building, Kuwait The interior is a demonstration of the unity of Islamic art. (p90)

Al-Corniche, Qatar A monument to 21st-century postmodern architecture, setting a benchmark for daring design. (p214)

Grand Mosque, Muscat Elegant, understated masterpiece reflective of the traditional restraint of Omani architecture. (p128)

Shibam, Yemen Called 'Manhattan of the Desert' by the traveller Freya Stark, this medieval town is where the art of high-rise began. (p375)

Kuwait Towers Used as target practice during the Iraqi invasion, these iconic towers have come to symbolise more than just water in the desert. (p85)

Yas Viceroy Hotel, Abu Dhabi The only hotel in the world to straddle a Formula One racetrack. (p330)

Mutrah Corniche A picturesque sweep of balconied houses, mosques and forts in the heart of Oman's capital. (p123)

Wildlife

With the exception of Bahrain, Qatar and Kuwait, the Arabian Peninsula countries offer spectacular wildlife experiences. Swim with dolphins, watch turtles lay their eggs or track oryx across the plains and you'll quickly realise that desert does not mean deserted.

Turtles Watch record numbers of turtles return to the beach of their birth at Ras Al-Jinz Turtle Reserve in Oman. (p150)

Dolphins Sail by dhow from the marina in Muscat and enjoy the company of acrobatic dolphins. (p126)

Whales In Muscat in December, look out for the gentle giants of the Indian Ocean. (p130)

Dugongs Go diving for pearls in Bahrain and you may well come face to face with the Gulf's own seacow. (p68)

Oryx Get up close to the endangered 'unicorn of Arabia' at Al-Areen Wildlife Park & Reserve in Bahrain. (p65)

Birds For a host of endemic species, head to Yemen's island of Socotra, dubbed the 'Galapagos of the Indian Ocean'. (p391)

Baboons Watch dawn unveil a frieze of silent baboons in Saudi's Asir National Park. (p264)

Hyrax Meet the unlikely relative of the elephant when the desert turns green in summertime southern Oman. (p188)

Gazelles Discover the indigenous inhabitants of Arabia without having to be David Attenborough to do so. (p192)

Camel riding in Sharqiya Sands, Oman

Adventure

Travellers have been attracted to the Peninsula for centuries in search of adventure. Follow the footsteps of Marco Polo, Richard Burton and Wilfred Thesiger in some of the best outdoor pursuits in the region.

Snorkelling and Diving Turn your eyes below the waterline anywhere along the Red Sea coast for one of the world's great underwater spectacles. (p274)

Wild camping Pitch a tent along the pristine Indian Ocean shore and listen to ghost crabs scuttling through the high-tide line. (p483)

Four-wheel drive excursions Take a high-altitude adventure through the Hajar Mountains in Oman (p169) or the Asir region in Saudi Arabia (p495) and discover gears you didn't know you had.

Sand driving Let down the tyres and get revving in the sand dunes of Qatar's Khor Al-Adaid (p226), Oman's Sharqiya Sands (p155) or the beautiful strawberry dunes of the UAE (p342).

Wadi walks Follow prehistoric hornbills as they screech through date oases in Yemen (p382) or plunge from pool to pool in Oman's Snake Gorge. (p169)

Camel riding Camels count as wildlife when lunging upright or 'couching' down for their rider; put your riding skills to the test in Oman's Sharqiya Sands. (p155)

Dhow rides Hold on to your wits as your captain steers you round the bend in the *khors* (creeks) of Musandam. (p178)

Skating and skiing If skiing through sand doesn't appeal, head for the cold stuff at Ski Dubai (p298) in the Mall of the Emirates or don skates in any of the Gulf capitals.

Month by Month

and is the world's richest long-distance running event. Details at www.dubaimarathon.org.

Qatar ExxonMobil Open

Qatar's sporting year begins with this international tennis event, which has included top players like Roger Federer. Details at www.qatartennis.org.

brings an intense and brief flourish of flowers and butterflies before the onslaught of summer scares them, and the last of the tourists, away.

Jenadriyah National Festival

Saudi Arabia's largest cultural event embraces the King's Cup camel race, falconry and traditional crafts. Details at www.saudiembassy.net.

January

Bitter cold in the mountains and at night on the desert plains but sublimely warm and sunny everywhere else, this is the peak season for visiting the Arabian Peninsula. Expect the odd rain shower though!

Muscat Festival

The Omani capital comes alive with top-class acrobatic acts, international craft shopping and Omani heritage displays in venues across the city for a month around January and February. Details at www.muscat-festival.com.

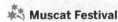

Dubai Marathon

This event, sponsored by Standard Chartered, attracts thousands of runners

February

Still cool by night and warm by day but without the rush of new-year visitors, February is one of the best months to enjoy the bustle of high season in the Gulf.

Shopping Festivals

Straddling January and February, the month-long Dubai Shopping Festival (www.dubaishoppingfestival.com) and the Hala Festival in Kuwait City offer big discounts in shops and firework displays.

March

A flush of lime green clads the desert as spring

Horse Racing

The Dubai World Cup is the world's richest horse race, is worth $10 million, and is a major event on the United Arab Emirates' social calendar. Details at www.dubairacingclub.com.
The Emir's Sword Race, held in Qatar, is one of the biggest international racing events of Arabian horses in the year. Details at www.qrec.gov.qa.

April

With the plains hotting up, this is a superb month to be in the mountains of Oman, Yemen or Saudi with wild and cultivated roses in full bloom, ready to be plucked for rosewater.

☆ **Formula One Bahrain**

This glamorous annual event is one of the biggest in Bahrain. Details at www.bahraingp.com.

May

Few visitors are brave enough to experience May in Arabia – it's intensely hot and overbearingly humid. Even temperate retreats, like Socotra, are plagued with high winds.

June

With miserable heat and humidity, the only good thing to be said for June is that hotels offer discounts. With Ramadan falling in June between 2014 and 2016, this is a month many people choose to avoid.

☆ **Power Boat GP, Doha**

Watch the wake being carved up by speed merchants in this championship grand prix. Details at www.qmsf.org.

🎆 **Ramadan**

The Holy Month of Ramadan is marked by fasting between dawn and dusk and visitors must take care to avoid eating or drinking in public. Ramadan evenings, however, are marked by socialising and seasonal delicacies. For dates, see p486.

🎆 **Eid al-Fitr**

Marking the end of the month of fasting, Eid al-Fitr is generally celebrated at home with the family with little of note for tourists.

(Above) Trained falcons can be seen at Jenadriyah National Festival
(Below) Fasting is followed by feasting during Ramadan

ISLAMIC HOLIDAYS

Ramadan, the month of fasting, and the two main Islamic holidays in the year, Eid Al-Fitr and Eid al-Adha (marked by feasting and festivities), are observed across the region. The dates are governed by the lunar calendar and therefore advance by roughly 10 days each year. See p486 for more.

July

Excessively hot in the desert, this is the season of the *khareef* (rainy period) in southern Oman and parts of Yemen. Regional visitors pour into the area to enjoy the contrast with home.

Turtle Nesting

Throughout the year, turtles return to the beach of their birth to lay their own eggs but July is the peak season in Oman when 100 green turtles lumber up the beach at Ras al-Jinz each night. Details at www.rasaljinz-turtlereserve.com.

August

High season in the misty, green, bug-laden haven of southern Arabia; the rest of the region pants in desiccating temperatures. Mountain areas offer some relief from the heat of the plains.

Salalah Tourism Festival

Regional visitors flock to the festival ground in Salalah to picnic in the drizzle and enjoy a program of international entertainment and Omani cultural shows. (p185)

September

With the return of blue skies, regional visitors return home from gloriously green southern Arabia, making this the perfect time for a lower-season visit. The sea remains too rough for swimming.

Classical Music

The season opens at the Royal Opera House in Muscat staging concerts, opera, ballet and jazz from internationally renowned companies. (p127)

October

The impact of millions of pilgrims heading to Mecca is felt at airports and on highways across the whole region and Saudi is closed to non-Muslim visitors.

Dance Festival

The Dubai International Dance Festival showcases renowned performing artists in this annual three-day event.

Eid al-Adha

Families gather to eat the fatted calf and celebrate the return of pilgrims from Mecca and Medina. For dates, see p486.

November

As the summer heat subsides, occasional rains help the wadis flow, and visitors begin to return to enjoy the reawakening of the Peninsula.

Formula One Abu Dhabi

Showcasing one of the most glamorous circuits in the world, the Abu Dhabi grand prix is now a highlight of the racing year. Details at www.yasmarinacircuit.com.

December

The end of the year marks the peak tourist season for good reason – the sea is still warm, the air is crisp and clear and evenings are warm enough for dining al fresco.

New Year

Although the Arab New Year falls on a different day each year, the region is never one to resist a party. From Dubai (www.mydowntowndubai.com) to Sana'a, fireworks are launched to celebrate 31 December.

Itineraries

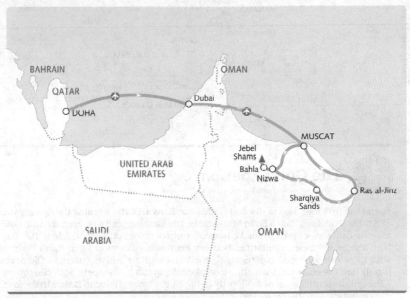

Best of Oman, UAE & Arabian Peninsula

For an introduction to the Peninsula that weaves between modern and ancient, begin your visit with two days in **Doha**, with its skyline of 21st-century architectural gems. Loiter with falcons in Souq Waqif and visit the exceptional Museum of Islamic Art to understand that the modern Gulf is built on inherited Arab values.

Fly to **Dubai** for three days to see a city obsessed with the newest, the biggest and the best, and visit that totem of superlatives, Burj Khalifa. Resurrect the past in a dhow trip along the Dubai Creek and visit Al Fahidi Historical Neighbourhood.

Fly on to **Muscat** for two days for a low-rise, understated experience of modern Arabia, catching a show in the city's magnificent Royal Opera House. See how 40 years of 'renaissance' has created a modern nation strongly underpinned by a respect for the past in a four-day tour of the heritage sites of **Nizwa** and **Bahla**. Forget history and think timelessness by hiking on top of lofty **Jebel Shams**, camel riding with the Bedu across **Sharqiya Sands** and watching turtles return to the beach of their birth at **Ras al-Jinz** en route back to Muscat.

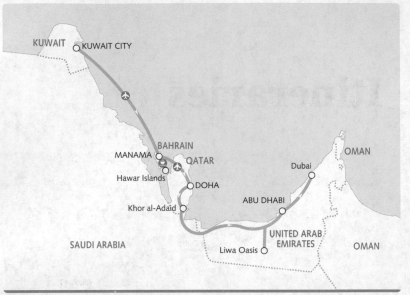

The Gulf Experience

3 WEEKS

Spend the first four days in dry and traditional **Kuwait City**, learning the sensory vocab of Arabia – the haggling in Souq Marbarakia, the haunting call to prayer, the wafts of *sheesha* (waterpipes used to smoke tobacco) from outdoor coffeeshops. Add to the Arabian lexicon by tracing similarities between Peninsula cultures at Tareq Rajab Museum with its priceless collection of regional jewellery, costumes and manuscripts. Old Arabia is only half the equation: leave time to explore the urban landscape of high-rise towers – the quintessential icons of modernity in the Gulf – before flying to **Bahrain** for four days (political situation allowing).

Oil is responsible for Arabia's rapid propulsion into the 21st century: see how in Bahrain's Oil Museum and enjoy some of the glamour of wealth at the Formula One racing circuit. Pearls gave the Gulf its former livelihood: buy a string at Gold City in **Manama** or dive for your own off the **Hawar Islands** before flying on to **Doha** for four days.

Both pearls and black gold have helped Qatar, with its commitment to hosting international sports, compete with the best. And what a venue Doha makes, with one of the most spectacular modern skylines in the world built on land reclaimed from the sea. Visit **Khor al-Adaid** in southern Qatar and watch the inland sea get its own back as it encroaches ever deeper into the interior sand dunes.

You can continue to walk on water – or rather, on reclaimed land – in **Abu Dhabi** where you will spend the next three days discovering how and why it has become the cultural as well as the political capital of United Arab Emirates. For contrast with the high-voltage Gulf city, escape to **Liwa Oasis** for two days. Here life moves at the pace of a camel's stride or a trade wind shunting sand across the tops of the dunes.

Unless you're a modern-day Thesiger, you'll soon be missing the dynamism of the urban experience, and in this respect the best has been kept until last. Spend your final four days in and around **Dubai**, discovering what makes it the most internationally famous city of the region. Swim with dolphins, shop with sharks, view the city from the world's tallest tower and dine underwater in the Gulf's most 'Yes we can' city.

Top: Mutrah Souq (p138), Muscat, Oman
Bottom: Royal Opera House Muscat (p127), Oman

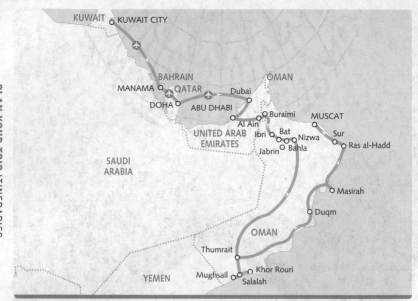

Pan-Peninsula: Five Countries in Five Weeks

Spend the first two weeks of the journey enjoying the Gulf experience with four days in each of the virtual city states of **Kuwait City**, **Manama** and **Doha**. Fly to **Dubai** and begin week three with your head in the clouds on top of the world's tallest tower, the Burj Khalifa, or admire this Dubai icon from another symbol of the vertical, Burj al-Arab. Cruise the Dubai Creek to see how height dominates the city. Transfer to the UAE's sophisticated capital **Abu Dhabi**: what the turrets of the Emirates Palace lack in height, they make up for in light bulbs.

With the city-centric part of the journey over, escape to the starry skies and apricot-coloured dunes of **Al Ain**. Allow time to wander through souqs of grumbling camels and listen for the ghost of intrepid desert explorer Thesiger, commemorated in the fort museum.

Begin week four by crossing the border via **Buraimi** to **Ibri** in Oman. This is the land of a thousand aged towers and fortifications, gracing mountain top and wadi's edge, and it's easy to feel the spirit of the ancients in their burial towers at **Bat**. Continue through the castle towns of **Jabrin** and **Bahla** to **Nizwa** where the mighty Jebel Shams towers over this heritage city.

Take a complete break from the vertical by journeying across the edge of the Empty Quarter on the flat and utterly featureless highway to **Thumrait**. The descent into **Salalah**, Oman's southern capital, after 10 hours of stony-plain monotony is sublime, especially during the rainy season when the desert turns green. End week four among the frankincense trees near **Mughsail** and see where the precious resin was traded at Al-Baleed and the ancient harbour of **Khor Rouri**.

With a car, begin week five by skirting the Arabian Sea from Salalah (via Hasik when the coast road is completed) to **Duqm**, pausing for a night on floating hotel Veronica. Complete a lap of **Masirah** to understand the true meaning of the term 'desert island' before continuing along the auburn edge of the Sharqiya sands to **Ras al-Hadd**. Spend a day in **Sur**, where the lighthouses of Ayjah guide dhows to safe haven, before heading to journey's end in the hospitable city of **Muscat**.

Easy Escape from Dubai

5 DAYS

Leave the city for a gentler pace by heading north to **Sharjah** with its historic wind towers of the Heritage Area and the cultural riches of the nearby Arts Area. Arrive for lunch at **Sharjah Desert Park** overlooking ostrich, oryx and gazelle. On day two, wind through the northern Emirates to the **Shams/Tibat border** and enter Oman's fabled Musandam Peninsula. Enjoy the spectacular drive along the cliff-hugging road to **Khasab** and time your arrival for a snorkel and sunset cruise on a dhow in Musandam's celebrated deep-water *khors* (creeks). Spend day three ascending by 4WD to **Jebel Harim** and descend to Rawdah Bowl for a picnic beside a 'House of Locks'. Retrace your steps to Khasab ready to board the evening fast ferry to **Muscat**: entering Mutrah harbour lit up with night lights is a magical experience. Visit Mutrah Souq and the old quarter of Muscat on day four. On day five, head west to the old capital cities of **Nakhal** and **Rustaq** with their magnificent forts. Break your journey back to Dubai at the beautiful beach resort at **Sawadi** or stretch into an extra day by staying overnight at the growing town of **Sohar**.

Easy Escape from Kuwait

1 WEEK

For the complete antithesis of life in Kuwait City, take a three-centre trip to Oman and the UAE. Fly on day one to **Muscat** and be immediately struck by the more tolerant attitudes towards dress and entertainment. Spend day two at a beachside hotel and enjoy a swim in a sea with waves, followed by sundowners and dancing in a local nightclub. On day three, be reminded of what mountains and orchards look like in a day trip to **Jebel Akhdar** and hike in that rare medium of pure, dry, fresh air. On day four, fly down to **Salalah** where the subtropical climate, rich greenery (especially in summer), cooler climate and more casual atmosphere will feel like another continent. On day five, relax with a spa and fresh papaya at your seaside resort, go snorkelling or visit the spectacular blowholes at **Mughsail**, located in a landscape untrammelled by oil pipelines and nodding donkeys. On day six, swap the rural idyll for the urban wild side by flying into **Dubai** for some extreme shopping, dining and partying. On day seven, button up the collar for the return to a very different Gulf experience in Kuwait.

Plan Your Trip

Expats

Some expats are drawn to the Arabian Peninsula in search of tax-free money and the expectation of an easy life. But the days of being paid well for doing little are over, while the realities of extreme temperatures and challenging cultural norms remain. So why consider an expat life? For many it's the excitement of being part of something experimental and optimistic in a region where the pace of change is unparalleled.

Key Differences

Bahrain
Extreme humidity in summer. Current political unrest. Tolerant of Western customs and manners.

Kuwait
A dry state. Very little greenery. Tolerant of non-Muslim religious expression. Current political unrest.

Oman
Slow pace of decision-making. Tolerant of Western customs and manners.

Qatar
Extreme humidity in summer. Quite conservative.

Saudi Arabia
A dry state. Highly conservative. Restricted movement outside city of residence. Women are not permitted to drive. Non-Muslim religious expression restricted.

United Arab Emirates
Liberal exterior hides a conservative core.

Yemen
Pockets of tribal, political and religious conflict throughout the country.

Everyday Life

Not So Different from Home

At first, the call to prayer five times a day, the heat, the homogenous clothing, the undisciplined driving and the ubiquitous aroma of *sheesha* (water pipe used to smoke tobacco) combine to create an overwhelming sense of difference. This difference is further emphasised by the barren desert landscape.

Give it a week, however, and the similarities start putting in an appearance and day-to-day life in Arabia appears not as 'foreign' as one had imagined. Western dress is worn in international-style malls (albeit under an *abeyya* – a woman's full-length black robe); Marmite and Heinz are on sale in familiar-looking shops; Western schools cater expertly for expat children; provision is made for non-Muslim worship; and most people speak English. The drinking of alcohol is tolerated in all countries except Kuwait and Saudi, and you can even buy pork in some supermarkets.

Many expats enjoy the fact that living in any of the Peninsula countries is like life in the West used to be, where it is safe to leave houses and cars unlocked, for children to play in the streets and talk to strangers, and where neighbours always have time for a chat. Times are changing in the big cities, but on the whole the friendly, safe and tolerant environment of all these countries (with the temporary exception of Yemen) is a major contributor to the quality of life. Even in Saudi Arabia, where public life is controlled by strict codes of conduct, expats enjoy a safe, relaxed and crime-free experience within their own compounds.

A Multicultural Experience

Expatriate populations outnumber national populations in all Gulf States. As such, the Arabian Peninsula is one of the most multicultural places on the planet. This is both a trial and a fantastic opportunity. The trial comes in learning to cope with another layer of cultural expectation. The opportunity comes in gaining an insight into richly different ways of life (expressed most noticeably through food, festivities and workplace practice).

Perhaps the most valuable aspect of the multicultural experience of the region is learning from the resident Iraqis, Afghans and Palestinians that there is another perspective on the politics of the region that is not often aired in the Western media.

Climate

Without doubt, one of the biggest challenges of living in the Peninsula is learning to cope with the weather. If you're from a cold, wet and windy place, it's hard to imagine you'd ever get bored of the endless blue skies. But in the summer, the sky isn't blue: it's white with heat and the extreme temperatures from April to October (which hover on average around 40°C and frequently rise to 45°C plus) require a complete life adjustment. Learning to live indoors in the air-conditioning for those months, to live life more slowly and find ways of exercising that don't involve going outside, is as difficult as coming to terms with winter in frozen climes. The upside is six months of magnificent, benign winter warmth that bid friends and relatives to visit. Here are some key ways to beat the heat:

Embrace local timing Working hours across the region tend to favour the mornings and late afternoons either with a 7am–2pm regime, or

a two-shift day from 7am to 7pm with a break between noon and 5pm.

Take a siesta If the job allows, follow local practice by eating your main meal at lunchtime and taking a nap in the heat of the day.

Drink plenty of water Expats often underestimate the amount of extra fluid intake they require in summer and become dehydrated and ill as a result.

Wear cotton clothing Excessive humidity in Gulf cities can make a temperature of 35°C feel more like 45°C and synthetic fibres stick to the skin, adding to the 'boil-in-the-bag' effect. Avoid excessive use of sunscreen for the same reason.

Wear a hat and sunglasses It's no accident that local costume includes some form of head covering for all. You should also cover your neck and protect your eyes from glare (off white buildings and the sea especially). Avoid sitting in the summer sun altogether if you want to maintain supple, unwrinkled skin.

Exercise with caution Half the activity takes twice the effort in extreme heat so follow the locals by exercising just before dawn or at an air-conditioned gym. There's often a slight cooling of temperature at dusk before the night-time heat explodes.

Escape to higher ground Temperature reduces by around 5°C for every 1000m of altitude gained. A weekend break (or summer retreat to drizzling Dhofar in Oman) may just keep you sane for the rest of the week.

The Law

In most Peninsula countries the law is based on Sharia'a law, which can lead to a wide interpretation of penalties for similar illegal activities from country to country and even from judge to judge, as there is no formal penal code.

Breaking the law in the Arabian Peninsula can have severe consequences for Westerners, and embassies have very little jurisdiction (or inclination) to help foreign nationals in breach of local laws.

Some things that are legal in the West, including public displays of affection, sex out of wedlock and consuming alcohol, are illegal in some Peninsula countries and can carry a harsh sentence. Illegal acts across the region include taking drugs, public drunkenness, driving after drinking

CULTURAL DOS AND DON'TS

Do...

It is not always easy, especially in the big cities of the Gulf, to interact with the local people – and especially with the indigenous Arabs who are often outnumbered in their own countries by expat residents. Some simple ways of engaging with the local culture, however, are listed below.

➡ **Visit the local museum or heritage village** Getting a feel for the region's Bedouin roots is a great way to understand differing concepts of time and hospitality. Visiting living heritage villages, especially during festivals and national days, provides insights into the rich song, dance, craft and cuisine inheritance of each country.

➡ **Learn Arabic** This is not necessary for survival, as English is so widely spoken, but just learning to read the street signs helps bring you closer to Arab culture.

➡ **Attend a wedding** Invitations to these will surely be forthcoming and, for women especially, it's the quickest way to learn that Arab women are not the oppressed creatures of Western perception.

➡ **Celebrate Eid, Diwali, Christmas and Arabic and Western new years** Peninsula people love a party and they are quick to give greetings at all religious festivals, not just those of Islam; joining them on such occasions is the best way to understand their strong sense of community.

➡ **Play football** Between acacia trees, on beaches or between mountain passes, showing interest in this regional obsession is the surest way to the Arab heart.

Don't...

Peninsula countries are, on the whole, very forgiving of the transgressions of foreigners (except in Saudi Arabia) but there is nothing to be gained by upsetting the citizens of your host country. To avoid giving offence or landing yourself in trouble with the authorities, don't do the following:

➡ **Wear revealing clothing** Even in liberal Dubai nothing causes more offence than exposing shoulders or thighs in shopping centres and other public spaces, or wearing tight and provocative clothing – that goes for men as well as women.

➡ **Show affection in public** Avoid holding hands, kissing or hugging with members of the opposite sex.

➡ **Indulge in excessive drinking** Being drunk in public is considered thoroughly reprehensible. In many countries in the region it will get you deported or even imprisoned. In Saudi, where alcohol is strictly prohibitted, the penalty is severe.

➡ **Drink and drive** Even in countries tolerant of alcohol consumption, there is zero tolerance for drinking and driving.

➡ **Take drugs** This is illegal in all countries of Arabia and can lead to severe penalties.

➡ **Eat, drink or smoke in public during daylight hours in Ramadan** Some countries also enforce a ban on gum chewing, singing and loud music.

➡ **Swear or use rude hand gestures** In some Arab countries this may not just be considered uncouth, it may also be illegal! It's also impolite to beckon with a finger or to use the left hand when touching, giving and eating.

➡ **Take photographs without permission** This is the case when photographing people, particularly women. You should also avoid anything military or 'strategic' (such as airports or bus stations).

➡ **Cohabit** Despite the low risk of detection if you are discreet, it is illegal to live with a member of the opposite sex (or have a baby) unless you are married. In Saudi, men and women may not travel together (including by car) unless related.

alcohol, lewd behaviour, adultery, cohabitation and homosexuality. Depending on the country you're in, breaking the law may lead to fines (for speeding and parking offences), jail (for causing accidental death), deportation (for cohabitation), public flogging (for adultery) or even a death sentence (for drug trafficking). Note that penalties, and even what's considered illegal, can change frequently in some countries. As such, it is vital that you thoroughly acquaint yourself with local laws before entering the country. Consult your HR manager and the embassy of the country in which you plan to work for guidance on legal matters before you take up employment.

Links to Legal Resources

The following resources can help throw light on the legal system in Gulf countries in particular.

Working in the Gulf (Explorer Group, 2011) List of legal services country-by-country.

Gulf Law (www.gulf-law.com) General introduction to Sharia'a and commercial law.

Expat Corner (www.expatcornergcc.com) Listing of Gulf Cooperation Council labour laws.

Working in the Region

Labour laws throughout the Gulf are extremely strict. It's illegal to seek work on a visit visa and there are severe penalties for those caught working illegally. Although some travellers take the chance of applying for ad-hoc work (in Dubai, for example), to remain within the law you should secure a position before arrival. Your 'sponsor' (usually your employer) acts as a kind of guarantor of your good conduct while you reside in the country and will help you obtain a visa.

Working and living conditions are usually of a high standard. Salaries, though not usually significantly higher than those in the West, carry the enormous advantage of incurring no personal taxation. It can be tricky, however, to change jobs if you decide you're not happy with the one you have. It can also be difficult to find long-term employment; many contracts are short term, renewable annually. While it's not necessary to speak Arabic (though it's

an advantage), good spoken and written communication in English is a prerequisite and many jobs require qualifications that would not be expected back home.

Those offering professional skills in much-needed services, such as translating, nursing, engineering and teaching (particularly English), stand the best chance of gaining employment; many administrative positions, on the other hand, are beginning to be filled by newly trained local professionals. Recruiting agencies in major European cities still head-hunt for positions in the Peninsula. Note that for English-language teaching, you will need at least a degree and teaching experience to be eligible for most job opportunities.

You can also inquire about job opportunities at your cultural centre (such as the British Council or Centre Culturel Français) and voluntary aid organisations

Applying the Right Attitude

The working life of an expat, which often involves confronting fundamental differences in outlook, culture and education between colleagues, can be quite a challenge. It helps, therefore, to identify these differences from the beginning and then to celebrate the 'other', rather than seek to change it. The host nations, of the Gulf in particular, do this very well, accepting the expat for who they are and rarely attempting to influence their religious or social beliefs and customs. By the same token, it is important for the expat to learn to appreciate the Arab way of doing things and not assume that the West always knows best. Indeed, the expat who listens to what people want – rather than anticipates what they want – is more likely to make a genuinely valuable contribution to the emerging but complex countries of the region than those who rush in with solutions that are inappropriate to the context and then feel defeated at the lack of application or implementation.

Business Etiquette

People from the Arabian Peninsula have been eminent merchants for centuries, with global trade in copper, frankincense, pearls and, latterly, oil running through their veins. Inevitably, they have developed highly refined customs and manners when it comes to commercial interaction and they are always a tad disdainful of their Western counterparts whose alacrity to get straight down to business shows, in their book, a lack of finesse in the fine arts of trade.

Though urbane enough to tolerate the mores of their overseas counterparts, Arab business people are impressed with good manners. Observing the following courtesies, therefore, may just help seal the deal.

Clothing Wear a suit (with a tie for men) but avoid silk or linen, which crease badly; women should cover knees, cleavage and shoulders. Attempts at dressing local-style (in *dishdasha* or *abeyya*, for example) are deemed ridiculous.

Timing Be on time for meetings but be tolerant of late arrivals (an accepted part of local custom). Avoid meetings or telephone calls on a Friday, which is the day of prayer and rest; during afternoon siesta (except in the UAE where the practice is dying out); and in the holy month of Ramadan.

Greeting Shake hands readily with men but wait for an Arab woman to proffer her hand first. Only use Arab greetings if you can master them, otherwise stick to formal English. Don't be surprised if people touch their heart after a greeting (as in Saudi), kisses on the cheek are exchanged between men (as in the Gulf States), noses are knocked or rubbed (as in areas of Oman) – equally don't try to do the same.

Addressing Use Arab given names, as opposed to family names. Instead of Mr Al-Wahabbi, it's Mr Mohammed. In the same way, expect to be called Mr or Ms plus your first name (Mr John or Prof Jane, for example) and don't attempt to change this polite form to your surname. The correct formal address (or equivalent of Mr) is usually *asayid* (meaning sir) or *asayida* (meaning madam).

Preliminaries Exchange pleasantries about the weather and ask after health and family for several minutes before turning to the subject in hand. It's considered rude to go straight to the point. Men, however, should never enquire after another man's wife or daughters. Exchange business cards (which are a must) with your right hand; do not use the left hand, which is reserved for ablutions.

Negotiating Bargaining is an important part of discovering value to the buyer weighed against worth to the vendor. The concept of a fixed price is a largely Western concept that is considered quite alien to the highly social and personal interaction of reaching a deal in the Middle East.

Agreement Although some of the gentility of reaching agreement has vanished during the recent global depression, an Arab word is his bond and, similarly, those who give a promise should keep it as a matter of honour.

Problem Solving Keep smiling, keep your temper and avoid raising your voice. Confrontation, criti-

PUTTING PEOPLE FIRST

Much of Arab life is underpinned by a sense of 'what will be, will be'. This fatalism stems from Islam and the belief that God determines fate and is reflected in the frequent conversational phrase, *insha'allah*, which literally means 'if Allah wills it'. A belief in God's will threads through all aspects of life; it informs the response to a car accident, a soured business deal or the death of a loved one, and it leads to a culture where personal accountability and the culture of blame (both closely held Western concepts) have limited meaning.

For the expat who is unaware of this difference, there are many frustrations involved in social and business interactions. For example, when rushing towards a deadline (a moveable concept across the region), it's not unusual to find colleagues have knocked off for a tea break. But then, from the Arab point of view, what can be more important than sharing time to discuss the day and swap family news? The deadline will be met if Allah wills it so in the meantime, take your rest and have a chat. More 'business' is conducted over a *chi libton* (cup of tea) than is ever concluded after a Powerpoint presentation because in Peninsula society, people come first. To enjoy as well as to succeed in living and working in the Arabian Peninsula, the expat has to learn to put people first, too, and the investment in good relations invariably pays unexpected dividends, smoothing the passage of daily life and opening up social and business opportunities.

cism, blaming and swearing are highly insulting in public as they involve loss of face for those concerned. Equally, making and forcing apology is a Western concept best avoided.

Socialising Take your cue from the host and avoid asking for alcohol unless it is offered. Never refuse a cup of tea or coffee as refusal may offend. Before any kind of transaction – at the checkout in a supermarket, if the traffic police stop you, before a meeting begins, even on the telephone between strangers – people greet each other thoroughly and preferably enquire after the other person's health.

Conversing Avoid politics, sex and religion as topics of conversation, and if you are drawn into such discussion, keep your comments general, not personal. Also, avoid any comparisons of people with animals, even in jest, especially dogs (which are considered unclean by many Muslims) and donkeys (used as a common insult).

Closing The exchange of gifts is an important aspect of conducting business in the region. Well-crafted tokens representing an aspect of your home country are the normal currency of leave-taking; poorly made items will do more damage to your agenda than good.

Women in the Workplace

In the workplace, opportunities for senior positions and pay are equal for both sexes (except in Saudi Arabia where women are only employed in certain sectors). It is the norm in most Gulf countries for men and women to work side by side in an office environment. Female professionals are respected for their qualifications and experience and although it's often harder for local women to break the glass ceiling, this is not the case for foreign female professionals who are accorded great respect.

General advice regarding business etiquette is the same for men and women with one exception: some devoutly religious men will not touch a woman's hand. The key is to take the cue from the other person when expecting to shake hands.

For general advice regarding challenges for foreign women in the region, see p480.

Expat Life for Children & Families

Arabs love the company of children and celebrate childhood through large families and varying indulgences. As such, expat children are assured of a welcome and may find that they have more freedom than they do back home, as parents feel safe in the knowledge that they are not going to be preyed upon in parks or offered drugs. The main concerns for a family are summarised below.

Activities There is little sophisticated child-oriented entertainment outside of the big cities, but a beach is never too far away, and there are often parks containing children's play areas (including swings and slides) even in small towns.

Birth & Maternity Leave Many expat women give birth in the region and it presents no special difficulties in the main cities. There are prenatal and postnatal groups on hand to help. Maternity leave is enshrined in law in most Arab countries.

Childcare Nannies (usually from the Subcontinent or the Phillipines) are one of the easily afforded perks of the region. Many mums opt for live-in home help and villas often cater for this with the provision of maid's quarters. In some cities, babysitting services are available in malls.

Coffee Mornings There are many groups, such as the Women's Guild in Oman (www.womensguild oman.com), which act as a forum for non-working expat women. These groups are a lifeline for many new arrivals in the region, providing local knowledge about everything from schooling, home help and health care to voluntary work and leisure activities.

Education The standard of international schools in the Arabian Peninsula is excellent, offering similar curricula to Western schools, enabling a smooth transition into university or college outside the region.

Healthcare The extreme heat can be debilitating for children, particularly babies. Obstetric and paediatric units in hospitals and clinics are generally of a high standard and most scourges of childhood in hot climates (such as polio, malaria and typhoid) are under control.

Hotels & Restaurants In top-end and some midrange hotels, children can usually share their parents' room for no extra charge. Extra beds or cots are normally available. High chairs are often only available in top-end restaurants.

Infants Disposable nappies are not always easy to come by outside large cities. Infant formula is widely available, however, as is bottled water.

Resources The international website Mums Net (www.mumsnet.com) is a useful forum for sharing advice and information on expat life in the Peninsula. For further advice on the dos and don'ts of taking the kids, see Lonely Planet's *Travel with Children*.

Special Needs Catering for the needs of children with disabilities is highly challenging in the region as often locals attach stigma to physical and especially mental disability. Even finding help or support with common childhood issues such as dyslexia, ADD and anorexia can be difficult.

Housing

Stories about wild parties on expat compounds where the residents never interact with people beyond the gates are largely a thing of the past. Company compounds do still exist in Saudi but many expats in the Gulf are these days given an allowance and expected to find their own accommodation. Some general advice regarding housing is as follows:

➡ Rental accommodation can be found, usually unfurnished, through embassies, cultural centres and newspapers.

➡ Villas with gardens, apartments with a shared swimming pool or a residency within a self-sufficient and gated compound are the preferred expat residency options. Many hotels offer long-stay arrangements.

➡ Check that air-con, maintenance of shared areas and mains water are included in the rent.

➡ Shaded, off-road parking is highly desirable.

➡ Unless you are a fan of early mornings, you may prefer to avoid neighbouring a mosque where a wake-up call will occur well before sunrise.

➡ Check your employment contract covers temporary accommodation while you house hunt.

➡ Relocation consultants as well as estate agents can be found in the telephone directories of most countries.

Health

Health care across the region is consistently of a high standard in all major cities. In smaller and especially rural communities health care may be confined to a visiting doctor at the local clinic. Health-care providers tend to be expats themselves, with many nurses from the Philipines and doctors from India.

Emergency treatment is often given free but you shouldn't rely on this. Ambulance services are available in cities but often a taxi is the best way to get to hospital in a hurry. Operations can be very expensive and many locals opt to have surgery in India or Thailand as they believe they will receive better care in those countries.

It's imperative to have health insurance for all the family. Carefully check the small print of any company-issued insurance as it may well exclude dental and eye care, prenatal, delivery and maternity care, as well as exempting pre-existing conditions.

Women's personal requirements (such as tampons and sanitary pads) can be found in the larger supermarkets of the bigger cities (which cater for expats). Contraception is readily available but abortion other than on health grounds is not readily supported.

'Red Tape'

The countries of the Middle East seem to have a passion for bureaucracy and have large public sectors in place to administer it. For the expat this entails various paperchases to ensure having the right permissions in place to work, own and drive a car, purchase alcohol and, in the case of Saudi, travel around the country. This isn't as daunting as it sounds as every company will have a fixer whose job it is to steer the employee over each bureaucratic hurdle. Note that for most countries in the region you need to test negative for AIDS and tuberculosis before you gain a residency permit; this is treated as a routine and perfunctory part of the visa-obtaining process.

You can speed up the obtaining of various permits by having a stock of passport-size photographs, some on plain white, and some on plain blue backgrounds;

multiple copies of an abbreviated CV (two pages maximum); copies of your tertiary qualifications and the original certificates attested by your embassy at the ready.

Take a number on entering queuing stations, carry a book to read, be patient and stay friendly and polite even when at your wit's end. When at length you get your residency card, driving licence or travel permit, carry it with you at all times – this is the law in most Peninsula countries.

Many countries will permit some nationalities to drive on a license from home. Other nationalities must pass the local driving test. Check with your embassy or HR manager.

Transport

In general, except in Dubai and Doha which have good public transport systems and Saudi where women can't drive, it is really useful to have a car for getting to work and/or running family errands. Cities are spread out and offices, services and entertainments far flung.

The Peninsula is a good place to buy a car but note that you can't buy one without a residency permit. Most mainstream makes and models are available, and prices are low (since there's no import duty). As when shopping for other items, bargaining is normal. A down payment of around 10% of the purchase price is usually expected if taking out a loan.

Because cars are cheap, they're also seen as disposable by the wealthy. There is a growing secondhand car market throughout the region. Note that change of ownership has to be completed with the local police. When buying a vehicle (or importing one), you usually have to register it with the police traffic department.

When secondhand car shopping it's essential you ensure that the car you're interested in purchasing has the following:

➡ an up-to-date test certificate

➡ a registration certificate (and that the engine and chassis numbers of the car matches the latter)

➡ a clean bill of health from a mechanic

➡ a clean record – fines outstanding on the car are usually transferred to the new owner.

Ramadan

The 'Holy Month of Ramadan' is a time of spiritual contemplation for Muslims. For the expat it can be a time of heightened frustration as everyone works more slowly and drives more quickly.

Muslims fast from sunrise to sunset during Ramadan. Foreigners are not expected to fast, but they should not smoke, drink or eat (including gum-chewing) in public during daylight hours in Ramadan. Business premises and hotels make provision for the non-fasting by erecting screens around dining areas.

Business hours tend to become more erratic and usually shorter and many restaurants close for the whole period.

With this change of routine and given the hardship of abstaining from water during the long, hot summer days, it's not surprising that tempers easily fray and the standard of driving deteriorates. Expats should make allowances by being extra vigilant on the roads and by being extra tolerant in all social interaction.

What to Wear

Nothing offends Arabs quite as much as inappropriate clothing. Topless or nude sunbathing on beaches or in wadi areas is strictly forbidden on the Peninsula; those

CHRISTMAS AS AN EXPAT

Christmas is celebrated with gusto in the Arabian Peninsula. In the malls and shopping centres, there are lights and carols, mangers with babies and neon cribs, cards with angels and the three wise men, and Arab Muslims queuing up to take the kids to see Santa. While it's common for locals to wish you a 'Happy Christmas', the best response is 'thank you' rather than a return of the same greeting. In the UAE provision is often made for vacations to be taken at Christmas but this is uncommon elsewhere in the region and 25 December is generally treated as a normal working day.

who flout this law are liable to be arrested. Here are a few tips on what travellers should wear to avoid offending anybody.

Men

Traditional dress has acquired complex nationalist connotations, visually setting apart natives of the region from the large population of foreigners. As such, Western men should avoid wearing local *thobes* or *dishdashas* (man's shirt-dresses) – at best, Arab people think it looks ridiculous. Locals dress smartly if they can afford to and visitors are similarly judged by their dress. Some hotel bars and nightclubs have a strict dress code and on the whole it's unacceptable to be seen anywhere in public, including hotel foyers and souqs, in shorts, vests and flipflops.

Women

Dressing modestly has the following advantages: it attracts less attention, gets a warmer welcome from the locals (who greatly appreciate a willingness to respect their customs), and proves more comfortable in the heat. Dressing 'modestly' means covering knees, upper arms, shoulders and neckline in loose, climate-suitable clothing. Wearing a bra, slips and petticoats under transparent clothing is a must. Carrying a hat or headscarf (which can be slipped on when necessary, such as when visiting a mosque) is also a good idea.

As with anywhere, take your cues from those around you: if you're in a rural area and all the women are in long, concealing dresses, you should dress conservatively. Dressing modestly doesn't mean wearing local clothes which may result in you being mistaken for a Muslim and the embarrassing consequences of that mistake. Women are only expected to wear an *abeyya* (but not cover their hair) in Saudi Arabia.

On public beaches, women will attract less unwanted attention in shorts and a loose T-shirt rather than in swimming costumes. Bikinis (except in tourist resorts) cause a local sensation.

MOSQUE ETIQUETTE

Some of the most impressive structures in the Arabian Peninsula are the Grand Mosques that grace each capital city. They are often open for visits by non-Muslims and can prove to be inspirational in terms of the cultural insights they afford. The following advice will help ensure no offence is unwittingly caused.

Do...

➡ Visit mosques that are explicitly open to visitors at the publicised times.

➡ Dress modestly in loose clothing, covering shoulders, arms and legs (and cleavage and hair if you are a woman); some mosques may request women to wear an *abeyya* (full-length black robe). Some mosques refuse admission to those wearing blue denim jeans, frayed jeans and any clothing deemed 'disrespectful'.

➡ Remove your shoes before stepping into the prayer hall.

➡ Sit on the carpet, enjoy the ambience and marvel at the usually lavish carpets, tiles, pillars, chandeliers and domes.

➡ Take photographs unless otherwise directed.

Don't ...

➡ Enter a mosque during prayer times unless you are Muslim.

➡ Enter the women's prayer hall if you are a man (women may enter the men's prayer hall in most public-opening mosques).

➡ Use the ablution area – this is reserved for the preparation of worship.

➡ Touch the Holy Quran.

➡ Extend your feet in front of you while sitting; tuck them underneath in a slouched kneeling position.

➡ Speak in a loud voice, sing or whistle.

➡ Take photographs of people praying.

WHAT TO WEAR

COVER WHAT?	WITH WHAT (WOMEN)?	WITH WHAT (MEN)?	WHERE?
face	• veil or mask	n/a	never, except for Muslims
whole body and hair	• *abeyya* • headscarf	n/a	outside the house in Saudi Arabia; in mosques elsewhere; some local weddings
lower leg, knees, shoulders and chest/ cleavage	• suit and tie • long trousers • long-sleeved shirt	• suit and tie • long trousers • long-sleeved shirt • no sandals	work environment in all countries
lower leg, knees, shoulders and chest/ cleavage	• suit and tie • long trousers • long-sleeved shirt	• suit and tie • long trousers • long-sleeved shirt	souqs and non-tourist frequented public areas, including beaches
lower leg, knees	• strappy gowns • party wear • smart-casual clothing	• jacket • no jeans • no sandals	weddings; dinner in five-star hotels; nightclubs
upper leg, back	• knee-length skirts • long shorts • T-shirts	• shorts • T shirts	all tourist-frequented public areas including malls, sights, restaurants, hotel lobbies and dining areas
stomach	• swimsuits • strappy vests • shorts	• shorts • string vests	tourist frequented public beaches
'vital bits'	• bikini • skimpy shorts • short skirts • transparent over-garments	• topless • skimpy trunks	beaches of international resorts and hotels
birthday suit	• g-strings • topless	• g-strings • skinny dipping	nowhere ever (including wadi bathing)

Further Reading

There are many informative books about the expat experience encompassing personal narratives and practical resources. In addition, there are some excellent expat websites with discussion forums dispensing advice and sharing experiences.

Internet Resources

The following websites provide an information service and networking opportunities exclusively for expats:

@llo Expat Middle East (www.middleeast. alloexpat.com)

British Expats (www.britishexpats.com)

Expat Exchange (www.expatexchange.com)

Expat Forum (www.expatforum.com)

Living Abroad (www.livingabroad.com)

Countries at a Glance

The term 'Arabian Peninsula' is such a cohesive one you could be forgiven for thinking that all the countries it comprises are alike. There are similarities between each country – the hot, arid desert, Bedouin roots, Islamic customs and the Arabic language – but the differences are just as pronounced. Head to the United Arab Emirates (UAE) and Gulf states to experience the quintessential modern Arabian city with cutting-edge museums, marble-clad malls selling the latest international fashions, avant-garde restaurants and landscaped resorts boasting every conceivable luxury. In marked contrast, Oman, Yemen and Saudi Arabia offer a glimpse of the old Arabia with characterful souqs, forts and ancient archaeological sites. At Arabia's desolate core, the Empty Quarter straddles Saudi, Oman and the UAE, giving opportunity for desert nights in organised camps in unparalleled landscapes.

Bahrain

Archaeology
Social Life
Culture

A Land of Burials

Riddling and honeycombing a surprisingly large proportion of the island, the enigmatic burial mounds at A'Ali and the tombs at Sar date back to the ancient Dilmun era and underline Bahrain's trading inheritance.

Cafe Culture

Sipping coffee shakes in Manama's fashionable Adliya district is one of the best ways to catch the social vibe of this vibrant and cosmopolitan city.

Pearling Trade

Bahrain's former wealth was built on pearls and whether you trace the new pearling path through Muharraq Island or dive with a nose-peg to harvest your own, you won't escape the significance of the pearl on Bahraini culture.

p46

Kuwait

Culture
Recent History
Shopping

Museums & Monuments

From the jewels and gems of the exquisite Tareq Rajab ethnographical museum to the landmark Kuwait Towers, Kuwait's identity is defined and preserved in diverse cultural riches.

Remembering the 1990s

The Iraqi invasion and the Gulf War at the end of the last century are hidden in the psyche of modern Kuwait – and exposed in moving memorials and landmarks scattered across the city.

Souqs & Malls

From souqs where the tumbling goods and produce go unlabelled to modern malls where nothing sells without the right label, Kuwait City offers a tantalising virtual history of shopping through the ages.

p78

Oman

Landscapes
Wildlife
History

Highs & Lows

Peering down from Jebel Shams (Oman's highest mountain) into Wadi Ghul, Arabia's 'Grand Canyon', is a vertiginous experience matched by driving through Sharqiya's almost vertical sand-dunes or diving in Musandam's cliff-hugging *khors* (creeks).

Not Deserted

Nesting turtles at Ras al-Jinz, breeding oryx and gazelles in the wilds of Jaaluni, leopards and wolves in Dhofar, and dolphins, whales and diverse Arabian Sea shells along Oman's pristine coast prove the desert is not deserted.

Forts & Castles

With over 2000 forts, castles and watchtowers, it's hard to pick a favourite Omani crenellation: at a push impressive Nakhal Fort wins it for location, location, location.

p116

Qatar

Landscapes
Architecture
Culture

Inland Sea

Beautiful Khor al-Adaid offers a dune for a pillow and stars for a blanket beside Qatar's fabled inland sea – a nostalgic landscape for camel treks, campfire barbecues and desert camps that evoke Qatar's Bedouin roots.

Urban Landscape

Competing for headroom in the clustered skies above West Bay, the creative high-rise towers of modern Doha prove that if an architect can think it, an engineer can built it.

Homes of Heritage

From Doha's superb Museum of Islamic Art to the modern revival of Souq Waqif with falcons, gold, antiques and incense on sale, Doha works hard to preserve its proud Arabian heritage.

p209

Saudi Arabia

History
Landscapes
Islam

History

Listen to the wind whistling around the ruins at Madain Saleh, Saudi's little Petra, and you can almost hear the ancient camel caravans grumbling across the desolate gravel plains of Arabia.

Landscapes

The Rub al-Khali, or Empty Quarter, has inspired travellers for centuries, but lesser known are the spectacular beauties of the fertile Asir Mountains in southern Saudi Arabia.

Islam

You don't have to be a Muslim to appreciate the power of Mecca and Medina on the national consciousness: the message of the holy cities is held in the hearts of the Saudi people and is obvious in their dress, customs and manners.

p241

United Arab Emirates

Architecture
Urban Culture
Landscapes

Urban Landscape

Dubai's Burj al-Arab building with its magnificent dhow-sail design, Abu Dhabi's opulent Emirate Palace, a Formula One race track riddling the core of Yas Hotel, Sharjah's culture and heritage zones – these are a few of the UAE's many modern-day wonders.

Superlatives

The iconic Burj Khalifa, the world's tallest building at 828m, sharks swimming in the middle of a Dubai mall and free-roaming oryx on an island illustrate the UAE's 'yes we can' culture.

Back to Basics

Lesser known than its modern alter ego, the UAE's ancient character is defined by magnificent dunes and desert retreats in the oases of Liwa and the sands of Al Ain.

p284

Yemen

Landscapes
Old Towns
Architecture

Mountain Terraces

Stunning mountain scenery in the Haraz illustrates the husbandry of the land by generations of terrace-building farmers – although the addictive qat (a mildly narcotic plant) is beginning to get the better of both local men and their crops.

Original Skyscrapers

The high-rise dwellings of ancient Shibam, a 2500-year-old city in dusty Wadi Hadramawt, is a precursor if not an inspiration for the modern-day craze for the sky-high tower block.

Traditional Life

The narrow-laned, gossipy, sociable souq is still at the heart of old Sana'a, with its toppling mud houses resplendent with coloured-glass windows – a theme repeated in ancient towns throughout Yemen.

p362

On the Road

Bahrain بحرين

Includes ➡

Why Go?

Like an oyster, Bahrain's rough exterior takes some prising open, but it is worth the effort. From the excellent National Museum in Manama to the extraordinary burial mounds at Sar, there are many fine sites to visit.

The country has long been defined by its relationship with water. Meaning 'Two Seas' in Arabic, Bahrain's focus is not the island's minimal land mass, but the shallow waters that lap its shores. The sweet-water springs that bubble off-shore helped bring about 4000 years of settlement, the lay-ers of which are exposed in rich archaeological sites around the island. The springs also encouraged lustrous pearls – the trade that helped to build the island's early fortunes.

Much of Manama's modern wealth, illustrated in high-profile building projects, rises proudly from land 'reclaimed' from the sea. With the projected effects of global warming, however, the sea may yet have the last laugh.

Best for Culture

➡ Bahrain National Museum (p49)

➡ Qala'at al-Bahrain (p62)

➡ Beit Sheikh Isa Bin Ali (p66)

➡ Sar (p63)

➡ A'Ali (p63)

Best for Nature

➡ Al-Areen Wildlife Park & Reserve (p65)

➡ Hawar Islands (p68)

➡ Dar Island (p68)

➡ Tree of Life (p66)

When to Go
Bahrain

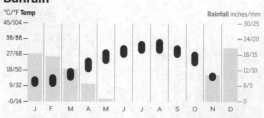

Nov–Mar Bask in the relative cool of a Gulf winter with daily blue skies.

Apr Join the ex-citement of life in the fast lane dur-ing the Formula One Grand Prix.

Apr Enjoy tradi-tional dancing at the annual Heritage Festival.

Daily Costs

Bahrain suits most pockets. With budget accommodation from US$70 (or less if you're prepared to share with dubious company!), cheap options for eating (around US$5) and free access to many of the main sites of interest, a minimum daily cost with transport comes to around US$120. This rises to US$170 if staying in midrange hotels and for a top-end hotel with car hire, US$350 is nearer the mark.

ITINERARIES

Stopover

Examine snapshots of the ancient and modern in **Bahrain National Museum** before wandering around the real thing in the wind-tower residences of neighbouring **Muharraq**. Share communal space with Islam at the giant **Al-Fatih Mosque** and pause for matters more corporal at one of Adliya's chic cafes. Get down and dirty in central Manama, drifting with street hawkers through **Bab al-Bahrain** and bargaining for local pearls in **Gold City**.

Three Days

After allowing day one for Manama, spend day two with the dead at **Bahrain Fort** and **Sar**. Admire the continuity with the ancient in the crafts of **Al-Jasra** and complete the burial circuit at **A'Ali** for sunset. Either pump up the pace on day three with a trip to the Formula One Racetrack or go slow at nearby **Al-Areen Wildlife Park & Reserve**.

For Expats

For those escaping the capital high life, cross the plains to the **Oil Museum** to see what the city's wealth is founded upon and visit the nearby **Tree of Life**, resting on even sparser foundations. If island fever sets in, dive off the edge with a nose-peg and sharp knife to collect pearls. Less painfully, take a weekend package to the **Hawar Islands** and ponder what a tidal rise of two inches might do to the islands' waistlines.

Essential Food & Drink

➡ **Makbus** Rice and spices with chicken, lamb or fish in sauce.

➡ **Rangena** Coconut cake.

➡ **Khabees** Dates in a variety of sizes, colours and states of ripeness.

➡ **Tap water** Safe to drink although most people stick to bottled water.

➡ **Alcohol** Available but discouraged through high tariffs.

➡ **Coffee** Any place called a 'coffeehouse' is usually a bar and intended for men only.

AT A GLANCE

➡ **Currency** Bahraini dinar (BD)

➡ **Mobile phones** SIM cards widely available

➡ **Money** ATMs widespread; credit cards widely accepted

➡ **Visas** Available on arrival for many nationalities

Fast Facts

➡ **Capital** Manama

➡ **Country code** 973

➡ **Language** Arabic (English widely spoken)

➡ **Official name** Kingdom of Bahrain

➡ **Population** 1.3 million

Exchange Rates

For current exchange rates see www.xe.com.

Australia	A$10	BD3.91
Euro zone	€10	BD4.87
Kuwait	KD1	BD1.34
Oman	OR1	BD0.98
Qatar	QR10	BD1.04
Saudi Arabia	SR10	BD1
UAE	Dh1	BD1.02
UK	UK£10	BD5.70
USA	US$10	BD3.77
Yemen	YR100	BD0.18

Resources

➡ **Al-Reem Tours** (www.alreem.com) A green site

➡ **Bahrain Tourism** (www.moc.gov.bh) Official site

➡ **Clickbahrain** (www.clickbahrain.com) Complete island guide

THE GULF

Muharraq · Bahrain International Airport
Beit Sheikh
Isa Bin Ali
③ Muharraq Island · Al-Hidd
Bahrain Fort
Karbabad
② ① Bahrain National Museum
Jidd Haffs
MANAMA
Juffair
Al-Budaiya · Mina Sulman
Bani Jamrah · Ad-Diraz
Jiddah Island
Al-Janabiya ④ Sar
Tubli Bay
King Fahd Causeway
A'Ali
Isa Town
Sitra
Al-Jasra
Umm al-Na'san
⑦ A'Ali
Hamad
Riffa
⑨ Dar Island
Awali
Jebel Lughaybirat (83m)
Al-Zallaq · 'Askar
Formula One ⑤ Racetrack
Jebel ad-Dukhan (134m)
⑩ Oil Museum
⑥ Al-Areen Wildlife Park & Reserve
Gulf of Bahrain
Ad-Dur
Al-Mamtalah
Ar-Rumaythah

N
0 ——————— 10 km
0 ——————— 5 miles

Hawar Islands ⑧

Bahrain Highlights

① Open the door on ancient Dilmun at **Bahrain National Museum** (p49).

② Take a 16th-century view of the sea from **Bahrain Fort** (p62).

③ Catch the whisper of a breeze under the windtowers of **Beit Sheikh Isa Bin Ali** (p66).

④ Visit **Sar** (p63) with its honeycombed burial chambers.

⑤ Sample life in the fast lane at Bahrain's **Formula One Racetrack** (p64).

⑥ Meet desert inhabitants at **Al-Areen Wildlife Park & Reserve** (p65).

⑦ Watch the sun set over the mysterious burial mounds of **A'Ali** (p63).

⑧ Wade with flamingos on the **Hawar Islands** (p68).

⑨ Dive from **Dar Island** (p68) and surface with pearls.

⑩ Visit the **Oil Museum** (p66), showcasing the foundation of Bahrain's modern wealth.

MANANA

منامة

POP 329,510

Manama means 'Sleeping Place', but with its central atmosphere, its late-night shopping, and its lively bars and nightclubs, it's hard to see when the city gets a chance to sleep. Manama is a night bird and people flock in on weekends for fine dining and an off-duty drink.

For those who prefer an early start to a late night, the city is sleepy enough by day, and it's unlikely there'll be much of a queue for the excellent Bahrain National Museum. That said, Manama's recent role as Arab City of Culture has led to a much greater emphasis on music, art and heritage events that has been of benefit to all.

History

On the face of it, Manama appears to be an entirely modern city, built quite literally from land reclaimed from the sea and typified by grand new building complexes such as the Bahrain World Trade Centre and the Financial Harbour. But appearances are deceptive and in fact Manama can trace its roots in Islamic chronicles as far back as AD 1345. In all likelihood, there were settlements on and around the best springs on the island for many centuries before that.

Invaded by the Portuguese in 1521 and then by the Persians in 1602, Manama then passed into the hands of Al-Khalifa, the current ruling family, in 1783. It became a free port in 1958 and the capital of independent Bahrain in 1971.

With a third of Bahrain's population living in the city, Manama continues to grow at a steady pace. A great way to gauge that growth is to enter the national museum and trace the myriad building projects across the satellite maps embedded into the floor. Together these projected public works, which include a soon-to-open 1000-seat National Theatre and a 'pearling pathway', make a fine foundation for the future of this easygoing city.

◉ Sights

All of Manama's main sights are located either along Al-Fatih Hwy or near (if not on) Government Ave. They are within an energetic walking distance of each other or a short taxi ride away. Note that opening hours change frequently – call in advance to avoid disappointment.

Walking between sights, you'll notice two sets of landmark buildings: the World Trade Centre with three wind turbines sandwiched between the segmented towers, and the gracefully sloping twin towers of the Financial Harbour. Completed before the global economic downturn of 2008, they have become symbols of the city's boom years and look spectacular when lit at night.

★ **Bahrain National Museum**   MUSEUM
(Map p54; ☑17 298 777; www.bnmuseum.com; Al Fatih Hwy; admission 500 fils; ⊗8am-8pm; ℗) Deserving its reputation as the most popular tourist attraction in Bahrain, the Bahrain National Museum is the best place to start for an intriguing, well-labelled introduction to the sights of the country. The museum, housed in a postmodern building with landscaping that brings the waterfront location up to the windows, showcases archaeological finds from ancient Dilmun. Among these finds are beautiful agate and carnelian beads and earthenware burial jars – used for the body as well as its chattels.

Don't miss the section on contemporary Bahraini culture – the reproduction souq on the 1st floor is particularly worth the stairs, as the barber could double for Sweeney Todd.

The museum also includes a wildlife hall, several gallery spaces used for contemporary exhibitions of art and sculpture, a shop selling Bahraini crafts, and a chic cafe. There's plenty to keep the family amused for several hours, but it will reward even a quick 10-minute visit and is particularly worthwhile if you want to gauge the progress of up-and-coming new attractions such as the national theatre, which is part of the museum complex.

Al-Fatih Mosque   MOSQUE
(Map p54; ☑17 727 773; www.alfateh.gov.bh; Al-Fatih Hwy; ⊗non-Muslims 9am-4pm Sun-Thu; ℗) A visitor wanting to learn more about Islam could not do better than to visit this grand mosque, with its informative guides. Built on reclaimed land in 1984, Al-Fatih Mosque is the largest building in the country and is capable of holding up to 7000 worshippers. The mosque was built with marble from Italy, glass from Austria and teak wood from India, carved by Bahraini craftspeople, and has some fine examples of interior design. The dedicated guides lead visitors through the mosque, explaining aspects of religious etiquette while pointing out special features of mosque architecture.

Bahrain

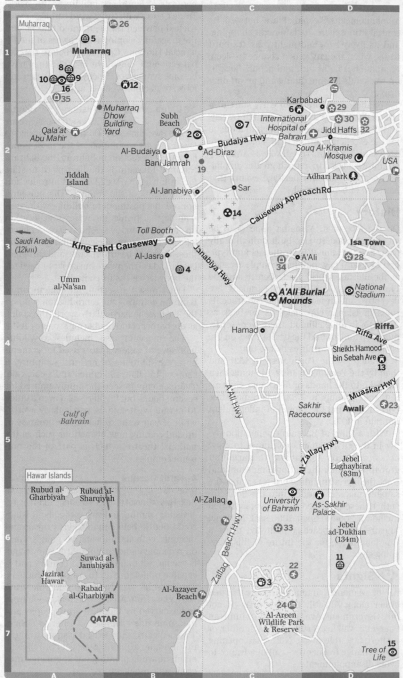

Muharraq

26

5 Muharraq

8 9
10 16
35

12

Qala'at Abu Mahir

Muharraq Dhow Building Yard

Subh Beach

2

Al-Budaiya

Bani Jamrah

Ad-Diraz

19

Al-Janabiya

Sar

7

Karbabad

6

29

30

32

International Hospital of Bahrain

Jidd Haffs

Souq Al-Khamis Mosque

27

USA

Adhari Park

Jiddah Island

14

Causeway Approach Rd

Saudi Arabia (12km)

King Fahd Causeway

Toll Booth

Al-Jasra

4

Janabiya Hwy

Umm al-Na'san

34

A'Ali

Isa Town

28

1 A'Ali Burial Mounds

National Stadium

Hamad

Riffa

Riffa Ave

Sheikh Hamood bin Sebah Ave

13

Gulf of Bahrain

A'Ali Hwy

Muaskar Hwy

Sakhir Racecourse

Awali

23

Al-Zallaq Hwy

Jebel Lughaybirat (83m)

Hawar Islands

Rubud al-Gharbiyah

Rubud al-Sharqiyah

Al-Zallaq

University of Bahrain

As-Sakhir Palace

Suwad al-Janubiyah

33

Jebel ad-Dukhan (134m)

Jazirat Hawar

Rabad al-Gharbiyah

QATAR

Zallaq Beach Hwy

22

11

Al-Jazayer Beach

3

24

20

Al-Areen Wildlife Park & Reserve

Tree of Life

15

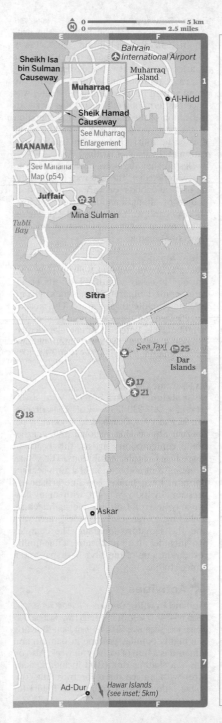

Bahrain

MANAMA FOR CHILDREN

Bahrainis welcome visiting children to their amenities, and a lively expat community means that kids are never short of something to do in Bahrain. Look out for a handy booklet published biannually called *Fab Bahrain*, available from bookshops, schools and Seef Mall. This free directory gives a full A–Z listing of what to do and where to go in Bahrain as a family, from the story-telling activities of 'Wriggly Readers' to waterskiing and wakeboarding. It also has an excellent website (www.fabbahrain.com).

The principal amusement area is Funland Bowling Centre (p52). An amusement park called **Kids Kingdom** (Map p54; King Faisal Corniche) has a few rides surrounded by the ongoing construction of the Financial Harbour projects.

Visitors begin their guided tour at the small library immediately to the right inside the main entrance, where women will be given a black cloak and headscarf to wear while visiting the prayer hall. Wearing shorts is prohibited. After the tour, visitors are welcome to free booklets in the *Discover Islam* series (published by the Muslim Educational Society of Bahrain), which help to dispel some of the commonly held misconceptions about Islam.

Beit al-Quran   MUSEUM
(Map p54; ☑ 17 290 101; Sheikh Hamad Causeway, access off Exhibition Ave; ☺ 9am-noon & 4-6pm Sat-Wed, 9am-noon Thu; ℗) With its wrapping of carved Kufic script, the distinctive Beit al-Quran is a fine example of modern Bahraini architecture. It houses a large and striking collection of Qurans, manuscripts and woodcarvings and functions as a good introduction to Islam in general, and Islamic calligraphy in particular. Look out for the miniature Qurans, the smallest of which (from 18th-century Persia) measures only 4.7cm by 3.2cm. The exhibits are well labelled in English and can be superficially perused within an hour. The bookshop in the foyer sells crafts. Visitors should dress conservatively. The building is next to the Bahrain Red Crescent Society, but the main entrance and car park are at the back. Tours are often organised – call ahead to check.

Bab al-Bahrain   MONUMENT
(Map p58; Government Ave) Built by the British in 1945, Bab al-Bahrain, the 'Gateway to Bahrain', was originally designed by Sir Charles Belgrave. It was redesigned in 1986 to give it more of an 'Islamic' flavour. The small square in front of the *bab* (gate) was once the terminus of the customs pier – an indication of the extent of land reclamation of the past two decades. The building now houses the Tourist Department (under renovation at the time of writing).

Despite having been moved back from the water's edge, the gateway is still aptly named, as goods of various description, people of all nationalities, street vendors, shoppers and workers pass under its arches in a constant pageant of activity in this, the heart of Manama.

Friday Mosque   MOSQUE
(Map p58; Government Ave) Built in 1938, this mosque is easily identifiable by its elaborately crafted minaret, the mosque's most interesting architectural feature. The mosque is reflected in the glass windows of the neighbouring Batelco Commercial Centre, providing a suggestive reflection of old and new Manama. The mosque is not open to tourists.

La Fontaine Centre
of Contemporary Art   GALLERY
(Map p54; ☑ 17 230 123; www.lafontaineartcentre. net; 92 Hoora Ave, Dhuwawdah; ☺ noon-10.30pm Tue-Sun) Showcasing regional and international contemporary artists, this beautiful space hosts regular exhibitions. The venue, a magnificent elaboration of a 19th-century Bahraini town house, is a fine artistic expression in its own right with many features typical of Gulf Islamic architecture, including covered colonnades, archways and the signature fountain. The complex also includes an amphitheatre, a fine-dining restaurant, one of the city's best spas and a dance studio.

🏃 Activities

Funland Bowling Centre   BOWLING, SKATING
(Map p54; ☑ 17 292 313; Al-Fatih Hwy, Marina Corniche; incl shoe hire BD2; ☺ 9am-1am) Bowling is a highly popular pastime in Bahrain and Funland is a hub of activity all week. Also on site is a skating rink (BD3 including skate hire) with an ice disco for travelling Travoltas – don't forget your white T-shirt for the ultraviolet lighting.

Dolphin Resort DOLPHIN WATCHING
(Map p54; ☎17 290 900; www.dpbahrain.com; Al-Fatih Hwy, Marina Corniche; adult/child BD4/2; ⊙3-11pm Mon-Sat) The arrival of dolphins and sea lions in Bahrain has been well received by Bahrainis who flock in large numbers to watch the daily 15-minute shows (check the website for current timings). The resort offers the chance to swim with the dolphins (BD20 per person) – call first to make an appointment.

Coral Bay BOAT TOUR
(Map p54; ☎17 312 700; http://coral-bay.net; Al-Fatih Hwy, Marina Corniche; ⊙9am-sunset Tue-Sun) Offering a wide range of water sports including short boat trips (BD5 per person), half- and full-day boat charter (BD175/325 including captain and soft drinks), jet skiing (BD20 for 30 minutes), waterskiing and banana boat, Coral Bay is one of the easiest ways to engage with the sea in Manama. Diving is also available (BD24 for a tank dive; BD65 for a PADI course). You can make a whole day of it at Coral Bay as there's a pleasant beach with facilities, Rayés (an excellent Lebanese restaurant) and Karma Lounge – a treat for serious nightclubbers.

Courses

Courses in traditional Bahraini and Arabic art and music are sometimes offered for a nominal fee by **Bahrain Arts Society** (Map p50; ☎17 590 551; www.bahartsociety.org.bh; Budayia Hwy). Arabic-language courses are run by **Berlitz** (☎17 827 847; www.berlitz-bahrain.com) for individual or group immersion.

Tours

Al-Reem Tours TOUR
(Map p54; ☎17 710 868; www.alreem.com; off Abdul Rahman Al-Dakhil Ave) If you're interested in ecotourism, it's well worth contacting Al-Reem Tours before your visit. This unique company specialises in environmental tours. It runs daily bird-watching and wildlife trips to remoter parts of the Hawar Islands and to the mainland desert. It also has a special six-day bird-watching package. Check the excellent website for more details.

Mathias Tourism TOUR
(☎17 786 484; www.mathiastours.com) One of the largest tour operators in Bahrain providing half- and full-day tours, including trips to the first oil well and Tree of Life.

Sleeping

There is a wide range of city accommodation on offer, particularly on or around Government Ave, in the heart of central Manama. Many of the budget and midrange hotels in this area entertain weekend visitors from Saudi Arabia – in more ways than one – so it may pay to spend a little more to enjoy one of the good-value, top-end hotels. Beautiful resort accommodation is available at the edges of the city, particularly on the causeway towards Muharraq Island and at Al-Seef, close to the shopping centre.

All of the budget hotels reviewed have air-con, TV (many with satellite) and a bathroom with hot water, but if you can stretch your budget to midrange, it's worth it.

Most of the midrange hotels listed have excellent-value rooms but you may never know it! If you are offered a carpetless broom cupboard, without windows, or a room overlooking the stairwell, ask to see another, or stipulate a room with a view.

Most of the top-end hotel prices listed include tax and breakfast.

Jindol Hotel HOTEL $
(Map p58; ☎17 227 227; www.jindolhotel.com; Municipality Ave; s/d BD15/25; 📶) If you manage to get beyond the tiny desk of this downtown hotel, the rooms and showers are clean and given an Arabic flourish.

Bahrain International Hotel HOTEL $
(Map p58; ☎17 211 313; www.bahrainhotel.com; Government Ave; s/d BD25/35; P📶) The curious mix of Parisian art deco (in the Al Banco Café) and the Lovely Gifts kiosk on the ground floor gives a certain character to the hotel but rooms vary widely from unacceptable with paper-thin walls, to comfortable and almost elegant with full-length drapes. Rockland Café Bar is a popular den.

City Centre Hotel HOTEL $
(Map p58; ☎17 229 979; www.city-centre-hotel.com; Government Ave; s/d BD25/35) This hotel has had its finger on the night-time pulse of Manama for years. The foyer doubles as a popular Lebanese restaurant that's always humming with locals, and the upper floors offer entertainment venues with a live band every night. As such, you'll be enticed to spend more time outside the room than in it – thankfully.

Adhari Hotel HOTEL $
(Map p58; ☎17 224 242; www.adhari-hotel.com; Municipality Ave; s/d BD25/35) The Adhari

Manama

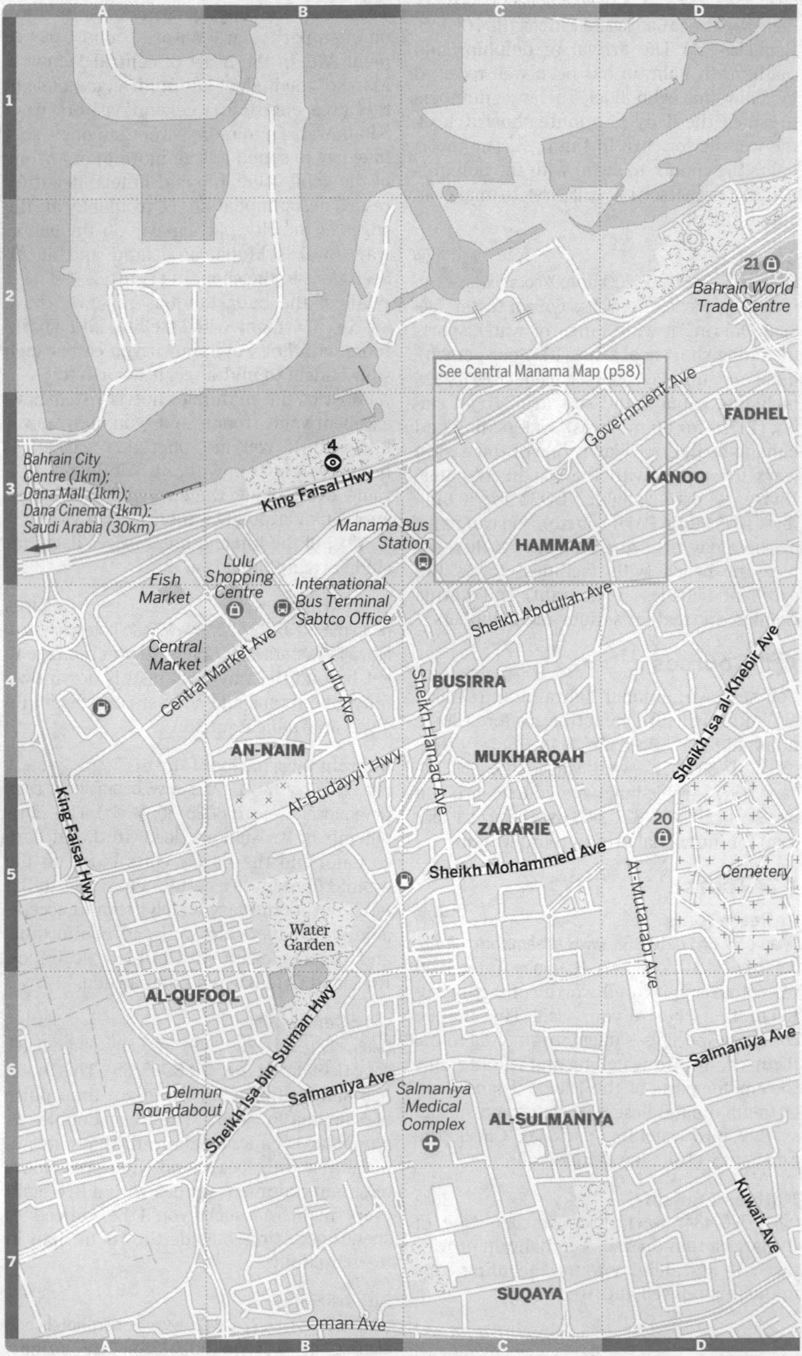

21 Bahrain World Trade Centre

FADHEL

See Central Manama Map (p58)

Government Ave

KANOO

Bahrain City Centre (1km);
Dana Mall (1km);
Dana Cinema (1km);
Saudi Arabia (30km)

4

King Faisal Hwy

Manama Bus Station

HAMMAM

Fish Market

Lulu Shopping Centre

International Bus Terminal Sabtco Office

Sheikh Abdullah Ave

Central Market

Central Market Ave

BUSIRRA

Lulu Ave

Sheikh Hamad Ave

AN-NAIM

Al-Budayyi' Hwy

MUKHARQAH

Sheikh Isa al-Khebir Ave

King Faisal Hwy

ZARARIE

20

Sheikh Mohammed Ave

Al-Mutanabi Ave

Cemetery

Water Garden

AL-QUFOOL

Sheikh Isa bin Sulman Hwy

Salmaniya Ave

Delmun Roundabout

Salmaniya Ave

Salmaniya Medical Complex

AL-SULMANIYA

Salmaniya Ave

Kuwait Ave

SUQAYA

Oman Ave

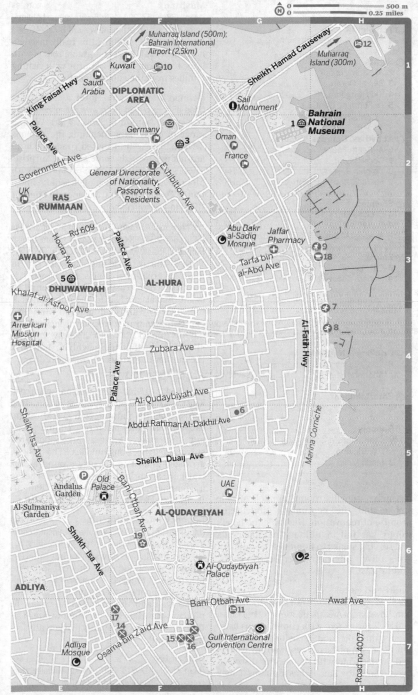

0 — 500 m
0 — 0.25 miles

Muharraq Island (500m);
Bahrain International
Airport (2.5km)

Sheikh Hamad Causeway

Muharraq
Island (300m)

12

Kuwait
10

King Faisal Hwy
Saudi
Arabia

DIPLOMATIC
AREA

Sail
Monument

Bahrain
National
Museum

1

Palace Ave

Germany

3

Oman

France

Government Ave

General Directorate
of Nationality,
Passports &
Residents

Exhibition Ave

UK

RAS
RUMMAAN

Abu Bakr
al-Sadiq
Mosque

Jaffar
Pharmacy

9

Rd 609

Hocia Ave

AWADIYA

Palace Ave

AL-HURA

Tarfa bin
al-Abd Ave

18

5

DHUWAWDAH

7

Khalaf al-Asfoor Ave

Al-Fatih Hwy

8

American
Mission
Hospital

Zubara Ave

Palace Ave

Al-Qudaybiyah Ave

Abdul Rahman Al-Dakhil Ave

6

Sheikh Isa Ave

Marina Corniche

Sheikh Duaij Ave

Andalus
Garden

Old
Palace

Bani Otbah Ave

UAE

Al-Sulmaniya
Garden

AL-QUDAYBIYAH

Shaikh Isa Ave

19

ADLIYA

Al-Qudaybiyah
Palace

2

Bani Otbah Ave

11

Awal Ave

17

13

Osama bin Zaid Ave

14

Adliya
Mosque

15

16

Gulf International
Convention Centre

Road no 4007

Manama

has noisy, no-frills rooms, a smell of stale smoke and the perennially undelivered promise of renovation. Hunter's, the hotel's trophy bar full of military paraphernalia and serving steaks to homesick US soldiers, gives a lively alternative perspective on the Middle East.

Gulf Pearl Hotel   HOTEL $$
(Map p58; ☎17 217 333; www.gulfpearl-manama.com; Government Ave; s/d BD30/40; @☀) Clean and well furnished, with commodious bathrooms, this is a good bachelor's choice. The 5th floor is supposedly reserved for women and families, but with its 1st-floor disco and lively Intensity Bar, it has dubious family appeal.

Mashtan   HOTEL $$
(Map p58; ☎17 224 466; www.mashtanhotelmanama.com; off Government Ave; s/d BD30/40; ☀) In a cavernous building, this really tasteless hotel has small but comfortable rooms with huge bathrooms. It's a favourite with visiting families from the subcontinent.

Delmon International Hotel   HOTEL $$
(Map p58; ☎17 224 000; www.delmonhotel.com; Government Ave; s/d BD35/45; ☎☀) With a range of seedy bars, including the dubious 'Diggers', the well-furnished rooms with giant mahogany beds come as some surprise. There's an excellent Arabic restaurant, with Moorish arches and cushioned sedans, and a family Friday brunch from noon to 5pm for BD10 in the coffeeshop.

★ Novotel Al-Dana Resort   RESORT $$$
(Map p54; ☎17 298 008; www.novotel.com; Sheikh Hamad Causeway; s/d from BD85/95; P☎☀) With distinctive style and character rare in many international hotels, the Novotel is built like a *qasr* (castle or palace) around elegant central courtyards, and punctuated at the edges by whimsical Bahraini wind towers. Commanding a wonderful view of the bay on Sheikh Hamad Causeway, you can almost forget that the neighbour has built the mother-of-all-tower-blocks next door.

Crowne Plaza   HOTEL $$$
(Map p54; ☎17 531 122; www.crowneplaza.com; King Faisal Hwy; s/d BD91/101; P☎☀) Situated across from the Bahrain National Museum, this low-rise hotel has a relaxed and pleasant atmosphere, with a large pool area surrounded by bougainvillea. The rooms, arranged almost motel-style around a central hub, are bright and attractive. There's a complimentary bus service to Bab al-Bahrain twice a day.

Regency InterContinental   HOTEL $$$
(Map p58; ☎17 227 777; www.intercontinental.com/manama; King Faisal Hwy; s/d BD95/105; P☎☀) In the middle of downtown but offering uptown accommodation, this old favourite has recently enjoyed a makeover. The hotel's contemporary black and grey elegance works well and the rooms make up for in pillows what they lack in window size. The Downtown Bar with nightly live jazz attracts the in-crowd.

Gulf Hotel   HOTEL $$$
(Map p54; ☎17 713 000; www.gulfhotelbahrain.com; Bani Otbah Ave; s/d BD98/108; ☎☀) De-

ⓘ IS BAHRAIN SAFE TO VISIT?

Until the Arab Spring of 2011 Bahrain had very little in the way of dangers and annoyances. With the possible exception of occasional greedy taxi drivers and the slightly nefarious nature of some of the city hotels, the worst that was likely to befall a visitor was a hangover or sunburn.

If truth be told, the same is pretty much the case today but what has changed dramatically is the *perception* of safety. With political tensions still running high at the time of writing, a ban on public demonstrations and distinguishable no-go areas around A'Ali and other towns outside the capital, there is an underlying feeling of unease. The slump in tourism will no doubt be exacerbated by the bombings in Manama in November 2012, injuring one and killing two Asian expatriates, and ongoing protests at the start of 2013.

As expert opinion suggests the political situation is likely to deteriorate, the best advice we can give to visitors is the following:

➡ monitor the situation in Bahrain through your consulate and the international media before booking your stay

➡ take local advice from the concierge at your hotel before venturing out

➡ avoid large gatherings of people

➡ restrict your visit to the main areas of tourist interest.

spite being 4km from the city centre, this veteran hotel is the most convenient for the Gulf International Convention Centre. With an extravagant foyer, velvet lounges and marble halls, the interior appears to belong to an Italian palazzo. The hotel's proximity to the most popular Western expat eating haunts of Adliya is an added bonus.

Movenpick Hotel Bahrain HOTEL $$$
(Map p50; ☑ 17 460 000; www.moevenpick-hotels. com; Muharraq Town; s/d BD100/112; P 🎧 🕿) It's usually hard to recommend a hotel near the airport but with the chain's usual inimitable feel for a landscape, this is one airport hotel that comes highly recommended. Built around an infinity pool that overlooks the tidal waters of the Gulf, the hotel whispers 'holiday' from the front door. Breakfast is not included.

Ritz-Carlton Bahrain
Hotel & Spa RESORT $$$
(Map p50; ☑17 588 000; www.ritzcarlton.com; Al-Seef; s/d from BD149/174; 🎧 🕿) Undoubtedly Bahrain's most luxurious and opulent hotel, boasting its own private beach and secluded island, though some may find the dark, polished interior of black marble and gilt-edged furniture oppressive and pretentious. The service is faultless, but staff are unfriendly. Nonetheless, if yours is a Bentley, you'll be in good company and the Friday brunch is worth saving your appetite for.

✗ Eating

There is a wide selection of restaurants in Manama to satisfy every palate, from a Full Monty of an English breakfast to a plate of French oysters overlooking the bay. For a good listing of what's on offer, it's worth getting hold of *TimeOut Bahrain* (www.time-outbahrain.com).

Quick eats are widespread with shwarma stands along Bani Otbah Ave in Adliya and in the centre of Manama (around the back of Bab al-Bahrain and in the souq). The large turnover of customers ensures the freshness of the snack.

There's a vibrant cafe culture in Manama, centred particularly on the Adliya district in the southeastern part of the city near the Convention Centre. The diverse venues offer a range of cuisines from breakfast to dinner and serve all day as popular meeting places. A stroll round this small and partly pedestrian district is a sure way to find your favourite flavours.

Charcoal Grill KEBAB $
(Map p58; Bab al-Bahrain; mains BD1.500-2.900; ⊙12.30-11pm) Plain, simple and clean, the meals in this no-frills grill are nonetheless spiced up by the panorama of life in the heart of the city. Tuck into a mixed grill while watching a procession of hawkers, streetwalkers, lurkers, shirkers and tourists as they cruise by the city's famous gate.

Central Manama

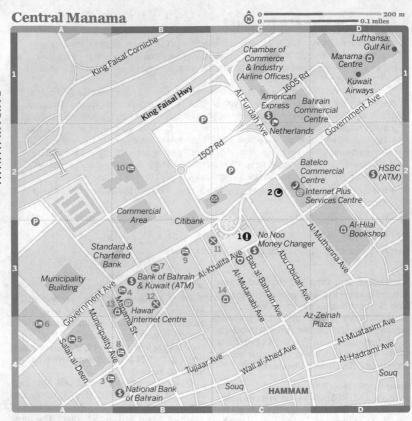

Habara Snacks & Fish
FISH & CHIPS **$**

(Map p54; ☑ 17 715 461; Osama bin Zaid Ave, Adliya; mains BD1.500-2.500; ☺ 8am-11pm) Staffed by cheerful men from Kerala, this nice little diner serves tasty fish and good fresh juices. If carrot with ice cream doesn't appeal, pop into Al-Jazeera supermarket next door for pudding.

Maria Corner
SHWARMA **$**

(Map p58; Al-Khalifa Ave; roll-up sandwiches 350 fils; ☺ 12.30-11.30pm) Near the rear of Bahrain International Hotel, this quick-eat establishment is safe for a roll-up sandwich and a mixed-fruit juice. There's no charge for the ringside view of life behind Government Ave.

Jim's
BRITISH **$$**

(Map p54; ☑ 17 710 654; Road No 3808, Adliya; breakfasts BD6, mains from BD8.500; ☺ 11am-midnight Thu-Sat, 11am-3pm & 6pm-midnight Sun-Wed) If you're British and homesick this place might cheer you up with regular roasts and a cosy cottage interior. It serves a 'Full Monty' breakfast on Friday with home-cooked eggs, bacon and black pudding. With a convivial atmosphere and legendary homemade chocolate vodkas, Jim's is popular with Western expats, so it's worth booking. The chef from Delhi serves up a curry just how the British love them!

The Conservatory
CAFE **$$**

(Map p54; ☑ 17 712 917; off Osama bin Zaid Ave, Adliya; high teas from BD10; ☺ 8.30am-6pm Sat-Thu; ☑) One of the oldest cafes in Manama, this place has earned a fine reputation for its excellent high teas and homely atmosphere. Step through the door of the town house and it feels like stepping into a secret garden. Good breakfasts too! Located behind Al-Jazeera Supermarket.

Rayés
LEBANESE **$$**

(Map p54; ☑ 17 312 700; www.coral-bay.net; Al-Fatih Hwy, Marina Corniche; mains BD4-BD14; ☺ noon-

Central Manama

lam) In one of the most attractive places to sample Lebanese food, right by the water's edge in the Coral Bay complex. The chef prides himself on the variety of the salads and cold mezze and the bread is baked on the premises. Buffets are offered from Thursday to Saturday and live Arabic music contributes to the convivial Middle Eastern atmosphere.

Café Lilou CAFE $$
(Map p54; ✆17 / 714 440; Yousef Ahmed Alshawi Ave, Adliya; lunches from BD12; ⊙8am-10.30pm Sat-Tue, to 11pm Wed-Fri; ⎘) This elegant balconied venue, with its velvet upholstery, wrought-iron banisters and polished wood floors, is reminiscent of a 19th-century Parisian brasserie and is the place for a trendy breakfast or a healthy lunch. Leave room for a signature handmade pastry (from BD2.100). It's located behind the Gulf Hotel, Adliya.

⭐ **Mezzaluna** INTERNATIONAL $$$
(Map p54; ✆17 742 999; Adliya; mains BD9.500; ⊙6-11.30pm Sat-Fri; ⎘) If you're looking for that 'somewhere special' but don't want to lose sight of the country you're in, then you can't do better than the atmospheric and sophisticated Mezzaluna. Occupying a stylish Bahraini courtyard house in a small

backstreet, the high-ceilinged restaurant is undoubtedly one of the best in Manama. It offers an international menu with an excellent wine list. Book to avoid disappointment. Signs show the way from neighbouring main roads.

La Fontaine INTERNATIONAL $$$
(Map p54; ✆17 230 123; www.lafontaineartcentre. net; 92 Hoora Ave; mains from BD10; ⊙noon-3pm & 6-11.30pm Tue-Sun; ⎘) ⎗ This fashionable restaurant, in the outstanding renovation project of La Fontaine Centre of Contemporary Art, is a magical place to enjoy dinner – in the illuminated courtyard in winter months. In the summer, the glass panel walls help capture the sense of this being a garden venue with the name-giving fountain in full view. The stunning architecture almost steals the show from the competent international dishes!

Self-Catering

Dozens of grocery stores (cold stores) are dotted around the residential areas, and are usually open from about 7am to 10pm. The French franchise Geant has a giant store in Bahrain Mall. Head to **Al-Jazeera Supermarket** (Osama bin Zaid Ave) or for fruit, spices, vegetables and meat, try the Central Market; for fish there's the Fish Market (no surprises here) – or a hook over the side, anywhere along the corniche, should do it.

🍸 Drinking & Nightlife

All top-end hotels have sophisticated bar areas, often with jazz or other live music, and usually featuring a 'happy hour' or cut-price cocktails. These include the generic **Clipper Room** (Map p58; Regency InterContinental, King Faisal Hwy), the bizarrely thematic **Sherlock Holmes** (Map p54; Gulf Hotel, Bani Otbah Ave) and the Polynesian-themed **Trader Vic's** (Map p50; Ritz-Carlton Bahrain Hotel & Spa, Alseef). There are bars in most of the midrange hotels too, but these can range from cosy to positively dire. The **Rockland Café Bar** (Map p58; Bahrain International Hotel, Government Ave) is one of the better ones.

Laialy Zaman CAFE
(Map p54; ✆17 293 097; Marina Corniche) One of the surprisingly few places to enjoy a sea view, this is an excellent place to catch the breeze, have tea and puff an apricot *sheesha*.

Hunter's Bar THEME BAR
(Map p58; ✆17 224 242; Adhari Hotel) Stepping into this bar is like walking back into 1970s

ⓘ WATER: SAFE TO DRINK?

Flouride is often considered to be a beneficial element of water, but in Bahrain you can get too much of a good thing – as the parlous state of teeth among the elderly testifies.

The abundant natural spring water contains double the normal levels of fluoride, which can lead to a disease called fluorosis. The condition is associated with a staining of the teeth and a fusion of bones, particularly of the spine.

Studies have revealed that many of the inhabitants of Bahrain's burial chambers suffered from the same disease. Since the installation of modern water-treatment techniques, fluorosis is thankfully becoming a thing of the past, however, and both tap and mineral water is now safe to drink.

'Nam: you expect the DJ to bellow above the rock music 'Good Morning, Bah-ha-rayn'. It's periodically packed with US military on R&R in the Gulf, so there's something rather poignant about the sober gloom when it's empty.

Nightclubs

Serious nightclubbers should pick up *Time-Out Bahrain* (www.timeoutbahrain.com) or consult the English-language newspapers to track down the in-crowd. The coolest nightspots at the time of research included the Karma Lounge (p53) at Coral Bay, which hosts international DJs, and **JJ's** (Map p54; ☑17 742 323; Road No 2607, Al-Bustan Hotel, off Bani Otbah Ave, Adliya), an old Bahrain favourite with Irish roots.

☆ Entertainment

To find out what's going on around Bahrain, see the 'What's On' listings of the *Gulf Daily News*, the *Bahrain this Month* magazine or *TimeOut Bahrain*, all of which are available in bookshops.

Cinemas

Show times often change, so check www.timeoutbahrain.com/films for current timings. Cinemas usually open around 10am and close at 1am. Tickets cost about BD3.

Dana Cinema (Map p50; ☑17 558 558; Sheikh Khalifa bin Sulman Hwy, Dana Mall) and **Al-Seef Cineplex** (Map p50; ☑17 582 220; Al-Seef Mall) regularly screen recent Western films.

Programs are advertised in the English-language newspapers. Special films are also shown at the Bahrain National Museum (p49) Sunday evening and the **Alliance Française de Bahrain** (Map p50; Building 51, Avenue 4109, opposite the Ministry of Education Hall, Isa Town; ⏱ evening Wed).

The Bahrain **Cinema Club** (Map p50; ☑17 725 959; Juffair Ave, Juffair, southern Manama) features Arabic and foreign films. All films are subtitled in English. For film lists and screening times, check the English-language newspapers or call the club for information about these popular events. It's next to Bahrain Archaeological Society.

Live Music

Bahrain International Exhibition Centre (Map p50; ☑17 558 800; www.bahrainexhibitions.com; Sheikh Khalifa bin Sulman Hwy) Often has recitals of Bahraini music.

🛍 Shopping

From markets to malls, central Manama has heaps of shopping opportunities – from characterful souqs to modern complexes, such as **Moda Mall** (Map p54; King Faisal Hwy, World Trade Centre) that are a showcase for designer outlets. Other malls include **Dana Mall** (Map p50; Sheikh Khalifa bin Sulman Hwy) and **Al-Seef Mall** (Map p50; Sheikh Khalifa bin Sulman Hwy), on opposite sides of Sheikh Khalifa bin Sulman Hwy and a short taxi ride into the suburbs. The giant Bahrain City Centre, also in Seef, is the biggest of the malls.

For regional souvenirs (most of which are imported from Yemen, India, Pakistan and Iran), there are many shops selling silver jewellery, brass coffee pots, lapis lazuli and coral beads, carpets and kilims in the streets of Adliya district (near the Gulf Hotel and Convention Centre), especially along Osama bin Zaid Ave.

Manama Souq   SOUVENIRS
(Map p58; behind Bab al-Bahrain; ⏱9am-1pm & 4-9pm Sat-Thu, 4-9pm Fri) Manama Souq, in the warren of streets behind Bab al-Bahrain, is the place to go for electronic goods, bargain T-shirts, nuts, spices, *sheesha* bottles and a plethora of other Bahraini essentials.

Bahrain Arts Society   ARTS & CRAFTS
(Map p50; ☑17 590 551; www.bahartsociety.org.bh; Budaiya Hwy) Just one of the many centres promoting local art and artists.

DON'T MISS

PEARLS

A highlight of shopping in Bahrain is looking for pearls. Pearls are created when grit enters the shell of, most usually, an oyster. The intrusive irritant is covered with a layer of mother-of-pearl, making it smooth and less irksome, and the longer the problem is nursed, the bigger it gets. Large pearls have attracted large sums of money throughout history but while size counts, it's not everything. Other factors taken into consideration are the depth and quality of lustre, perfection of shape and the colour, which ranges from peach to iron.

Commercial pearling was halted with the pioneering (in Japan) of the cultured pearl in the 1930s. Created through the artificial injection of a bead into the shell of an oyster, cultured pearls are more uniform and created more quickly. Nonetheless, at the heart of the gem is a piece of plastic.

In Bahrain, on the other hand, natural pearls are still garnered from the island's healthy oyster beds in a revival of this heritage industry. Occasionally, the sea bed renders up the larger, uniquely coloured pearls that once made the area so famous, but more usually, Bahraini pearl jewellery features clusters of tiny, individually threaded, ivory-coloured pearls, set in 21 carat gold.

Visit the gold shops of central Manama to see how pearls continue to inspire local jewellers. A perfect pearl can fetch thousands of dollars but a pair of cluster earrings or a ring can start at a reasonable US$100. Prices for pearl jewellery are more or less fixed but there's no harm in asking for a discount for oyster shells (US$60 including growing pearl – or free for those willing to dive for their own).

Crafts Centre Gallery and Workshop CRAFT (Map p54; ☑17 254 688; 263 Sheikh Isa al-Khebir Ave; ☺8am-2pm Sun-Thu) Home to a variety of studios and workshops, promoting the contemporary revival of traditional crafts, such as weaving, palm-leaf papermaking, pottery and ironwork. All the work is for sale.

Gold City JEWELLERY (Map p58; Government Ave) Bahrain is the only country in the world to sell almost exclusively natural pearls. While the odd imported, artificial pearl creeps in, shop owners are very quick to tell you which ones are and which ones are not genuine, natural Bahraini pearls; when it comes to Bahrain's most famous heritage item, it is more than their license is worth to mislead the customer.

ℹ Information

EMERGENCY
Ambulance, Fire & Police (☑999)

INTERNET ACCESS
There are many internet centres scattered around Manama.

Hawar Internet Centre (Manama St; per hour 400 fils; ☺8am-1am) Centrally located alongside Gold City, this facility has voice chat with webcam.

Internet Plus Services Centre (Government Ave, 1st fl, Batelco Commercial Centre; per hour 500 fils; ☺8am-8pm)

MEDICAL SERVICES
Medical treatment is easy to obtain in Bahrain and the standard of care is high. Medical services or supplies are available at the following facilities:

American Mission Hospital (☑17 253 447; www.amh.org.bh; Sheikh Isa al-Khebir Ave) Over 100 years old, this is the oldest and smallest hospital in Manama, but it is well equipped.

International Hospital of Bahrain (☑17 598 222; www.ihb.net; just off Budaiya Hwy)

Jaffar Pharmacy (☑17 291 039; Tarfa bin al-Abd Ave; ☺24hr) Located near McDonald's, off Exhibition Ave.

Salmaniya Medical Complex (☑17 288 888; Salmaniya Ave) Emergency treatment is available for residents and expats at a nominal fee of BD3.

MONEY
There are a number of banks and money changers on Government Ave between Bab al-Bahrain and the Delmon International Hotel. There are ATMs at most banks including HSBC.

American Express (Al-Furdah Ave, ABN-Amro Bank Bldg; ☺7.30am-3pm Sun-Thu) Exchanges currency.

No Noo Money Changer (behind Bab al-Bahrain Ave) Don't be put off by the name; this establishment has grown from a hole in the wall to a fully fledged office. It still keeps late but unspecified hours.

POST

Central Post Office (Government Ave, opposite Bab al-Bahrain Ave; ⊙7am-7.30pm Sat-Thu) Poste restante facilities are available.

TELEPHONE

There are phone booths and payphones for local and international calls located all over the city. **Batelco Commercial Centre** (☑17 881 111; www.batelco.com.bh; Government Ave) International calls can also be made from here.

TOURIST INFORMATION

Tourist information can be obtained at the airport and on the causeway between Saudi Arabia and Bahrain. The Tourist Department is more of an administrative rather than information centre. Hotels, *TimeOut* guides and the **ClickBahrain** (www.clickbahrain.com) website provide the best information.

ⓘ Getting There & Away

AIR

Most airline offices are situated around Bab al-Bahrain, in the Chamber of Commerce & Industry building, or inside the Manama Centre, which is where you'll find Gulf Air (p76), the main national carrier.

Bahrain International Airport (☑17 321 013, flight information 17 339 339; www.bahrainairport.com; Muharraq Island) is one of the busiest airports in the Gulf.

ⓘ Getting Around

TO/FROM THE AIRPORT

The airport is on Muharraq Island, approximately 6km from central Manama. A metered taxi from central Manama to the airport should cost about BD4. For trips *from* the airport there is a BD2 surcharge. Many hotels offer a shuttle-bus service.

There are ATMs for a range of bank cards, including Amex, in the transit lounge of the airport; and car-hire outlets in the arrivals hall.

BUS

Most people get around town by car or taxi, despite there being a rudimentary bus service. The bus system is largely designed for the use of expat construction workers and routes seldom relate to tourist destinations. Locals consider the use of buses rather eccentric but if you are determined to, then call into the **Manama bus station** (Government Ave) for ad hoc information.

TAXI

Taxis are easy to find, and there are taxi stands outside Bab al-Bahrain and many hotels. Taxis in Bahrain have meters and the flag fall is BD1 for the first 2km. Thereafter the meter ticks over in increments of 200 fils for every subsequent kilo-metre. Fares officially increase by 25% between 10pm and about 6am. For a better guarantee of meter use, try **Radio Taxis** (☑17 682 999). Alternatively, for a far more comfortable experience, try **Bahrain Limo** (☑toll free 17 266 266), which charges BD1.200 for 2km and 250 fils per each half-kilometre thereafter.

AROUND BAHRAIN ISLAND

Although dominated by its capital city, there's more to Bahrain Island than Manama, as those coming for the Grand Prix are sure to discover. The island is particularly rich in archaeological sites. Bahrain is small so the main sights make easily accessible day trips from the capital by car, and some can even be visited by bus. It's hard to get lost, because all road signs point to Saudi!

Bahrain Fort Complex   قلعة البحرين

◎ Sights

★ **Qal'at al-Bahrain**   ARCHAEOLOGICAL SITE (⊙8am-8pm; P; ⊑5 from Manama, then half-hour walk) A 10-minute drive from central Manama, and standing guard on an ancient tell (a mound created by centuries of urban rebuilding) overlooking the northern coast, Bahrain Fort was built by the Portuguese in the 16th century as part of a string of defences along the Gulf. The moated fort is particularly attractive at night, when the surrounding history of the site seems to rise out of the excavations and linger between the floodlights.

The site was occupied from about 2800 BC and there are seven layers of history represented in the digs surrounding the fort, including the remnants of two earlier forts.

The fort is well signposted about 5km west of Manama. There is no public transport directly to the site.

Fort Museum   MUSEUM (Map p50; Bahrain Fort; admission 500 fils; ⊙8am-8pm Tue-Sun; P) This excellent museum helps bring Bahrain Fort alive. How can you fail to enjoy exhibits labelled 'Looking for a Tylos Necropolis?'. Displays about snake bowl sacrifices and stamp seals from the Dilmun period help unravel some of the complexities of a site that spans nearly 5000 years.

WORTH A TRIP

ARCHAEOLOGICAL SITES NEAR MANAMA

For archaeology enthusiasts with a keen imagination, it's worth visiting **Barbar** (Map p50; suggested donation BD1; ☺ daylight hours), a complex of 2nd- and 3rd-millennium BC temples, dedicated to Enki, the God of Wisdom and the Sweet Water From Under the Sea. The excavated complex can be seen from a series of walkways; a detailed map (such as *In Bahrain: A Heritage Explored* by Angela Clark) or a knowledgeable tour guide are needed to make sense of the site. Nearby **Ad-Diraz Temple** (Map p50; ☺ daylight hours) FREE also dates from the 2nd millennium BC.

The two temple sites are best visited on a guided tour. There is no public transport but the the sites are signposted along Budaiya Hwy from Manama (but not if you're driving in the other direction) near the village of Bani Jamrah. The village is famous for **textile weaving** and workshops sell handloomed cloth.

🍴 Eating

Museum Café   CAFE
(Map p50; Bahrain Fort; ☺ 10.30am-7pm) With the best sea view on the island, this cafe's terrace is a magical place to sit with a divine cake from nearby Le Chocolat Gourmet Bakery and watch the mudflats bubble with lowlife.

A'Ali   عالي

POP 57,000

A'Ali is distinguished by the extraordinary burial mounds that surround the town. At the time of writing, the area had also acquired something of a reputation for unrest and there was a heavy police presence and roadblocks restricting access. Ask locally before venturing out and be guided by the advice of your taxi driver: if he won't go there, then perhaps neither should you!

⊙ Sights

★ **A'Ali Burial Mounds**   ARCHAEOLOGICAL SITE
(Map p50; daylight hours; P) To gain an idea of the significance of the **burial mounds** that dominate the approach to A'Ali, it's worth spending time at the Bahrain National Museum in Manama beforehand. The mounds, which date from the Dilmun period, encase burial chambers used for all members of society, young and old.

At 15m in height and 45m in diameter, the tallest of the mounds are referred to as the 'Royal Tombs'. It's easy to see why they deserve the name, as they give A'Ali, a scruffy town of potters and bakers, a regal presence.

From Manama, take the Sheikh Sulman Hwy south past Isa Town, then turn west along A'Ali Hwy and follow the signs to the mounds; the journey takes 20 minutes by car. Keep your eyes open either side of the highway for other burial mounds: there are more than 100,000 of them in Bahrain. An erratic bus service links Manama and A'Ali.

Pottery Workshop   CRAFT
(Map p50; ☺ 9am-1pm & 4pm-6pm Sat-Thu) A'Ali is the site of Bahrain's best-known pottery workshop and ceramics are on sale at several stalls nearby. Look out for the votive display of curiosities in the workshop and the traditional mudbricked kilns. In kilns of a different kind, flat bread is baked in traditional ovens nearby.

A'Ali townsfolk seem to be fond of their pigeons – there are some elaborate dovecotes around town, particularly near the pottery.

Sar   سار

The excavations at Sar have revealed a honeycomb of **burial chambers** (Map p50; ☺ daylight hours) dating from the Dilmun period. They have all long since been plundered, but the systematic removal of the coping stones has at least revealed the inner sanctum of the site and there is still a feeling that this is 'hallowed ground'. When excavations are finished, there are plans to turn the site into a major tourist attraction, including a museum. For now, while the explanatory heritage board is not very illuminating, there is a special privilege in being able to wander unchecked among the cradles of the dead.

Although the site is visible from the main road, there is no access from the Causeway Approach Rd. Instead, follow signs for the village of Sar, heading south from Budaiya Hwy, or from Janabiya Hwy, and then look for heritage signs that lead to the site. Sar is 10km from Manama. There's no public transport.

King Fahd Causeway معبر الملك فهد

There is something immensely evocative about a border and there could be few more impressive heralds of a border than the 26km causeway that links Saudi Arabia with Bahrain. Built in a series of humpbacked rises and long flat stretches across the shallows of the Gulf, this remarkable piece of engineering, completed in 1986 at a cost of US$1.2 billion, is worth a visit just to marvel at the construction. On either side of an island, roughly in the middle of the causeway, are two observation towers that invite visitors as close to the border as visas allow. For an egg roll-up and chips while watching the sun dip behind the Saudi mainland at sunset, try the King Fahd Causeway Restaurant (☑17 690 674; admission 500 fils; ⊘ 9am-11pm), halfway up the tower on the Bahraini side. Leave enough time to queue for the tiny lift that services the viewing platform near the top of the tower. From there it's possible to see the 26km, four-lane causeway in full, with its 12,430m of viaducts and its five separate bridges, all made from 350,000 sq metres of concrete and reinforced by 147,000 tonnes of steel.

All drivers (and passengers in taxis) must pay a toll at a toll booth (per vehicle BD2) along the Causeway Approach Rd, whether going to Saudi or not. The island in the middle of the causeway is 25km from Manama and it takes 30 minutes to drive there.

Al-Jasra الجسرة

A pleasant, leafy suburb, Al-Jasra is most often visited for the handicraft centre. It is worth sparing some extra time to amble past villas and small, private plantations to gain a feel of this typical Bahraini community.

◉ Sights

Al-Jasra House　HISTORIC BUILDING
(Map p50; ☑17 611 454; admission 500 fils; ⊘ 9am-6pm Sat-Thu, 3-6pm Fri; ℗) One of several historic homes around Bahrain that has been restored to its original condition, Al-Jasra House was built in 1907 and is famous as the birthplace in 1933 of the former emir, Sheikh Isa bin Sulman al-Khalifa. It is constructed in the traditional way from coral stone, supported by palm-tree trunks. The gravel in the courtyard is made up of a 'hundreds and thousands' mixture of tiny mitre

and auger shells. Opening times are erratic, so call ahead to confirm.

From the Causeway Approach Rd, look for the exit to Al-Jasra (before the toll booth); the house is well signposted. The town is 15km from Manama and takes 20 minutes to travel by bus or car.

Al-Jasra Handicraft Centre　HANDICRAFTS
(Map p50; ☑17 611 900; ⊘ 10am-4pm Sat, 8am-2pm Sun-Thu) In the residential area of Al-Jasra is the government-run Al-Jasra Handicraft Centre. This collection of workshops specialises in textiles, woodwork and basket weaving. Bus 12 from Manama stops outside, so this is one destination reasonably accessible by public transport, but timings are unreliable.

Riffa Fort قلعة ريفا

Commanding the only piece of high ground overlooking the Hunanaiya Valley, this **fort** (Sheikh Salman bin Ahmad Al-Fatih Fort; Map p50; ☑17 322 549; admission 500 fils; ⊘ 8am-2pm Sun-Wed, 9am-6pm Thu & Sat, 3-6pm Fri) was originally built in the 19th century. It was completely restored in 1983. The limited captions and explanations are in Arabic, and the rooms are mostly empty, but it's interesting enough and the views over a valley of a golf course, nodding donkeys and tree-lined highways is appealing.

The fort is easy to spot from several main roads near the town of Riffa and is well signposted. Access to the fort is only possible along Sheikh Hamood bin Sebah Ave, which is off Riffa Ave. Riffa is 25km from Manama and a 30-minute ride by car. Along the journey, note all the magnificent avenues of palms, orange-flowering cordias and topiaried citrus trees that line the suburban part of the highways.

Bahrain International Circuit

The distinctive Al-Sakhir Tower of the **Formula One Racetrack** (Map p50; ☑17 450 000; www.bahraingp.com; tours BD6; ⊘ 10am & 2pm Sun, Tue & Thu) rises above the surrounding desert like a beacon. If you are curious to see what a state-of-the-art race track looks like, then join a 40-minute tour of the grounds, including the media centre and race control room, and even take a lap around the circuit. Tours are offered every Sunday, Tuesday and Thursday; you can book online.

There are also opportunities to see drag racing at the circuit and to experience four-wheel driving (BD12 for 25-minute ride; BD65 for self-drive). Go-carting (BD10 for 15-minute drive) is available daily.

From Manama, just about all roads point to the circuit. The circuit is 30km from Manama and it takes around 35 minutes to get there by car. There is no public transport.

Al-Areen العرين

Al-Areen was once little more than empty desert with a few forlorn native species roaming inside some random enclosures. Over the past few years, however, the escarpment has been transformed into a major tourist attraction with the arrival of the wildlife reserve, a resort and spa, and a water park.

Al-Areen's attractions are signposted off the Zallaq Hwy, 35km from Manama (40 minutes by car). There is no public transport.

◉ Sights & Activities

Al-Areen Wildlife
Park & Reserve   WILDLIFE RESERVE
(Map p50, ☑ 17 845 480, www.alareen.bh; off Zallaq Hwy; adult/child BD1/500 fils; ◷ 8am-6pm Sat-Thu, 1-6pm Fri; ℗) ❡ This interesting 10 sq km reserve, in the southwest of the island, is a conservation area for species indigenous to the Middle East and North Africa. After a short introductory film (in Arabic only), a small bus leaves roughly every hour for a tour (with commentary in Arabic and English) past some of the 240 species of birds and mammals housed in the park. There are several herds of mature oryx with fabulous horns that make it easy to appreciate, firstly, how this gracious animal could be mistaken for a unicorn and, secondly, what an enviable choice of national animal it makes.

As the park is prone to changing its opening times at regular intervals, it's best to check the website before heading out.

Lost Paradise of
Dilmun Water Park   WATER PARK
(Map p50; ☑ 17 84 5100; www.lpodwaterpark.com; off Zallaq Hwy; adult/child BD15/7; ◷ 10am-6pm Wed-Mon) With dozens of water-themed amenities, including slides, fountains and a wave pool, you can hear the squeals of delight for miles. There's even a sandy beach.

Al-Jazayer Beach   BEACH
About a five- to 10-minute drive west from the Lost Paradise of Dilmun Water Park is

CIRCUIT FACT FILE

With more than a billion people in worldwide audiences, the highlight of Bahrain's sporting calendar is undoubtedly the Grand Prix. Authorities insist on a respect for local sensibilities so winners are sprayed not with champagne but with *warrd*, made from locally grown pomegranate and rosewater, and pit girls wear Gulf outfits rather than hotpants. The magnificent Arabian-style stadium, 'tented' grandstands and allusions to the country's wind towers make a fine showcase for modern Bahrain as well as the sport. Below are the 'fast facts' to date:

Where A 30-minute drive south of Manama.

When Completed in 2004.

How much US$150 million.

How many workers Over 1000 people employed to build the venue.

How many hours An estimated 3.5 million hours of work clocked up on the project.

Capacity of stadium 70,000 people.

Number of tracks Six, including a 1.2km drag strip and a 2km test oval.

Barriers A total of 4100m of tyre barriers using 82,000 tyres around the circuit.

First winner Michael Schumacher for Ferrari.

Al-Jazayer beach, which has shady palm trees and reasonable swimming, though the water, like the entire coast of Bahrain, is very shallow.

🛏 Sleeping

Al-Areen Palace & Spa   RESORT $$$
(Map p50; ☑ 17 845 000; www.alareenpalace.com; Al-Areen; s/d from BD335/355; ℗ 🛜 🛋) When the sun sets in the descending pools of the resort's inner courtyards, it is obvious why the resort was built on the country's only elevated ground. The atmosphere is hallowed and apart from the soft-slippered masseurs padding from the spa to poolside, there's little to interrupt the sense of exclusive calm.

Tree of Life شجرة الحياة

And the Lord God planted a garden eastward in Eden; and there He put the man whom He had formed. And out of the ground made the Lord God to grow every tree that is pleasant to the sight, and good for food; the tree of life also in the midst of the garden, and the tree of knowledge of good and evil.

Genesis 2:8-9

The Tree of Life (Map p50) is a lone and spreading mesquite tree, famous not because it survives in the barren desert (plenty of trees and thorn bushes do that) but because it has survived so long. No one is sure what sustains this knot of thorny branches, but it has presumably tapped into an underground spring – a miracle that has led some to suggest it is the last vestige of the Garden of Eden. It won't be a change in the climate, however, that will signal its downfall, but the all-too-visible change in the kind of visitor it attracts, as daubs of spray paint all over the venerable old bark forewarn.

When standing under the spreading limbs of this tree that graces a patch of Bahrain's southern desert, with earth movers scraping the escarpment for cement, and oil and gas pipelines riddling alongside, it's hard to imagine anywhere less deserving of the name 'Garden of Eden'. And yet, modern scholars point to several ancient sources that suggest Bahrain may have been the locus of paradise. In the Babylonian creation myth, the Epic of Gilgamesh, Dilmun (Bahrain's ancient incarnation) is described as the home of Enki (the god of wisdom), the Sweet Water From Under the Sea, and Ninhursag (goddess of the Earth). In the Old Testament, it is possible that Hebrew and Sumerian traditions of paradise are similarly conflated. On encountering this Tree of Life, however, you may well urge archaeologists searching for Eden to keep looking!

Follow signs to the tree along the Muaskar Hwy. It is just off the sealed road (take a right turn by Khuff Gas Well 371 and turn right again along the power lines). There's no need for a 4WD, but take care not to drive into soft sand. There is a signboard at the site telling visitors how to get there. The Tree of Life is 40km from Manama and a 45-minute drive away. Note the wind-eroded forms in the escarpment near the site.

Oil Museum

Built in 1992, to mark the 60th anniversary of the discovery of oil, this museum (Map p50; ☑17 753 475; ⊙10am-5pm Fri) FREE is housed in a grand, white-stone building quite out of keeping with the surrounding nodding donkeys and sprawling pipelines. In the shadow of Jebel ad-Dukhan, or Mountain of Smoke – Bahrain's highest point at a very modest 134m – the building is befitting as a landmark of the country's wealth, for it marks the point at which 'Black Gold' was struck for the first time on the Arabic side of the Gulf. The museum has exhibits, photographs and explanations about the oil industry in Bahrain. A few metres away, you can see the country's first oil well, which was constructed in 1932.

Ring to check opening times, as the museum is seldom visited despite being clearly signposted along an unmarked road south of Awali. There is no bus service to this region. By car, it's about 40 minutes to the museum, which is 35km south of Manama.

Muharraq Island محرق

POP 189,114

Just over the causeways from Bahrain Island, Muharraq Island could in many respects belong to a different country. With some interesting old houses, a fort and a shore full of moored dhows and lobster pots, there's enough to keep visitors occupied in the atmospheric back streets for at least half a day. The more recent addition of cultural centres, focused on preserving Bahrain's fast-disappearing heritage, may well detain you longer.

The attractions are easy to reach by taxi from central Manama (around BD3) and are within walking distance of each other.

◉ Sights

Beit Sheikh Isa Bin Ali HISTORIC BUILDING
(Map p50; ☑17 293 820; Central Muharraq; admission 400 fils; ⊙8am-6pm) Offering a fascinating look at pre-oil life in Bahrain, Beit Sheikh Isa Bin Ali was built around 1800. The chief sitting room downstairs was kept cool in summer by the down draft from the wind tower, the shutters on which could be closed in winter. There is some fine gypsum and woodcarving throughout the house. While the rooms are bare, the different sections of the house are well captioned in English and

DON'T MISS

HERITAGE PATHWAY IN MUHARRAQ

A 3.5km pedestrian 'pearling pathway', tipped for Unesco world heritage status, is being built by the Ministry of Culture to link some of the top sites across Muharrq Island and to offer insights into Bahrain's pearling heritage. Parts of that pathway have now been completed in the labyrinthine alleyways of central Muharraq. From an unpromising opening next to Latifa Laundry (alongside Beit Seyadi), Lane 917 leads past renovated buildings, en-plein-air art, an urban water feature and craft workshops. Don't miss the following:

➜ **Sheikh Ebrahim bin Mohammed Al-Khalifa Centre for Culture and Research** (📞 17 322 549; ⊙ 9am-1pm & 4-7pm) FREE Inspired by the early-20th-century intellectual of the same name, it hosts recitals, lectures and exhibitions every Monday evening. At other times it delivers a synopsis of Bahrain's history and heritage through the pages of a giant electronic book: a mere wave of the hand turns the pages on Dilmun, pearling and the Tree of Life. One page reads: 'Like gold our talents are precious', which is a fitting expression of all the arts works on display along the pearling pathway.

➜ **Abdullah Al-Zayed House** FREE Dedicated to the country's press heritage with an old typewriter and a copy of Bahrain's first newspaper on display.

➜ **Al-Korar House** FREE The gathering point for Muharraq craftswomen intent on preserving the craft of gold-thread weaving. Three generations of a local Muharraq family have saved the art of *al-korar* from extinction. Once, the intricate golden thread work was the occupation of all resident women; now only a handful of people know how to weave the elaborate braid that once adorned all Bahraini ceremonial gowns. All works the ladies make in this house are sold before they are even made so you will have to be lucky to see one of the finished, gossamer-thin gowns.

➜ **Saffron 2** (⊙ 9am-noon & 5-8pm) Keeping the ancient art of conversation alive over the sale of excellent coffee and bakes, this new coffeeshop is set in a beautifully restored old house, next to Al-Korar House.

None of these enterprises has quite filled the boots of their splendid venues yet, but they are a sign that the culture of 'out with the old and in with the new' has run its course at last as architects and interior designers find inspirational ways of making the past relevant to modern generations. Check the Ministry website (http://www.moc.gov.bh/en) for updates on this path of progress.

a good half-hour could be spent rambling up and down the different staircases.

From Sheikh Hamad Causeway turn right at the roundabout on Sheikh Abdullah bin Isa Ave. Brown signs indicate the way.

Beit Seyadi   HISTORIC BUILDING
(Map p50; Central Muharraq) FREE A traditional house from the pre-oil period, Beit Seyadi once belonged to a pearl merchant. The house is closed for restoration but the fine exterior, with its peculiar rounded corners decorated with emblems of stars and crescent moon, makes it worth a visit. An old mosque is attached to the house.

While you are in the neighbourhood, look across the car park outside Beit Seyadi at the **house of Aleh Sultan Sameen Bak** – that's if you can find it! It's hard to differentiate the front door from the panels of corrugated iron, mirrors, plastic flowers and other 'life collectibles' that have accrued in the entrance way.

Bin Matar House   MUSEUM
(Map p50; 📞 17 322 549; Sheikh Abdullah Bin Isa Ave, Central Muharraq; ⊙ 9am-1pm & 4-7pm Sat-Thu) This traditional house, built in 1905 in the heart of Muharraq, was saved from demolition by the Sheikh Ebrahim Centre for Culture and Research. Once the home of a pearl merchant, and later a clinic of Dr Bandar Kab, a renowned physician in the 1940s, it has been reinvented as a museum devoted to the history of pearling and a gallery displaying contemporary art.

Vertical Garden   LANDMARK
(Muharraq Green Gate; Map p50; Sheikh Abdullah Bin Isa Ave) Along Sheikh Abdullah Bin Isa Ave is a 'vertical garden' that acts as a landmark for entrance to the old quarter of the

island. Created by European artist Patrick Blanc, and the first of its kind in the Middle East, it is home to 200 species of plants in what Blanc describes as a 'living laboratory'. It comprises a single wall with an arch, planted with salt- and heat-tolerant plants including aloe.

Qala'at Arad
FORT

(Arad Fort; Map p50; ☑17 672 278; admission 500 fils; ⊙9am-6pm; ℗) Built in the early 15th century by the Portuguese, Qala'at Arad has been beautifully restored. There is little to see inside except the old well and the date-palm timbers used to reinforce the ceiling. Nonetheless, the location overlooking the bay makes it well worth a trip, especially at sunset, when the neighbouring park comes alive with local strollers.

From Manama, take the Sheikh Hamad Causeway and follow the signs along Khalifa al-Khebir Ave and Arad Hwy.

Al-Oraifi Museum
MUSEUM

(Map p50; ☑17 535 112; off Airport Avenue; admission BD1; ⊙8am-noon & 4-8pm Sat-Thu, 8am-noon Fri) Dedicated to the art and artefacts of the Dilmun era, this private collection of art and sculpture has over 100 works of art from this era. Inspired by these artefacts, the artist owner paints Dilmun-related canvases which he displays in the museum's gallery. From Manama, take the Sheikh Isa bin Sulman Causeway and follow the signs along Airport Ave.

🛍 Shopping

Suq al Qaisariya
SOUQ

(Souq Muharraq; Map p50; ⊙10am-1pm & 4-7pm Sat-Thu, 4-7pm Fri) This newly renovated collection of traditional old shops is burried in the heart of Souq Muharraq and has already become a popular site for visitors. It will eventually form part of the heritage pathway being built through the old quarters of the island in celebration of the pearling trade.

Other Islands

Hawar Islands
جزيرة حوار

The 16 virtually uninhabited islands known collectively as the Hawar Islands are very close to Qatar. The islands are home to a large number of flamingos and cormorants, about 2000 Bahraini troops and the attractive **Tulip Inn Hawar Beach** (☑17 532 272;

www.tulipinnhawarbeach.com; s/d BD60/72; ❄). Closed at the time of writing, the resort normally offers a range of wildlife tours and water activities. If service resumes, the boat to the Hawar Islands leaves from the Ad Dur jetty on the southeast coast of Bahrain Island, a 25-minute drive from Manama.

Dar Island
جزيرة الدار

Just off the coast south of Sitra, Dar Island offers a great retreat from the city. The main attraction is the sandy beach, but water sports are also available, and there is a restaurant and bar at **Al-Dar Islands Resort** (Map p50; ☑17 704 600; www.al-darislands.com; s/d BD50/80; ⊙7am-5pm; ❄) ⁄. The resort is eco-conscious and protects the island by limiting the number of visitors per day so it is important to book ahead. Rooms can be rented by the day, overnight or for 24 hours.

Several excursions operate from the resort, including fishing, dolphin-watching and dugong-watching. One of the most popular trips is **pearl collecting**, which involves snorkelling to harvest oysters in shallow waters followed by a demonstration of how to find out if they are pearl-bearing. The trip costs BD30 per person per hour for a minimum of two people.

Transport to Dar Island leaves from the scruffy harbour in Sitra, on the east side of Bahrain Island. To get there, take Ave 1, the road that ends at Al-Bander Resort (private members only) and the Yacht Club, which welcomes tourists. Turn left at the sign for Gulf Ports and Harbour Services. Sea taxis for Dar Island are available from here, leaving any time daily between 9am and sunset. The trip costs BD5 return for adults and BD3 for children. Remember to bring your passport as photo ID is necessary for boarding the boat.

UNDERSTAND BAHRAIN

Bahrain Today

Until the Arab Spring of 2011, the red-and-white flag of Bahrain fluttered along the main thoroughfares of the country's tree-lined highways as a symbol of a seemingly contented nation – a nation confident of its place as an offshore banking centre and commercial hub and a valued member of the UN,

Arab League and Gulf Cooperation Council (GCC). But dissatisfaction has simmered resolutely under the surface of this apparent quiet for more than a decade, partly based on the slow pace of political development but also largely due to sectarian differences.

On 14 February 2002, Bahrain was declared a constitutional monarchy where both men and women are eligible to vote and stand for office in a fully elected parliament. But the fact remains that a Sunni monarch, Sheikh Hamad bin Isa al-Khalifa, is at the helm of a country where Shiites form the majority of the population. In 2006 Al-Wifaq, a Shia political party, won the largest number of seats in parliamentary and municipal elections. This helped pacify the political aspirations of the Shia majority until 2011, when tension erupted in street demonstrations and major disturbances. After Eid Al-Adha in November 2012, the government banned public gatherings in an attempt to quell the rising tensions, but at the time of writing there is a real fear that the prolonged period of civil unrest may spiral out of control. The death of an Indian expat in November 2012 in roadside bombs, and regular attacks on schools, has added to the growing sense of unease.

The continuing unrest threatens to destabilise Bahrain's diversified economy, with debate as to whether the Grand Prix should take place in the current climate, and a further slump experienced in international tourism. Regional tourism continues to play a significant role in the economy with many visitors, from Saudi Arabia in particular, intent on enjoying Bahrain's relative tolerance of 'liberal behaviour' regardless. Bahrain's role as an offshore banking centre and commercial hub is more fragile, however, and some commentators suggest it won't take much to threaten international investment – much-needed to complete the ambitious projects started in the pre-2008 building frenzy.

History

Dilmun – The Ancient Garden of Eden

Anyone with the mildest interest in history cannot help but be curious about the civilisation that left behind 85,000 burial mounds that lump, curdle and honeycomb 5% of the island's landmass. Standing atop a burial mound at A'Ali, it is easy to imagine that the people responsible for such sophisticated care of their dead were equally sophisticated in matters of life. And, indeed, such was the case.

Although Bahrain has a Stone Age history that dates back to 5000 BC, and evidence of settlement from 10,000 BC, it has recently been confirmed by archaeologists as the seat of the lost and illustrious empire of Dilmun, the influence of which spread as far north as modern Kuwait and as far inland as Al-Hasa Oasis in eastern Saudi Arabia.The Dilmun civilisation lasted from 3200 to 330 BC, during which time, according to Sumerian, Babylonian and Assyrian inscriptions, the island's residents were not only commercially active, plying the busy Gulf waterways, but were also attentive to matters at home. The proper burial of the sick, handicapped and young in elaborate chambers, together with their chattels of ceramic, glass and beads (meticulously displayed at the Bahrain National Museum), suggest a civilisation of considerable social and economic development, assisted by the perpetual abundance of 'sweet', or potable, water on the island.

Little wonder, then, that Dilmun (which means 'noble') was often referred to as the fabled Garden of Eden and described as 'paradise' in the Epic of Gilgamesh (the world's oldest poetic saga). Dilmun's economic success was due in no small part to the trading of Omani copper, which was measured using the internationally recognised 'Dilmun Standard' (the weights can be seen in the Bahrain National Museum).

When the copper trade declined, in around 1800 BC, Dilmun's strength declined with it, leaving the island vulnerable to the predatory interests of the surrounding big powers. By 600 BC Dilmun was absorbed entirely by the empire of Babylon and was subsequently ceded to Greece. The Greeks called the island 'Tylos', a name it kept for nearly a thousand years (from 330 BC to AD622) despite Greek rule enduring for less than 100 years. Little distinguishes the history of Bahrain from the rest of the Gulf thereafter until the 16th century.

Pearls & the Founding of Modern Bahrain

Take a stroll along the 'pearling path' in Muharraq and you'll quickly learn the significance of the pearl trade to Bahrain. The presence of sweet-water springs under the sea, mingling with the brackish waters of the shallow oyster beds, contributes to the peculiar colour and lustre of Bahrain's pearls, and it was upon the value of these pearls that Bahrain grew into one of the most important trading posts in the region.

A 'fish eye' (the ancient name for pearl) dating back to 2300 BC, found in the excavations at Sar, suggests that pearling was an activity dating back to the days of Dilmun but despite the beauty of the catch, pearling was an unglamorous industry. It entailed local 'divers' working with little more than a nose-peg and a knife in shark-infested waters, and being hauled up with their bounty by 'pullers' working long and sun-baked shifts from June to October. At the height of the pearling industry, some 2500 dhows were involved in the industry and loss of life was common.

The rich pearl industry was something of a mixed blessing in other ways as well as it attracted the big naval powers of Europe, which wheeled about the island trying to establish safe passage for their interests further east. In the early 1500s the Portuguese invaded, building one of their typical sea-facing forts on Bahrain's northern shore (Qala'at al-Bahrain) – the coping stone on seven layers of ancient history. Their rule was short-lived, however, and by 1602 the Portuguese were ousted by the Persians.

Pearls played a hand in the country's modern incarnation: this lucrative trade attracted the Al-Khalifa, the family that now rules Bahrain, to the area from their original stronghold in Al-Zubara, on the northwestern edge of the Qatar peninsula. The Al-Khalifa were responsible for driving out the Persians from Bahrain in about 1782. They were themselves routed by an Omani invasion, but returned in 1820 never to leave again.

Relationship with the British

It only takes a walk through Adlya, with its emphasis on full English breakfasts and high teas, to discover that the British are part and parcel of the island's history. The origin of that special relationship can be traced to the 19th century when piracy was rife in the Gulf.

Although piracy never gained a foothold in Bahrain as such, the island gained something of a reputation as an entrepôt, where captured goods were traded for supplies for the next raid. The British, anxious to secure their trade routes with India, brought the Al-Khalifa family, who were professedly opposed to piracy, into the 'Trucial system' (the system of protection against piracy that operated throughout the old Trucial States; that is, the Gulf states that signed a 'truce' or treaty with Britain against piracy and which largely make up today's United Arab Emirates).

In hindsight, this could almost be dubbed 'invasion by stealth', as by 1882 Bahrain could not make any international agreements or host any foreign agent without British consent. On the other hand, as a British protectorate, the autonomy of the Al-Khalifa family was secure and threats from the Ottomans thwarted.

To this day, a special relationship can be felt between the Bahrainis and the sizable expatriate British community that extends well beyond the landscaping of public parks and the building of roundabouts. Bahrain regained full independence in 1971.

Oil – Bahrain's Black Gold

In the middle of the desert, roughly in the middle of the island, stands a small museum sporting marble pillars and a classical architrave, wholly unbefitting of the landscape of nodding donkeys in the vicinity. But the museum has a right to certain pretensions of grandeur; it marks the spot where, in 1932, the Arab world struck gold – black gold, that is – and with it, the entire balance of power in the world was transformed forever.

The first well is in the museum grounds, with polished pipes and cocks worthy of the momentousness of its role in modern history. The discovery of oil could not have come at a better time for Bahrain as it roughly coincided with the collapse of the world pearl market, upon which the island's economy had traditionally been based. Skyrocketing oil revenues allowed the country, under the stewardship of the Al-Khalifa family, to steer a course of rapid modernisation that was a beacon for other countries in the region to follow well into the 1970s and '80s.

When the oil began to run out, so did the fortunes of the government, and in the last decade of the 20th century the country was shocked by sporadic waves of unrest. The troubles began in 1994 when riots erupted after the emir refused to accept a large petition calling for greater democracy, culminating in the hotel bombings of 1996 (at the Diplomat and what is now the Ritz-Carlton Bahrain). Despite many concessions, including the establishment of a constitutional monarch in 2002, the political tensions have yet to be fully resolved.

People & Society

The National Psyche

Bahrain is so close to the mainland it is joined by a causeway to Saudi Arabia. Bahrain is nonetheless an island, and there is something of an island mentality to be felt in Manama and microcosmically in Muharraq, too. It is difficult to pinpoint the differences between Bahrainis and other *jizari* (people of the Gulf) inhabitants, but perhaps it lies somewhere in the Bahraini identification with the wider world, a feeling engendered by the centuries of international trade and, in more recent times, by the earliest discovery of oil in the region. This latter fact enabled Bahrain to engage in an international dialogue well before its neighbours, and as such helped in developing a sense of greater affinity with Western nations, as well as a tolerance and even acceptance of many (and some would argue not altogether the best) Western practices. Even a one-time visitor cannot fail to notice the many bars serving alcohol, the largely unchecked social freedoms and the general party atmosphere that engages the streets of Manama.

Naturally enough, a greater degree of conservatism prevails outside the capital area, but this is still not the land of the censorious: on the far-flung Al-Jazayer Beach, there is a notice that asks the beachgoer to be quiet out of respect for visitors wishing to escape the noise of the city. In a beach hut, not 5m away and with the door shut against the wind, the fully amplified, Afro-Arabic beat of an ad-hoc jam session bulges against the surrounding austerity of the desert. It speaks volumes.

Lifestyle

It's the prerogative of the inhabitants of busy seaports to select from the 'customs and manners' that wash up on the shore. Watching young Bahraini men on the nightclub floor in one of Manama's central hotels, for example, sporting a crisp white *thobe* (floor-length shirt-dress) or the international uniform of jeans and leather jacket, a visitor could be forgiven for thinking that the young have sold out to the West. These same young men, however, would probably have been to the barber, aged three to six years old, one auspicious Monday, Thursday or Friday in spring, and come out clutching their coins – and loins. These same young men will no doubt send their sons on similar rituals of circumcision and maturation, because beneath the urbane exterior, the sweet waters of the island run deep.

As for Bahraini women, while Islam requires surrender to the will of God, it does not imply surrender to the will of man. Bahraini women take their place in many walks of public life, and, as such, 'surrender' is the last word that comes to mind. Only an outsider considers it contradictory that women who choose to cover their hair in the presence of men should at the same time give them instructions on all matters of life, cardinal and profane.

Bahraini people have enjoyed the spoils of oil for over half a century and it's tempting to think wealth has created a nation of idlers; you won't see many Bahrainis engaged in manual labour, for example, nor waiting on tables. But a modern, enterprising, wealthy nation isn't built on money alone, and the burgeoning financial sector is proof that the locals have chosen to invest their energies and creativity in their traditional trading strengths while importing labour for the jobs they no longer need to do themselves.

As for most Arab nationals, 'home is where the heart is' for Bahrainis. Despite the imperatives of international business, time with the family is cherished, and the sense of home is extended to the Bahraini community at large through many public-funded amenities and educational opportunities. After Ramadan, for example, Al-Fatih Mosque opens its doors to free feasting for non-Muslims during *eid:* in some countries this would be interpreted as proselytising; here it is a symbol of the infectious sense of home shared with non-nationals.

Multiculturalism

Behind Bab al-Bahrain, at the heart of Manama, there is little besides shop signs in Arabic to indicate that this is indeed part of Arabia. There are Indian and Pakistani shop owners, Jewish money exchangers, Filipino hotel workers and occasional groups of US servicemen. The same could be said of Al-Seef, where the manicured gardens and bars of the Ritz-Carlton Bahrain Hotel & Spa and the international chain stores of Al-Seef Mall are peopled largely by Western expatriates.

Indeed, in a country where nearly 32% of residents (44% of the workforce) are non-Bahrainis or expatriates (Western expats

LOCAL CRAFTS

On the face of it, Bahrain is a modern country that looks forward more often than it looks back. This is changing, however, and Manama's recent post as Capital of Arab Culture has led to a revival of interest in Bahrain's artistic heritage. Several cultural centres, such as the Crafts Centre Gallery and Workshop (p61) in central Manama, and workshops, such as Al-Jasra Handicraft Centre (p64), have been set up to encourage the continuation of skills. Crafts are generally carried out in cottage industries or co-operatives with people working from the privacy of their own inner courtyards. If you head out to the following places, especially in the company of a local guide, however, you may be lucky to see these crafts in progress.

➡ **Pottery and ceramics** Village of A'Ali.

➡ **Traditional weaving** Villages of Ad-Diraz and Bani Jamrah.

➡ **Basket weaving with palm leaves** Village of Karbabad.

➡ **Pearl jewellery** Gold souq, Manama.

➡ **Al-Kurar metal thread work** (for decorating ceremonial gowns) Al-Kurar House, Muharraq.

comprise about 10% of the resident population), it is surprising to find that such a strong sense of local identity has survived. This imbalance, while harmonious for the most part, has been a source of political agitation too. In 1997, for example, a series of arson attacks were carried out by unemployed Bahrainis, angry that jobs were being taken by workers from Asia. While the government has since actively pursued a policy favouring the indigenous workforce, tensions continue to prevail as educated Bahrainis find it difficult to compete in sectors with entrenched (and often experienced and skilled) expatriate workforces.

In common with other Gulf nationals, and despite a free and excellent education system, many Bahrainis choose to study abroad, particularly in the USA and UK. They generally come back, however!

Arts

There's a vibrant contemporary-arts scene in Bahrain. Exhibitions of local paintings regularly take place at the Bahrain National Museum and at La Fontaine Centre of Contemporary Art. There are also a few private galleries, often showcasing the work of the owner. These include the Rashid al-Oraifi Museum in Muharraq and the Muharraqi Gallery in A'Ali, which features the surreal works of Abdullah al-Muharraqi.

The lanes surrounding Beit Seyadi on Muharraq Island are slowly developing into a centre for the preservation of traditional arts, crafts and social customs under the patronage of the Sheikh Ebrahim bin Mohammed Al Khalifa Centre for Culture and Research.

The best way to find out what's going on where is to consult the listings in *TimeOut Bahrain* or the English-language newspapers.

Environment

The Land

Most people think of Bahrain (741 sq km) as a single flat island with a couple of low escarpments in the middle of a stony desert and surrounded by a very shallow, calm sea. In fact, such is the description of Bahrain Island only, which, at 586 sq km, is the largest in an archipelago of about 33 islands, including the Hawar Islands, and a few specks of sand that disappear at high tide. When crossing any of the causeways, including the King Fahd Causeway, which links Bahrain with the Saudi mainland, it is easy to see how the whole archipelago was once attached to the rest of the continent.

Wildlife

Bahrain's noteworthy wildlife includes the Ethiopian hedgehog, Cape hare, various geckos and the endangered Rheem gazelle, which inhabits the dry and hot central depression. The Hawar Islands, with their resident cormorant and flamingo populations, give a staging post to winter migrants. The

Rheem gazelle, terrapin, sooty falcon and the seafaring dugong all appear on the endangered species list but some of them can be seen, along with a beautiful herd of oryx, at Al-Areen Wildlife Park & Reserve.

The deserts of Bahrain may look sparse, but various twigs turn up in the souq to be applied in poultices or pastes in a rich tradition of herbal medicine. Applying the sap of al-Liban tree or inhaling incense is an apparent cure for measles; for a skin infection, there's rock salt or the bark of the *dawram* tree; or for jaundice there's *agool* soup made of boiled wild thorns. Another useful plant is the endangered mangrove, which provides a rich habitat for a variety of birds and molluscs among its scaffolding of aerial roots.

A unique ecosystem in Bahrain is created by the seagrass *Halodule uninervis*. Important for the dugong and a large number of migrating birds, this tough plant is remarkably resilient against extreme temperatures and high salinity.

National Parks

Located in the middle of Bahrain Island, Al-Areen Wildlife Park & Reserve was set up to conserve natural habitats in order to support research projects in the field of wildlife protection and development. In common with most Gulf States, the 20th-century passion for hunting left the island virtually bereft of natural inheritance. At least at Al-Areen, visitors can see well-looked-after specimens of indigenous fauna, such as gazelles and bustards (large ground-living birds). The park also provides a free-roaming natural habitat for certain native Arabian species, including the endangered oryx.

In addition to Al-Areen, there are two other protected areas in Bahrain: the mangroves at Ras Sanad (Tubli Bay) and the Hawar Islands. With a huge residential development project underway in one and oil exploration around the other, it's hard to see what is meant by 'protection'.

Environmental Issues

Bahrain has made a big effort to clean up its act environmentally and beautification projects have brought a touch of greenery back to the concrete jungle. But these measures are largely cosmetic, and the main threats to the environment remain unrestrained development; perpetual land reclamation; an inordinate number of cars (about 200 per sq km); rampant industrialisation; and pollution of the Gulf from oil leakages and ocean acidification. In addition, little appears to have been done to curb emissions from heavy industry (such as the aluminium smelting plant) to the east of Bahrain Island.

During the stand-off between Bahrain and Qatar over ownership of the Hawar Islands, the wildlife, which includes dugongs and turtles and many species of migratory bird, was left in peace. Immediately after the territorial dispute was resolved, however, Bahrain invited international oil companies to drill for oil. The impact of this is a source of great topical debate.

SURVIVAL GUIDE

🛈 Directory A–Z

ACCOMMODATION

Bahrain's main sights are all within day-trip distance of the capital. As a result, most visitors stay in the large selection of hotels available in Manama and its suburbs. The following notes may be helpful in determining what type of accommodation to book:

➡ Bahrain has accommodation to fit most pockets, although travellers will find it difficult to find single/double rooms for less than BD15/25 per night.

➡ Many of the cheaper hotels (and some midrange hotels) double as brothels for visiting Saudi patrons. The cheaper the room, the more overt the night-time activity.

➡ Midrange accommodation usually implies a carpet, minibar, satellite TV and view of something other than an internal stairwell.

➡ Bahrain has some excellent top-end accommodation, including resorts. These often offer substantial discounts to the published rack rate.

➡ Camping is not a recommended option.

SLEEPING PRICE RANGES

The following price ranges refer to a double room with bathroom and air-con in high season (November to March). Taxes are included in the price. Listings are arranged by price and then by author preference within a price category.

$ less than BD40 (US$106)

$$ BD40–BD80 (US$106–US$212)

$$$ more than BD80 (US$212)

ℹ️ DUBIOUS BUDGET HOTELS

You don't have to be Richard Gere to know that pretty women hanging around a hotel foyer does not bode altogether well for a quiet night's sleep. Indeed, many male visitors have reported being harassed with phone calls in the middle of the night, and the paper-thin walls of some of the more budget accommodation leave little to the imagination. Ask the price of a night's sleep in the infamous Hotel Bahrain, for example, and you may well receive the same reply given to us: 'this hotel no-sleep – sleep cost more'.

Ironically, the Muslim holidays – when a wave of Saudi tourists floods over the causeway – seem to turn even the midrange hotels into a rendezvous for mostly discreet and unobtrusive liaisons. One word of warning: when a hotel says it has a floor especially for women, it often means just that, with a variety of women of the night plying their trade. As such, women travelling on their own are better off avoiding it. Despite Manama's alter ego, however, solo women are unlikely to feel threatened on the capital's streets, which are so a-throng with people engaged in 'no-sleep' they seem disinclined to mess with yours.

ACTIVITIES

The main activities in Bahrain focus around the sea, although very shallow coastal waters mean that swimming, snorkelling and boating are all best carried out well offshore. On land, golf is popular. Expats will find membership of a club offers big savings and a ready-made social life.

➡ **Dolphin watching** Contact **Bahrain Yacht Club** (Map p50; ☑17 700 677; www.thebahrainyachtclub.com; ⊘8am-11pm Sat-Wed, 8am-midnight Thu & Fri) or Coral Bay (p53) for boat trips.

➡ **Golf** Both **Awali Golf Club** (Map p50; ☑17 756 770; www.awaligolfclub.com; ⊘7am-8pm) and **Royal Golf Club** (Map p50; ☑17 750 777; www.royalgolfclub.com; ⊘7am to 11pm, last 9-hole tee 9pm) have beautiful greens – not a given in the desert!

➡ **Horse riding** Both **Dilmun Club** (☑17 693 766; www.dilmun-club.com; ⊘Sat-Thu) in Sar and **Bahrain Riding School** (☑39 566 809; twinpalmsridingcentre.com) offer lessons.

➡ **Pearl diving** Al-Dar Islands Resort (p68) provides the nosepeg – you just bring the stamina.

➡ **Running** For those who prefer to share their pain, contact the **Bahrain Hash House Harriers** (☑17 862 620; www.bahrainhash.com).

➡ **Water sports** In addition to Bahrain Yacht Club and Coral Bay, there's **Al Bander Hotel & Resort** (Map p50; ☑17 701 201; www.albander. com) and **Bahrain Sailing Club** (Map p50; ☑17 836 078)

BOOKS

➡ *Bahrain Island Heritage* by Shirley Kay – useful and informative.

➡ *Resident in Bahrain* by Parween Abdul Rahman and Charles Walsham – helpful for businesspeople.

➡ *Looking for Dilmun* by Geoffrey Bibby – celebrated book on Bahrain in the 1950s and '60s.

➡ *Bahrain Through the Ages* by Sheikh Haya Ali al-Khalifa and Michael Rice – in-depth coverage of Bahrain's archaeology.

CUSTOMS REGULATIONS

➡ Importation, purchase and consumption of alcohol is permissible.

➡ Non-Muslim visitors can import 1L of wine or spirits, or six cans of beer duty-free.

➡ If you're returning to Saudi via the causeway, don't forget to empty the coolbox!

EMBASSIES & CONSULATES

The nearest embassies representing Australia, Canada and Ireland are in Riyadh, Saudi Arabia. Most of the embassies are in the Diplomatic Area in Manama, between King Faisal Hwy and Sheikh Hamad Causeway.

Opening hours are usually 8.30am to noon. The Saudi Embassy is only open from 9am to 11am. All embassies and consulates are closed Thursday and Friday.

French (☑17 298 600; www.ambafrance.com. bh; Al-Fatih Hwy)

Dutch (☑17 530 704; fax 537 040; Al-Furdah Ave, ABN Bldg) Handles Benelux countries.

German (☑17 530 210; www.manama.diplo.de; Sheikh Hamad Causeway, Al-Hassaa Bldg)

Kuwaiti (☑17 534 040; fax 536 475; King Faisal Hwy)

Omani (☑17 293 663; fax 293 540; Al-Fatih Hwy)

Saudi Arabian (☑17 537 722; fax 533 261; King Faisal Hwy)

UAE (☑17 723 737; fax 17 717 724; Road 4007, off Awal Ave, Juffair)

UK (☑17 574 100; www.ukinbahrain.fco.gov.uk; Government Ave)

USA (☑17 272 400; www.bahrain.usembassy. gov; just off Sheikh Isa bin Sulman Hwy, Al-Zinj)

FOOD
For an overview of Bahrain's cuisine, see p47 and the Flavours of Arabia chapter (p459).

INTERNET ACCESS
The main internet service provider is Batelco (p62). There are many wi-fi hot spots around town, especially in Starbucks and McDonald's and in most hotels. Prepaid wi-fi cards cost BD1 (two days).

There are many internet centres in Manama.

LEGAL MATTERS
Breaking the law can have severe consequences. For more information, see the Expats chapter (p33) and consult your embassy.

MAPS
The *Bahrain Map & Pocket Guide* (BD1), published in cooperation with Tourism Affairs, Ministry of Information is available from the airport, Bahrain National Museum and bookshops. It has useful up-to-date information on the reverse, together with a good map of Manama.

MONEY
Bahrain's currency is the Bahraini dinar (BD). One dinar is divided into 1000 fils. There are 500 fil and 1, 5, 10 and 20 dinar notes. Coins come in denominations of 5, 10, 25, 50, 100 and 500 fils. The Bahraini dinar is a convertible currency and there are no restrictions on its import or export.

ATMs & Credit Cards
Major credit cards are widely accepted throughout Bahrain. Most banks have ATMs that accept Visa, Cirrus and MasterCard cards, while the Bank of Bahrain & Kuwait (BBK) has ATMs that take Visa, MasterCard, Cirrus, Maestro and Amex cards.

Money Changers
Money (both cash and travellers cheques) can be changed at any bank or moneychanging office. There is little to choose between banks and money changers in terms of exchange rates and it's rare for either to charge a commission. Currencies for other Gulf States are easy to buy and sell.

Tipping & Bargaining
A service charge is added to most bills in restaurants and hotels in Bahrain, so tipping is at your discretion. An appropriate tip for good service would be around 10%. Airport porters expect 200 fils per bag despite their services being covered by the airport tax. Taxi drivers do not expect a tip for short journeys. For longer journeys (over 5km), 10% would be appropriate.

Bargaining in the souqs and in most shops, together with asking for a discount, is expected.

OPENING HOURS
The weekend in Bahrain is on Friday and Saturday for most commercial and government organisations.

Banks 7.30am to 3pm Sunday to Thursday
Government offices 7am to 2pm Sunday to Thursday
Internet cafes 8am to 1pm and 4pm to 10pm
Post offices 7am to 2pm (and 4pm to 6pm at alternating offices)
Restaurants 11am to 3pm and 6pm to 1am
Shopping centres 9am to 10pm Saturday to Thursday, 10am to 10pm Friday
Shops 8am to noon and 3.30pm to 7.30pm Saturday to Thursday

PHOTOGRAPHY
Plenty of shops in Manama, and elsewhere around Bahrain, sell batteries and memory cards for cameras. Many camera shops can burn photos onto a CD and print digital pictures.

POST
Sending postcards to Europe/North America and Australasia costs 150/200 fils. Letters cost 200/250 fils per 10g. Parcels cost a standard minimum of BD3 for the first 500g to all Western countries, and BD1/1.500 for every extra 500g.

PUBLIC HOLIDAYS
In addition to the main Islamic holidays, Bahrain celebrates a number of public holidays.
New Year's Day 1 January
Ashura Tenth day of Muharram (month in the Hejira calendar; date changeable) – Ashura marks the death of Hussein, grandson of the Prophet. Processions led by men flagellating themselves take place in many of the country's predominantly Shiite areas.
National Day 16 December

TELEPHONE
Bahrain's telephone country code is 973 and there are no area or city codes. The international access code (to call abroad from Bahrain) is 00. There are several help lines including local directory assistance (181) and international directory assistance (191).

PRACTICALITIES

➔ **Magazines** The monthly *Bahrain This Month* and *TimeOut Bahrain* have comprehensive local listings.

➔ **Newspapers** The *Gulf Daily News* and the *Bahrain Tribune* are the main English-language dailies. International newspapers are available in major hotels and bookshops the day after publication.

➔ **Radio** *Radio Bahrain* broadcasts in English on 96.5FM and 101FM.

➔ **TV** Bahrain TV broadcasts Channel 55 in English (from late afternoon), and the BBC World Service is shown in English on Channel 57. Most satellite programs, such as CNN and MTV, are available at many hotels.

➔ **Smoking** Widespread but top-end hotels reserve rooms for nonsmokers.

➔ **Weights & Measures** Bahrain uses the metric system.

Bahrain's telecommunications system is run by the government monopoly, Bahrain Telecommunications Company (Batelco). International calls from Bahrain cost BD0.180 per minute to Europe, Australia and North America. Rates are reduced to BD0.160 between 7pm and 7am every day, as well as all day Friday and on public holidays. Local calls anywhere within Bahrain cost 20 fils per minute.

Blue payphones take coins. Red payphones take phonecards, which are widely available from most grocery stores in denominations of BD1, BD3, BD5 and BD10.

Mobile Phones

Bahrain's mobile-phone network runs on the GSM system through Batelco and Zain. Visitors can also purchase SIM cards for BD1, BD5 and BD10 at all Batelco and Zain outlets. Recharge cards come in many denominations up to BD20.

VISAS

Visas are needed to visit Bahrain. For people of many nationalities, these can be conveniently obtained at Bahrain International Airport or at the border with Saudi Arabia. A two-week visa on arrival costs BD5 and is payable by credit card only. You can check your eligibility for a visa on arrival online (www.evisa.gov.bh) as there are some restrictions currently in place (for example, for certain professions).

Multiple-entry business visas are available for citizens of many nationalities. Valid for five years with maximum stays of 28 days; cost is BD20.

Visa Extensions

Two-week visa extensions can be obtained by visiting the **General Directorate of Nationality, Passports & Residents** (☑17 530 902; www.evisa.gov.bh; Sheikh Hamad Causeway). The cost is currently BD5 and they take 72 hours to process. Foreigners overstaying their visas are rigorously fined.

WOMEN TRAVELLERS

Bahrain is fairly liberal compared to some other Gulf countries, which can be both a blessing (less of the staring) and a nuisance (more of the hassle).

ℹ Getting There & Away

AIR

Bahrain International Airport (p62) is on Muharraq Island, 12km from the centre of Manama, and handles frequent services to many intercontinental destinations as well as other countries in the region.

The national carrier is **Gulf Air** (☑ call centre 17 373 737, flight information 17 339 339, sales 17 222 820; www.gulfair.com; Manama Centre, bldg 58, Government Rd, Manama), which flies to destinations worldwide. It has a good safety record and reliable departure times.

Airlines Flying to/from Bahrain

Air Arabia (☑17 505 111; www.airarabia.com) Hub: Sharjah.

Bahrain Air (☑17 463 330; www.bahrainair.net) Hub: Muharraq, Bahrain.

British Airways (☑17 589 600; www.ba.com) Hub: Heathrow, London.

Emirates (☑17 588 700; www.emirates.com) Hub: Dubai, UAE.

Etihad Airways (☑17 540 066; www.etihadairways.com) Hub: Abu Dhabi, UAE.

Kuwait Airways (☑17 223 332; www.kuwaitairways.com) Hub: Kuwait City.

Lufthansa (☑17 828 763; www.lufthansa.com) Hub: Frankfurt, Germany.

Oman Air (☑17 500 020; www.omanair.com) Hub: Muscat, Oman.

Qatar Airways (☑17 505 150; www.qatarairways.com) Hub: Doha, Qatar.

Saudi Arabian Airlines (☑17 211 550; www.saudiairlines.com) Hub: Jeddah, Saudi Arabia.

LAND
Border Crossings

The only 'land' border is with Saudi Arabia, across the King Fahd Causeway.

Tourists are not permitted to drive between Saudi and Bahrain in a hired car. Residents of Saudi who have their own cars may use this crossing providing they have car insurance for both countries. For those coming from Saudi this can be purchased at the border. A transit visa must be obtained from the Saudi authorities for those driving by car between the UAE and Bahrain. This is not easy to obtain.

Bus

The **Saudi Bahraini Transport Co** (Sabtco; ☑17 252 959; www.sabtco.biz) runs an upmarket car and bus service between Manama and Dammam in Saudi Arabia. It also acts as the agent for the Saudi bus company, **Saudi Arabian Public Transport Co** (Saptco; ☑17 263 244; www.saptco.com.sa) (Saptco), with regular services to Dammam. From Dammam there are regular connections to Riyadh (Saudi Arabia) and Doha (Qatar) for those who have a Saudi transit visa.

From Manama, Saptco also has daily buses as far as Amman (Jordan) and Damascus (Syria), Abu Dhabi, Dubai and Sharjah (UAE) and Kuwait City, all for under BD20. All departures are from the **international bus terminal** in Manama, where the Sabtco office is located.

You must have a valid transit visa for Saudi Arabia in advance and an onward ticket and visa for your next destination beyond Saudi's borders.

Car & Motorcycle

All drivers (and passengers in taxis) using the causeway to Saudi must pay a toll of BD2 at the toll booth on the western side of the inter section between Causeway Approach Rd and Janabiya Hwy.

Anyone crossing the border from Bahrain to Saudi will be given a customs form to complete, and drivers entering Bahrain from Saudi must purchase temporary Bahraini insurance and also sign a personal guarantee.

SAMPLE FLIGHTS & FARES

FLIGHT	PRICE	FREQUENCY
Manama to Doha (Qatar)	BD36	daily
Manama to Muscat (Oman)	BD45	daily
Manama to Kuwait City	BD48	daily
Manama to Abu Dhabi (UAE)	BD48	daily
Manama to Riyadh (Saudi Arabia)	BD57	daily
Manama to Sana'a (Yemen)	BD100	3 times weekly

Prices quoted are taken from standard Gulf Air rates. Cheaper fares may be available on Air Arabia and Bahrain Air, the region's low-cost airlines.

DEPARTURE TAX

Departure tax is included in the price of your ticket.

SEA

Valfajr 8 Shipping Company runs a weekly ferry service between Manama and the Iranian port of Bushehr. A one-way fare, including two meals, costs BD38. The ship departs from the Mina Sul man port in Manama and the agent in Bahrain is **International Agencies Company** (☑17 727 114; www.intercol.com). For useful additional information, check out www.irantravelingcenter.com.

ⓘ Getting Around

BUS

Bahrain has a public bus system linking most of the major towns and residential areas but it is designed primarily for the expatriate workforce. As such, it is of limited use to tourists, with a lack of route guides and timetables, and destinations that do not coincide with places of tourist interest. If you are determined, however, then visit Manama bus station (p62) for information.

CAR & MOTORCYCLE

Driving around Bahrain is straightforward and roads are well signposted to the main sites of tourist interest.

Speed limits, the wearing of seat belts and drink-driving laws are rigorously enforced. Speed limits are 60km/h in towns, 80km/h in the outer limits of suburbs and 100km/h on highways. Petrol stations are well signposted, especially along highways.

Hire

Car-hire companies have offices in Manama and at the airport, charging from BD17/68 for one day/week for the smallest four-door sedan.

Rates exclude petrol, but include unlimited mileage and insurance. To avoid the excess of BD100 to BD200 in case of an accident, it's wise to pay the extra BD2 Collision Damage Waiver (CDW) per day. Rates are for a minimum of 24 hours. Companies normally only accept drivers over 21 years old (over 25 for more expensive models), and foreigners must (theoretically) have an International Driving Permit, although a driving licence is often sufficient. There is nowhere to rent a motorcycle.

LOCAL TRANSPORT

Most visitors get around Bahrain by taxi although persistence is needed to persuade drivers to use their meters. If visiting more than one tourist attraction outside Manama and Muharraq, it's cheaper to hire a car.

Kuwait الكويت

Includes ➜

Best for Culture

➜ Tareq Rajab Museum (p84)

➜ Kuwait Towers (p85)

➜ Al-Hashemi Marine Museum (p91)

➜ Sadu House (p92)

➜ Souq (p89)

Best for Nature

➜ Scientific Center (p85)

➜ Scientific Center Aquarium (p85)

➜ Planetarium (p88)

➜ Falaika Island (p99)

➜ Mutla Ridge (p100)

Why Go?

Kuwait, in the cradle of one of the most ancient and most-contested corners of the world, is best described as a city state. For centuries Kuwait City has been like a magnet attracting Bedouin people from the interior, in search of a sea breeze and escape from recurring drought. Today the metropolis is still an oasis in a land of desert plains, but rather more of the cultural and culinary kind. Excellent museums, a corniche of combed beaches and lively restaurants, malls and souqs mark the Kuwait City experience.

Outside the capital there are few attractions other than coastal resorts. Oil excavation dominates the flat desert plains and there are few distinctive geographical features. That said, there is always something to see in a desert, with a bit of patience and an eye for detail; when it comes to the ritual camping expedition, Kuwaitis have plenty of both.

When to Go

Kuwait

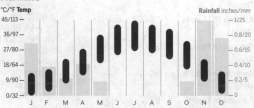

Nov–Jan Experience the relief of cool evenings after the burning heat of summer.

Feb Pick up a bargain in Kuwait's Halla shopping festival.

Feb–Mar During spring, the desert is laced in a gossamer of lime green.

Daily Costs

Kuwait is an expensive country to visit. With budget accommodation from US$100, cheap options for eating (around US$20) and museum admission charges, a minimum daily cost with transport comes to around US$200. This rises to US$380 if staying in midrange hotels and for a top-end hotel with car hire, US$450 is nearer the mark.

ITINERARIES

Stopover

Come eye to eye with the incoming tide at the Scientific Center's **aquarium**. Potter the length of the **corniche** (Arabian Gulf St), pausing at Kuwait Towers for an aerial view of the city. Get a feel for the country's Bedouin history at **Sadu House**, take lunch in one of the few remaining heritage houses at **Beit 7**, and sample local desserts in the city's most traditional souq, **Souq Marbarakia**. Return to the water (or dry dock to be exact) for dinner on the dhow at **Al-Boom**.

Three Days

After day one exploring the corniche, head inland on day two to **Tareq Rajab Museum** – a hidden gem of a collection displaying ethnographic treasures from across the Islamic world. Spend the afternoon shopping for brands in fashionable **Salmiya** district and end the day enjoying the bustle of promenading locals at nearby **Marina Crescent**.

For Expats

Spare a thought for the events of the past two decades by visiting the diminished **National Museum**, sense the still-smarting scars of war in the Kuwait House of **National Memorial Museum** and drive out to Al-Jahra's **Mutla Ridge**. Brighten up a sobering day at the **Hilton Kuwait Resort**, on a silky stretch of coastline with sequined waters, explore **Wafra Farms** to enjoy some greenery in the unremitting desert or get away from it all on **Falaika Island**.

Essential Food & Drink

➡ **Baked fish** Blended with coriander, turmeric, red pepper and cardamom.

➡ **Hamour or pomfret** Fish stuffed with herbs and onions.

➡ **Gulf prawns** Available late autumn and early winter.

➡ **Alcohol** Not available nor permissable.

➡ **Mixed fruit cocktails** Served in rainbow combinations.

➡ **Tap water** Safe to drink although most people stick to bottled water.

AT A GLANCE

➡ **Currency** Kuwaiti dinar (KD)

➡ **Mobile Phones** SIM cards widely available

➡ **Money** ATMs widespread; credit cards widely accepted

➡ **Visas** Available on arrival for many nationalities

KUWAIT

Fast Facts

➡ **Capital** Kuwait City

➡ **Country code** ☎965

➡ **Language** Arabic; English widely spoken

➡ **Official name** Kuwait

➡ **Population** 2.6 million

Exchange Rates

Australia	A$10	KD2.95
Bahrain	BD1	KD0.75
Euro zone	€10	KD3.69
Oman	OR1	KD0.73
Qatar	QR10	KD0.77
Saudi Arabia	SR1	KD0.08
UAE	Dh1	KD0.08
UK	UK£10	KD4.31
USA	US$10	KD2.81
Yemen	YR100	KD0.13

For current exchange rates see www.xe.com.

Resources

➡ **Complete Guide to Kuwait** (www.kuwaitah.net) Great general guide

➡ **Live Work Explore** (www.liveworkexplore.com/Kuwait) Comprehensive expat site

Kuwait Highlights

1 Appreciate the life of a mudhopper in the magnificent display of marine life at the **Scientific Center Aquarium** (p85)

2 Compare regional headdresses in the **Tareq Rajab Museum** (p84) – a gem of an ethnographic collection that escaped the Iraqi invasion

3 Take an eagle's eye view of the city and the Gulf from the iconic **Kuwait Towers** (p85)

4 Dine in a dhow at **Al-Boom restaurant** (p96), in the shadow of the largest wooden boat on earth, Al-Hashemi II.

5 Revisit the Gulf War and its heroes in the **Kuwait House of National Works: Memorial Museum** (p90)

6 While away an evening in the company of crowds at **Souq Marbarakia** (p95)

7 Go shopping in Salmiya (p97) and pick up the latest fashions

8 Enjoy R & R on the beach at the **Hilton Kuwait Resort** (p94)

9 Make a weekend of it on the island of Failaka (p99)

10 Take the **Bridge to Nowhere** (p100) and stop to camp before you get there!

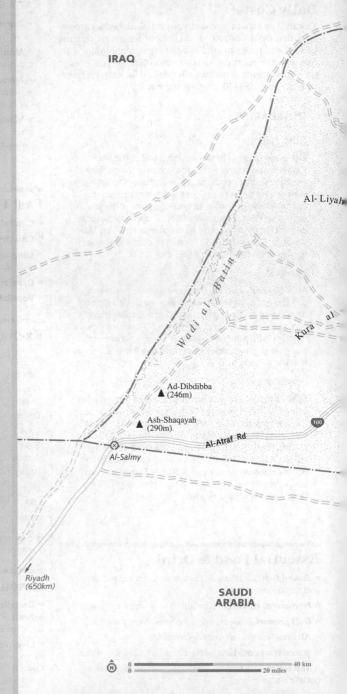

IRAQ

Al-Liyah

Wadi al-Batin

Kura al

▲ Ad-Dibdibba (246m)

▲ Ash-Shaqayah (290m)

⊗ Al-Salmy

Al-Atraf Rd

100

Riyadh (650km)

SAUDI ARABIA

0 ————— 40 km
0 ————— 20 miles

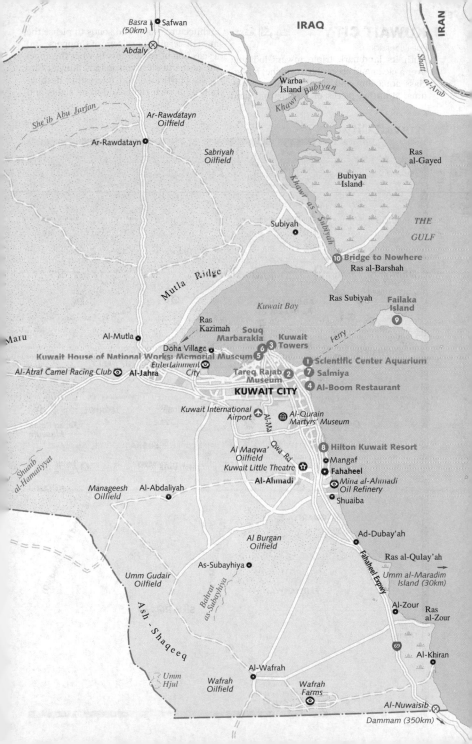

IRAQ

IRAN

Basra
(50km) ● Safwan

Abdaly

Warba
Island

Bubiyan

She'ib Abu Jarfan

Ar-Rawdatayn
Oilfield

Ar-Rawdatayn ●

Sabriyah
Oilfield

Khawr

Khawr as-Subiyah

Bubiyan
Island

Ras
al-Gayed

Maru

Al-Mutla ●

Mutla Ridge

Subiyah ●

Kuwait Bay

Ras Subiyah

**THE
GULF**

10 **Bridge to Nowhere**
Ras al-Barshah

Failaka
Island
9

Ras
Kazimah

Souq
Marbarakla
6 **5**

Kuwait
3 Towers

ferry

Doha Village

Kuwait House of National Works: Memorial Museum

Entertainment
City

1 **Scientific Center Aquarium**

Al-Atraf Camel Racing Club ●
Al-Jahra

Tareq Rajab
Museum **2**

7 **Salmiya**

KUWAIT CITY

4 **Al-Boom Restaurant**

Kuwait International
Airport

Al-Qurain
Martyrs' Museum

Al Maqwa'
Oilfield

Kuwait Little Theatre

Al-Ahmadi

Al-Ma Owa Rd

8 **Hilton Kuwait Resort**

● Mangaf

Fahaheel

Mina al-Ahmadi
Oil Refinery

● Shuaiba

Shuaib
al-Hamatiyyat

Manageesh
Oilfield

Al-Abdaliyah ●

Al Burgan
Oilfield

As-Subayhiya ●

Ad-Dubay'ah

Ras al-Qulay'ah

Umm al-Maradim
Island (30km)

Umm Gudair
Oilfield

Ash - Shaqeeq

Bahrat
as-Subayhiya

Fahaheel Expwy

Al-Zour
69

Ras
al-Zour

Al-Khiran ●

Umm
Hjul

Wafrah
Oilfield

Al-Wafrah ●

Wafrah
Farms

Al-Nuwaisib

Dammam (350km)

KUWAIT CITY

مدينة الكويت

POP 1.5 MILLION

With its landmark triple towers looming over a clean and accessible corniche; a first-class aquarium and some excellent museums; stunning pieces of marine and land architecture; malls and souqs to please the most discerning or eclectic of shoppers; and a selection of restaurants to whet the appetite of the fussiest gourmands, Kuwait City is a sophisticated and interesting destination in its own right. Add to its sights and

Kuwait City

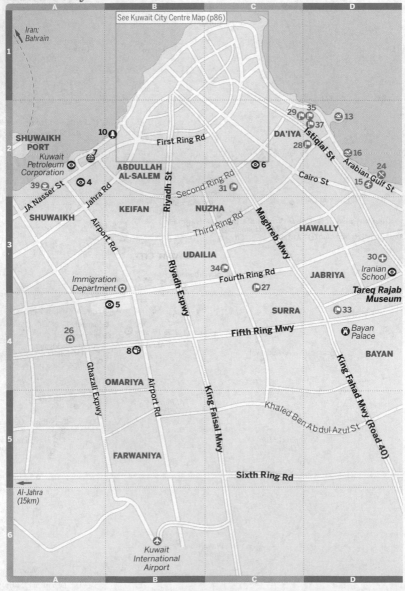

attractions a harrowing layer of modern history, the effects of which rumble invisibly below the surface, and there is enough to keep all but the dedicated nightclubber intrigued for days.

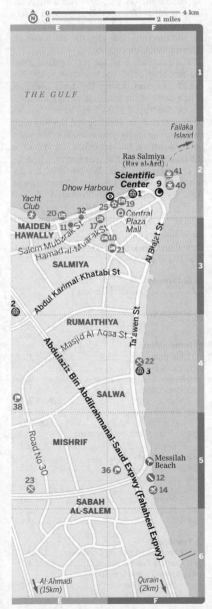

THE GULF

Failaka Island

Ras Salmiya (Ras al-Ard)

Scientific Center

Dhow Harbour

Yacht Club

MAIDEN HAWALLY

Central Plaza Mall

SALMIYA

Abdul Karimal-Khatabi St

RUMAITHIYA

Masjid Al Aqsa St

SALWA

Abdulaziz Bin Abdirrahmanai-Saud Expwy (Fahaheel Expwy)

MISHRIF

Road No 30

Messilah Beach

SABAH AL-SALEM

Al-Ahmadi (15km)

Qurain (2km)

History

As improbable as it seems today, Kuwait City was until recently a nomadic port town and Salmiya consisted of a few mud huts around a tree – and that is within the living memory of the older generation. Suddenly, within the past two decades, a booming Middle Eastern metropolis has burst from its skin and the gates are all that remain of the redundant city walls. Three successive master plans have tried to give direction to this capital growth, allowing for generous mortgages and free housing for the needy, but the growth is organic and unstoppable.

One of the few things that hasn't changed is the city's name. The capital evolved from a collection of Bedouin tents around a well into a small military outpost with a *kout* (small fort adjacent to water). This *kout* was built in 1672 by the Bani Khalid tribe who came from the Arabian interior to escape drought. The word *kout* evolved to give the city (and indeed the country) its name.

Something else that hasn't changed is the city's relationship with the sea. Its natural harbour made it an ideal location for a port. Indeed, it proved such an excellent port that it soon came to handle a lucrative trade in frankincense from Oman, pearls from Bahrain, spices from India, textiles from China and dates from just about everywhere. The port also facilitated the trans-shipment of goods across the desert to the Syrian port of Aleppo, a journey of two to three weeks. Pilgrims returned in the other direction, great caravans taking sustenance for the onward journey to Mecca. Today the city's port continues to play a vital role in the capital's fortunes.

The Iraqi invasion in 1990 tore a piece of the city's heart out, but remarkably most of the landmark buildings remain standing. A visitor today is never likely to know how much the city suffered.

◉ Sights

Many of Kuwait's sights are concentrated along the corniche (Arabian Gulf St) and around the National Museum area. While some of the downtown sights are within walking distance of each other, the most convenient way of visiting outlying attractions, or of covering longer stretches of the corniche, is by taxi.

One of the best new sights in Kuwait is the night-time display of lights on the new tower blocks dominating the Dasman area of town. Architects seem intent on outdoing each other in ingenuity of design, colour and motion of these lighting displays which combine to make downtown look much more dynamic and complete than it appears by day!

After the Tareq Rajab Museum, the following sights are listed geographically along or just off Arabian Gulf St from the Scientific Center to Yaum Al-Bahhar Village.

★ **Tareq Rajab Museum** MUSEUM
(Map p82; ☎ 2531 7358; www.trmkt.com; Street 5, House 22 Block 12, Jabriya; admission KD2; ☺4-7pm Sat-Thu) Housed in the basement of a large villa, this exquisite ethnographic museum should not be missed. It was assembled as a private collection of Islamic art by Kuwait's first minister of antiquities and his British wife. A pair of ornate doors from Cairo and Carl Haag's 19th-century painting of Lady Jane Digby el-Mesreb of Palmyra, who lived in tents in the winter and a Damascus villa in the summer, mark

the entrance to an Aladdin's cave of beautiful items. There are inlaid musical instruments suspended in glass cabinets; Omani silver and Saudi gold jewellery; headdresses, from the humble prayer cap to the Mongol helmet; costumes worn by princesses and by goatherds; necklaces for living goddesses in Nepal; Jaipur enamel; and Bahraini pearl. Despite all these superbly presented pieces from around the Muslim world, it is the Arabic manuscripts that give the collection its international importance.

The museum is all the more prized given the fate that befell the treasures in the National Museum during the Iraqi invasion. When news of the invasion spread, the owners bricked up the doorway at the bottom of the entry steps and strewed the way with rubbish. The Iraqis questioned why the stairs led to nowhere, but mercifully didn't pursue the issue and the collection survived intact.

The museum is in Jabriya, near the intersection of the Fifth Ring Motorway and the Abdulaziz Bin Abdilrahman al-Saud

Expressway (also known as the Fahaheel Expressway). Although there is no sign on the building, it is easily identified by its entrance – a carved wooden doorway flanked by two smaller doors on each side. All four of the door panels are worked in gilt metal.

Allow an hour to visit, although anyone with a passion for textiles will inevitably want to stay longer. Buses 102 and 502 stop at Hadi Clinic. Walk south along the Fahaheel Expressway for five minutes and turn right just before the Iranian School. Walk for a further 50m and the museum is on the left.

★ **Scientific Center**   MUSEUM
(Map p82; ☑184 8888; www.tsck.org.kw; Arabian Gulf St, Salmiya; adult/child KD3.500/2.500; ⏱9am-9.30pm Sun-Tue, 9am-10pm Thu, 2-10pm Fri; ℗) Housed in a fine, sail-shaped building on the corniche, the Scientific Center's mesmerising **aquarium** is the largest in the Middle East. The unique intertidal display, with waves washing in at eye level, is home to shoals of black-spotted sweetlips and the ingenious mudskipper. But the most spectacular part of the display (with giant spider crabs at 3.8m leg to leg, a living reef and fluorescent jellyfish coming in at a close second) is undoubtedly the wraparound, floor-to-ceiling shark and ray tanks. Ring ahead to check feeding times (currently 7pm Monday for sharks and 11am Sunday to Wednesday for fish).

There's an **IMAX cinema** and an interactive learning centre called **Discovery Place** where children can make their own sand dunes or roll a piece of road. The **dhow harbour** is home to *Fateh al-Khair,* the last surviving dhow of the pre-oil era. Admission prices vary, depending on which parts of the centre are visited.

Salmiya bus stop, for buses 15, 17, 24, 34 and 200, is a short 10-minute (shaded) walk away.

Al-Corniche   CORNICHE
(Arabian Gulf Street; ℗) Comprising over 10km of winding paths, parks and beaches on Arabian Gulf St (sometimes referred to locally as Gulf Rd), the corniche is marked at its southern end by the Scientific Center and at its northernmost point by the Kuwait Towers. Stop off at any one of the many beaches, restaurants or coffeehouses to watch a desert sunset, or, on hot summer evenings, enjoy being part of the throng of people flocking to the sea to catch the breeze.

★ **Kuwait Towers**   MONUMENT
(Map p86; www.kuwaittowers.com; Arabian Gulf St, Dasman; ℗) Kuwait's most famous landmark, the Kuwait Towers, with their distinctive blue-green 'sequins', are worth a visit for the prospect of sea and city that they afford.

Designed by a Swedish architectural firm and opened in 1979, the largest of the three towers rises to a height of 187m, and houses a two-level revolving observation deck, gift shop and cafe. The lower globe on the largest tower stores around one million gallons of water. The middle tower is also used for water storage, while the smallest tower is used to light up the other two.

A **collection of photographs** show how the so-called 'barbarian invaders' tried to destroy the symbol of Kuwait during the Iraqi invasion.

The towers are currently closed for major refurbishment with an expected reopening by mid-2013.

Beit Dickson   HISTORIC BUILDING
(Map p86; ☑2243 7450; Arabian Gulf St; ⏱8am-12.30pm & 4.30-7.30pm Mon-Thu, 8.30-11am & 4.30-7.30pm Fri & Sat) **FREE** A modest, white building with blue trim, Beit Dickson was the home of former British political agent Colonel Harold Dickson and his wife Violet whose love of and contribution to Kuwait is documented in the various archives inside the house.

Freya Stark spent most of March 1937 in the house and, while she adored Kuwait, she described the house as a 'big ugly box'. Nonetheless, a collection of photographs taken during Kuwait's British protectorate era; a replica museum of the Dicksons' living quarters; and an archive of Kuwaiti–British relations that dates from the 19th century to the 1960s, when Kuwait was granted independence, make the museum an interesting place in which to spend an hour.

Maritime Museum   MUSEUM
(Map p86; Arabian Gulf St, Qibla; ⏱8.30am-12.30pm & 4.30-8.30pm Mon-Sat, 4.30-8.30pm Fri; ℗) **FREE** Giving an excellent insight into the seafaring heritage of Kuwait, the entrance of this new museum is graced with three magnificent dhows. Dhows and boons like these brought water from the Shatt al-Arab waterway near Basra to the bone-dry city, making a tidy profit from thirsty inhabitants. Photographs inside the museum show the transport of water from boon to home

Kuwait City Centre

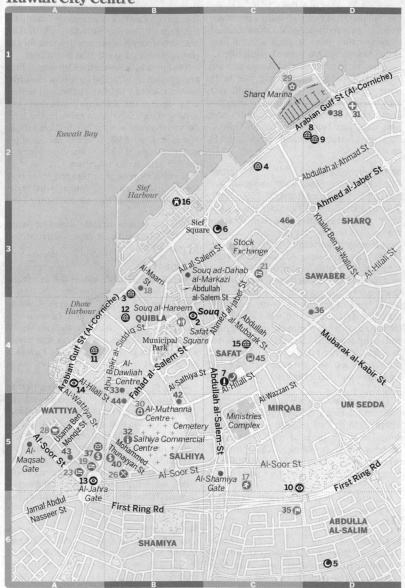

before desalination plants brought water to the taps of all householders.

The pearling displays upstairs comprise a fascinating collection of daily-use objects such as a heavy lead weight, turtle-shell nose peg, leather finger ends and a wool suit to guard against jelly fish. These objects speak volumes about the deprivations of a life spent prising pearls from a reluctant seabed. The sieves of tiny mesh used to sift pearls according to size, show that the effort was barely worth the dangers involved.

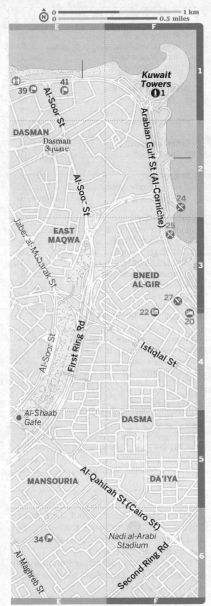

Modern Art Museum GALLERY

(Map p86; ☑ 2246 8348; www.artkuwait.org; Arabian Gulf St, Sharq; ⊘ 9am-1pm & 5-8pm Sun-Thu; Ⓟ) Adjacent to the Maritime Museum on Arabian Gulf St, this attractive, traditional-style building hosts a number of exhibitions of contemporary art throughout the year. Check the Art Kuwait website for a calendar of events.

Sief Palace PALACE

(Map p86; Arabian Gulf St) This is the official seat of the emir's court. The L-shaped Sief Palace that faces the roundabout is the original palace dating from the early 20th century, while the new and ponderously opulent palace, complete with lake, helipad and dock for visitors' yachts, was completed around the beginning of 2000. Neither palace is open to the public and photography is prohibited.

Grand Mosque MOSQUE

(Masjed Al-Kabir; Map p86; ☑ 2241 8447; www.the-grandmosque.net; Mubarak al-Kabir St) Located opposite Sief Palace, the Grand Mosque was opened in 1986 and cost KD14 million to construct. The largest of the city's 800 mosques, it boasts Kuwait's highest minaret (74m) and can accommodate up to 5000 worshippers in the main hall, with room for another 7000 in the courtyard. Tours, best organised through a local tour operator, are provided by the knowledgeable mosque staff. For information on what to wear in a mosque and other courtesies, see p40.

National Museum Complex MUSEUM

(Map p86; ☑ 2245 1195; Arabian Gulf St, Qibla; ⊘ 8.30am-12.30pm & 4.30-8.30pm Mon-Thu, 4.30-8.30pm Fri, 8.30-11.30am Sat; Ⓟ) FREE Once the pride of Kuwait, the National Museum remains a shadow of its former self. The centrepiece of the museum, the **Al-Sabah collection**, was one of the most important collections of Islamic art in the world. During the Iraqi occupation, however, the exhibition halls were systematically looted, damaged or set fire to.

Following intense pressure from the UN, the majority of the museum's collection was eventually returned, but many pieces had been broken in transit, poorly stored and, some suggest, deliberately spoiled. Nonetheless, this beleaguered collection has since been displayed in London's British Museum and the Metropolitan Museum of Art in New York while waiting to be restored in its entirety to Kuwait's National Museum.

The museum is marooned in the middle of the *bondu* (waste ground) off Arabian Gulf St, opposite Sharq Mall and next to the Modern Art Museum. There is currently no website nor permanent telephone contact.

Kuwait City Centre

Over 2000 items are now on display, covering various aspects of Kuwait's national heritage, including ancient treasures from Failaka Island, stamps and seals from the Bronze Age, axe heads and a wonderful Hellenistic limestone dolphin. The dhow in the courtyard (a replica of *Muhallab II* that was destroyed by the Iraqis) makes a good photo opportunity at sunset.

The quaint **Popular Traditional Museum** (Map p86; ☑2272 9158) variously described as the Heritage Museum and Culture Museum – is in Building 2, in the rear of the museum complex. It illustrates daily life in pre-oil Kuwait through a diorama of full-sized figures going about their various businesses – be sure to see the bead maker and what the museum booklet describes as the 'men's over-robe tailor'.

Buses 12 and 16 (departing from the main bus station) stop a couple of blocks from the museum complex.

Planetarium   PLANETARIUM
(Map p86; ☑2245 1195; Arabian Gulf St, Qibla; ⊙9.30am-noon & 5.30-6.30pm Mon-Thu, 5-6.30pm Fri, 9.30-10.30am Sat; ℗) FREE Forming part of the National Museum complex, the wonderful, modern Planetarium has regular shows.

Beit al-Badr
HISTORIC BUILDING

(Map p86; Arabian Gulf St, Qibla; ☉8am-1pm & 4-7pm Sat-Wed; P) **FREE** A traditional mud-built house, with heavy carved doors, Beit al-Badr was built between 1838 and 1848 and is one of the last examples of pre-oil residential architecture in the city. It is located alongside Sadu House. Opening times are erratic so, as there is no phone number, visitors have to take pot luck.

National Assembly Building
HISTORIC BUILDING

(Map p86; Arabian Gulf St, Qibla) Close to the National Museum, this interesting white building with its distinctive canopy was designed by Jørn Utzon, the Danish architect who also designed the Sydney Opera House, and was completed in 1985. The two sweeping roofs were designed to evoke Bedouin tents and the building is befitting of the first parliament of the region. The building is not generally open to the visiting public.

Old Kuwaiti Town
NOTABLE BUILDINGS

(Map p86; Arabian Gulf St, Qibla) Situated just southwest of the National Assembly Building on Arabian Gulf St, the houses in this complex of replica 19th-century dwellings gives a good idea of what Kuwait City would have looked like before the discovery of oil. The neighbouring blocks are being redeveloped to approximate traditional 20th-century dwellings – now there's progress!

★ Souq
SOUQ

(Map p86; btwn Mubarak al-Kabir, Ahmad al-Jaber & Ali al-Salem Sts; ☉9am-1pm & 4-9pm Sat-Thu, 4-9pm Fri) True to its origins, Kuwait City has retained the old souq in all of its complex, bustling and convoluted glory in the city centre. Albeit partly housed now in a smart, modern building, complete with cubby-holes of lockable wooden shutters, it nonetheless exudes antique practices, from the sharp haggling over ribands of offal and tails of ox, to the quick-witted trading of olives and dates in the extensive food halls of **Souq Marbarakia**. It's a wonderful place to idle a few hours, and indeed an entire lunchtime could be spent sampling delicacies without ever setting foot in one of the numerous snack shops that line the outer rim of the souq.

The souq also comprises the small, covered **Souq al-Hareem**, where Bedouin women sit cross-legged on cushions of velvet selling kohl (black eyeliner), pumice stones and gold-spangled dresses in the red, white and green livery of the Kuwaiti flag. Beyond the covered alleyway, the souq opens out into lanes stocked with woollen vests and Korean blankets.

The close-by **Souq ad-Dahab al-Markazi** is the city's central gold market and many shops spangle with wedding gold and local pearls along the perimeter of Souq Marbarakia.

Liberation Tower
TOWER

(Map p86; ☎2242 9166; Abdullah al-Salem St, Safat) Not to be confused with the distinctive Kuwait Towers, Liberation Tower in the city centre is the tallest building in the city, and at a height of 372m claims to be the fifth-tallest communications tower in the world. Started before the invasion, the tower took its new name when it was completed in 1993. Panoramic lifts ascend to a viewing balcony and revolving restaurant.

Science & Natural History Museum
MUSEUM

(Educational Science Museum; Map p86; ☎2242 1268; Abdullah al-Mubarak St, Safat; ☉9am-noon & 4.30-7.30pm Sun-Thu) **FREE** For an eclectic range of exhibits from electronics and space paraphernalia to fossils, stuffed animals and an 18m whale skeleton, this museum, near Liberation Tower, also has a **planetarium** with a Galaxy Skyshow.

Yaum Al-Bahhar Village
PARK

(Map p82; Arabian Gulf St, Shuwaikh; ☉5pm-11.30pm) **FREE** With traditional wind-tower architecture, this small area of craft workshops is part of a development along the coast that includes walking paths and fountains. The workshops are open at variable times and some of the items are for sale. Some not-for-the-faint-hearted crafts include stuffed bustard (an endangered bird) and shell decorations that you wouldn't wish on your enemy.

This is a good place for male visitors to enjoy a mint tea in a traditional coffeeshop and listen to the clack of bone on board as locals play backgammon.

Old City Gates
LANDMARK

(Map p86) **Al-Shaab, Al-Shamiya, Al-Jahra** and **Al-Maqsab** are the names of Kuwait City's gates in Safat on Al-Soor St, the street that follows the line of the old city wall ('soor' is the Arabic word for 'wall'). Despite their ancient appearance, the wall and gates were only constructed around 1920. The wall was demolished in 1957.

DON'T MISS

KUWAIT'S MODERN ARCHITECTURE

Kuwait's extraordinary modern wealth has been expressed in many pieces of architectural civic pride. If you're in town for a while, don't miss at least a drive-by of the following fine buildings.

➡ **Kuwait Towers** (p85) There are few buildings in the region as iconic as these water towers. Their slender columns and plump reservoirs are symbolic of the way in which a city has blossomed from humble beginnings.

➡ **Liberation Tower** (p89) The fifth-largest communication tower in the world, illustrates how the city, despite the troubles of the past 20 years, has aspired to compete with regional neighbours.

➡ **National Assembly Building** (p89) Designed by Jørn Utzon of Sydney Opera House fame, this landmark building resembles a piece of unfurled silk, evoking both the canopy of a Bedouin tent and a sail-furled dhow, while expressing modernist concepts of negative space and the sculpture of light and shade.

➡ **Arab Fund Building** (p90) With its expression of the integrity of space and function, light and communication, and combining modern interior design, this superb building remains true to a traditional Islamic aesthetic.

➡ **Grand Mosque** (p87) Across from Sief Palace on Arabian Gulf St, Kuwait City's main mosque is graced with the tallest minaret in the country.

➡ **Fatima Mosque** (Map p86) Considerable wealth has been channelled into religious architecture, with some 60% of Kuwait's mosques financed and built by individuals, including this distinctive green-and-white domed mosque in Abdullah al-Salem.

➡ **Shaikh Nasser al-Sabah Mosque** (Map p82) In Ras Salmiya (also known as Ras al-Ard) this pyramid-shaped mosque is another example of exceptional modern mosque design.

➡ **Sharq Souq** (p97) This flight of fancy, with its wind-tower design and adjoining marina, is an expression of the city's humble Bedouin and seafaring beginnings both metaphorically and literally.

Kuwait House of National Works:
Memorial Museum MUSEUM
(Map p82; ☑ 2484 5335; Block 7, 71 St, opposite Prime Minister's residence, Shuwaikh; admission KD1; ⊘ 8.30am-1pm & 4.30-8.30pm Sun-Thu, 4.30-8.30pm Sat) This innovative museum encapsulates the horror of the Iraqi invasion and honours the sacrifices that Kuwaiti citizens, the Kuwaiti military and the allies made in order to beat back Saddam's forces. The exhibits comprise a set of well-crafted models of the city that are illuminated in time with an audio recording in English. Despite the nationalist propaganda, the experience of walking through the darkened corridors, lit only by simulated gun blasts and mortar attacks, and focusing on the heroism of the few for the safety of the many, has a contemporary resonance that transcends the exhibit's narrow remit.

The museum is best reached by taxi and can be combined with a visit to the nearby Arab Fund Building. Alternatively, take bus 13 along Arabian Gulf St to the airport and get off at KPC, the steel and concrete headquarters of Kuwait Petroleum Corporation (KPC). As the road bends sharply inland from here, take the first lane on the left.

Arab Fund Building BUILDING
(Map p82; ☑ 2484 4500; www.arabfund.org/aohq; Airport Rd, Shuwaikh) **FREE** Although not strictly open to the casual caller, the impressive Arab Fund Building, with a host of exceptionally beautiful rooms, is worth the trouble of gaining access. Call first to request an appointment and explain that you wish to see the building's interior and you'll be given a guided tour by one of the employees.

The gravity of the exterior belies the light and airy interior, designed upon Arabic architectural principles of integrity of space, decoration and function. The magnificent eight-storey atrium with wooden lattices, opening onto a transparent corridor or an exquisite hidden *majlis* (meeting room), is an exciting reinterpretation of a familiar theme. Traditional craftsmanship from around the Arab world is represented in lavish concoctions of ceramic, carpet and woodwork in one of the most extraordinary expressions of postmodern eclecticism in the Gulf.

Friday Market   SOUQ

(Souq al-Jum'a; Map p82; south of 4th Ring Rd & west of Airport Rd, Shuwaikh; ⊙8am-4pm Fri) For a plastic pot plant, a secondhand dress, an Afghan coat or a smuggled antique from Iran, this enormous weekly, semi-covered market is more than a shopping extravaganza – it offers an insight into contemporary Kuwaiti culture and cross-border relations. Five minutes of shuffling between dusty textiles and sipping on the good-natured coffee of a friendly vendor delivers more in the way of insight into the complex web of Kuwaiti affairs, domestic and international, than one could absorb in a month of lectures on Arabic culture.

House of Mirrors   HOUSE

(Map p82; ☑2251 8522; Street 94, House 17 Block 9, Qadisiya) FREE For a quirky art-in-action experience, visit this small museum in a residential house in the suburbs of Qadisiya. Reputedly, 77 tons of mirror and 102 tons of white cement have been used in the creation of the mirror mosaics that spangle the entire house – both inside and out. The creation of Lidia al-Qattan, the widow of Khalifa al-Qattan, a renowned Kuwaiti artist, the project was inspired by the decorating of an old piece of dining room furniture and grew to incorporate epic scenes, as in the Room of the Universe (bedroom) and the Basin of the Sharks (hallway). Ring ahead to request a tour.

Al-Qurain Martyrs' Museum   MUSEUM

(☑2543 0343; House 61, St 3, Block 4, Qurain; ⊙8.30am-noon & 4.30-8.30pm Mon-Thu & Sat, 4.30-8.30pm Fri) FREE Located in the residential suburb of Qurain, a 20-minute taxi ride southeast of the city centre, this small museum is a memorial to a cell of young Kuwaiti patriots who tried to resist arrest in February 1991.

To understand what invasion meant to the ordinary Kuwait family, allow half an hour to visit this sobering museum, if only to see copies of documents issuing instructions to 'burn and destroy' homes and 'fire

on demonstrations'. Bus 101 stops within a 10-minute walk of the museum, but it is difficult to find the precise location without assistance. Go by taxi.

Al-Hashemi Marine Museum   MUSEUM

(Map p82; ☑2567 3000; www.al-hashemi2.com; Ta'awen St, behind Radisson Blu Hotel, Salwa) FREE For proof that the Vikings made it to the Middle East, albeit only model ones, it's worth visiting this museum with its impressive collection of large, scaled-model dhows. A novel shop sells 21 piece knot boards and Gipsy Moth lanterns among other nautical souvenirs, such as barometers and sextants. You can even buy your own Nelson figurine, incomplete with one arm.

On the wall of the museum is a certificate, dated 2002, from Guinness World Records announcing that **Al-Hashemi II**, the huge and unmissable wooden dhow adjacent to the museum, is the largest wooden boat on earth, measuring a world-record-breaking 80.4m long, 18.7m wide and weighing an estimated 2500 tonnes. The vision of Husain Marafie, owner of the Radisson Blu Hotel, the dhow was completed in 1998 from mahogany and ekki logs from Cameroon, planks from the Ivory Coast and pine logs from Oregon. It's worth taking a five-minute walk inside the lavish, parquet-floored interior, used for conferences and banqueting.

A smaller dhow in the complex, called **Al-Boom**, is a restaurant (p96); it's a great place for dinner. The complex is next to the Palm Gardens Hotel inside the grounds of the Radisson Blu Hotel (currently under reconstruction).

🏃 Activities

Kuwait City's location on the seafront provides many opportunities for fun with water – in it (swimming), on it (water sports and ice skating), alongside it (jogging along the corniche) and through it (ferry rides). Contact **Touristic Enterprises Company** (TEC; ☑2562 2600; www.kuwaittourism.com) for current details of many activities in Kuwait.

Swimming

All the way along Arabian Gulf St there are splendid beaches and there is nothing to stop a committed paddler from taking a dip from most of them, though the water tends to be on the shallow side for serious swimming and worries prevail as to the state of pollution in the water.

Green Island
SWIMMING

(Map p82; ☑2257 3542; Arabian Gulf St, Dasman; adult/child 500/250 fils Sun-Wed, adult/child KD1 Thu-Sat; ☺9am-11pm) For activities ranging from strolling in the gardens, swimming in a lagoon, cycling or listening to an impromptu concert, this artificial island – joined to the mainland by a pedestrian causeway – houses a 700-seat amphitheatre and a game park for children. On Friday, the increased entrance fee covers the cost of an open-air concert of Arabic music.

Messilah Water Village
SWIMMING

(Map p82; ☑2565 0642; Ta'awen St, Messilah; adult/child KD1/500 fils; ☺8am-11pm) For those who prefer facilities to the sea, Messilah Water Village, 20km south of the city centre, has a good range of pools, floats and slides. The water is chilled in summer and heated in winter. Between April and August the beach is reserved for women only on three days of the week. The same company manages the centrally located Aqua Park (p93) beside the Kuwait Towers – call first, as the park is not always open.

TEC Swimming Pool Complex
SWIMMING

(Map p82; ☑2562 3154; Arabian Gulf St, Dasman; KD1) If the turquoise sea doesn't tempt, this complex has three large pools, two for men only and one for families.

Diving & Other Water Activities

Dive Caroline
DIVING

(Map p82; ☑6690 4201; www.divecaroline.com; Fahaheel Sea Club) This is a well-established centre at the Fahaheel Sea Club offering day trips and night dive trips (from KD20/15) to Donkey Reef. It also offers sailing, windsurfing, kayaking and other water sports.

Ice Skating

Ice-skating Rink
SKATING

(Map p86; ☑2241 1151; Al-Soor St & First Ring Rd, Shamiya; admission 500 fils, skating incl boots KD1.500; ☺8.30am-10pm) One of the best in the region, this Olympic-sized rink has a spectator capacity of 1600. It's home to the Kuwaiti Falcons, the country's official ice-hockey team, and the only Arab team to win membership of the International Ice Hockey Federation.

🍵 Courses

Beit Lothan
CULTURAL CENTRE

(Map p82; ☑2575 5866; www.baytlothan.org; Arabian Gulf St, Salmiya; ☺9am-1pm & 5-9pm Sun-Thu, 5-9pm Sat) This cultural centre promotes the work of Kuwaiti and Gulf artists and craftspeople through regular exhibitions in a 1930s house that was originally the home of the country's late emir, Sheikh Sabah al-Salem al-Sabah. Apart from cultural activities, the centre acts as a conduit for the energies of Kuwaiti youth. It offers a range of courses, including crafts, poetry, drawing and painting.

Sadu House
CULTURAL CENTRE

(Map p86; ☑2243 2395; www.alsadu.org.kw; Arabian Gulf St; admission free; ☺8am-1pm & 4-8pm Sat-Thu) Forming part of the National Museum complex, Sadu House is a cultural foundation dedicated to preserving Bedouin arts and crafts. It is the best place in Kuwait to buy Bedouin goods, such as cushion covers and bags. The house is built of gypsum and coral, with fine decorations in the courtyard and an elegant use of light and space making it a great venue to study a course in weaving. The Bedouin craftswomen teach *sadu* (Bedouin-style) and other weaving techniques. Check with the Kuwait Textile Arts Association (ktaaworkshop@yahoo.com) for details.

🍵 Tours

Kuwait Tourism Services Company
TOUR AGENCY

(Map p86; ☑2245 1734; www.ktsc-q8.com; Ice-skating Rink, Al-Soor St & First Ring Rd, Shamiya) Runs tours around the various city sights and out to the oilfields. It mainly caters for large tour groups, but can also arrange similar tours for individuals. Excursions, which start from KD10 per person, include half- and full-day city, coastline, diving and Gulf cruising tours.

Nuzha Tourist Enterprises
TOUR AGENCY

(☑2575 5825; www.nuzhatours.com) Can organise tours and offers camel and horse rides, desert safaris, climbing tours and many other activities. You'll need to use a translation facility to access the website.

🎊 Festivals & Events

Hala Festival
SHOPPING

(www.hala-feb.com) During the month of February, the city goes crazy with the annual shopping festival. There are lots of draws giving away valuable prizes in the shopping centres, and special promotions lure customers in. Many shops offer discounts of up to 70%. Ask your hotel reception where to go for the best bargains.

KUWAIT CITY FOR CHILDREN

Kuwait is a safe, easygoing, family-oriented country, and children are welcome and catered for everywhere. Many of the city's family entertainment activities are organised by Touristic Enterprises Company (p91), known as TEC. The TEC information centre can advise on facilities in town and at its resorts, and take reservations.

Shaab Leisure Park (Map p82; ☎ 2561 3777; www.shaabpark.com; Arabian Gulf St, Salmiya; admission 500 fils; ☉ 4pm-midnight Sun-Thu, 10am-midnight Fri & Sat) Occupying a large, open area, this leisure park offers around 70 rides, bungee jumping and pony riding. Some of the attractions are free, others cost from KD2. For a unique souvenir, try the video cinema, where visitors can make their own music video.

Aqua Park (Map p86; ☎ 2243 1960; www.aquaparkkuwait.com; Arabian Gulf St, beside Kuwait Towers) The centrally located Aqua Park is managed by the same people who run Messilah Water Village. Call first, as it is not always open.

Kuwait Zoo (Map p82; ☎ 2473 3389; cnr Airport Rd & 5th Ring Rd, Omariya; Omariya; ☉ 8am-8pm Oct-Apr, 8am-noon & 4-8pm May-Sep, Sun-Fri) The Kuwait zoo has 65 species with an emphasis on desert dwellers.

Music & Water Display (Map p86; ☎ 2242 8394; Al-Soor St & First Ring Rd; admission KD1 Wed-Thu, free Fri-Tue; ☉ 4pm-midnight Oct-Apr, 3-10.30pm May-Sep, Sun-Fri) Located next to the ice-skating rink, this outdoor display is said to have the fourth-largest set of fountains in the world.

The festival coincides with National Day on 25 February and Liberation Day on 26 February. During this time, there are often fireworks displays and the city is draped in lights. Arts, sports, a carnival and other activities make this an exciting time to be in town. Check the festival website and 'What's On' listings in the English-language daily papers for details.

🛏 Sleeping

All of the hotels mentioned here have aircon, bathrooms, satellite TVs and minifridges. Prices quoted are inclusive of the 15% service charge that most hotels add to their tariff, though it's always worth asking for a discount. Breakfast is not generally included.

Top-end prices quoted here are rack rates: with a bit of persuasion, you can usually negotiate some sort of 'corporate' rate and a range of rates are available online.

International Hotel
HOTEL $

(Map p82; ☎ 2574 1788; inter-hotel@hotmail.com; Dumna St, behind Al-Fannar Complex, Salmiya; s/d KD20/25) This 1970s hotel, in its distinctive round building and period-piece lobby of varnished wood and mirror, is something of a Kuwaiti institution. The oddly shaped rooms with their curved balconies, chocolate brown carpets and grilled radiators, are dated but spacious. There is 24-hour room service and a restaurant. The hotel is tucked in the lanes behind Hamad al-Mubarak St.

Oasis Hotel
HOTEL $

(Map p86; ☎ 2246 5489; www.oasis.com.kw; cnr Ahmad al-Jaber & Mubarak al-Kabir Sts, Sharq; s/d KD30/35; 🛜) This lime green hotel, with its sea-green reception area, has simple, clean rooms and is in a prime downtown location, just five-minutes' walk from the souq. The upper floors have expansive views.

Ibis Hotel
BUSINESS HOTEL $

(Map p82; ☎ 2573 4247; www.ibishotel.com; Salem Al-Mubarak St, Salmiya; r KD39.100; 🅿🛜) Intended primarily as a business hotel (ask for the lower rates offered at the weekend), this modern hotel in the heart of shoppers' paradise represents exceptional value for money. The bright, glass-fronted coffeehouse and lobby, on the third floor of the hotel, allows for a lofty survey of the busy heart of Salmiya. There's a National rental car agency in the foyer.

Ritz Salmiya
HOTEL $$

(Map p82; ☎ 2571 1001; www.ritzkuwait.com; Qatar St, Salmiya; r from KD42; 🛜) With the opportunity of using the facilities (including a pool and sauna) of the sister Ritz hotel on the corniche, this good value, bright and friendly hotel, opposite the City Center shopping mall, has an appealingly busy atmosphere. Rooms are modern and bright.

Kuwait Palace Hotel HOTEL $$
(Ghani Palace; Map p82; ✆ 2571 0301; infor@kuwaitpalace.net; Salem Mubarak St, Salmiya; s/d KD35/45; @ ≋) One of the few hotels you don't have to check the address to remember you're in Arabia. Located in a Yemeni-style building near Central Plaza mall, the hotel sports furniture from Syria, lanterns from Morocco and local plaster work. Each wood-panelled room is split level with kitchenette and balcony and gives in character what it lacks in finish.

The sister hotel, Ghani Palace, which shares the same building, offers monthly rentals.

Le Royal BOUTIQUE HOTEL $$
(Map p86; ✆ 2251 0999; www.leroyalkuwait.com; Al-Khalij Al-Arabi St, Bneid al-Qar; r from KD55; P ≋ ≋) This small and tasteful boutique-style hotel, on a slip road off Arabian Gulf St, offers wonderful sea views, a French rococo foyer and a bright and intimate atmosphere. The rooms, with their CD players, polished floors, floral-design bedsteads, huge bolster pillows and enormous luxury bathrooms are state-of-the-art. There's a cosy wicker-chair cafe in the foyer.

Plaza Athenee Hotel BOUTIQUE HOTEL $$
(Map p86; ✆ 184 6666; www.plazaatheneekuwait.com; Port Said St, Block 18, behind Al-Manar Complex, Bneid al-Qar; s/d KD34.500/57.500) If you're wondering at the discrepancy in price between single and double in this boutique hotel, it is not a printing error! The singles are pigeon-sized, with tiny, angular shower rooms and linoleum floors. In contrast, the doubles, with heavy Arabian-style furniture and thick wooden doors all have marble-topped kitchenettes, balconies and separate sitting areas.

Le Meridien Tower Kuwait BOUTIQUE HOTEL $$
(Map p86; ✆ 183 1831; www.lemeridienkuwait.com; Fahad al-Salem St, Wattiya; r from KD60 (KD40 Thu-Fri); ≋ ≋) This stylish downtown hotel prides itself as being the first 'art and tech' hotel in the Gulf with designer features including powered showers and interactive TV. The illuminated glass panels behind the bedstead and the glass washbasin in the bathrooms help complete the impression of 22nd-century living.

Live cooking shows in the Cascade Restaurant (named after the water feature in the foyer) cater for individual guests.

Hilton Kuwait Resort RESORT $$$
(✆ 2225 6222; www.hilton.com; Coast Rd, Mangaf; from KD80; P ≋ ≋) Situated on 1.8km of white-sand beach with spotless water, this resort, 35km from the city, provides the perfect antidote to the proverbial 'hard day in the office', whether 'office' equates with a business meeting, a day of committed shopping or sightseeing, or even a day of peacekeeping over the border.

Seashell Jalai'a Hotel & Resort RESORT $$$
(✆ 2325 0004; www.seashell-kuwait.com; Rd 245, Fahad Motorway, Jalai'a; r from KD80; P @ ≋) Located about 70km south of Kuwait City, this is definitely not what one could call 'conveniently located'. If you are looking to get away from the city for a weekend, however, this palm tree, pool and beach complex, with its desert-castle architecture, ayurvedic centre and health club could be just the thing.

With a spa, water-sports facilities, cinema, entertainment centre and bicycle hire, it's unlikely you'll notice that's there's precious little surrounding the resort but desert.

Sheraton Kuwait LUXURY HOTEL $$$
(Map p86; ✆ 2242 2055; www.luxurycollection.com/kuwait; Safat Tower, Fahad Al-Salem St; r from KD100; P ≋ ≋) This old war-horse of a central hotel has been given a recent makeover and now it glitters with dazzling chandeliers and mirror-polished treacle-coloured marble. Afternoon tea here is a top expat experience. What the hotel lacks in friendly staff it makes up for in glamour.

★ **Marina Hotel** LUXURY HOTEL $$$
(Map p82; ✆ 2223 0030; www.marinahotel.com; Arabian Gulf St, Salmiya; s/d KD110/124; P ≋ ≋) Situated on the edge of bustling Marina Crescent and within walking distance from the shopping district of Salmiya, this low-rise hotel floats like a lily on the water's edge and offers many rooms with direct access onto the beach. Sophisticated, elegant and modern, this is one boutique hotel that succeeds in being practical as well as aesthetically pleasing.

If you get bored of gazing at the sea outside your bedroom window, you could always sit in the lobby and enjoy the aquarium behind reception instead. The hotel's Atlantis restaurant, in the shape of a ship's prow, is an excellent place to sample the catch of the day.

Eating

Perhaps the city's best-loved activity, dining out is something of an institution, and there are literally hundreds of restaurants to suit all wallets and palates. The eateries listed below represent an eclectic hotchpotch of choices that have a flavour of the region either in the cuisine or in the ambience.

One of the liveliest places to enjoy the night breeze over a chilled fruit juice – and a choice of grilled, baked and fried fishy delights – is in and around Marina Crescent in Salmiya. The plaza and its many cafes and restaurants is attached by footbridge to the Marina Mall in Salmiya and is a relaxed meeting place of Kuwaiti families throughout the weekend.

Sultan Centre
SUPERMARKET $
(Map p86; Arabian Gulf St, Sharq Souq, Sharq; ☺24 hr) This modern chain of supermarkets has all the wherewithal for a budget picnic. The closest store to central Kuwait City is in Sharq Souq.

Restaurant 99
CAFE $
(Map p86; Al-Soor St; sandwiches from 350 fils; ☺7am-1pm & 4-8pm Sat-Thu, 4-8pm Fri) Near Al-Jahra Gate, this is one of the city's traditional cheap and cheerfuls for a quick bite. Hummus, *shwarma* (meat sliced off a spit and stuffed in a pocket of pita-type bread with chopped tomatoes and garnish) and a wide variety of Arabic-bread fillings are on offer for a few hundred fils.

★ Souq Marbarakia
KEBAB $
(Map p86; btwn Mubarak al-Kabir, Ahmad al-Jaber & Ali al-Salem Sts, safat; kebabs around KD2; ☺11am-midnight) One of the best ways to get a feel for the heart of the city is to pull up a chair at one of the casual tables strewn around the western edge of the old souq on the semi-pedestrianised Abdullah al-Salem St. If you order kebabs, a generous helping of green leaves, pickles, hummus and Arabic bread arrives to garnish the meat.

Layali al-Helmeya
KEBAB $
(Map p82; ☎2263 8710; Arabian Gulf St, Salmiya; snacks 500 fils-KD2; ☺7am-3pm) A block north of the New Park Hotel, this is a lovely place to sit and enjoy the view overlooking Kuwait Bay with a fresh mango juice. A modern version of a traditional Egyptian coffeehouse, it offers kebabs and falafel sandwiches, and *shish tawouk* (chicken kebab). A *sheesha* costs KD1.600.

Breadz
BAKERY $
(Map p86; ☎2240 7707; Arabian Gulf St, Ground fl, Sharq Souq, Sharq; sandwiches & salads from KD2.250; ☺10am-10pm) Breadz offers a deliciously fresh selection of pastries, sandwiches and salads, as well as fresh fruit juices, tea and coffee. The outdoor terrace overlooking the Sharq marina makes this a pleasant spot for a snack. The decadent dessert bar is worth a look.

Burj Al-Hamam
LEBANESE $
(Map p86; ☎2252 9095; www.kfg.com.kw/bur-jalhamam; Arabian Gulf St, Dasman; mains KD2-5; ☺9am-midnight; ☎) This square restaurant at the end of a pier is like a piece of punctuation along the corniche but don't let the rather unattractive steel exterior put you off. Burj Al-Hamam is a great place to sample Middle Eastern fare in a thoroughly convivial atmosphere among local families. There's an outer terrace with 270 degrees open to the sea.

Restaurant Assaha
LEBANESE $$
(Lebanese Traditional Village; Map p86; ☎2253 3377; www.assahavillage.com; Al-Khalij Al-Arabi St, Rneid al-Qar; mains KD5; ☺noon-11.30pm; ☎) This place offers an atmospheric dining experience in a restaurant that has been built to resemble an old Kuwaiti villa so convincingly, you'll be surprised to learn it's brand new. With snugs and a *majlis* area, tiled floors and antiques, this is the Oriental experience that is all too hard to find in the tower block cities of the Gulf.

Beit 7
INTERNATIONAL $$
(Map p86; Usama Ben Monqiz St, Behbehani Houses No 7 off Al-Soor St; mains KD5.500; ☺9am-11pm) With tables tucked around the interior courtyard of this old coral-and-gypsum house, dating from 1949 and included on the government's list of heritage sites, this restaurant, with its beaded lanterns, palm fans and wicker chairs, has retained the feeling of house and home. It serves international fare and is a firm favourite with the expat community.

Le Notre
FRENCH $$
(Map p86; ☎180 5050; Arabian Gulf St; meals KD5-9; ☺noon-midnight) Fantastic views of the Kuwait Towers, a discerning menu, an exclusive chocolatier and a landmark building of steel and glass make this restaurant one of the chicest in town.

★ Al-Boom
SEAFOOD $$$

(Map p82; ☑ 2575 6000; Ta'awen St, Radisson SAS Hotel, Rumaithiya; set 3-course meal KD15; ⊙ 7-11.30pm) Located in the hull of a boat, this inventive restaurant takes some beating, particularly as this isn't just any old boat: this is *Mohammedi II*, built in Culicut, India in 1979. A replica of the largest dhow ever built (*Mohammedi I*, 1915), it took three years to construct from teak wood and 2.5 tonnes of copper, and was completed with 8.8 tonnes of handmade iron nails.

Not that one spares much thought for the 35,000 days of labour that was invested in one of the most characterful cargo holds in the history of boat building: when ensconced in the curving hull, under a ship's lantern hung from the beams, the attention is much more carefully focused on the set-piece of grilled grouper or sirloin, delivered sizzling to a personalised brass dinner setting. As the ship is dry, in all senses of the word, seasickness is not a prime concern. As this is a very popular venue, it's advisable to make a reservation; there are two sittings, one at 7pm and one at 9pm.

Ayam Zamar
LEBANESE $$$

(Map p82; ☑ 2473 2100; Crowne Plaza Hotel, Farwaniya; meals KD7-15; ⊙ noon-midnight) Perched in an eyrie high in the atrium of the 'happening' Crowne Plaza Hotel, this Lebanese restaurant is spread over a number of split levels, taxing the dexterity of the waiters who have to climb dozens of steps per serving. Somehow they still manage to bring the mezze steaming hot from the kitchens. Book for the Arabian Friday brunch.

♥ Drinking & Nightlife

There are a number of Arabic cafes around town where mostly men go to chat over a *sheesha* and many small cups of sweet, black coffee. The coffeehouses mentioned below are the equivalent of a commercial *diwaniya* (gathering) and business preliminaries are often conducted informally on the premises.

Souq Marbarakia
COFFEEHOUSE

(Map p86; btwn Mubarak al-Kabir, Ahmad al-Jaber & Ali al-Salem Sts; ⊙ 4pm-midnight) Women may feel rather uncomfortable in the covered inner courtyard of the old souq, near the cafes on the western edge of the souq, but men will love the convivial atmosphere.

Beit Lothan
COFFEEHOUSE

(☑ 2575 5866; Arabian Gulf St, Salmiya; ⊙ 10am-10pm) Coffee, tea and a *sheesha* are available in a quiet garden, adjacent to the Beit Lothan cultural centre.

Casper & Gambini's
CAFE

(Map p86; ☑ 2243 0065; www.casperandgambinis. com; Usama Ben Monqiz St, Behbehani Houses, off Al-Soor St, Wattiya; meals KD5-8; ⊙ 10am-11pm) More cafe than coffeehouse, this award-winning coffee specialist serves up 100% Arabica coffee beans where solo women will feel perfectly at home. The Espresso Freeze is reason enough to visit this atmospheric, wooden-floored venue in an old Kuwaiti townhouse.

English Tea Lounge
LOUNGE

(Map p86; ☑ 2242 2055; Sheraton Kuwait Hotel, Wattiya; high tea from KD8; ⊙ 10am-1pm & 4pm-midnight Sat-Thu, 4pm-midnight Fri) The

---

WATER, WATER EVERYWHERE BUT NOT A DROP TO DRINK

Kuwait has long been known for its fine natural harbour but, like so many places in the Middle East, it is chronically short of water. Indeed, from 1907 until 1950, traders had to buy fresh water from the Shatt al-Arab waterway near Bubiyan Island, at the head of the Gulf, and ship it by dhow to Kuwait. The trade peaked in 1947 when it was estimated that 303,200L of water per day was arriving in Kuwait by boat – thankfully the country didn't have a golf course.

Early investment of oil revenues into the search for ground water was unsuccessful, but the country's first desalination plant in 1950 signalled the end of the sea trade in water. An exorbitant way to acquire fresh water, desalination nonetheless satisfies the country's huge thirst for water, which (according to some local water resource experts) has grown to the highest consumption of water in the world.

Natural resources are precious and, as every Bedouin knows (and any mid-summer visitor can guess at), water in the desert is far more valuable than oil. In Kuwait, it's also more expensive.

Sheraton, with its multiple marble pillars, record-breaking crystal chandeliers and extravagant Persian carpets, looks like the last place to find a Welsh tea with rarebit. But if scones and cucumber sandwiches beckon, choose from a Yorkshire tea with fruit cake, or a Royal Windsor tea with smoked salmon.

☆ Entertainment

In the absence of bars, entertainment in the city is pretty much confined to shopping and dining, although film and theatre are popular with locals. Check Bazaar (www.bazaar-magazine.com) for 'What's On' and 'Where'.

Cinemas

Considering its size, Kuwait has an overwhelming number of cinemas, which unfortunately show the same films (usually heavily edited to exclude kissing, nudity and sex – violence, however, is left uncensored). The more popular and modern of the cinemas are in the malls, such as at Sharq Souq (p90) and in the **Al-Fanar Shopping Complex** (Map p82; ☎ 2575 9306; Salem Mubarak St, Salmiya).

Cinemas are run by the **Kuwait National Cinema Company** (☎ 2461 0545, 24hr service 180 3456; cinema admission KD2.500-KD5; ☉ 10am-midnight Sat-Thu, 2pm-midnight Fri) and single men are segregated from women and families. Women are not expected to go to the cinema alone.

There is also an **Imax cinema** in the Scientific Center (p85).

Theatre

Arabic theatre has enjoyed a long history in Kuwait, dating back to 1922 when the first amateur plays were performed, and are highly popular with Arab audiences.

Two groups perform in English. The Kuwait Players began in 1952 and stage about 10 productions per year, from pantomime to Shakespeare. The other company is **Kuwait Little Theatre** (☎ 9937 3678, 2398 2680; www.theklt.com; Main St, Al-Ahmadi), which has been performing comedies and dramas in its own venue in Al-Ahmadi since 1948 – visit the website to find out more.

For performance times and venues, check 'What's On' listings in the local papers.

🔒 Shopping

Salmiya is undoubtedly *the* shopping district of Kuwait. The main street, Hamad al-Mubarak St, is known as the 'Champs-Élysées' of the Middle East and is filled with dazzling shopping malls.

For something traditional and locally produced, the Kuwaiti Bedouin weavings at Sadu House (p92), a cultural foundation dedicated to preserving Bedouin art, are recommended. Alternatively, some 'old lamps for new' often turn up at the Friday Market. The old souq in the heart of Kuwait City is a great place to shop for anything from olives to blankets – or just to snack and watch the world go by.

Sharq Souq MALL
(Map p86; www.souksharq.com; Arabian Gulf St, Sharq; ☉ 10am-10pm) A modern complex that boasts its own marina.

The Avenues MALL
(Map p82; ☎ 2259 7777; www.the-avenues.com; Fifth Ring Rd, Al-Rai; ☉ 10am-10pm) With its six-star hotel and valet parking, this is worth a visit just for the architecture.

Kuwait Bookshop BOOKS
(Map p86; ☎ 2242 4289; kbs1935b@qualitynct. net; Fahad al-Salem St, Basement, Al-Muthanna Centre, Safat; ☉ 9am-12.30pm & 5-9.30pm Sat-Thu, 9am-noon & 5-9pm Fri) With a wide selection of bestsellers, books on current affairs and local-interest, this is the best place to look for English-language books.

ℹ Information

EMERGENCY
Ambulance, Fire & Police (☎ 112)

INTERNET ACCESS
Many of the top-end hotels offer free Internet access to guests. There are internet cafes in the city centre and in Salmiya.
Kuwait Internet Café (Map p86; Fahad al-Salem St, 2nd fl, Al-Dawliah Centre; per hr KD2; ☉ 8am-10pm) Located behind the Kuwait Airways building, it offers reasonably fast connections.

MEDICAL SERVICES
Services in an emergency are provided free or at a minimal charge on a walk-in basis in most city hospitals. The biggest hospital is **Al-Amiri Hospital & Casualty** (Map p86; ☎ 2245 0005; Arabian Gulf St).

MONEY
Banks are evenly distributed throughout the city. Moneychangers can offer slightly better rates than banks (and usually charge lower commissions); try some of the side streets that

run from Safat Sq. Travellers cheques can be changed at the following places:

Al-Ghanim Travel (Map p86; 2nd fl, Salhiya Commercial Centre, Fahad al-Salem St; ☉8am-1pm & 4-7pm Sat-Thu) American Express is found here and card holders can cash personal cheques, but the office will not hold mail for Amex clients.

Al-Muzaini Exchange (Map p86; Fahad al-Salem St; ☉8am-1pm & 4-7pm Sat-Thu)

UAE Exchange (Map p86; Fahad al-Salem St, Basement, Burgan Bank Bldg; ☉8am-1pm & 4-7pm Sat-Thu)

POST

Kuwait City Post Office (Fahad al-Salem St; ☉8am-1pm Sun-Thu) By the intersection with Al-Wattiya St.

TELEPHONE & FAX

Main Telephone Office (cnr Abdullah al-Salem & Al-Hilali Sts; ☉24hr) Located at the base of the telecommunications tower. Prepaid international calls can be booked, but international cardphones are cheaper. Fax services are also available.

TOURIST INFORMATION

There is still no official tourist information office in Kuwait despite rumours to the contrary. However, the **Kuwait Touristic Enterprises Company** (☎ 180 6806; www.kuwaittourism.com; Ice-skating Rink, Al-Soor St & First Ring Rd, Shamiya) is a private company with many years of experience in supplying tourist information and is an oracle of entertainment in the city. The **Kuwait Government Online** (www.e.gov.kw) website also has some useful information for visitors. The website of **Kuwait Tourism Services Company** (www.ktsc-q8.com) includes information on the Kuwaiti lifestyle.

TRAVEL AGENCIES

Lots of small travel agencies, including Al-Ghanim Travel, are to be found on Fahad al-Salem and Al-Soor Sts, between Al-Jahra Gate and the Radio and TV building.

Al-Hogal Travels (Map p86; ☎ 2243 8741; Al-Dawliah Centre, Fahad al-Salem St)

Sanbouk Travels & Tours (Map p86; ☎ 2241 6642; Arabian Gulf St) Located opposite Sharq Souq.

❶ Getting There & Away

Kuwait is more or less a city-state so the information for getting to and from Kuwait City is the same as that for getting to Kuwait in general, and is located under the Survival section (see p114).

❶ Getting Around

TO/FROM THE AIRPORT

Orange taxis charge a flat KD7 between the airport (16km south of the city) and the city centre. It's a 20- to 30-minute journey. Buses 13 and 501 run between the main bus station and the airport every half-hour from 5.30am to 9pm daily (250 fils). Car-rental agencies have booths on the ground floor of the airport.

BUS

Two main public bus services operate in Kuwait City: **Kuwait Public Transport Company** (KPTC; ☎ 2232 8501; www.kptc.com.kw) and **City Bus** (KPTC City Bus; ☎ 2232 8501; www.transportkuwait.com/citybus.html). They both run air-conditioned buses with fares ranging from 200 fils to 350 fils between the hours of 5am to 10pm.

Note that the front seats of these buses are reserved for women.

City Bus offers 15- or 30-day passes for KD7.500 and KD13.500 respectively. Route maps for both companies are available online, from the bus station and on the buses.

The **main bus station** (Map p86) is near the intersection of Al-Hilali and Abdullah al-Mubarak Sts in the Safat district. On printed timetables the station is referred to as 'Mirqab' or 'Mirgab' bus station'.

TAXI

There are several types of taxis operating in Kuwait City, including call taxis (which are 24hr radio-controlled with the fare agreed in advance), orange cabs (which can be shared from 250 fils plus 50 fils per kilometre, or privately engaged from KD1.500) and white cabs (which have negotiable fares). It's easy to hail a taxi from the road or from taxi ranks near malls and hotels.

AROUND KUWAIT

Kuwait, to all intents and purposes, is a city-state wherein most of the attractions and activities are centred in the capital. There are few towns outside Kuwait City and even less in the way of physical attractions in the oil-producing interior.

Despite these drawbacks, however, Kuwait is comprised of a long and beautiful stretch of coast, and future tourist developments include the multi-billion-dollar holiday resort and entertainment complex on Failaka Island, expected to take 10 years or so to complete.

Failaka Island جزيرة فيلكا

Failaka Island has some of the most significant archaeological sites in the Gulf. With a history dating from the Bronze Age, evidence of Dilmun and Greek settlements, a classical name to die for (the Greeks called it 'Ikaros') and a strategic location at the mouth of one of the Gulf's best natural harbours, this island could and should be considered one of Kuwait's top tourist attractions.

Alas, recent history has deemed otherwise. First, the Iraqis established a heavily fortified base on Failaka, paying scant regard to the relics over which they strewed their hardware, and then the island was billeted by Allied forces with equally pitiful regard for antiquities.

Thanks to the new resort, the island is once again open to visitors and is beginning to assume its rightful importance at last.

🛏 Sleeping

Ikaros Hotel RESORT $$
(☑ 2224 4988; www.failakaheritagevillage.com; s/d KD35/50, 📧) If you like Failaka Island enough to stay, this hotel has a range of facilities in the so-called Failaka Heritage Village, including a children's zoo, lake, horse-riding, camel rides and various water sports. Home-made crafts are produced in the living heritage village and are available for sale.

The hotel, which has made a good job of refurbishing the old police station, offers traditional houses that sleep five to 15 people. The resort also offers day rates of KD13 per adult and KD10 per child on Friday, Saturday and public holidays and operates a catamaran service from Marina Crescent (next to Starbucks). You need to book ahead and must arrive at least 45 minutes before departure.

❶ Getting There & Away

Kuwait Public Transport Company Ferries (KPTC Ferries; Map p82; ☑ 2232 8814; Arabian Gulf St, Salmiya) Ferries to Failaka Island depart from Ras Salmiya (also known as Ras al-Ard). The trip takes one hour, costs KD3 and leaves daily except Saturday at 8.15am, returning at 12.30pm. A guide would be handy for interpreting the various ruins. If you take your own vehicle it costs KD20 (rental car KD37) for the return fare. The ferry terminal in Kuwait City can be reached via buses 15, 24 and 34.

Fahaheel فحاحيل

POP 100,000

The traditional town of Fahaheel was, until quite recently, a distinct village in its own right. It now merges into the city suburbs but retains a distinctive atmosphere, reminiscent of its Bedouin roots. The fish souq and dhow harbour are more characterful, in many ways, than their modern counterparts in the city centre. The oil refinery at neighbouring Mina al-Ahmadi is one of the largest in the world.

The Hilton Kuwait Resort is just north of here.

Buses 40, 101, 102 and 502 run to Fahaheel. The town can be reached by car on the Fahaheel Expressway, 39km from the city centre.

Al-Ahmadi الاحمدى

POP 742,011

Built to house the workers of Kuwait's oil industry in the 1940s and '50s, the town of Al-Ahmadi, close to Fahaheel, was named after the emir of the day, Sheikh Ahmed. It remains, to some extent, the private preserve of the Kuwait Oil Compnay (KOC). There are some pleasant public gardens and performances in English at the Kuwait Little Theatre.

The **Oil Display Centre** (☑ 2386 7703; www.kockw.com; Mid 5th St; ⊙ 7am-3pm Sun-Thu) **FREE** is a well-organised introduction to KOC and the business of oil production.

Bus 602 runs from Fahaheel to Al-Ahmadi (passing by the oil display centre as it enters the town). To get here by car from Kuwait City, take the King Fahad Motorway south until the Al-Ahmadi exit. First follow the blue signs for North Al-Ahmadi and then the smaller white signs for the Oil Display Centre.

Ras Al-Zour رأس الزور

Around 100km and an hour's drive south of the capital, Ras al-Zour (also spelt Ras Azzor) is one of the most pleasant beach areas in Kuwait. The Saudi Texaco compound is only open to guests of members, but the public beach alongside is clean and attractive too.

OFF THE BEATEN TRACK

BRIDGE TO NOWHERE

By following signs to Subiyah from Mutla Ridge, you'll eventually reach the **Bridge to Nowhere**, some 50km northeast of Al-Jahra. There's a checkpoint in front of it, preventing further excursion, but the bridge spans more than just the narrow passage to Bubiyan Island: it also reinforces Kuwait's claim to the island in the face of erstwhile claims by both Iraq and Iran. So keen was Kuwait to maintain its claim to the uninhabited, flat and barren island and its neighbouring water supply, when the Iraqis blew up the middle section of the bridge, the Kuwaitis quickly rebuilt it even though it goes to nowhere.

A brand new, three-lane highway now goes to nowhere as well. Eventually, it will lead to the mega port planned for completion over the next decade. In the meantime, if you fancy getting off the beaten track, this is one way to do it without leaving the tarmac!

Wafrah Farms

While not the most obvious of tourist destinations, Wafrah Farms, about a 1½-hour drive south of the capital, on the Saudi Arabian border, is a soothingly green oasis of vegetable gardens and papaya trees. It makes a pleasant excursion from Ras al-Zour.

Entertainment City

Located in Doha Village, this huge **park** (☑ 2487 9455, 2487 9545; admission KD3.500; ⊙ 3-11pm Sun-Wed, 10am-10pm Thu-Fri Oct-Apr, 5pm-1am Sun-Fri May-Sep) is 20km west of Kuwait City. It comprises three theme parks (Arab World, International World and Future World), a miniature golf course, a small lake with landscaped parkland and railway, a small zoo and a variety of restaurants. The entrance fee covers most of the rides but there is an additional charge for some of the more elaborate rides. Admission times vary slightly from season to season, so call ahead. Monday is generally reserved for women only. There is no public transport to the park

and a taxi (KD7 from the city centre) is not easy to hail for the return journey.

Al-Jahra الجهراء

POP 480,322

Al-Jahra, 32km west of Kuwait City, is the site where invading troops from Saudi Arabia were defeated (with British help) in 1920. It was also the site of the Gulf War's infamous 'turkey shoot' – the Allied destruction of a stalled Iraqi convoy as it lumbered up Mutla Ridge in an effort to retreat from Kuwait. The highway and surrounding desert are now completely clear of evidence, picked over by scrap-metal dealers and dubious souvenir hunters.

⊙ Sights & Activities

Red Fort FORT
(☑ 2477 2559; ⊙ 8.30am-12.30pm & 4.30-7.30pm Sun-Thu, 8.30-11am & 4.30-7.30pm Fri & Sat) FREE The town's only sight is the Red Fort, which played a key role in the 1920 battle where invading troops from Saudi Arabia were defeated (with British help). Also known as the Red Palace, this low, rectangular, mud structure is near the highway: coming from Kuwait City, take the second of the three Al-Jahra exits from Jahra Rd. The Red Fort is on the right, about 200m south of Jahra Rd.

Al-Atraf Camel Racing Club CAMEL RACING
(☑ 2539 4014; Salmi Rd; ⊙ from 7am) FREE Between November and April camel racing can be seen early in the morning on Friday and Saturday (races start around 7am or 8am). Phone ahead for details of races, or check the 'What's On' listings in the English-language daily papers. The track is 7km west of Al-Jahra.

❶ Getting There & Away

Al-Jahra can be reached conveniently by bus 103 from Kuwait City, which passes directly in front of the Red Fort. By car, take the Sixth Ring Rd west out of Kuwait City. For the racing club take the turn-off where there is a faded sign of a camel, after skirting Al-Jahra.

Mutla Ridge مطلا

While not a particularly spectacular line of hills, Mutla Ridge is about as good as it gets in Kuwait. The ridge at least offers a wonderful view of the full expanse of Kuwait Bay. Although the land mines have been cleared, you should stick to the paths in case of explosive remnants.

For a taste of the desert, take the road to **Bubiyan Island** that runs along the south-eastern flank of the ridge. Either side of the road, large numbers of camels roam along its edge, grazing on the coarse grass that is common to the area. In spring, the slope down to the coastal marshes is pale green with new shoots and full of wild flowers. It is also a popular area for camping, both for Bedu (look for their black tents and goats) and city dwellers (who use white tents and aerials) keen to touch base with nature for a while.

UNDERSTAND KUWAIT

Kuwait Today

Relationship with Iraq

It's not possible to talk about Kuwait as it is today without factoring in its strategic importance at the oil-rich end of the Gulf. At the time of the Iraqi invasion of Kuwait in 1990, there was some speculation, in Western countries at least, as to why such an unprepossessing splinter of desert should be worth the trouble. Of course, anyone watching the retreating Iraqi army, under skies black from burning wells, could find an easy answer: oil. But oil was only half of the story. Kuwait is not, nor has it ever been, simply a piece of oil-rich desert. Rather, it represents a vital (in all senses of the word) piece of coast that for centuries has provided settlement, trade and a strategic staging post.

The latter is a point not lost on US military forces, who until relatively recently camped out on Failaka Island. Two decades ago, the same island, at the mouth of Kuwait Bay, was occupied by the Iraqis. Roughly 2300 years before that, it was the turn of the ancient Greeks, attracted to one of only two natural harbours in the Gulf; and 2000 years earlier still, it belonged to the great Dilmun empire, based in Bahrain. The country has a curious way of cleaning up history once the protagonists have departed, and just as there's very little evidence of recent events without some determined (and ill-advised) unearthing, the same could be said of the rest of Kuwait's 10,000 years of history.

In fact, between one glamorous development and another, it's almost possible to overlook the Iraqi invasion – almost, but not quite. Over two decades have passed, but the devastating experience lurks under the national consciousness and visible reminders of the war remain to this day, not least in museums of commemoration. Despite this, there's little ostensible animosity between Kuwaitis and their northern neighbours; in fact, a good deal of sympathy passes between the two as Iraq continues to pay a heavy price for former conflicts.

The Arab Spring & Quest for Reform

On 15 January 2006, the respected Emir of Kuwait, Sheikh Jaber al Sabah, died, leaving Crown Prince Sheikh Sa'ad al-Sabah at the helm. Poor health, however, led to Sa'ad's abdication (he died in May 2008) and the prime minister, Sheikh Sabah al-Ahmad al-Sabah, took over.

Under Kuwait's 1962 constitution, the emir is the head of state. By tradition the crown prince used to serve as prime minister but since 2003 the post has emerged as a separate entity. The prime minister recommends cabinet appointments for the emir's approval, usually reserving key portfolios (such as the interior, and foreign affairs and defence) for other members of the ruling family.

In the Arab Spring of 2011, youth activists targeted the prime minister and his cabinet for removal amid allegations of corruption and he was forced out of office in late 2011. Opposition groups were joined in their discontent by the *bidoon*, stateless Arabs who demanded citizenship, jobs and benefits afforded to Kuwaiti nationals. A year later, electoral reform prompted even more widespread protest and the elections of December 2012 were boycotted by Sunni Islamists, certain tribal groups and youth groups, resulting in a larger representation of Shiites in the National Assembly.

Nascent Democracy

Kuwait has an elected National Assembly, the role of which is only just beginning to live up to the hopes of those who support a more Western-style democracy. The powers of the emir, crown prince and cabinet are tempered by the increasingly-vociferous 50 members of the Assembly, which must approve the national budget and can question cabinet members. That said, the emir has the power to dissolve the assembly whenever he pleases (and he has done so five times since 2006), but is required by the constitution to hold new elections within 90 days of any such dissolution (a requirement that, historically, has not always been honoured).

In May 2005, after years of campaigning, women were at last enfranchised and permitted to run for parliament and in 2009 four women were elected to the National Assembly – a move viewed by many as a sign of a new era of transparent government. Despite the reticence of hard-line clerics and traditional tribal leaders, women now hold positions of importance in both private and public sectors.

The country's parliament is still viewed with some scepticism as it is considered to stall rather than achieve reforms, but slowly and surely democracy is developing.

Economic Challenges and Strengths

During the late 1970s Kuwait's stock exchange (the first in the Gulf) was among the top 10 in the world, but a decade later the price of oil collapsed together with a not-entirely-legal parallel financial market, leaving hundreds of people bankrupt. The scandal left behind US$90 billion in worthless post-dated cheques and a mess that the Kuwaiti government is still trying to sort out. The invasion of the 1990s was an unmitigated financial disaster and the country is still paying back its military debts, while trying not to count the cost of rebuilding the country. As such, it is remarkable to see how spectacularly the economy has bounced back over the past decade.

With the country home to 10% of the world's oil reserves, oil and oil-related products naturally dominate the economy and, with more than 100 years' worth of remaining oil, the need to diversify has not been as urgent as it has been in neighbouring countries. Tourism, for example, is a negligible part of the economy.

Given its enormous wealth in natural resources, boosted by the discovery in March 2006 of 35 trillion cubic feet of natural gas, the country has been able to buffer the economic turbulence of the recent global recession. Indeed, large scale construction projects across the city continue unabated.

History

Early History

Standing at the bottom of Mutla Ridge on the road to Bubiyan Island, and staring across the springtime grasslands at the estuary waters beyond, it's easy enough to imagine why Stone Age man chose to inhabit the area around Ras Subiyah, on the northern shores of Kuwait Bay. Here the waters are rich in silt from the mighty river systems of southern Iraq, making for abundant marine life. Evidence of the first proper settlement in the region dates from 4500 BC, and shards of pottery, stone walls, tools, a small drilled pearl and remains of what is perhaps the world's earliest seafaring boat indicate links with the Ubaid people who populated ancient Mesopotamia. The people of Dilmun also saw the potential of living in the mouth of two of the world's great river systems and built a large town on Failaka Island, the remains of which form some of the best structural evidence of Bronze Age life in the world.

The Greeks on Failaka Island

A historian called Arrian, in the time of Alexander the Great, first put the region on the map by referring to an island discovered by one of Alexander's generals en route to India. Alexander himself is said to have called this, the modern-day island of Failaka, Ikaros, and it soon lived up to its Greek name as a Hellenistic settlement that thrived between the 3rd and 1st centuries BC. With temples dedicated to Artemis and Apollo, an inscribed stele with instructions to the inhabitants of this high-flying little colonial outpost, stashes of silver Greek coins, busts and decorative friezes, Ikaros became an important trading post on the route from Mesopotamia to India. While there is still a column or two standing proud among the weeds, and the odd returning Kuwaiti trying to resettle amid the barbed wire, there's little left to commemorate the vigorous trading in pearls and incense by the Greeks. There's even less to show for the Christian community that settled among the ruins thereafter.

Growth of Kuwait City

Over time, Kuwait's main settlements shifted from island to mainland. In AD 500 the area around Ras Khazimah, near Al-Jahra, was the main centre of population, and it took a further 1200 years for the centre of activity to nudge along the bay to Kuwait City. When looking at the view from the top of the Kuwait Towers, it's hard to imagine that 350 years ago this enormous city was comprised of nothing more illustrious than a few Bedouin tents clustered around a storehouse-cum-fort. Like a tide, its population swelled in the intense summer heat as nomadic families drifted in from the bone-dry desert and then receded as the winter months stretched good grazing across the interior.

Permanent families living around the fort became able and prosperous traders. One such family, Al-Sabah, whose descendants now rule Kuwait, assumed responsibility for local law and order, and under their governance, the settlement grew quickly. By 1760 when the town's first wall was built, the community had a distinctive character. It was comprised of merchant traders, centred around a dhow and ocean-going boon fleet of 800 vessels, and a craft-oriented internal trade, arising from the camel caravans plying the route from Baghdad and Damascus to the interior of the Arabian Peninsula.

Relations with the British

By the early 19th century, as a thriving trading port, Kuwait City was well in the making. However, trouble was always literally just over the horizon. There were pirates marauding the waters of the Arabian coast; Persians snatched Basra in the north; various Arab tribes from the west and south had their own designs, and then, of course, there were the ubiquitous Ottomans. Though the Kuwaitis generally got on well with the Ottomans, official Kuwaiti history is adamant that the sheikhdom always remained independent of them, and it is true that as the Turks strengthened their control of eastern Arabia (then known as Al-Hasa), the Kuwaitis skilfully managed to avoid being absorbed by the empire. Nonetheless, Al-Sabah emirs accepted the nominal Ottoman title of 'Provincial Governors of Al-Hasa'.

Enter the British. The Kuwaitis and the British were natural allies in many regards. From the 1770s the British had been contracted to deliver mail between the Gulf and Aleppo in Syria. Kuwait, meanwhile, handled all the trans-shipments of textiles, rice, coffee, sugar, tobacco, spices, teak and mangrove to and from India, and played a pivotal role in the overland trade to the Mediterranean. The British helped to stop the piracy that threatened the seafaring trade, but were not in a position to repel the Ottoman incursions – that is until the most important figure in Kuwait's modern history stepped onto the stage. Sheikh Mubarak al-Sabah al-Sabah, commonly known as Mubarak the Great (r 1896–1915), was deeply suspicious that Constantinople planned to annex Kuwait. Concerned that the emir was sympathetic towards the Ottomans, he killed him, not minding he was committing fratricide as well as regicide, and installed himself as ruler. Crucially, in 1899, he signed an agreement with Britain: In exchange for the British navy's protection, he promised not to give territory to, take support from or negotiate with any other foreign power without British consent. The Ottomans continued to claim sovereignty over Kuwait, but they were now in no position to enforce it. For Britain's part, Prussia, the main ally and financial backer of Turkey, was kept out of the warm waters of the Gulf and trade continued as normal.

Rags to Riches in the 20th Century

Mubarak the Great laid down the foundations of a modern state. Under his reign, government welfare programs provided for public schools and medical services. In 1912, postal and telegraphic services were established, and water-purification equipment was imported for the American Mission Hospital. According to British surveys from this era, Kuwait City numbered 35,000 people, with 3000 permanent residents, 500 shops and three schools, and nearly 700 pearling boats employing 10,000 men.

In the 1920s a new threat in the guise of the terrifying *ikhwan* (brotherhood) came from the Najd, the interior of Arabia. This army of Bedouin warriors was commanded by Abdul Aziz bin Abdul Rahman al-Saud (Ibn Saud), the founder of modern Saudi Arabia. Despite having received hospitality from the Kuwaitis during his own years in the wilderness, so to speak, he made no secret of his belief that Kuwait belonged to the new kingdom of Saudi Arabia. The Red Fort at Al-Jahra, was the site of a famous battle in which the Kuwaitis put up a spirited defence. They also hurriedly constructed a new city wall, the gates of which can be

AL-QURAIN MARTYRS' MUSEUM

Early one morning during the Iraqi invasion in the early 1990s, a minibus (the one that is still parked outside) drew up outside an ordinary house in the suburbs – the house that today has been converted into the Al-Qurain Martyrs' Museum (p91). When no one answered the door, Iraqi militia parked outside and began firing at the doors and windows trying to rout a cell of the Kuwaiti resistence interred inside. They bombarded the house for hour upon hour with machine guns, bombs and eventually a tank waiting for the young patriots to surrender. Eventually, they got tired of waiting. Nine of those under siege were captured and tortured to death, while four hid in a roof space.

General Schwarzkopf, who visited the house on 14 April 1994, commented that 'when I am in this house it makes me wish that we had come four days earlier then perhaps this tragedy would not have happened'. The Iraqi occupation lasted for seven long months, during which time many similar raids on the homes of Kuwait families were made.

For anyone interested in recent history and wanting to gain a measure of what invasion may feel like for the civilian population, then a visit to this sobering monument of a house (or what's left of it) is worth the difficulty in finding it.

seen today along Al-Soor St in Kuwait City. In 1923 the fighting ended with a British-brokered treaty under which Abdul Aziz recognised Kuwait's independence, but at the price of two-thirds of the emirate's territory.

The Great Depression that sunk the world into poverty coincided with the demise of Kuwait's pearling industry as the market became flooded with Japanese cultured pearls. At the point when the future looked most dire for Kuwait, however, an oil concession was granted in 1934 to a US–British joint venture known as the Kuwait Oil Company (KOC). The first wells were sunk in 1936 and by 1938 it was obvious that Kuwait was virtually floating on oil. WWII forced KOC to suspend its operations, but when oil exports took off after the war, Kuwait's economy was launched on an unimaginable trajectory of wealth.

In 1950, Sheikh Abdullah al-Salem al-Sabah (r 1950–65) became the first 'oil sheikh'. His reign was not, however, marked by the kind of profligacy with which that term later came to be associated. As the country became wealthy, health care, education and the general standard of living improved dramatically. In 1949 Kuwait had only four doctors; by 1967 it had 400.

Independence

On 19 June 1961, Kuwait became an independent state and the obsolete agreement with Britain was dissolved by mutual consent. In an act of foreboding, the President of Iraq, Abdulkarim Qasim, immediately claimed Kuwait as Iraqi territory. British forces, later replaced by those of the Arab League (which Kuwait joined in 1963), faced down the challenge, but the precedent was not so easily overcome.

Elections for Kuwait's first National Assembly were held in 1962. Although representatives of the country's leading merchant families won the bulk of the seats, radicals had a toehold in the parliament from its inception. Despite the democratic nature of the constitution and the broad guarantees of freedoms and rights – including freedom of conscience, religion and press, and equality before the law – the radicals immediately began pressing for faster social change, and the country changed cabinets three times between 1963 and 1965. In August 1976 the cabinet resigned, claiming that the assembly had made day-to-day governance impossible, and the emir suspended the constitution and dissolved the assembly. It wasn't until 1981 that the next elections were held, but then parliament was dissolved again in 1986. In December 1989 and January 1990 an extraordinary series of demonstrations took place calling for the restoration of the 1962 constitution and the reconvening of parliament.

The Invasion of Iraq

Despite these political and economic tensions, by early 1990 the country's economic prospects looked bright, particularly with an end to the eight-year Iran–Iraq war, during which time Kuwait had extended considerable support to Iraq. In light of this, the events that followed were all the more shocking to most people in the region. On 16 July 1990, Iraq sent a letter to the Arab League accusing Kuwait of exceeding its Organization of Petroleum Exporting Countries (OPEC) quota and of stealing oil from the Iraqi portion of an oilfield straddling the border. The following day Iraqi president Saddam Hussein hinted at military action. The tanks came crashing over the border at 2am on 2 August and the Iraqi military was in Kuwait City before dawn. By noon they had reached the Saudi frontier. The Kuwaiti emir and his cabinet fled to Saudi Arabia.

On 8 August, Iraq annexed the emirate. Western countries, led by the USA, began to enforce a UN embargo on trade with Iraq, and in the months that followed more than half a million foreign troops amassed in Saudi Arabia. On 15 January, after a deadline given to Iraq to leave Kuwait had lapsed, Allied aircraft began a five-week bombing campaign nicknamed 'Desert Storm'. The Iraqi army quickly crumbled and on 26 February 1991, Allied forces arrived in Kuwait City to be greeted by jubilant crowds – and by clouds of acrid black smoke from oil wells torched by the retreating Iraqi army. Ignoring demands to retreat unarmed and on foot, a stalled convoy of Iraqi armoured tanks, cars and trucks trying to ascend Mutla Ridge became the target of a ferocious Allied attack, nicknamed 'the turkey shoot'.

Physical signs of the Iraqi invasion are hard to find in today's Kuwait. Gleaming shopping malls, new hotels and four-lane highways are all evidence of Kuwait's efforts to put the destruction behind it. However, the emotional scars have yet to be healed, particularly as hundreds of missing prisoners of war are yet to be accounted for, despite the fall of Saddam Hussein.

Kuwait After the Demise of Saddam Hussein

In March 2003 the Allied invasion of Iraq threw the country into paralysing fear of a return to the bad old days of 1990, and it was only with the death of Saddam Hussein (he was hanged on 30 December 2006) that Kuwaitis have finally been able to sigh with relief. Without having to look over its shoulder constantly, Kuwait has lost no time in forging ahead with its ambitious plans, including that of attracting a greater number of regional tourists. The annual Hala Shopping Festival in February is proving a successful commercial venture, attracting visitors from across the region, and resorts offer R & R mostly to the international business community. More significantly, cross-border trade with Iraq (particularly of a military kind) has helped fuel the economic boom of this decade, a boom barely impacted by the global recession.

DEWANIYA – KUWAITI GATHERINGS

An important part of life in Kuwait, *dewaniya* refer to gatherings of men who congregate to socialise, discuss a particular family issue or chew over current affairs. The origins of these gatherings go back centuries but the rituals remain the same – a host entertains family, friends or business acquaintances in a room specially intended for the purpose at appointed times after sundown. Guests sit on cushions and drink copious cups of tea or coffee, smoke, snack and come and go as they please.

In the early 20th century, on the edge of Souq Mabarakia, Mubarak the Great held a famous daily *dewaniya*, walking each day from Sief Palace through the old souq to an unprepossessing building amid random coffeehouses. Here he would sit incognito, talk to the people and feel the pulse of the street. Sitting near the same place today (a renovated traditional building without signage may mark the spot), with old men nodding over their mint teas, city types trotting to work, merchants hauling their wares to Souq Marbarakia and groups of women strolling in the shade, it's easy to see why he chose this spot.

For any male visitor wanting similarly to get under the skin of the local Kuwaiti culture, the *dewaniya* around town offer the opportunity to rub shoulders with local dignitaries and generally form alliances.

People & Society

The National Psyche

It's easy to imagine that recent events have fashioned a suspicious and bitter mind-set among Kuwaitis: young Kuwaiti men (together with family heirlooms) snatched from homes; national treasures ripped from the nation's museum; the Kuwait Towers used for target practice – these and countless other horrors marked the Iraqi invasion. And then there was the almost as agonising threat of the same occurring only a decade later.

Despite the trauma, it is a credit to the national temperament that life in Kuwait is characterised not by suspicion and bitterness but by affable handshakes, courteous business meetings and spending sprees in the capital.

Of course, Kuwaitis haven't forgotten the invasion; indeed, in the past few years, there has been an increase in the number of memorials and plaques appearing around the city as if, since the demise of Saddam, people are daring to look back and place the event in a historical context at last, rather than trying to forget about the possibility of a repeat occurrence. Groups of school children can be seen shepherded through the Kuwait House of National Memorial Museum knowing this was their parents' war and not a threat they need to feel defensive about for their own sake.

Kuwaitis are an ambitious and sophisticated people, determined to grasp the commercial opportunities that the 21st century has laid at the doorstep of their continuing wealth but mindful, as Muslims, that what is written will be. As such, there's not much point in fretting about the future.

Lifestyle

In common with the rest of the Gulf, Kuwaiti people value privacy and family intimacy at home, while enjoying the company of guests outside. In many instances, 'outside' is the best description of traditional hospitality: while female guests are invited into the house, men are often entertained in tents on the doorstep. These are no scout camp canvases, however, but lavish striped canopies made luxurious with cushions and carpets.

Any visitor lucky enough to partake in tea and homemade delicacies in these 'majlis al fresco' may be inclined to think that life in Kuwait has retained all the charm and simplicity of its Bedouin roots.

Kuwaitis take a different view, however. Some blame the war for a weakening of traditional values: theft, fraudulent practice, a growing drug problem, higher rates of divorce and incidents of suicidal driving have all increased. Others recognise that the same symptoms are prevalent in any modern society. With a cradle-to-grave welfare system, where 94% of Kuwaiti nationals are 'employed' in government positions, and an economy that has run ahead faster than the culture has been able to accommodate, many Kuwaitis feel their society has become cosseted and indulgent, leaving the younger generation with too much time on their hands to wander off course.

Life in Kuwait has changed out of all recognition in the past decade: women work, couples hold hands in public, taboo subjects find expression, and people spend money and raise debts. Indeed, the galloping pace of change is proving a divisive factor in a country of traditionally conservative people. It would be ironic if a society that had survived some of the most sophisticated arsenal of the 20th century fell under the weight of its own shopping malls.

Population

The last census, at the end of 2007, put Kuwait's population at 3.4 million. Of these, about 31% are Kuwaitis, many of Bedouin ancestry, and the remaining 69% are expats. After liberation, the government announced that it would never again allow Kuwaitis to become a minority in their own country, implying a target population of about 1.7 million. With an unquenchable desire for servants and drivers, and an equal antipathy for manual labour, it is unlikely the Kuwaitis will achieve this target any time soon.

There are small inland communities but, to all intents and purposes, Kuwait is a coastal city-state.

A generation of young men are missing after the Iraqi invasion.

Multiculturalism

The origin of the non-Kuwaiti population has changed considerably in the last two decades. Before the Iraqi invasion, 90% of the expat population was from Arab countries, with large volumes of Egyptian labourers, Iranian professionals and over a million Palestinian refugees who arrived after the creation of the State of Israel in 1948. Since the invasion, Arab nationalities make up less than 15% of the expat population, with large numbers of Palestinians, in particular, being forced to return to their country of origin – a bitter phrase in the circumstances. As Yasser Arafat was widely regarded as a supporter of the invasion, all Palestinians were tarred with the same brush; some were even court martialled on charges of collaboration.

Today Kuwait resembles other parts of the Gulf in its mix of mainly Indian and Filipino immigrants. Alas, a two-tier society appears to have developed wherein some immigrant workers (Filipino maids, in particular) are subject to virtual slave labour. Talk to many Pakistani or Indian traders, taxi drivers, pump attendants or restaurant workers, however, and they evince a warmth towards the country that is somewhat surprising to the Western bystander: just as the friendly reflections regarding the Iraqi man in the street comes as a surprise when speaking to elder Kuwaitis. In comparison with other countries in the region, Kuwait has a relatively small Western expat population, working almost exclusively in higher-paid professions.

Religion

Most Kuwaitis are Sunni Muslims, though there is a substantial Shiite minority. During the 1980s there was considerable tension, mostly inspired by Iran, between the two communities, a worry that has returned with sectarian violence over the border in Iraq.

Before the Iraqi invasion, Kuwait was still governed by a strict code of conduct, steered by a devout following of Islam. The invasion shook belief in all kinds of areas, including religious observance. Materialism is beginning to exert as strong an influence on the young as religion used to affect the customs and manners of their Bedouin or seafaring ancestors. Kuwaiti society certainly can't

GROWING A SOCIAL CONSCIENCE

Mindful of the pitfalls of a modern, affluent life, several eminent Kuwaitis have introduced initiatives to help the young rediscover deeper, traditional values of self-discipline and caring for others. One such project, **Lothan Youth Achievement Center** (Loyac; Map p82; 2572 7399; www.loyac.org; Beit Lothan), gives the privileged youth of Kuwait City the opportunity to interact with poorer communities. Organisers find this kind of community service helps young people channel their energies into positive, character-building activity. The coordinator of Loyac's International Programs told us about the scheme and the contribution it is making.

Motivation in starting the project After September 11, the founder, Fare'a al-Saqqaf, recognised one of the problems leading to extremism was the lack of alternative activities to help keep the young gainfully occupied. To address this, Loyac was designed to help secondary school children and college students to build their personalities, raise their morale and identify goals to help them become caring individuals within society.

Kinds of activities Participants are involved in summer internships in companies, voluntary work experience, global outreach, computer and language development, summer camps, performing arts and sporting activities.

Willing participants Loyac's programs are fully booked and the message has spread to young people of all nationalities across Kuwait. It apparently comes as a shock to many youngsters in Kuwait that there are people who live quite different lives from themselves, without the benefit of wealth and modern convenience, but they are keen to learn and to help in the community service projects Loyac runs both nationally and abroad.

Long-term benefits The projects aim to foster the so-called '7 Habits', encompassing increased self-confidence, self-esteem, greater control of life, and finding a reasonable life-work balance. They also stress the need to see and experience life from other people's perspectives. By internalising these habits, youngsters develop grounded personalities and life-long values of community service and the understanding of the needs of others.

be described as permissive, but the veil in many areas of social exchange is discernibly slipping.

A tolerance towards other religions is evinced through the provision of services at Coptic, Anglican, Evangelical and Orthodox churches in Kuwait City. Kuwait is the only Gulf country to have a strong relationship with the Roman Catholic Church.

Arts

Kuwait's artistic endeavours are influenced by the country's Bedouin roots and its seafaring tradition.

The Bedouin arts of weaving, folk tales, songs and dancing are to less and less an extent passed on in the daily lives of modern Kuwaitis, but attempts to preserve them by the activities of cultural centres such as Sadu House are reassuring.

Kuwait's seafaring tradition has manifested artistically in the form of sea shanties and seafaring folklore. Shipbuilding developed into an art form, too, in its 18th-century heyday, as can be seen at the Al-Hashemi Marine Museum. Two modern wooden sailing boats, *Mohammedi II* and *Al-Hashemi II,* on the same site as the museum, showcase the aesthetic side of shipbuilding. A tradition of lavish feasting upon the return of ships, which were often out pearling for months at a time, is also heartily alive.

Kuwait City has also developed a lively contemporary art scene with a growing regional reputation for the quality of exhibitions shown at venues such as the Modern Art Museum. (p87)

Environment

The Land

It has to be said that Kuwait is not the most well-endowed patch of earth, either in terms of the sublime or the picturesque. The interior consists of a mostly flat, gravelly plain with little or no ground water. Its saving grace is the grassy fringe that greens up prettily across much of the plain late in the spring, providing rich grazing for the few remaining Bedu who keep livestock. The only other geographic feature of any note in a country that measures 185km from north to south and 208km from east to west is Mutla Ridge, just north of Kuwait City. The coast is a little more characterful, with dunes, marshes and salt depressions around Kuwait Bay and an oasis in Al-Jahra.

Of the nine offshore islands, the largest is Bubiyan Island, while Failaka Island is the most historic: there are plans afoot to develop a container port on the former and a vast tourist complex on the latter, but at present there is not much to see on either island.

Wildlife

The anticlockwise flow of Gulf currents favours Kuwait's shoreline by carrying nutrients from the freshwater marshes of Shatt al-Arab and the delta of the Tigris and Euphrates in southern Iraq. The result is a rich and diverse coastline, with an abundance of marine life that even the poisoning of spilt oil has failed to destroy.

ANIMALS

Pearly goatfish, the oddly spiked tripod fish and the popular dinner fish of silver pomfret are just some of the myriad species of fish that frequent the fishermen's nets along Kuwait Bay. Crabs tunnel in the mud flats near Doha Village, surviving in extreme temperatures and aerating the mud for other less durable bedfellows – such as the tiny mudskipper that sorties out for a mouthful of mud and water with which to build the walls of its castles in the sand. Propped up on their fins for a gulp of oxygen, they provide a tasty titbit for black-winged stilts, teals, lesser-crested terns and huge nesting colonies of Socotra cormorants, which share the coastline, and they trap algae in their geometric homes that feed the flamingos.

Inland, birds of prey, including the resident kestrel and the short-toed eagle, roam the escarpments. The desert comes alive at night with rare sightings of caracal, and hedgehog, big-eared fennecs – the smallest canines in the world – and jerboas, which gain all the liquid they need from the plants and insects they eat. It is easier to spot the dhobs, a monitor lizard with a spiny tail, popular as a barbecue snack. And, of course, no Arab desert is the same without the diligent dung beetle or the scorpion.

In terms of endangered species, given the events of the past few years, it's remarkable that a few more species have not been added to the familiar list of desert mammals, like oryx and gazelle, made regionally extinct through hunting. The desert wolf has made something of a comeback in recent years and has been spotted near residential areas.

PLANTS

After the winter rains, corridors of purple-flowered heliotrope bloom everywhere, and the highways are decorated with borders of assorted wild flowers. There are about 400 plant species in Kuwait. One of the most common is the bright-green *rimth,* which, along with red-flowered *al-awsaj,* is a favourite of grazing camels. The Bedu still use herb poultices for snake bites. In spring, truffles sprout through the cracked ground in desert wadis, as if remembering that Kuwait was once a delta land of the long-extinct Arabian River.

AN ENVIRONMENTAL CATASTROPHE

A coalition of 28 nations fought to drive Iraq's military out of Kuwait in January and February 1991. In the months that followed, an equally impressive international effort helped clean up the ensuing mess.

An Unprecedented Oil Spill

The environmental damage caused by the war occurred on an unprecedented scale. On 20 January 1991, the third day of the war, Iraqi forces opened the valves at Kuwait's Mina al-Ahmadi Sea Island Terminal, intentionally releasing millions of litres of oil into the Gulf. The resulting oil slick was 64km wide and 160km long. Between six and eight million barrels of oil are thought to have been released, at least twice as much as in any previous oil spill. At least 460km of coastline, most of it in Saudi Arabia and Bahrain, was affected, with devastating consequences for the region's cormorants, migratory birds, dolphins, fish, turtles and large areas of mangrove.

Fire and Devastation of Wildlife

The systematic torching of 699 of the emirate's oil wells contributed to the environmental disaster. By the time the war ended, nearly every well was burning. At a conservative estimate, at least two million barrels of oil per day were lost – equivalent to about 5% of the total daily world consumption. One to two million tonnes of carbon dioxide streamed into the air daily, resulting in a cloud that turned day into night across the country.

Like the slick, the fires devastated wildlife throughout the region, but they also had a direct impact on public health. Black, greasy rain caused by the fires was reported as far away as India, and the incidence of asthma increased in the Gulf region.

Efficient and Collaborative Clean-Up

The slick was fought by experts from nine nations and oil companies managed to recover, and reuse, about a million barrels of crude oil from the slick. Initial reports that it would take five years to put all the fires out proved pessimistic. A determined international effort, combined with considerable innovation on the part of the firefighters, extinguished the fires in eight months. The crews did the job so fast that one well had to be reignited so the emir of Kuwait could 'put out the final fire' for reporters in November 1991.

Blooms of Hope in the Desert

Cleaning up the 65 million barrels of oil, spilt in 300 oil lakes covering around 50 sq km of desert, was not so speedily effected. In a joint project between the Kuwait Institute of Scientific Research (KISR) and the Japanese Petroleum Energy Center (JPEC), a bio-remediation project was launched to rehabilitate the oil-polluted soil. Through a variety of biological processes, which included composting and bioventing, more than 4000 cubic metres of contaminated soil were treated, resulting in soil of such high quality that it was good enough for landscaping and could be used as topsoil.

The **Japanese Garden in Al-Ahmadi** is a showcase for the miracle 'oil soil'. The garden's 'blooms of hope' are a testimony to international cooperation and the ability of man and nature to outwit the worst that disaster can throw at them. The gardens are currently undergoing rejuvenation.

A particular blow to the country's ecology was the loss of many kilometres of black mangrove roots and beds of seagrass to oil spillage. These precious and endangered species help to stabilise and extend the country's shoreline, and their damage has been devastating.

National Parks

Larger than the state of Bahrain, the 863 sq km nature reserve on the northern end of Bubiyan Island is home to many species of birds and animals. Comprised of marshland and creeks, it is a haven for waders. It was heavily mined during the Gulf War and the causeway destroyed. The future could be just as alarming with a port and residential complex planned for the southern part of the island.

Environmental Issues

While Kuwait shares many of the same environmental concerns as its Gulf neighbours, it has also had to contend with the extraordinary circumstances inflicted by war. Over a decade later, the casual visitor is unlikely to detect any signs of war either in the desert or along the coast. A thorough cleanup by Pakistani and Bangladeshi troops, and subsequent diligence with regard to the removal of unexploded ordnance, means that Kuwaitis can once again enjoy the ritual camping expedition without fear of danger. Perversely, however, it is now the campers who are threatening the environment with discarded rubbish and heavy use of delicate grazing lands. In addition, relaxed standards with regard to waste and oil dumping have led to concerns about polluted seas along Kuwait's shoreline.

Every year on 24 April, the country observes Regional Environment Day, with school competitions and raised public awareness regarding marine and land resources.

SURVIVAL GUIDE

❶ Directory A–Z

ACCOMMODATION

There are few options for budget travellers in Kuwait but some good value choices in the mid-range category.

The northern shore of Kuwait Bay is a popular camping spot with locals: just look for the tents

from October to April. Alternatively, there are some good places to camp on the coast near the Saudi Arabian border. Camping equipment is available in the many sporting goods shops in the city malls. This isn't camping on a budget, mind: a 4WD is necessary to find a suitable spot.

ACTIVITIES

Most activities are either organised, or take place, in Kuwait City.

For swimming outside of Kuwait City, there are many public beaches along the coast, particularly to the south. One-piece swimsuits for women are encouraged.

Fishing and boating are offered to visitors by **Kuwait Offshore Sailing Association** (☑ 9973 1859; www.kosaq8.com). Camel racing takes place just outside Al-Jahra.

BOOKS

➡ *Pearling in the Arabian Gulf* by Saif Marzooq al-Shamlan – an interesting collection of memoirs and interviews on Kuwait's pearling industry.

➡ *Women in Kuwait* by Haya al-Mughni – paints a clear and illuminating picture of the lives and roles of Kuwaiti women, as well as society's attitudes towards them.

➡ *Traditions & Culture* by Sheikha Altaf al-Sabah – a beautifully produced coffee-table book, with excellent photographs depicting old Kuwait, its people and traditional culture.

➡ *Welcome Visitors' Guide to Kuwait* published by the Ministry of Information – updated regularly and includes lovely photos.

➡ *Days of Fear* by John Levin – the definitive work in English on the Iraqi invasion. Levin, an Australian long-term resident of Kuwait, lived through the Iraqi occupation.

CUSTOMS REGULATIONS

➡ No alcohol or pork-related products permitted in the country.

➡ Up to 500 cigarettes and 500g of tobacco permitted.

→ Duty-free items are on sale at the duty-free shop in the arrivals and departures section of the airport.

EMBASSIES & CONSULATES

Many embassies are in the Diplomatic Area. Embassies are usually open from about 8am to 1pm Sunday to Thursday. A more complete list appears on www.kuwaitiah.net/embassy.html.

Bahraini (Map p82; ☎ 2531 8530; fax 2533 0882; Surra St, Villa 35, Block 6, Surra)

Canadian (Map p82; ☎ 2256 3025; www.canadainternational.gc.ca; Al-Mutawakil St, House 24, Block 4, Diplomatic Area, Da'iya) Adjacent to the Third Ring Rd.

Dutch (Map p82; ☎ 2531 2650; www.kuwait.nlembassy.org; Street 1, House 76, Block 9, Jabriya)

Egyptian (Map p82; ☎ tel 2251 9956; fax 2256 3877; Street 58, Villa 1, Block 5, Diplomatic Area, Da'iya)

French (Map p86; ☎ tel 2257 1061, fax 2257 1051; Street 13, Villa 24, Block 1, Mansouria)

German (Map p86; ☎ 2252 0827; www.kuwait.diplo.de; Street 14, Villa 13, Block 1, Abdulla al-Salim)

Iranian (Map p82; ☎ tel 2256 0694; fax 2252 9868; Block 5, Diplomatic Area, Da'iya)

Jordanian (Map p82; ☎ tel 2531 2293; fax 2531 2291; Akkah St, Villa 20, Block 3, Nuzha)

Lebanese (Map p82; ☎ 2256 2103; fax 2257 1628; Block 6, Diplomatic Area, Da'iya)

Omani (Map p82; ☎ 2256 1956; fax 2256 1963; Street 3, Villa 25 Block 3, Udailia) By the Fourth Ring Rd.

Qatari (Map p82; ☎ 2251 3606; fax 2251 3604; Istiqlal St, Diplomatic Area, Da'iya) Off Arabian Gulf St.

Saudi Arabian (Map p86; ☎ 2255 0021; www.embassy.saudi.com/kuwait; Arabian Gulf St, Sharq)

Syrian (Map p82; ☎ 2539 6560; fax 2539 6509; Al-Khos St, Villa 1, Block 6, Mishref)

Turkish (Map p82; ☎ 2253 1785; www.turkishembassy.org.kw; Istiqlal St, Block 5, Diplomatic Area, Da'iya) Opposite Green Island.

UAE (Map p82; ☎ 2252 8544; fax 2252 6382; Istiqlal St, Plot 70, Diplomatic Area, Da'iya) Off Arabian Gulf St.

UK (Map p86; ☎ 2259 4320; www.ukinkuwait.fco.gov.uk; Arabian Gulf St, Dasman) West of Kuwait Towers.

US (Map p82; ☎ 2539 5307; www.kuwait.usembassy.gov; Al-Masjid al-Aqsa St, Plot 14, Block 14, Bayan) About 17km south of the city centre.

FOOD & DRINKS

For an overview of Kuwait's cuisine, see p79 and the Flavours of Arabia chapter (p459).

Kuwait is a dry state where the consumption of alcohol is strictly forbidden. Penalties if caught in possession of alcohol or appearing under the influence of alcohol are high. If you happen to be a hip-flask traveller, make sure you tip the contents away before arriving at the airport.

INTERNET ACCESS

Internet access is easy for those travelling with a laptop as many hotels and cafes are now wi-fi enabled. Prepaid dial-up internet cards are available in denominations of KD2, KD5, KD13 and KD17, and can be purchased at *bakalas* (corner shops) and supermarkets. A KD13 card gives around 150 hours of internet access. Why it is such an obscure denomination is a mystery!

There are also many internet cafes in Kuwait City.

LEGAL MATTERS

Breaking the law can have severe consequences. For more information, see the Expats chapter (p33) and consult your embassy.

MAPS

GEO Projects publishes a good country map on the reverse of two useful maps of Kuwait City in its Arab World Map Library, available from car-rental offices, hotels and bookshops.

MONEY

The currency used in Kuwait is the Kuwaiti dinar (KD). The dinar is divided into 1000 fils. Coins are worth five, 10, 20, 50 or 100 fils. Notes come in denominations of 250 fils, 500 fils, KD1, KD5, KD10 and KD20. The Kuwaiti dinar is a hard currency and there are no restrictions on taking it into or out of the country.

ATMs & Credit Cards

Visa and Amex are widely accepted in Kuwait, and all major banks accept most credit cards and are linked to the major networks. Most banks accept Visa (Electron and Plus), MasterCard and Cirrus.

Moneychangers

Moneychangers are dotted around the city centre and main souqs, and change all major and regional currencies. Only banks and the larger money-exchange facilities will change travellers cheques which are rapidly becoming obsolete.

EATING PRICE RANGES

The following price ranges refer to a standard main course. Service charge and tax is included in the price.

$ less than KD5 (US$18)
$$ KD5–KD10 (US$18-US$36)
$$$ more than KD10 (US$36)

The dinar is no longer pegged to the dollar but this has made little difference to exchange rates, which remain consistent from one money-changer to the next.

Tipping & Bargaining

A tip is only expected in the upmarket restaurants where 10% for service is often already added to the bill. For longer journeys, 10% is a suitable tip for a taxi driver.

Bargaining is de rigueur in Kuwait's souqs but also in many Western-style shops and some hotels. It is always acceptable to ask for a discount on the original price offered, particularly as discounts have generally already been factored into the quoted price.

OPENING HOURS

These opening hours prevail throughout Kuwait.
Banks 8am to 1pm and 5pm to 7.30pm Sunday to Thursday
Government offices 7am to 2pm (summer), 7.30am to 2.30pm (winter), Sunday to Thursday
Internet cafes 8am to 10pm
Post offices 8am to 1pm Sunday to Thursday
Restaurants 11am to 3pm and 7pm to 11pm
Shopping centres 10am to 10pm
Shops 8.30am to 12.30pm and 4pm to 7pm or 8pm Saturday to Thursday

PHOTOGRAPHY

Any photo lab can print digital images, and memory cards and an assortment of batteries are obtainable throughout the city. Small photo studios throughout the city centre process passport photos for about KD4. Bear in mind the following tips:

➡ Feel free to photograph obvious 'tourist' sites, such as the Kuwait Towers or the Red Fort in Al-Jahra.
➡ Avoid aiming a camera at military installations, embassies or palaces.
➡ Avoid taking pictures of people without seeking their permission first.
➡ Refrain from taking photographs of local women – this is considered haram (forbidden).

POST

The postal rate for aerograms and for letters or postcards weighing up to 20g is 150 fils to any destination outside the Arab world.

Postage for cards or letters weighing 20g to 50g is 280 fils. Ask at the post office for parcel rates as these vary significantly from country to country.

There is no poste restante service in Kuwait. Large hotels will usually hold mail, but only for their guests.

PUBLIC HOLIDAYS

In addition to the main Islamic holidays, Kuwait celebrates three public holidays:
New Year's Day 1 January
National Day 25 February
Liberation Day 26 February

SAFE TRAVEL

Traffic Accidents The many spectacularly twisted bits of metal left by the roadside are testament to the fact that Kuwait has one of the highest road accident rates in the world. Indeed, one third of all deaths in Kuwait are driving-related. The horrifying scenes on TV have not deterred Kuwait's drivers, despite

PRACTICALITIES

Magazines The *Kuwait Pocket Guide* covers everything from doing business in the country to where to find horse-riding lessons, and is essential for anyone intending to spend any length of time in the country. International glossy magazines, complete with large tracts of blackened text courtesy of the government censor, or even with pages torn out, are also available from hotels.

Newspapers The *Arab Times*, *Kuwait Times* and *Daily Star* are Kuwait's three English-language newspapers. They include useful 'What's On' listings. International newspapers are available (usually a day or two late) at major hotels.

Radio Radio Kuwait – also known locally as the Superstation – broadcasts on 99.7 FM; it plays mostly rock and roll, with some local news and features. The US military's Armed Forces Radio & TV Service (AFRTS) can be heard on 107.9 FM; it broadcasts a mixture of music, news and chat shows.

TV Kuwait TV's Channel 2 broadcasts programs in English each evening from around 2pm to midnight. Many hotels, even the smaller ones, have satellite TV.

Smoking Much more prevalent than in neighbouring Gulf countries on buses, in taxis, at the airport, and in restaurants and hotel rooms.

Weights & Measures Kuwait uses the metric system.

government efforts to slow the pace down with radar surveillance. As such, it's hard to recommend driving in Kuwait unless you're confident of holding your own in the face of sheer lunacy. A police sign at traffic lights speaks volumes: 'Crossing the red signal leads to death or prison'.

Discarded Ordinance Although the country has now been cleared of mines after the Gulf War, you should still remember *not to pick up any unfamiliar object* in the desert and to stick to established tracks.

TELEPHONE

Some useful telephone information:

➜ Country code for Kuwait: ☎965 plus local eight-digit number.

➜ No area codes.

➜ International access code (to call abroad from Kuwait): ☎00.

➜ Local calls are free.

➜ International calls cost (per minute) to Australia 200 fils, Canada 150 fils, Japan 190 fils, Netherlands 170 fils, New Zealand 210 fils, UK 170 fils and USA 120 fils.

➜ Dwindling cardphones take cards in units of KD3, KD5 and KD10.

Mobile Phones

According to the British Ambassador in Kuwait, Kuwaitis are committed users of smartphone and have one of the highest incidences of Tweat use in the world.

Users of mobile phones can link into the GSM services of Wataniya or Zain. Prepaid SIM cards are widely available in malls and from Zain (there's a booth at the airport).

Fax

Fax services are available from government communications centres, though there are usually long queues. The best bet is the business centres in the larger hotels, which charge according to their IDD rates.

VISAS

Visas on arrival Available at Kuwait International Airport for nationals of 34 countries including Australia, Canada, the EU, New Zealand and the USA (KD3, valid for 90 days, 30 days maximum stay). Take a number from the Fast Service Desk and buy stamps worth KD3 from the neighbouring machine (free for British passport holders). There's no need to wait again at the immigration desk downstairs.

Israeli Connection Anyone holding a passport containing an Israeli or Iraqi stamp may be refused entry to Kuwait.

Multiple-entry visas Only available for business requirements (valid for 12 months, apply in advance).

 IS KUWAIT SAFE?

At the time of writing, pro-democracy protests, rumbling on into a second year after the Arab Spring of 2011, were still an issue the government was trying to resolve. Tourists were neither involved or threatened by the demonstrations nor by the government's attempts to curb the gatherings. As such, there is no reason for tourists to avoid the country at present but it would be prudent to check goverment travel advisory websites for updates before committing to a visit. Refer to the Safe Travel chapter for more information.

Transit Visas

A transit visa can be obtained from any Kuwaiti consulate or from the Kuwait Port Authority if you arrive by sea; it is valid for a maximum of seven days and costs KD2. To be eligible, applicants must have a valid visa for their next destination and a confirmed onward ticket.

Visa Extensions

Up to two one-month visa extensions are possible. To do this, an application needs to be made to the **Immigration Department** (28 Street, off Airport Rd) in Shuwaikh before the existing visa expires. Alternatively, hop on a plane to Bahrain for the weekend and re-enter on a new visit visa. There is a hefty fine (KD10 per day) for overstaying once the visa has expired.

WOMEN TRAVELLERS

Women travellers may find the increased attention from men in Kuwait a nuisance. From being tailgated while driving to being followed around shopping centres, expat women are frequently the targets of young men's harmless but irritating fun. Despite dressing conservatively, refusing to respond to approaches and avoiding eye contact with men, it's still hard to avoid attracting unwanted attention.

Generally, if the situation becomes uncomfortable, the best way to defuse it is to stop being an object and become a foreign person: this can be accomplished by turning towards the men in question, giving them a firm but frosty greeting (all the better in Arabic) and offering the right hand for shaking. Ask the offending parties where they come from and to which family they belong. This is usually so unexpected and traumatising for these men that the threat disappears.

❶ Getting There & Away

AIR
Airports & Airlines
Kuwait International Airport (☑ flight information 161; www.dgca.gov.kw) is due for an upgrade. Visas are obtained from a counter on the upper storey of the airport (take a ticket and wait in line), before descending to passport control and baggage claim. Given the limited attractions of the airport and the heavy smoking of regional users, waiting around for a flight can seem like a long time.

Kuwait's national carrier is **Kuwait Airways** (Map p86; ☑ 2434 5555; www.kuwait-airways. com; cnr Abu Bakr al-Siddiq St & Al-Hilalli St, Safat) which flies to many destinations in the Middle East, Europe (including London, Paris and Frankfurt), Asia and the USA. It has an excellent safety record and is reliable and punctual.

Kuwait also has a no-frills, private carrier called **Jazeera Airways** (☑ 177; www.jazeeraairways.com; Kuwait International Airport) with flights to 30 destinations within the Middle East and the Indian subcontinent.

Airlines flying to/from Kuwait
British Airways (☑ 2242 5635; www.ba.com) Heathrow, London

Emirates Airlines (Map p86; ☑ 2242 5566; www.emirates.com; Al Jawahara Tower, First Floor, Al Salhiya Ali Al Salim St) Dubai

Fly Dubai (☑ 2241 4400; www.flydubai.com) Dubai

Gulf Air (Map p86; ☑ 2224 3777; www.gulfair. com; Khaleej Tower, Abu Baker Al Sadeeq St, Qibla) Bahrain

Lufthansa (☑ 2224 0160; www.lufthansa.com) Frankfurt

Oman Air (☑ 2226 0250; www.omanair.com) Muscat

Qatar Airways (☑ 2242 3888; www.qatarairways.com) Doha

Saudi Arabian Airlines (Map p86; ☑ 2242 6310; www.saudiairlines.com; Securities Group Building, Ahmed Al Jaber St, Al Sharq) Jeddah

Yemen Airways (☑ 2245 7962; www.yemenia. com) Sana'a

Fares
Kuwait is not a particularly cheap place to fly into or out of. The airlines and travel agents control prices tightly, and few discount fares are available. The following fares represent walk-in prices from Kuwait City with Gulf Air, one of the most flexible and comprehensive airlines in the region.

FLIGHT DESTINATION	PRICE	FREQUENCY
Abu Dhabi (UAE)	US$310	daily
Doha (Qatar)	US$330	daily
Manama (Bahrain)	US$210	daily
Muscat (Oman)	US$390	daily
Riyadh (Saudi Arabia)	US$430	daily
San'a (Yemen)	US$250	five times per week with one Gulf stop

LAND
Border Crossings
Kuwait has borders with Iraq (currently closed to visitors) and Saudi Arabia. The crossings with Saudi Arabia are at Al-Nuwaisib (for Dammam) and Al-Salmy (for Riyadh). You must have a valid visa for Saudi Arabia or a transit visa, an onward ticket and a visa for your next destination beyond Saudi's borders before you can cross the border. You cannot obtain these at the border.

Bus
Kuwait Public Transport Company (KPTC; ☑ 2232 8501; www.kptc.com.kw) operates comfortable, modern buses to a number of different destinations beyond Kuwait's borders. Buses also operate between Kuwait and Cairo, via Aqaba in Jordan and Nuweiba in Egypt. Agents specialising in these tickets (the trip takes about two days) are located in the area around the main bus station.

Modern, air-con buses, operated by the Saudi bus company **Saptco** (www.saptco.com.sa) and handled in Kuwait by **Kuwait & Gulf Transport Company** (☑ 2484 9355), travel between Kuwait and Dammam (Saudi Arabia) and costs around KD7. The trip takes six hours.

Car & Motorcycle
For those planning on driving through Saudi Arabia, a three-day transit visa is required. Enquire at the **Saudi Embassy** (☑ 2255 0021; Arabian Gulf St, Sharq) for more details.

SEA
The **Combined Shipping Company** (Map p82; ☑ 2483 0889; www.cscq8.com; 1st flr, Office 119, Kuwait Port Authority Bldg, Jamal Abdul Nasser St, Shuwaikh) operates a return service twice a week from Kuwait's Shuwaikh Port to the Iranian port of Bushehr. A one-way/return economy passage costs around US$70/140; an extra US$250 is required to take a car but check for seasonal variations in price. You can book online (www.irantravelingcenter.com).

Speedboat services leave from Shuwaikh Port for Manama (five hours) in Bahrain. The easiest way to book tickets for these services is through one of the city travel agents.

Nuzha Touristic Enterprises (☎ 2575 5825; www.nuzhatours.com) runs charter trips to Manama and Doha but this is not likely to be a cheap way of getting to those countries.

ⓘ Getting Around

BOAT

Kuwait Public Transport Company Ferries (p99) go to Failaka Island from Kuwait City. Nuzha Touristic Enterprises (p115) run half- and whole-day boat trips.

BUS

Kuwait has a cheap and extensive local bus system but it's designed for the convenience of local residents rather than for visiting tourists. The routes therefore don't often coincide with the places of tourist interest. Nonetheless, if a 10-minute walk either side of the bus stop isn't a problem, pick up a bus timetable from the main bus station in the city centre or from inside the bus.

Most bus routes are operated by Kuwait Public Transport Company (p98), which has comfortable, air-conditioned vehicles. Intercity trips cost just a few fils per ride. Route 101 runs from the main bus station in the city centre to Al-Ahmadi and Fahaheel. Route 103 goes to Al-Jahra. The Citybus (☎ 2232 8501; www.transportkuwait.com/citybus.html) alternative follows KPTC routes but doesn't always go the full nine yards;

a route map can be obtained from the bus – by which time it may be too late! Better still, you can check the routes on the website. Both services are used primarily by lower-income workers travelling to their place of work.

CAR & MOTORCYCLE

If you have an International Driving Permit (IDP), or a licence and residence permit from another Gulf country, driving in Kuwait is possible, without any further paperwork, for the duration of your visa.

Fair warning is given of the dangers of driving on Kuwait's roads. For more information, see p112.

Hire

Costs of car rental ranges between KD10 (for a Toyota Corolla) to KD30 (for a Toyota Prado) per day for car hire. This rate usually includes unlimited kilometres and full insurance. Given the very high incidence of traffic accidents in Kuwait, it is worth paying the extra for fully comprehensive insurance. **Al-Mulla** (☎ 2444 8590; www.autoalmulla.com) is one of the better local agencies, with desks at the airport and in many of the city hotels.

LOCAL TRANSPORT
Taxi

Taxis are a useful and popular way of getting around, though they are comparatively expensive when travelling outside the city area, when costs can increase to KD10 per hour. If you want to do some exploring around Kuwait by taxi, it's better to agree on a half- or full-day rate in advance.

Oman عمان

Best for Culture

➡ Bahla Fort (p169)
➡ Mutrah Souq (p123)
➡ Rustaq Fort (p174)
➡ Bayt al-Zubair (p125)
➡ Khasab Fort (p177)

Best for Nature

➡ Jebel Shams (p167)
➡ Sharqiya Sands (p155)
➡ Wadi Dharbat (p188)
➡ Ras al-Jinz (p150)
➡ Wadi Shab (p148)

Why Go?

In Muscat's Grand Mosque, there is a beautiful hand-loomed carpet; it was once the world's largest rug until Abu Dhabi's Grand Mosque, in the United Arab Emirates, pinched the record. This is poignant because Oman doesn't boast many 'firsts' or 'biggests' in a region obsessed by vanity. What it does boast, with its rich heritage and embracing society, is a strong sense of identity, a pride in an ancient, frankincense-trading past and confidence in a highly educated future.

For visitors, this offers a rare chance to engage with the Arab world without the distorting lens of excessive wealth. Oman's low-rise towns retain their traditional charms and Bedouin values remain at the heart of an Omani welcome. With an abundance of natural beauty, from spectacular mountains, wind-blown deserts and a pristine coastline, Oman is the obvious choice for those seeking out the modern face of Arabia while wanting still to sense its ancient soul.

When to Go

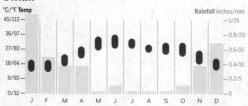

Jan–Feb Muscat Festival brings cultural shows and shopping to the capital.

Jul–Aug Salalah Tourism Festival celebrates the rainy season in southern Oman with shows and shopping.

Nov–Mar Cooler air and fresh winds herald the high season for tourism.

Daily Costs

Oman is an expensive country to visit with limited accommodation and transport options outside the capital. Budget accommodation, where it is available, averages US$50 for single occupancy but there are cheap options for eating (around US$5) and minimal entry fees to many of the main sites of interest; with a combination of public transport and taxi, a minimum daily cost comes to around US$100. This rises to US$230 if staying in midrange hotels with car hire and US$450 for a top-end hotel with 4WD hire.

ITINERARIES

Muscat Stopover

Rise with the dawn to see the weird and wonderful at Mutrah's **fish market**. Join the ebb and flow of the city's residents by strolling the **corniche** and ducking into **Mutrah Souq**. Spare an hour for the sights of **Muscat proper**, the walled heart of the capital, before an extravagant dinner at **Al-Bustan Palace Hotel**.

Two weeks

Begin a mountain tour in the old city of **Nizwa**. Climb to **Jebel Akhdar**, famed for giant pomegranates. Hike the rim of Oman's Grand Canyon for some carpet-buying on **Jebel Shams**. Engage with *jinn* (genies) at the tombs and forts of **Bat**, **Bahla** and **Jabrin**. Take the long way home to Muscat via a dizzying mountain drive to Rustaq, and dive in a sparkling sea at **Sawadi**.

Three weeks

Go in search of wild places from Muscat to Salalah. Follow the coast road to **Sur**, home of the dhow (Arab boat), pausing to explore the celebrated wadis (desert valleys) of **Shab** and **Tiwi**. Learn about turtles at **Ras al-Jinz** before cutting inland to the **Sharqiya Sands**. Acclimatise to nights under the stars before the camping journey to beautiful **Salalah** via **Duqm**.

Essential Food & Drink

⇒ **'Lobster'** Local, clawless crayfish.

⇒ **Harees** Steamed wheat and boiled meat.

⇒ **Shuwa** Marinated lamb cooked in an underground oven.

⇒ **Halwa** Gelatinous sugar or date-syrup confection.

⇒ **Tap water** Safe to drink but most folk drink bottled water.

⇒ **Alcohol** Available at hotels and tourist-oriented restaurants.

⇒ **Coffee** Laced with cardamon and served with dates, it's an essential part of Omani hospitality.

AT A GLANCE

⇒ **Currency** Omani rial (OR)

⇒ **Mobile phones** SIM cards widely available

⇒ **Money** ATMs widespread; credit cards widely accepted

⇒ **Visas** Available on arrival for many nationalities

Fast Facts

⇒ **Capital** Muscat

⇒ **Country code** ☎968

⇒ **Language** Arabic; English widely spoken

⇒ **Official name** Sultanate of Oman

⇒ **Population** 3.1 million

Exchange Rates

The rial is pegged to the US dollar and rarely fluctuates. For current exchange rates see www.xe.com.

Australia	A$10	OR4
Bahrain	BD1	OR1.02
Euro zone	€10	OR4.93
Kuwait	KD1	OR1.35
Qatar	QR10	OR1.05
Saudi Arabia	SR10	OR1.02
UAE	Dh1	OR1.04
UK	UK£10	OR5.84
USA	US$10	OR3.85
Yemen	YR100	OR1.79

Resources

⇒ **Destination Oman** (www.destinationoman.com) Practical information

⇒ **Oman Tourism** (www.omantourism.gov.om) Official tourist website

OMAN

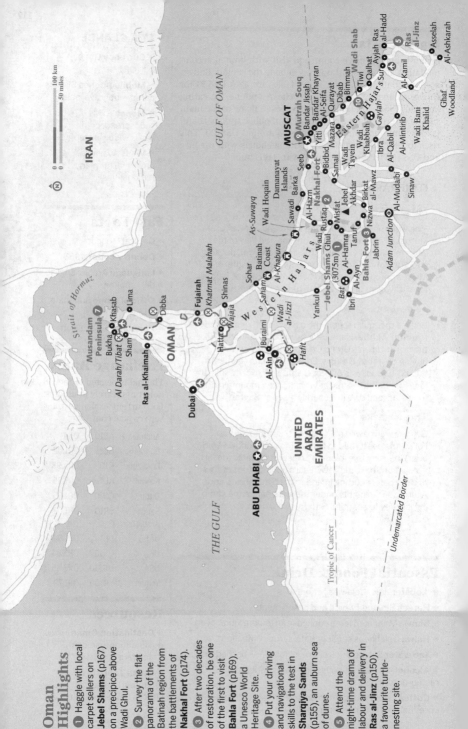

Oman Highlights

❶ Haggle with local carpet sellers on **Jebel Shams** (p167) on a precipice above Wadi Ghul.

❷ Survey the flat panorama of the Batinah region from the battlements of **Nakhal Fort** (p174).

❸ After two decades of restoration, be one of the first to visit **Bahla Fort** (p169), a Unesco World Heritage Site.

❹ Put your driving and navigational skills to the test in **Sharqiya Sands** (p155), an auburn sea of dunes.

❺ Attend the night-time drama of labour and delivery in **Ras al-Jinz** (p150), a favourite turtle-nesting site.

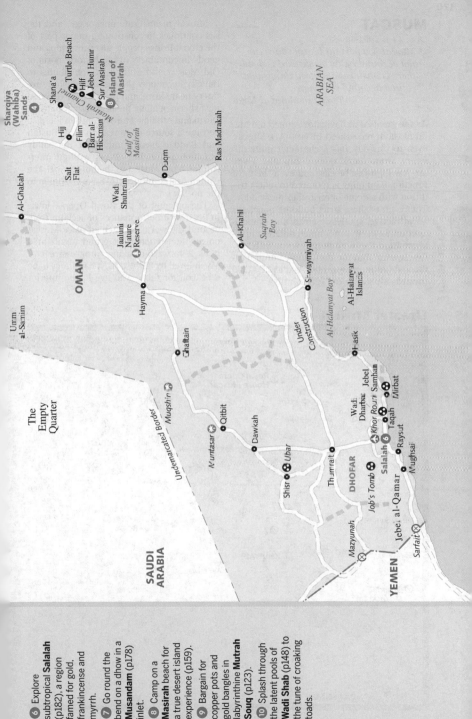

6 Explore subtropical **Salalah** (p182), a region famed for gold, frankincense and myrrh.

7 Go round the bend on a dhow in a **Musandam** (p178) inlet.

8 Camp on a **Masirah** beach for a true desert island experience (p159).

9 Bargain for copper pots and gold bangles in labyrinthine **Mutrah Souq** (p123).

10 Splash through the latent pools of **Wadi Shab** (p148) to the tune of croaking toads.

MUSCAT مسقط

♪ 24 / POP 1 MILLION

Muscat is a port the like of which cannot be found in the whole world where there is business and good things that cannot be found elsewhere.

Ahmed bin Majid al-Najdi

As the great Arab navigator Ahmed bin Majid al-Najdi recognised in 1490 AD, Muscat, even to this day, has a character quite different from neighbouring capitals. There are few high-rise blocks, and even the most functional building is required to reflect tradition with a dome or an arabesque window. The result of these strict building policies is an attractive, spotlessly clean and whimsically uniform city – not much different in essence from the 'very elegant town with very fine houses' that the Portuguese admiral Alfonso de Alburqueque observed as he sailed towards Muscat in the 16th century.

Muscat means 'safe anchorage', and the sea continues to constitute a major part of the city: it brings people on cruise ships and goods in containers to the historic ports of Old Muscat and Mutrah. It contributes to the city's economy through the onshore refinery near Qurm, and provides a livelihood for fishermen along the beaches of Shatti al-Qurm and Athaiba. More recently, it has also become a source of recreation at Al-Bustan and Bandar Jissah, and along the sandy beach that stretches almost without interruption from Muscat to the border with the United Arab Emirates (UAE), over 200km to the northwest.

The opening of the Royal Opera House in 2011, with performances of acclaim from around the world, has helped place Muscat on an international stage and highlighted it as a forward-thinking, progressive city. Much loved by its citizens, it continues to be a beacon for those who live in the interior

OMAN MUSCAT

Greater Muscat

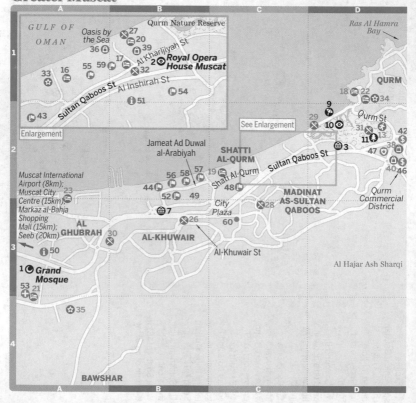

and a role model of understated calm in a region of hyperbole.

History

Muscat became the capital of Oman in 1793, and the focus of the country's great seafaring empire of the 18th and 19th centuries. Having been party to the control of much of the coast of East Africa, its 20th-century descent into international oblivion, under Sultan Said bin Taimur, was all the more poignant. The tide is turning on history, however, and the capital is once more at the centre of life in Oman.

Perhaps the first documented reference to Muscat is by the 2nd century geographer Ptolemy who mentioned a 'concealed harbour', placing the sea at the centre of Muscat's identity where it remains today. In fact, surrounded on three sides by mountains, it remained all but inaccessible from the land for centuries, and the Arab tribes from Yemen who supposedly first settled the area almost certainly approached from the sea.

A small port in the 14th and 15th centuries, Muscat gained importance as a freshwater staging post, but it was eclipsed by the busier port of Sohar – something the people of Sohar's Batinah region hope may well happen again. By the beginning of the 16th century, Muscat was a trading port in its own right, used by merchant ships bound for India. Inevitably it attracted the attention of the Portuguese, who conquered the town in 1507. The city walls were constructed at this time (a refurbished set remains in the same positions), but neither they nor the two Portuguese forts of Mirani and Jalali could prevent the Omani reconquest of the town in 1650 – an event that effectively ended the Portuguese era in the Gulf.

Muscat became a backwater for much of the 20th century and the city gates remained resolutely locked and bolted against the encroachments of the outside world until 1970.

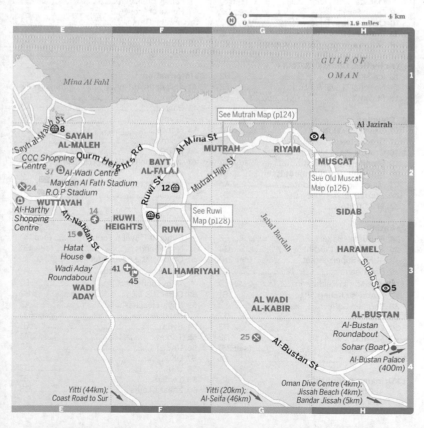

Under the auspices of the current Sultan Qaboos, the city reawakened. To facilitate the growing number of cars needing access to the city, a hole was driven through the city walls. Goods and services flooded in and Muscat flooded out to occupy the surrounding coastline. Touchingly, the city gates continued to be locked at a specific time every evening, despite the adjacent hole in the wall, until the gates were replaced with an archway. In many respects, that little act of remembrance is a fitting metaphor for a city that has given access to modern conveniences while it continues to keep the integrity of its traditional character.

◉ Sights

Wedged into a relatively narrow strip of land between the mountains and the sea, Muscat comprises a long string of suburbs spanning a distance of 50km or so from the airport to Al-Bustan. Visiting the sights can therefore take a bit of planning, and during rush-hour periods (7–8.30am, 12.30–3.30pm and 5.30–7pm Saturday to Wednesday) you may need to add an extra 45 minutes to get to your destination.

Muscat is sometimes referred to as the 'three cities': Ruwi, Mutrah and Old Muscat (a small area with few shops and no hotels, comprising the diwan – or palace administration – and many of the capital's sights of interest). The neighbouring port of Mutrah has the most budget accommodation, while shopping centres and transport terminals are in the commercial district of Ruwi and the suburbs with their lovely beaches.

◉ Mutrah   مطراح

The recommended sights listed below are ordered geographically along the corniche.

★ Corniche   CORNICHE
Mutrah stretches along an attractive corniche of latticed buildings and mosques; it looks spectacular at sunset when the light casts shadows across a serrated crescent of mountains, while pavements, lights and fountains invite an evening stroll.

Despite being the capital's main port area, Mutrah feels like a fishing village. The daily catch is delivered to the **fish market** (Map p124; ☺6-10am), by the Marina Hotel, from sunrise every day. A lengthy refurbishment is nearing completion.

Bait al-Baranda   MUSEUM
(Map p124; ✉ 24 714262; Al-Mina St, Mutrah; adult/child OR1/400 baisa; ☺9am-1pm & 4-6pm Sat-Thu) Located in a renovated 1930s house, this excellent museum traces the history and prehistory – of Muscat through imaginative, interactive displays and exhibits. A 'cut-and-paste' dinosaur, using bones found in Al-Khoud area of Muscat and topped up with borrowed bones from international collections, is one of the many striking exhibits. The ethnographic displays help set not just Muscat but the whole of Oman in a regional, commercial and cultural context. The ground floor of the museum is used as an exhibition space. There is a branch of the popular Khargeen Café in the entrance.

★ Mutrah Souq   SOUQ
(Map p124; Mutrah Corniche, Mutrah; ☺8am-1pm & 5-9pm Sat-Thu, 5-9pm Fri) Many people

come to Mutrah Corniche just to visit the souq, which retains the chaotic interest of a traditional Arab market albeit housed under modern timber roofing. There are some good antique shops selling a mixture of Indian and Omani artefacts among the usual textile, hardware and gold shops. Bargaining is expected but the rewards are not great, as any discount will be small. Entrance to the souq is via the corniche, opposite the pedestrian traffic lights. Take care not to wander into the historic Shiite district of Al-Lawataya by mistake, as the settlement is walled for a good purpose. A sign under the archway requests that visitors keep out. Turn right immediately inside the entrance and follow your nose along to the **gold souq**; or walk straight ahead, fork right at the first junction and left at Muscat Pharmacy for Al-Ahli Coffeeshop. You'll pass a traditional coffeehouse at the entrance but this tends to be a locals-only meeting point for elderly men.

Mutrah

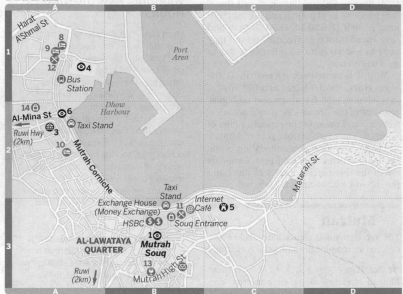

OMAN MUSCAT

Mutrah Fort
FORT

(Map p124) Built by the Portuguese in the 1580s, this fort dominates the eastern end of the harbour. Used for military purposes, it is generally closed to visitors although you can scale the flank of the fort for a good view of the ocean.

Al-Riyam & Kalbuh Bay Parks
PARK

(Map p120; ☉4-11pm Sat-Wed, 9am-midnight Thu & Fri) Beyond Mutrah Fort, the corniche leads to the leafy Al-Riyam Park, with fine photo-worthy views of the harbour from the giant ornamental incense burner (worth a snapshot in its own right). There's also a small funfair. Further along the corniche, Kalbuh Bay Park juts into a sea that's full of large shoals of sardines. The park is a good place for an evening stroll from Mutrah.

Watchtower
TOWER

(Map p124) The restored Portuguese watchtower sitting proudly on a promontory out to sea, halfway along the corniche, affords a lovely view of the ocean. The area is a popular place to catch the evening breeze and is decorated with colourful fountains at night.

◉ Old Muscat

The main road leads via the corniche to the tiny, open-gated city of Muscat, home to the palace and diwan. It sits cradled in a natural harbour surrounded by a jagged spine of hills and makes a fascinating place to spend half a day. It is the site of Oman's brandnew national museum (opposite the palace entrance), the opening of which is expected in 2015.

Muscat Gate Museum
MUSEUM

(Map p126; ☑99 328754; Al-Bahri Rd, Mutrah; ☉9.30-11.30am & 4.30-7pm Sat-Thu) **FREE** Straddling the road between the corniche and the old walled city, this museum, with the original gates used until the 1970s to keep land-bound marauders out, marks the position of the old city wall and introduces Muscat proper. It is also a vantage point for the corniche and the diwan. A drive up to the aerial mast on the neighbouring hill gives an even better view of Mutrah and Muscat.

★ Sultan's Palace
PALACE

(Al-Alam; Map p126; off Al-Saidiya St, Muscat) If you stand by the harbour wall on Mirani St, the building to the right with the delightful

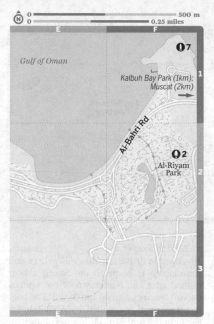

0 —————— 500 m
0 —————— 0.25 miles

Gulf of Oman

Kalbuh Bay Park (1km);
Muscat (2km)

Al-Bahri Rd

Al-Riyam
Park

Mutrah

◎ Top Sights

◎ Sights

⊜ Sleeping

⊗ Eating

⊔ Drinking & Nightlife

⊜ Shopping

mushroom pillars in blue and gold is the Sultan's Palace. Built over the site of the former British embassy, there used to be the stump of a flagpole in the grounds: the story goes that any slave (Oman was infamous for its slave trade from East Africa) who touched the flagpole was granted freedom. On the inland side, an avenue of palm trees leads to a roundabout surrounded by grand royal court buildings and the yet-to-open national museum. Pause in front of the colonnaded approach to the palace for a quintessential photograph of Muscat. The palace is closed to the public.

Al-Jalali Fort
FORT

(Map p126) Guarding the entrance to the harbour to the east, Al-Jalali Fort was built during the Portuguese occupation in the 1580s on Arab foundations.

The fort is accessible only via a steep flight of steps. As such, it made the perfect prison for a number of years, but now it is a museum of Omani heritage, open only to visiting dignitaries and heads of state.

Neither this fort nor Al-Mirani Fort is open to the public, but photos are permitted. During palace military occasions, bagpipers perform from the fort battlements, and the royal dhow and yacht are sailed in full regalia into the harbour. With fireworks reflected in the water, it makes a spectacular sight.

Al-Mirani Fort
FORT

(Map p126) Al-Mirani Fort was built at the same time as Al-Jalali Fort. It contributed to the fall of the Portuguese through a curious affair of the heart: legend has it that the Portuguese commander fell for the daughter of a Hindu supplier, who refused the match on religious grounds. On being threatened with ruin, he spent a year apparently preparing for the wedding, but in fact convinced the commander that the fort's supplies needed a complete overhaul. Instead of replacing the removed gunpowder and grain, he gave the nod to Imam Sultan bin Saif, who succeeded in retaking the defenceless fort in 1649. The Portuguese were ousted from Muscat soon after. The fort is not open to the public.

Bayt al-Zubair
MUSEUM

(Map p126; ☎24 736688; www.baitalzubairmuseum.com; Al-Saidiya St; adult/child OR2/1; ⊙9.30am-6pm Sat-Thu) In a beautifully restored house, this museum exhibits Omani heritage in photos and displays of traditional handicrafts and furniture.

Old Muscat

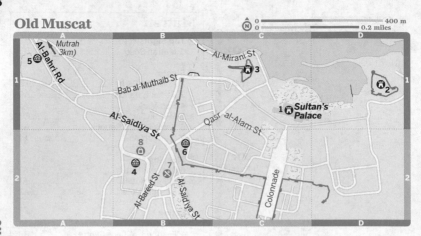

Omani-French Museum   MUSEUM
(Map p126; ☎24 736613; Qasr al-Alam St; adult/child 500/200 baisa; ⊗8am-1.30pm Sat-Wed, 9am-1pm Thu year-round, 4-7pm Sat-Thu Oct-Mar) With galleries detailing relations between the two countries, this museum provides an interesting snapshot of mostly 19th-century colonial life in Muscat.

◎ Al-Bustan   البستان

Al-Bustan Palace   NOTABLE BUILDING
(off Sidab St, Al-Bustan) Set in lush gardens, this sumptuous hotel was built as a venue for the Gulf Cooperation Council (GCC) summit in 1985. Remarkable for its enormous domed atrium, the hotel is worth a visit just to admire the building's interior and the location.

Al-Bustan Roundabout   LANDMARK
Just outside Al-Bustan Palace Hotel, a small roundabout is home to the *Sohar*, a boat named after the hometown of the famous Omani seafarer Ahmed bin Majid. The boat is a replica of one sailed by Abdullah bin Gasm in the mid-8th century to Guangzhou in China. It was built in the dhow yards of Sur from the bark of over 75,000 palm trees and four tonnes of rope. Not a single nail was used in the construction. Tim Severin and a crew of Omani sailors undertook a famous voyage to Guangzhou in this boat in 1980 – a journey of 6000 nautical miles that took eight months to complete.

Marina Bandar al-Rowdha   HARBOUR
(Map p120; ☎24 737288; Sidab St) Marina Bandar al-Rowdha is primarily of interest to those who are interested in water sports as it offers a full range of boating amenities. That said, it's also a pleasant place to enjoy harbour activity and relax at the Blue Marlin restaurant (p136). The marina offers free use of its pool for those dining at the restaurant, making it a potential day trip when combined with a boat trip to see the dolphins. The journey to the marina, along the coast road from Old Muscat to Al-Bustan, offers spectacular mountain and sea views and a glimpse of local life.

◎ Ruwi   روي

Oman's 'Little India' is the commercial and transport hub of the capital, with plenty of budget-priced places to eat, shop (especially along Souq Ruwi St) and socialise.

National Museum MUSEUM
(Map p120; ☑24 701289; An-Noor St; admission 500 baisa; ⊙8am-1.30pm Sat-Wed) With displays of jewellery, costumes and dowry chests, this museum has its moments. A mural and collection of boats celebrating Oman's seafaring heritage are probably the best part of a tired collection that is soon to be completely revamped and given superb new quarters opposite the Sultan's palace in Old Muscat.

Sultan's Armed Forces Museum MUSEUM
(Map p120; ☑24 312648; Al Mujamma St, Ruwi; admission adult/child OR1/500 baisa; ⊙8am-1.30pm Sat-Wed, 9am-noon & 3-6pm Thu, 9-11am & 3-6pm Fri) Despite its name, this excellent museum is far more than just a display of military hardware. The museum is housed in Bayt al-Falaj, built in 1845 as a royal summer home but used mostly as the headquarters of the sultan's armed forces. The lower rooms give a comprehensive outline of Oman's history, and the upper rooms explore Oman's international relations and military prowess. The museum is on the itinerary of visiting dignitaries and you'll be given a mandatory military escort. There's a *falaj* (irrigation channel) in the grounds outside.

⊙ Qurm القرم

Most of this area comprises modern shopping centres and residences, but there are several places to visit and a great beach.

PDO Oil & Gas Exhibition MUSEUM
(Map p120; ☑24 677834; Sayh al-Malih St; ⊙7am 3pm Sat-Wed, 8am-noon Thu) **FREE** Petroleum Development Oman (PDO) is responsible for much of the rapid growth of infrastructure throughout the country, as outlined in the PDO Oil & Gas Exhibition. The interactive displays are a must for anyone interested in science in general and the oil and gas industry in particular. To reach the museum from Qurm, follow the signs for the Crowne Plaza Hotel and take the first right turn along Sayh al-Malih St.

Planetarium PLANETARIUM
(Map p120; ☑24 675542; Sayh Al-Malih St, Sayah Al-Maleh) The Planetarium is open for two shows per week in English (at 7pm Wednesday and 10am Thursday) but book one day ahead. To reach it from Qurm, follow the signs for the Crowne Plaza Hotel and take the first right turn along Sayh al-Malih St.

Qurm Nature Reserve OUTDOORS
(Map p120) Protects a rare stretch of mangrove. Although it is closed to visitors, it's possible to sit in adjacent coffeeshops and do some birdwatching over a latte.

Qurm Park PARK
(Map p120; Qurm; ⊙10am-10pm; P) ✔**FREE** Large and attractive park that boasts a lake, shade for picnics and a heritage village that is active during Muscat Festival.

Qurm Beach BEACH
(Map p120) A road runs along the edge of Qurm Nature Reserve towards the Crowne Plaza Hotel, giving access to a long, sandy beach – a popular place for cruising in the latest on four wheels and for family picnics on the sand. Women bathing on their own have been accosted here, so avoid skimpy swimwear. There are cafes along the beachfront with a view out to sea.

⊙ Shatti al-Qurm & Al-Khuwair شاطي القرم و الخوي

Near the Hotel InterContinental Muscat, along Way 2817, there is a small shopping complex that has become the teeming heart of modern Muscat. This is where you will find young Omanis cruising the loop in their new VWs, families strolling along the beach amid five-a-side footballers, and expats enjoying the Western-style cafe culture and shops.

It's worth driving around the **ministry and embassy buildings** bunched in this area. Make time to stop at the beachside **Grand Hyatt Muscat** to enjoy a Yemeni prince's flight of fancy; love it or hate it, tea in the foyer is a delight.

★ Royal Opera House Muscat NOTABLE BUILDING
(Map p120; ☑24 403300; www.rohmuscat.org.om; Sultan Qaboos St, Shatti Al-Qurm; P) The arrival of the Royal Opera House Muscat in 2011 was a high point in the capital's cultural life. Built by the same architects as the Grand Mosque, the understated marble exterior belies the magnificent interior of inlaid wood and arabesque designs.

Some of the most famous names in opera and ballet performed in a world-class program in the opera house's inaugural year and the quality of production has already won international acclaim. There's a strict dress code for attending a performance:

Ruwi

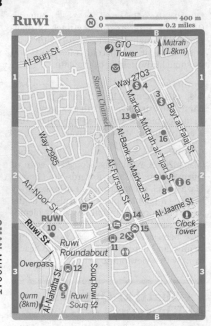

Ruwi

Sleeping
1 Sun City Hotel.....................................B3

Eating
2 Al-Bulbul Restaurant &
   Coffeeshop......................................B3

Information
3 Citibank B1
4 HSBC B1
5 Mustafa Jawad Exchange
   Company (Money
   Exchange) A3
6 Thomas Cook (Bahwan Travel
   Agencies) B2

Transport
7 Bin Qasim Transport........................A2
8 Emirates...B2
9 Europcar...B2
10 Gulf Air...A3
11 Intercity Microbus Station................B3
12 Microbus Station (Local)..................A3
13 Oman Air...B1
14 ONTC Bus Station B2
15 Taxi Stand B3
16 Thrifty Car Rental B2

jeans are not permitted. Even if you're not intending to catch a show, stop by to admire the beauty of the building and enjoy window shopping in the adjacent Opera Galleria arcade. Call the box office to check the availability of tours.

Natural History Museum   MUSEUM
(Map p120; ☑ 24 641374; Way 3413; adult/child 500/100 baisa; ☉ 8am-1.30pm Sat-Wed, 9am-1pm Thu) The Ministry of National Heritage houses the small but lovely Natural History Museum. The museum is a must for anyone interested in the local flora and fauna, and there are some excellent displays on Oman's geography and geology, together with information about environmental protection.

⊚ Al-Ghubrah & Ghala

الغبرة و غلا

★**Grand Mosque**   MOSQUE
(Map p120; Sultan Qaboos St; ☉ non-Muslims 8-11am Sat-Thu) This glorious piece of modern Islamic architecture was a gift to the nation from Sultan Qaboos to mark the 30th year of his reign. Quietly imposing from the outside, the main prayer hall is breathtakingly rich. The Persian carpet alone measures 70m by 60m wide, making it the second-largest

hand-loomed Iranian carpet in the world; it took 600 women four years to weave. The mosque can accommodate 20,000 worshippers, including 750 women in a private *musalla* (prayer hall).

Children under 10 are not permitted. It's important to dress modestly when visiting. See p40 for more information.

Al-Ghubrah and Ghala lie some 8km west of Al-Khuwair. If you are visiting the mosque from Muscat in the summer, it's easier to take a taxi (OR5) rather than catch the bus: it is a hot walk crossing the highway via the overpass. Plenty of buses bound for Ruwi stop outside the mosque.

⭧ Activities

The sea and the mountains dominate Muscat, giving plenty of amenities for water-related sports and some independent hiking. **Muscat Diving & Adventure Centre** (☑ 24 485663; www.holiday-in-oman.com) can help with activity-based trips in the capital area and beyond.

Four-Wheel Drive Excursions
Muscat's rocky mountains and soft-sand dunes offer some exciting and challenging 4WD driving. Close to the city there are plen-

ty of places to explore, especially near Yitti and en route to Al-Seifa. For more adventurous routes in Oman, pick up a copy of *Off-Road in the Sultanate of Oman,* by Lonely Planet author Jenny Walker and Sam Owen.

Many people refer to this activity as 'wadi-bashing' as taking a 4WD into remote terrain can lead, through careless or insensitive driving, to irreparable degradation of the environment. With care and concern for the desert, however, going off-road is easily one of the highlights of visiting Oman.

It's also possible to take 4WD tours to many off-road destinations.

Beaches

Although all beaches in Oman are public, many of the big hotels have attractive beach-side facilities (pools, restaurants, gardens) open to non-guests for a fee. Women may feel more comfortable swimming in this environment than in the sea at public beaches. The Crowne Plaza Hotel is at the head of a beautiful, sandy bay and has access to a secluded scrap of beach. Admission costs OR8 per day for an adult, OR6 for children. InterContinental Muscat (p132) offers an adult day rate of OR10 (OR6 for children). A taxi from Mutrah should cost around OR5. At present, all beaches in Muscat are 'public', so there's nothing to stop a keen walker starting at Qurm Nature Reserve and walking all the way to Seeb, a distance of some 20km or so.

Birdwatching

There are several birdwatching opportunities in Muscat and over 450 bird species to look out for in Oman. Contact the **Oman Bird Group** (www.birdsoman.com) for specialist information. A new reserve with hides is being planned at Al-Ansab lagoons, part of the city's waste-water facility.

Hiking

There are some rewarding mountain walks in the Muscat area. Several two- to three-hour walks in and around Mutrah and Old Muscat afford excellent views of the two port areas and take the rambler up past ruined villages. These walks are covered in Anne Dale and Jerry Hadwin's *Adventure Trekking in Oman,* with good maps, directions and safety precautions. Their Muscat–Sidab route is a one-hour walk that could be added, for those energetic walkers, onto our walking tour (p132).

The **Ministry of Tourism** (☑24 588700; www.omantourism.gov.om) has developed a set of walking tours and a booklet describing some great routes across Muscat and beyond. Brown information signs mark the trailheads of some routes. One, the C38 from Al-Riyam Park to Mutrah (a walk of 2km taking about 1½ hours), is an option on our walking tour. Be prepared for rough conditions in remote territory on all trails: stout walking shoes, water and a hat are essential at any time of year, even on the shortest route.

MUTRAH SOUQ

Describing Mutrah's attractions, a local said 'you must visit the souq-or-market'. Thinking he said 'supermarket', it was a surprise to find a warren of alleyways with no checkouts – but there are some similarities. For a start, just when you thought you'd fathomed where to find the frankincense, you find that alleyway now stocks Thai clothing. Secondly, though you fully intended to look for a present for Aunt Alice, you came out with a toy helicopter, two melamine trays and an armful of fairy lights instead. Thirdly, even though you definitely didn't want to buy a *dishdasha* (man's shirt-dress), there was a special offer for three. And finally, although all alleyways seem to be heading for the exit, you can't actually get out.

Mind you, getting a little lost is part of the fun of the souq, as that is the most likely time you'll stumble on the 'special offers' – the ones unique to 'that place' at 'this time'. And Mutrah Souq has plenty of those – like the old picture frames, complete with woodworm, from the wood-crafting town of Ibra; antique *mandoos* (wedding chests) with brand-new thumbtacks brought down from the Hajar Mountains; rope-twined muskets that saw action in the Dhofar wars of the 1970s; an alleyway of sandals that complete the men's smart Omani costume; and another of aluminium serving dishes for the traditional Omani *shuwa* (marinated lamb cooked in an underground oven).

In summary, from a camel with an illuminated hump to a mosque alarm clock, Mutrah Souq sells all the things you never wanted but can afford to buy (plus a few you did and can't) and is an experience not to be missed.

Horse Riding

There are two horse-riding schools in Muscat that are open to the public: Al-Sawahil Horse Riding (☎ 95 177557; ahmad-565@hotmail.com) and Qurm Equestrian School (☎ 99 832199).

Water Sports

Water sports in Muscat include diving and snorkelling. There are also boat trips around scenic Bandar Khayran and the nearby rock arch. Stars of the show are the highly popular dolphin- and whale- watching trips. Kiosks along Mutrah Corniche advertise these boat rides for OR15 for a two-hour boat trip, leaving at 8.30am, noon, 1pm and 3.30pm every day from Marina Bandar al-Rowdha.

Eurodivers (☎ 24 737293; www.euro-divers.com; Sidab St) offers diving and snorkelling from Marina Bandar al-Rowdha. The marina itself offers a full range of boating amenities, and has an excellent on-site restaurant, with an outdoor terrace, called the Blue Marlin (p136).

Other companies operating from the marina offer dolphin boat trips (for two hours leaving at 8am and 10am), glass-bottom boat trips (Sea Tours Oman; ☎ 99 425461; www.seatoursoman.com), sunset cruises and a two-hour semi-submersible boat trip (☎ 97 307877; www.alkhayran.com; per trip OR25; ☉ 8am, 9am, 10am & 11am May-Sep) for a close-up of the coral gardens without getting wet.

🐾 Courses

Muscat isn't a great place to learn Arabic, as many people speak English proficiently and relish the chance to practise.

For the determined, however, Polyglot (Map p120; ☎ 24 666666; www.polyglot.org; off Wadi Aday roundabout, Ruwi; per course OR140) runs 10-week courses in six different levels of Arabic proficiency, from beginners to advanced. The teachers are usually from Sudan and the courses concentrate on classical Arabic rather than the Omani dialect.

For a much more personal experience in very small class sizes, the Center for International Learning (☎ 24 551041; www.omancenter.org; Beach Rd, Al-Hail; from OR415 for a two-week Arabic course) comes highly recommended.

🧭 Tours

As Muscat's attractions are so spread out, a tour is recommended. Generally, tours can be organised on a bespoke basis by any of the main tour operators.

Big Bus Tours   CITY TOUR

(☎ 971 4340 7709; www.bigbustours.com; adult/child/family US$52/$26/$130; ☉ 11am & 2pm) This new service runs air-conditioned, open-top double-decker bus tours through the capital on a hop-on, hop-off basis, taking in 12 of the major sites from Mutrah and old Muscat to Qurm and offering a free shuttle to the Grand Mosque. Buses leave from outside Mutrah Souq and the whole tour takes 1½ hours with an extra 30 minutes for a free walking tour of the palace area of old Muscat. A guide gives an on-board commentary in English. Tickets can be bought on the bus or from hotels and a discounted combination ticket for Muscat and Dubai or Abu Dhabi is available.

National Travel & Tourism   CITY TOUR

(Map p120; ☎ 24 660300; www.nttomantours.com; Ar-Rumaylah St, Wattayah; ☉ 8.30am-6pm Sat-Thu) Can arrange half-day city tours for OR45 for a car of up to three people with an English-speaking driver.

✨ Festivals & Events

Lasting for a month from around the end of January, Muscat Festival has become a highlight of the capital's year. The event is organised around several main venues – one usually in Qurm Park and others in the suburbs of All-Amerat and Naseem Gardens along the Muscat to Barka Hwy near Seeb.

In the main venue, there are nightly fireworks about 8pm, a 'living' replica of an Omani village with *halwa*-making and craft displays, exhibitions from regional countries and events such as laser shows and traditional dancing. There is also a funfair, international pavillions selling crafts, bargain clothing and bedding and a range of items from cheap imports to inlaid furniture from Pakistan. International dance troupes perform on the open-air stages and fashion shows take place nightly; other acts, such as high-wire acrobatics, occupy the periphery. In addition, many shops in Muscat offer grand draws and discounts. Check the English-language newspapers and Muscat FM radio for the festival program.

On 18 November, National Day is marked with fireworks, city buildings are draped with strings of colourful lights, and Sultan Qaboos St is spectacularly lit and adorned with flags. Petunia planting along highway verges, roundabouts and city parks is timed for maximum blooming, transforming the city into a riot of floral colour.

🛏 Sleeping

Muscat is not a cheap city to sleep in, but it does have some splendid hotels. Some are almost holidays in their own right. The hotels of Qurm, Shatti al-Qurm and Al-Khuwair are all on or near the same stretch of sandy beach. Alternatively, for a location within walking distance of the capital's main attractions, try the less-expensive hotels in Mutrah.

Top-end prices quoted here are rack rates and you can almost certainly arrange a discount of some sort. Disconcertingly, rates change by 20% or more from one day to the next. Nonsmoking rooms are available.

Marina Hotel
HOTEL $
(Map p124; ☑ 24 713100; Mutrah Corniche, Mutrah; s/d OR18/25; 🖻) For those wanting to discover Muscat's soul, then the Marina Hotel, overlooking the fish market and participating in the character of the corniche, offers a very good vantage point. You can feel the city's pulse over breakfast on the terrace of the popular Al-Boom Restaurant. The rooms are on the cramped side but it remains a local favourite.

Naseem Hotel
HOTEL $
(Map p124; ☑ 24 712418; naseemhotel@gmail.com; Mutrah Corniche, Mutrah; s/d OR18/25) In need of a makeover, this tired old Mutrah favourite has large rooms, four or five with stunning views of the harbour. Given its prime location, plum in the middle of the city's finest row of merchant houses, it's remarkable that this hotel has survived. What it lacks in decor (and clean carpets), it makes up for in friendly, helpful service.

Al-Fanar Hotel
HOTEL $
(Map p124; ☑ 24 712385; alfanarcorniche@hotmail.com; Mutrah Corniche, Mutrah; s/d OR12/18) Near the fish market and neighbouring the Marina Hotel, this travellers' haunt is in dire need of a facelift. If you can ignore the down-at-heel interior, the basic rooms are clean and the cheapest in town. Ask for a room that doesn't face a brick wall. Breakfast is not included.

Sun City Hotel
HOTEL $
(Map p128; ☑ 24 789801; hotel.suncity@hotmail.com; Al-Jaame St; s/d OR20/25; 🖻) Beside Ruwi bus station, this hotel – with its bright lobby,

enormous plastic potted orange trees, and large rooms with shiny floor tiles and big windows – is recommended if you have an early bus to catch. Friendly staff can help you navigate the vagaries of the bus station.

Qurm Beach House
HOTEL $$
(Map p120; ☑ 24 564070; qbhotel@omantel.net.om; Way 1622, Qurm; s/d OR20/45; 🖻 @) In a quiet location within walking distance of a beach, this hotel is on the approach to the Crowne Plaza Hotel. Don't be put off by the appearance of the lobby; the rooms are appealingly quirky with an ill-assortment of furniture. Next door is Rock Bottom Café (p137), one of the hottest nightclubs in town.

Beach Hotel
HOTEL $$
(Map p120; ☑ 24 696601; www.beachhotelmuscat.com; Way 2818, Shatti al-Qurm; s/d OR40/45; 🖻) In a pristine white building with tiled blue trim, big rooms with armchairs, balconies and a lobby with sky blue domes, this is a rare residential-style hotel. The breakfast menu includes *fuul medamas* (beans) and *khubz* (Arabic flat bread) and with hospitable, helpful Omani staff and an easy walk to the beach, this hotel offers a genuine Omani experience.

Majan Continental Hotel
BUSINESS HOTEL $$
(Map p120; ☑ 24 592900; www.majanhotel.com; Al-Ghubrah St; s/d OR40/50; 🖻 🖻 🖻) Perched on top of a hill overlooking the pearly white suburbs of Muscat, this comfortable, Arabic-style hotel is popular with Omanis. If you think of Muscat as a prudish city, then think again: quiet and decorous by day, the hotel reinvents itself at night into the city's liveliest nightspot. Best suits male travellers wanting to feel the pulse of local life.

Beach Bay Hotel
BOUTIQUE HOTEL $$
(Map p120; ☑ 24 692121; www.beachbaymuscat.com; Way 3040, off Al-Saruj St, Shatti al-Qurm; s/d OR65/76; 🖻 🖻) Fun and quirky, and with a nautical theme, this ship's-bow–shaped hotel is only a seagull's glide from the sea. With sailor-suited staff and compass-patterned carpets, ships' wheel banisters and a dhow-shaped reception, guests will be glad to learn that rooms bear little resemblance to cabins.

★ The Chedi
LUXURY HOTEL $$$
(Map p120; ☑ 24 524400; www.ghmhotels.com; Way No 3215, off 18th November Street, Al-Ghubrah North; r from OR230; 🖻 🖻 🖻) With a hint of the kasbah (desert castle) combined with Asian minimalism, the Chedi has been designed

to make the best of its mini sand-dune location. Don't let the occasional groan of aircraft at Muscat International Airport put you off: usually, the only audible sound from the poolside of Muscat's most stylish hotel is the chink of wine glasses.

The gardens, rhythmically punctuated by Zen ponds, raked pebbles and a pool virtually contiguous with the sea, are satisfying to the soul. Hanging suits and accommodating the etceteras of working life may be difficult in the minimally furnished rooms, but if all you brought is a swimsuit and a good book, then very little will intrude on your sense of getting away from it all.

Hotel InterContinental Muscat   RESORT $$$
(Map p120; ☎ 24 680000; www.ichotelsgroup. com; off Way 2817, Shatti al-Qurm; s/d OR140/150; P ≈ ≋) If anything is 'happening' in Muscat, chances are it is doing so at the 'Inter-Con' – an excellent hotel in terms of service and amenities. While not the prettiest building in town, this hotel has a fine interior, quality rooms, shady gardens and access to the beach. Jawaharat Al-Shatti Complex – a happening shopping complex, one of the liveliest in town, including coffeehouses and restaurants – is within walking distance.

Grand Hyatt Muscat   LUXURY HOTEL $$$
(Map p120; ☎ 24 641234; www.muscat.grand.hyatt. com; Way 3033, Off Al-Saruj St, Shatti al-Qurm; s/d OR150/159; P ≈ ≋) This hotel is pure kitsch! Allegedly designed by a Yemeni prince, the exterior owes much to Disney, while its stained-glass and marble interior is a cross between art deco and a royal Bedouin tent. With luxurious, balconied rooms, Muscat's best Italian restaurant, Tuscany, water sports and limitless walks along the sandy beach, this hotel has more than one angle.

Al-Bustan Palace   LUXURY HOTEL
(Ritz-Carlton Hotel; ☎ 24 799666; www.ritzcarl-ton.com; off Sidab St, Al-Bustan; r from OR200; P ≈ ≋) In a secluded bay ringed by spectacular mountains, Al-Bustan is more palace than hotel. It has an atmosphere and class of its own, partly engendered through the Arabian-style interior and top-quality restaurants. The hotel grounds are like a Garden of Eden with infinity pools and shady lawns backing onto a pristine beach. A Six Senses Spa is due to open in late 2013.

🏃 City Walk
Muscat Coastline

START FISH MARKET, MUTRAH
END AL-BAHRI RD, OLD MUSCAT
LENGTH 8KM; FOUR TO FIVE HOURS

This walking tour follows the sea through the ancient ports of Mutrah and Muscat. Pack a snack and take lots of water. The walk can be segmented if time, energy or summer heat forbids the whole circuit.

Begin where the morning tide beaches fishermen and their catch at the ❶ **Fish Market** (p123). Stop for something fishy at nearby La Brasserie (p136), with delicious seafood on the menu.

Turn right at ❷ **Samak roundabout**, which means 'The Fish' in Arabic and is decorated with a pair of generic pisces. Call into nearby ❸ **Bait al-Baranda** (p123) and learn about the history of Muscat's relationship with the sea and the origin of the city's name, meaning 'safe anchorage'. Return to the corniche and head towards the fort. Cast your eye out to sea: His Majesty's Dhow is generally harboured here, cruise ships dock by the harbour master and the ferry to Musandam sits proudly in its own berth. Inland, the merchants' houses of the Lawataya people, who built their fortunes on the seafaring trade, sport balconies that allow the inhabitants a nostalgic glance across the Arabian Ocean.

Turn into ❹ **Mutrah Souq** (p123), where items such as handmade models of silver dhows and ship chandlery are on sale; this souq grew from seaborne cargo and to this day many of the wares (Indian spices and textiles, Egyptian plastic, Iranian crafts and Chinese toys) are shipped in by sea. Ward off scurvy with a fruit juice at ❺ **Al-Ahli Coffeeshop** (p137) in the heart of the souq. Return to the corniche and turn right towards 16th-century ❻ **Mutrah Fort** (p124), built by the Portuguese who were unwittingly led to Muscat by the kindness of Ahmed bin Majid, a famous sailor from Sohar.

At the ❼ **goldfish monument and fountains**, a heron often snacks in view of the royal yacht and the visiting navies of other nations. Continue towards the giant incense burner; Oman's former prosperity was built on Dhofar frankincense, which

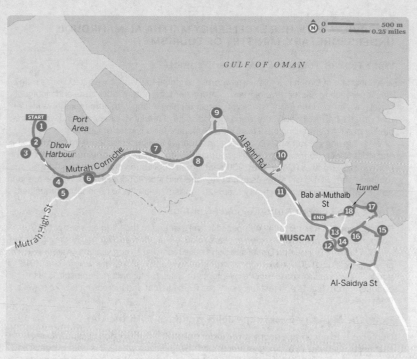

left the shores of Oman with other precious cargo such as Arabian horses.

On reaching ❽ **Al-Riyam Park** (p124) you could, with stout shoes, head back to Mutrah on the Ministry of Tourism's walking route C38, past panoramic views. Alternatively, continue along the corniche to the ❾ **watchtower** (p124) and scan for dolphins – some real and some carved from marble.

After a rest at ❿ **Kalbuh Bay Park** (p124) cut inland via Al-Bahri Rd and enter the 'city proper' via ⓫ **Muscat Gate Museum** (p124). Every night until the 1970s the doors to the city were locked at this point, keeping tradition in and those from the interior out.

Turn right towards Sidab on Al-Saidiya St and visit ⓬ **Bayt al-Zubair** (p125) for photographs showing the sea's influence on Muscat. Buy a souvenir of your tour in ⓭ **Bait Muzna Gallery** (p138) opposite.

Continue along Al-Saidiya St, still heading for Sidab. Pause for fried fish at ⓮ **Muscat Light Restaurant & Coffeeshop** (p135) on the corner before turning right along an avenue of date palms.

At the roundabout, march left through the colonnade towards the grand front entrance of the ⓯ **Sultan's Palace** (p124). Follow the palace walls left, past beautiful gardens and mature trees (a favourite roost of myna birds) on Qasr al-Alam St.

At the junction, you can turn left for the ⓰ **Omani-French Museum** (p126) and a display on shipbuilding, or right for Muscat Harbour. The Portuguese built forts, such as ⓱ **Al-Mirani** (p125), towering to the left, and **Al-Jalali** (p125, across the bay), to protect their maritime interests. Look across the harbour for a graffiti log book etched into the promontory rocks, left by the visiting navies of Great Britain and other countries. This is a good place to admire the back garden of the palace and imagine the spectacle of the military banquets held annually here, complete with ice sculptures on the lawn, a band on each of the surrounding forts, lights from Oman's fully-rigged tall ship moored in the harbour for the occasion, and fireworks mirrored in the calm waters of the bay.

Turn left at the harbour wall, and duck under the tunnel before the modern naval base. Turn right under the ⓲ **old city gate** onto Bab al-Muthaib St. This soon runs into Al-Bahri Rd – and from here, it's an easy taxi ride back to Mutrah.

INTERVIEW WITH HER EXCELLENCY MAITHA AL-MAHROUQI: UNDERSECRETARY, MINISTRY OF TOURISM

What Type of Tourism Does Oman Promote?

The Sultanate of Oman is a relative newcomer to global tourism so we have taken a managed approach to sector development. Cultural heritage, nature, adventure and indulgent travel have formed the cornerstones of our positioning. Along with authenticity, we feel that Oman's natural beauty, the grandeur and scale of our landscapes, and the warm hospitality make a compelling case to visit the Sultanate for business or leisure.

We are giving greater emphasis to regional touring and business tourism. Accompanied and independent tours are growing in popularity, with much of this originating from the United Arab Emirates (UAE). The 3000-seat Oman Convention and Exhibition Centre (opening early 2017) will allow us to host regional and international events. We see pre- and post-event tours as an opportunity to spread tourism's benefits to regional communities.

How Safe is Oman Amid Regional Conflict?

Regional conflict has certainly dampened travel demand to the Middle East, but the Gulf Cooperation Council (GCC) region appears relatively unaffected. Our neighbouring mega-aviation hubs in Dubai, Abu Dhabi and Doha have recorded strong year-on-year growth. We are awaiting end of 2012 data, but our expectation is a 16% increase in arrival over 2011, and a 26% increase in passenger movements to Salalah. Musandam Peninsula is also benefiting from flights and fast ferry services from Muscat and increasing leisure travellers from the UAE.

Does the Ministry Encourage Joint Holidays With the UAE?

Our focus is to encourage people to consider holidaying in the region because we see sustainable benefits in building awareness in the region as a whole. It is both dynamic and diverse, and includes manufactured and natural destinations. We see Oman as complementary to the mega-aviation hubs. There are frequent daily flights and our discounted tourism visa is attractive for those driving from the UAE. We are also seeing more business people and holidaymakers on Oman Air taking the opportunity of an Oman stopover.

✖ Eating

There are lots of opportunities for fine dining in Muscat, particularly at top-end hotels. Equally, it's hard to go 10 paces without tripping over a stand selling *shwarma* (meat sliced off the spit and stuffed in pita-type bread with chopped tomatoes and garnish).

Dozens of what are locally termed 'coffee-shops' abound in Muscat selling a variety of largely Indian snacks, such as omelettes rolled up in Arabic bread with chilli, samosas and curried potatoes. It is more difficult to eat typical Omani food – the best options are Ubar, Khargeen and Bin Ateeq. For a comprehensive round-up of Muscat's restaurants and cafés, it's worth buying a copy of *Time Out Muscat* (OR2). Following is a selection of restaurants that give a flavour of the region, either in menu or venue, and some of Muscat's favourite cafes.

Al-Daleh Restaurant INTERNATIONAL $
(Map p120; ☑ 24 813141; An-Nuzha St, National Hospitality Institute, Al-Wadi al-Kabir; 3-course lunch OR4; ⊙ 1-3pm Sat-Wed) 🍽 Nervous Omani hospitality students practise their culinary and waiting skills at this exceptionally good-value restaurant. Menus comprise mostly top-notch international dishes. Encouraging these youngsters on their chosen career path is a great way to make your visit to Muscat count. Ring to book a table as it gets busy.

Al-Boom MIDDLE EASTERN $
(Map p124; ☑ 24 713100; Marina Hotel, Mutrah Corniche, Mutrah; breakfast OR4, dishes OR4; ⊙ 7.30-10.30am, noon-3pm & 6pm-1am) This intimate, licensed restaurant, with large windows and a terrace overlooking the harbour, is a good place to get a feel of Muscat's age-old relationship with the sea.

Is it Possible to Balance Tourism's Demands with Oman's Natural Values?

Oman's natural values and beauty are among its great assets. The Ministry of Tourism is working with community groups and government agencies to find ways to safeguard the environment. We have a lot to do, but the main drive is to ensure that our education system addresses these issues. Young people must value the outdoors (organisations such as Outward Bound have been highly effective in this respect) and treasure cultural heritage – this means teaching them to notice petroglyphs in Wadi bani Kharus, or to be inquisitive about ancient archaeology sites such as Khor Rouri.

Any New Attractions on the Way?

The rate of progress is spectacular. We have over 2000 new resort and hotel rooms opening this year. Niche resorts at Khasab and Jabel Akhdar will make a significant contribution to regional tourism. The spectacular road from Hasik to Shwaymiya (Dhofar) will soon complete the coastal drive from Muscat to Salalah. In addition, six international-standard airports are planned or in construction, and our fast ferry service to Musandam now operates from both Muscat and Shinas.

Insider Tips for Our Readers?

I spent much of my younger life outside Oman and coming back home, I've noticed the pace of change. But some things don't change – the friendliness and openness of the Omani people. So my top tips would be to take time to do things the local way – sit and chat with elders in a village, or share coffee and dates with them. Drink tea with shop vendors while bargaining for Omani crafts. These are good ways to maximise the positive impact of each visit. As for minimising negative impact, visitors are politely reminded to respect our culture – particularly when it comes to covering up in public places.

In a Nutshell, Why Should People Visit Oman?

The strapline *Beauty has an address* features in all our promotions for good reason!

Fastfood 'n' Juice Centre SHWARMA $
(Map p124; Mutrah Corniche, Mutrah; sandwiches 400 baisa; ⊙9am-10pm) Left of the entrance to Mutrah Souq, with tables on the pavement, this local-style restaurant is an ideal place to people-watch over a *shwarma* and a *chi libton* (tea-bag tea with sweet condensed milk). If it's full, there are a couple of neighbouring eateries that will do just as nicely.

Muscat Light Restaurant & Coffeeshop SANDWICHES $
(Map p126; Al-Saidiya St, Old Muscat; shwarma 350 baisa; ⊙9am-9pm) Have an egg roll-up in view of Fort Al-Mirani in this corner street cafe, ideal as a rest stop on a walking tour of Muscat.

Al-Bulbul Restaurant & Coffeeshop KEBAB $
(Map p128; Al-Jaame St, Ruwi; snacks 350 baisa; ⊙8am-11pm) Just across the road from Ruwi bus station, this 'Arab and Turkish' street-side cafe is a good place for a quick *shwarma* before catching the bus.

Bin Ateeq OMANI $$
(Map p120; ☑24 478225; Al-Khuwair St, Al-Khuwair; meals OR5; ⊙10am-midnight) 🍴 One of the few places in Muscat to serve local Omani dishes. Caters mainly for homesick Omani traders, with seating on old carpets in private rooms with a television. Forgiving the the unglamorous surroundings, the food is generally good quality and authentic; try *harees*, a glutinous Omani dish that's often mixed with chicken.

★ **Kargeen Caffe** MIDDLE EASTERN $$
(Map p120; ☑24 692269; Medinat Qaboos complex; mains OR4; ⊙7.30am-midnight Sat-Thu, 5pm-midnight Fri; 🍴) 🍴 With a choice of open-air and *majlis*-style dining (on sedans in small rooms), this excellent restaurant has spilt into a courtyard of illuminated trees to create a thoroughly Arabian experience. Sustaining local heritage in the choice of decor, music and cuisine, this is one venue where it's easy to remember your location.

Make sure you try the traditional Omani *shuwa* – one of the few places to sample this succulent banana leaf–wrapped lamb dish. Also worth a try are the hibiscus drinks and avocado milkshakes.

Ubhar OMANI $$

(Map p120; ☑ 24 699826; Bareeq Al-Shatti Mall, Shatti Al-Qurm; mains OR5; ⊘ noon-3.30pm & 6.30-11pm) 🍴 This Omani restuarant (with seating at tables rather than on the floor) offers an avante-garde menu. Camel features among other traditional meats. Leave room for dessert – the frankincense ice cream and *halwa* pastries are delicious. Within walking distance of the Royal Opera House Muscat, it's ideal for a post-show dinner.

La Brasserie FRENCH $$

(Map p124; Corniche; mains OR7; ⊘ noon-3pm & 7-11pm Mar-Nov, 7-11am Dec-Feb) Serving delicious French food in a small, wooden den of a restaurant opposite the fish market in Mutrah, La Brasserie is the perfect venue for coffee and a pastry on a walking tour of Muscat.

Blue Marlin Restaurant INTERNATIONAL $$

(Map p120; ☑ 24 740038; Marina Bandar al-Rawdar; meals OR6; ⊘ 8.30am-11pm) With cheerful cloth-covered tables under umbrellas alongside the harbour, Blue Marlin Restaurant offers consistently delicious light bites at lunch time – perfect after a boat trip from the marina. Breakfast aficionados take note: this place serves real bacon! Diners are offered free access to the marina's pool.

D'Arcy's Kitchen BREAKFAST $$

(Map p120; ☑ 24 600234; Way 2817, Shatti al-Qurm; dishes from OR5; ⊘ 9am-10pm; ☑) Next to the Omani Heritage Gallery, this friendly, award-winning establishment serves Western favourites at reasonable prices and is open when most other cafes are taking a siesta. An English breakfast for OR5 will set you up well for a 'constitutional' along the nearby beach. Cash only.

★ The Beach SEAFOOD $$$

(Map p120; ☑ 24 524400; The Chedi Muscat, Al-Ghubrah North; meals from OR45; ⊘ 7-10.30pm Sep-May; ☑) 🍴 This top-class restaurant, with superb Arabian ambience created by fire pits and subtle lighting, serves exciting, complex fare in a luxurious beachside location. The French pastry chef at the hotel's indoor restaurant makes wicked confections, including delectable homemade chocolates,

if your sweet tooth tempts you. The four-course degustation menu is excellent.

Mumtaz Mahal INDIAN $$$

(Map p120; ☑ 24 605907; Way 2601, Qurm; meals from OR10; ⊘ noon-3pm Sat-Thu, 7pm-midnight, 1-3pm & 7pm-midnight Fri; ☑) Specialising in northern Indian Mughlai cuisine, Mumtaz Mahal is more than just the best Indian restaurant in town – it is part of the landscape of Muscat. Perched on a hill overlooking Qurm Nature Reserve, with live sitar performances, traditional seating at low tables, and lantern-light, this restaurant is a local legend.

La Mer SEAFOOD $$$

(Map p120; ☑ 24 662924; Al-Shatti St, Shatti al-Qurm; mains OR6; ⊘ noon-11pm) Pick your own selection of Arabian Sea fish from the ice-table and ask the chef in the show kitchen to prepare it in a Moroccan-style tagine or lightly grilled with garlic, lemon and butter. One of the few restaurants with a magnificent view of the sea, making it a great place for lunch.

Al-Kiran Terrace INTERNATIONAL $$$

(☑ 24 799666; Al-Bustan Palace, Al-Bustan; Friday brunch buffet incl glass of champagne OR26; ⊘ 12.30-3.30pm Fri; ☑) For Muscat's best Friday brunch – in gorgeous surroundings and with a bar licence after 2pm – this is more of a day out than just an excellent dining experience.

Self-Catering

The ubiquitous **Al-Fair supermarket** (Map p120) chain is the perfect shop for picnic ingredients with an expansive fruit and vegetable counter and items to suit Western palates; the one in Medinat Qaboos makes excellent bread. Another good place to buy bread and savoury pastries is **Al-Bustan Bakery** (Map p120) in the Qurm Commercial District.

Lulu's (Map p120) is the region's favourite supermarket chain and its food halls include many Middle Eastern favourites such as hummus and *muttabel* (smoked aubergine dip). There is a convenient branch off Sultan Qaboos St in Al-Khuwair. You can pick up a cool box and freezer packs while you're at it to keep the picnic edible in the searing summer temperatures.

🍷 Drinking & Nightlife

Arabic coffee is surprisingly hard to find in Muscat outside an Omani home or a hotel lobby. The so-called 'coffeeshops' all over town are oriented more to snacking than sipping coffee. International cafe chains have become an addictive part of the local culture.

Each of the top hotels has an elegant cafe and a bar where alcohol is unrestricted but expensive.

★ Trader Vic's   COCKTAIL BAR
(Map p120; ☑24 680080; Hotel InterContinental Muscat, Shatti al Qurm; ☺6pm-2am) When it comes to cocktails (try the Samoan Fogcutter or the Honi Honi), nowhere competes with this fun and lively Polynesian-style venue. Resident stirrer and shaker Hubert Fernandes, assistant bar manager, has been making 'em how you like 'em for a decade and is an undoubted expert. With live Latin music (except Fridays) and wafts of Mongolian barbecued choice cuts, you'll probably be seduced into staying for dinner.

Al-Ahli Coffeeshop   JUICE BAR
(Map p124; ☑24 713469; Mutrah Souq; large mixed juice 900 baisa; ☺10am-1pm & 4-10pm Sat-Thu, 4-10pm Fri) In the middle of Mutrah Souq, this is the best place for delicious, layered fruit juices of pomegranate, custard apple and mango. There is a traditional coffeehouse on the left, just inside the souq, where Omani elders (men) trade news.

Al-Ghazal Bar   PUB
(Map p120; ☑24 680000; Hotel InterContinental Muscat, Shatti al-Qurm; ☺noon-2am Sat-Tue, noon-3am Wed-Thu, 2pm-2am Fri) More of a pub than a bar, this is a popular expat meeting place, with live music, a quiz night, televised sport and excellent Western-style bar food.

Grand Hyatt Muscat   HIGH TEA
(Map p120; ☑24 641234; Way 3033, off Al-Saruj St, Shatti al-Qurm; afternoon tea OR9; ☺3-8pm) If you sit sipping tea long enough in the extravagant foyer of this sumptuous hotel, chances are you'll worry that the tea was laced: the statue of the *Arab on Horseback* that graces the central podium moves just slowly enough to make you suspect you've joined the flight of fancy that inspired the architects.

John Barry Bar   LOUNGE
(Map p120; ☑24 641234; Grand Hyatt Muscat, Shatti al-Qurm; ☺2pm-1am Tue & Fri, to 2am Wed & Thu) Named after the raised ship and its booty of silver treasure that made the fortunes of the Hyatt's owner, this bar is a so-

phisticated setting for some live piano music and a cocktail.

☆ Entertainment

For classical music lovers, a show at the Royal Opera House Muscat (p127) is a must if only to enjoy the wonderful Arabian ambience of this superb new venue. Online bookings can be made or call in on a weekday night if you've packed your glad rags.

Muscat is rather thin on other entertainment options, although the five-star hotels and some of the smaller ones have bars and nightclubs, usually with live acts. Local 'live acts' often take the form of gyrating women (typically from India, Russia or North Africa) in skimpy outfits worn over thick leggings; the women are sometimes contained behind wire mesh in case the locals find the Arab pop irresistible and insist on dancing along.

For Muscat's perennial hot spot, try **Rock Bottom Café** (Rockies; Map p120; ☑24 564443; Way 1622, Ramee Guestline Hotel, Qurm; ☺7pm-3am), which has live music every night except Sundays. *Time Out Muscat* is the best source of information for current favourites.

There are several cinemas in town including **Al-Shatti Plaza** (Map p120; ☑24 692656) in Shatti al-Qurm, and **Al-Bahja Cinema** (☑24 540856) in the mall of the same name.

You can take in a football (soccer) game at **Sultan Qaboos Sports Complex** (Map p120; ☑24 592197; Al-Ghubra St, Al-Ghubra South).

🔒 Shopping

Muscat doesn't have the exhaustive range of shopping options on offer in other parts of the region, nor is it particularly cheap. However, with one of the most characterful old souqs in the region, a few classy shops such as those in Opera Galleria adjacent to the Royal Opera House Muscat, and some big sprawling malls (Qurm City Centre, Muscat City Centre near Rusayl roundabout and nearby Markaz al-Bahja), there's enough to keep a dedicated shopper happy.

Souq Ruwi St is worth visiting for all manner of cheap and cheerfuls – from souvenir T-shirts to don't-ask DVDs and gold from India.

Crafts, Souvenirs & Gifts
Some popular Omani-produced items include highly worked silver *khanjars* (curved daggers) that start at OR30 for a tourist replica to OR500 for an exquisite genuine item;

baskets worked with pieces of camel or goat hide (from OR5); *kuma* (Omani hats), which start at OR2 for a machine-made one to OR50 for a highly crafted handmade piece; hand-loomed goat-hair rugs (from OR15); frankincense (from 500 baisa) and a range of local and imitation perfumes; and dates (from 600 baisa per 500g).

Mutrah Souq
SOUQ

(Map p124; Mutrah Corniche, Mutrah; ☺ 9am-1pm & 5-10pm Sat-Wed, 5-10pm Fri) From *khanjars* to framed silverwork, gold and spices, this labyrinth of alleyways under a *barasti* (palm leaf) roof is the top spot in town for crafts and souvenirs.

Omani Heritage Gallery
HANDICRAFTS

(Map p120; ☑ 24 696974; www.omaniheritage.com; Way 2817, Jawaharat Al-Shatti Complex, Shatti al-Qurm; ☺ 10am-1pm & 4-9pm Sat-Wed, 4-9pm Fri) For guaranteed 'Made in Oman' crafts, try the Omani Heritage Gallery, a nonprofit organisation set up to encourage cottage industries through the sale of handicrafts. Prices are high, but so is the quality.

Omani Craftsman's House
HANDICRAFTS

(Map p120; ☑ 24 568553; Qurm shopping complex) Opposite the Sabco Centre in Qurm. Opening hours are erratic to say the least!

Sabco Centre
SHOPPING CENTRE

(Map p120; Qurm shopping complex; ☺ 10am-10pm Sat-Thu, 4.30-10pm Fri) A surprisingly comprehensive little souq located inside the Sabco Centre sells crafts (mostly from India and Iran), pashmina shawls and Omani headdresses. Bargaining is recommended, but prices are reasonable. The souq's excellent

cobbler can repair any leather item. Some shops in the souq close at lunchtime.

Bateel
DATES

(Map p120; ☑ 24 601572; www.bateel.ae; Oasis by the Sea complex, Shatti al-Qurm; ☺ 10am-1pm & 5-10pm Sat-Thu, 2-11pm Fri) For a regional gift with a difference, the chocolate dates from Bateel are utterly world class.

Amouage
PERFUMERY

(Map p120; Sabco Centre, Qurm shopping complex; ☺ 9.30am-1pm & 4.30-9.30pm Sat-Thu, 4.30-10pm Fri) Amouage sells the most expensive (and exquisite) perfume in the world, produced from frankincense, musk and other exotic ingredients in premises near Rusayl. You'll find the ultimate Arabian gift here.

Bait Muzna Gallery
CONTEMPORARY ART

(Map p126; ☑ 24 739204; www.baitmuznagallery.com; Al-Saidiya St, Old Muscat; ☺ 9.30am-1.30pm & 4.30-8.30pm Sat-Thu) ✆ Contemporary paintings and jewellery are exhibited and sold in this gallery opposite Bayt Al-Zubair.

Jawahir Oman
JEWELLERY

(Map p120; ☑ 24 563239; Al-Wilaj St, Qurm; ☺ 9.30am-1pm & 4-8pm Sat-Thu) ✆ Selling prized Omani silver, this shop's exclusive contemporary jewellery and gift items are handcrafted in a workshop in Muscat.

Camping Equipment

Most of what you will need for a night under the stars is sold at Al-Fair supermarkets. For more specialised equipment, try **Ahmed Dawood Trading** (Map p124; ☑ 24 703295; Al-Mina St, Mutrah) or Muscat Sports in Markaz al-Bahja.

MUSCAT FOR CHILDREN

Muscat is a safe and friendly city with a few attractions for children.

Children's Museum (Map p120; ☑ 24 605368; off Sultan Qaboos St, Qurm; admission 500 baisa; ☺ 8am-1.30pm Sat-Wed, 9am-1pm Thu year-round, 4-6pm Mon Oct-Mar) This well-signposted domed building has lots of hands-on science displays.

Ice Skating (Fun Zone; Map p120; ☑ 24 662951; Qurm Park, Qurm; admission incl skate hire OR4; ☺ 9am-midnight) A good way to beat the summer heat. Sessions last 90 minutes. Women-only sessions on Monday from 9am to 6pm. The rink is closed between 8pm and 10pm on Saturday to allow the ice hockey team to practice.

Markaz al-Bahja (Foton World Fantasia; ☑ 24 537061; near Seeb) A fair way out of town, this covered play area with themed rides is in a shopping mall, 5km northwest of Muscat International Airport on the highway towards Seeb.

Marah Land (☑ 24 562215; Qurm Park, Qurm; admission 300 baisa plus 250-750 baisa per ride; ☺ 8am-1pm & 4pm-midnight Sat-Thu, 4pm-midnight Fri) Set inside the attractively landscaped Qurm Park, this funfair with Ferris wheel is a local favourite.

Bookshops

Most large hotels stock a wide range of coffee-table books, specialist guides and a selection of Lonely Planet guides. The following are also worth a visit:

Family Bookshop BOOKS
(Map p120; ☑ 24 604245; Madinat Sultan Qaboos; ⊙10am-1pm & 4.30-8pm Sat-Thu, 4.30-8pm Fri) One of the few remaining bookshops in Muscat, this Omani-run stalwart stocks a good selection of English-language titles on Oman, including Lonely Planet guidebooks, and a few bestsellers.

House of Prose BOOKS
(Map p120; ☑ 24 564356; Al Wadi Centre, Qurm; ⊙9.30am-1pm & 4.30-8pm Sat-Thu, 6-8pm Fri) Stocks secondhand paperbacks with a great buy-back scheme.

🛈 Information

EMERGENCY

Ambulance, Fire & Police (☑999) Emergency services.

Royal Oman Police (☑24 560099) Organises emergency care at the scene of an accident.

INTERNET ACCESS

Internet cafes can be found all over Muscat. The standard rate is around 500 baisa per hour.

Fastline Internet (Al-Jaame St, ONTC bus station, Ruwi; per hour 500 baisa; ⊙10am-midnight Sat-Thu, 2pm-midnight Fri; ☎)

First Internet Café (CCC Shopping Centre, Qurm; per hour 800 baisa; ⊙9.30am-1.30pm & 5-10pm Sat-Thu, 5-10pm Fri; ☎)

Internet Café (Corniche, Mutrah; per hour 400 baisa; ⊙9.30am-1.30pm & 4pm-midnight, ☎)

MEDICAL SERVICES

International-standard health care is available at the main city hospitals. Initial emergency treatment may be free, but all other health care is charged. English is spoken in all hospitals and clinics in Muscat.

Pharmacies rotate to provide 24-hour coverage in all regions; check the English dailies to learn which ones are on duty on a given day. Pharmacies can advise which local doctors or dentists are on duty.

Al-Nahdha Hospital (Map p120; ☑24 837800; Al-Nahdha St, Wattiyah) Emergency cases are generally brought here.

MONEY

The big banks are centred in Ruwi's central business district, although one or two bank headquarters are drifting up towards the airport into what is being dubbed as Muscat's new centre. There are numerous branches with ATM facilities throughout Muscat. Most are able to give cash advances on international credit cards and will exchange travellers cheques (though they charge a large commission for this service). Most banks are closed on Friday and Saturday.

The most convenient money changers are in Qurm, along Souq Ruwi St in Ruwi and on the Mutrah Corniche at the entrance to Mutrah Souq. Most of these places are open from 8am to 1pm, and some from 5pm to 7pm; all are open Sunday to Thursday. Some open on Saturdays too.

Amex (Map p120; ☑24 573555; Al-Walaj St, Ernst & Young Bldg, Qurm; ⊙8.30am-5pm Sun-Thu) Trying to make a comeback in Oman but still not widely used.

HSBC (Map p128; Markaz Mutrah al-Tijari St, CBD Ruwi; ⊙8am-1pm Sun-Thu) The HQ and one of many branches in Muscat.

POST

Branch post office (Markaz Mutrah al-Tijari St, CBD Ruwi; ⊙8am-1.30pm Sat-Wed, 8-11am Thu)

Main post office (Al-Matar St; ⊙8am-1.30pm Sat-Wed, to 11am Thu) Located by the airport, but on the opposite side of the highway. There are also branches in Old Muscat and Mutrah.

TELEPHONE

There are numerous cardphones around the city for making local and international calls. Hayyak cards (OR3 with OR1 of credit), for making international and local calls from a mobile phone, can be bought at the airport or at Omantel counters in malls and at most supermarkets and corner shops.

Telephone office (Al-Burj St, CBD Ruwi; ⊙8am-2pm & 4-6pm) Faxes can be sent from here.

TOURIST INFORMATION

Brochures and maps are available from foyers in larger hotels.

Ministry of Tourism (Map p120; ☑24 588700; www.omantourism.gov.om; ⊙7.30am-1.30pm Sat-Wed) Staff can answer limited telephone enquiries but this is a ministry rather than a tourist centre and staff are not prepared to receive visitors. However, they sometimes give out brochures and their website is very informative.

National Travel & Tourism (☑24 660376; www.nttoman.com; Ar-Rumaylah St, Wattayah; ⊙8am-1pm & 4-7pm Sat-Thu) Next to the Kia showroom in Wattayah, this is one of the best places to ask for information. Staff are experienced and helpful.

ℹ Getting There & Away

AIR

Situated 37km west of Mutrah is **Muscat International Airport** (☑ 24 519223; www.omanairports.com). The only domestic flights available at the time of writing were with **Oman Air** (Map p128; ☑ 24 531111) between Muscat and Salalah (one way/return OR32/64, 1½ hours, four daily at variable times), and Muscat and Khasab (one way/return OR24/48, one hour, every morning at variable times). Airports are being built in a number of locations and flights will eventually be offered to Sohar, Ras al-Hadd, Duqm and Masirah. Chartered flights are offered to Jaaluni near Duqm three times a week but check with a travel agent before relying on this and note that the return flight to Muscat is often oversubscribed as this service is used mostly by port workers.

BUS

The national bus company **Oman National Transport Copmany** (ONTC; ☑ 24 490046; www.ontcoman.com) provides comfortable intercity services throughout Oman. Its main depot is the **ONTC bus station** (Map p128; ☑ 24 708522) in Ruwi. Timetables in English (with fares) are available on the website; a summary is printed in the *Oman Observer*.

ONTC buses run to Salalah (one way/return OR7.500/13, 12 hours, twice daily at 7am and 10am). However, there is some competition on this route from **Bin Qasim Transport** (Map p128; ☑ 24 785059; Way 2985), which has a daily bus at 6pm (one way/return OR6/11). This company is around the corner from the bus station, near Moon Travels.

TAXI & MICROBUS

Taxis and microbuses leave for all destinations from Al-Jaame St, opposite the main (ONTC) bus station in Ruwi. There is an additional departure point at Rusayl roundabout (also known as Burj al-Sahwa – the Clock Tower), west of the airport interchange.

Some sample taxi/microbus fares:

TO	SHARED (OR)	ENGAGED (OR)	MICRO-BUS (OR)
Barka	1	5	1.500
Buraimi	15	75	n/a
Nakhal	2	10	1.500
Nizwa	2	10	2.500
Rustaq	2.500	12.500	n/a
Samail	1	5	1.500
Sohar	2.500	12.500	2
Sur	4	20	3.500

CAR

Car hire can be arranged with several agencies in Ruwi, including **Alwan Tour Rent-a-Car** (☑ 99 833325; www.alwantour.com) and **Mark Tours** (☑ 24 782727; www.marktoursoman.com/rentacar), as well as at the usual desks in hotels and at the airport in Muscat and Salalah.

ℹ Getting Around

TO/FROM THE AIRPORT

Taxis running between the airport and Qurm, Al-Khuwair, Ruwi, Mutrah, Muscat and Seeb cost a fixed rate of OR10; it's OR18 to Barr al-Jissah. Taxis are blue-striped and have 'airport taxi' on the side. These will soon have meters. Alternatively, you can walk 500m to the highway outside the airport and wait for a microbus. Microbuses pass the airport fairly frequently between 7am and 10pm, and cost 800 baisa to Ruwi, Mutrah or Muscat. Buses heading in this direction leave from the other side of the footbridge. There is no direct bus service to/from the airport.

MICROBUS & TAXI

In Mutrah, local microbuses cruise the corniche and congregate around Mutrah bus station. In Ruwi they park en masse along Al-Jaame St, opposite the main bus station. Trips from one suburb to the next cost 200 to 300 baisa. No microbus journey within greater Muscat should cost more than one rial.

Muscat's non-airport taxis are orange and white and do not have meters. Even if you bargain you will inevitably pay two or three times the going rate for locals – be sure to fix the rate before you get in. A taxi between suburbs in Muscat should cost no more than OR10 engaged or OR3 shared (getting to/from the airport excepted). Expect to be charged double the going rate to/from hotels.

A shared taxi from Ruwi to Rusayl roundabout costs OR3 (OR12 engaged). Microbuses charge OR1.200 for the same trip. From Mutrah Corniche to Rusayl roundabout, the microbus/taxi fare should be OR4/1.800 (OR15 engaged).

If you're in town for a while, collect the card of a taxi driver who proved satisfactory and call them as required.

It's best to navigate by reference to landmarks (for example the HSBC in Qurm, the Clock Tower roundabout in Rusayl) rather than street addresses when travelling by public transport or taxi.

AROUND MUSCAT

For an easy and rewarding day trip from Muscat, a trip to the *khors* (rocky inlets) is recommended. The area, southeast of the city, is a popular snorkelling spot for weekend boat trips but it's also possible to reach many of the *khors* by car.

Peaceful alternatives to staying in Muscat include the traditional town of Seeb, to the west of Muscat, and the spectacular resort of Bandar Jissah, to the east of Muscat. Both are well worth considering.

Seeb   السيب
☑ 24 / POP 302,000

If you are looking to experience a typical Omani town close to Muscat that barely sees a tourist, you can't do better than a trip to Seeb. A 20 minute drive northwest of the airport, this thriving coastal town has much to offer: there's a watchtower, a lively souq with a colourful textiles market, a gold souq with competitive prices, traditional Omani hat shops, *halwa* for sale, a magnificent stretch of sandy beach and some of the best squid kebabs in Oman.

◉ Sights & Activities

There are no 'tourist' sights as such but Seeb is a great place to experience everyday Omani life. The wonderful 8km corniche has a landscaped area for walking, enjoying sea views, sniffing drying sardines and watching the fishermen mending nets.

One place to get a feel for the culture is on the main one-way road that runs in a circle through the heart of the town, flanked with banks, the **gold souq** (look out for fine displays of Omani bridal gold), supermarkets and tailors. The main **souq** is between the main road and the sea in a purpose-built sandy-coloured complex of buildings near the main mosque; it includes a fruit and vegetable area and a fish market.

The road doubles back on itself just after shops selling Arabic-style sofas and sedans and Omani honey. On the return section of the loop are outlets selling Omani-style **traditional ladies' clothing** with colourful anklets and embroidered smocking. Interspersed with the tailors are 'wedding services' shops selling strings of lights and outrageous bridal thrones. Towards the end of the street, and completing the loop, there are many **carpentry workshops** selling *mandoos* (bridal chests). Usually black or terracotta-red and decorated with brass tacks, these make a fun souvenir. A small box costs OR10 or a large chest OR50 with many sizes in between.

Seeb is an excellent place to find a tailor. Bring a favourite shirt or skirt and buy some material in a Seeb textile shop. The cloth merchant will advise you which tailor to visit to make a replica in half a day for under OR20. If you've been invited to a special 'do' in Muscat and forgot to pack the dinner jacket, this is the place to get one made for a bargain OR65, including material.

The other drawcard in Seeb is the beach. For shell enthusiasts, the long flat sands at low tide make a great place to see horn, turret and auger shells. While you're on the corniche, step into **Al-Abnah Freish Antiques & Gifts** for a small selection of silver souvenirs and camel sticks.

🛏 Sleeping & Eating

There are a couple of pleasant places to stay in Seeb that make an alternative to the busy hotels of Muscat.

Al-Bahjah Hotel   HOTEL $
(☑24 424400; bahjahsb@omantel.net.om; Seeb High St; s/d OR23/28; @) Right in the heart of town (turn towards the sea by Oman International Bank) and with a dhow and a giant coffee pot in the foyer, this is a traditional Omani hotel. It has a characterful and cosy Indian restaurant with a license. Try *palak paneer* (spinach and cottage cheese) with rice, roti and pickles for a bargain OR2.500

Ramee Dream Resort   HOTEL $
(☑24 453399; www.rameehotels.com; Dama St; s/d OR35/40; 🖥🕊) There's not much to dream about at this hotel although the sea is only a five-minute walk away and guests can watch herons parachute into the tidal pools in front of the hotel. The rooms have split-level 'duplex' options for families. A nightclub features live music from Africa. The resort is 1km west along the corniche from Seeb fish market.

There are many places to eat in town, such as the beachside **Seeb Waves Restaurant** (☑24 425556; Corniche; mains OR2; ⏱10am-1pm & 4-10pm Sat-Thu, 4-10pm Fri) with tasty chilli chicken, and a couple of more Western-style cafes. One of the best options is to buy squid kebabs (300 baisa per stick) from the vendors on the corniche (opposite the souq) and eat them sitting on the sea wall. The neighbouring juice shop, **Al-Hamael Trading**, has a small sea-facing terrace from where you can watch boats entering the new harbour,

OMAN SEEB

a project that has helped to protect Seeb's thriving fishing industry.

❶ Getting There & Around

A taxi from the highway near Muscat International Airport takes 20 minutes along Sultan Qaboos Hwy (OR2). Frequent minibuses connect Muscat with Seeb (OR1.200).

Bandar Jissah   بندر الجصة

📌 24

Once, Bandar Jissah was a rocky promontory with a small, inaccessible beach. It is now home to Muscat's most prestigious resort and some excellent water sports facilities.

◉ Sights & Activities

Picturesque **Jissah beach** (sometimes referred to as Qantab Beach) offers perfect bathing on weekdays (it gets too crowded on the Omani weekend). For OR10 per boat (five people), entrepreneurial fishermen will take visitors on a 30-minute tour to see the famous **sea arch** that is now almost incorporated into the resort.

If you have your own transport, pause at the spectacular **viewing point** between Bandar Jissah and the long descent into Al-Bustan. On the opposite side of the road, those after serious exercise can ascend to Muscat's hidden **40km cycle and walking track** that snakes above Bandar Jissah. A road cut spectacularly through the mountains links Bandar Jissah with Yitti.

🛏 Sleeping & Eating

Oman Dive Center   CABIN **$$**

(📌 24 824240; www.omandivecenter.info; Bandar Jissah; half-board in cabin s/d OR59/84; 🅿 @ 🏊) 🐾 Offering simple *barasti* (palm-leaf) huts with attached shower room on the beach, the Oman Dive Center is in a lovely location on a sandy bay. Perhaps one of the most easygoing places to enjoy some water sports, the centre offers half-day snorkelling trips (OR20, including equipment hire; OR15 for afternoon trips) and dolphin-watching trips (OR18) with the chance of seeing whales between December and February. You can enjoy the peaceful, secluded beach (and club facilities) for the day for a nominal OR4 for adults and OR2 for children (OR2/1 Saturday to Wednesday). It also makes a good place for lunch (try the camel burger). You'll need your own transport or a taxi to get here (about OR7 from Mutrah).

Shangri-La's Barr Al Jissah Resort & Spa   RESORT **$$$**

(📌 776666; www.shangri-la.com; off Al-Jissah St; 🅿 🛜 🏊) Shangri-La's Barr Al-Jissah Resort & Spa comprises three kasbah-style hotels around a magnificent shared beach and landscaped garden. **Al-Bandar Hotel** (r from OR163) is the more business-oriented of the three hotels. The sophisticated six-star **Al-Husn Hotel** (r from OR216) is perched on the headland, and **Al-Waha Hotel** (r OR220), the easygoing, family accommodation, is accessed via a tunnel through the cliff.

Meandering between the hotels, a lazy river offers a fun way of getting from one watering hole to another. The richly carpeted foyers, marble corridors and designer bedrooms and bathrooms in all three hotels make choosing one over the other a matter of whim. The resort includes some of the country's top restaurants: the Bait al-Bahr (seafood), Samba (international buffet) and Al-Tanoor (Middle Eastern fare).

There is a complimentary bus service from Muscat International Airport, or it is a 15-minute drive by car from Mutrah.

Yitti   يتي

📌 24

About 25km from Muscat, Yitti boasts a beautiful, sandy **beach** surrounded by craggy mountain scenery. The beach is at the end of a large, muddy inlet that is regularly picked over by wading waterbirds.

If the tide is low, you can wade to a sandbar and look left for a great view of Bandar Jissah's famous **sea arch**. You'll notice a clump of serrated rocks at the end of the inlet. It was believed these rocks were inhabited by *jinn* (genies) and offerings used to be left at their base. Alas, the spirits have gone somewhere more private, according to the local fishermen, due to the disfiguring earthworks on the far side of the creek. A large resort is planned for the entire bay but has been postponed due to the economic downturn, and Yitti remains, for now at least, a peaceful backwater.

There is no public transport to Yitti, which is about a half-hour drive from Mutrah. There are three routes to Yitti from Muscat. The shortest way is to follow the signs through a deep cut in the mountains from the roundabout in Bandar Jissah. To make an enjoyable round trip, return through Wadi Mayh.

Wadi Mayh   وادي مياح

For a taste of a typical Omani wadi within an afternoon's drive of Muscat, look no further than Wadi Mayh. With towering limestone cliffs, sand-coloured villages, back-garden date plantations, straying goats and feral donkeys – not to mention a compulsory watchtower or two – Wadi Mayh has it all. Look out for a pair of stout *falaj* (traditional irrigation channels) that have been shored into either side of the wadi, and carry water from one village plantation to the next.

The wadi has areas where multicoloured layers of rock have been forced into a vertical wall. The steep sides of the wadi make it vulnerable to fierce flash flooding that often washes out part of the road.

The entrance to the wadi is about 24km from Wadi Aday roundabout in Muscat. To reach the wadi, follow the Qurayat road from the roundabout. After 16km, turn left at the roundabout with the gold eagle. Turn left at the sign for Yitti (at 24km) and the road eventually leads into the wadi. The wadi can be negotiated by car although the last section of road (about 10km) towards Yitti is not sealed. There is no public transport. Wadi Mayh is signposted off the Bandar Jissah–Yitti road.

Bandar Khayran   بندر خيران

It's worth driving for at least 30 minutes along the Yitti to Al-Seifa road to get a flavour of the inlets or *khors* that make this part of the Muscat coastline so memorable.

The first *khor* is popular with fishermen, but the second *khor* (at 4.8km) is one of those rare entities – a tidal football pitch, giving a new meaning to the term Mexican wave, perhaps, especially as the spectators of this busy pitch include crabs and mud creepers.

An Oberoi Resort is planned for the next *khor* at Shatti Masgour.

Thereafter (at 6km), the road hugs the side of Bandar Khayran, a large, mangrove-fringed lagoon, more usually visited by boat from Muscat. It is a beautiful spectacle late in the afternoon when the sandstone, and its reflection in the water, seem to vibrate with colour. Turn right at the mosque in the middle of Khayran village, taking care to dodge the goats and the small boys selling seashells. Turn left at the junction for Safait Al-Shaikh (at 12.5km) for some excellent **snorkelling** (watch out for seahorses), or continue to Al-Seifa.

Al-Seifa   السيفا

There's not much to the scenically appointed village of Al-Seifa, resting in the shadow of the Hajar Mountains. Nearby beaches to the east, however, offer protected camping for those who bring equipment and provisions. The beaches are worth a closer look as they are a lapidary's dream: in between the sandy bays, pebbles of yellow ochre, burnt sienna and olive green beg to be picked up. For those interested in bugs, the giant-skipper butterfly frequents the surrounding wadis in spring. The whole bay is now the location of an ambitious but not yet wholly complete nor successful tourist development complex called Al-Muriya.

Al-Seifa is clearly signposted off the Bandar Jissah to Yitti road. It is only about 25km but it takes a good 40 minutes to drive because of the winding road and some steep descents. You will need 10 minutes more and preferably a 4WD to find your own beach beyond Al Seifa along unpaved tracks. There is no public transport.

🛏 Sleeping & Eating

Sifawy Boutique Hotel   BOUTIQUE HOTEL **$$$**
(☑24 749111; www.sifawyhotel.com; Al-Seifa; r around OR100; P 🛜 ☒) Wrapped around a new marina with a backdrop of mountains, this boutique hotel, designed by renowned Italian architect Alfredo Freda, will no doubt come into its own once the surrounding residential complex is complete. For now it remains marooned in splendid isolation among a cluster of half-finished villas and unpaved roads. The hotel's water taxi service (child/adult OR4/8) contributes to the sense of arriving in a remote location.

The speed boats depart at 10am, noon and 4pm, Thursday to Saturday, from Marina Bandar al-Rowdha, and make the return journey at 11am, 3pm and 5.30pm. A taxi to or from Mutrah costs OR15, or OR10 from Bandar Jissah.

As-Sammak   SEAFOOD **$$**
(☑24 749111; Al-Seifa; mains OR7; ⊙noon-10.30pm) This atmospheric open-air restaurant on the beach, next door to the Sifawy Boutique Hotel, is a casual venue for sampling quality food. Ask for the catch of the day and the chef's choice of preparation.

OMAN WADI MAYH

Qurayat

قريات

📱 24 / POP 44,900

There are a number of features to enjoy in this attractive fishing village an hour's drive east of Muscat. Sights include the 19th-century **fort** and a unique triangular **watchtower** overlooking the corniche. The sandy **beach** to the east of the tower extends for many kilometres with only the occasional football team to interrupt it.

The town was once an important port, famous for exporting horses that were reared on the surrounding plains. Sacked by the Portuguese in the 16th century, the town never regained its importance, although it retains a lively fishing industry and is celebrated for its basket makers. The large, porous baskets are made from local mangrove, and are used for keeping bait fresh aboard the small boats that pack the harbour.

Qurayat is well signposted from the Wadi Aday roundabout in Muscat, a pretty and at times spectacular 82km drive through the Eastern Hajar foothills on a fine highway. Look out for Indian rollers (blue-winged birds) in the palm trees lining the avenue into town. Shared taxis cost OR2.5 and microbuses OR1.500 from the Wadi Aday roundabout. A taxi costs OR15.

There are no places to stay in Qurayat, but it makes a pleasant day trip from Muscat if combined with Mazara, or a good stop-off before continuing along the coastal highway to Sur.

Mazara

مزارع

📱 24

Positioned halfway along Wadi Dayqah, protected by a fort perched on a rocky outcrop, surrounded by copper-toned mountains and half-buried in thick plantations, the picturesque village of Mazara makes for an interesting day out from Muscat. A loose assemblage of toads, kingfishers and goats congregate in the semi-permanent pools that gather in the bottom of the wadi.

Looming over the village is the enormous **Wadi Dayqat dam**, the largest in Oman. A road winds up to the reservoir, the edges of which have been pleasantly landscaped and provide opportunities for a picnic. The vista of mountains reflected in the plate-glass water is a rare sight in the desert. A seasonal coffeeshop opens up at peak times and plans for further tourist amenities are afoot.

Brown signs indicate 'Wadi Dayqat Dam' 19km off the Muscat–Sur Hwy. To reach the crumbling fort in Mazara, follow the road through the village and across the wadi. There is no public transport.

SUR & THE EASTERN COAST

This easternmost region of the Arabian Peninsula holds some of Oman's main attractions, including beautiful beaches, spectacular wadis, turtle-nesting sites and the strawberry blond Sharqiya sand dunes. As many of the sites of interest lie en route rather than in the towns, it's worth having your own vehicle, although tours cover the whole area.

The main artery into the region is the Qurayat–Sur coastal highway which runs along the scenic base of the Eastern Hajar Mountains. There are no hotels between Muscat and Sur, but plenty of beaches for camping for those with equipment and supplies.

The route along the coast road to Sur ideally forms the first day of a two- or three-day circular tour, returning to Muscat via Al-Mintirib and the Sharqiya Sands. Alternatively, it makes the first leg of an epic camping trip along the coast to Masirah or Salalah; the road cuts across the sand dunes in a remarkable feat of modern engineering.

Sur

سور

📱 25 / POP 64,900

With an attractive corniche, two forts, excellent beaches nearby and a long history of dhow-building, there is much to commend Sur to the visitor. In addition to its attractions, Sur is a convenient base for day trips to Wadi Tiwi and Wadi Shab and the turtle reserve at Ras al-Jinz. It also makes a good halfway rest point on a round trip from Muscat via the desert camps of the Sharqiya Sands.

History

Watching the boat-builders at work in the dhow yards in Sur, hand-planing a plank of wood, it is easy to recognise a skill inherited from master craftsmen. Sur has long been famed for its boat-building industry and even in the 19th century – when the Portuguese invasion and the division of Oman

Sur

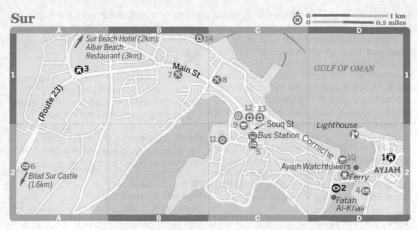

Sur

into two separate sultanates had delivered a heavy blow to the port town's trading capability – Sur still boasted an ocean-going fleet of 100 or more vessels. Demand for ocean-going boats declined once the British India Steamer Navigation Company became pre-eminent in the Gulf and the town's fortunes declined correspondingly. Sur is currently enjoying a resurgence, however, thanks to a state-of-the-art liquid gas plant and a fertiliser factory, which have generated lots of new jobs.

◉ Sights

Bilad Sur Castle
CASTLE

Built to defend the town against marauding tribes from the interior, 200-year-old Bilad Sur Castle boasts unusually shaped towers. It has been closed for an extended period for restoration. To reach the castle, turn left off Main St, 1.3km from the clocktower

roundabout at the Muscat end of town, at an elaborately kitsch residence.

Sunaysilah Castle
CASTLE

(Main St; admission 500 baisa; ⏰ 7.30am-6pm Sun-Thu) Perched on a rocky eminence, this 300-year-old castle is built on a classic square plan with four round watchtowers. It was the most important part of the defensive system of Sur, a town that was greatly fortified to protect its illustrious overseas trade. A few artefacts help bring some of the rooms to life. You can't miss the castle as its presence looms over the town centre. The entrance is off Main St.

Corniche & Dhow Yards
CORNICHE

The corniche affords a wonderful view across to the picturesque village of **Ayjah**. Dhows used to be led to safe haven by Ayajh's three **watchtowers**, which mark the passage into the lagoon. It is still possible to see the boats being made by hand alongside this passage.

To reach the dhow yards, turn left at the souq end of Main St and follow the road in a crescent past the corniche to the great lagoon. The road circles back eventually to the new souq, passing by **Fatah al-Khair**, a beautifully restored dhow built in Sur 70 years ago and brought back from retirement in Yemen. A small open-air museum (open during daylight hours) in the grounds houses other traditional vessels. Look out for a small workshop opposite the dhow: Sur is famous for carpentry and some finely crafted model dhows are on sale here (opening hours are at the whim of the owner).

🛏 Sleeping

There are only three places to stay in Sur so it is worth booking accommodation in the high season (November to February) and during public holidays.

Sur Hotel   HOTEL $
(☑ 25 540090; surhotel@live.com; off Souq St; s/d/tr OR18/24/31; 🗺) In the middle of the souq, rooms are noisy but the bus stop, cinema and corniche are within walking distance. Turtle-watching trips can be arranged through the hotel (OR25 for minimum of two people) as well as trips to Wadi Tiwi (OR40) or Wadi Bani Khalid (price negotiable). A booking and transport service to camps in Sharqiya Sands is available.

★Sur Beach Hotel   HOTEL $$
(☑ 25 542031; http://surhotelsoman.com; Beach Rd; s/d OR40/45; P 🗺 🏊) This beachside hotel benefits from its location along a shoreside path. It receives many visitors at weekends during the winter season so booking is advisable. The rooms have balconies overlooking the sea from which you can watch for phosphorescent waves at night. Try the excellent Indian fish dishes and fresh *japathi* in the restaurant. Picnic boxes (OR4.500 and OR6) save the bother of self-catering.

Sur Plaza Hotel   HOTEL $$
(☑ 25 543777; www.omanhotels.com; off Main St (Route 23, Ibra-Sur Hwy); s/d OR55/65; P 🗺 🏊) With the Captain's Bar (6pm to 3am) offering live entertainment (usually a Filipino band), this hotel is popular with tour groups despite being inland. Oyster's Restaurant serves delicious local kingfish. There is a Budget rental agency in the foyer and turtle-

watching trips can be arranged (OR18 per person), departing at 7.45pm and 3am for the dawn excursion.

🍴 Eating

For international-style food, the restaurants inside the Sur Beach Hotel and Sur Plaza Hotel offer the best choices. Lonely Planet has reviewed the more local options.

There are many small grocery shops in the New Souq area of town. Nabras al-Afia shopping centre, opposite Sur Hotel, sells everything needed for a picnic.

★Zahrat Bilad al Sham Restaurant   KEBABS $
(Main St; mains OR2; ⊘ 11am-1am) Right on the main road, this popular venue offers sizzling kebabs marinated in the chef's best spices, reputedly from Ottoman origin, and naughty triple-decker fruit juices. If these aren't hitting the spot, then the freshly baked baklavas right next door from the Bab Al-Hara sweet shop surely will.

Albar Beach Restaurant   MIDDLE EASTERN $
(Beach Rd; snacks from OR1.500; ⊘ 2pm-2am; 🚗) One of the few restaurants beside the sea, this simple eatery – with plastic chairs on a terrace and an air-conditioned interior for the hotter months – offers friendly service on the beachfront near the Sur Beach Hotel.

Zaki Restaurant   ROTISSERIE $
(Main St; mains OR1; ⊘ noon-1am) Located next to the Oman Oil petrol station, this place serves the best rotisserie chickens in town, complete with Arabic bread, chopped salad and tasty dhal. If the roadside location doesn't appeal, then ask for a takeaway and park at one of the picnic shelters near the Sur Beach Hotel.

Sur Sea Restaurant   SEAFOOD $
(☑ 99 746423; off Souq St; mains OR2; ⊘ 7am-3am) On the ground floor of the Sur Hotel (the entrance faces the other side of the block), this is a popular and lively local restaurant.

🍷 Drinking & Nightlife

Restaurant & Coffeeshop   CAFÉ
(Corniche; ⊘ 10am-midnight) With old men singing sea shanties under the tree outside and dhows wafting into the lagoon, this coffeeshop is a good place to tap into the heart of traditional Sur.

Bawadi al-Aija Coffeeshop and Restaurant
CAFE

(☑ 25 3601030; Souq St; ☺ 1pm-3am) From the outdoor seating area of this place, with a cup of mint tea or a mixed fruit juice in hand, it's fun to watch the residents of Sur amble past the brightly lit shops of the town's liveliest street.

Captain's Bar
BAR

(☑ 25 543777; Main St; ☺ 8pm-2am) This is the best place to meet other tourists or Western expats. It's cosy and has live entertainment, usually in the form of a Filipino band.

☆ Entertainment

City Cinema
CINEMA

(☑ 25 540666; www.citycinemaoman.net; opposite Fish Market; English film OR2.500) Screens films in English from 5.30pm daily and is a non-smoking establishment.

🔒 Shopping

Sur has grown considerably in the past few years, largely as a result of the nearby gas and fertiliser plants. The souqs of Sur reflect the town's greater prosperity and there are some interesting shops to explore.

Ladies' Souq
SOUQ

(Main St; ☺ 10am-noon & 5-10pm) There are many textile shops in the Ladies' Souq, some selling braided ankle parts for women's trousers.

Al-Haramain Perfumes
PERFUMERY

(Souq St; ☺ 10am-1pm & 4.30-9pm) Adjacent to the Ladies' Souq. The elaborate bottles alone are temptation enough to enter the shop, and being daubed in exotic musk and ambergris is one of Arabia's great experiences.

Safen Al Khaleej
CRAFT

Between the Flamingo roundabout and the new harbour, this workshop sells handcrafted model wooden dhows. You'll have to take pot luck with opening hours.

ℹ Information

There are numerous banks, most with ATMs, along Main St and Souq St.

Internet Café (Souq St; per hour 500 baisa; ☺ 8am-1pm & 4-10pm Sat-Thu, 4-10pm Fri) Occupies the upper floor of the Digital Photo Express shop.

ℹ Getting There & Around

Public transport leaves from near the Sur Hotel. Buses to Muscat via Ibra (OR4, 4¼ hours) depart at 6am and 2.30pm; via the coastal highway (OR3, 2½ hours) they depart at 7am. Shared taxis to the Rusayl roundabout in Muscat via the coastal highway cost OR4 (engaged cost OR20).

Taxis cost 200 baisa per ride anywhere in Sur.

Ayjah
العيجة

Lying on the other side of the lagoon from Sur, the pretty, whitewashed village of Ayjah is worth a visit. The renovated **Al-Ayjah Fort** (admission 500 baisa; ☺ 8.30am-2.30pm Sun-Thu) seems to have been built as part and parcel of the surrounding merchant houses with their elaborately carved doors and lotus-pillared porches. If you wander over to the old **lighthouse**, there is a fine view of Sur.

Ayjah boasts its own hotel, **Al-Ayjah Plaza Hotel** (☑ 25 544433; www.alayjahplaza-hotel.com; s/d OR41/47; ℗ ☎). Located on the edge of the lagoon, across the water from Sur, it offers good-value modern rooms with big windows. The hotel's Turkish restaurant (open from 11am to midnight) is a pleasant place to enjoy watching dhows beaching at low tide in the lagoon.

To reach Ayjah, you can either cross the bridge (Oman's first and only suspension bridge) or drive 10km around the lagoon.

Sinkhole Park (Hawiyat Najm Park)

The blue-green, brackish water at the bottom of this peculiar 40m by 20m limestone hole invites a swim and a snorkel. The intrepid can inch round the ledges that surround the pool and dive into the deep unknown. It's known locally as Bayt al-Afreet (House of the Demon); you could come face to face with more than you bargained for in the water, the depth of which is still uncertain. If the demon eludes you, look out for the equally elusive blind cavefish instead.

The sinkhole is beside the Muscat–Sur Hwy, near the village of Dibab. Follow the signposts off the highway towards a green oasis. There are toilets but no changing or other facilities at this picnic spot.

From the sinkhole, you can drive along the old coast road for a closer look at the sea and rejoin the highway at the next junction in either direction.

OMAN AYJAH

Mountain Road to Jaylah

Along the Muscat–Sur coastal highway, you'll notice several roads zigzagging up the mountainside into the clouds that often top the Eastern Hajar range. They mostly connect with small villages, such as Umq, in the heart of the mountains from where there is no onward route except by foot.

One exception, however, is the graded track carved out of the rock face that leads to the cliff-hugging village of **Qaran**. The route is strictly 4WD and is not for the faint-hearted as the last part of the ascent is a near-vertical climb with sharp hairpin bends. The ascent offers a panoramic view of the coastal plain and an idea of the arid plateau that characterises the top of the Eastern Hajar range. If you're feeling brave, have a good sense of direction and spare petrol, you can follow the road across the plateau to the tombs at Jaylah and descend towards Ibra on the other side of the mountains.

Look out for a brown sign to 'Qaran' or 'Kbaikab Graveyard and Al Jayla Village' off the Muscat–Sur Hwy, 5km northwest of Wadi Shab. Beware, there are no facilities whatsoever on top of this desolate plateau and the nearest petrol station is in Sur (or along Hwy 23 on the Ibra side of the mountains). Watch for grazing gazelle along the route.

Wadi Shab   وادي شعب

Aptly named in Arabic the 'Gorge Between Cliffs', Wadi Shab is still one of the most lovely destinations in Oman – despite the ugly Muscat–Sur Hwy slung across the entrance. The wadi rewards even the most reluctant walker, with turquoise pools, waterfalls and terraced plantations; kingfishers add glorious splashes of colour and all year round trusses of pink oleander bloom by the water's edge.

While swimming in the lower pools is forbidden (they are a source of drinking water), there is an opportunity for discreet swimming in the upper reaches of the wadi where you can duck into a partially submerged cave.

To begin the walk, take the boat (200 baisa each way) across the deep water at the entrance of the wadi, organised by enterprising locals, and follow the path through plantations, crossing and recrossing the wadi several times before reaching a small pumping station. Be prepared to wade up to your knees in places and beware of slipping on algae-covered rocks. After heavy rains, bring a bag for your camera and some dry clothes just in case you are obliged to swim.

The path has been concreted (not very sympathetically) for part of the way and passes close to several villages that are hidden away in the plantations. At times the path follows an impressive *falaj* (traditional irrigation system) complete with underground sections and laced with ferns. The wadi eventually broadens into an area of large boulders and wild fig trees with many pools of deep water. Look for a ladder descending into one of these pools as Wadi Shab bends to the left. If you duck through a short underwater channel in this pool, you will find the partially submerged cavern. Allow up to two hours of walking to reach this pool.

It's possible to walk beyond the pools to other small villages clustered along the wadi floor but the paths are not so well-trodden and they follow, sometimes steeply, goat tracks over the wadi cliffs. Walking shoes and plenty of drinking water are necessary. The wadi becomes drier the higher you climb into the mountains.

Wadi Shab is signposted off the Muscat–Sur coastal highway. You can't miss Wadi Shab: the vista of mountains opening into a pea-green lake is sublime after the barren plain.

Vehicles, thankfully, cannot navigate the wadi beyond a small parking area. Toilets, open from 7am to 7pm in the parking lot, are intended to disuade visitors from urinating in the wadi.

Camping and lighting a barbeque are not permitted in the wadi. As with all wadis in Oman, flash flooding can make them impassable for a time. Check with any of the tour companies reviewed by Lonely Planet (see p205) for up-to-date information on Wadi Shab's accessibility, especially after rains.

Tiwi   طيوي

♪ 25

There's not much to the little fishing village of Tiwi, but being flanked by two of Oman's beauty spots, Wadi Shab and Wadi Tiwi, it has found itself very much on the tourist map. Not that it has made many concessions to tourism – there's no hotel and no public transport, either to Muscat or to Sur. The locals are nonetheless forbearing of the convoys of passing 4WDs and are delighted when a driver bothers to stop for a chat. If you do stop, ask about Ibn Mukarab. The story goes that this Saudi fugitive paved the steps from his house (the ruins are still visible on the hill) to his tomb in gold. As anticipated, the locals dug the steps up for the booty, making the tomb inaccessible. Ibn Mukarab has since been able to enjoy the peace in death that he couldn't find in life.

Just 48km from Sur, Tiwi and the two flanking wadis make an easy day trip from Sur; the Muscat–Sur Hwy passes the very doorstep of the town. You might be able to persuade a taxi driver from Sur to take you to Tiwi (OR15) and wait for an hour or so while you explore either Wadi Shab or Wadi Tiwi. Alternatively, hotels in Sur can arrange a tour.

There is plenty of ad-hoc camping along nearby beaches. The most popular is Tiwi Beach (White Beach), a large sandy bay 9km northwest of Tiwi towards Dibab, accessed via the old coast road.

Wadi Tiwi وادي طيوي

With its string of emerald pools and thick plantations, Wadi Tiwi almost rivals Wadi Shab in beauty, especially in the spring when the allotments turn a vivid green. Known as the 'Wadi of Nine Villages', there are excellent walking opportunities through the small villages that line the road. For the more ambitious hiker, there is a strenuous but rewarding two-day hike that begins at Sooee, the last of the nine settlements. Indeed, the route over the mountain to Wadi Bani Khalid has become a popular camping excursion with walking groups.

Wadi Tiwi can be accessed by car but villagers prefer visitors to approach on foot. The road is narrow and steep in parts towards the upper reaches and it is easy to get a large vehicle stuck between the plantation walls.

To reach the wadi by car, turn towards the mountains at a small junction with a brown signpost for Tracking Path E35 at the Sur end of Tiwi village. Donkeys and herons share the knee-deep grass at the mouth of the wadi. Unfortunately, you will also spot the giant highway pylons that now stride across the once picturesque wadi entrance. The road is paved for part of the way. At the point where it meanders into the date plantations it is best to park and walk. There is no public transport but tours can be arranged from hotels in Sur.

Qalhat قلهات

The 2nd-century settlement of Qalhat is one of the most ancient sites in Oman. There's not much left to see except the ruined **Tomb of Bibi Miriam** but if you pay the site a visit, you'll be in excellent company; both Marco Polo in the 13th century and Ibn Battuta in the 14th century stopped here on their travels. You'll also have the satisfaction of knowing that your journey to Qalhat was a tad more adventurous than theirs. In their day, Qalhat was a 'very good port, much frequented by merchant ships from India' and a hub for the trade in horses from the

OMAN'S ANCIENT IRRIGATION SYSTEM

As you travel around northern Oman, be sure to look out for Oman's ancient irrigation system – an engineering highlight of such sophistication and complexity that it has earned Unesco heritage status.

Comprised of channels, known locally as *aflaj* (plural) or *falaj* (singular), cut into mountainsides, running across miniature aqueducts and double-deckering through tunnels, this irrigation system is responsible for most of the oases in Oman. The precious water is diverted firstly into drinking wells, then into mosque washing areas and at length to the plantations, where it is siphoned proportionally among the village farms. Traditionally, a *falaj* clock, like a sun dial, was used to meter the time given to each farm; nowadays, some *aflaj* are controlled by automatic domes.

There are more than 4000 of these channels in Oman, some of which were built more than 1500 years ago. The longest channel is said to run for 120km under Sharqiya Sands. Although they can be seen throughout the mountains, the best, most easily accessible examples are in Nizwa, Tanuf, Wadi Bani Awf, Wadi Dayqah and Wadi Shab.

interior. Today only the tomb, water cistern and remnants of city walls are visible, and in place of barques and dhows, all that the sea brings to the shore are sharks, sardines and rays. If you camp nearby, the water is often spangled at night with green phosphorous.

The site was closed for maintenance at the time of writing and is unlikely to open soon. Until the site is redeveloped for tourism, you can spot the tomb from the highway.

Ras al-Jinz رأس الجنز

Ras al-Jinz (Ras al-Junayz), the easternmost point of the Arabian Peninsula, is an important **turtle-nesting site** for the endangered green turtle. Over 20,000 females return annually to the beach where they hatched in order to lay eggs.

Oman has an important role to play in the conservation of this endangered species and takes the responsibility seriously, with strict penalties for harming turtles or their eggs. The area is under government protection and the only way to visit the site is by joining an escorted tour. For further information about conservation measures in place to protect Oman's turtles, contact the **Environment Society of Oman** (☑24 482121; www.environment.org.om).

While the tour is intended for the well-being of the turtle, at peak holiday times large volumes of people flock to the reserve.

Thankfully groups are limited to 20 people per guide with no more than five guides in each session. Despite the reserve's best efforts, there is something immensely intrusive about large, noisy groups gawping at such an intimate act, especially when flippers are lifted out of the way for better viewing and the frightened turtles are chased down the beach by mobile-phone wielding individuals. As such, the experience may not be to everyone's taste.

🏃 Activities

★ **Ras al-Jinz Turtle Reserve** ECOTOUR (Visitors Centre; ☑96 550606; www.rasaljinz-turtlereserve.com; adult/child OR3/1; children under 5 yrs free; ☉ 9am-8pm) 🐢 Turtles do not approach the beach during the day so for the best chance of seeing a turtle, you must join a night tour (from 9pm each evening) bookable in advance online or by calling the reserve. If you turn up without a reservation, you may miss the opportunity as maximum visitor numbers are adhered to.

The beach is a 900m, 15-minute walk from the visitors centre across soft sand. Cars are not permitted beyond the visitors centre: a shuttle bus is provided for the elderly and those with special needs. Note that photography is not permitted during the night visit.

There is an excellent museum at the visitors centre (adult/child OR1/500 baisa) with

LOCAL KNOWLEDGE

SPOTTING TURTLES – BEST TIME TO GO

Turtle-watching aficionados time their visit to Ras al-Jinz to witness maximum traffic on the beach. This is what they recommend:

Go in July This is the peak laying season for the green turtle when more than 100 females come ashore each night.

Go between September and November Although at least one turtle arrives on the beach every night of the year, this is the best time to witness both laying and hatching at Ras al-Jinz.

Go at new moon Although full-moon nights make it easier to walk and to witness the spectacle, turtles prefer dark nights so as not to attract the unwanted attentions of predators, which often dig up the eggs as soon as they are laid.

Go at dawn There is a tour at 4am perfect for seeing the last of the latecomers. At this time of day, there are fewer visitors and you can set your own limits of discretion around the few remaining laying turtles.

Go regardless If the turtles have already departed, then don't be too disappointed: at dawn the sandstone cliffs are burnished rose-red by the rising sun, and the turtle tracks of last night's heavy traffic inscribe the sand like ancient calligraphy – a rare sight that few people get to enjoy.

a video in English and German, a 3D cinema and an audio guide to displays and relics charting the history of local interaction with turtles since ancient times.

Between 8am and 1.30pm you can enjoy the magical bay without an escort and it's often possible to spot turtles between the waves, waiting for nightfall before approaching the beach.

🛏 Sleeping & Eating

Desert Discovery Tours   DESERT CAMP $
(☑24 493232; www.desert-discovery.com; half board per person OR25, with shared bathroom OR20; 🅿) Offering a number of *barasti* huts and portacabins with beds, A'Naseem Tourism Camp is 4km outside the turtle reserve on the approach road to Ras al-Jinz – handy for a dawn visit to the beach. Children between six and 12 years of age are accommodated at half price, and children under six can stay free of charge.

Ras al-Jinz Turtle Reserve   HOTEL $$
(☑96 550606; www.rasaljinz-turtlereserve.com; s/d OR65/85; 🅿@) Don't be put off by the ugly façade of the visitors centre at the turtle reserve: the sea-facing part is in keeping with the weather-eroded cliffs that flank the bay. The room rate (payment in cash only) includes the cost of an evening and dawn guided tour of the turtle beach.

A restaurant serves international-style cuisine (the buffet costs OR9.500) and there is a shop selling a range of Omani handicrafts. The reserve is soon to open a dozen tents in the grounds; check the website for details.

ℹ Getting There & Around

Ras al Jinz can be visited as an evening or dawn trip from Sur, organised through Sur Hotel (p146) and Sur Plaza Hotel (p146). The journey time is 40 minutes each way. There is no public transport.

If you have your own vehicle, follow the signs to Ayjah and Ras al-Hadd. Ras al-Jinz can also be reached from Al-Kamil, on the Muscat–Sur Hwy, via Al-Ashkarah (about an hour's drive).

Ras al-Jinz airport is expected to open in 2014.

Ras al-Hadd   راس الحد
☑ 25

A **fort** (admission 500 baisa; ⊙7.30am-6pm Sun-Thu) built between 1560 and 1570 AD, some shops and attractive lagoon scenery nearby

make this fishing village a useful supply point or alternative stopover for visiting Ras al-Jinz.

🛏 Sleeping & Eating

Ra's al-Hadd Beach Hotel   HOTEL $
(☑25 569111; surbhtl@omantel.net.om; cabin OR35, r OR42; 🅿) Offering good-value accommodation on the edge of a flat, calm lagoon, the hotel has a great location. At dawn and dusk wading birds abound in the lagoon and the sea bobs with the backs and heads of turtles, queuing up to come ashore in the dark. For their protection, it's not permitted to camp or picnic at night on this beach.

The hotel restaurant offers simple Indian fare or a buffet of international-style dishes. To reach the hotel, turn off the main road, by the castle in Ras al-Hadd, and follow the signs. Two-hour dhow trips are available for OR30 per boat for up to six people.

Turtle Beach Resort   DESERT CAMP $
(☑25 543400; www.tbroman.com; half board s/d from OR45/50, s/d without bathroom OR35/42) Offering accommodation in *barasti* and concrete huts of varying degrees of comfort, this camp is located on a glorious lagoon side beach. The only drawback is that the huts are so close together you are at the mercy of noisy neighbours. The open-air dining area, in the shape of a wooden dhow, is a sociable spot, and there is a bar.

The camp is signposted left immediately after entering Ras al-Hadd. A one-hour dolphin-watching trip in a fibreglass boat costs OR35 per boat (up to eight people); a one-hour dhow trip is OR60 per boat (up to 16 people).

ℹ Getting There & Around

To reach Ras al-Hadd, follow the signs for Ras al-Jinz but veer left after Khor Garami. It is clearly signposted. There is no public transport to this area.

Al-Ashkarah   الأشخرة
☑ 25 / POP 10,000

Wedged between two beautiful white-sand beaches, Al-Ashkarah is a lively fishing village and important supply point for the Bedouin communities of the Sharqiya Sands. Umbrellas on the beaches on the southern side of town provide camping opportunities. The sea here is much rougher and more characterful than on the beaches

ⓘ TURTLE-WATCHING ETIQUETTE

Watching labour and delivery on Oman's sandy beaches can be an awe-inspiring sight. Serene and patient, the female turtles that quietly lumber up the beach are sure to win the hearts of anyone lucky enough to see the spectacle of egg-laying. Witnessing these gentle giants slip back into the darkness of the returning tide is one those unforgettable wildlife experiences – at least, that is, if the turtles are permitted to make their exit *after* rather than *before* the job is done and without the disheartening spectacle of bullish tourists trying to take a photograph at any cost.

Turtles are no land lovers, and they are very easily dissuaded from making the journey up the beach. In fact, any disturbance during the turtle's approach to the shore will most probably result in a U-turn and it may be days before the turtle plucks up the courage to try again. Once the digging of pits is over and the laying has begun, however, the process cannot be interrupted. Nonetheless the following actions should be avoided:

➡ touching or approaching a moving turtle

➡ standing in front of a nesting turtle

➡ riding or sitting on a turtle (it happens)

➡ lighting a fire or using a torch near a turtle beach

➡ taking photographs with a flash or a mobile phone (cameras are not permitted on the beach at Ras al-Jinz)

➡ leaving litter – turtles often mistake plastic bags for jellyfish, a favourite food.

north of town and if you choose to break your journey here, you can look forward to large waves and flocks of gulls itching to join your picnic.

🛏 Sleeping & Eating

⭐ **Arabian Sea Resort** HOTEL $$
(☑ 97 794244; www.arabiansea.com; off Ras Al-Hadd to Al-Ashkarah Rd, Asselah; s/d with sea view OR30/40) In a superb location at the top of the high tide, where turtles lumber up the beach at night, this low-rise hotel looks more like a government school from the distance. The rooms, however, have salted linen, huge windows, *rondelles*, plasterwork and equestrian paintings that give them a rococo flourish. The hotel is in Asselah, close to Al-Ashkarah.

The owner can arrange 4WD and camel safaris into the interirior. The trips last from 5pm to 7pm (OR30 for children, OR70 for adults) and culminate in a sunset vista of a desert castle that belongs to the owner's family.

Al-Ashkarah Hotel HOTEL $
(☑ 25 566222; Main Rd, Al-Ashkarah; s/d OR10/12) If you arrive too late to set up camp, Al-Ashkarah Hotel, with pink doors and ill-fitting carpets, is just about clean. The Golden Beach Restaurant next door can rustle up rice and dhal or an egg roll-up for breakfast.

The hotel is on the main road, on the edge of town.

Al-Ashkarah to Shana'a Road

Dubbed the 'Dunes Rd', this remarkable feat of engineering cuts a corridor through the auburn Sharqiya Sands and is almost a destination in its own right. The road links Al-Ashkarah with Shana'a, the ferry terminal for Masirah. Crossing some of the most inhospitable terrain in the country, it passes small fishing villages, outcrops of aeolite (fossilised sand) blown into extraordinary formations, and the tracks of the Bedu, which ignore the road and continue across it as if it were a minor interruption to age-old caravan routes.

Fill up with petrol and supplies in Al-Ashkarah as the road takes about two hours to drive (excluding photo stops).

Jalan Bani Bu Hassan & Jalan Bani Bu Ali

جعلان بني بو حسن و جعلان بني بو علي

☑ 25 / POP 30,000

These towns comprise a conglomeration of watchtowers, old fortified houses, forts and ancient plantation walls, all of which lie crumbling in various states of beloved dereliction. There has been little attempt to court the modern world and none at all to woo the visitor, making a visit to these sites all the more rewarding.

It's worth trying to stumble on **Jami al-Hamoda Mosque** in the middle of Jalan Bani Bu Ali, with its unique structure of 52 domes and a *falaj* used for ablutions running through the courtyard. To get to the mosque, follow the signs for Jalan Bani Bu Ali at the roundabout off the Al-Kamil to Al Ashkarah road. Drive along the main street towards the fort (closed to the public but obvious above the palm trees), and pass into a housing area. Turn left immediately after the fort just before reaching a brown sign that wistfully states 'you are on the fringe of the sands' and warning you not to go further without 4WD (tracks lead from here into the Sharqiya Sands but should not be attempted without a guide as these routes are seldom explored by visitors). Follow the tarmac road for half a kilometre and the mosque appears on the left. Look out for elaborately painted metal doors on the surrounding houses – a feature of the region.

If the quiet authenticity of the two towns or their gateway location on the edge of the Sharqiya Sands appeal, then consider staying at **Al Dabi Jalan Bani Bu Ali Tourist Motel** (25 553307; d/tr OR20/25; P). With fancy tiling, arched corridors and carved doors, the hotel has pretensions above its ability to deliver (as you can see from the drab chocolate-brown foyer with frayed chairs) but it does at least offer a clean bed for the night. There's a small restaurant next door for tasty *biryani* (OR2.500).

The twin towns are 17km from Al-Kamil and 36km to Al-Ashkarah and make a good diversion en route to/from Ras al-Jinz.

Al-Kamil الكامل

25 / POP 22,800

Despite some interesting old **architecture**, including a **fort** and **watchtowers**, this small town is more commonly known as an important junction with Al-Ashkarah Rd and the Muscat–Sur Hwy, punctuated by local-style **cafes**. It is something of a rarity in Oman, however, for being one of the few towns in the country surrounded by trees. The low-lying **acacia and ghaf woodland** is a special feature of the area, much prized by the Bedouin who use the wood for shade,

shelter (as props for their tents) and firewood. Their camels nibble the nutritious new shoots and livestock lick the moisture from the small leaves in the early morning.

Al-Kamil, an important staging post between Muscat, Ibra and the Sharqiya Sands, and Wadi Bani Khalid, Sur, Al-Ashkarah and Ras al-Jinz, is a good place to break a long journey. There are no hotels in the town of Al-Kamil but the **Oriental Nights Rest House** (99 006215; info@onrh-oman.com; r from s/d OR20/25; P), on the Muscat–Sur Hwy opposite the junction for Wadi Bani Khalid, offers very friendly, simple accommodation in clean rooms. There are better grades of rooms at slightly higher costs. If you're looking for a sands experience but don't fancy the big desert camps, ask about the hotel's overnight camping with the Bedu (OR55 per person); the price includes a barbecue, bedding and breakfast. The hotel's dining room offers a choice of home-cooked Indian curries, dhal and spicy soups.

There is a bus to Al-Kamil from Sur (OR1, 45 minutes) and Muscat (OR3.500, three hours and 40 minutes), but note that there is no reliable public transport to Ras al-Jinz from Al-Kamil, nor to Wadi Bani Khalid.

Wadi Bani Khalid وادي بني خالد

Justly famed for its natural beauty, this wadi just north of the town of Al-Kamil makes a rewarding diversion off the Muscat–Sur Hwy or as a destination in its own right. The approach road, which climbs high into the Eastern Hajar Mountains, zigzags through some spectacularly colourful rock formations, green with copper oxide and rust-red with iron ore, and passes by an *ayn* (natural spring), which is signposted by the side of the road.

Wadi Bani Khalid comprises a long series of plantations and villages that lie in or close to the wadi floor. All year round, water flows from a natural spring in the upper reaches of the wadi, supporting the abundant vegetation that makes it such a beautiful spot. Most people visiting Wadi Bani Khalid head for the source of this water, which collects in a series of deep **pools** in the narrow end of the wadi, and **Moqal Cave**. Both are well signposted from the Muscat–Sur Hwy.

The pools have been developed into a tourist destination with a small (too small) car park, a concrete pathway and a series of picnic huts. Swimming is possible here but only if clothed in shorts and a T-shirt over the top of a swimming costume. The site is rather unattractive but at least efforts have at last been made to enhance access to this beauty spot. It is heavily crowded at weekends and during public holidays, but it is possible to escape the visitors relatively easily by going in search of the cave or by climbing above the wadi on the marked path. The path eventually leads to Tiwi by the coast. It takes three days to walk (with donkeys carrying camping equipment) and is a popular hike organised by tour agents in Muscat.

To reach the cave, look for a lower path above the picnic area and walk along the bottom of the wadi. You will have to scramble over and squeeze under boulders and ford the water several times. For precise directions, ask the goat herders. If they don't tell you the right place, it's because they don't like tourists swimming deeper into the wadi. Then again, they may just be worried you'll be lured into the land of gardens and cool streams revealed to all who strike the rocks of Moqal Cave and utter the magic words 'Salim bin Saliym Salam'. The cave, however, is more likely to reveal evidence of bats and previous visitors. The narrow entrance is finally accessed by a concrete stairway. A torch is needed to see anything, and to find the underground pools, you will need to be prepared to scramble and slither through the mud. To reach the cave, walking shoes are advisable, together with a reasonable level of fitness. If the water levels are high, the route should be avoided. It's inadvisable to enter the cave alone.

For a panoramic view of the wadi plantations, stop at the **Tourist Service Centre** (☉ 7am-7pm) on the approach road to Moqal Cave. It's currently closed, but hopefully this cafe will open again soon as it overlooks a sea of palm trees and is blissfully peaceful at sunset when most day trippers have gone home. You can at least bring your own picnic and enjoy the view from the terrace of the car park.

Jaylah   الجيلة

This exciting destination on top of the Eastern Hajar Mountains is worth the effort as much for the journey through crumbling cliffs and past remote mountain villages as for the reward of seeing ancient tombs on the summit.

The route, which can only be negotiated by 4WD, begins at a right turn for Souqah, just before the town of Ash-Shariq (also known as Simayiah – located at the entrance of Wadi Khabbah). The start of the track moves each time it rains: look for a track on the other side of the wadi or ask locally. Make sure you have water, a map, compass and a full tank of petrol. At 3.1km after you leave the sealed road, take the right fork for Jaylah (sometimes spelt Gaylah or Al-Gailah). The track traces a precarious route through walls of unhinged black shale, waiting for a good storm to collapse. The last 6km of the ascent to the plateau, past shepherd enclosures, is currently poorly graded and progress is slow. At 21.4km, turn steep left by the water filling 'station' and follow the road to the top of the plateau.

Myriad car tracks thread from village to village on the top of the plateau and numerous little communities survive on very little on the more or less barren plain. Until recently, the only access to many of these villages was by foot with an occasional helicopter visit bringing supplies and/or health officials.

The 90 or so tombs scattered across the hilltops date back to the Umm an Nar culture of 2000 to 2700 BC and, if you've been to Bat, you'll recognise the meticulous stone towers, carefully tracing the ridges of the high ground. Local belief has it that they were built by the spirit Kebir Keb, which is as good a way as any of describing the collective consciousness of the ancients.

If you are feeling adventurous, you can continue over the unmapped plateau to the village of Qaran and drop down to the Muscat–Sur coastal highway, 5km northwest of Wadi Shab. This road is not for the fainthearted, though, with near vertical descents.

Wadi Khabbah & Wadi Tayein   وادي كبه و وادي الطائين

These two wide and luscious wadis meander along the western base of the Eastern Hajar Mountains and provide a fascinating alternative route between Muscat and Sur. A 4WD is needed to navigate the off-road sections, which invariably involve fording water. The picture of rural wadi life that unfolds as you meander through the spectacular mountain scenery is a highlight. There are numerous plantations and small villages in these wadis and it's much appreciated if you travel through the wadis with sensitivity.

Near the point where Wadi Kabbah runs into Wadi Tayein is the village of Tool. Tool is also the gateway to Wadi Dayqah; you can park outside the village and wade across the wadi entrance. Deep pools invite a swim but don't for a minute think that you're alone – the steep ravine is a favourite with silent-walking shepherds. Tool lies 10km east of the town of Mehlah, at the end of the sealed road through Wadi Tayein.

Al-Mintirib   المنترب

📞 25 / POP 10,000

This small village on the edge of the dunes is an important navigational landmark for visits to the Sharqiya Sands. Camp representatives often meet their guests here and help them navigate (by 4WD only) the route to their site – usually impossible to find independently. Al-Mintirib has a picturesque old quarter of passing interest for those breaking the drive from Muscat, 220km to the northeast. The village is 10km southeast of Al-Qabil Rest House on the Muscat–Sur Hwy.

👁 Sights

Al-Mintirib Fort   FORT
(admission 500 baisa; ⊙ 7.30am-2.30pm Sun-Thu) In the days before the housing of Al-Mintirib encroached on its space, this solid-walled fort with its sunken door must have been an impressive sight, holding back the dunes in one direction, and repelling marauding tribes from the mountains. Opening hours are rather erratic.

Bidaya Museum   MUSEUM
(admission OR1; ⊙ 9am-2pm) This quirky little museum on the edge of the sands preserves the history of the Hijri Tribe, written in Arabic on goat skins. A collection of old spears and swords that date back 300 years or more, together with Chinese ginger jars and dishes (an essential part of all Omani households in the last century), household implements and clothing are well displayed in a cavernous old house, restored for the purpose. Located across the road from the fort in Al-Mintirib, it's worth a 20-minute stop before heading into the dunes.

🛏 Sleeping & Eating

Al-Qabil Rest House   HOTEL $
(📞 25 581243; www.desert-discovery.com; Route 23, Al-Qabil; s/d OR25/30) Located on the Ibra–

Sur Hwy 10km northwest of Al-Mintirib, the hotel offers simple rooms around a landscaped courtyard. Doors close by 10pm. For those wanting to experience the dunes as a day trip rather than an overnight experience, the hotel offers escorted access to the dunes.

Book a 4WD and driver by the hour online through the Desert Discovery website. A three-hour trip allows time for scrambling up dunes or visiting Bedu families.

Travellers Oasis   INTERNATIONAL $
(Route 23, Mintirib; meals OR2; ⊙ 9am-9pm) In an area of few tourist amenities, this new restaurant serving simple international fare offers a welcome break along the Ibra–Sur Hwy on the outskirts of the desert hub of Mintirib. It looks set to serve as a meeting point for those planning an excursion into the sands and a chance to discuss driving tactics over a coffee.

Sharqiya (Wahiba) Sands   رمال الشرقية

A destination in their own right, or a diversion between Muscat and Sur, these beautiful dunes, formerly known as Wahiba Sands, could keep visitors occupied for days. Home to the Bedu, the sands offer visitors a glimpse of a traditional way of life that is fast disappearing as modern conveniences limit the need for a nomadic existence. The Bedu specialise in raising camels for racing and regular **camel races** take place throughout the region from mid-October to mid-April. Contact the **Ministry for Camel Affairs** (📞 26 893804) for details.

The sands are a good place to interact with Omani women whose Bedouin lifestyle affords them a more visible social role than many other rural women. They wear distinctive, brightly coloured costumes with peaked masks and an *abeyya* (full-length robe) of gauze, and are accomplished drivers, often coming to the rescue of tourists stuck in the sand. They are also skilful craftspeople and may well approach you with colourful woollen key rings and camel bags for sale.

It is possible, but highly challenging, to drive right through the sands from north to south, camping under the seams of native *ghaf* trees or tucking behind a sand dune. There are, however, no provisions available, petrol stations or any other help at hand in the sands beyond the desert camps at the northern periphery. As such, it is imperative that you go with a guide. Off-road guidebooks describe this route but all will advise you not to venture through the sands alone. In the summer the sands rage with heat so avoid exploring too far off the beaten track between April and October: if you get stuck at this time of year, chances are you won't be able to carry enough water to walk to safety, even if you can find the way through the disorienting high dunes of the south.

For the casual visitor, the best way to explore the sands is by staying at one of the desert camps. If you don't have a car, then the owners of the camp will meet you at the Muscat–Sur Hwy, and guide you, usually in convoy, across the sands. Some now have graded tracks and even tarmac roads approaching the camp gates, making for a less hair-raising driving experience. Needless to say, it is essential to have a 4WD, and prior knowledge of off-road driving is very helpful if you try to reach some of the more remote camps on your own.

If you don't fancy the prospect of getting your vehicle stuck in the sand, there are plenty of tours available and some camps will come and collect their non-driving guests for an extra fee (usually around OR40 return with a sunset drive thrown in).

Alternatively, if you want to enter the sands without the drama of going off-road, you can drive through the sands on a sealed road from Al-Ashkara to Shana'a – a desert experience unique to Oman.

Sleeping

Accommodation in the sands takes the form of tented or *barasti* camps that offer the full desert experience, including camel and horse rides (OR30/20 per hour), dune-driving (OR40 to OR60 per hour), sand-boarding and trips to Bedouin settlements. Don't confuse camping here with budget accommodation. The camps are often quite expensive for what they offer. The best-value camps are as follows and prices shown include breakfast and a barbecue dinner.

Al-Raha Tourism Camp   DESERT CAMP $
(☑99 551155, 99 343851; www.alrahaoman.com; half board per person OR20, with air-con OR25; ℗) Located deep in the dunes, this friendly, efficient camp offers concrete huts decorated with *barasti* at the end of a long corridor of orange sand. There's a play area and

discounted accommodation for children (children under two years old stay for free; children between two and 12 years old pay OR10). Particularly recommended as a base for exploration deeper into the sands.

Access is via Mintirib along 18km of graded track. Although some car owners choose to bring a saloon car, car-hire insurance will not cover you for going off-road without a 4WD, and the washboard (ridged bars across the track) will damage an ordinary car's suspension.

Al-Areesh Camp   DESERT CAMP $
(Desert Discovery Tours Camp; ☑99 450063, 24 493232; www.desert-discovery.com; half board tent per person with/without bathroom OR25/OR20; ℗) ✿ This lovely camp lies on the edge of a silver sand dune with local Bedouin villages nearby. Accommodation is in tents of various sizes with charpoys (lightweight bedsteads) for optional outside sleeping. A sealed road makes access easy. Call the camp for help along the last portion of track. The camp offers camel and 4WD rides with profits going to local Bedu.

★1000 Nights   DESERT CAMP $$
(☑99 448158; www.1000nightscamp.com; half board tent without bathroom s/d OR25/45, with bathroom s/d OR57/67; ℗ �🛜 🏊) ✿ This magical camp is a haven of Bedouin-style tents, breezy Arabian-style seating areas and a swimming pool! Despite this oddity, this is one camp where you are genuinely in the heart of the dunes and the challenge of getting there, 19km over a sand ridge from Al-Raha camp on the valley floor, is part of the excitement.

A retired Bedford brought the resident dhow here in three pieces; now reassembled as a bar, it makes a fun place to watch those other ships of the desert lope by. Unique, all-day horse-riding or camel-riding adventures with a Bedouin guide are OR90 per day with lunch. Dinner in the carpeted open-air *majlis* (seating area) is a simple buffet jollied along with the hypnotic rhythms of Bedouin drummers and dancers. If the tour guides join in, the entertainment can last all evening. Like all the desert camps it can be noisy and very busy on a Wednesday or Thursday evening but for the rest of the week, the silence of the sands is reclaimed. If you can't bear to be that far from normal life, there's free wi-fi and internet facilities.

SURVEY OF THE SANDS

If you drive through the Sharqiya Sands in the spring, when a green tinge settles over the dunes, you'll notice that they are not the static and lifeless heap of gold-coloured dust that they might at first appear. Not only do they move at quite a pace (up to 10m a year) but they are also home to a surprising number of mobile inhabitants.

The Royal Geographical Society of London, in cooperation with the Omani government, conducted a survey in 1986 and concluded that among the 180 species of plants, there were 200 species of mammals, birds, reptiles and amphibians in the sands. The best way to spot these inhabitants is to look for the prints that slither, wriggle and otherwise punctuate the sand early in the evening and then lie in wait above the point where the tracks end. Sooner or later, the animal will burrow to the surface and scuttle off for twilight foraging.

While each animal has its place in the delicate ecosystem of the sands, the health of the environment as a whole is largely due to one six-legged, black-boxed insect called a dung beetle. Rolling its prize up and down the dunes, it can cover many acres of land and in so doing helps fertilise the fragile plants in its path.

Nomadic Desert Camp DESERT CAMP $$
(☑99 336273; www.nomadicdesertcamp.com; s/d without bathroom OR49/76; ℗) ✆ This intimate camp, run by a Bedouin family, offers personal service in the heart of the dunes. Accommodation is in *barasti*-style huts with shared bathrooms. Included in the price is transport to and from Al-Wasil on the Muscat–Sur Hwy, a camel ride and visit to a Bedouin village. There is no generator and therefore no air-con, which makes for a peaceful and authentic experience.

Desert Nights Camp DESERT CAMP $$$
(☑92 818388; www.desertnightscamp.com; half board s/d OR164/199; ☉Aug-May; ☎) This camp offers what might best be described as 'bush chic' for those who want to see the sands but don't really want to engage with them. The compact, canvas-roofed cabins are impeccably designed with boutique furnishings and the *majlis* (seating area), bar and reception area are decked with Omani antiques. However luxurious the camp, the noise from quad bikes is irritiating despite the sunset curfew.

There is 24-hour electricity, year-round air-conditioning and hot-water showers so you can pretend you are anywhere but the desert. Just 11km from Al-Wasil, a sealed and then a graded road leads up to the camp gate. There's free transport from the road for those without 4WD.

ⓘ Getting There & Around

To get to the edge of the Sharqiya Sands by public transport, take a Muscat–Sur bus (from Muscat/Sur OR3/2) and ask to be dropped off at Al-Qabil Rest House. It takes three hours from Muscat and 1½ hours from Sur. There are six buses per day in either direction.

The sands run parallel to the Muscat–Sur Hwy and the easiest access into the sands (with your own vehicle) is at Al-Mintirib.

Ibra إبرا

☑25 / POP 27,200

Ibra, the gateway to the Sharqiya Region, enjoyed great prosperity during Oman's colonial period as the aristocratic locals set sail for Zanzibar and sent money home for plantations and luxury residences, still in evidence in the old quarter of town. The tradition of farming is continued today, with rich plots producing vegetables, bananas, mangos and, of course, dates. A watchtower punctuates the top of each surrounding hill, indicating the prior importance of the town – an importance it is beginning to enjoy again with the arrival of a university and large regional hospital. Ibra makes a pleasant stop-off for those heading to Sharqiya Sands.

◎ Sights & Activities

Ibra has a lively **souq** that is at its most active on a Wednesday morning. Arranged around a double courtyard, the greengrocery takes pride of place in the centre, with local melons and aubergines making colourful seasonal displays. A working silver souq, where *khanjars* (tribal curved daggers) and veil pins are crafted, occupies several of the shops around the outer courtyard, muscling in between carpentry shops where

ⓘ DRIVING TO THE DESERT CAMPS

If you're driving a 4WD to a camp through soft sands it can be an exhilirating but also an unnerving experience. Here are a few tips to make sure you get there in one piece.

➡ Deflate your tyres slightly at the edge of the sands to help with traction.

➡ Avoid driving on graded desert tracks with deflated tyres – this is the quickest way to a puncture.

➡ Strap down any loose luggage in the car to avoid it taking flight as you rev over a sand dune.

➡ Engage 4WD but only use low ratio if you can feel the vehicle labouring.

➡ Keep the speed up, especially on inclines, and avoid steering over high dunes – this is for play only.

➡ Don't stop! Aim for pockets of hard ground between soft sand if you need a break to gather your wits.

➡ If a Bedu suggests an alternative route to your camp, it may well be a better route but it will cost you. Expect to tip OR15 for a short guiding service. Don't follow vague instructions like 'round that dune and just over there' – you'll never find the way!

➡ Remember to reinflate your tyres at the nearest village before driving too far on sealed roads after leaving the sands.

elaborately carved doors are still made. Look out for a shop called 'Sale and Maintenance of Traditional Firearms & Rifle Making': there's always an energetic huddle of old men engaged in comparing ancient weaponry around the tables outside. You will probably also notice piles of flattened and dried fish – a local delicacy, still prized despite the modern road system that brings fresh fish to Ibra via the neighbouring wet fish market.

To reach the souq by car, turn right off the Muscat–Sur Hwy at a sign for Al-Safalat Ibra, just past the Sultan Qaboos Mosque; the souq is about 500m on the right. If coming by bus, say you're heading for the souq and ask to be set down near Al-Yamadi turning.

Women may be tempted to visit on a Wednesday morning when the nearby **women's souq** attracts women-only buyers and sellers from all over the region, selling a variety of handicrafts such as baskets, woven cushions and camel bags. Men are not welcome and photographs are prohibited.

If you continue past the souq area and turn right at a brown sign for the local villages of Al-Munisifeh and Al-Kanatar, you'll come to one of the old parts of Ibra with plenty of crumbling **mud-built houses** of two or three storeys. You can reach them either by walking across the wadi, or by taking the long way round, following the brown signs. There's a paved walkway of several kilometres through some of the best parts of the old village, accessed by a double archway; note the well on the right of the entrance and the old **Al-Qablateen Mosque** 500m along the narrow lane. Several of the houses have been restored by local residents and it makes an intriguing place to take a stroll – cars may struggle to get round the corners.

🛏 Sleeping & Eating

There are a few accommodation options in Ibra. Eating outside these is confined to small coffeeshops. Opposite the souq is a large supermarket called Al-Najah shopping centre and there are lots of small groceries, *shwarma* stands and rotisseries dotted along the main street.

Ibra Motel HOTEL $
(☑ 25 571666; www.ibramotel2.com; Naseeb Rd; s/d OR15/17) It's cheap and central and for the price, not much more can be expected of it. Nonetheless, this modest hotel with a fancy foyer of outlandish plastic flowers has clean rooms and smartly tiled bathrooms. Breakfast is provided (from 500 baisa) in the adjoining **Fahad bin Saleh Al-Hooti Restaurant** (☑ 92 416105). The hotel is just off the Muscat–Sur Hwy, behind the Omanoil station.

Nahar Tourism Oasis DESERT CAMP $
(☑ 99 387654; www.nahartourismoasis.com; r OR15/25/36; ℗) A pleasant place to experi-

ence the surrounding rock desert, this camp feels remote despite being only 3km from Ibra. Accommodation is in traditional mud-built rooms with decorative wind-towers, although a generator supplies air-con during the summer. Guests must bring their own food. Transport from the town centre and to its excellent 1000 Nights (p156) desert camp can be arranged.

Al-Sharqiya Sands Hotel HOTEL $
(☑ 25 587000; fax 99 207012; Route 23, Ibra; s/d OR32/37; ℗ ▥) On the Ibra–Sur Hwy just south of Ibra, this hotel is arranged around an unappealing pool. The rooms are adequate but have seen better days and the whole hotel looks unloved at present There is a loud 'local' bar and a more family-oriented licensed restaurant with an international menu. The chef is from Morocco – try his excellent fare before he moves on to better things!

Rawazen Restaurant TURKISH $
(☑ 98 077980; mixed grill OR3; ⊙ 8am-2am) With small cubicles, this new restaurant on the main highway in Ibra (opposite the Ibra Motel) offers cosy dining for good-value prices.

❶ Getting There & Around

The Muscat–Sur Hwy passes through the modern town centre. The Muscat to Sur bus stops in Ibra (from Muscat OR3.700, about 2¼ hours, six times daily both ways). A shared taxi costs OR2.500 to Ruwi in Muscat.

Sinaw سناو
☑ 25 / POP 10,000

The reason most people pay a visit to Sinaw is to see its rather wonderful **souq**, which, like most other souqs in the country, is at its most active early on a Thursday morning. What makes this particular souq such fun to visit is that it attracts large numbers of Bedouin from nearby Sharqiya Sands who throng to the town to trade livestock for modern commodities. Local ladies wearing bronze peaked masks and transparent gauzy *abeyyas* add to the exoticism of the spectacle. Just before *eid* (Islamic feast) the centre of town comes to a virtual standstill as camels are loaded (with inordinate difficulty) onto pick-up trucks and goats are bartered across the street. Spirals of smoke emanating from almost every house in the vicinity over the holiday period indicate that the livestock are not traded in vain.

The souq is on the edge of the town, on the Sinaw to Hijj (also known as Hay) road. It is arranged around a central courtyard and the souq gates are decorated with a green car for some reason. If you pass this gate on your left and veer around to the right, a left turn after about 500m takes you up the hill towards a **cemetery**. After a couple of kilometres more, you'll come to the old town of Sinaw. Well-preserved multi-storey **mud houses** make this a fascinating place to wander around and give an idea of how this town has always been an important trading post.

Sinaw is 65km west of Ibra. Although you can catch a bus from Muscat (OR3, three hours), it's not very useful as it leaves late in the afternoon and there's nowhere to stay.

Masirah مصيرة

With its rocky interior of palm oases and gorgeous rim of sandy beaches, Masirah is the typical desert island. Flamingos, herons and oyster-catchers patrol the coast by day, and armies of ghost crabs march ashore at night. Home to a rare shell, the Eloise, and large turtle-nesting sites, the island is justifiably fabled as a naturalist's paradise. Expats stationed here affectionately termed Masirah 'Fantasy Island' – not because of the wildlife, but because anything they wanted during the long months of internment was the subject of fantasy only.

Little is known about the history of the island, except through hearsay. At one point it was inhabited by Bahriya tribespeople, shipwrecked from Salalah. Wiped out by an epidemic 300 years ago, their unusual tombstones can still be seen at Safa'iq (p160). The island has been used variously as a staging post for trade in the Indian Ocean, and as home to a floating population of fishermen attracted by the rich catch of kingfish, lobster and prawn.

Masirah, 63km long, 18km wide and lying 15km from the mainland coast, is still remote, with minimal facilities, but the island's splendid isolation is under threat with hotel chains negotiating for a portion of the eastern shore. For now, though, Masirah continues to offer a rare chance to see nature in the raw: if you can get there it promises a rare trip on the wild side.

A sealed road runs around the entire island but without a 4WD it is hard to get a close-up of the coast without a long walk.

The northwestern tip of the island is a military zone and is off limits.

If you miss the last ferry to Masirah, there are two places to stay on the mainland that are relatively nearby. The sparkling **Al-Jazeera Tourist Guesthouse** (📞 99 820882; s/d/ste OR12/15/25) is in Mahout (also spelt Mahoot and Mahouth), 63km from the ferry, at the Hijj junction on the Sinaw–Duqm road. Or, if you are desperate, there is the **Mahouth Guesthouse** (📞 95 288177; r OR15) in Hijj, 45km from the ferry.

Hilf هيلف

📞 25 / POP 8500

The small town of Hilf, a 3km string of jetties, shops and fish factories in the northwest, is home to most of Masirah's population. Car ferries from the mainland dock at any of the three main jetties that line up along the corniche, which runs parallel with the main street in town.

There are no shops or petrol stations beyond the town, but Hilf caters for most basic needs from food stuff to simple camping and fishing gear, and the town has hotels, banks, ATMs, an internet cafe (without the coffee), post office, pharmacy and modern hospital, all within walking distance of the crossroads on the main street through town.

SHIPWRECKED!

Masirah must be the only place in Oman without a fort – unless the air base counts. The local population tolerates the overseas militia with good grace, but outsiders have not always been welcome. In 1904 a British ship called the *Baron Inverdale* was wrecked off the rugged eastern coast. Her crew struggled ashore expecting Arab hospitality, but found a very different reception. A monument to their massacre in the shape of a concessionary Christian cross is all that remains of the luckless crew.

There were rumours of cannibalism and as a result the sultan decreed the destruction of all local houses – there are surprisingly few permanent settlements, even for the tiny population. A royal pardon was only granted to the islanders in 2009. You'll be glad to know that nowadays the only meat on the kebabs is likely to be camel or goat.

Beyond Hilf

You'll notice as you drive around the island that the rough Indian Ocean contrasts with the calm and shallow Masirah Channel, lending a different character to the island on either side. There are few attractions to draw the visitor away from the beach, but it is worth visiting the 300-year-old **grave sites** at Safa'iq, just inland from the island road (look for a red flag 6km north of Sur Masirah). Two rocks are usually the only indication of a grave for men, three rocks for women, but some of the Safa'iq graves have surprisingly elaborate headstones.

The **Baron Inverdale Monument** is at the far northwest of the island and is currently off limits. **Jebel Humr** (274m) is the highest point of Masirah's hilly backbone and a climb up this flat-topped mountain is recommended for the wonderful view of the island it affords, especially at sunset. The plateau is strewn with fossils. Wear good shoes as the scree can be quite dangerous towards the top. To get there, head out of Hilf in the direction of Sur Masirah, turn left at the sign for A'Samar and scout around the wadi until the mountain comes into view. It takes about 30 minutes to hike up the left rump of the mountain and scramble over the rim.

Masirah is internationally renowned for its turtles: four species frequent the island, including the hawksbill, olive ridley and green, but the most numerous are the loggerheads. Thirty thousand come ashore each year, making Masirah the largest **loggerhead turtle-nesting site** in the world . The favourite nesting beach is near the Masira Island Resort.

For their sheer diversity, the shells of the island are hard to beat. Spiny whelks (murex) used to be harvested here for their purple dye, and ancient shell middens near Sur Masirah indicate that clams were an important food source for early settlers. Latterly, the island has become famous for the 'Eloise', a beautiful, rare shell unique to Masirah. The collection of live specimens of mollusc and coral is strictly prohibited.

Nightlife on Masirah is limited to 'labour and delivery' among the turtle population – all other entertainment is left to the imagination. High tide on the southwestern shore offers idyllic **swimming**, but the other coast should be treated with caution due to strong currents.

Bait is available from the fish factories – during winter you can expect to catch something using the simplest hand line.

🛏 Sleeping

With a 4WD, camping in any of the deserted bays on the west coast or at the southern tip is recommended. If you choose the east coast, don't forget you cannot light fires on a turtle beach.

There are now four hotels on the island, three of which are in Hilf and within walking distance of the ferry jetties.

Danat Al-Khaleej Hotel HOTEL $
(☑25 501533; www.danat-hotel.com; Main Rd, Hilf; r OR25; ☏) The 10 rooms of this new little hotel, 1km from the jetties on the road leading southeast out of town, sport large, fancy rooms with exotic repro furniture. The custard-yellow walls and red carpet are an unusual design choice but the management is friendly.

Serabis Hotel HOTEL $
(☑99 446680; dira2008@omantel.net.om; Corniche, Hilf; s/d OR18/25) The gloomy lobby of this Egyptian-run hotel is a bit dispiriting, as are the basic, cavernous rooms. It is clean, however, and the location at the end of the corniche (next to Al-Maha petrol station) is convenient for night-time strolls in the town.

Masirah Hotel HOTEL $
(☑25 504401; booking@omantel.net.om; Main Rd, Hilf; r OR21; ☑☏) With multiple beds, commodious bathrooms and a lot of Arabic chintz, you can forgive the goats sitting on the doorstep. This is the biggest and most established of Hilf's three budget hotels and it has a reasonable in-house restaurant.

Masira Island Resort RESORT $$
(☑25 504274; www.masiraislandresort.com; Cross-Island Rd; r OR75; ☏🏊) 🍴 This attractive, landscaped resort is a 10-minute walk across soft sand to the water's edge; turtles nest on the beach. The restaurant is the only place on Masirah for international cuisine and there's a bar. You need your own transport to reach the hotel.

🍴 Eating & Drinking

Under the guise of the ubiquitous coffeeshop, you can find Indian, Chinese and seafood, in addition to the usual Arabic fare, peppering the main street through Hilf. Ask at your hotel for current recommendations

as the restaurants change as quickly as the expat staff marooned on the island. For Turkish kebabs, Shatti Masirah Coffeeshop, between the crossroads and Masirah Hotel, is an old favourite.

Basic provisions can be found in the souq in Hilf. Abu Shabeeb is the most comprehensive supermarket in town but if you require any 'must-haves', bring them with you.

ℹ Information

Limited information about the island is available from the hotels. Alternatively, try asking in **Explore Masirah** (☑98 186161, 25 504442; ⊗8am-9pm) next to the Serabis Hotel – Masirah's first and only tourist operator.

ℹ Getting There & Away

Getting to the ferry terminal at Shana'a is theoretically feasible by public transport but not practical as there is no direct service from Muscat and unhelpful connections mean that you can easily get marooned in the interior without a hotel. It's incomparably better to drive; consider hiring a car in Sur and making a round trip from there if you don't fancy the long slog from Muscat.

A left turn off the Sinaw–Duqm road at Mahout leads, after 18km, to Hijj (also known as Hay). Shana'a is a further 45km away along a sealed road. Turn right across the salt flats (which turn a stunning red when the algae is in bloom) at a sign saying 'Hijj 43km, An-Najda 13km'. Muscat to Shana'a takes about five or six hours by car. Alternatively, take the stunning new coast road across the edge of the Sharqiya Sands – the closest you can get to the desert experience from a sealed road anywhere on the Arabian Peninsula (five hours from Muscat, three hours from Sur).

The trip by ferry from Shana'a, near the desolate salt flats of Barr al-Hickman, is certainly characterful. The journey to Hilf usually takes 1½ hours – a lot longer when the boat gets beached on a sand bar – and the cost is OR10 each way per car; foot passengers travel free. Ferries run from morning until evening, but only during high tide. They run roughly every two hours but leave when full. The last guaranteed boat in either direction is at 5pm. Tickets are bought on the ferry. From Hilf, be aware that the ferries leave from all three jetties: ask locally, or spot the smoke, to guess which ferry will leave first and from where. During weekends and holidays the queue for the ferry on the mainland can be very long and entail chaotic waits of up to three hours or more with no opportunity to reverse out if you change your mind about waiting. There's no booking service. A new high-speed ferry service is promised for 2014.

ⓘ Getting Around

The only way to explore the island is by car or on foot – the taxis only service Hilf. There is no car-hire service on Masirah so the most feasible option for getting around is to bring your own vehicle. A sealed road circumnavigates the island but you'll need a 4WD to get close enough to the sea to enjoy it or to camp by it.

NIZWA & THE MOUNTAINS

This dramatic, mountainous region is one of the biggest tourist destinations in Oman, and for good reason. The area has spectacular scenery, including Jebel Shams (Oman's highest mountain), Wadi Ghul (the Grand Canyon of Arabia) and Jebel Akhdar (the fruit bowl of Oman). In addition, some of the country's best forts can be seen in Nizwa, Bahla and Jabrin.

Many of the sights from Nizwa to Jabrin can be managed on a long day trip from Muscat, and all tour companies in the capital organise such trips. The region deserves more than just a fleeting visit, however, especially if adding 4WD excursions into the jebel (mountain).

With a 4WD, an exciting three-day round trip from Muscat can be made via Nizwa, crossing over the mountains from Al-Hamra and descending to Rustaq and the Batinah Plain.

Nizwa نزوى

☑ 25 / POP 84,500

The historic town of Nizwa, two hours from Muscat along a good highway, lies on a plain surrounded by a thick palm oasis and some of Oman's highest mountains. It forms a natural gateway to the historic sites of Bahla and Jabrin, and for excursions up Jebel Akhdar and Jebel Shams.

Only half a century ago, British explorer Wilfred Thesiger was forced to steer clear of Nizwa: his Bedouin companions were convinced that he wouldn't survive the ferocious conservatism of the town and refused to let him enter. He'd have been amazed to find that Nizwa is now the second-biggest tourist destination in Oman. The seat of factional imams until the 1950s, Nizwa, or the 'Pearl of Islam' as it's sometimes called, is still a conservative town, however, and appreciates a bit of decorum from its visitors.

◉ Sights

Nizwa Fort FORT

(admission 500 baisa; ☉9am-4pm Sat-Thu; ℗) Built over 12 years in the 17th century by Sultan bin Saif al-Yaruba, the first imam of the Ya'aruba dynasty, the fort is famed for its 40m-tall round tower. It's worth climbing to the top of the tower to see the date plantations encircling the town and the view of the Hajar Mountains.

★**Nizwa Souq** SOUQ

(☉9am-1pm & 5-8pm Sat-Thu, 5-8pm Fri; ℗) The fruit and vegetable, meat and fish markets are housed in new buildings, behind the great, crenulated piece of city wall that overlooks the wadi. If you're not put off by the smell of heaving bulls and irritable goats, the livestock souq (in full swing between 7am and 9am on Friday) is worth a look. It occupies a small plot of land beyond the souq walls, left of the entrance.

You'll have to try hard to find a bargain for antiques and silver at the other end of the souq (nearest the fort), but local craftsmanship is good. Nizwa is particularly famous for crafting silver khanjars. Today Indian or Pakistani silversmiths often work under an Omani mastercraftsman, especially for pieces designed for tourists, but the workmanship is exquisite. Prices range from OR50 for a tourist piece to over OR500 for an authentic piece.

🛏 Sleeping

All of Nizwa's hotels are located along Hwy 15 between Birkat al-Mawz and Nizwa. You need to book ahead between October and April.

Majan Guesthouse HOTEL $

(☑25 431910; www.majangh.com; s/d OR25/30) With Arab decor, carved wooden doors with brass fixtures and a gift shop in the foyer, this hotel makes a genuine effort for the tourist trade. Next to the Hungry Bunny fast-food outlet, the hotel is 5km from the khanjar roundabout.

Tanuf Residency HOTEL $

(☑25 411601; fax 25 411059; s/d OR18/20) This one-star hotel attempts some frivolity with festoons of plastic flowers hanging from the ceiling but the effort would be better spent keeping the simple accommodation clean. With so little accommodation in town, it may be better than nothing. The hotel is 4.5km from the khanjar roundabout.

★**Falaj Daris Hotel** HOTEL $$
(☑25 410500; www.falajdarishotel.com; s/d OR58.500/64; P⊛⛱) This delightful hotel, wrapped around two swimming pools and a bar and with a vista of toothy mountains beyond, is the most characterful hotel in Nizwa. The rooms are more pleasant in the new block, but the older courtyard and pool have some welcome shade under which is arrayed the evening buffet – a friendly, tasty affair with long tables for tour groups.

Wi-fi is available (OR1 for one hour) in the business centre. The hotel is 4km from the *khanjar* roundabout.

Al-Diyar Hotel HOTEL $$
(☑25 412402; www.aldiyarhotel.com; s/d OR35/45; ⊛⛱) There is some charm in the gypsum and marble foyer, complete with gift kiosk, but that charm doesn't extend to the plain, large, no-nonsense rooms. In a popular town with very few beds, however, this no criticism. The hotel, which has a large restaurant and wi-fi (OR2 for 24 hours), is 3.5km from the *khanjar* roundabout.

Golden Tulip Nizwa Hotel HOTEL $$
(☑25 431616; www.goldentulip.com; s/d OR82/94; P⊛⛱) This rather pretentious, marble-clad hotel has a vast foyer but somehow misses the feeling of Omani hospitality, despite often hosting members of the royal family. Contrary to first impressions, the internal bar with the dancing damsels offers an innocent form of entertainment and tourists are welcome. The hotel is near the Jebel Akhdar junction, 18km from the *khanjar* roundabout.

✕ Eating

★**Al-Zuhly Restaurant** SHWARMA $
(meals OR2.500; ⊙noon-11pm) This is a simple venue with outdoor seating on the pavement but it has one of the best night-time views in Oman. Situated opposite the souq, the cafe overlooks the fort and mosque, both of which are lit up spectacularly at night. It sells *shwarma* and kebabs, and is always busy with locals who generally pull up in the car and toot for a takeaway.

Al-Masharef Turkish Restaurant TURKISH $
(☑95 605335; meals OR3; ⊙11am-midnight) On the Muscat–Nizwa Hwy, next to Tanuf Residency, this friendly restaurant has indoor seating, welcome in the summer after a dusty day's drive in the jebel. Kebabs and mezze are the most popular fare.

Bin Ateeq Restaurant OMANI $
(☑25 410466; off Main St, Nizwa; meals OR3; ⊙5-10pm) Part of a small chain of Omani-style restaurants, this is one of the few places where you have the opportunity to sample local dishes. It is just a pity that the restaurant hasn't risen to the challenge of increased tourists looking for an authentic experience because the rather grubby private rooms are not the best ambience for dinner on the ground. Still, it's worth a try.

❶ Information

Banks and money changers are along the main street that runs from the fort complex to the book roundabout. The post office is inside the souq.

For those with a special interest in Nizwa, a website (www.nizwa.net) offers interesting insider information.

❶ Getting There & Away

ONTC buses run from Muscat to Nizwa Souq (OR1.900, two hours 20 minutes, 8am and 2.30pm daily). Buses for Muscat from Nizwa leave at 8am and 5.30pm.

You can catch the bus from Muscat to Salalah at 8.30am, noon and 9pm. The fare from Nizwa to Salalah is OR6, and the journey takes 10 hours. Telephone the **Ruwi bus station** (☑24 701294) in Muscat to reserve a seat and check times.

Engaged-taxi/shared-taxi/microbus fares from Nizwa to Rusayl roundabout in Muscat are OR20/4/2 (to Ruwi add OR1.500/1). Nizwa to Ibri costs OR20/3/2 by engaged taxi/shared taxi/microbus.

Coming from Muscat, the bus stop and taxi stand are in the middle of the wadi in front of the fort complex, 800m past the *khanjar* roundabout. When the wadi is flowing, the road is impassable at this point, hence the bridge further upstream that leads to the book roundabout. Buses for Ibri leave from the book roundabout. Buses for Salalah leave from the outskirts of Nizwa at the Farq roundabout.

Microbuses (300 baisa) link the hotels that lie along Hwy 15, the old Muscat–Nizwa road, with the town centre.

Around Nizwa

About a 30-minute drive from Nizwa, there are a number of fine destinations that can be visited on a day trip from the town, including Al-Hoota Cave, Misfat and Al-Hamra.They all lie up against the sloping shoulder of the Hajar Mountain range and can be reached by turning right off the Nizwa–Bahla road, 30.6km from Nizwa, at the Omanoil petrol station. Brown signs lead from there to each of the Lonely Planet–reviewed destinations. There's no public transport.

★ **Al-Hoota Cave** CAVE
(☑ 244 98 258; www.alhootacave.com; adult/child OR5.500/3; ☺ 9am-1pm & 2-6pm Sat, Sun & Tue-Thu, 9am-noon & 2-6pm Fri; ℗) This cave, which is embellished with stalactites and stalagmites, has developed into a popular attraction. The interactive on-site geological museum explores some of the features that have made Oman internationally renowned among geologists. There is also a gift shop, pleasant restaurant and outdoor cafe with a fine view of pale hills.

A train takes you into the cave and a 40-minute walking tour passes by an underground lake with blind cave-fish. The last tour in the morning and afternoon is 45 minutes before closing time. If you turn left when leaving the cave complex, the road takes you (after 2km) to a small park next to a wadi with flowing water: it makes a good place for a picnic.

Prebooking is required as the cave can only accommodate 750 visitors per day and is often closed due to flooding after rains. No cameras are allowed in the cave – they must be deposited in safety boxes.

Al-Hamra الحمراء
☑ 25 / POP 19,500

This venerable village at the foot of the Hajar Mountains is one of the oldest in Oman, and is interesting for its wonderfully well-preserved row of two- and three-storey mudbrick houses built in the Yemeni style. There are many abandoned houses in the upper parts of the village and it's easy to gain an idea of a lifestyle that has only changed in the past three decades.

To reach the old part of town, follow the main road, past the turning for Misfat. The road skirts uphill above the old buildings until it reaches a tree-filled roundabout. Park near the large, square mud building and explore the town and plantation on foot.

⊙ Sights

Bilad al-Sifah MUSEUM
(admission OR3; ☺ 9am-5.30pm) This quirky museum is more open house than historical display. Three ladies accompany guests around their traditional house (half of which is missing the roof) in the aged and crumbling village of Al-Hamra. They demonstrate the culinary arts of juniper oil production, Omani bread-making and coffee bean grinding and there's an opportunity for a photoshoot in traditional regional costume. Sitting cross-legged in the *majlis* (seating area), surrounded by photos of local sheikhs, sampling coffee and dates and exchanging sign language with the ladies, is an experience not to be missed.

The museum is in the old part of Al-Hamra. Park by the roundabout at the western end of town and walk along the street past the historic old Yemeni-style buildings. The ladies will spot you before you see them in the interior gloom of the downstairs entrance.

🛏 Sleeping & Eating

★ **The View** ECOLODGE $$
(☑ booking office 24 400873, at the lodge 97 748031; www.theviewoman.com; half board r with/without view OR80/70; ℗) ✿ High above Al-Hamra, this comfortable tented accommodation boasts a superb location hovering over the Al-Hamra basin. A competent restaurant, boasting its own kitchen garden, and excellent staff have won this lodge many regular visitors so reservations are necessary. You can bring your own wine.

To reach the lodge, follow the brown signs from the village of Al-Hamra, a dizzying 1400m below. The 7.5km ascent is steep and 4WD is essential. A 1km walk from the View leads to some interesting villages.

Misfat مسفاه
☑ 25

There is a sealed road from Al-Hamra up to this mountain-hugging village (which is sometimes spelt Misfah), making it one of the few mountain villages that is easily accessible without a 4WD. The mountain flank, draped in date plantations and a terraced sequence of stone houses in the foreground, is very picturesque and often seen in promotional literature on Oman. For the best view of the entire village, turn right by the tourist park, pausing to read the informative Ministry of Tourism signboards. The boards indicate a number of great hikes in the area, ranging from an easy 30-minute stroll through the village to a nine-hour hike in the mountains.

Accommodation is available at Misfah Guest House (☑ 99 338491; bandb.misfah@

gmail.com; half board s/d OR30/50). This family-run enterprise, in the heart of Misfat village, is housed in a wonderful old building – it's a family heirloom. One of the few places to sample genuine Omani home-cooked dishes, it's possible to call in just for lunch (OR5). Beware though: once you have descended through the village and entered the enchanted garden of date, lemon and mango trees, you won't want to leave.

Reservations are essential – not least to ensure you find the way from the car park, a five- or 10-minute walk through a labyrinth of alleys, tunnels and plantations paths.

Mountain Road via Hatt & Wadi Bani Awf

الحمراء الرواد بني عوف

This truly spectacular road over the Western Hajar Mountains affords some of the best views in Oman. It can be accomplished as a long round trip from Muscat or as a more leisurely outing from Nizwa to Rustaq. With two sleeping options along the route, and a third nearing completion on the summit, the road could enable a major exploration of the mountains. Although the mountain part of the route is only 70km long, it takes about four hours to drive and a 4WD is essential to negotiate the sustained, off-road descent into Wadi Bani Awf. This route passes through remote, rugged country and you should take the necessary precautions (spare tyre, jack, water, warm clothing, walking shoes and basic provisions). Check weather conditions before you leave and do not attempt the journey during or after rains.

Follow the signs for Al-Hoota Cave from the Nizwa–Bahla road. You'll see a brown sign, just before reaching the cave, indicating Bilad Sayt (Balad Seet). The road, zig-zagging up the mountain in front of you, is sealed for the entire ascent. Look out for wild palms and clumps of aloe.

Zero your vehicle's odometer at the base of the road and at 23.9km you will come to the Sharfat Al-Alamayn viewpoint, on the saddle of the ridge: this is the highest point in the road. It's worth spending time here to enjoy the scenery and to look for wolf traps (piles of stone with a slate trap door) before the long descent into the village of Hatt.

After Hatt, the road continues for another 6km, skirting past **Bilad Sayt**, which is off the road to the left. The village is well worth a detour. With its picture-postcard perfection of terraced fields and sun-baked houses, it's one of the prettiest villages in the area. The villagers prefer visitors to park outside and walk in or simply view the village from a distance.

At 43.8km, the road passes the entrance to aptly named **Snake Gorge**, a popular destination for adventure hikers and climbers, and through the middle of a football pitch. From here the main track meanders around the mountain to the exit of Snake Gorge at 49.6km, signalled by a neat row of trees. If you're here in the spring, look out for a beautiful yellow-flowering tree (*Tecomella Al-Zamah*) that some say is indigenous to the area.

Continue along the main track into Wadi Bani Awf ignoring the left fork at 57.2km that leads into Wadi Sahten. At 59.4km you will pass through the small wadi village of

MISFAT – AT THE HEART OF THE HAJAR MOUNTAINS

For a magnificent introduction to life among the date palms on the flank of Oman's highest mountain, a walk through the picture-perfect village of Misfat is highly recommended. Understandably, locals insist on visitors parking on the edge of the village and you'll see why as you begin to walk through the narrow alleyways of the village and along the edge of the encompassed plantations on the well-marked trails. This is one of the few villages that actively welcomes tourists but in return visitors are requested to respect marked no-go areas and to refrain from picking fruit – the village's main livelihood.

If you're not keen on finding your own way between the flowing *aflaj* and abundant terraces of crops, the village guest house offers a three-hour guided walking tour (OR20) with a local resident. This is quite the best way of learning about life in a traditional Omani community at the heart of the Hajar Mountains.

Al-Teekah and eventually arrive at Hwy 13 at 69.7km. Turn left for Rustaq, or right for Nakhal and Muscat. Road construction in Wadi Bani Awf may mean you need to detour through Wadi Sahten to Rustaq.

🛏 Sleeping & Eating

Al-Hoota Resthouse   HOTEL $

(☑ 92 822473; hootaoman@hotmail.com; r OR20, chalet OR30; P) 🅿 Run by the local Al-Abri family, this simple guesthouse has a range of comfortable, uncomplicated rooms and chalets near Sharfat al-Alamayn, the highest point on the mountain road to Hatt. A buffet dinner (OR5) can be rustled up with some notice. A 3km, four-hour trek to a local village is one of many walking options from the guesthouse.

Tourist Village Resort Motel   HOTEL $

(☑ 97 588818; r OR25; P) This no-frills guesthouse at the opening of Wadi Bani Awf has 11 simple rooms and an occasional swimming pool (usable only when water is available) set in a semi-wilderness of flowering trees and shrubs. A restaurant is planned but in the meantime, dinner is a 'bring your own' affair.

Birkat Al-Mawz   بركة الموز

☑ 25 / POP 10,000

The name of this village roughly translates as 'Banana Pool' – a suitable name, as a quick drive through the village plantation will reveal.

Although there is a fort, **Bait al-Radidah** (admission 500 baisa; ⊙ 8am-4pm Sat-Thu, to 11am Fri), and some interesting old buildings, most people only venture into Birkat al-Mawz to begin the drive (or strenuous day hike) up Wadi Muaydin to the Saiq Plateau on Jebel Akhdar. It's a good place to buy provisions as these are not readily available from Jebel Akhdar.

To hire a 4WD for the ascent to Jebel Akhdar, visit **Al-Mousel Rent-a-Car** (☑ 92 311173, 25 443767; almouseltourism@hotmail.com; ⊙ 7.30am-8pm). It charges OR35 for a vehicle that can be hired between 7.30am and 8pm. Staff can arrange camping trips for a minimum group of four to Jebel Akhdar from OR19 per person.

Birkat al-Mawz lies on the old Muscat–Nizwa Rd, 111km from the Rusayl roundabout in Muscat and 24km from the *khanjar* roundabout in Nizwa.

Jebel Akhdar   الجبل الأخضر

☑ 25

Without a guide or some inside information, Jebel Akhdar (Green Mountain) may seem something of a misnomer to the first-time visitor. Firstly, Jebel Akhdar refers not to a mountain as such, but to an area that encompasses the great **Saiq Plateau**, at 2000m above sea level. Secondly, the jebel keeps its fecundity well hidden in a labyrinth of wadis and terraces where the cooler mountain air (temperatures during December to March can drop to -5°C) and greater rainfall (hailstones even) encourage prize pomegranates, apricots and other fruit. With a day or two to explore this 'top of the beanstalk', the determined visitor will soon stumble across the gardens and **orchards** that make this region so justly prized. Ask your hotel for a hand-drawn map picking out some of the highlights of the area.

◉ Sights & Activities

It helps to think of Jebel Akhdar as two separate areas – an upper plateau, and a lower plateau on which the main town of **Saiq** is located. In a weekend, you can spend one day exploring each. On the edge of the lower plateau, in a south-facing crescent high above Wadi al-Muaydin, are spectacularly arranged terraced villages, where most of the market-gardening takes place and where old men and young boys sell honey and fruit by the roadside. Head for **Diana's Viewpoint** – named after the late Diana, Princess of Wales, who visited this vertiginous vista – with its natural pavement of fossils and dizzying view of the terraces below. The viewpoint is en route to the dangling village of Al-Aqor. **Wadi Bani Habib** with its old ruined village and abundant walnut trees is also located on the lower plateau and is a popular and picturesque place for a walk. For a longer hike, after allowing time to adjust to the thin, high-altitude air, walk from Al-Aqor to Seeq around the edge of the crescent. This is particularly rewarding during spring when the fragrant, pink roses from which rosewater is made are in bloom.

The upper plateau is accessed via a right turn up the mountain near Jebel Akhdar Hotel. Here you can picnic among magnificent mature **juniper trees** in a perfect campsite about 2km after the sultan's experimental farm. The farm, which is closed to the public, develops strains of vegetable and fruit suitable to the extreme Omani climate. From the campsite, hike through wild olive and fig trees to sunset point (a left turn before the school). A vast mountain resort is under construction on the edge of the jebel, offering spectacular views across the mountains.

You are only permitted to approach Jebel Akhdar by 4WD. There have been many fatal accidents caused by people trying to make the long descent in a 2WD, using their brakes rather than changing gears.

The only alternative to a 4WD is a walking trail through the terraced villages of Wadi al-Muaydin to the Saiq Plateau. You'll need a guide and you should allow six hours from Birkat al-Mawz at the bottom of the wadi to reach the plateau (12 hours return). Beware: it's an unrelenting uphill slog!

🛏 Sleeping

⭐ **Sahab Hotel** HOTEL **$$**
(☑ 25 429288; www.sahab-hotel.com; r from OR83; P@🛜🌁) 🍴 Blending in with the local stone, this lovely hotel boasts spectacular views across the horseshoe crescent of Jebel Akhdar. It's a travesty that competitors have chosen to build a far-less sympathetic hotel right next door. As such, it's worth paying the extra for a deluxe room (from OR97) overlooking the hotel's wilderness herb garden rather than the construction site.

To reach the hotel, follow signs for Al Aqor 500m from the Al Maha petrol station in Saiq.

Jebel al-Akhdar Hotel HOTEL **$$**
(☑ 25 429009; www.jabalakhdharhotel.com.om; s/d OR42/55; P) Perched like an eyrie on the edge of Saiq Plateau, this hotel feels empty even when full. With an open fire in the lobby in winter and a wind howling around the wacky stained-glass domes, it at least has character. It's easy to spot on the main road, 2km before the town of Saiq.

ℹ Getting There & Around

Access to Jebel Akhdar is via the town of Birkat al-Mawz. Follow the brown signs for Wadi al-Muaydin, off Rte 15, and head for the fort. After 6km you will reach a checkpoint where you will have to satisfy the police that your car has 4WD. Saiq is about 30km beyond the checkpoint and the main road, after a series of steep switchbacks up the mountainside, leads straight there.

As yet there is no public transport to the area, but several tour companies, including **National Travel & Tourism** (Map p120; ☑ 24 660376), offer day trips from OR130 per person. It is cheaper and possibly more rewarding to hire a 4WD in Birkat al-Mawz and stay at one of the two hotels.

Jebel Shams جبل شمس

Oman's highest mountain, Jebel Shams (Mountain of the Sun; 3075m), is best known not for its peak but for the view into the spectacularly deep Wadi Ghul lying alongside it. The straight-sided Wadi Ghul is known locally as the Grand Canyon of Arabia as it fissures abruptly between the flat canyon rims, exposing vertical cliffs of 1000m and more. Until recently, there was

---

ROSEWATER

If you are lucky enough to find yourself in the small village of Al-Ayn on Jebel Akhdar in April, then you will be sure to have your nose assailed by the redolent Jebel Akhdar rose. Each rose has a maximum of 35 petals, but if you spend time counting them, you may well be missing the point. The point in cultivating these beautiful briars is not for the flower but for the aroma. For hundreds of years, the rose petals have been harvested here to produce rosewater (*attar* in Arabic) – that all-important post-dinner courtesy, sprinkled on the hands of guests from slender, silver vessels.

The yellowing bottles lined up in the sticky shed of a rosewater workshop suggest the petals have been boiled and discarded. This in fact is not the case. While the exact production of the precious perfume is kept a family secret, anyone on Jebel Akhdar will tell you the petals are not boiled but steamed over a fire with an arrangement of apparatus that brings to mind home chemistry sets. But the alchemy, according to Nasser 'bin Jebel', whose father's hands are ironically blackened each spring with rosewater production, is not so much in the process of evaporation but in the process of picking. If you see people dancing through the roses before dawn, chances are they are not calling on the genies of the jebel to assist the blooms, but plucking petals when the dew still lies on the bushes and the oil is at its most intense.

nothing between the nervous driver and a plunge into the abyss, but now an iron railing at least indicates the most precipitous points along the track and a couple of rough car parks along the rim pick out some of the best viewpoints into the canyon.

While there is nothing 'to do' exactly at the top, the area makes a wonderful place to take photographs, have a picnic (there are no shops or facilities so bring your own), enjoy a hike...or buy a carpet.

You need only step from your vehicle and you'll find **carpet sellers** appear from nowhere across the barren landscape clutching piles of striped red-and-black goat-hair rugs. Weaving is a profitable local industry, but don't expect a bargain. A large rug can cost anything from OR30 to OR80, depending on the colours used and the complexity of the pattern. Weaving is men's work on Jebel Shams: spinning the wool is women's work. If you can't find room for a carpet, a spindle made from juniper wood makes a more portable souvenir.

Jebel Shams is a feasible day trip from Nizwa (or a long day trip from Muscat), but to savour its eerie beauty, consider staying overnight on the plateau near the canyon rim at one of the low-key accommodations.

🛏 Sleeping & Eating

Jabal Shems Heights
Guest House   MOUNTAIN CAMP **$**
(☑92 721999; www.jabalshems.com; half board in tent or cabin OR40; P) Situated at the start of the walking route to the summit of Jebel Shams (route W4, seven to 12 hours), this camp offers rooms that are little more than a concrete shell with air-con and lino floors. There's hot water in the attached shower cubicle, however, and a small restaurant on site. Be warned, it is freezing in winter.

Sunrise Camp   MOUNTAIN CAMP **$$**
(☑97 100791; www.sunriseresort-om.com; half-board in Arabic tent OR50, chalet OR60 ; P) In a dramatic location overlooking a mountain precipice, 50-minutes' drive from Al-Hamra, this remote camp makes for a peaceful retreat. Beds are offered in Arabic-style tents or concrete chalets (all with private bathrooms). Guests retreat inside the dining room during bitter winter nights. Pitch your own tent for OR10 including supper and breakfast. A three-hour marked trail offers fine views of Rustaq, thousands of kilometres below.

To reach the camp, follow the directions to Jebel Shams but turn left at the camp's signboard a few kilometres after the end of the sealed road, before you reach the Jebel Shams plateau. The graded road (4WD essential) zigzags up a neighbouring flank of the mountain.

Jebel Shams Resort   MOUNTAIN CAMP **$$**
(☑99 382639; www.jebelshamsresort.com; half board tents s/d OR35/50, cabins s/d OR55/70; P❄) Offering cosy stone cabins with bathroom, verandah and heater and some Arabic tents popular with Omanis at weekends, this camp is so close to the canyon rim, you'll have to be strapped down if you're a sleepwalker. Mountain-bike hire (OR5 per hour), pitch and putt, and air-rifle practice (OR1 for 10 shots) are available. Pitch your own tent for OR4 (OR16 with food).

The camp is signposted from the Shell petrol station in Al-Hamra, 39km (40 minutes' drive) up the flank of Jebel Shams.

ℹ️ Getting There & Away

The junction for Jebel Shams is clearly signposted off the Nizwa–Bahla road, 30.6km from the book roundabout in Nizwa. Turn right at the Omanoil petrol station then left after 11.8km at a Shell petrol station and follow the sealed road along the bottom of the wadi. At 9.1km after the Shell petrol station, the road passes the vacant **village of Ghul** at the entrance of the Wadi Ghul canyon (you can access the canyon for a short distance only), providing a good photo opportunity.

The road climbs through a series of sharp hairpin bends to the top of Jebel Shams. The road then gives way to a well-graded track that climbs eventually to the military radar site on the summit (closed to visitors). There's a right turn just before the summit that leads, after 10 minutes' drive or so, to the canyon rim, 28km from the Shell station.

It is possible but foolhardy to attempt the drive without a 4WD, and car-hire agencies won't thank you for the uninsurable abuse of their car. There is no public transport here.

For a rewarding drive with spectacular views, you can continue up the graded track towards the summit of Jebel Shams (the very top is a restricted area, closed to the public) and follow the signs for Krub and Al Marrat. Continue around the loop via the Sunrise Resort, passing the ruins of ancient burial sites. A graded road from this area is under construction and by the end of 2013 will lead to Rustaq, cutting 90 minutes off the current drive time.

Bahla بهلا

☑ 25 / POP 58,200

Ask anyone in Oman what Bahla means to them and historians will single it out for its fort, expats for its potteries; but any Omani not resident in the town will respond with *'jinn'*. These devilishly difficult spirits are blamed for all manner of evil-eye activities, but you're unlikely to encounter them unless you understand Arabic, as they are considered a living legend in the folklore of the country.

☉ Sights

★ Bahla Fort   FORT
(www.virtualbahla.com; admission 500 baisa; ☺9am-4pm Sat-Thu, 8-11am Fri) A remarkable set of battlements is noticeable at every turn in the road, running impressively along the wadi and making Bahla one of the most comprehensive walled cities in the world. These walls extend for several kilometres and are said to have been designed 600 years ago by a woman. Part and parcel of the battlements is the impressive 12th-century fort, built by the Bani Nebhan tribe and one of the most extensive in Oman. After many years of restoration it has finally opened to the public and has easily proved why it was granted Unesco World Heritage Site status in 1987. As yet there are no interpretative panels or other tourist information but you can gain an idea of the purpose of each room by referring to the website. A booklet is planned.

OMAN BAHLA

OFF THE BEATEN TRACK

ADVENTURE IN THE HAJAR MOUNTAINS

Most people would be content with peering gingerly over the rim of Wadi Ghul (Oman's Grand Canyon) but there are those for whom this isn't close enough. If you are the kind who likes to edge to the ledge, then try some of the following adventure activities in the Hajar Mountains.

Hike the Balcony Walk The return hike along route W6 from the rim village of Al-Khateem (3km beyond Jebel Shams Resort) to the well-named hanging village of Sap Bani Khamis is a favourite with thrill-seekers. Abandoned more than 30 years ago, it is reached along the popular but vertiginous balcony walk: one false step in this five-hour 'moderate hike' will send you sailing (without the 'ab') 500m into the void.

Cycle at High Altitude For those with lungs built to withstand punishing altitude, try Bike & Hike Oman's (p205) high-altitude tour that pedals between 1600m and 2300m with two canyons thrown in.

Climb in Snake Gorge If you're comfortable with an extreme angle of dangle, then you might like the climbing opportunities in the upper reaches of this narrow gorge. Enthusiasts have thrown up 'via ferrata' lines allowing those with a head for heights to pirouette on a tightrope 60m above certain death.

Rappel into Majlis al-Jinn The 158m drop into this cavern is like a descent into Hades. Fabled as the second-largest cavern in the world – bigger than St Peter's Basilica in Rome, bigger than Cheops' pyramid in Giza – this is one mighty hole. Don't count on *jinn* (genies) for company; the only spirit you're likely to feel is your own, petering out with the rope as you reach for rock bottom. Named after the first person to descend into the shaft of sunlight at the bottom of the cavern, Cheryl's Drop is the deepest free-fall rappel in Oman.

Drive the Mountain Road to Hatt You don't need to see the mangled heaps of metal at the bottom of the vertical cliffs to realise that this is one off-road route that needs extreme concentration. If impossible inclines, narrow gaps and heart-stopping drop-offs appeal, this five-hour route is for you.

With dozens of challenging hikes, 200 bolted climbing routes, and an almost uncharted cave system, Oman is one adrenalin rush still pretty much waiting to happen. If you want to be in with the pioneers, contact the mountain camps on Jebel Shams (guided hikes cost from around OR50 from the camps for a maximum of four people). Alternatively, contact Muscat Diving & Adventure Centre (p128) which tailor-makes trips for the extremely edgy or Bike & Hike Oman (p205) which offers exciting pedal-power tours.

Bahla Potteries
CRAFT

(◷8am-1pm & 4.30-6pm Sat-Thu) All over Oman you'll spot terracotta pots with simple ribbed decorations at the entrances to smart villas and hotels. The famous potteries where these beloved vessels are made are humble in comparison, buried in the backstreets of Bahla.

To reach the potteries, follow the main road through the town centre towards the plantations. After 500m you will come to a number of potteries; the traditional unglazed water pots cost a couple of rials. A large 'Ali Baba' pot fetches around OR40. Beware, the streets are very narrow here and it is easy to get a 4WD stuck. It's better to walk if you're not planning to make a big purchase.

Old Souq
SOUQ

(◷6-10am) Bahla has a traditional souq with homemade ropes and *fadl* (large metal platters used for feeding the whole family) for sale, and a beautiful tree shading the tiny, central courtyard. To find the souq, turn off Hwy 21, the main Nizwa–Ibri road, opposite the fort; the souq entrance is 100m on the right.

🛏 Sleeping & Eating

Jibreen Hotel
HOTEL $

(☑ 25 363340; www.jibrenhotel.com; s/d OR30/40; P⊚) Conveniently situated on the main Bahla–Ibri road by the Jabrin junction. With sky-blue *rondelles* in the ceiling, rag-rolled walls, Egyptian gilt-edged furniture and luxurious drapes in the wi-fi equipped bedrooms, Jibreen Hotel is often full. With no other accommodation nearby, it's worth calling ahead.

ⓘ Information

There is a branch of the Nizwa-based **Al-Huzaily Travel** (Travel City; ☑ 25 419313; www.alhuzaily. com) opposite the bus stop on the corner of the road that leads to the souq. It acts as an ad-hoc information centre.

ⓘ Getting There & Away

Microbuses to/from Nizwa cost OR1 and shared taxis cost OR2 (OR10 engaged). The trip takes about 45 minutes. The bus stop outside the fort advertises services at 10.55am and 5.25pm to Ibri and 8.05am and 5.12pm to Ruwi in Muscat. Probably of less interest are the services to Dubai at 2.10am and Salalah at 8.10pm.

Jabrin جبرين

Rising without competition from the surrounding plain, **Jabrin Castle** (admission 500 baisa; ◷9am-4pm Sat-Thu, 8-11am Fri) is an impressive sight. Even if you have seen a surfeit of forts at Nizwa and Bahla, Jabrin is one of the best preserved and most whimsical of them all.

Built in 1675 by Imam Bil-arab bin Sultan, it was an important centre of learning for astrology, medicine and Islamic law. Look out for the **date store**, to the right of the main entrance on the left-hand side. The juice of the fruit would have run along the channels into storage vats, ready for cooking or to assist women in labour. Note the elaborately **painted ceilings** with original floral motifs in many of the rooms.

Head for the flagpole for a bird's-eye view of the **latticed-window courtyard** at the heart of the keep. Finding these hidden rooms is part of the fun and the defensive mechanism of Jabrin. Try to locate the **burial chambers**, remarkable for their carved vaults. The **falaj** was not used for water but as an early air-con system. There is even a room earmarked for the sultan's favourite horse.

Jabrin is clearly signposted 7km off the Bahla–Ibri road. Beware of hitching from the junction, as it is an exposed 4km walk if you're out of luck. It may be better to engage a return taxi (OR7) from Bahla.

Bat & Al-Ayn بات و العين

Unlike the discreet modern cemeteries of Oman, where a simple, unmarked stone indicates the head and feet of the buried corpse, the ancient tombs of Bat and Al-Ayn rise defiantly from the tops of the surrounding hills, as in a bid for immortality. Not much is known about the tombs except that they were constructed between 2000 and 3000 BC, during the Hafit and the Umm an Nar cultures.

Known as 'beehive tombs' (on account of their shape) these free-standing structures of piled stones were designed to protect the remains of up to 200 people. There is barely a hilltop without one, and because of the extent of the site, which lies on an ancient caravan route, the whole area has been declared a Unesco World Heritage Site.

While Bat has the largest concentration of tombs, the best-preserved tombs are near

Al-Ayn. If you time your visit for an hour or so before sunset, **Jebel Misht** (Comb Mountain) makes the most stunning backdrop for the highly atmospheric site.

To reach Bat, take the road signposted for Ad Dariz off Hwy 21 in Ibri and zero your odometer. At 6.2km, look out for the **ruined village** of Al-Ghabbi on the left of the road. After 16.2km, turn right for Bat and left at the small roundabout. Veer right to Al-Wahrah at 17.7km through fertile Al-Hajar Wadi and at 31.6km turn left for Wadi al-Ayn on the graded road that tends southeast through russet-coloured foothills. If you find yourself in the village of Bat, you've missed the turning! It takes a while to recognise the tombs, but once you've spotted one, you will see them on almost every hilltop either side of the track.

If you continue to the end of the graded road (about 55km) you'll come to a T-junction. A right turn here will take you back to Hwy 21. A left turn here takes you to Al-Ayn, beside the distinctive, triangular, tooth-edged Jebel Misht (one of the Oman 'Exotics' – a limestone mass that is out of sequence with the surrounding geology). The tombs are arranged in a line along a low ridge on the flank of this mountain. A two-bay parking slot opposite a mosque helps focus your eye in the right place; from here you can walk through the foreground plantation and up the hillside into the unfenced site.

Further along the road, signs lead up a winding paved road to the beautiful **mountain village** of Sint (Sant on some maps). With a 4WD and an off-road guide, there are some exciting mountain drives in this area. There is no public transport.

Ibri   ابرى

📞25 / POP 116,400

Ibri is the capital of the northern Al-Dhahirah Region. A modern town with a major highway, Hwy 21, linking it to the border town of Buraimi in the north, it has a few sights to keep a visitor busy including a newly renovated fort. The town also makes a friendly stopover en route from the UAE to Nizwa and a base for visiting the Unesco-protected tombs at Al-Ayn and Bat. If you have plenty of time to explore Oman, a loop can be made from Muscat via Nizwa, Bat and Ibri, through the mountains along the newly sealed Hwy 8 to Sohar and back along

the coast to Muscat – a trip of at least three days.

There are literally dozens of *shwarma* and rotisserie-chicken restaurants along Hwy 21 if you want to get a feel for local life. Banks and supermarkets are clustered around the central roundabout at the turning for Ibri Castle.

To reach Ibri by public transport, two daily buses leave Muscat at 8am and 2.30pm for Ibri (OR3.700, 4½ hours), passing through Nizwa at 10am and 4pm (OR1.500, 2½ hours). Buses leave for Muscat at 4pm. Microbuses cost OR2 from Nizwa and take two hours.

⊙ Sights

Ibri Castle   CASTLE
(admission 500 baisa; ⊙9am-4pm Sat-Thu, 8-11am Fri) Currently the more interesting and complete of the town's two forts, this imposing building has been restored recently and has brought the old quarter of Ibri to life. There is not too much to see inside but the views from the battlements are grand and the neighbouring gold souq and livestock markets are fun for wandering around.

⊨ Sleeping & Eating

Ibri Oasis Hotel   HOTEL $
(📞25 696172; iohotel@omantel.net.om; Hwy 21; s/d OR28.300/38.900; P🛱) The Ibri Oasis Hotel is on the Buraimi side of town. With a polished marble staircase and stained-glass windows, the hotel is mainly used by local dignitaries. Breakfast is OR3.700 and the dinner menu tends towards Indian cuisine.

Buraimi   البريمي

📞25 / POP 75,000

For many years the inseparable twin of Al-Ain, in the UAE, Buraimi is now divided from its alter ego by a large barbed-wire fence. This shouldn't be interpreted as a cooling of relations between Oman and its neighbour, just an attempt to sort out a border that leaked in both directions.

Buraimi has a large and interesting **fort** (admission 500 baisa; ⊙9am-4pm Sat-Thu) with decorations that give it a Saharan flourish in comparison with the austere exteriors of most of Oman's interior forts. The market opposite sells *barasti* (plaited palm fronds traditionally used for roofing and fencing) while just along the road a lively souq trades in locally grown fruit and veg from neighbouring plantations, dates and honey from the mountains, and a handful of crafts (including camel sticks and Bahla pottery) from around Oman. There are lots of local eateries in this area too.

Despite these attractions, it's fair to say that there's not much reason to make a special visit other than if you're using the UAE border for Al-Ain and Abu Dhabi. If you do visit, take your passport: you cannot pass through the border post (which is in Wadi Jizzi – 50km *before* the UAE border) without it.

There are several simple places to stay in town, the best of which is **Al-Buraimi Hotel** (fax 25 642010; r OR25; @ ≋), along the road to Sohar on the edge of town. It's dated, with lime green walls and cavernous corridors, but it is also clean and friendly. Three daily buses leave Muscat at 6.30am, 1pm and 4pm for Buraimi (OR4.200, 4½ hours).

SOHAR & BATINAH PLAIN

This flat and fertile strip of land between the Hajar Mountains and the Gulf of Oman is the country's breadbasket and most populous area. Interesting sites include the old castle towns of Nakhal and Rustaq, exhilarating off-road destinations such as Wadi Bani Awf and Wadi Hoqain, the fishing towns of Barka and Sohar, and an attractive resort at Sawadi.

Many of the sights can be managed on day trips from Muscat, with a tour company or even by public transport. A more enjoyable way of visiting, however, is to hire a car and visit Nakhal and Rustaq en route to Sohar, returning via Sawadi and Barka on a two- or three-day trip. This is difficult to accomplish if relying only on public transport, particularly as there is limited accommodation. With a 4WD (even better with camping equipment), side trips into Wadi Bani Awf or Wadi Hoqain open the door to some of the most dramatic landscapes in the country.

It's also possible to combine the above route with a visit to (or preferably *from*) the Western Hajar Mountain region by using the 4WD mountain road via Hatt and Wadi Bani Awf. In addition, there are many other spectacular wadis with remote villages and superb desert mountain scenery, accessible to those with a 4WD, an off-road guide and a sense of adventure.

On the Muscat-Sohar Hwy, elaborately decorated mosques reflect the Persian influence of the Farsi people who have settled in the region. Also look out for forts guarding the coastal strip at As-Suwayq, Al-Khabura and Saham. None particularly warrant getting off a bus for, but they may be worth a leg stretch from your own vehicle. Note that large portions of the highway are being widened and flyovers constructed over the main intersections in place of roundabouts. This means that until 2014 there are likely to be considerable delays eastbound around the construction sites between 6am and 8am and from about 4pm to 6pm westbound.

Sohar صحار

⏱ 26 / POP 140,000

The rumoured home of two famous sailors, the historical Ahmed bin Majid and the semifictional Sinbad, Sohar is one of those places where history casts a shadow over modern reality. A thousand years ago it was the largest town in the country: it was even referred to as Omana, though its ancient name was Majan (seafaring). As early as the 3rd century BC, the town's prosperity was built on copper that was mined locally and then shipped to Mesopotamia and Dilmun (modern-day Bahrain).

The town boasts one of the prettiest and best-kept seafronts in the country, but little more than legend – and a triumphal arch over the Muscat–Sohar Hwy – marked its place in history until a decade ago when a vast port-side industrial area transformed the town into a city. The port has brought jobs, an influx of expatriates, new residential areas, giant malls, a five-star hotel, a regional hospital complex and a new university illustrative of Sohar's new wealth. In fact, rumour on the street is that Sohar has pretensions of grandeur that more than match its copper-mining heyday. Watch out Muscat!

Most of Sohar's sites of interest lie along or near the corniche, 3km from the Muscat-Sohar Hwy. Note that there is a lot of construction along the Muscat-Sohar Hwy, where dangerous junctions and roundabouts are being replaced with flyovers. Work is likely to continue into 2014.

☉ Sights

Sohar's glorious **beach**, with glossy-smooth strands of sand, runs without interruption into the distance. Access to the beach is easiest from a car park next to Sohar's **municipal park** (☉ sunrise-sunset) **FREE**. Look under the hedges for the mighty minotaur, the largest beetle in Arabia. This nicely maintained park is next to Sohar Beach Hotel, north along the sea front.

The **fish market**, built in the shape of a dhow, punctuates the northern end of the corniche and is fun to visit early in the morning. Also worth a visit is the **traditional handicraft souq** (☉ 8am-noon Sat-Thu). Only half the workshops in this modern arcade are open but there's a few mat-weaving establishments and an apothecary, where you can pick up some *bukhoor hassad,* a mixture of natural ingredients to ward off the evil eye. Try sage for sore throats, frank incense for constipation and myrrh for joint pains. The opening to the souq is at a bend in Sohar Rd by Al-Jadeeda Stores.

Built in the 13th century, Sohar's distinctive white **fort** allegedly boasts a 10km tunnel intended as an escape route during a siege. Easier to find is the small **museum** in the fort's tower, which outlines local history, and the **tomb** of one of Oman's 19th-century rulers, Sayyid Thuwaini bin Sultan al-Busaid, the ruler of Oman from 1856 to 1866. The fort has been closed for several years for restoration. Neighbouring the fort is Sohar's newly revamped **heritage souq**: the addition of a covered walkway, arcade and wooden doors for the shops has made it a more interesting and attractive place for a wander.

Sohar is in the heart of a fertile **oasis**, and a pleasant hour can be spent wandering through the local plantations and farms. To reach the plantations, drive beyond Sohar Beach Hotel and turn right on Al-Nuz'ha St to find a string of fishing settlements.

🛏 Sleeping & Eating

There are numerous places to eat in town and along the highway. For a partial sea view and newly caught hamour from the fish market opposite, **Wardat al-Fatah Trading** (mains OR2.500) on Sultan Qaboos St serves delicious Turkish food at simple, outdoor plastic tables. Lulu's Hypermarket, selling everything you might need for tomorrow's journey, is on Sohar roundabout.

★ Sohar Beach Hotel
HOTEL $$

(☑ 26 841111; www.soharbeach.com; Sultan Qaboos St; r from OR75; 🛜 ⛲) Situated northwest of the corniche on a long sandy beach, the Sohar Beach Hotel has made the most of its traditional-style building to bring a bit of local character to Sohar accommodation. With a good restaurant, coffeehouse, pretty gardens and a pool, it makes a peaceful retreat while being a few minutes' drive from the town's attractions.

Al-Wadi Hotel
HOTEL $$

(☑ 26 840058; www.omanhotels.com; Al-Barakah St; s/d OR41/53; 🛜 ⛲) With a lively atmosphere (due partly to the enormously popular 'taxi bar' – frequented almost exclusively by local male taxi drivers), Al-Wadi has nicely refurbished poolside rooms and a welcoming foyer with *majlis*-style seating. The Sri Lankan chef musters a buffet (OR9–OR12) when occupancy is high. The hotel is on a service road off Sallan Roundabout on the main Muscat–Sohar Hwy, 10km from the town centre.

Crowne Plaza Sohar
HOTEL $$$

(☑ 26 850901; www.ichotelsgroup.com; Sohar-Buraimi Hwy; s/d OR115.800/126; @ ⛲) Tiers of bougainvillea lead to the domed porch and grand foyer of this glossy hotel, on the new highway to Buraimi about 15km from the centre of town. It overlooks desolate gravel plains but work will soon begin on Sohar airport in the vacant land opposite. A jazz festival hosted by the hotel in November is tipped to become an annual event.

Dhow Marine Restaurant
SEAFOOD $$

(☑ 22 024077; mains OR3.500; 🍴) In the heart of the busy fish market, this attractive, bright-windowed restaurant serves up the best of the catch fresh from the incoming fishing boats. Preparations range from Indian and Chinese to fish and chips with plenty of non-fish and vegetarian options.

❶ Getting There & Away

ONTC buses from Muscat (OR2.600, three hours, departs 6am, 6.30am, 1pm, 3pm, 4pm) drop passengers off at the small hospital near the centre of town and then continue to Buraimi or Dubai.

Microbuses and taxis come and go from a car park across the street from the hospital. Microbuses charge OR3.500 for the trip to Rusayl roundabout in Muscat and OR4.500 to Ruwi. Shared taxis charge OR8 to Rusayl roundabout and OR10 to Ruwi (OR50 engaged).

Nakhal نخل

📞 26 / POP 18,000

Nakhal is a picturesque town dominated by the Hajar Mountains and one of Oman's most dramatic forts. Built on the foundations of a pre-Islamic structure, the towers and entranceway of this **fort** (admission 500 baisa; ⊙ 9am-4pm Sat-Thu) were constructed during the reign of Imam Said bin Sultan in 1834. There are excellent views of the Batinah plain from the ramparts, and the *majlis* (seating area) on the top 'storey' of the fort makes a cool place to enjoy the tranquillity. The windows are perfectly aligned to catch the breeze, even in summer.

There are many features to look for: gaps where boiling cauldrons of honey would have been hinged over doorways; spiked doors to repel battering; round towers to deflect cannon balls; *falaj* in case of a siege. The entire structure is built around a rock; this is a common feature of Omani forts, which saves the problem of having to construct sound foundations.

Continue past Nakhal Fort through date plantations for 2.5km to find the **Ath-Thowra hot spring**. The spring emerges from the wadi walls and is channelled into a *falaj* for the irrigation of the surrounding plantations. There are usually children and goats splashing in the overspill. Look out for the flash of turquoise-winged Indian rollers, among other birds, attracted to the oasis. Picnic tables with shelters make it a popular place on Thursday and Friday.

Microbuses and taxis are the only viable transport to Nakhal and leave from the junction with the main road and in the area below the fort. Microbuses charge OR1 for the trip to Rusayl roundabout (a journey of about an hour), and 500 baisa to/from the Barka junction (30 minutes). A taxi charges about OR5 for the same trip if you can find one that doesn't only travel locally.

Wadi Bani Awf وادي بني عوف

This spectacular wadi often flows year-round and looks particularly gorgeous when mountain rain causes the *falaj* to cascade over its walls. That said, the trip (currently 4WD only) should be avoided if there is any hint of stormy weather. It is possible to reach the **rock arch** (a fissure in the cliff, about 17km into the wadi) as a day trip from Muscat or Sawadi. If you follow the graded road through the rock arch into neighbouring **Wadi Sahten**, you will eventually emerge in Rustaq but beware, this is a long journey. If treating the wadi as a side trip en route from Muscat to Sohar, you probably won't have time to penetrate the wadi for more than 5km or 6km.

To reach Wadi Bani Awf, turn left 43km from Nakhal, off the Nakhal–Rustaq road. There is no access by public transport. Discreet wild camping is possible in the upper reaches of the wadi but this may soon change. Major construction has begun on a sealed road through the entire length of the wadi which will in turn lead to greater development around the upper wadi villages, making camping inappropriate.

Wadi Bani Awf can also be reached via the mountain pass from Al-Hamra on the other side of the Western Hajar Mountains.

Rustaq الرستاق

📞 26 / POP 79,700

Some 175km southwest of Muscat, Rustaq is best known today for its imposing **fort** (admission 500 baisa; ⊙ 9am-4pm Sat-Thu), though it enjoyed a spell as Oman's capital in the 17th century. The fort was closed for restoration at the time of writing. There is an **old souq** opposite the fort used for livestock and a smart **new souq** on the main street, about 1.5km from the highway. If you've time to spare, you could visit Ayn Al-Khasfar. To reach these **hot springs**, turn right at the traffic lights on the way into town and you will find them beside the mosque at the end of the road.

The only place to stay in the area is the simple but friendly **Shimook Guesthouse** (📞 26 877071; alshomokh88@yahoo.com; r OR25, with breakfast OR30), at the start of the road from Rustaq to Ibri, opposite Mecca Hypermarket. The rooms are basic to say the least and the bathroom taps drip irrepressibly, but the waft of extravagant incense makes up for these shortcomings. You can ask for dinner (freshly cooked and tasty) in the front yard or go for kebabs at one of the small restaurants on the corner (a two-minute walk towards the great Sultan Qaboos Mosque).

Microbuses can be found a few hundred metres from the fort on the main road to Nakhal (OR1) or the Barka roundabout (OR2). For Muscat, you must change taxis in Barka.

OMAN'S GEOLOGICAL HERITAGE

If geology seems like a frankly 'anorak' pursuit, then a trip through the wadis of the Western Hajar Mountains might change your mind. Seams of iridescent copper minerals; perfect quartz crystals glinting in the sun; stone pencils and writing slates loose in the tumbling cliff; walls of fetid limestone that smell outrageously flatulent when struck; pavements of marine fossils, beautiful for their abstract design and the pattern of history they reveal – these are just a few of the many stone treasures of Batinah's wild wadis.

Although many of these features can be spotted in Wadi Bani Awf, it is neighbouring Wadi Bani Kharus that excites geologists. They go in search of the classic unconformity that is revealed halfway up the canyon walls a few kilometres into the wadi. At this point, the upper half of the cliff is a mere 250 million years old while the lower half is over 600 million years old. What created this hiatus, and what it reveals about tectonic forces, is the subject of speculation in numerous international papers. For the layperson, what makes Wadi Bani Kharus remarkable is that it appears to have been opened up as if for scientific study: the opening of the wadi comprises the youngest rocks, but as you progress deeper into the 'dissection', some of the oldest rocks in Oman are revealed, naked and without the obscuring skin of topsoil and shrubs. While you're inspecting the rocks, look out for petroglyphs – the ancient images of men on horseback are a common feature of all the local wadis.

All the main wadis in the area – Wadi Mistal, Wadi Bani Kharus, Wadi Bani Awf and Wadi Sahten – have their share of geological masterpieces and can be easily accessed with a 4WD, a map and an off-road guidebook. Take along Samir Hanna's *Field Guide to the Geology of Oman*, too, to help identify some key features. Note that there are currently major roadworks in each of the wadis – the good news is that this means they will soon by accessible without 4WD.

Wadi Hoqain وادي الحوقين

This fertile wadi, accessible only by 4WD, offers one of the easiest off-road experiences of the region and an intimate view of life under the date palms. A reasonable graded road meanders through wadi-side plantations and villages, bustling with activity in the late afternoon. Add copper-coloured cliffs and a stunning castle to the rural mix, and it's a wonder that this wadi has remained a secret for so long.

To reach the wadi, take the Rustaq–Ibri road. Zero your odometer at the great mosque roundabout in Rustaq at the start of the road and after 15km look for a bridge over a wadi. Turn right here for Neyobet Wadi bani Henai and follow the track to the wadi bottom. At 17km, you will reach the fortified 'castle' in the middle of the wadi. On closer inspection, you'll find the castle is better described as a walled settlement. The best view of the fortification is the approach, with watchtowers and date plantations in the foreground and the wadi escarpment behind.

The track climbs out of the wadi and leads past an abandoned settlement at 24.5km. It crosses the wadi once or twice more, and follows a falaj channel for part of the way. Eventually the track emerges in a plantation and block-making village at 35km. The local industry of concrete block-making for construction is a feature of many small towns in Oman. If you get lost in the village, locals will steer you to the other side of town, which eventually meets up with a sealed road at about 60km. Turn right for Al-Hazm (where there is yet another magnificent fort – currently closed for repair) 20km from Rustaq, or left to reach the Muscat-Sohar Hwy. The whole route from Rustaq to Al-Hazm takes about three hours.

Barka برقح

☑ 26 / POP 96,400

The main reason for visiting Barka, 80km west of Muscat, is to see bull-butting. This is where great Brahmin bulls, specially raised by local farmers, are set nose-to-nose in a push-and-shove that supposedly hurts neither party. To get to the bullring by car take the turning for Barka off the Muscat–Sohar Hwy and turn left at the T-intersection in the centre of town. After 3.4km you will see the concrete enclosure on your right. Bull-butting rotates from village to village along the Batinah coast on selected weekends. Ask locally to find out when and where, or chance your luck at the bullring on a Friday between November and March from 4pm to 6pm. There's no admission charge.

Barka's fort has an unusual octagonal tower. It has been closed for restoration for some time but is still impressive from the outside. To reach the fort from the town centre, turn right at the T-intersection; it's 300m on the left.

Barka's other point of interest is the 18th-century Bayt Nua'man (admission 500 baisa; ☉ 8.30am-1.30pm Sun-Thu; P), a restored merchant house that was closed at the time of writing. The turn-off for the house is signposted off the Muscat–Sohar Hwy, 7km west of Barka roundabout. There's no public transport to the house.

Barka is famous for its halwa, a unique, laboriously made Omani confection that, served with small shots of Omani coffee, is an essential part of hospitality on formal occasions. The gelatinous sweet is quite distinct from the sesame confection known as halvah, found across the rest of the region. A pot from dedicated halwa shops in town costs from OR8.

There's nowhere to stay in Barka, but the town makes an easy diversion en route for Sawadi or Sohar.

❶ Getting There & Away

ONTC buses run between the Barka roundabout and Muscat's Ruwi bus station (OR1, five times daily). Taxis and microbuses can be found around the T-intersection in town and at the Barka roundabout on the highway. A shared taxi from Rusayl roundabout to Barka costs OR3 per person and around OR12 engaged. Microbuses charge OR1.500.

Sawadi   السوادي
☑ 26

A sandy spit of land and some islands scattered off the shore make Sawadi a popular day trip, an hour or so drive west of Muscat. At low tide, you can walk to a watchtower on one of the islands, but beware: the tide returns very quickly. There's good snorkelling off the islands and local fishermen will take you around for OR5.

There is an abundance of shells at Sawadi. The resort shop sells a handy volume called Collectable Eastern Arabian Sea-shells, by Donald Bosch, if you want help identifying the booty on the beach.

One of the largest developments in the Middle East is taking shape at Sawadi, transforming the surrounding desert into a housing and tourist complex. The global recession has slowed the rate of progress but new tourist facilities are likely to be available within the next three to five years. In the meantime, the construction is far enough away from Sawadi's main beach area not to spoil the peace.

🏃 Activities

Extra Divers   DIVING
(☑ 26 795545; www.alsawadibeach.com) A variety of water sports, snorkelling and diving (OR33 for two dives plus OR4 for the permit and OR15 for equipment hire) is on offer from the professional and experienced Extra Divers, including boat trips to the nearby Damanayat Islands. The dive centre operates from the resort's beach. In the winter months, this is a good place to learn to dive; a three- to four-day open water course costs OR175 (plus OR38 for book and certificate). Kite-boarding, jet skiing and kayaking (OR6 for one hour) are also on offer.

Horse-Riding   HORSE RIDING
(☑ 26 795535, ext 215; 30min/1hr OR10/15; ☉ 7am-1pm & 2-6pm) A local enterprise manages a small stable of horses (and an occasional camel) from the Al-Sawadi Beach Resort. Galloping along the beach at sunset is possible for experienced riders. Short trips on a horse or camel are available for children (OR5 for 15 minutes).

🛏 Sleeping

★ Al-Sawadi Beach Resort   RESORT $$
(☑ 26 795545; www.alsawadibeach.com; half board r with garden view OR76, with seaview OR81; P@⊛) Forty minutes west of Muscat International Airport, Al-Sawadi Beach Resort makes a peaceful alternative to city accommodation. With a limitless beach peppered with pink top-shells, bungalow-style rooms set in landscaped gardens of cacti and aloe, and lots of user-friendly services and amenities including a spa (a three-treatment package costs OR65), gym and tennis courts, this old favourite offers good value for money.

There are several bars, including a beach bar – almost unheard of in Oman! Sawadi makes a good base for outdoor activities. The resort is run by Extra Divers who also organise 4WD excursions into the nearby wadis through an in-house tour agency.

ℹ Getting There & Away

From the turn-off to Sawadi off the Sohar–Muscat Hwy, it's a further 12km to the coast. The resort is 1km before the end of the headland. There is no public transport to Sawadi. An engaged taxi from Muscat is OR25.

Damanayat Islands
جزيرة الدمنيات

These government-protected rocky islands about an hour's boat ride off the coast of Sawadi are rich in marine life and make an exciting destination for snorkelling and diving. Turtles feed off the coral gardens here and at certain times of the year can be found congregating in large numbers. Angel and parrot fish are commonly seen and colourful sea snakes are another feature of the area – though be warned, the latter are highly dangerous if disturbed. Day trips (from OR18 for snorkelling, OR37 for diving with your own equipment) can either be arranged through Extra Divers at Al-Sawadi Beach Resort or through one of the dive centres in Muscat.

THE MUSANDAM PENINSULA

Separated from the rest of Oman by the east coast of the UAE, and guarding the southern side of the strategically important Strait of Hormuz, the Musandam Peninsula is dubbed the 'Norway of Arabia' for its beautiful *khors*, small villages and dramatic, mountain-hugging roads. Accessible but isolated in character, this beautiful peninsula with its cultural eccentricities is well worth a visit if you're on an extended tour of Oman, or if you're after a taste of wilderness from Dubai.

Khasab
خصب

📋 26 / POP 18,000

The capital of the province is small but far from sleepy. Its souq resounds to a babble of different languages, including Kumzari (a compound language of Arabic, Farsi, English, Hindi and Portuguese), and its harbour bursts with activity, much of it involving the smuggling of US cigarettes to Iran in return for goats. The smugglers are distinguished

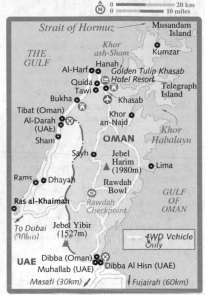

Musandam Peninsula

OMAN DAMANAYAT ISLANDS

by their souped-up fibreglass boats with outboard motors that line up along the creeks waiting for dusk to make the mad dash 55km across the strait to Iran. They bring money and character into town, so no one seems in a hurry to get rid of them; besides, piracy has been a tradition in these parts for well over 200 years and locals respect a good piece of tradition.

◎ Sights

Forget what you read about 'city tours', Khasab is still just a town where the biggest event of the past three years has been the building of a Lulu's supermarket. That said, it makes a pleasant place to wander around and it boasts an excellent museum and a lively shopping area. If you drive past Lulu's on the left and take the first right towards Khmazera Castle, you'll circuit some grand modern villas with nautical themes: one house has a scale model of a dhow over the entrance while another sports fine Iranian tiles with a seafaring theme. The whole town is partially buried in date plantations.

⭐**Khasab Fort**   FORT
(admission 500 baisa; ⊙9am-4pm Sat-Thu, 8-11am Fri) With its command of the bay sadly diminished since Lulu's was built on

WAJAJA & KHATMAT MILAHAH

الوجاجة و خطمة الملاحة

These two **border crossings** are the most common entry and exit points for the UAE. Wajaja is the post that buses use (it takes about an hour for a full bus to clear customs) while Khatmat Milahah is more useful for those with their own transport wanting to explore the eastern coast of the UAE. A good tip when using either border is to bring a photocopy of your passport and a pen; you may find that this helps speed up the process, which can be lengthy at weekends and on public holidays. Don't try to take beer in your coolbox in either direction! The rules regarding entry and exit formalities change frequently so check with the Royal Oman Police (p139) before travelling.

reclaimed land, Khasab Fort nonetheless cuts quite a dash with its four stone turrets and fine set of crenulations. Built by the Portuguese in the 17th century around a much older circular tower, this well-preserved fort now houses one of the best little ethnographic museums in Oman.

Allow an hour to do a visit justice and to explore the *bait al qufl*, literally the 'house of locks', built by a master craftsman in the courtyard. Typical of the region, these houses were built with a floor well below ground level – one of several features keeping the house safe during the empty summer months when the occupants moved to the shore to fish and harvest dates. You can see remnants of these houses in Rawdah Bowl, a two-hour off-road drive through the mountains. Also on display is *'arish*, a summer house built on stilts to allow for ventilation in the sweltering summer months.

The central tower of the fort houses the best part of the museum with displays on the peninsula's flora and fauna and a video highlighting the famous sea chants of local fishermen.

Khmazera Castle
CASTLE
(⊙8am-2pm Sat-Wed) **FREE** Buried in the heart of town (brown signs show the way), this small fortified house sports two cannons at the doorway, a renovated well in the courtyard and giant oyster shells in one of

the rooms. It's underwhelming after Khasab Fort but worth a pause during a walk or drive around town.

🏃 Activities

In addition to dhow rides and diving, Khasab is a good place for a swim. There is a lovely sandy beach with palm umbrellas and toilets on the town's outskirts and beautiful shells often wash up here when the weather is rough. Follow the road from the port towards Bukha for 2km or so. Don't be alarmed by the 1.8m sharks that often circle in the shallow bays near Khasab – apparently they're not interested in human flesh.

Dhow Trips

A key activity from Khasab is to explore the coastline with its rugged inlets on board a traditional wooden fishing vessel known locally as a 'dhow'. A boat ride is easy to arrange either through your hotel or through one of the many agencies in town. The trips are a fantastic way not just to enjoy the spectacular fjord-like scenery, but also to watch the great flocks of Socotra cormorants and bridled terns that inhabit the *khors*' vertical cliffs. Equally rewarding are the antics of humpback dolphins that invariably accompany boats around the neck of each inlet. Deep-sea fishing is popular off the most northen tip of the peninsula, especially around Musandam Island.

Musandam Sea Adventure Tourism
BOAT RIDE
(☑ 26 730424; www.msaoman.com; ⊙9am-4pm) Dhow trips can be booked through this highly recommended agency. The owner is proud of being local and employs knowledgeable Omani captains who speak a variety of languages. If you have a specific interest (such as birdwatching) the guides will be happy to tailor a trip for you. A popular trip is to camp overnight on a beach in one of the *khors*; the trip costs OR40 per person (for a minimum of two people) and includes all equipment, dinner and breakfast.

Khasab Sea Tours
BOAT RIDE
(☑26 731123; www.kstoman.com; ⊙9am-4pm) This agency, almost opposite Al-Maha petrol station near the port, offers half-day dhow rides from 9am to 1pm to Telegraph Island for OR15 per person. Whole-day trips (9am to 5pm) press on to Seebi Island and cost OR20 and include lunch. Snorkelling equipment is provided on board.

Diving & Snorkelling

Extra Divers   DIVING
(☑99877957;   www.musandam-diving.com;
⊙8am-6pm) Musandam has a reputation as
an exciting destination for diving but conditions are suitable mainly for experienced
divers. Extra Divers, at the Golden Tulip
Khasab Hotel Resort, organises full-day
dive trips for a range of capabilities. The
cost is OR53 for two dives, including equipment hire. Snorkelling costs OR19 including
equipment.

Mountain Safaris

The most cost-effective and easiest way to
explore the peninsula is to take a tour on
what is locally called a 'mountain safari'.
About 10 different operators offer similar
trips that include a half-day 4WD to Khor
an-Najd and Jebel Harim (from OR30 per
person) and a full-day drive to Rowdah Bowl
(OR60). All companies offer dhow trips if
you're looking for a 'one-stop' service. Book
online, through your hotel or at the offices
in Khasab.

Khasab Travel & Tours   TOUR
(☑26 730464; www.khasabtours.com; ⊙8am-1pm
& 4-7pm) Situated in the old souq and at the
Golden Tulip Khasab Hotel Resort, Khasab
Travel & Tours is well established if rather
brusque with customers. On offer is a two-
night B&B package at the Golden Tulip Hotel; pick-up service from Dubai (or from the
airport, port or the border); exit tax from
UAE and road permit for Oman; full-day
dhow trip, a half-day mountain safari and a
city tour for OR180 per person.

🛏 Sleeping & Eating

In peak season, October to April, you need to
book accommodation as Khasab is a popular
weekend trip for UAE visitors. All the hotels
offer a pick-up service from the airport.

Camping is not officially permitted in
Musandam (there are security issues) but
authorities usually turn a blind eye if you're
discreet. Khor an-Najd is the best place to
head for but as there are no facilities, you'll
need to bring all your own equipment.

The Lake Hotel   HOTEL $
(☑26 731664; maideltour@yahoo.com; r OR25; ℗)
Within walking distance of the fort (towards
the port end of town), this Omani-run hotel
offers basic, shabby rooms with views over
the town. Payment is with cash only.

Khasab Hotel   HOTEL $$
(☑26 730267; www.khasabhotel.net; s/d Sat-Wed
OR28/38, Thu & Fri OR38/47; ℗@✉) A kilome-
tre south of the town centre towards the air-
port, this long-established hotel offers bright
rooms with views of the mountains. There's
a cosy restaurant on site with a Filipino chef.
Payment is cash only. Arrangements can be
made for guests wanting to visit the bar at
the Golden Tulip for OR3 return.

★**Golden Tulip Khasab
Hotel Resort**   HOTEL $$$
(☑26 730777; www.goldentulipkhasab.com; s/d
OR117/141; ☎✉) Perched on a headland just
outside Khasab, on the Khasab–Tibat road,
this old favourite is surrounded on three
sides by water with a terrace making the
most of the crystal-clear water and mountain scenery. At sunset the cliffs on the opposite side of the bay dissolve like liquid
gold. There is a variety of rooms, some with
split levels, windows for walls and balconies
aligned to the sunset. The terraced restaurant offers a buffet three times a day. Wi-fi
costs OR2.300 for 30 minutes.

There are a number of restaurants around
the souqs selling similar fare of roast chick-
en, kebabs and fresh juices from around
OR1.500. Expect to keep company with a
smuggler or two. Alternatively, pop into the
Golden Tulip for a sumptuous breakfast,
lunch or dinner buffet (from OR8/11/14). At
the weekend, a buffet with a live cooking station at the Golden Tulip costs OR16.380.

Lulu's Hypermarket (⊙9am-11.45pm)
sells excellent fresh biryani, roasted and tandoori chicken, salads and pastries – all the
ingredients needed for a picnic.

🛍 Shopping

Walking sticks make an unusual souvenir of
the region. With their axe-tops, used traditionally for cutting wood, killing snakes and
keeping children in order (at least according
to one local), these sticks are the emblem of
the Shihuh tribespeople – the main ethnic
group in the Musandam Peninsula. They
carry them in place of the camel stick on
formal occasions. Ones with silver decoration cost OR55-plus and the easiest place to
find one is at the gift shop just inside Lulu's.

ℹ Getting There & Away

The Musandam Peninsula can easily be visited
as a long weekend trip from either Muscat or

Dubai (two hours by road). From Muscat, a great way to visit is to fly to Khasab for an eagle-eyed view of the mountains and take the memorable high-speed ferry around the *khors* on the way back. Another option offered by **Oman Air Holidays** (www.omanair.com) is to fly both ways for OR145 per person including two nights at the Golden Tulip Hotel in Khasab.

AIR

Oman Air (☑ in Khasab 26 731592, in Muscat 24 531111; www.omanair.com) has flights between Khasab and Muscat (OR24 each way, 1¼ hours) every morning at variable times. The office in Khasab is on the main roundabout opposite the grand mosque, and flights depart and arrive from the military air base.

BOAT

National Ferries Company (☑ in Khasab 26 731802, in Muscat 24 715252; www.nfc.com) operates a service to/from Muscat at 3pm (one way/return OR23/44, five hours). There are two services per week. To enjoy the journey in style, consider paying the extra for business class (OR45/85). You can take a car (including car rental) on the ferry for an extra OR50 return. The trip is punctuated with dinner, a film channel and attendant dolphins that can't quite keep up with the fastest catamaran in the world. The journey through one of the busiest shipping lanes in the region is worth taking for the spectacular cruise into the harbour at either end.

CAR

Driving to and from Muscat (eight hours in either direction) involves getting a road permit (for some residents – check with your sponsor or HR manager), insurance for two countries, and passing through checkpoints no fewer than eight times. On an Omani visit visa, this is not the best use of time.

It is a feasible drive, however, from Dubai. The only border post allowing access to the Musandam Peninsula is at Al-Darah/Tibat, on the western coast of the UAE. Expat residents in Oman and the UAE cannot currently drive through Wadi Bih to or from Dibba although this is rumoured soon to change. There is a Dh35 road tax to leave the UAE and OR5 road tax to enter Musandam Peninsula. Visas on arrival are available.

A 4WD is necessary to explore the mountains. You can bring a car (including a rented car) from Muscat on the ferry.

LONG-DISTANCE TAXI

There is no public transport operating in Musandam. You can book a taxi, though, through your hotel to Bukha (OR20), Tibat, Khor an-Najd or Jebel Harim (OR30), and Dubai (OR60).

ⓘ Getting Around

TO/FROM THE AIRPORT

It's best to arrange transfers with your hotel in advance as there are no taxis near the airport. The airport is 2km from the souq and 6km from the harbour if you'd rather walk.

CAR

Car hire (2WD/4WD OR13/39) is available from the ever-obliging Omani owner of **Khasab Rent-a-Car** (☑ 99447400). A 4WD with a driver costs OR60 per day. Cars can be delivered to your hotel and dropped off at the ferry terminal. You can also try **Rahaal Khasab** (☑ 99 441700; hayatix5@hotmail.com) for cheap 4WD deals from OR25 per day.

TAXI

The orange-and-white taxis in town are owned by locals running errands and are not useful as public transport. If you want to go into town, or beyond, ask the hotel or an agency to arrange transport for you.

Khasab–Tibat Road طريق خصب - طيبات

The cliff-hugging 42km, 90-minute drive from Khasab to Tibat is a highlight of a trip to Musandam. The sealed road is a feat of engineering and affords spectacular views across the Strait of Hormuz. There are a few sites of interest along the way and you could spend a day pottering along the road, enjoying a swim at one of the many glorious sandy beaches – and watching very large sharks basking in the shallows.

About 8km from Khasab harbour lies the village of Tawi, site of a few **prehistoric rock carvings** of boats, houses and warriors on horseback. To reach these petroglyphs, follow a track up Wadi Qida, just before Qida village, for 2.3km. The petroglyphs are etched into two rocks on the left, just before a large white house with outdoor ovens.

Scenically positioned **Bukha Fort** commands a good view of the bay halfway along the Khasab–Tibat road. Prisoners used to be pegged to the lower courtyard and drowned by the incoming tide. The view from the fort (closed to visitors) above town shows the classic Musandam landscape of steep-sided cliffs sheltering 'bowls' (cul-de-sac plains) of flat-topped acacia trees. Often the beachside settlements are inundated by the listing flanks of sand dunes blown back from the shore.

The road ends in Tibat at Al-Darah border with the UAE; the post is open 24 hours and passing through customs on either side is quick and efficient.

The Musandam Khors

أخوار المسندم

A dhow trip around the *khors* (inlets) of Musandam, flanked by dolphins, is a must and well worth the expense. Trail a fishing line from the back of the traditional Arabic boat, and your skipper will cook what you catch for lunch. So remote are some of these *khors* that people still have their water delivered by boat and speak a dialect almost unrecognisable to Arabic speakers from Muscat.

Note that you will need a permit (which can be arranged by pre-booking with a tour company) to enter any village in the Musandam *khors*.

Khor ash-Sham

خور الشم

This beautiful inlet is interesting for its stone fishing villages, accessible only by boat, and for Telegraph Island, which you can land on at high tide. Snorkelling and swimming in the pristine surrounding waters is a highlight as are the dolphins which swim alongside the boat. It is the most popular dhow tour from Khasab.

Khor an-Najd

خوورنجد

At 24.5km southeast of Khasab, this is the only *khor* accessible by vehicle (preferably 4WD). You can camp on the rim of this wild bay although it's often too shallow and muddy for a good swim. The viewpoint at the top of the graded road, however, is stunning and worth the visit for its own sake. This is the view that is most often chosen in tourist literature to promote Musandam.

To reach the *khor* from Khasab, head inland past the airport for 15km and follow the sign for 'Khor an-Najd 10km'. After 5.6km turn left and head for the graded road that winds up the mountain. After 2.3km you come to the pass, from where a steep 2.8km descent brings you to the water's edge.

From the base of the track, a road leads to Sal Ala'a and Al-Khaldiyah, an inland bowl full of mature trees that makes for a pleasant and rare shaded picnic spot.

Kumzar

كمذار

✔ 26

Set on an isolated *khor* at the northern edge of the peninsula, the surprisingly modern town of Kumzar is accessible only by boat. The villagers speak their own language, known as Kumzari – a combination of Farsi, Hindi, English, Portuguese and Arabic.

There is nowhere to stay in Kumzar, and there are no sights of special interest in the town. It is nonetheless fascinating to wander around the old stone houses and the souq area to see how this outpost has developed its own unique character.

Water taxis travel between Khasab and Kumzar, charging a rather outrageous OR120 (and in excess of OR200 at weekends) for the harrowing trip in a speedboat with no seats and a maximum clearance between deck and gunwale of 15cm. It's much better to organise a day trip through a tour company (OR30 per person for a 9am to 4pm dhow ride with a minimum of four people).

OMAN THE MUSANDAM KHORS

GOING ROUND THE BEND

Ever wondered about the term 'going round the bend'? If you take a trip to Khor ash-Sham, you'll learn first-hand what the saying means.

In the middle of the *khor* (inlet), a tiny island, not much bigger than a postcard and considerably less attractive, was home to a British telegraphic relay station in the 19th century. The utter isolation of the island, tucked around the bend of this remote inlet, with no diversions other than sleeping and swimming, drove many of the workers stationed there to madness. The saying 'going round the bend' persists to this day...and so perhaps does the associated implication of being 'driven round the bend'.

From time to time, the military set up camp on the rocks and see how long it takes to run out of things to do. Personnel stationed there run straw polls estimating the number of days endurable at a stretch. One volunteered the improvement of their fishing skills, and Captain Ahmed Saif said, 'We get very good at counting cormorants.'

Jebel Harim   جبل حارم

If you have a 4WD, the mountain scenery around Jebel Harim (Mountain of Women) makes a rewarding day trip, especially in spring when the mountains are full of delicate blooms such as wild geraniums and miniature iris.

The graded road switchbacks through limestone formations until it reaches the Sayh plateau, a startling patchwork of fields and grazing donkeys surrounded by stone settlements. The road climbs a further 8km to a pass below the telecommunications tower (off limits to the public) that marks the top of the mountain. Even if you don't intend to make the descent to Rawdah Bowl, it's well worth unravelling the helter-skelter of road for a few kilometres beyond the pass: the views of improbable homesteads, clinging to the crescent-shaped canyons, with terraces in various states of livid green or grey abandonment, are spectacular.

Rawdah Bowl   مدرّج الروضة

From Jebel Harim, the descent towards Dibba is via a narrow ridge with remarkable views of striated sedimentary rock.

At the bottom of the descent, a right turn leads towards Dibba via the Omani checkpoint (no access for non-Omanis) while a left turn crosses the wadi bottom and meanders into the Rawdah Bowl – a beautiful depression of mature acacia and *ghaf* trees. The bowl has several interesting features including the local stone-built houses known as *bait al qufl*, or the 'house of locks'. So called on account of the elaborate locking mechanism, the homes (which are left empty during the summer months) are built low to the ground and the floor is excavated to about 1m below the door with beds and an eating area raised on platforms. The furniture and vital earthenware water jars are often placed inside before the house is roofed, ensuring that no one makes off with the contents during migration. Some of the rocks used in these buildings are 1m thick and take six to eight men to lift. One good example still exists in the middle of the bowl, near the road and a grave site. Note the roof made of tree trunks and insulated against the heat and cold by mud.

The area has a long history of settlement, as can be seen from the pre-Islamic tombstones (lying close to the road) made either from luminous yellow sandstone or grey limestone and etched with script or pictographs. The entire area, with its diagonal slants of sandstone, takes on a surreal quality at sunset.

DHOFAR, SALALAH & SOUTHERN OMAN

The southernmost province of Oman is a world away from the industrious north and is separated geographically by an interminable gravel desert. With its historic frankincense trade, great beaches, a laid-back atmosphere and an interesting ethnic mix, it's a fascinating place to visit, particularly during or just after the *khareef* (mid-June to late August season of mists and light rains).

There are many intriguing sites to visit as day trips from Salalah, including Job's Tomb; the heroic town of Mirbat with its beautiful beaches; and Mughsail, famed for the violent blowholes in the undercliff and for nearby groves of wild frankincense.

If you are travelling during the *khareef* and can put up with the unremittingly tedious journey from Muscat or Nizwa, it is worth going overland to Salalah across the largely featureless Al-Wusta Region and returning by plane. This is the best way to sense the full spectacle of the *khareef* across the top of the jebel; after eight hours of gravel plains, Dhofar seems like a little miracle.

Salalah   صلاله

☑ 23 / POP 172,000

Salalah, the capital of the Dhofar region, is a colourful, subtropical city that owes much of its character to Oman's former territories in East Africa. Flying into Salalah from Muscat, especially during the *khareef*, it is hard to imagine that Oman's first and second cities share the same continent. From mid-June to mid-August, monsoon clouds from India bring a constant drizzle to the area and, as a result, the stubble of Salalah's surrounding jebel is transformed into an oasis of misty pastures. Year-round, Salalah's coconut-fringed beaches and plantations of bananas and papayas offer a flavour of Zanzibar in the heart of the Arabian desert.

The giant Salalah Port at Raysut has brought new wealth to the city, not to mention thousands of day-visit cruise-

Salalah

OMAN SALALAH

ship passengers. As a result, the city has undergone a beautification process and lots of helpful brown signs help steer visitors around Salalah and surrounding sights of special interest.

Sights & Activities

★ Museum of the Frankincense Land
ARCHAEOLOGICAL SITE
(admission OR2; ⊙8am-2pm & 4-8pm Sat-Wed, 4-8pm Thu & Fri) The main point of interest in Salalah is the ancient site of **Al-Baleed**. The comprehensive set of ruins, which are well labelled and atmospherically lit at night, belong to the 12th-century trading port of Zafar. From here, frankincense was shipped across the sea to India in exchange for spices. The surrounding plantations of coconut, papaya, sugar cane and banana illustrate the fecundity of the region and it is little wonder that the port was a prosperous one. Little is known about the port's demise but the

excellent on-site **museum** charts the area's settlement since 2000 BC and illustrates the maritime strength of the nation, including its recent renaissance through the port projects at Salalah, Duqm (tipped to be the largest port in the Arab world) and Sohar. The site includes at least 3km of beautifully landscaped walking paths (open until 8pm each evening) alongside the *khor* and into the adjoining reed beds where an observation tower makes for good birdwatching.

Plantations   GARDENS

Salalah is famous for its plantations of coconuts, papayas and bittersweet, small bananas. Stroll through the plantation roads near the corniche (2km from the town centre); for refreshment, stop off at the many colourful fruit stands that stay open until late in the evening.

Al-Husn Souq   SOUQ

(Sultan Qaboos St; ⊙10am-1pm & 4.30-9.30pm) Head for this souq to rub shoulders with the jovial Dhofari people. The alleyways next to the sultan's palace flap with colourful cotton headdresses, smoke with aromatic frankincense and sparkle with imitation jewellery. This is a good place to see how the Omani hats are made.

Extra Divers   DIVING

(☑ 92 873560; www.divesalalah.com; Crowne Plaza Resort Salalah, Al-Khandaq St; ⊙4-6pm Oct-May) For diving and snorkelling opportunities in the region, contact the highly competent Extra Divers. A day trip (two dives) including transport, equipment and permit costs OR60. Note that it is not possible to dive or snorkel in the summer months (June to September) due to dangerous currents.

⮞ Tours

Zahara Tours   TOURS

(☑ 24 400844; www.zaharatours.com; ⊙8am-1pm & 4-7pm Sat-Thu) The Frankincense Trail explores the mountains (OR141), the castle tour covers Taqah and Mirbat (OR136) and there's a city tour (OR120) operating on Saturdays and Wednesdays. All prices quoted are for a whole-day excursion in a vehicle with an English-speaking driver and a maximum of three people.

✱ Festivals & Events

During the *khareef*, the Ittin road is the main location of the Salalah Tourism Festival. Arab families from across the region come to picnic in paradise. Their favourite haunt is under the streetlights of Ittin Rd where a large festival complex includes funfairs, clothes stalls, cultural villages, a theatre, restaurants and lots of small stands selling kebabs and *shwarma*. Check *Oman Today* for a program of nightly concerts (from around OR7), among other activities.

🛏 Sleeping

During the *khareef*, all accommodation in Salalah is heavily booked, so reservations are essential. Prices during the *khareef* may be significantly greater than those quoted here. Camping is possible around Mirbat, but you'll need to bring your own equipment. Alternatively, you can buy supplies in any of the major shopping centres in Salalah.

★ Salalah Beach Villas   HOTEL $

(☑23 235999; www.beach-villas-salalah.com; Beach Rd, off Ad-Dahariz St; s/d sea view with balcony OR30/38; P🛜🖵) On the beach one block east of the Crowne Plaza, this welcoming family-style hotel has lovely views: the sea is so close you can taste it through the window. Walk off breakfast along the magnificent white-sand beach and hazard a splash in the surf on calmer days. Don't leave without trying the house speciality: Mr and Mrs Kumar's fish curry (OR6) is a legend among travellers.

The veteran landlord can organise overnight desert tours to Ayoun Pools and the Empty Quarter from OR130, and full-day tours east or west of the Dhofar plain from OR80. Car hire (2WD/4WD from OR14/37, including 200km free mileage) is available with discounts for week-long rentals. This guesthouse also runs the 65-room hotel block next door (singles/doubles OR40/56 for sea view with balcony), which has the benefit of an all-day restaurant. Note that the neighbouring Arabian Sea Villas is not run by the same landlord despite the proximity of the villas.

Haffa House   HOTEL $

(☑23 295444; www.shanfarihotels.com; cnr Al-Matar & Ar-Robat Sts; s/d OR30/35; 🛜🖵) Located within a small commercial complex near the clock-tower roundabout, the hotel is one of the city's main landmarks. Don't be put off by the rather cavernous, gloomy foyer: the rooms are old-fashioned but comfortable, the bathrooms and corridors sport marble and Arabian tiles, and there is a pool. The restaurant, with views of the hills, serves tasty Asian-style fare among less appealing international dishes.

Al-Hanaa Hotel
HOTEL $

(☑23 290274; msarawas@omantel.net.om; 23 July St; s/d OR13/17; P) This Arabic-style hotel with a tiled foyer is recommended for its bright, clean rooms. It is situated in the middle of town, within walking distance of the bus station and the main shopping areas.

Salalah Hotel
BUSINESS HOTEL $

(☑23 295332; fax 23 292145; Al-Souq St; r OR15; P @) Almost opposite the ONTC bus station, this good-value hotel has large, comfortable rooms and friendly staff. It is close to the new souq area and attracts an interesting mixture of Omani salespeople and regional travellers.

Crowne Plaza Resort Salalah
RESORT $$$

(☑23 238000; www.cpsalalah.com; Al-Khandaq St; s/d from OR90/100; P🛜🏊) The main rendezvous for Western expats, this sociable and highly competent hotel, with *rondallas* of local scenes and coloured glass, is the most characterful of the large hotels in and around Salalah. It has a small golf course, beach and terraced restaurants overlooking a magnificent sandy beach, with waves illuminated each evening beneath the palms

Hilton Salalah Hotel
RESORT $$$

(☑23 211234; www.hilton.com; As-Sultan Qaboos St; s/d from OR80/90; P🛜🏊) It was a surprise when the Hilton chose Salalah instead of Muscat. It was an even greater surprise when the hotel was built 12km along the highway to Mughsail, within view of the enormous Raysut Port. Despite the cargo boats queuing up on the horizon, and camels charging by the rather cramped grounds, the hotel is a hit with Nordic holidaymakers.

Juweira Boutique Hotel
BOUTIQUE HOTEL $$$

(☑23 239600; www.juweirahotel.com; Salalah Beach; s/d 88/105; P🛜🏊) It's hard to wholly embrace the vision of this new hotel, marooned in the middle of lonesome Salalah Beach, some 13km from town. It will make better sense when other parts of the surrounding tourism and residential complex are open and it's less of a ghost town. In the meantime, the hotel and its quality amenities offer a peaceful retreat.

✖ Eating

There are plenty of small Indian restaurants along As-Salam St and Sultan Qaboos St near the Crowne Plaza Resort. All the top-end hotels have good restaurants and cafes, with Western menus and prices to match.

There are numerous cold stores, supermarkets and hypermarkets, including Lulu, all over town for picnic items.

Zakri Restaurant
SHWARMA $

(☑23 236234; Sultan Qaboos St; shwarma 300 baisa; ⊙4pm-3am) This no-frills restaurant, one in a string of cheap and cheerful eateries 1km from the Crown Plaza Resort, serves very good fruit juices and *shwarma*. Stroll along the same road for dessert from the fruit stands.

Café de Paris
CAFE $

(Corniche; snacks from OR1; ⊙10am-2am) To learn all you need to know about life in Oman's laid-back second city, sit on the corniche at this cafe and watch the fishermen reel in their bait, young Dhofaris play dominos and old men congregate in huddles on the sand as the sun sets.

The Cascade
INDIAN $

(☑23 292382; 23 July St; mains OR1.500-2.500; ⊙11am-3.30pm & 6.30pm-midnight) This atmospheric venue serves Indian meals and an Arabic-Indian buffet dinner on Thursday. It also has private dining areas for Omani-style food. Needless to say it is always abuzz with locals and is a good place to gain a flavour of cultural exchange – such as has been occurring in Dhofar for centuries.

Bin Ateeq
OMANI $

(☑23 290232; 23 July St; mains OR2.500; ⊙9.30am-1am) 🍴 This chain of restaurants provides a rare opportunity to sample Omani food in a country where going out for dinner usually means eating Indian cuisine. Eating Omani cuisine is beginning to catch on among regional guests, though, and Salalah boasts four branches of Bin Ateeq with two on 23 July St.

★ Dolphin Beach Restaurant
INTERNATIONAL $$

(☑23 238000; Crowne Plaza Resort Salalah, Al-Khandaq St; buffet OR6; ⊙noon-3pm & 6pm-midnight) One of the few restuarants to offer dining with a sea view, this open-air restaurant under the coconut palms offers a different themed buffet each night. Call ahead to reserve a beach-side table if you want to watch the waders dash in and out of the floodlit waves, finding their supper as you eat yours.

☆ Entertainment

Both the Crowne Plaza Resort Salalah and the Hilton Salalah Hotel offer live music.

Shopping

Among Dhofar's most distinctive souvenirs are small, bead-covered kohl (black eyeliner) bottles (OR4 to OR10) from Al-Hosn Souq. Baskets made of rush and camel's leather, from the fishing village of Shwaymiyah, make another good souvenir (OR5 to OR30), together with colourful woven rice mats. These can be bought at the **Handycrafts Bazaar** (Al-Tanmiyah St; ⊙ 9am-1pm & 4-10pm Sat-Thu, 4-10pm Fri) near the new souq.

Don't visit Dhofar without treading in the paths of ancient traders! A small bag of locally harvested frankincense in any souq costs from 500 baisa, and a decorative, locally made pottery incense burner costs OR1.500 to OR10. There are different grades of incense: Somali frankincense is cheaper but not so aromatic while the milky, greenish resin from Dhofar is highly prized. A whole kit with burner and charcoal costs OR1, or buy a local perfume made from frankincense (OR5 to OR50 per bottle).

Salalah has some master silversmiths. Ash-Sharooq St, behind Al-Husn Souq, is a good place to buy a new silver *khanjar*. They are beautifully crafted and cost OR100 to OR250. Visit the gold souq on An-Nahdah St for Salalah's distinctive silver necklaces and bracelets, which cost around OR25 (depending on weight).

Halwa shops selling Oman's traditional confection monopolise the corner of Al-Hafah and Sultan Qaboos Sts.

For camping equipment and supplies, visit Lulu Shopping Centre, south of Haffa House.

Information

There is no information centre as such, but the travel agencies on An-Nahdah St are helpful and some of them can arrange local tours. For a map, **The Family Bookshop** on the same street is the best bet.

Banks with ATMs, including HSBC, and a few exchange houses can be found around the intersection of An-Nahdah and Al-Salam Streets.

There are several internet cafes on 23 July St, charging around 800 baisa per hour. The most convenient is **Internet Café and Computer Services** (⊙ 9am-2am) opposite the ONTC bus station.

The entrance to the **Main Post Office** (An-Nahdah St; ⊙ 8am-2pm Sat-Wed, 9-11am Thu) is at the rear of the building. The **Telephone Office** (cnr An-Nahdah & Al-Montazah Sts; ⊙ 8am-2.30pm & 4-10pm) offers fax facilities.

Muscat Pharmacy is on An-Nahdah St and Salalah has excellent medical facilities at **Sultan Qaboos Hospital**.

Getting There & Away

AIR

The national carrier, **Oman Air** (✆ Muscat 24 531111, Salalah 23 295747; Haffa House), flies to Muscat (one way/return from OR32/64, 1½ hours) up to four times daily at variable times.

BUS

ONTC (✆ 23 292773; www.ontcoman.com) buses to Muscat (one way/return OR7.500/12, 12 hours, three daily) via Nizwa leave from the bus station in the new souq at 7am, 10am and 7pm. You can store luggage in the adjoining ticket office free of charge. There is also a service to Dubai (one way/return OR11/18) at 3pm. ONTC runs air-conditioned, non-smoking coaches with toilet and TV on this service. Private bus companies ply the route with less reliability. Bin Qasim (p140) offers a service at 4pm and leaves from the market area near ONTC.

Getting Around

CAR

Hiring a car in Salalah is recommended for exploring, especially during the *khareef*. You don't strictly need a 4WD unless you want to enjoy some of the country's best camping, or explore the more rugged roads, but beware of the soft sand on the beaches.

The main car-hire companies can be found on arrival at the airport and Budget is represented at the Crowne Plaza Resort. Many local companies offer cars for hire, especially along 23 July St. For competitive rates and help with where to explore, **Salalah Beach Villas** (✆ 23 235999) hires 2WD/4WD from OR14/37, with 200km free and reductions for week-long rental.

During the *khareef* the roads into the jebel are notoriously dangerous. They are slippery and local drivers fail to make allowances for the fog. Camels often cause accidents by wandering onto the road – if you hit one, you can be sure it will be an extremely expensive female, prize-winning, racing camel.

TAXI & MICROBUS

Salalah's taxis and microbuses hang out behind HSBC on Al-Salam St. Microbus fares from Salalah include Mirbat (OR2) but most routes are inconvenient as they drop passengers off at the junction with the main road and there's a long walk into town.

Taxis will generally only make trips beyond Salalah on an engaged basis (OR10 to Taqa and OR15 to Mirbat, OR25 to the Salalah Marriott Resort, for example). There is no public transport from the airport. Taxis charge a fixed price of OR3 from the airport to anywhere in Salalah. A microbus ride within the city costs around 500 baisa and a taxi about OR1. Taxis cost OR3 to the Crowne Plaza Resort Salalah and OR3.500 to Hilton Salalah Hotel from the city centre.

Around Salalah

Salalah is sandwiched in the middle of a plain between the mountains and the Indian Ocean. This plain, with its horseshoe crescent of hills, extends east towards Jebel Samhan, and west towards the Yemeni border. For a day trip, it's feasible to go east or west, but not to tackle both!

The hillsides at any time of year are a fascinating product of human interaction with centuries of livestock grazing (mostly camels, cows and goats) helping to shape the contours, while nature takes care of the rest. Ancient trees and striking limestone formations are just some of the unique natural wonders of the region.

Many facilities at Dhofar's sights, such as restaurants and teashops, are only open in the *khareef*.

Beaches & Springs

There are glorious white-sand beaches along the entire coastal plain of Salalah, extending from the corniche in the heart of the city. Beware of strong currents anywhere along the coast during the *khareef*: swimming is prohibited at this time and challenging for weak swimmers at any time of year.

The whole area surrounding Salalah is dotted with *ayns* (fresh water springs), and any of these make a good half-day trip from the city. To reach them, follow the brown signs from the Salalah–Mirbat road. Some of the most picturesque springs include Ayn Razat, set in gardens; Ayn Tabraq and Ayn Athum, in the heart of a subtropical thicket; and Ayn Garziz, which can be visited off the Ittin Rd on the way to Job's Tomb. With eccentric limestone cliffs, gnarled with wild fig-tree roots and hanging with maidenhair ferns, this is a good spot to appreciate the transformation brought about by a drop of water.

Job's Tomb قبر النبي أيوب

In religious terms, this **tomb** (admission 500 baisa; ☉ daylight) is probably the most important site in Dhofar. Regardless of your religious convictions, the tomb, situated on

an isolated hilltop overlooking Salalah, is a must-see for the beautiful drive, especially during the *khareef*, and for the excellent view over the Salalah plain on a clear day.

Surrounded by bright-yellow weaver birds and their tunnel-like nests, the tomb is just over 30km northwest of Salalah. Take the main westbound road towards Mughsail and follow the signs along the Ittin Rd. Turn left at the signpost for An-Nabi Ayyub after 22km. A small restaurant below the tomb has wonderful views but precious little else! There is no public transport.

If you are visiting Job's Tomb during the *khareef*, return to the main road and turn right to Ayoon. If you continue along here for another 10km or so, through a grove of frankincense trees, you'll reach the end of the monsoon catchment. The contrast between the green slopes and the desert floor beyond is remarkable. You can continue along this road until you meet the Thumrait road where a right turn brings you back to Salalah.

East of Salalah

Taqah طاقة

This pretty fishing village, at the end of the magnificent white-sand beach that extends from Salalah, has recently smartened itself up for tourists. It has several attractions, including a landscaped *khor*, a fine corniche, a fort on the hill (closed to visitors) and, for some inexplicable reason, a multi-storey branch of Bank Dhofar. The star of the show, however, is the small but well-preserved 19th-century **Taqah Castle** (adult/child OR500/200; ☉ 9am-4pm Sat-Thu, 8-11am Fri). With a furnished interior, video display, excellent signage, craft shop and an accompanying booklet explaining the history of this sardine-producing town, this is one of the best fort museums in Oman.

Khor Rouri خور روري

Looking across one of Dhofar's prettiest bays at peacefully grazing camels and flocks of flamingos, it's hard to imagine that 2000 years ago Khor Rouri was the trading post of the frankincense route and one of the most important ports on earth. Today little remains of the city except the painstakingly excavated ruins of **Sumhuram Archaeological Park** (admission OR1; ☉ 9am-6pm); you can wander around the ruins and watch the archaeologists at work. Visit the gallery within the site to see some of the 1st century BC to 3rd century AD finds from the site including some evocative Kursi inscriptions. There are toilets but no other facilities here.

Khor Rouri is about 35km east of Salalah. Take the Mirbat road and follow the brown signs. A microbus to the junction on the highway is 500 baisa.

marks the entrance). A sealed road leads to the top of the waterfall and eventually to an unlikely lake (which shrinks to a pond after a poor rainy season) with a tea shop open in the *khareef*. Don't be tempted to swim as bilharzia is present here. A sealed road at the bottom of the cliff leads to the seasonal pool at the base of the waterfall, a haven for butterflies.

Wadi Dharbat وادي دربات

A popular picnic site during the *khareef* and a great place to enjoy the jebel in any season, Wadi Dharbat is the source of the estuary that flows into Khor Rouri. During a good *khareef,* an impressive waterfall spills over the cliff face, 300m to the plain below. Above the falls, water collects in luminous limestone pools. In the dry months, October to May, the Jibbali tribespeople set up their camps in this area. The surrounding caves were used by the sultan's forces, together with the British SAS, to infiltrate areas of communist insurgency in the mid-1970s. Now the most surreptitious activity you are likely to see is the scuttling away of a small, fur-clad rock hyrax (an unlikely relative of the elephant) that lives among the rocks. Chameleons share the same territory and are equally clandestine, changing colour when abashed.

To get to Wadi Dharbat, follow the signs off the Mirbat road and climb 3km to the Wadi Dharbat junction (a small coffeehouse

Mirbat مرباط

☑ 23 / POP 13,900

The town of Mirbat, just over 70km east of Salalah, has seen better days, but it has considerable historical significance. The town's main **fort** is now derelict despite being the site of the well-documented Battle of Mirbat in which nine soldiers kept 300 insurgents from taking Mirbat in July 1972 during the Dhofari insurrection. Two British Victoria Crosses were earned by the SAS but not awarded, to help keep the war out of the public eye. A much older fort, by the shore, has recently been restored.

Notice the old **merchant houses** with their wooden, latticed windows. The onion-domed **Bin Ali Tomb**, 1km off the main road, marks the entrance to the town.

Glorious beaches stretch east and west of Mirbat, though a 4WD is necessary if you want to get close enough to the sea for wild camping (there are no facilities). Snorkelling (OR20 for a trip from 9am to 2.30pm) and diving trips (OR56 for dives including

---

ⓘ TOURS OF DHOFAR

Given the lack of useful public transport and the difficulty of driving in the *khareef* (rainy season), Dhofar is one region that repays the expense of taking a tour. This can be organised through hotels, or the travel agencies along An-Nahdah St in Salalah offer similar tours around Salalah and the Dhofar region.

Most tours take you either east of Salalah (to Khor Rouri, Taqa and Mirbat) or west (to Job's Tomb and Mughsail blowholes) and cost from around OR80 for a day trip. For the romantic, there is 4WD visit to the lost city of Ubar, 175km from Salalah (OR120), but be warned, you'll need a lively imagination or Ranulph Fiennes' book *Atlantis of the Sands* to make any sort of sense of the site. For a more-rewarding experience, spend the night in the Empty Quarter at a camp near Al-Hashman (from OR160 including half board). All prices quoted are for a vehicle with an English-speaking driver and a maximum of four people.

For help with more-adventurous Empty Quarter expeditions, contact the desert specialist Mussallem Hassan who runs an experienced agency called **Arabian Sand Tours** (☑ 23 235833; www.arabiansandtours.com). He can organise five-day trips for OR130 per day for one to three people. For a modern-day Thesiger experience, driving along the whole Saudi–Oman border to the UAE costs from OR200 per day and takes 10 days. You'll find Mussallem Hassan at the Arabian Sea Villas, next to Salalah Beach Villas on the beachfront in Salalah.

MUSCAT TO SALALAH OVERLAND

Inland Route

It comes as some surprise to see a sign off the Rusayl roundabout in Muscat that says 'Salalah 998km'. Salalah may be Oman's second city, but it would be inconceivable to see a sign pointing to Edinburgh from the outskirts of London, or Washington from New York. The signs imply that there is precious little in between – that once on the lonely Hwy 31 from Nizwa, there is nothing between you and Salalah. And that's pretty much the case! The eight-hour journey between Nizwa and Thumrait across Al-Wusta Region is punctuated by one lone limestone hump near Adam, the excitement of a small town at Hayma and little else. One Thorn Tree correspondent called it 'the least memorable journey in the world' and, as you gaze across the big sky, midpoint along Hwy 31, without a rock, a bush, or any kind of interruption of the level plain, it's hard not to agree.

With your own 4WD, however, there are a few points of interest en route, summarised below. If the prospect of exploring this 'Road Across Nowhere' appeals, you can make the interminable drive more bearable by stopping off at the friendly, simple, courtyard guest houses of Al-Ghabah Hotel, Al-Ghaftain and Qitbit. There's no need to book ahead!

Oases of Muntasar (near Qitbit) Famous for the daily fly-by of thousands of sand grouse.

Oasis of Muqshin Relatively easy access to the magnificent *ghaf* woodlands and seams of Sodom's apple that decorate the edge of the Empty Quarter.

Shisr Chance to exercise the imagination at the supposed site of the fabled gold-pillared city of Ubar (p191), a shortish detour along Hwy 43.

Coastal Route

There is an altogether more scenic way of getting to Dhofar along the shores of the beautiful Arabian Sea but it is not for those in a hurry. The coastal trip from Muscat to Salalah takes at least three days and the beauty of the coast will make you wish you'd allowed more time. There are hotels at Ashkara, Mahout and Duqm along this route but you'll need camping equipment or be prepared for a very long drive (at least six hours) between Duqm and Thumrait or Salalah. A spectacular coast-hugging road from Shwaymiyah to Salalah will shave two hours off this journey time on completion in 2014. If you want to explore the best of the route, you'll need a 4WD so you can reach the shore or explore a wadi. For full descriptions of how to make the best of this area, refer to an off-road guide. Some of the highlights of this route include:

Film Traditional Barasti fishing villages.

Wadi Shuhram Ancient rock formations such as blue-green algae (the earth's original animate form) in the laminations of Wadi Shuhram (near Shital).

Duqm Wind-eroded sandstone in the rock garden at Duqm.

Ras Madrakah Superb shells and cosy camping in the coves of this headland.

Al-Kahil Pink lagoons and flamingos.

Shwaymiyah Basket-weaving and a long bay: under the looming presence of Jebel Samhan, lair of the leopard, this is one of the most beautiful sights in Oman.

Top Tip:

Try to time your arrival in Salalah in daylight. If you drive either route in summer (between July and mid-September) you will enter Salalah on Hwy 31. There is a point along that road, just after Thumrait, where you will notice something quite remarkable: the jebel, suddenly, unexpectedly and with rulerlike precision, turns green. After 10 hours or three days of hard desert driving, it is an unforgettable, almost Zen-like experience that can only be fully experienced through the force of contrast. In the words of the Bedu, 'There's nothing sweeter than water after drought.'

equipment and permit) are easily organised through **Extra Sports** (☑ 99 895457; www.dive salalah.com; ⊕ 8-9am & 3-6pm), a competent dive centre at the Salalah Marriott Resort. Don't forget to rest at sea level for a day if you intend to visit Jebel Samham after diving.

The **Salalah Marriott Resort** (☑ 23 268245; www.marriottsalalahresort.com; half board r OR66; @ ⊠) has brought luxury and comfort to the coastal experience for those who'd rather not camp, but the intended concrete city planned for the vicinity may not please everybody. Discount is available for those resident in Oman. The resort is a 10-minute drive east of the town of Mirbat; signposts from the main Salalah–Mirbat road indicate the direction. Transport is free from the airport and there's a complimentary hotel shuttle to town at 3.30pm, returning at 8.45pm, every day except Friday.

Microbuses to Mirbat charge OR2 for the trip from Salalah. Taxis cost around OR15.

Jebel Samhan   جبل سمحان

Although you need a permit and a good reason to visit the leopard sanctuary at Jebel Samhan, the sealed road up to the reserve entrance makes a rewarding day trip from Salalah. The road passes the entrance to Tawi Attair, a deep sinkhole known as the 'Well of Birds' which has a viewing platform but is really only accessible with a guide. Further up the Jebel Samhan road, signs lead to Taiq Cave, a vast limestone complex deep in the hills. En route to the cave, you'll pass lots of low-lying *jebbali* roundhouses, traditionally constructed with sticks and more recently covered with tarpaulins and tyres.

Continuing towards Jebel Samhan, the road climbs up through a variety of different flora, including rocky fields of desert roses. Sometimes known as elephant plants, they have huge bulbous trunks and beautiful pink flowers in spring. As you near the summit (around 1300m) drive towards the cliff edge for a panoramic view of the coast. There are many exceptional vistas in Oman and this is one of them. If you're wondering about the odd spiky tree on the plateau, it's called a dragon tree and is confined to high, semi-arid elevations. The road ends at a couple of ad hoc teashops.

To reach any of these sights, take the Tawi Attair road after the fishing town of Taqah, and follow the brown signs. If you return to the coast from Tawi Attair following the signs to Mirbat, you'll pass (on the right of the descent) a wadi of tall, bulbous **baobab trees** – the only such trees in Arabia.

Hasik   حاسك

Positioned at the most eastern end of the Dhofar coast before the cliffs of Jebel Samhan interrupt, Hasik is worth the two-hour drive from Salalah for the journey more than the destination. The road is sealed and not particularly exceptional in winter, but in summer luminous clouds billow down from the jebel and high winds whip across the water, sending the surf backwards as the waves roll inexorably forwards. Glossy cormorants cluster like oil slicks in the coves and waders shelter from the seasonal fury amid the drifts of pink top shells.

There is not much to see in Hasik itself, but if you continue along the road towards Hadraban, look out for a spectacular limestone formation overhanging the sandstone cliffs. A small car park marks the spot. Construction of a road around the base of Jebel Samhan, linking Hasik to Shwaymiya, will cut two hours off the coastal journey from Duqm to Salalah and be a tourist attraction in its own right.

Hasik is clearly signposted from Hwy 47, just before the town of Mirbat.

West of Salalah

Mughsail   مغسيل

Mughsail is 48km west of Salalah on Oman's most spectacular bay, ending in a set of sheer cliffs that reaches towards the Yemeni border. Immediately below the start of the cliffs (turn left opposite Al-Maha petrol station) the rock pavement is potholed with **blowholes** that are active year-round, but particularly volatile during the high seas of the *khareef*. An enterprising teashop has opened at the entrance offering magnificent views of the coast from a shady terrace. Toilets are available here too.

Sarfait Road   طريق صرفيت

If you have your own transport, it's worth continuing from Mughsail towards the Yemeni border. The road is an impressive feat of engineering, zigzagging 1000m to the top of the cliff. Look out for a wadi full of

LOST CITY OF UBAR

In early 1992 the British explorer Ranulph Fiennes, together with a group of US researchers, announced that they had found (with the use of satellite imagery) the remains of Ubar, one of the great lost cities of Arabia. According to legend, Ubar, otherwise known as the Atlantis of the Sands, was the crossroads of the ancient frankincense trail. Scholars are fairly certain that the place existed, that it controlled the frankincense trade and was highly prosperous as a result, but therein lies the end of the certainties. The Quran states that God destroyed Ubar because the people were decadent and had turned away from religion, but archaeologists are more inclined to believe that it fell into a collapsed limestone cavern. Ongoing studies are hopeful of a more definitive reason for the city's demise.

Predictably, there are many who dispute the rediscovery of Ubar. At the time of writing, excavations at the site were proceeding slowly and nothing of sufficient age had surfaced to verify the claims. So is it worth the effort of bouncing along a graded track into the middle of nowhere to see not very much? For the historian, the romantic, or the plain curious, the discomfort of getting to this barren site is justified by the chance to peer through a hole in the desert at a legend laid bare.

OMAN UEAR

frankincense trees 8km from Mughsail. Three or four kilometres after the top of the road, there are stunning views back towards Mughsail and inland across some of the wildest wadis in Arabia. The vegetation in this area is entirely different from that on the Salalah plain, with yuccas and succulents clinging to the limestone ledges.

At 13.5km from Al-Maha petrol station in Mughsail, there is a small sign for **Fizayah**, 6km down the cliff face from the Sarfait Rd. It's just about possible in a 2WD in the dry season. The effort will be rewarded by one of the most dramatic spectacles in Dhofar: lunging cliffs and limestone pinnacles, decorated at the base with perfect sandy coves and grazing lands for the numerous camels owned by *jeballi* (the indigenous residents of Dhofar's mountains).

The Sarfait road continues to the Yemeni border, a two-hour drive from Salalah along a sealed road, passing the endearingly dubbed **Sea Overlooking Site**, 31km from Al-Maha petrol station. There is no accommodation between Salalah and the border crossing and no facilities at the border itself. It wasn't advisable to use this route to Yemen at the time of writing.

Ubar اوبار

Ubar (also spelt Wubar), near the town of Shisr, is an archaeological site of potentially great importance. Lost to history for over a thousand years, the rediscovery of the remains of this once mighty city caused great archaeological excitement in the 1990s. It may be hard for the ordinary mortal to appreciate what all the fuss is about: there is almost nothing to see at present except a small, dusty museum, and the fabled golden pillars of antiquity are still only the stuff of dreams.

If legend gets the better of you, however, you can reach Ubar via the main Salalah–Thumrait Hwy. At just over 10km north of Thumrait, turn left to Shisr (72km) on a graded road (4WD necessary). On entering Shisr, the site is on the right.

The equally legendary Empty Quarter beckons beyond. Ask tour companies in Salalah about overnight camping trips to the edge of these famous sands from the settlement of Al-Hashman.

Duqm الدقم

☑ 23 / POP 11,200

Set to become the location of the largest port in the Middle East, and second in the world only to Singapore, this once tiny fishing community is being slowly transformed out of all recognition. The construction teams are being mindful to preserve the town's main attraction, the fabulous **rock garden** of wind-eroded forms between the town and Ras Duqm, which has been chosen as the location for a cultural centre. In case you're wondering, the stone plug out to sea is called **Nafun Island**.

Major tourist resorts are planned on nearby beautiful beaches, including the newly opened **Crowne Plaza** (☑ 25 214444;

DON'T MISS

OMAN'S ONE & ONLY FLOATING HOTEL

If you've always fancied the glamour of a cruise ship but didn't trust your sea legs to make the experience pleasant, then the new floating hotel moored at Duqm may just be what you're looking for. **Veronica** (Floating Hotel; ☑ 25 212300; www.veronicaduqm. com; s/d OR45.600/59.700) is a retired cruise ship built on the Clyde in the UK in 1965 for a Swedish American line – hence the Nordic mural located midships. Towed to Duqm as an inventive solution for the need to provide immediate quality accommodation to service dock crew, the ship provided over 20,000 room nights in its first year of operation – remarkable when you consider it is sitting adjacent to a tiny fishing village in the middle of one of the most remote stretches of coast in Oman.

With nightly films shown in the tiered cinema at 9.30pm, free 30-minute guided tours of decks and engine room, lavish set meals of international quality, a below-Plimsolline swimming pool on the Emerald Floor, a library and the cosy Mariner's Bar, this old dame of a cruise liner has more by way of entertainment than offered by the entire region of Al-Wusta. That's all soon to change as construction of a city of 200,000 people, scheduled flights into a brand-new airport and tourist development along the Duqm coast slowly bring rival interest. For now, however, enjoying the fading glory of *Veronica* has to be one of the most unique accommodation experiences in Oman.

www.ihg.com/crowneplaza; r from OR83; (P ⊛ ☒) on a sandy bay south of the port complex. Prices at the time of writing reflected the 'soft opening' status of the hotel and are likely to increase. The only other places to stay in Duqm are **City Hotel Duqm** (☑ 25 214900; www.cityhotelduqm.com; s/d OR55/70), a modern, low-key business hotel signposted off the highway with friendly, helpful management, and *Veronica*, a retired cruise ship resting in the dock.

Hayma   هيما

☑ 23 / POP 10,400

This is the chief town of the region and an important transit point between the interior and the coast. Although there is little to commend the town itself, it does have basic accommodation and makes a good base for visiting the oryx reserve in Jaaluni.

The **Hayma Motel** (Himah Motel; fax 23 436061; Hwy 31; r OR18), on the highway opposite the main road turning into town, primarily caters for Asian businesspeople and has possibly the worst beds in the country with springs that sprung years ago. A better bet is the newer **Arabian Oryx Hotel** (☑ 23 436379; arabianoryxhotel@gmail.com; r OR20; P ⊛) 1km further up the road, which also offers basic Indian cuisine.

There are a number of unremarkable chicken-and-rice restaurants dotted around the petrol station opposite the motel.

Jaaluni   جالوني

The return of the oryx is one of the great wildlife success stories of the region and watching these magnificent animals paw the dust in the summer heat, or slip gracefully through the dawn mists in winter, makes the long journey to the desolate Jiddat al-Harasis plain worthwhile.

A permit is needed to visit the reserve; this is easily organised through the **Office of the Advisor for Conservation of the Environment** (Map p120; ☑ 24 693537, 24 593537; acedrc@omantel.net.om; per party OR20; ⊙7am-6pm) in Muscat. The permit covers the cost of a mandatory guide, usually a member of the Harsusi tribe, who will show you the on-site portacabin **museum**, the resident, captive breeding herd and help you spot a wild oryx if you're lucky. You will definitely see gazelle – they linger around the reserve offices, nibbling the grass in the parking lot. If you ask, the guide will also take you to the remarkable windblown formations of the Huqf Escarpment, an hour deeper into the reserve. Unfortunately most guides don't speak English. Alternatively, tour operators can arrange trips with English-speaking guides.

You can camp in the reserve at a designated site but you will need to bring your own food. Keep your clothes under canvas as there is always a heavy dew by the morning – this is how the animals survive in the absence of surface water.

The reserve is 50km off the Hayma–Duqm road (Hwy 37) on a poorly graded track. The track can be identified by a blue sign for Habab, 96km from Duqm and 13km from the only housing complex on Hwy 37. After 23km along the track, veer right at the blue sign for Jaaluni. It takes about an hour to drive from Hayma to the reserve. The guard at the security gate by the reserve fence will want to see your permit.

UNDERSTAND OMAN

Oman Today

The Rebirth of Oman

'Renaissance' is a term any visitor to Oman will hear, as it refers to the current period under Sultan Qaboos, a leader held responsible by most of the population for easing the country into modernity. Before he came to the throne in a bloodless coup in 1970, Oman had no secondary and only two primary schools, two hospitals run by the American mission and a meagre 10km of sealed roads. In addition, the country was in a state of civil war.

The country has since caught up with its more affluent neighbours. It now boasts efficient, locally run hospitals, universities, electricity to remote villages and an ever-improving infrastructure of roads. In January 1992 an elected Majlis ash-Shura (Consultative Council) was convened as a first step towards broader participation in government. Female representation on the council is growing (they were the first in the Arab Gulf states to participate in this way) and women continue to hold high office in government, including at ministerial level. The country enjoys an enviably low crime rate and a well-trained and highly educated workforce.

It is perhaps this latter point that led to the Arab Spring of 2011 in Oman which took its toll on the country's stability. Oman fell 20 points on the Global Peace Index 2012, published by the US Institute for Economics and Peace, although it still ranks among the most peaceful countries in the Arab world. Local protests, particularly in the northern town of Sohar, focused less on calls for greater democracy (the sultan is the ultimate authority, with jurisdiction over even minor policy decisions) than on the lack of opportunities for job seekers and the slow progress of Omanisation – the process of replacing expatriates with Omani nationals.

Despite these disturbances, Sultan Qaboos remains a popular leader whose reign is celebrated with due pomp and ceremony each year. His 'meet the people' tour, where he and his ministers camp in different regions of the country to listen to local requests, is a good metaphor for his success. These tours, during which any visiting dignitaries are obliged to go camping too, are often marked by pennant-carrying camel riders bringing their petitions across the desert with gifts of goats for His Majesty. Requesting lighting in their village on day two of the sultan's visit, petitioners may well expect to see the pylons delivered by day four of the same trip. It is this accessibility on the part of the sultan, together with his reputation for delivering promises, and for promoting tolerance and dialogue in a region not wholly typified by either quality, that makes him a national treasure.

Sultan Qaboos is not married and has no children. As he celebrates over 40 years of a benign and enlightened reign, thoughts inevitably are turning to what the country will do without him.

Education & Diversification

In building a modern state, Sultan Qaboos' chief strategy has been to create a highly trained local workforce through intensive investment in education. Schooling is free, even partially at tertiary level, and provision is made (until recently by helicopter) for children of even the remotest villages. There has been no distinction in this approach between the genders. Indeed, girls account for almost half of the students in public and private schools while around half of the students at Sultan Qaboos University, the country's leading educational establishment, are women. Women are outperforming male students even in engineering and medicine, traditionally male disciplines: the first female flight engineer in the region is from Oman.

With limited oil revenues, Oman cannot sustain costly expatriate labour, so a policy of 'Omanisation' in every aspect of the workforce is rigorously pursued. In contrast to the rest of the region, it is refreshing to find locals – often of both sexes – working in all sections of society, from petrol-pump attendants to senior consultants.

Two central planks of the economy are self-sufficiency in food production, realised through intensive agriculture along the Batinah coast, and diversification of the economy. These schemes include the export of natural gas from a successful plant near Sur; an enormous port project in Duqm, which is predicted to be one of the biggest in the world when it is complete; and other important port projects that are undergoing expansion at Salalah and Sohar. The decision to disperse new economic initiatives across the regions has helped keep local communities buoyant and helped slow the exodus of villagers migrating to the capital.

Much investment continues to be made in Oman's infrastructure – no mean feat given the challenges presented by the country's size, remoteness and terrain. It is now possible to drive on sealed roads to most towns and villages across the country. A similar surge in IT infrastructure is ensuring that Oman is connected effectively to the world's information highways, with e-government and telecom developments revolutionising the way business is conducted at home and abroad.

History

Gold, Frankincense and...Copper

The term 'renaissance' applied to the current sultan's reign is an appropriate one, as it suggests equally rich periods through Oman's long history.

As far back as 5000 BC, southern Oman (now called Dhofar) was the centre of the lucrative frankincense trade. This highly prized commodity, produced from the aromatic sap of the frankincense tree, was traded for spices with India and carried by caravans across all of Arabia. While the trees grew in Yemen and one or other two locations, they grew best in the monsoon-swept hills of Dhofar, where they continue to be harvested to this day. So precious was the sap of these trees that even the part-mythical Queen of Sheba hand-delivered Dhofari frankincense to King Solomon (p389). Equally legendary, of course, are the gifts borne by the three wise men of biblical report.

The Bible also mentions the golden-pillared city of Ubar, built by the people of Ad. This fabled city, which has excited the curiosity of explorers for hundreds of years, grew out of the frankincense trade to become one of the most powerful cities in the region. The remains of the city were reputedly rediscovered in the 1990s by English explorer Ranulph Fiennes. Nonetheless, it is hard to believe this claim, looking at the virtually barren plot near Thumrait. Much more persuasive is the fact that the presumed descendents of the remarkable civilisation of Ad still occupy the surrounding desert, speaking the distinct and ancient language of Jibbali, whimsically known as the 'language of the birds'.

Oman enjoyed further prosperity in pre-Islamic times through the trading of copper. Indeed, Oman is referred to in some sources as 'the Mountain of Copper', and the Bahrain National Museum provides evidence of vigorous trading in copper between Oman and its Gulf neighbours. The country then slipped into a long period of isolation that prevailed until the 7th century AD when Islam was introduced by Amr ibn al-As, a disciple of the Prophet Mohammed. Oman was quick to embrace the new faith – it even gained a reputation for its proselytising zeal.

For about the next 500 years Oman came under the leadership of the Bani Nabhan dynasty (1154–1624).

Hostilities: the Portuguese

Frequent civil wars during the Bani Nabhan dynasty, between the sultan's forces and tribal factions, left the country vulnerable to outside hostilities that eventually came in the form of the Portuguese.

Alarmed by Oman's naval strength and anxious to secure Indian Ocean trade routes, the Portuguese launched a succession of attacks against Omani ports; by 1507 they managed to occupy the major coastal cities of Qalhat (near Sur, and mentioned in the journals of Ibn Battuta and Marco Polo), Muscat and Sohar. Ironically, it was a talented sailor from Sohar, Ahmed bin Majid, who unwittingly helped Vasco da Gama navigate the Cape of Good Hope in 1498, leading to the Portuguese invasion a few years later.

Over the next 150 years Oman struggled to oust the occupying forces. Eventually, under the guidance of the enlightened Ya'aruba dynasty (1624–1743), Oman was able to build up a big enough fleet to succeed. The Portuguese were interested in Oman only as a sentry post for their maritime adventures and had barely ventured into the country's interior. They were therefore easy to rout, given Oman's newly established naval might. Other than Al-Jalali Fort, Al-Mirani Fort and Mutrah Fort, all of which dominate the centre of Muscat, the Portuguese left little behind, although their legacy of military architecture shaped fort construction in Oman.

Unified & Wealthy

By 1650 Oman became a settled, unified state of considerable wealth and cultural accomplishment, with influence extending as far as Asia and Africa. Many of Oman's other great forts were built during this period, including the impressive, round-towered Nizwa Fort.

By the 19th century, under Sultan Said bin Sultan (r 1804–56), Oman had built up a sizcable empire controlling strategic parts of the African coast, including Mombasa and Zanzibar, and parts of what are now India and Pakistan. Today it is easy to see the influence that Oman had on the coastal areas of those countries, and even more tangibly the extent to which its own culture and population was enriched by the contact. The Batinah coast, for example, is home to the Baluchi people originally from Pakistan; as a result, mosque design along the highway between Barka and Sohar bears more resemblance to the florid architecture across the neck of the Gulf than it does to the more austere Ibadi tradition of Oman's interior.

When Sultan Said died, the empire was divided between two of his sons. One became the Sultan of Zanzibar and ruled the African colonies, while the other became the Sultan of Muscat and ruled Oman. The division of the empire cut Muscat off from its most lucrative domains, and by the end of the century, the country had stagnated economically, not helped by British pressure to end its slave and arms trading.

Coastal Versus Interior: Isolation

The new century was marked by a rift between the coastal areas, ruled by the sultan, and the interior, which came to be controlled by a separate line of imams (religious teachers). In 1938 a new sultan, Said bin Taimur, tried to regain control of the interior, sparking off the Jebel Wars of the 1950s. Backed by the British, who had their own agenda, Said successfully reunited the country by 1959.

In all other respects, however, Said reversed Oman's fortunes with policies that opposed change and isolated Oman from the modern world. Under his rule, a country that a century earlier had rivalled the empire builders of Europe became a political and economic backwater. While neighbours such as Bahrain, Qatar and Kuwait were establishing enviable welfare states and sophisticated modern patterns of international trade, Oman slumped into poverty, with high rates of infant mortality and illiteracy. Even the communist insurgency in Dhofar during the 1960s failed to rouse Said from his reclusive palace existence in Salalah, and by the end of the decade his subjects, the most powerful of which had been either imprisoned or exiled, lost patience and rebellion broke out across the country.

The unrest led to a palace coup in July 1970 when Said's only son, Qaboos, covertly assisted by the British, seized the throne. With a face-saving shot in the foot, Said was spirited off to the Grosvenor Hotel in London, where he spent the remainder of his days. Some suggest that Said was not a greedy or malicious leader, just fiercely protective of his country's conservative traditions, which he feared would be eroded by the rapid modernisation experienced in neighbouring countries. Perhaps the country's contemporary balance between old and new, so skilfully maintained by his son, owes something to Said's cautious approach to Western influence.

People & Society

The National Psyche

Since the sultan came to power in 1970, Oman has trodden a careful path, limiting outside influence while enjoying some of the benefits that it brings. The result has been a successful adoption of the best parts of the Gulf philosophy, marked by a tolerance of outside 'customs and manners', without the sacrifice of national identity that often characterises rapid modernisation. Oman takes pride in its long history, consciously maintaining customs, dress, architecture and rules of hospitality, as well as meticulously restoring historical monuments. With relatively modest oil revenues, Omani people have had to work hard to make their country what it is today, and perhaps that is why the arrogance that may be seen in neighbouring countries is conspicuously absent here. It is refreshing to find Omani nationals in all walks of life, from taxi drviers to university professors.

Lifestyle

It would be hard to imagine any country that has changed so dramatically in such a short space of time. Within the living memory of most middle-aged people outside Muscat, travelling to the next village meant hopping on a donkey or bicycle, education meant reciting the Quran under a tree, and medication comprised of a few herbs (very effective ones) from the mountainsides. Modern farmers contemplate genetically modified crop rotations, yet also look at the cloudless sky and realise that their grandmothers and children haven't been praying loudly enough. Little wonder that some families have buckled under the pressure of such an extraordinary pace of change; alcoholism, divorce, drug abuse and manic driving are all social ills that have increased proportionately.

On the whole, however, Oman is a success story; it has embraced the new world with just enough scepticism to allow people to return to their villages on the weekend, park their Toyotas at the end of the tarmac and walk the rest of the way to see grandfather.

It's possible to recognise people's ethnic origins, even the regions from which they hail, by observing women's clothing. Heads, arms and legs are always covered, but outfits range from a patterned cotton cloth to a transparent *abeyya* (woman's full-length black robe), worn with a peaked face mask. In the capital, the silk *abeyya,* often worn over Western clothing, has become a fashion item. During festivals, sisters and even friends often wear clothes cut from the same cloth with elaborately embroidered trouser cuffs. Men wear a *dishdasha* (shirt-dress, usually white) and a white hat, traditionally embroidered by a loved one. On official occasions, they wear a turban (made of pashmina and usually imported from Kashmir) and tuck a silver *khanjar* (ceremonial dagger) into their belt. For an especially formal occasion, they may wear a silk outer garment with gold trim and carry a short, simple camel stick.

Multiculturalism

Oman's population is predominantly Arab, although the country's imperial history has resulted in intermarriage with other groups, particularly from East Africa. As such, some Omanis speak Swahili better than Arabic. An Indian merchant community has existed in Muscat for at least 200 years, and people of Persian or Baluchi ancestry inhabit the Batinah coast. The Jibbali people form a separate group in Dhofar. Many Jibbali live a mostly nomadic life with their own distinct customs; their language, completely distinct from any other, is dubbed 'the Language of the Birds'. Kumzari, the compound language spoken in parts of the Musandam Peninsula, is a mixture of Portuguese, Arabic and Farsi. Omani people have a strong sense of tribe and their tribal names (for example, al-Nabhani, al-Wahaybi, al-Balushi) indicate very clearly to which area they belong. Some families, such as Al-Abris from Wadi Sahten, can be pinpointed to specific wadis in the Hajar Mountains.

Attracted by work and modern amenities, many people are moving to the capital, Muscat, which is spreading along the coast towards Seeb. In an effort to stem this flow, graded roads, electricity and water have been supplied to even the smallest *willayat* (village). It is not unusual in even these farflung outposts of the country to see expatriates (mostly from India) working in shops and clinics.

Religion

About 75% of Omanis follow the Ibadi sect of Islam, an austere form of Islam that eschews decadence of any kind, even in mosque architecture. That said, modern Omanis tend to be pragmatic in their interpretation of religion, are tolerant of other forms of Islamic worship and allow expats to express their own religions in and around Muscat.

Magic plays a tangible role in the spiritual life of many Omanis. The 'evil eye' is not mere superstition; it is regarded as a hazard of everyday life. Amulets containing verses from the Quran, or hung around the necks of infants, are considered an effective way of warding off such problems. An expat member of the Magic Circle (an exclusive and international society of professional magicians which vows never to reveal to the public the tricks of its trade) was once invited to do a magic show in a village: when he conjured a white rabbit from his hat, his entire audience ran away.

Arts

In a village between Dibab and Tiwi on the old Qurayat–Sur coast road, the porches of several houses sport splendid pink or lime-green bathroom tiles, complete with fern motifs. Next door to one of these houses, the remains of an intricately hand-carved door lay disintegrating for years until weather, or an entrepreneur from Muscat, or both, put paid to it. It's not a case of out with the old and in with the new, but a demonstration of Oman's commercial relationship with art: a job lot of Indian tiles for a camel-bag of incense (or the modern-day equivalent) is the kind of international exchange that has characterised the pragmatic nature of Omani arts and crafts for centuries. It's not unusual, for example, to find the family silver (particularly grandmother's jewellery) making the journey to Muscat because wife number two prefers gold. Before they became items of tourist value, exquisite pieces of silver were readily melted down and returned in kind from the gold souq. In fact, for centuries most silver jewellery was fashioned from Oman's old currency (smelted Maria Theresa dollars, or *thalla*), prized for its 80%-plus silver content.

Oman's arts and crafts are all the more wonderful for being about the living rather than the dead, the practical rather than the purely decorative. Whether this heritage can withstand rapid modernisation is another matter.

Traditional Crafts

There are many crafts in Oman, all of which have been meticulously documented through the Omani Craft Heritage Documentation Project, under the auspices of His Highness Seyyid Shibah bin Tariq al-Said and endorsed by Unesco.

Each region of Oman is associated with a different craft – Bahla is famous for pottery, Nizwa for silver jewellery, Jebel Shams for rug-weaving, Sur for boat-building, Shwaymiyah for basket-making. For a definitive survey of Omani crafts, the twin-volume *The Craft Heritage of Oman,* by Neil Richardson and Marcia Dorr, makes a superb souvenir. Avelyn Forster's book *Dis-*

appearing Treasures of Oman focuses on the silver Bedouin jewellery of Oman.

For more information on Oman's rich craft industry, see the website of the **Public Authority for Craft Industries** (☑24 525944; www.paci.gov.om).

Music & Dance

There are dozens of traditional song and dance forms in Oman, over 130 of which have been documented by the **Oman Centre for Traditional Music** (☑24 602127; www.octm-folk.gov.om), which was established in 1984 to preserve the country's musical heritage. Oman was the first Arab country to become part of the International Council for Traditional Music, under Unesco.

Oman's music is diverse, due to the country's seafaring and imperial heritage. The *naham* is a particularly famous call to crew members to pull together during a long sea voyage.

Sultan Qaboos is a Western classical-music lover. The Royal Oman Symphony Orchestra set up in his honour has been a surprising success, given the difficulties involved in learning a completely different musical idiom. The opening of the magnificent Royal Opera House Muscat (p127) in 2011, to mark the occasion of the 40th anniversary of the sultan's reign, has enabled the hosting of world-class opera, ballet and classical-music orchestras from around the world. There is an efficient online reservation system with collection of tickets at the door. The season extends from September to May.

Each branch of the armed forces has a band of international calibre, including the highly popular bagpipe contingent – no official ceremony in Oman would be the same without the pipes and drums. The massed bands perform annual tattoos, giving lavish horse- and camel-back displays. Some of the military bands have regularly participated in the Edinburgh Tattoo.

Architecture

Oman may no longer boast pillars of gold like the fabled city of Ubar, but it does have another architectural trump card: its forts. There is barely a village without one.

The country has mercifully largely escaped the skyscraping obsession of its neighbours, settling for more restrained public buildings in keeping with a more modest budget. However, what the buildings lack in multiple floors, they make up for in imaginative design. Muscat, in particular, abounds with serene and elegant examples, such as the ministry buildings and embassy buildings in Al-Khuwair. The Grand Mosque in Al-Ghubrah, completed in 2001, is the ultimate expression of restraint, with the simplicity of its exterior masking an exuberantly rich interior.

Not all of Muscat's buildings are grave, however; take the whimsical Grand Hyatt Muscat, with its confection of arabesques and crenulations, or the venerable but distinctly quirky Al-Bustan Palace Hotel. Whatever individual flights of fancy are indulged in by the architect, the result is a harmonious affair of whitewashed or sand-coloured buildings that illustrates a respect for traditional architectural values.

Barasti (palm-leaf) and other palm-constructed housing is still common along the coast from Duqm to Shwaymiyah. In the Sharqiya Sands, Bedu use goat-hair tents, and many people on the mountains live in caves with an improvised front door. The round houses made from constructed, interlocking sticks that cling to the hills of Dhofar are interesting. They were once thatched but these days are more likely to be covered in bright plastic.

Environment

Oman is blessed with a remarkable environment of spectacular landscapes and a wealth of flora and fauna. However, it doesn't render up its treasures easily and a 4WD is required to visit many of the places of natural beauty and interest. Accommodation near these places is often restricted to ad-hoc camping, but many regard this as a joy in its own right. Indeed, waking up to the sound of a turtle retreating down the beach, or falling asleep to the croak of toads, is an unforgettable experience. To help explore these places, *Off-Road in the Sultanate of Oman,* by Sam Owen and Lonely Planet author Jenny Walker, describes how to reach just about every corner of the country.

If hiring a vehicle is not an appealing option, there are plenty of tours available from Muscat and Salalah that will reveal the country to the visitor.

The Land

Geographically, Oman is large and diverse, with an untrammelled coastline over 3000km in length, rugged mountains, a share of the Empty Quarter and a unique monsoon catchment. It extends from the fjords of the Musandam Peninsula to the intermittently green Dhofar region.

Most of the country's population is concentrated on the Batinah coast, a semifertile plain that runs from the border with the UAE to Muscat, and is separated from the rest of Arabia by the Hajar Mountains. These mountains are internationally famed for their geological heritage and even the layperson will enjoy the candy-striped rocks. The highest peak is Jebel Shams (Mountain of the Sun) at 3075m, alongside which runs Wadi Ghul, dubbed the Grand Canyon of Arabia. On the slopes of nearby Jebel Akhdar (Green Mountain), temperate fruits are grown.

Much of the country between the Hajar Mountains and Dhofar is flat and rocky desert, but there are also areas of sand dunes. Most notable are the Sharqiya Sands, formerly known as Wahiba Sands, and the less-accessible sands of the Rub al-Khali (Empty Quarter). Oman is not as rich in oil as its neighbours, but it does have some extensive fields in the gravel plains around Marmul in Al-Wusta Region and Fahood in Al-Dakhiliyah Region.

Thriving and diverse marine life exists off Oman's long coastline and there are many islands, the chief of which is the desert island of Masirah.

Wildlife

ANIMALS

Oman's isolated mountains and wadis provide a haven for a variety of animals. These include over 50 types of mammals, such as wolves, foxes, hedgehogs, jerboas and hares. The largest land mammal that a visitor is likely to see is the gazelle, a herd of which lives in a protected area along the Qurayat–Sur coast highway.

There are 13 different species of whale and dolphin in Omani waters, including the world's biggest living creature, the blue whale. Oman also has an important biodiversity of molluscs. Indeed, the rich variety of shells adds to the pleasure of visiting the coast.

The *Oman Bird List* is updated regularly and published by the Oman Bird Records Committee (ORI, available in Muscat bookshops); there are over 400 recorded species. Spoonbills and flamingos frequent salt lagoons, even in Muscat, but the country is internationally renowned for its migrating raptors. For more information, it's worth buying *Birdlife in Oman*, by Hanne and Jens Eriksen. Keen ornithologists should contact the Oman Bird Group (p129).

There is a wide diversity of insects in Oman – from the mighty minotaur beetle to the fig tree blue, orange pansy and other butterflies – attracted to Oman's fertile wadis or desert acacias.

ENDANGERED SPECIES

Oman is of global importance to the survival of the endangered green turtle and has one of the largest nesting sites in the world at Ras al Jinz. There are five endangered species of turtle supported by the coasts of Oman, all protected by royal decree.

Oman's varied terrain is home to a large number of endangered species, including houbara bustard, ibex, *tahr* (an Omani species of a goatlike animal) and Arabian leopard. The latter frequents Jebel Samhan in Dhofar and has even been known to stroll onto the runway at Salalah. There are also declining numbers of sand cat, caracal, honey badger and mongoose.

The Arabian Oryx Sanctuary in Jiddat al-Harasis protects a herd of wild oryx.

PLANTS

Oman built an empire on the frankincense trees that grow in Dhofar. The trees are still bled for the aromatic sap, but dates, covering 49% of cultivated land, have overtaken them in economic importance. Oman has a very rich plant life thanks to its fertile wadis, many irrigated year-round by spring water. It is common to see tall stands of pink oleander flowering in the wadis throughout the year.

A government-sponsored herbal clinic in Muscat uses many locally occurring plants and shrubs to treat a wide range of illnesses, most commonly diabetes and hypertension.

A national collection of plants is being assembled as part of the world-class **Oman Botanic Garden** (www.oman-botanic-garden. org), the first of its kind in Arabia. When complete (in 2014), every habitat in Oman will be represented in two giant biomes.

National Parks

While there are several reserves, such as the Qurm Nature Reserve in Muscat, set up to protect the endangered mangrove, and the Arabian Oryx Sanctuary, there are no formal national parks. The Damanayat Islands are designated as a national nature reserve and access to this pristine marine environment is controlled.

Environmental Issues

Oman has an enviable record with regard to its protection of the environment – a subject in which the sultan has a passionate interest. His efforts have been acknowledged by the International Union for the Conservation of Nature (IUCN), which awarded him the John C Philips Prize in 1996, and cited Oman as a country with one of the best records in environmental conservation and pollution control. The sultanate's first environmental legislation was enacted in 1974, and in 1984 Oman was the first Arab country to set up a ministry exclusively concerned with the environment. The prestigious Sultan Qaboos International Prize for Environmental Preservation, first awarded

> ### RETURN OF THE ORYX
>
> In 1962 the Fauna Preservation Society captured the last remaining oryx close to the border with Yemen and sent them to a zoo in the USA. By 1982, protected by new laws banning the hunting of wild animals, a herd of 40 Arabian oryx was returned to Jiddat al-Harasis. Despite intermittent bouts of poaching the program has met with success, in part due to the commitment of the Harasis tribe designated to look after them.
>
> The return of the oryx to Oman was the occasion of great rejoicing, which prompts the question: what it is about this antelope that provokes such emotion? Perhaps it's the uncanny resemblance of a mature bull, with rapier-like antlers, to the mythical unicorn. This is not as far-fetched as it seems. The ancient Egyptians used to bind the antlers of young oryx so they would fuse into one. Seeing a white, summer-coated herd-bull level up to a rival in profile, it's easy to confuse fact with fiction.

in 1991, is given every two years to a conservation body or individual chosen by Unesco for environmental performance.

On 8 January each year the sultanate celebrates Environment Day, when children learn about habitat erosion, rubbish dumping and depletion of freshwater reserves. One of the environmental problems that visitors will notice is the amount of oil washed up on Oman's beaches, dumped illegally from container ships. Despite heavy penalties if caught, offenders often get away with it, as it's almost impossible for Oman's military services to police such a long and exposed coastline.

Until recently, Oman's shores were otherwise pristine. Unfortunately, the sudden influx of tourists has led to previously unknown problems including dirty beaches where people insist on leaving their litter behind. Plastic bags are fast becoming a serious environmental hazard, mistaken by land and marine animals for food.

By far the most upsetting issue, however, has been the insensitivity of tourists towards the turtle population at Ras al-Jinz. The government has put the protected area under strict management and this is beginning to help minimise the disruption of the celebrated nesting sites.

To find out more about the steps Oman is taking to preserve the environment and the unique flora and fauna within it, contact the Environmental Society of Oman (p150). There is also an Outward Bound initiative to bring environmental awareness to the nation's youth.

Food & Drink

While local cuisine outside the Omani home tends to be of Lebanese origin, home cooking is nutritious and varied, reflecting Oman's ethnic diversity. Cardamom, saffron and turmeric are essential ingredients, but Omani cooking is not exceptionally spicy.

With access to a long coastline, Omanis are particularly fond of fish – sardines can be seen drying in noisome piles from Sohar to Salalah. Until recently, however, shellfish, including the local lobster (actually a large,

---

OMAN'S FAVOURITE SWEETS

Omanis have a decidedly sweet tooth, which they indulge during every important social occasion. Little surprise then that Oman has a particularly high incidence of diabetes. What is more surprising is that most Omanis have a fine set of teeth. If offered, you'll be expected to sample the traditional treats so don't forget to use only your right hand in receiving or offering the following sweetmeats.

Halwa At official ceremonies, such as graduations and National Day celebrations, *halwa* is offered to guests. Lumps of the sticky, glutinous confection are pinched out of a communal dish between the right finger and thumb, much to the chagrin of those who forgot to bring a hanky. This sweetmeat is made of sugar or dates, saffron, cardamom, almonds, nutmeg and rosewater in huge copper vats heated over the fire and stirred for many hours by men wielding long, wooden pestles; it's hard and hot work and its production is displayed as an entertainment during *eids* (Islamic feasts) and festivals. Every region thinks it produces the best *halwa* but Barka is generally understood to have the edge and many outlets around the town sell it piled up in colourful plastic bowls or glazed ceramic dishes.

Dates If no one quite got round to making the *halwa* for a party, then dates will suffice. Dates are not only an indispensable part of a meal, but also of Omani hospitality. Dates are always served with one or two cups of strong *qahwa* (Arabic coffee laced with cardamom) and it is impolite to refuse to share at least one date with at least two cups with a host (but not too many more).

Honey Dubbed by some as the 'liquid gold' of the region, honey costs OR10 to OR70 a kilo. As such, it's easy to see why apiculture is on the increase. It's not a new trend, however: boiling honey was used in Oman as a weapon against enemies – just look for the holes above fort doors. The most expensive honey is still collected in the traditional way from wild beehives in the upper reaches of the Hajar Mountains. Pale, golden honey indicates the bees were raised on date-palm pollen; deep amber suggests sumar-tree blossom; while *sidr*, a mountain shrub, produces a molasses-coloured honey.

clawless crayfish), were not considered fit for eating.

Perhaps the most typical Omani dish is *harees,* made of steamed wheat and boiled meat to form a glutinous concoction. It is often garnished *ma owaal* (with dried shark) and laced with lime, chilli and onions, and is a popular dish used to break the fast during Ramadan.

Visitors should try *shuwa* (marinated meat cooked in an earth oven) if given the chance. It is the dish of parties and festivals, and comprises goat, mutton, calf or camel meat, prepared with date juice and spices, and wrapped in banana leaves. The result, at least 12 hours later, is a mouth-wateringly tenderised piece of meat, aromatically flavoured with wood smoke and spices. It is served with *rukhal* (wafer-thin Omani bread) and rice on a *fadhl* (giant, communal eating tray), and eaten, of course, with the right hand only. Guests traditionally eat first, followed by men, who are expected to reserve the best pieces for women.

A delicious traditional dish from southern Oman is *rabees*. It is made from boiled baby shark, stripped and washed of the gritty skin, and then fried with the liver.

Fruit is an important part of an Omani meal, usually served before the meat course. Oman grows its own prize pomegranates, bananas, apricots and citrus fruit on the terraced gardens of Jebel Akhdar.

Camel milk is available fresh and warm from the udder in Bedouin encampments. Like mare milk, it's an experience many prefer to miss! Alcohol cannot be purchased 'over the counter' in Oman without a resident permit. It is available, however, in most of the more expensive hotels and restaurants.

SURVIVAL GUIDE

ⓘ Directory A–Z

ACCOMMODATION

In general, accommodation in Oman is limited and expensive. The following notes may be helpful when booking accommodation:

➡ Discounts can often be negotiated in the low season (May to September, except in Salalah where peak season is June to August).

➡ In many places, there's no alternative to the single midrange to top-end hotel, and smaller towns often have no hotels at all.

SLEEPING PRICE RANGES

The following price ranges refer to a double room with bathroom and air-con in high season (November to March). Taxes and breakfast are included in the price. Listings are arranged by price and then by author preference within a price category.

$ less than OR45 (US$120)

$$ OR45–OR100 (US$120–US$265)

$$$ more than OR100 (US$265)

➡ Room rates for accommodation reviewed by Lonely Planet include the mandatory 17% tax and include breakfast unless otherwise stated.

➡ The only official campsites in Oman are at Ras al-Jinz, and some expensive 'camping experience' resorts in Ras al-Hadd and Sharqiya Sands.

➡ Wild camping is one of the highlights of Oman, providing you are discreet, outside urban areas and don't require creature comforts. Finding somewhere suitable to camp can be difficult without a 4WD vehicle.

ACTIVITIES

Oman is a large country with a sparse population. There are still vast tracts of land without a road that are virtually unmapped. This is excellent news for anyone interested in the outdoors, as you have the chance of coming across an unmapped wadi or hidden cave system, finding a bed of undisturbed fossils, or discovering a species unnamed by science – the possibilities are endless. However, there is a responsibility, firstly, to avoid getting into a dangerous situation (rescue services are either not available or stretched to the maximum in taking care of road traffic accidents) and, secondly, to limit the negative impact of each activity on the environment.

Off-Road Exploration

One of the highlights of visiting Oman is off-road exploration of its mountains, wadis, sand dunes and coastline, particularly in a 4WD with some camping equipment. Hiring a 4WD can be expensive, but tour companies offer all the main off-road destinations as day trips or on overnight tours.

Hiking, Rock Climbing & Caving

With a pair of stout boots, a map, water and *Adventure Trekking in Oman,* by Anne Dale and Jerry Hadwin, you can access superb walking territory all over the country. Unless you are an accustomed outbacker, however, it is advisable to take a tour that can help tailor a trip to suit your interests.

Rock climbing and caving are increasingly popular activities in Oman, but they tend to be conducted on a 'go-it-alone' basis. *Rock Climbing in Oman,* by RA McDonald, lists some exciting routes, but you need a climbing partner and equipment.

Oman has some rich cave systems, many of which have never been explored. *Caves of Oman,* by Samir Hanna and Mohamed al-Belushi, gives an excellent account of speleology in Oman and points out some local safety advice.

Other Activities

Fishing Muscat Game Fishing Club (☏ 99 322779; www.mgfa-oman.com) Organises deep-sea outings. Game fish is tag and release but tuna you can take home for supper. The competitive angler might like to try a line in the three-day Sinbad Classic, held in Muscat each winter.

Dolphin-watching Oman is a great country for naturalists, with dolphins and whales found in large numbers off the coast: early-morning boat trips from Marina Bandar al-Rowdha (p126) are the best way to spot them.

Turtle-watching Important turtle-nesting sites are found near Sur; informative tours of a nesting beach can be arranged through Ras al-Jinz Turtle Reserve (p150).

Water sports There are some excellent snorkelling and diving opportunities in Oman, and the vast coastline is virtually unexplored in many places. Diving courses are available in Muscat, Al-Sawadi Beach Resort (p176) and Salalah. Various water sports are offered through the five-star hotels in Muscat and at Oman Dive Center (p142).

BOOKS

➤ *The Doctor and the Teacher: Oman 1955–1970,* by Donald Bosch – includes an interesting account of life before the 'renaissance'.

➤ *On the Track of the Early Explorers,* by Philip Ward – combines modern travel narrative with the accounts of earlier travellers.

➤ *Arabian Sands,* by Wilfred Thesiger – the final part of Thesiger's 1959 classic describes Oman's interior.

➤ *Atlantis of the Sands,* by Ranulph Fiennes – an account of the Dhofar insurgency in the 1960s, and also describes the search for the lost city of Ubar. On the same subject, *The Road to Ubar,* by Nicholas Clapp, is worth a read.

➤ *Off-Road in the Sultanate of Oman,* by Lonely Planet author Jenny Walker and Sam Owen – a must for 4WD exploration in Oman. It covers the entire country, highlights special interests and has a useful set of maps.

➤ *Adventure Trekking in Oman,* by Anne Dale and Jerry Hadwin – lists some great hikes.

➤ *Oman – a Comprehensive Guide,* published under the auspices of the Directorate General of Tourism. Includes interesting anecdotal information.

CHILDREN

Oman is a friendly and welcoming place for children. For younger children, beachcombing, sandcastle building and paddling make Oman a dream destination. That said, there are few specifically designed amenities for children, except for a park with swings in most town centres.

CUSTOMS REGULATIONS

➤ Non-Muslims travelling by air can bring in one bottle of alcohol.

➤ It is illegal to cross by land from Oman into the UAE and vice versa carrying alcohol.

➤ A 'reasonable quantity' of cigars, cigarettes and tobacco can be imported.

DANGERS & ANNOYANCES

Oman is a very safe country. Three dangers that may escape the attention of visitors, however, are high volumes of traffic accidents due to tailgating and speed, flash floods and the isolation of many off-road destinations.

EMBASSIES & CONSULATES

Unless indicated otherwise, all the embassies listed are on Jameat ad Duwal al-Arabiyah St in the district of Shatti al-Qurm, Muscat. The British embassy looks after Irish nationals, processes visas and handles emergencies for Canadian citizens. Australians should contact the Australian embassy in Riyadh, Saudi Arabia.

Consular sections of the embassy often close an hour or two earlier than the rest of the embassy, so try to go as early in the day as possible or ring first to check. Embassies include:

Bahraini (Map p120; ☏ 24 605133; bahrain@ omantel.net.om; Way No 3017, Shatti al-Qurm; ⊙ 8am-2.30pm Sat-Wed)

Dutch (Map p120; ☏ 24 603706; www.oman. nlembassy.org; Way 3017, Villa 1366, Shatti al-Qurm; ⊙ 9am-noon Sat-Wed)

Egyptian (Map p120; ☏ 24 600411; fax 24 697366; ⊙ 9am-12.30pm Sat-Wed)

French (Map p120; ☏ 24 681800; www.ambafrance-om.org; ⊙ 9am-2.30pm Sat-Wed)

German (Map p120; ☏ 24 832482; www. maskat.diplo.de; An-Nahdah St, Ruwi; ⊙ 9am-noon Sat-Wed)

Iranian (Map p120; ☏ 24 696944; fax 24 696888; ⊙ 7.30am-4pm Sat-Wed)

Jordanian (Map p120; ☏ 24 692760; fax 24 692762; ⊙ 8am-noon Sat-Wed)

Kuwaiti (Map p120; ☏ 24 699626; fax 24 600972; ⊙ 8am-12.30pm Sat-Wed)

Lebanese (Map p120; ☏ 24 695844; fax 24 695633; Way No 3019, Shatti al-Qurm; ⊙ 8am-2.30pm Sat-Wed)

Qatari (Map p120; ☑ 24 691152; fax 24 691156; ⊙ 8am-2.30pm Sat-Wed)

Saudi Arabian (Map p120; ☑ 24 601744; fax 24 697058; ⊙ 8.30am-2pm Sat-Wed)

Syrian (Map p120; ☑ 24 697904; fax 24 603895; Al-Inshirah St, Madinat as-Sultan Qaboos; ⊙ 9am-2pm Sat-Wed)

Turkish (Map p120; ☑ 24 697050; Way No 3047, Shatti al-Qurm; ⊙ 8am-noon Sat-Wed)

UAE (Map p120; ☑ 24 400000; uaeoman@ omantel.net.om; ⊙ 8am-1.30pm Sat-Wed)

UK (Map p120; ☑ 24 609000; www.britishembassy.gov.uk; ⊙ 7.30am-2.30pm Sat-Wed)

USA (Map p120; ☑ 24 643400; www.oman.usembassy.gov; ⊙ 8am-4pm Sat & Mon-Wed)

Yemeni (Map p120; ☑ 24 600815; fax 24 605008; Way No 2840, bldg No 2981, Shatti al-Qurm; ⊙ 9am-1.30pm Sat-Wed)

FOOD

For information about Oman's cuisine, see p117, p200 and the Flavours of Arabia chapter (p459).

INTERNET ACCESS

Internet access is available throughout Oman and many of the larger towns have at least one internet cafe. Prepaid cards are available.

LEGAL MATTERS

Breaking the law can have severe consequences. For more information, see the Expats chapter (p33) and consult your embassy.

MAPS

Up-to-date maps are hard come by in Oman. The *Apex Map of Oman*, available from bookshops and hotel foyers, has city maps as well as a large, reasonably accurate road map of Oman. Hildebrand's *Oman* road map has been recommended by travellers, but is not available in Oman.

MONEY
ATMs & Credit Cards

ATMs are widespread in Oman and many of them, particularly those belonging to HSBC, are tied into international systems. The most popular credit card in Oman is Visa, but MasterCard is also widely accepted. Amex is not accepted in many shops, and you may incur a fee of 5% for using it in some restaurants and hotels.

Currency

The official currency is the Omani rial (OR but widely spelt RO). One rial is divided into 1000 baisa (also spelt baiza and shortened to bz). There are coins of 5, 10, 25, 50 and 100 baisa, and notes of 100 and 200 baisa. There are notes of a half, 1, 5, 10, 20 and 50 rials.

Exchanging Money

Most banks will change US-dollar travellers cheques for a commission. Money changers keep similar hours to banks, but are often open

---

EATING PRICE RANGES

The following price ranges refer to a standard meal. Service charge and tax is included in the price.

$ less than OR5 (US$14)

$$ OR5–OR10 (US$14-US$28)

$$$ more than OR10 (US$28)

---

from around 4pm to 7pm as well. They usually offer a slightly more competitive rate than the banks, and most charge only a nominal commission of 500 baisa per cash transaction.

Tipping & Bargaining

A tip of 10% is customary only in large hotels and restaurants if a service fee hasn't been included in the bill. It is not the custom to tip taxi drivers or smaller establishments.

Discounts are available for most items in all shops other than supermarkets and Western-style chain stores. Haggle for taxi fares and souvenirs but don't expect too much of a bargain!

PHOTOGRAPHY

Memory cards and batteries are widely available in Muscat. Most studios can print digital photos from a memory card and transfer photos to a CD. It is important to be discreet photographing people, especially women, as it can cause great offence, especially in rural and remote areas.

POST

Sending a postcard to any destination outside the Gulf Cooperation Council costs 150 baisa. Postage for letters is 250 baisa for the first 10g and 400 baisa for 11g to 20g. For parcels of up to 1kg it is around OR5.

PUBLIC HOLIDAYS

In addition to the main Islamic holidays, Oman observes these public holidays:

Lailat al-Mi'raj (Ascension of the Prophet) The exact date is dependent on the sighting of the moon – the date is never given until the last minute.

Renaissance Day (23 July) A day's holiday is given to mark the beginning of the reign of Sultan Qaboos, generally credited for the modern rebirth of the country.

National Day (18 November) Marked by at least two days of holiday, camel-racing, military parades and flags decorating the highway.

RESPONSIBLE TRAVEL

Westerners are often seen wandering around supermarkets or hotel foyers in shorts, dressed in bikinis on public beaches and skinny-dipping in wadis. These practices are highly resented, though Omanis are too polite to say as much. In order to respect local customs, knees, cleavage and shoulders should be covered in public.

It's tempting when exploring off-road destinations to drive straight through the middle of villages. This is about as sensitive as taking a lorry through a neighbour's garden back home. If you want to see the village, it's better to park outside and walk in, preferably with permission from a village elder.

In addition, Oman's wild environment requires special consideration. Tyre tracks leave marks on the desert floor, often forever, and litter does not biodegrade in the hot, dry climate.

SHOPPING

Oman is a great centre for handicrafts, with expertise in silversmithing. Exquisitely crafted *khanjars* can cost up to OR500 but tourist versions are available from OR30. Genuine Bedouin silver is becoming scarce (read *Disappearing Treasures of Oman*, by Avelyn Foster). Silver Maria Theresa dollars, used as Oman's unit of currency for many years, make a good buy from OR3. Wooden *mandoos* (chests) studded with brass tacks cost from OR10 for a new one and start at OR100 for an antique.

Other items commonly for sale include coffeepots (not always made in Oman), baskets woven with leather, camel bags, rice mats and cushion covers. Many are imported, as per centuries of tradition, from India and Iran.

Frankincense is a 'must buy' from Salalah, together with a pottery incense burner (both available in Muscat). Amouage (from OR50), currently the most valuable perfume in the world, is made in Muscat partially from frankincense and comes in different fragrances and preparations. A visit to one of the outlets (at city centre, Qurm or the airport) is a treat in itself. Omani dates make another excellent gift.

SOLO TRAVELLERS

Travelling beyond Muscat and the main towns of Nizwa, Sohar, Sur and Salalah can be a lonely experience. The interior is sparsely populated and, with no established circuit of travellers' meeting places, bumping into other foreigners is rare outside the holiday period. While Omani people are very friendly and hospitable, they are also private and you are unlikely to be invited to stay for longer than the customary bread and salt. If you hitchhike to somewhere remote, you may have a very long wait before you find a ride

OPENING HOURS

At the time of writing Oman's weekend was on Thursday and Friday; opening hours used throughout this chapter reflect this. In a recent announcement, the weekend has changed to Friday and Saturday. As we go to press, it is unclear what Oman's new business hours will be. As a rule of thumb, many sights and activities will continue to be closed or have reduced hours on a Friday, especially during the morning which is typically dedicated to prayer. Below are the opening hours at the time of writing and the anticipated new opening hours.

PLACE	AT TIME OF WRITING	CHANGES AFTER 1 MAY 2013
banks	• 8am to noon Sunday to Thursday • some reopen between 5pm and 8pm	• no change anticipated • no change anticipated
government departments & ministries	• 7.30am to 2.30pm Saturday to Wednesday • closing 1.30pm during Ramadan	• 7.30am to 2.30pm Sunday to Thursday • closing 1.30pm during Ramadan
post offices	• 8am to 1.30pm Saturday to Wednesday • 8am to 11am Thursday	• 8am to 1.30pm Sunday to Thursday • 8am to 11am Saturday
restaurants	• 8am to 11am Thursday • 5pm to midnight Friday	• no change anticipated • no change anticipated
shops	• 8am to 1pm and 4pm to 7pm Saturday to Thursday • 5pm to 7pm Friday • Mutrah Souq and upmarket Muscat shopping centres open to 9pm or 9.30pm	• no change anticipated • no change anticipated • no change anticipated
sights	• 9am to 4pm Saturday to Thursday • closed or reduced hours on Friday	• no change anticipated • no change anticipated

out again. On the whole, as with any country with large expanses of remote territory, it's better to have backup in the form of a vehicle, a companion, or at least water, a map and compass.

TELEPHONE & FAX

Each area of Oman has its own code (for example, 24 is the prefix for Muscat). Note that you need to use this code even if calling from within the same area.

Central public-telephone offices offer fax services in Muscat and Salalah, though the latter only has cardphones. Phonecards are available from grocery stores and petrol stations. International phone calls can be made with a phonecard by dialling direct from most public phone booths throughout Oman. The cost of a two-minute call to Europe and the USA is approximately 200 baisas.

Mobile Phones

Temporary local GSM connections can be made through the purchase of an **Omanmobile** (www. omanmobile.om) Hayyak SIM card (OR3), which includes OR1 worth of call time. Alternatively, **Nawras** (www.nawras.com.om) and **Friendi Mobile** (www.friendimobile.om) offer a similar service. These cards can be purchased on arrival at the airport and from shopping centres in Muscat.

TOURS

Tours in Oman are generally tailor-made for the customer in private vehicles with an English-speaking driver-guide. This is great for your itinerary, but painful on the pocket unless you can muster a group of three or four to share.

The following are average prices per vehicle for a full-day tour from Muscat. Picnic lunch costs an extra OR5.

TOUR	COST (OR)
dhow cruise	25 (per person)
dolphin-watching	20 (per person)
Jebel Shams	130
Nakhal & Rustaq	90
Nizwa, Bahla & Jabrin	100
Sharqiya Sands	130
Wadi Shab & Wadi Tiwi	110

Tour companies abound in Muscat, Salalah and Khasab; they offer camel safaris, 4WD touring, camping, city tours, caving, rock climbing, dhow rides, dolphin-watching and combinations thereof. Some recommended agencies are as follows:
Alive Oman (☑ 97 300007; gordon@alive-oman.com) Offers a personal service for adventure tourism and specialises in sourcing Omani guides.

Bike & Hike Oman (☑ 24 400873; www. bikeandhikeoman.com) Offers a number of spectacular cycling and hiking tours in the Hajar Mountains.

Desert Discovery (☑ 24 493232; www.desert-discovery.com) For trips to the Sharqiya Sands.

Explore Oman (www.exploreoman.com) An experienced UK-based company.

Mark Tours (☑ 24 782727; www.marktours-oman.com) A popular and experienced company that can tailor-make study tours and adventure trips.

Muscat Diving & Adventure Centre (☑ 24 485663; www.holiday-in-oman.com) The best company through which to organise activities such as caving, hiking and other outward-bound activities.

National Travel & Tourism (NTT; ☑ 24 660376; www.nttoman.com) Offers an excellent, friendly and comprehensive tour service, including trips to the Oryx Sanctuary at Jaaluni National Reserve.

Sea Tours Oman (☑ 99 425461; www. seatoursoman.com) Specialises in boat trips including glass-bottom boats in Muscat.

TRAVELLERS WITH DISABILITIES

Oman does not cater particularly well for the needs of disabled travellers with ramps and disabled parking being the exception rather than the rule except in Muscat. The **Oman Association for the Disabled** (☑ 99 329030; www.oad-oman.org) primarily assists nationals but they may be able to help if you call with enquiries.

VISAS

A visit visa, required by all nationalities except for citizens of Gulf countries, can be obtained by many foreign nationals (including those from the EU, the Americas, Australia and New Zealand) at Muscat International Airport. For a visit of 10 days or less it costs OR5 and for 10 days up to one month it costs OR20. You may be refused admission if you have an Israeli stamp in your passport.

It is also possible to obtain a visa at those border crossings that are open to foreigners. Currently those with a UAE tourist visa may visit Oman overland without paying for an Omani visa (you must travel with your passport though).

Visa regulations change freqently so check the official Royal Omani Police (ROP) website (www. rop.gov.om).

Multiple-entry visas cost OR50 and are only given to those who can prove they are on business. They are valid for one year with maximum stays of three weeks.

OMAN DIRECTORY A–Z

Visa Extensions

A one-month extension (OR20) is available for those on a one-month visit visa from the ROP Visa Information counter at Muscat International Airport between 7.30am and 1pm Saturday to Wednesday. Overstaying a visa will incur charges on departure (OR10 per day).

WOMEN TRAVELLERS

Women travelling alone are a novelty in Oman and you may feel uncomfortable, particularly on public transport, eating in restaurants and when visiting public beaches. Omani men mostly ignore women (out of respect) and it's hard to meet Omani women. Many of the country's attractions lie off-road where travelling solo (for either sex) is inadvisable unless you are highly resourceful and, if driving, strong enough to change a tyre.

Harassment is not a big problem, except near hotels where attitudes are, rightly or wrongly, influenced by the sight of women in bikinis. Outside hotels, it helps (in addition to being more culturally sensitive) to be discreetly dressed in loose-fitting clothing, and to wear shorts and a T-shirt for swimming.

WORK

To work in Oman you have to be sponsored by an Omani company before you enter the country (ie you have to have a job). Although it is illegal to work on a tourist visa, some expats take a short-term contract and hope their employer will arrange a labour card for them. The reality is a fretful experience best avoided.

❶ Getting There & Away

ENTERING OMAN

Entering Oman at Muscat International Airport (p140) is straightforward. The small airport is efficient, queues are kept to a minimum (outside holiday periods), staff are friendly and your luggage is often waiting on the carousel before immigration is complete. Most visitors require a visa upon arrival. This is easily expedited by filling in a form (in the immigration hall) and taking it to the clearly marked visa-collection counter before queuing up to have your passport stamped. A new airport should be open by 2015.

AIR
Airports & Airlines

There is only one truly international airport in Oman, and that is Muscat International Airport in Muscat. That said, Oman Air is due to run direct flights between Dubai and Doha and Salalah airport.

Regional Flights

There are direct flights to each of the destinations below daily, except for Sana'a which is serviced by a weekly flight. Frequent single-stop flights connect all these destinations.

FLIGHT DESTINATION	PRICE (OR)
Abu Dhabi (UAE)	62
Doha (Qatar)	130
Kuwait City (Kuwait)	95
Manama (Bahrain)	135
Riyadh (Saudi Arabia)	100
Sana'a (Yemen)	(suspended)

Airlines Flying to/from Oman

British Airways (☑24 568777; www.ba.com) Hub: Heathrow, London.

Emirates (Map p128; ☑24 404444; www.emirates.com) Hub: Dubai. Has an office in Ruwi.

Gulf Air (Map p128; ☑24 482777; www.gulfairco.com) Hub: Bahrain. Office in Ruwi.

Oman Air (☑24 531111; www.omanair.com) Hub: Muscat. Office in Ruwi.

Qatar Airways (☑24 162700; www.qatarairways.com) Hub: Doha, Qatar.

Saudi Arabian Airlines (☑24 789485; www.saudiairlines.com) Hub: Jeddah, Saudi Arabia.

Sri Lankan Airlines (☑24 785871; www.srilankan.com) Hub: Colombo, Sri Lanka.

LAND

Oman borders the UAE, Saudi Arabia and Yemen. Current practicalities mean, however, that you can only enter UAE. The situation changes frequently and it's worth checking with the **Royal Oman Police** (www.rop.gov.om; Muscat International Airport) before planning your trip to see which crossings are open to non-GCC visitors. Visas are obtainable at all Oman border posts.

Border Crossings

➡ **UAE** There were four border posts open 24 hours to foreigners at the time of writing: these are at Wajaja; Khatmat Milahah; Tibat; and Buraimi.

➡ **Yemen** There are two border posts with Yemen at Sarfait and Mazyunah. Both were closed to tourists at the time of writing.

Bus

➡ **UAE** The **Oman National Transport Company** (ONTC; ☑24 490948; www.ontcoman.com) has buses on the Oman–Dubai express service at 6am (OR5.500, 5½ hours, daily) departing from **Ruwi bus station** (☑24 701294) in Muscat.

➡ **Yemen** The Gulf Transport Company has buses to Mukhalla in Yemen from Salalah bus station. However, this service was suspended for foreigners at the time of writing.

PRACTICALITIES

→ **Electricity** The mains electricity in Oman is 220V to 240V. Adaptors are widely available at hotel shops and from supermarkets such as Al-Fair.

→ **Magazines** *Oman Today* is a monthly pocket-sized handbook, with listings and features of interest to the tourist. It conducts a thorough and locally revered review of restaurants each year. *What's On in Muscat* gives a useful listing of events.

→ **Newspapers** *The Times of Oman* and *Oman Daily Observer* are local English-language newspapers. Foreign newspapers are available (three days old) from hotels and major supermarkets.

→ **Radio** The local English-language radio station broadcasts on 90.4FM (94.3FM from Salalah) from 6.30am to midnight daily, with news bulletins at 7am, 2.30pm and 6.30pm. High FM (95.9FM) is Oman's most popular English-language commercial radio station.

→ **TV** Oman TV broadcasts the news in English nightly at 8pm and shows English-language films two or three nights a week. Satellite TV is also widely available.

→ **Smoking** A no-smoking policy is enforced in interior public places. This includes inside restaurants and on public transport.

→ **Weights & Measures** Oman uses the metric system.

Car

It's possible to drive through any of the borders in your own vehicle if you obtain insurance to cover both countries.

You need extra insurance if you wish to take a hired car over the border to/from the UAE and you must return the car to the country in which you hired it (unless you're willing to pay a huge premium).

SEA

There are no passenger services to/from Oman, although Muscat is a port of call for cruise liners.

❶ Getting Around

AIR

Besides Muscat International Airport in Muscat, the only functioning airports in Oman are at opposite ends of the country in Salalah and Khasab; both of these handle domestic flights only but connections with Dubai and Doha are rumoured to begin in 2013. Four new airports are being built at Ras al-Hadd, Sohar, Adam and Duqm, which will help open up the country for visitors.

The national carrier is Oman Air (p206). It services the domestic airports, as well as a selection of Middle Eastern and subcontinental destinations. Tickets can be booked through any travel agent or online.

The only domestic flights available in the country at the time of writing are on Oman Air as follows:

Between Muscat and Salalah (One way/return OR32/64, 1½ hours, up to four times daily at variable times.)

Between Muscat and Khasab (One way/return, OR32/64, 1¼ hours, once daily at variable times.)

BUS

The intercity buses are operated by ONTC (p140), which has daily services to/from most of the main provincial towns for less than OR8. Buses are usually on time, comfortable and safe. It is worth making reservations for longer journeys. Tickets are available from the bus driver.

CAR

→ Road signs are written in English (albeit with inconsistent spelling), as well as in Arabic, throughout Oman.

→ Helpful brown tourist signs signal many sites of interest.

→ Petrol, all of which is unleaded, is widely available.

→ Al-Maha petrol stations usually have modern, well-stocked shops and clean toilets.

Driving Licence

Most foreign driving licences are accepted in Oman but an International Driving Permit is preferable. Some foreign residents of Oman need a road permit to leave or re-enter the country by land. This regulation does not apply to tourists.

Hire

International car-hire chains in Oman include Avis, Budget, Europcar and Thrifty, but dozens of local agencies offer a slightly reduced rate. Rates for 2WD cars start at about OR16 and 4WD vehicles at OR30. Always carry water with you (a box of a dozen 1.5L bottles costs OR1.700 from petrol stations) and a tow-rope (OR4 from any large supermarket). 'Freezer packs' (600 baisa each) will keep your cool box cold for a day, even in summer, and you can ask hotels to refreeze the packs at night.

Insurance

Check the small print on all car-hire documents to see if you are covered for taking the vehicle off-road.

Road Conditions

Travellers comment that some roads indicated in this book as '4WD only' are passable in a 2WD. Often they are right, until something goes wrong; 2WDs are not built to withstand potholes, washboard surfaces and steep, loose-gravel inclines, let alone long distances to the next petrol station.

If travellers' letters are anything to go by, who knows over what terrain the previous driver dragged your hire car! Bear in mind, you'll get no sympathy from hire companies if your 2WD breaks down off-road (and don't forget you're not insured to be off-road in a 2WD). With virtually zero traffic on some routes you are very vulnerable, especially in extreme summer temperatures.

In short, saving on the expense of a 4WD might cost more than you bargained for.

Road Hazards

Watch out for the following potential problems on the road:

➡ Aggressive tailgating and fast, inappropriate driving particularly in the capital area.

➡ Camels and goats wandering onto the road, with disastrous consequences in Dhofar during the *khareef* (rainy season) when locals continue to drive at the same speed regardless of the fog.

➡ Exceptionally slippery conditions after rain (a hazard of all dry, hot areas).

➡ Failing brakes on mountain roads (low gear is a must).

➡ Beguiling soft sand and a salty crust called *sabkha* (that looks and feels hard until you drive on it). As a rule, always stick to the tracks: if they suddenly stop, it's time to reverse!

➡ Flash-flooding – occurs frequently in wadis.

Road Rules

The following traffic laws are strictly enforced, especially in Muscat:

➡ Seatbelt use is mandatory for passengers and there is a fine of OR10 for not wearing one.

➡ You are not permitted to drive while using a hand-held mobile phone.

➡ Drink-driving is completely forbidden.

➡ Most vehicles are fitted with a beeping device for Oman's maximum speed limit of 120km/h and there are many speed cameras to encourage drivers to comply. Punitive fines for speeding are being introduced in an effort to reduce accidents.

➡ Note that it's illegal to drive a dirty car – the fine is OR5!

Responsible Driving

Before heading off over uncharted territory, it's worth asking if you really need to be the person who scars this piece of desert. It's better, generally, for your safety and for the environment if you stick to previous tracks.

HITCHING

Hitching is possible but inadvisable as most roads outside the capital area have low volumes of traffic. Bear in mind that you may often get left between towns while the driver turns off-piste to his or her village. You therefore need to be self-sufficient enough to survive the hottest part of a day – even a night or more in some parts of the interior – without any prospect of an onward or return ride.

Always carry water and avoiding hitching off-road. It is the custom to offer the driver some remuneration. If you're driving, you will often be asked to give a ride to locals but do this with caution.

LOCAL TRANSPORT

Oman has a comprehensive system of cheap but rather slow long-distance shared taxis (painted orange and white) and microbuses. Oman's shared taxis and microbuses do not wait until they are full to leave. Instead, drivers pick up and drop off extra passengers along the way.

To visit certain places of interest, you'll often have to take an 'engaged' taxi (ie private, not shared) – generally four times the price of a shared taxi as you have to pay for all the seats. Bargain hard before you get in and try to avoid hailing a taxi from a hotel. Fares quoted by Lonely Planet for Oman are for shared taxis unless otherwise stated.

Beware that public transport isn't networked, so a bus or taxi may go from A to B and B to C but not from C to A. This means it's easy to get stranded in a town with no onward connections.

Qatar قطر

Best for Culture

➡ Museum of Islamic Art (p215)

➡ Souq Waqif (p216)

➡ Falcon Souq (p216)

➡ Qatar National Museum (p216)

➡ Katara (p223)

Best for Nature

➡ Khor al-Adaid (p226)

➡ Bir Zekreet (p229)

➡ Al-Shahaniya (p227)

➡ Jebel Jassassiyeh (p228)

Why Go?

Ask the Qataris, Bedouin roots notwithstanding, what they are most proud of and they will undoubtedly say Doha. And indeed you can see why: the modern capital with its spectacular tapering towers, elegant corniche and extravagant malls, makes Doha arguably the finest stop over in the Gulf.

But there's more to Qatar than a shopping spree. The whole country, with its heritage souqs, world-class Museum of Islamic Art, and lyrical sand dunes, offers an excellent introduction to the Arab world but without the tensions often associated with the Middle East.

The success of this booming nation is more than just skin deep. Rapid economic expansion, barely brooked by the global recession, international sports tournaments, and Education City: these are some of the many hallmarks of Qatar's sophistication. Chances are, if you spend a night in the vibrant city of Doha, you'll be lobbying the relatives to stay a whole lot longer in Qatar.

When to Go

Qatar

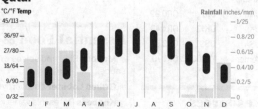

Nov–Mar Enjoy a break from the intense heat and humidity of summer.

Apr Cheer on the favourite at the Emir's Cup event – camel racing at its best.

Jun Watch the grand prix of power boat racing slice up the waters of Doha Bay.

QATAR

Fast Facts

➡ **Capital** Doha

➡ **Country code** ☎ 974

➡ **Language** Arabic (English widely spoken)

➡ **Official name** Qatar

➡ **Population** 1,699,435

Exchange Rates

The riyal is pegged to the US dollar. For current exchange rates see www.xe.com.

Australia	A$1	QR3.79
Bahrain	BD1	QR9.66
Euro zone	€1	QR4.66
Kuwait	KD1	QR12.92
Oman	OR1	QR9.45
Saudi Arabia	SR1	QR0.97
UAE	Dh1	QR0.99
UK	UK£1	QR4.43
USA	US$1	QR3.64
Yemen	YR100	QR1.70

Resources

➡ **Al-Jazeera** (www.aljazeera.com) Arab-world equivalent of the BBC

➡ **Experience Qatar** (www.experienceqatar.com) Official website of Qatar

Daily Costs

Qatar is a relatively expensive destination. With the few budget hotels being swept away in the name of development, accommodation is hard to find below US$100. Factoring in cheap options for eating (around US$10) and the cost of a sight or an activity, a minimum daily cost with transport comes to around US$150. This rises to US$230 if staying in midrange hotels and for a top-end hotel with car hire, US$400 is nearer the mark.

Qatar Stopover

Spend a morning absorbing the best of Doha in a promenade along the **corniche**, watching the city's stellar skyline dance in the heat. Use the afternoon in cooler contemplation at the **Museum of Islamic Arts**, Doha's priceless treasure house. Seek out silks and spices for sale in **Souq Waqif**, and admire the feathered plumage on display in the neighbouring **Falcon Souq**. Dine at one of the souq's teeming restaurants.

Three Days

After day one exploring modern central Doha, recharge on day two by the beach at **InterContinental Doha** before a sunset **dhow trip**. On day three hire a car and tour the peninsula, stopping off at **Al-Khor** for lunch at Al-Sultan Beach Resort. Head north to explore the ancient **rock carvings** at Jebel Jassassiyeh and end the day at **Al-Zubara**, visiting this far-flung fort.

For Expats

Camp out under the escarpment at **Bir Zekreet** and search for a pearl on a shore full of washed-up oysters. Cast an eye over the historic interior at **Umm Salal Mohammed**, or enjoy some R & R at **Sealine Beach Resort**. Stay overnight at the enchanting inland sea of **Khor al-Adaid** and sleep on a magic carpet of sand.

Essential Food & Drink

➡ **Makbus** Rice and spices with chicken, lamb or fish in a rich sauce.

➡ **Grilled Lobster** Local crayfish are a popular favourite.

➡ **Khabees** Dates in a variety of sizes, colours and states of ripeness.

➡ **Tap water** Safe to drink although most people stick to bottled water.

➡ **Alcohol** Available only in top-end hotel restaurants and bars.

➡ **Coffee** Traditionally served pale and spiked with cardamon or dark, strong and with plenty of sugar.

Qatar Highlights

1 Step into the future by walking along **Al-Corniche** (p214), Doha's über-modern seafront

2 Immerse yourself in the region's rich heritage at the **Museum of Islamic Art** (p215)

3 Step into the past in the cardamon-scented alleyways of **Souq Waqif** (p216)

4 Ruffle feathers at the **Falcon Souq** (p216) by bidding for a peregrine

5 Take a dune for a pillow and the stars for a blanket at beautiful **Khor al-Adaid** (p226)

6 Pretend you're on a gondola in Venice at **Villaggio Mall** (p224)

7 Find fish inland at the rock carvings of **Jebel Jassassiyeh** (p228)

8 Visit an exhibition, enjoy opera or dine at **Katara** (p223)

9 Set up camp under a desert mushroom at **Bir Zekreet** (p229)

10 Be the first to visit the **National Museum** (p216) after its extensive refurbishment

DOHA

الدوحه

POP 796,947

It's rare to see a great city in the making these days. While it would be misleading to represent Doha as a latter-day New York (much of the new development has been given a heart but hasn't yet acquired a soul), Doha is nonetheless well on its way to realising the grand vision of its founding fathers. Whether you go giddy looking down from the 56th floor of the InterContinental, or glide past the exotic skyline from a dhow in the bay, you can't help but be struck by the

Greater Doha

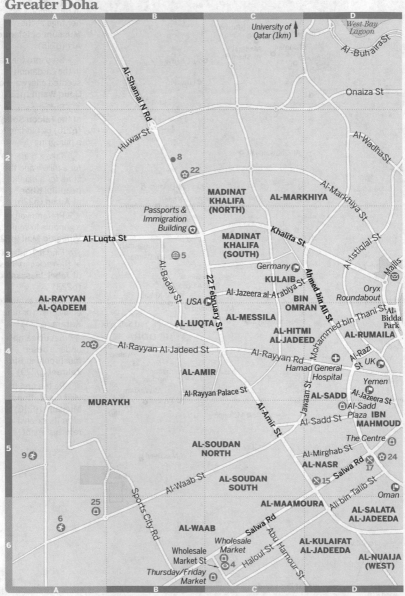

QATAR DOHA

beauty of Doha's buildings. Or should that be Buildings, with a capital 'B', for these new goliath-like structures capture the intangible sense of prosperity and optimism you feel when walking around renovated souqs and new malls alike, or while watching Doha families strolling the grounds of the city's opulent resorts.

'Watch this space' was a good motto for Doha a few years ago; 'enjoy this space' is a better motto for today as the city begins to fill its own shoes, leaving plenty of gorgeous green spots to kick off your own.

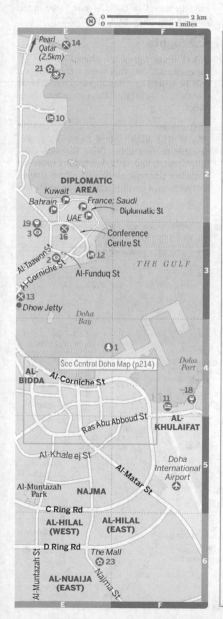

QATAR DOHA

Greater Doha

🎯 Sights
Animal & Bird Market	(see 4)
1 MIA Park	E4
2 Ministry of Education	E3
3 Ministry of Justice	E3
4 Omani Market	C6
5 Weaponry Museum	B3

🎯 Activities, Courses & Tours
Arabian Adventures	(see 12)
6 Gondolania	A6
Jungle Zone	(see 25)
7 Katara Beach	E1
8 Qatar Guest Centre	B2
9 Racing & Equestrian Club	A5
Winter Wonderland	(see 16)

💤 Sleeping
10 InterContinental Doha	E1
11 Sharq Village & Spa	F4
12 Sheraton Doha Hotel & Resort	E3

🍴 Eating
13 Al-Mourjan	E3
14 Al-Sayyad	E1
Al-Shaheen	(see 12)
15 Batteel Café	D5
Carrefour	(see 16)
16 City Centre Doha	E3
17 Eli France	D5
Fish Market	(see 10)
Giant Stores	(see 25)

🍷 Drinking & Nightlife
Paloma	(see 10)
18 Pearl Lounge	F4
19 Strata Lounge	E3

🎭 Entertainment
City Center-Doha	(see 16)
20 Doha Players	A4
21 Katara	E1
22 Landmark Shopping Mall	B2
23 Mall	E6
24 The Laughter Factory	D5

🛍 Shopping
City Centre Doha	(see 16)
25 Hyatt Plaza	A6
Landmark Shopping Mall	(see 22)
Villaggio Mall	(see 6)

History

With more than half of the population of Qatar residing in the capital, one would expect Doha to have an ancient and powerful history. On the contrary, Doha was a small and inconsequential fishing and pearling village up until the mid-19th century, when the first Al-Thani emir, Sheikh Mohammed bin Thani, established his capital at Al-Bida, now the port area of town. From a notorious safe haven for Gulf pirates, it became the British administrative centre in 1916 and the capital of the independent state of Qatar in 1971.

The University of Qatar (1973) and Qatar National Museum (1975) brought education and culture to the city, and slowly the shape of Doha changed, one ringroad at a time, from an ugly concrete rash to the elegant city of today. The masterstoke was the early construction of Doha Bay, carved out of reclaimed land, and giving harbour to Doha's shrimp industry, leisure for inhabitants and

a vantage point that architects have exploited to the full in West Bay.

With the new airport nearing completion, served by the world's 'five star airline', with a whole new town centre growing alongside Souq Waqif, and with ambitious construction and beautification projects well underway, the secret of Doha is sure to be outed well before the World Cup in 2022.

◉ Sights

Doha's main sights are along and just off the corniche. Note that some attractions can only be visited by prior appointment. This is most easily facilitated through a tour company.

Al-Corniche　　　　　　　　　CORNICHE
(ⓟ) 🌿 The highlight of Doha is unquestionably the corniche. Doha Bay was carefully constructed with landfill to make an attractive crescent, along which runs shaded footpaths and cycling tracks. One great way

Central Doha

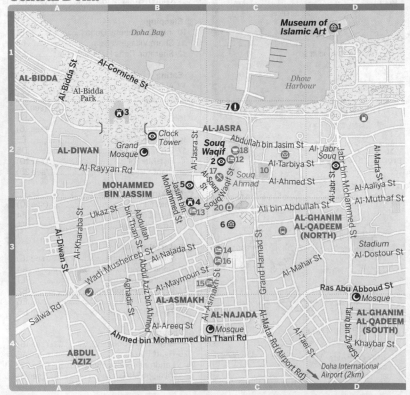

to gain an introduction to the city is to begin at the Ras Abu Abboud St Flyover at the southeastern end of the corniche and either walk or drive around to the Sheraton Doha Hotel & Resort, looking out for the prominent landmarks.

⭐ **Museum of Islamic Art**　　MUSEUM
(Map p214; 📞 44 224 444; www.mia.org.qa; just off Al-Corniche; 10.30am-5.30pm Sat-Mon, Wed & Thu, 2-8pm Fri; Ⓟ) **FREE** Rising from its own purpose-built island and set in an extensive landscape of lawns and ornamental trees, this is a monument of a museum. It was designed by the renowned architect IM Pei (architect of the Louvre pyramid) and is shaped like a postmodern fortress with minimal windows (to cut down on energy use) and a 'virtual' moat.

The museum houses the largest collection of Islamic art in the world, collected from three continents. Exquisite textiles, ceramics, enamel work and glass are showcased conceptually: a single motif, for example, is illustrated in the weave of a carpet, in a ceramic floor tile or adapted in a piece of gold jewellery in neighbouring display cases allowing visitors to gain a sense of the homogeneity of Islamic art.

This is the kind of museum that is so rich in treasure that it rewards short, intense visits. Pace yourself by visiting the cafe downstairs or punctuate your visit with a browse in the extensive museum shop to avoid sensory overload. Avoid strappy tops and shorts or you may be refused admission.

MIA Park　　PARK
(Map p212; Corniche, Adjacent to the Museum of Islamic Arts; ⊙10.30am-11pm; Ⓟ) One of many beautiful green spaces in Doha, MIA Park is home to Richard Serra's vertical steel sculpture – the first public piece of art by this celebrated artist in the Middle East. On the first Saturday of every month from October to March, stalls sell arts and crafts, clothing

QATAR DOHA

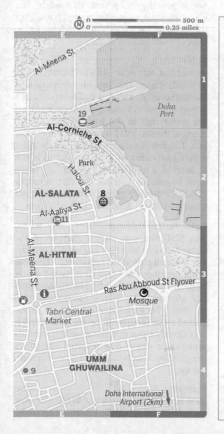

0　　　500 m
0　　　0.25 miles

and souvenirs form the Park Bazaar (noon-7pm).

★ Souq Waqif
SOUQ

(Map p214; bounded by Al-Souq St & Grand Hamad St; ☉10am-noon & 4-10pm; P) Reincarnated in the last decade as the social heart of Doha, Souq Waqif is a wonderful place to explore, shop, have dinner or simply idle time away in one of the many attractive cafes. There has been a souq on this site for centuries, as this was the spot where the Bedu would bring their sheep, goats and wool to trade for essentials. It grew into a scruffy warren of concrete alleyways by the end of the last century and at one point was almost condemned for demolition. Thankfully, someone spotted its tourist potential and the entire market area has been cleverly redeveloped to look like a 19th-century souq, with mud-rendered shops and exposed timber beams and some beautifully restored original Qatari buildings. Such has been the success of this venture that the souq keeps growing to accommodate new 'old alleyways' and is one of Doha's top attractions.

Despite the slight 'Disneyfication' of the area (quite literally with the Disney turrets given to Doha Fort at the souq's entrance), the chief business of the souq continues unabated and it remains one of the most traditional market places in the region. This is the place to look for the national Qatari dress, including beautifully embroidered *bukhnoq* (girl's head covering), spices, perfumes and oud (an exotic incense made from agarwood). For a fun souvenir, take an empty glass jar and ask the spice traders to fill it with layers of colourful cumin, fenugreek, turmeric and ginger. If you get tired wandering round the antique shops and contemporary art galleries, stretch out on a divan and cushions at **Coffee Asherg** and watch the world go by.

Most of the shops in the souq close around noon and reopen at 4pm but the many cafes and restaurants remain open all day.

Falcon Souq
SOUQ

(Map p214; Adjacent to Souq Waqif; ☉9am-1pm & 4-8pm, 4-8pm Fri; P) This fascinating new souq, next to Souq Waqif, is worth a visit just to see the kind of paraphernalia involved in falconry. All kinds of equipment, such as *burkha* (hoods) and *hubara* (feathers), are on sale. During falcon season (October to March) you will also see dozens of peregrines and other assorted falcons

patiently aperch their stands. A truculent falcon costs about QR2000, but a well-mannered bird can be many times that figure and usually changes hands privately. The shop owner is quite happy to show off the birds to anyone who shows some interest. The best part of the experience, however, is seeing young Qatari lads buying their first falcon under the beedy eyes of an uncle or grandfather, keen to hand down the family heritage of bird-handling skills.

Gold Souq
SOUQ

(Map p214; adjacent to Souq Waqif; ☉10am-noon & 4-10pm) This pageant of glorious design and spectacular craftsmanship is fun to see even without the intention to buy. The souq comes alive later in the evening, especially before a holiday, when men traditionally express the value of their relationships through buying 22kt gold bangles, or a 'set' comprised of earrings, necklace and bracelet for the women in their family. Qatari bridal jewellery can cost thousands, but sometimes pieces can be traded back after the wedding for something more readily usable, or even just for cash.

Doha Fort
FORT

(Al-Koot Fort; Map p214; Jasim bin Mohammed St; P) Built during the Turkish occupation in the 19th century, this fort has been used as a prison and an ethnographic museum. During restoration in the late 1970s, however, many of the original features of the fort were lost. The fort is now used as a backdrop for events happening in Souq Waqif and is still in need of a modern mission in life. Often open to curious tourists, the fort is empty inside. Camels are grazed outside during *eid* to remind city kids of their Bedouin roots.

Qatar National Museum
MUSEUM

(Map p214) You can catch a glimpse of the Qatar National Museum just off Al-Corniche but it is still closed for renovation. The museum occupies the **Fariq Al-Salata Palace**, built in 1901 and used by Sheikh Abdullah bin Mohammed, Qatar's ruler from 1913 to 1949. The lengthy refurbishment is expected to be completed by the end of 2014; it is already clear that the museum, with its remarkable desert-rose inspired structures designed by Jean Nouvel, will be worth waiting for.

Mathaf
GALLERY

(Arab Museum of Modern Art; ☑44 028 855; www.mathaf.org.q; Off Al Luqta St, Education City; admis-

FALCONRY

If you want a glimpse of heritage alive and well today, don't miss the Falcon Souq (p216). You only have to see the scale of the souq, afforded its own traditional arcaded building off Souq Waqif, to understand the place of falconry in Qatari society. It can be quite unnerving entering a falcon shop. Birds, some hooded in black leather, others watching intelligently with wary eyes, perch on the open railing at a hand's distance, waiting to be taken home, fed less than a square meal and put straight to work.

Falconry is an ancient art that dates at least from the 7th century BC. The first falconer, according to Arabic tradition, was a violent king of Persia who was so entranced by the grace and beauty of a falcon taking a bird on the wing that he had it captured so he could learn from it. What he learnt, according to legend, changed him into a calm and wise ruler.

It is no easy task to train birds of prey. Bedu, the falconers par excellence, traditionally net their falcons (usually saker or peregrine) during their migration, using pigeons as bait. They train the birds through complex schedules of sleep deprivation and sparse feeding, retain them for as long as it takes to harvest fresh meat, and then set them free again at the onset of summer.

It is estimated that 2000 falcons are still employed on the Arabian Peninsula each year. Today, birds are more usually bred and 'imprinted' from hatchlings to create a bond that lasts a lifetime. Sporting achievement is measured not through the number of quarry caught but in the skill of the catch – and in the wisdom of leaving enough prey for tomorrow.

sion to exhibitions QR25; ☺11am-6pm Sat-Thu, 3-9pm Fri; P) This exceptional new exhibition space was opened in 2010 providing a home for international art with an Arab connection. Housed in an old school near Education City, the building was redesigned by French architect Jean-Françoise Bodin. The venue hosts a variety of exhibitions, workshops and lectures through the winter months.

Heritage House   HISTORIC BUILDING
(Map p214, Al-Najada Shopping Centre courtyard, just off Grand Hamad St) Formerly an ethnographic museum, this restored traditional house was built in 1935 and offers the best chance to see a *badghir* (wind tower). The square wind tower was commonly used as a form of pre-electric air-conditioning throughout the Gulf, sucking fresh air into the house and channelling it into the ground-floor rooms. It is closed to visitors but is worth a look from the outside.

Weaponry Museum   MUSEUM
(Map p212; ☎44 867 473; btwn Al-Luqta St & Makkah St; ☺by prior arrangement) FREE This small museum has an impressive collection of arms and armour, some from the 16th century. However, what makes this museum worth a visit is the dazzling array of gold and silver swords and daggers, including a *khanjar* (ceremonial dagger) that belonged to Lawrence of Arabia. The museum is open to the public by prior appointment or with a tour guide.

Omani Market   SOUQ
(Map p212, Wholesale Market St; ☺10am-1pm & 4-7pm) This small market, near the Thursday/Friday Market, offers a curious mishmash of items, such as Saudi dates and hand-woven baskets, Omani dried fish, tobacco and lemons, Iranian honey and pots, camel sticks and incense, and fronds of pollen-bearing date flowers (to fertilise the female date palms). Buying anything here renders the satisfaction of taking part in a trade that has existed between Oman and the Gulf for centuries.

Animal & Bird Market   SOUQ
(Map p212; Salwa Rd; ☺10am-1pm & 4-7pm) Located behind the colourful Wholesale Market (selling wholesale fruit, vegetables, meat and fish), it comes alive with local Qatari families just before the *eid* holidays.

🏃 Activities

Dhow Ride   BOAT TOUR
(Corniche; adult/child QR20/10; ☺8am-4pm) For a chance to see the corniche from the sea, consider taking a dhow ride around Doha Bay. These local fishing boats leave from the jetty near Al-Mourjan restaurant on the cor-

niche. All the tour companies offer three- to four-hour evening dhow cruises with dinner, traditional music and entertainment for around QR330 per person.

Doha Golf Club
GOLF

(☑ 44 960 777; www.dohagolfclub.com; West Bay Lagoon; ☺ 6.30am-11pm) A sight to behold amid the surrounding barren desert, the green Doha Golf Club has an internationally recognised 18-hole course, which hosts the annual Qatar Masters in March. Open to nonmembers, it also has a flood-lit, nine-hole academy course for those in a hurry.

Katara Beach
SWIMMING

(Map p212; ☑ 44 081 017; www.katar.net; Katara Cultural Village; child/adult QR25/100; ☺ 9.30am-sunset) If you fancy a swim but don't want to go too far from the city for it, the 1.5km beach at Katara Cultural Village offers a whole day out to visitors with the chance of dinner and a show at the adjoining arts centre when the sun goes down. Children under six gain free admission to the beach and there's a ladies-only section. One-piece costumes are advised.

Racing & Equestrian Club
HORSE RACING

(Map p212; ☑ 44 803 016; www.qrec.gov.qa; Al-Furousiya St) FREE For a chance to meet and mingle with the locals, consider attending one of the weekly horse races that occur throughout the season (October to May). Horses are in the hearts of most Qataris, and every Thursday at 4pm races of pure-bred Arabian horses take place at the Racing & Equestrian Club.

Courses

Thanks to the vibrant expatriate community in Doha, there are many courses available, from line dancing to karate, ice-skating and scuba diving. Anyone in town for a while and interested in any of these activities is advised to pick up a copy of *Marhaba, Qatar's Premier Information Guide*, available from some hotels, supermarkets and bookshops, and consult its 'Leisure Activities' section.

Language & Culture

Qatar Islamic Cultural Center
LANGUAGE

(Map p214; ☑ 44 250 175; www.fanar.gov.qa/TrainingCenter.aspx; Medinat Khalifa South; ☺ 7.30am-1.30pm & 5-8pm Sun-Thu) Near the Doha English Speaking School. Courses in Arabic language and culture (QR300).

Qatar Guest Centre
LANGUAGE

(Map p212; ☑ 44 620 191 44 862 390; www.qgc.com.qa; Kab bin Malek St, Airport Rd, Doha) Three month Arabic courses, free of charge. Useful for those interested in Islam. Call or email first to check availability.

University of Qatar
LANGUAGE

(☑ 44 034 584; www.qu.edu.qa; Jelaiah St, Tarfa, Doha) Runs a year-long course in Arabic.

Sailing

Regatta Sailing Academy
SAILING

(☑ 44 424 577; www.regattasailingacademy.com; InterContinental Doha, West Bay; ☺ 7am-9pm) Offers a variety of casual and certified sailing courses from beginner to advanced levels for all ages.

Tours

There are several excellent companies that organise tours around Doha, to the desert, camel farms and Khor al-Adaid. They are often able to arrange access to private museums, private zoos and other interesting sights that are not open to the independent traveller. They all offer similar sorts of packages, but some of the better ones include:

Arabian Adventures
CULTURAL

(Map p212; ☑ 44 361 461; www.arabianadventureqatar.net) Has a desk at the Sheraton Doha Hotel & Resort. Only tour operator managed by Qatari nationals.

Gulf Adventures
ADVENTURE

(Map p214; ☑ 44 221 888; www.gulf-adventures.com; Aspire Zone Street, off B Ring Rd) Offers friendly and knowledgeable advice.

Qatar International Tours
CULTURAL

(☑ 44 551 141; www.qittour.com) Desert safaris with overnight camping offered. Historical heritage tours a strong point.

Festivals & Events

Doha hosts a huge variety of events and entertainment with sports high on the agenda. The sports event of the decade for Qatar was the Asian Games held in December 2006 with 45 nations participating in 423 events. The games prompted the building of a new marina, hotels, beaches and major infrastructure which have enhanced Doha's image as a top venue for international sporting events. The games also left a legacy of high-level international competitions, tournaments and meets, many of which take place in the **Aspire Zone**, an international stand-

A PROMENADE UNDER THE PALMS

If you want an encapsulation of Doha in a day, try threading through the palm trees of Doha's beautiful corniche. The 8km trip around Doha Bay affords some spectacular views of a growing city and invites plenty of rest-stops along the way. Beware, it will feel more like a hike across the Sahara if you attempt the trip in summer.

Begin at Ras Abu Abboud St Flyover, where a small park with ornamental wind towers introduces the 'heritage' zone of the corniche. The collection of white-washed, traditional-style buildings on the far right belongs to the exquisite five-star **Al-Sharq Village Resort & Spa**. Have breakfast there and you won't want to bother with the rest of the promenade. Sip coffee instead in the traditional Halul Coffeehouse (p223) and watch the wind rustling the Washington palms amid the national maroon and white flags that decorate this part of the corniche. The traditional Qatari building on the opposite side of the main road is the newly refurbished National Museum (p216); when complete (predicted by the end of December 2014), the new buildings comprising the museum complex, inspired by the desert-rose, promise to be a remarkable feat of engineering.

Continue into the 'sea' zone of the corniche, passing Doha's busy port marked by the monumental anchors on the shore and the cream-coloured flour mills at the end of the jetty. Notice also the first of the corniche's unique contemporary buildings – a brooding black glass construction with dramatic overlapping planes like a storm at sea. In contrast, looming from the water at 1.3km, the marble-clad Museum of Islamic Art (p215) rises out of the Gulf like an iceberg, with far more hidden beneath the surface than is hinted at by its understated exterior. Continuing the nautical theme, at 1.8km, look inland for a ministry building shaped like a ship's bridge. The **dhow harbour** is the next point of interest, the entrance of which is marked by the famous **pearl monument** (Map p214) (2.3km), a popular spot for photos. Enjoy the spectacular view of West Bay from the end of a jetty full of lobster pots and lazy dhows, moored up between night time fishing trips. It's hard to believe that this remarkable skyline of futuristic towers was built entirely on land reclaimed from the sea.

If you've had enough of the sea, turn inland on Grand Hamad St towards the elegant spiral-tapered building (Qatar Islamic Cultural Centre) for must-see Souq Waqif (p216) or walk along the 'garden' zone of the corniche, where water cascades down the steps of the **Diwan Building** (Map p214) (2.7km), an enormous grass lawn defies the elements and winter petunias decorate the approach to the Ministry of Interior. **Rumeilah (Al-Bidda) Park** (Al-Corniche) is next on the left, offering leafy shade for a halfway nap.

The honeycombed post office (5.1km) marks the start of the 'highrise' zone at the northwestern end of the corniche. Have lunch at Al-Mourjan Restaurant (p222) for a close up view of the newly built West Bay towers. From here to the end of the corniche is a cluster of spectacular buildings including the **Ministry of Justice** (Map p212), with a pair of scales over the doorway, the **Ministry of Education** (Map p212), featuring a mosque dome set in the glass frontage, the candy-twisted **Al-Biddar Tower** that defies gravity and the snow-flake clad **World Trade Centre** among many other show-stopping towers. Reward your efforts at the end of the corniche with coffee and cake in Al-Dafra Park next to the Sheraton Doha Hotel & Resort, or smarten up for dinner at the top of the Sheraton pyramid. The stunning views from Al-Shaeen Restaurant allow you to retrace the route you've just travelled from the comfort of an armchair.

ard sports facility. The 12th Pan Arab Games was held in Doha in December 2011, the FINA World Swimming Championships will be held here in 2014, and of course there's the 2022 FIFA World Cup to look forward to.

Qatar's annual **Tribeca Film Festival** (DTFF; www.dohafilminstitute.com), held in November at a number of venues around Doha, is the highpoint of a regular calendar of cinema promoted by the Doha Film Institute. Katara (p218) is the main hub of activities during the festival.

Check 'What's On' listings in the newspapers, and especially in *Marhaba, Qatar's Premier Information Guide* (published quarterly) for a month-by-month guide to Doha's busy calendar.

DOHA FOR CHILDREN

Qatar is a safe, easygoing, family-oriented country, and children are welcome and catered for everywhere. Even the Gulf, with its gently sloping shores and flat, waveless seas is more conducive to paddling about and building sand castles than it is to extreme sports. The large resorts all have plenty of activities for young children and Doha has a heap of attractions to keep even the most overactive kids amused.

Midway along the corniche, the unfenced Rumeilah (Al-Bidda) Park (p219) has attractions for children, including a heritage village.

Winter Wonderland (Map p212; ✆ 44 839 163; Conference Centre St, City Centre Doha, West Bay; ☉10am-9pm Sat-Wed, 10am-11pm Thu, 1-10pm Fri), located at City Centre Doha, features an ice-skating rink. Inside the popular Villaggio Mall, **Gondolania** (Map p212; ✆ 44 519 993; www.playlandco.com; Villaggio Mall; ☉ 9am-11pm Sat-Wed, 9am-midnight Thu, 2pm-midnight Fri) offers rides, a 4D cinema, go-karts and a bowling alley. The mall itself offers gondola rides on a Venetian canal where you can almost believe the gondoliers are putting some effort in – thankfully, they don't sing.

Housed in the Hyatt Plaza mall, **Jungle Zone** (Map p212; ✆ 44 694 848; www.hyattplaza.com; Hyatt Plaza; admission Thu-Sat QR55, Sun-Wed QR40; ☉1-10pm Sun-Thu, 10am-10pm Sat) offers 3500 sq m of animal-themed children's attractions.

🛏 Sleeping

There is some excellent accommodation in Doha, particularly at top-end resorts, which offer wonderful views and beach locations, especially in the West Bay area. Cheaper accommodation is conveniently located near Souq Waqif, although none of the options could be termed genuinely 'budget'. The basic men-only budget hotels are intended largely for Asian expats and are not reviewed by Lonely Planet.

All rooms at the hotels reviewed have air-conditioning, a TV (normally satellite), fridge and bathroom but do not include breakfast unless stated.

Top-end prices quoted are rack rates. Discounts and special deals can often be negotiated, especially during summer.

Qatar Palace Hotel HOTEL $
(Map p214; ✆ 44 421 515; www.qatarpal.com.qa; 44 Al-Asmakh St; s/d QR370/450; ☏) The commodious rooms in pastel shades with large sofas are homely and comfortable but beware, some rooms are virtually windowless. The Maharajah Restaurant, with a chef from Mumbai, is a local favourite.

Al-Nakheel Hotel HOTEL $
(Map p214; ✆ 44 283 221; www.alnakheel-hotel.com; 101 Al-Asmakh St; s/d QR350/450) With the proposed expansion of Souq Waqif, this basic hotel with mirrored ceilings in the corridors, may soon be given a new lease of life. Ask to see a room to avoid a view onto a brick wall.

Al-Bustan Hotel BOUTIQUE HOTEL $$
(Map p214; ✆ 44 328 888; www.albustanhotel.qa.com; Al-Muthaf St; s/d incl breakfast QR450/550; ☏) One block inland from the corniche and identifiable in a row of similar hotels by its filigree gypsum exterior, this small hotel, with its potted bonsai and Islamic-patterned flooring in the foyer, is often fully booked so ring ahead.

Royal Qatar Hotel BUSINESS HOTEL $$
(Map p214; ✆ 44 249 444; www.royalqatarhotel.com; Al-Asmakh St; s/d QR500/550; ☐☏) If you can look past the pompous management, this circular tower-block hotel is in walking distance from Souq Waqif and offers comfortable rooms – most with good views across the city. It organises city tours for QR60 per hour.

Al-Khariss Hotel BOUTIQUE HOTEL $$
(Map p214; ✆ 44 310 786; alkharisshotelt@gmail.com; Souq Waqif; r QR600; ☏) Buried in the heart of the souq, this little hotel has only eight rooms. The smell of spices drifting in on the trade winds, and the sound of haggling from the souq below, will transport the guest to the Arabia of old. The entrance is off the main pedestrian street in Souq Waqif, opposite an antique shop with a huge model dhow.

Sheraton Doha Hotel & Resort HOTEL $$$
(Map p212; ✆ 44 854 444; www.sheraton.com/doha; Al Funduq St; r from QR1100; ☏☷) The Sheraton Doha is more than a place to stay: it's an institution. It's the oldest of Doha's

five-star hotels, and still boasts one of the best locations, with wonderful views from attractive, split-level rooms with balconies, and a private beach. Rates include breakfast delivered to the room in silver salvers.

InterContinental Doha   RESORT $$$
(Map p212; ☑44 844 444; www.intercontinental. com; r QR1200; P⃣🛜🏊) This genteel luxury hotel has been dwarfed by lofty neighbours in recent years but it continues to thrive regardless. InterCon hotels have an excellent reputation in the Gulf for the 'common touch' – providing high-quality facilities and the best-in-town entertainment without being snooty. This resort, with its attractive beach area and lively bars, is no exception and is a great choice for a family getaway.

★Al-Najada
Boutique Hotel   BOUTIQUE HOTEL $$$
(Map p214; ☑44 336 444; www.cwbh.com; Souq Waqif St, Souq Waqif; r from QR1250; 🛜) ⦿ This superb new hotel, at the opening of Souq Waqif, is part of a set of six exclusive boutique hotels in the heart of the old souq. Al-Najada, with its courtyard design, wattle-and-daub rooms and wooden beamed ceilings, is the most traditional. The architect has recreated a rambling Qatari style building but added stylish modern features such as granite flooring and walls of water.

With a spa and an inspiring rooftop view, it offers a haven of quiet in the heart of the bustling souq.

Sharq Village & Spa   RESORT $$$
(Map p212; ☑44 256 666; www.ritzcarlton. com/sharqvillage; Ras Abu Abboud St; r QR1450; P⃣🛜🏊) With its Arabian-heritage style of architecture, exquisite desert planting in the gardens and beach location, this is one superb hotel. The intimate, super-luxurious rooms with four-poster beds and diaphanous silken drapes are arranged around sand-coloured courtyards and cacti gardens. Lanterns, shadows dancing across the marble and Ali Baba pots bubbling with water, all play their part in creating an Arabian Nights experience.

✖ Eating

If you're a serious foodie, make sure you pick up a copy of *Mahaba Dining Guide* before selecting where to eat. If you're still undecided after you've read our reviews, take a stroll along Souq Waqif's central thoroughfare and choose a restaurant to suit your mood. Alternatively, head for Katara (p223) with a variety of smart restaurants strung along the promenade.

Quick eats are available in all the big malls such as **City Centre Doha** (Map p212; ☑44 839 990; Conference Centre St; ⊙10am-10pm Sat-Thu) and Villaggio Mall (p224) – but beware that on a weekend at lunchtime, they're not particularly quick!

Café-Tasse   ITALIAN $
(Map p214; ☑44 447 017; Souq Waqif; mains QR40; ⊙8am-2am; 🌿) If you've reached the limit of your fascination for Middle Eastern food, one venue that is worth singling out is this Italian-style restaurant. Offering all-day dining of pasta, salads and snacks, a quick bite generally turns into something a bit longer as diners enjoy the Souq Waqif pageant flow past the cafe doors.

Battool Café   CAFE $
(Map p212; ☑44 441 414; www.batteel.com; Salwa Rd; snacks QR50; ⊙8am-midnight) With a range of delicious freshly baked pastries, homemade ice creams and sorbets, and some innovative sandwiches, this cafe, set in a traditional Qatari house with Arabic cushions and *barasti* (palm leaf) ceilings, is a firm favourite with residents.

Tent   MIDDLE EASTERN $$
(Map p214; ☑44 328 888; Al-Muthaf St, Al-Bustan Hotel; mains QR60; ⊙noon-midnight) Located under a Bedouin-style tent, this popular restaurant is a relaxed place to try delicious Arabic fare or a puff of *sheesha* (water pipe used to smoke tobacco) under swinging Arabian lamps. The waiters are accustomed to helping people find their way around a Middle Eastern menu of mezze (small preparatory dishes).

★Al-Tawash Restaurant   QATARI $$
(Map p214; ☑44 982 002; Souq Waqif; mains QR80; ⊙noon-midnight) In the heart of Souq Waqif, this beautifully resurrected Qatari building (on the corner of the main thoroughfare and the lane leading to the car park) is an atmospheric venue for sampling traditional Qatari fare. Seating areas include a Bedouin tent enclosure, open terrace and private cubbyhole, lavished with Syrian tables and upholstered cushions and lit with lanterns.

The name may change soon with the new management but the restaurant will remain as one of the few venues to specialise in Qatari food.

Al-Mourjan
LEBANESE $$

(Map p212; 44 834 423; Al-Corniche, Balhambar Bldg; mains QR100; Noon-1am;) This elegant, gypsum-walled seafront restaurant serving Lebanese food has a great location, in full view of the West Bay skyline. If the hot and cold mezze don't win you over, there's an international menu. There's a minimum spend of QR100 per person. The adjoining terrace cafe serves light bites and fresh mango juice in the only open-air venue along the corniche.

L'Wzaar
SEAFOOD $$$

(Seafood Market; 44 080 711; Katara; mains QR150) There's a separate fish and chip shop in this glamorous, choose-your-own fish restaurant. Near the auditorium in the cultural village of Katara, it gives a rare opportunity to mingle with local Qatari families.

Fish Market
SEAFOOD $$$

(Map p212; 44 844 444; InterContinental Doha; mains QR150; 6pm-midnight Sat-Thu, 12.30-3.30pm Fri) Visit the Fish Market and pick the fish you fancy from the display and tell the chef how you'd like it cooked. With a resident belly dancer and skipping lanterns, count on an evening of entertainment as well as excellent supper.

Al-Shaheen
INTERNATIONAL $$$

(Map p212; 44 854 071; Al-Funduq Rd, West Bay, Sheraton Doha Hotel & Resort; mains QR180; 7pm-1am Sun-Fri;) Boasting great views of the city and the sea, this sophisticated restaurant, with its bedevilling Arabic music, is a local favourite. Apart from its nightly à la carte menu, it also offers a Mediterranean Brunch on Friday (noon to 4pm) from QR190.

Al-Sayyad
MIDDLE EASTERN $$$

(Map p212; 44 847 420; www.thediplomaticclub.com; Diplomatic Club; set menu from QR235; noon-midnight;) Al-Sayyad is worth visiting just for a walk through the jewel-like Diplomatic Club, with its inlaid furniture and strawberry-coloured carpets. With views of the West Bay high-rises on one side and the Pearl on the other, the restaurant catches the best of the sea breeze. A choice of set menus are helpful for those new to Middle Eastern cuisine.

Self-Catering
One of the best bakeries in town, **Eli France** (Map p212; 4435 7222; Salwa Rd; 8am-11.30pm) is next to the Ramada Junction on Salwa Rd; it also has a branch in the City Centre Doha.

There are dozens of grocery stores and supermarkets dotted around town. **Carrefour** (Map p212; 4484 6265) in City Centre Doha has a very good fresh fish and vegetable counter. For a cheaper variety of edible goods, try **Giant Stores** (Map p212; 4469 2994) in the Hyatt Plaza.

Drinking & Nightlife

Bars
In the absence of nightclubs or pubs, hotel bars double as nightlife in Doha. They are generally only open to hotel residents and 'members' (who pay a nominal annual 'membership'). These rules, however, are continually relaxing and even Qataris can now be seen in some of these establishments (once strictly forbidden).

★ Strata Lounge
COCKTAIL BAR

(Map p212; 44 015 888; West Bay, InterContinental Doha – The City; 6pm-2am) On the 56th floor of this brand new hotel, this is already a head-spinning venue – and that's more to do with the mixologist's concoctions than the vertiginous views. The only challenge is working out which 'vertical bus' delivers you to the top floor.

Habanos
LOUNGE

(44 848 000; Ritz-Carlton Doha; 6pm-late) Cigar and fine wine lounge with happy hour between 6pm and 8pm.

Paloma
BAR

(Map p212; 44 844 444; West Bay, InterContinental Doha; 6pm-2am) One of the most lively bars in town is the Paloma. It's the best place for live music and doubles as a Tex-Mex restaurant. The Lava Lounge, also here, is another hip spot.

Pearl Lounge
COCKTAIL BAR

(Map p212; 44 298 888; Ras Abu Abboud St, Doha Marriott Hotel; 9pm-3am Mon-Sat, 5-8pm Sun) Draped across two floors of an opulent central hotel. Has a large menu of tasty temptations to accompany the bangs, sours and fizzes.

Coffeehouses
The private *majlis* (meeting room) is popular around town, where men congregate over tea or coffee for a chat, or to share news or watch TV together.

★ **Coffee Asherg** COFFEEHOUSE
(Map p214; ✉ 44 367 776; Souq Waqif) On the eastern (sea-facing) edge of the souq, this traditional rooftop coffeehouse is welcoming of all-comers. Stretched on a divan under the stars, sipping mint tea and listening to the muezzin call prayers at dusk while the city lights sparkle into life, is the quintessential Arabic experience.

Halul Coffeehouse COFFEEHOUSE
(Map p214; Al-Corniche) On the corniche, this local-style coffeehouse has somehow escaped the modernisation of the area and makes a suitable place to pause for a *chi libton* (tea) on a hike round the corniche.

☆ Entertainment

With the burgeoning number of luxury hotels in Qatar, there is plenty of entertainment on offer. Jazz evenings, live entertainment and international food promotions are held frequently. Check the 'What's On' listings in *Time Out Doha* and *Marhaba, Qatar's Premier Information Guide*, as well as the English-language newspapers for anything from line dancing at the rugby club to cookery classes at the Ritz-Carlton Doha.

Katara ARTS CENTRE
(Cultural Village; Map p212; ✉ 44 080 000; www.katara.net) FREE This extensive collection of new Qatari-style buildings, with the superb modern coliseum at the hub, provides a fantastic venue for art exhibitions, opera, concerts and other live entertainment. The website gives a helpful listing of events and booking options. There is no charge for admission to the grounds which are home to varied restaurants and a beach.

Cinemas & Theatre

The best cinemas are in **City Centre Doha** (Map p212; ✉ 4483 9990), the **Mall** (Map p212; ✉ 4467 8666; cnr D Ring Rd & Najma St) and the **Landmark Shopping Mall** (Map p212; ✉ 4488 1674; cnr Al-Shamal N Rd & Al-Markhiya St) shopping complexes. They show the latest Hollywood blockbusters and the occasional film from Iran or Europe. Tickets cost about QR30. For current information on cinemas in Qatar, visit www.movies.theemiratesnetwork.com.

Doha Players THEATRE
(Map p212; ✉ 44 474 911; www.dohaplayers.com) In existence for 50 years, the Doha Players stages amateur productions.

The Laughter Factory COMEDY
(Map p212; ✉ 4428 1673; www.thelaughterfactory.com; Salwa Rd, Radisson Blu Hotel) The Laughter Factory organises monthly tours of professional comedians from the international circuit around the Gulf . Tickets sell like hot cakes.

🔒 Shopping

Doha is full of wonderful shopping opportunities, and you can buy anything from a camel to a racing car, an Armani suit to a sequinned *abeyya* (woman's full-length black robe), and a fishing rod to a peregrine falcon. While there aren't many locally produced crafts, half the fun of shopping in Doha is ambling through the souqs or brand-new shopping malls, stumbling over things you couldn't imagine people would want to buy and then buying one anyway, like a house for the garden birds (complete with letter box), or a dyed-pink hair extension made of ostrich feathers – the possibilities are endless.

One of the joys of shopping in Doha's traditional souqs is that the shopkeepers take the time to chat with their customers, whether buying or not, making shopping one of the best ways to engage with the locals. Despite a bit of push and shove when it's crowded, all the souqs are safe places to visit and bargaining is expected. The traditional souqs are reviewed under 'Sights'.

Malls

There is a kind of subversion of expectation inside the great shopping malls of the Gulf. They appear to be even more opulent versions of American malls, complete with themed entertainment and Starbucks, but then you'll find an *abeyya* shop selling women's cloaks or a prayer bead counter next to a waffle stand that confirms that you are, indeed, shopping in the Middle East. In the heat of summer, they become much more than a place to shop as people congregate there to escape the ravages of the sun and to be entertained by the prospect of other worlds. Each of the malls has some form of entertainment for the family, from skating rinks to cinemas and as such, they make for a popular day's outing.

City Centre Doha MALL
(Map p212; ⊙ 44 839 990; www.citycenterdoha.com; ⊙ 10am-10pm Sat-Thu, 2-10pm Fri) A veritable pantheon of the shopping world. With its 350 shops, from Debenhams to the Family

WORTH A TRIP

LIVESTOCK MARKET

If you find yourself with an hour to spare and you're looking for an induction to local life, then head to to the wholesale market on Salwa Road. The market is the main hub for sales of fruit and vegetables, fish and meat. There is also a livestock market which may be of interest to anyone who hasn't seen pink, yellow and lime green chicks before. Why the birds are dyed is a mystery of the region. Fortunately, they leave the spotted guinea fowl, ring-necked parakeets, African greys and cut-throat zebra finches untinged – possibly because the plumage of these domestic birds is outrageous enough already.

The day before an *eid* (Islamic feast), the market heaves with goat-buyers, camel-traders and sheep-shoppers, all looking for a suitable *eid* supper, but the animals are well shaded and watered, and respect for the livestock is shown by much inspection of teeth and smoothing of coats. It's worth visiting the market just for the sideshows: cockerels unbagged in a flourish, children tugging at rabbit ears, hooded peregrines balancing on a white-*thobed* arm and women in black picking their way through the mayhem of one of the great bazaars of modern times. It's a world away from the sanitised experience of a Western supermarket meat counter but it is very much part of the Middle East, repeated in similar scenes from Yemen to Kuwait.

Development Centre (top floor, selling local crafts); its tented architecture, marble flooring and glass-fronted lifts; its ice-skating rink, bowling alleys and climbing walls; its congregations of juice-sipping Qataris and huddles of homesick expatriates; and trolleys laden with eggs, packets of *khobz* (Arabic flat bread) and Egyptian olives, it's more an event than an errand.

Villaggio Mall   MALL
(Map p212; ☑ 44 135 222; www.villaggiodoha.com; ⊗ 10am-11pm Sat-Thu, 1-11pm Fri) In this Venetian-themed mall, next to Aspire Zone, you can shop under a diorama of fluffy white clouds, eat pizza at Paul's and take a ride on a gondola along the grand canal. It includes lots of entertainment opportunities, including cinema.

Landmark Shopping Mall   MALL
(Map p212; ☑ 44 875 222; www.landmarkdoha.com; cnr Al-Shamal N Rd & Al-Markhiya St; ⊗ 9am-10pm Sat-Wed, 9am-11pm Thu, 1-11pm Fri) This enormous shopping centre, with a multiplex cinema, Marks & Spencer department store and Virgin Megastore, is home to dozens of other international chain stores.

Hyatt Plaza   MALL
(Map p212; ☑ 44 999 666; www.hyattplaza.com; Al-Waab St; ⊗ 10am-10pm Sat-Thu, 2-10pm Fri) Located alongside the Khalifa Sports Stadium, this houses over 100 outlets.

ⓘ Information

DANGERS & ANNOYANCES

Doha is one of the safest cities in the Middle East. Even women travelling on their own late in the evening are unlikely to feel threatened, providing they are dressed appropriately. The only danger worth commenting on is the volume of traffic, and the speed, as drivers don't always obey the rules.

EMERGENCY

Fire, Police & Ambulance (☑ 999) Emergency number.

INTERNET ACCESS

Internet access costs from QR30 per hour at the business centres of all the top-end hotels. There are also easy-to-use internet cafes in the City Centre Doha, open from 10am to 1am. Qtel hotspots allow access with prepaid cards in many cafes including Eli France, and in malls such as Landmark Shopping Mall. Free access is available in some city parks.

Free wi-fi is available at Café Tasse (p221) and Starbucks in City Centre Doha (p223).

MEDICAL SERVICES

Hamad General Hospital (☑ 44 394 444; www.hmc.org.qa; Al-Rayyan Rd) Subsidised medical and dental treatment is available for tourists on a walk-in basis.

MONEY

There are plenty of moneychangers just south of Doha Fort. ATMs are available throughout Doha that take Visa, MasterCard, Cirrus, Maestro and Amex cards.

POST

General Post Office (☎44 464 446) Located in a large building off Al-Corniche near the Oryx roundabout.

Post Office (Abdullah bin Jasim St)

TELEPHONE

Qtel Main Office (☎44 200 700; Wadi Musheireb St; ⏲24hr) Fax and telephone services are available.

TOURIST INFORMATION

There are no tourist information centres as such, but the **Qatar Tourism Authority** (www.experienceqatar.com) provides good general information on its website.

Local travel agencies are the best in situ source of information regarding Doha.

Getting There & Away

Qatar's only public airport is **Doha International Airport** (☎44 656 666; www.dohaairport.com) which has recently been upgraded while awaiting the completion of the new airport in 2015. A number of airlines including **Qatar Airways** (www.qatarairways.com), the country's main airline, and Gulf Air (p239) have offices at the airport. Many airlines have offices in the **Airline Centre** (Ras Abu Abboud St) and **Al-Sadd Plaza** (C Ring Rd), south of the city centre.

Getting Around

TO/FROM THE AIRPORT

Most top-end hotels and resorts provide free transport to/from the airport. Karwa taxis (turquoise in colour) are regulated by the government. They are clean, safe and metered. The journey between the airport and central Doha costs a minimum of QR25. Avoid taking unofficial taxi rides from the touts at the airport who illegally claim business for their private car. Karwa buses between the airport and the Al-Ghanim bus station leave every hour between 5.50am and 11.50pm from Saturday to Thursday. The service starts an hour later on Friday.

BUS

The national bus company provides comfortable city services around Doha in environmentally friendly, battery-powered and LPG-fuelled vehicles. Timetables are displayed at each of the sheltered bus stops.

Karwa Public Bus (☎44 588 588; www.eng.mowasalat.com; ⏲4.30am-10.30pm) This government-run service operates buses every 15 to 30 minutes along many different routes around the city. All routes start from Al-Ghanim bus station and have stops every 750m. There is a minimum charge of QR2 and a maximum charge of QR3 for inner city rides. Services to Al Wakra, Wukair, Al Khor, Dukhan, Mesaieed and Al-Shahaniya are also available with a maximum charge of QR9. To travel by bus, you must purchase a Karwa Smartcard. Without a card, there's a QR10 fee for a single journey. Cards are available at the bus station and at some supermarkets. Check online for details (www.karwasmartcard.com).

Al-Ghanim Bus Station (☎44 588 888; www.eng.mowasalat.com) All public buses begin their route at this station.

CAR

There are a string of car-rental companies in the arrivals area of the airport.

Driving in Doha is easy enough if you watch out for impatient drivers overtaking on both the left and right, honking the horn at roundabouts and free-roaming pedestrians. Parking, except in the souq areas, is not too much of a problem: most hotels and malls have car parks or parking services. A lack of street signs can make navigation difficult and most people navigate by landmark not by road sign.

TAXI

Despite the efficient bus system, most people get around Doha by taxi. The best taxi service is run by **Mowasalat Karwa** (☎458 8888). Journeys cost QR4 plus QR1.800 per kilometre. Waiting time costs QR8 for each 15 minutes. The minimum fare is QR10. The bright turquoise cars can be hailed by the side of the road or found at the airport, outside malls and hotels.

AROUND DOHA

While Qatar isn't exactly blessed with sights and activities outside the capital of Doha, it does have several attractions that justify the cost of hiring a vehicle for a day or two, including a few coastal villages where life still revolves around fishing and the local mosque.

The land is arid in the extreme but that is not to say it is featureless: there are some beautiful beaches, interesting wind-eroded escarpments and large areas of sand dune. The country's biggest natural attraction is undoubtedly Khor al-Adaid, a saltwater inlet in the south surrounded by a magical landscape of sand and salt.

Camping at Khor al-Adaid or at Bir Zekreet is a reminder of the achievement of the Qataris (which they have in common with their Gulf neighbours) in fashioning a complex modern state from a virtually barren plot of land.

Al-Wakrah & Al-Wukair

الوكرة و الوكير

POP 141.222

The old pearling villages of Al-Wakrah and Al-Wukair are rapidly stringing out to meet the Doha suburbs. They make a pleasant afternoon outing from the capital, however, and there are several interesting old mosques and traditional houses in and around the gracious modern villas. The old souq along the shoreline is being given a makeover following the success of Souq Waqif in Doha.

The beaches south of Al-Wakrah offer glorious stretches of sand, interspersed with the odd *khor* (creek). The shallow water makes paddling a better option than swimming. At least the determined wader is in good company: flocks of flamingos roost along the coast between Al-Wakrah and Mesaieed during winter, and groups of six or seven flamingos are a familiar sight, sieving the water with their beaks, or with neck and one leg tucked up, taking a nap. Fishing is a popular pastime in the area, as the limestone shallows act as fish traps when the tide goes out.

Both Al-Wakrah and Al-Wukair are an easy 15-minute drive by car from Doha, following Al-Matar Rd past the airport and heading south. The bus from Doha leaves every 20 minutes and costs QR5.

Mesaieed

مسعيد

POP 14,800

Mesaieed is an industrialised town about 45km south of Doha, but although it's not particularly attractive in itself, the nearby beaches with deep water make for some of the best swimming in Qatar.

🛏 Sleeping

Sealine Beach Resort   RESORT $$

(☑ 44 765 299; www.qnhc.com; r QR750 Sun-Wed, QR900 Thu-Sat; ⓟ@⊠) Sealine is a lovely, understated, low-rise resort built on a beach just south of Mesaieed. It's far enough away from the industrial area to be unaffected by the heavy industry, and the ring of glorious amber sand dunes doubles the resort's entertainment opportunities. The beach shelves quite steeply, allowing for good swimming, and desert quad bikes can be hired from the resort to explore the local dunes, known as the 'singing sands'. The latter are particularly beautiful at sunset, although purists may be disappointed by myriad bike tracks that spoil the dunes' pristine curves. Day visitors are welcome to use the hotel facilities, including pools and the beach; camel and horse rides are available; and there is a clown to entertain the children, as well as activities like face painting. Admission costs QR25 for children and QR50 for adults from Sunday to Wednesday and QR75 and QR125 respectively from Thursday to Saturday.

To reach Mesaieed from Doha, follow the road past the airport and through Al-Wakrah. A taxi to the resort from Doha costs around QR200.

Khor Al-Adaid

خور العديد

Without a doubt, the major natural attraction in Qatar is the beautiful 'inland sea' of Khor al-Adaid, near the border with Saudi Arabia. Often described as a sea or a lake, the *khor* is in fact neither: rather it is a creek surrounded by silvery crescents of sand (known as *barchan*). All sand dunes look wonderful in the late afternoon sun, but those of Khor al-Adaid take on an almost mystical quality under a full moon when the *sabkha* (salt flats) sparkle in the gaps between the sand.

While a night under the stars on a camping expedition is a special experience in the right company, not everyone goes to the area to enjoy the tranquillity. Sand skiing, quad-biking and 4WD racing compete with the time-honoured picnic and a song, much to the consternation of some and the pleasure of others. The area is big enough, thankfully, to satisfy both, although environmental concerns are being expressed as more and more travel agencies make the area the central attraction of their tours.

This region is *only* accessible by 4WD, and independent travellers should accompany someone who knows the area and really can drive a 4WD. Being stuck in the sand is no fun after the first hour and in summer is very dangerous. If you're determined to do it yourself, make sure you have at least a box of water bottles on board for each passenger, a map and compass, very clear directions of the best route currently navigable, a tow rope and a shovel. If you get stuck don't dig: let out the air in the tyres and return to the nearest petrol station immediately to reinflate.

Going on an organised tour is probably the safest way to see Khor al-Adaid; overnight tours often include folkloric entertainment and a barbecue, as well as camping equipment. Rates vary but a six- to seven-hour day excursion usually costs around QR625 per person for two people; add another QR100 per person for an overnight trip.

Umm Salal Mohammed
ام صلال محمد

POP 60,509

There are several old buildings dating from the 19th and early-20th century dotted around this small, modern residential district. The ruined **Umm Salal Mohammed Fort** (⊙8am-1pm & 4-7pm) `FREE` was built for military and civil use. Neighbouring **Barzan Tower** is possibly more interesting as the triple-decker, T-shaped construction is unique in the Gulf; however, this whitewashed building was closed to the public at the time of research and is unlikely to reopen any time soon.

Umm Salal Mohammed is about 22km north of Doha, just west of the main highway to Al-Ruweis. It's impossible to give directions to the fort or tower as there are no street signs, but it's easy enough to stumble across both as they are visible above the surrounding houses.

Umm Salal Ali   أم صلال على

A small field of six 'Iron Age' **grave mounds**, dating from the 2nd millennium BC, is worth a visit in Umm Salal Ali if you're visiting nearby Umm Salal Mohammed, especially if you have a guide. If not, look for rounded bumps in otherwise flat land just north of the town; more mounds are scattered among the buildings in the town centre. Umm Salal Ali is clearly signposted off the main highway north to Al-Ruweis, about 27km from Doha.

Al-Khor   الخور

POP 193,983

Al-Khor, once famous as a centre for the pearling industry, is a pleasant town with an attractive corniche, small dhow yard and lively fish market. The small **museum** (if it ever reopens) displays archaeological and cultural artefacts from the region including traditional clothing. Several old **watchtowers** are scattered around town; many have been restored to their original form.

The nearby **mangroves** are a good place for birdwatching.

If the relative tranquillity of the town appeals, you can extend your stay at **Al-Sultan Beach Resort** (☑44 722 666; www.alsultanbeachresort.com; r incl breakfast QR1140; @☒). Situated just off the corniche, it is a quirky place with cast iron horses in the drive, tigers in the foyer and paintings of camels decorating the rooms. With comfortable rooms, an infinity pool, and sea views there's not much to detract from the peace and quiet.

Al-Khor is a drive of around 45 minutes, or 40km from Doha.

WORTH A TRIP

CAMELS AT AL-SHAHANIYA   الشحانية

If you've come to the Middle East hoping to see camels, then there's one place guaranteed to find them. At Al-Shahaniya, 60km west of Doha along the Dukhan Rd, camels roam freely around the desert or you can see them being exercised before the famous local **camel races**.

Camel races (known as the 'sport of sheikhs'), can be seen from a purpose-built stadium. If you have a car – a 4WD is not necessary – it's fun to drive along the 8km racetrack during the race. It can be quite an event, as female camels can maintain a speed of 40km/h for an entire hour, and are often better at keeping in their lane than the motorists. Check the English-language daily newspapers for race times or contact a tour company, most of which organise trips to the races during the season (October to May).

It's easy to spot the stadium, as long before it comes into view the approach is marked by 5km of stables, exercise areas, lodgings for the trainers and breeders, and all the other facilities required of a multimillion-dollar sport, not to mention a national passion befitting Qatar's Bedouin origins.

THE PETROGLYPHS OF JEBEL JASSASSIYEH   جبل الجساسية

It's probably fair to say that despite appearing in tourist literature, the petroglyphs of northern Qatar have been seen by very few visitors. This is largely because until very recently their whereabouts was all but a secret and only those in the know with a 4WD could find them.

So what are these elusive petroglyphs? About 60km north of Doha there is a low-lying rocky outcrop known as Jebel Jassassiyeh. This unpromising piece of desert is remarkable for its rock carvings – there are over 900 strewn across 580 sites. Some of these ancient incisions in the rocks are said to depict aerial views of boats, which is interesting given that in an utterly flat country, on a usually utterly flat sea, there would have been no opportunity for people to have an aerial view of anything.

And where exactly are they? To reach the main concentration of petroglyphs, take the road to Jassassiyeh off Highway 1 and then the first (unmarked) road on the left. After eight kilometres you will come to some fenced-off areas with warnings not to trespass. The gates are left open, however, and you are free to wander around providing you are sensitive to the antiquity and importance of the sites. There are no signs so look for uniform grooves and incisions on top of flat rocks: once you have spotted one, you'll find you are surrounded by many similar carvings.

Al-Ghariya   الغورية

Since Qatar has such a picturesque coastline, it's rather surprising that there are not more resorts like **Al-Ghariya Resort** (☑44 728 000; www.alghariyaresorts.com; villa from QR3000 Thu-Sat, QR1800 Sun-Wed; ▣). With apartment-style accommodation and a kitchen area for self-catering, it is popular with Doha families – be warned, the noise of children on sand buggies can be deafening. There's an indoor private pool for ladies and an outside pool for men; swimming in the sea is only possible at the neighbouring beach.

All round Al-Ghariya there are excellent **birdwatching** possibilities (4WD or a strong pair of boots permitting).

Al-Ghariya is signposted off the northern highway from Doha, some 85km from the capital.

Al-Ruweis   الرويس

POP 3400

Situated at the northern tip of the peninsula (at the end of the northern highway about 90km from Doha) is Al-Ruweis, a typical fishing village where the age-old industries of net-mending and fish-pot cleaning take place on board the stranded dhows, while waiting for the tide to return.

Several **abandoned villages**, like Al-Khuwair and Al-Arish, mark the road between Al-Ruweis and Al-Zubara. They were vacated in the 1970s as the inhabitants were drawn to new areas of industry.

The lovely, unspoilt **beaches** around the northern coast are a joy, but access is really only possible in a 4WD; extreme care should be taken to follow previous driving tracks, both for environmental and safety reasons.

Al-Zubara   الزبارة

POP 860

Al-Zubara occupies an important place in Qatari history, as it was a large commercial and pearling port in the 18th and 19th centuries when the area was under the governance of Al-Khalifa (now the ruling family in Bahrain).

Al-Zubara Fort (☉5.30am-5.30pm) was built in 1938 and used by the military until the 1980s. The archaeology and pottery exhibits have sadly been neglected, but the fort is still worth visiting for the bleak views from the battlements. The fort is at the intersection of a road from Doha and Al-Ruweis, 2km from Al-Zubara.

Nearby, work is underway to open up the on-going excavations of an old pearling village to visitors. There's not too much to see but the enthusiasm of the archaeologists is infectious.

Al-Zubara is 105km northwest of Doha along Highway 1.

Bir Zekreet بِر زكريت

There is not much in the way of altitude in Qatar, which only serves to exaggerate the little escarpment on the northwest coast of the peninsula, near Dukhan. The limestone escarpment of Bir Zekreet is like a geography lesson in desert formations, as the wind has whittled away softer sedimentary rock, exposing pillars and a large mushroom of limestone. The surrounding beaches are full of empty oyster shells with rich mother-of-pearl interiors and other assorted bivalves. The shallow waters are quiet and peaceful and see relatively few visitors, making the area a pleasant destination for a day trip Camping is possible either along the beach or less conspicuously under the stand of acacia trees near the escarpment. There are no facilities or shops nearby, so campers should come prepared, bringing water especially in the summer months.

To reach Bir Zekreet from Doha, head west past Al-Shahaniya and take the signposted turn-off on the right about 10km before Dukhan. A new road is under construction which will make reaching the area easier, but a 4WD is advisable for exploring the escarpment area. To reach the desert mushroom, turn right 1.5km past the school at a gap in the gas pipes and bear left before the trees.

The remains of the 9th-century **Murwab Fort**, about 15km further up the northwest coast from Dukhan, may be worth a visit with a guide. Five groups of buildings, including two mosques and an earlier fort, have been partially excavated but a lack of information makes the sight of limited interest.

UNDERSTAND QATAR

Qatar Today

Benign Dictatorship

Since June 1995 when Sheikh Khalifa al-Thani was replaced as emir by his son Hamad in a bloodless coup, Qatar has tried to court friendship with odd bedfellows – allowing American troops to launch its operations in Iraq and Afghanistan from Qatar, for example, while courting the Taliban and Hamas. Equally, it has been quick to side with rebels against authoritarian regimes (for example in calling for the resignation of President Assad in Syria) while failing to implement democratic reform at home.

This dichotomous approach to international and domestic affairs has attracted consternation among Arab League members and is viewed with apparent exasperation from the West. But when a country has the world's largest gas fields and is consistently among the world's three richest countries in per capita terms, there's little appetite for rocking the boat by pointing out such inconsistencies.

Besides, the lack of democracy in Qatar has not proved too much of an issue among the native population. In 2011, Qatar was notable among regional neighbours for the lack of Arab Spring protests despite having no elected representatives in government and despite the key government posts being occupied by members of the emir's family. This is not to say there has been no political reform. Since assuming power, the emir has accelerated the modernisation of the country through encouraging education and training (in which women comprise the majority of university students), investing in independent media, and opening the country to tourism.

Punching Above its Weight

When Hosni Mubarak, former president of Egypt, visited Qatar in 2000 he commented, in reference to the coverage of Al-Jazeera news channels: "All this noise is coming out of this little matchbox!" Emboldened by extraordinary wealth, Qatar is far bigger in terms of influence in the region than its small size (geographically and in population) would suggest.

On National Day, 3 September, the country flutters with the maroon-and-white national flag, symbolising the bloodshed of past conflicts (particularly those of the latter half of the 19th century) and subsequent peace. Over the past two decades, Qatar has earned a reputation as one of the most politically stable countries in the region and enjoys international confidence in its ability to host successful high-level events. In 2001 Qatar hosted the World Trade Organization Conference and the 15th Asian Games in 2006. In 2022 it will host the FIFA World Cup.

QATAR BIR ZEKREET

AL-JAZEERA TV: THE BLOOM OF A THORN TREE

What Makes Al-Jazeera so Unique?

One of the 'blossoms' produced by the freedom of the press in Qatar in 1995 was the establishment of Al-Jazeera Independent Satellite TV Channel in November 1996. Free from censorship or government control, it offered regional audiences a rare opportunity for debate and independent opinion, and opened up an alternative perspective on regional issues for the world at large. Its call-in shows were particularly revolutionary, airing controversies not usually open for discussion in the autocratic Gulf countries.

Al-Jazeera's Origins

Al-Jazeera, which means 'The Island' in English, was launched as an Arabic news and current affairs satellite TV channel, funded with a grant from the Emir of Qatar. It has been subsidised by the emir on a year-by-year basis since, despite the airing of criticism towards his own government. The station was originally staffed by many former members of the BBC World service, whose Saudi-based Arabic language TV station collapsed under Saudi censorship; a close relationship with the BBC continues to this day.

The station has always been viewed with suspicion by ruling parties across the Arab world: its website notes one occasion in the early days (on 27 January 1999), when the Algerian government pulled the plug on the capital's electricity supply to prevent the population from hearing a live debate that alleged Algerian military collusion in a series of massacres. Critics closer to home accuse Al-Jazeera of boosting audience ratings through sensational coverage.

International Significance

Al-Jazeera only became internationally significant after the September 11 attacks on New York in 2001. The station broadcast video statements by Osama bin Laden (incidentally earning the station $20,000 per minute in resale fees) and other Al-Qaeda leaders who defended the attacks. The US government accused the station of a propaganda campaign on behalf of the terrorists; however, the footage was broadcast by the station without comment and later parts of the same tapes were shown by Western media channels without attracting condemnation. Al-Jazeera continued to air challenging debate during the Afghanistan conflict, bringing into sharp focus the devastating impact of war on the lives of ordinary people. In 2003 it hired its first English-language journalist, Afshin Rattansi, from the BBC's *Today Programme*. It has since been accused by American sources of sustaining an anti-American campaign, something the channel denies.

Al-Jazeera has earned its spurs on the frontline of journalism and is today the most widely watched news channel in the Middle East. In November 2006 a 24-hour, seven-day-a-week news channel called Al-Jazeera English was launched and it currently broadcasts to more than 260 million households in more than 130 countries, making it one of the most widely watched channels in the world. It has won many international awards for risk-taking journalism both on TV and through its website (www.aljazeera.net in Arabic and aljazeera.net/english – with 20 million visits every month, one of the most frequented websites in the world), launched in January 2001. In 2012 Al-Jazeera won the prestigious Royal Television Society Award for news channel of the year.

Unafraid of controversy, the stated aim of Al-Jazeera is to seek the truth through contextual objectivity (in as much, of course, as that is ever possible): 'Truth will be the force that will drive us to raise thorny issues, to seize every opportunity for exclusive reporting'. For many Western governments at least, that's proving to be an unexpected thorn among the first blossoms of democracy.

Qatar is a member of many international organisations such as the UN, the Organisation of Petroleum Exporting Countries (OPEC), the Arab League, the International Monetary Fund (IMF) and the World Bank, and the Gulf Cooperation Council (GCC).

Within the space of 80 years, Qatar has emerged from the virtual anonymity of its past to become a regional force to be reckoned with. Monuments to that achievement are found symbolically in the country's modern infrastructure and its social welfare programs. But also, perhaps for the first time in its history, they're also found in a tangible sense, by the growing ring of magnificent buildings that grace Doha's corniche, and in the high-profile events the country hosts.

History

Early Inhabitants

The written history of Qatar begins in grand fashion with a mention by the 5th-century Greek historian Herodotus, who identifies the seafaring Canaanites as the original inhabitants of Qatar. Thereafter, however, Qatar appears to be the subject more of conjecture than history. Although there is evidence, in the form of flint spearheads, pottery shards (in the National Museum), burial mounds near Umm Salal Mohammed and the rock carvings of Jebel Jassassiyeh of the early inhabitation of Qatar (from 4000 BC), the Peninsula has surprisingly little to show for its ancient lineage.

Take Al-Zubara, for example: the famous ancient Greek geographer Ptolemy tantalisingly includes 'Katara' in his map of the Arab world. This is thought to be a reference to Al-Zubara, Qatar's main trading port right up until the 19th century. A visitor to the small modern town, however, would have difficulty imagining a dhow dodging the sandbanks at low tide, let alone a fleet of cargo ships moored in the harbour and, bar a few minor archaeological remains, the surrounding desert is marked by absence rather than by historical presence.

History as a Living Inheritance

The history of Qatar, in many respects, is the history of the Bedouin, who traverse a land 'taking only memories, and leaving only footprints', footprints that are dusted away by frequent sandstorms. As such, history in Qatar is easier to spot in the living rather than the dead, for example, by the racing of camels at Al-Shahaniya, the trading of falcons in Doha's souqs, the hospitality towards guests in the coffeehouses of the city, and the building of camps (albeit with TV aerials and 4WDs) in the sand dunes of Khor al-Adaid.

Documents indicate that Qatar played an important role in the early spread of Islam through the assembling of a naval fleet used to transport the warriors of the Holy Jihad. Again, however, Islam is carried rather more stoutly in the conservatism of the modern people than in any monuments to that era.

Even the Portuguese, who left forts in every country in the Gulf like modern businessmen leave calling cards, bequeathed only hearsay to Qatar's coast line. The Turks helped drive out the Portuguese in the 16th century and Qatar remained under the nominal rule of the Ottoman Empire (and the practical governance of local sheikhs) for more than four centuries. Yet the comings and goings of even that great empire have made little impression on Qatar's sands of time, metaphorically or physically. Indeed, what is remarkable about the history of Qatar is not what has been left behind but the almost magical erasure of any visible sign of 6000 years of its human evolution.

Al-Thani Family Dynasty and the British

The transience of historical record changes in the mid-18th century with the arrival of the ruling Al-Thani family. Al-Khalifa (the current ruling family of Bahrain) controlled much of the Peninsula until the arrival, in the mid-18th century, of the charismatic Al-Thani family, which remains in power to this day.

Al-Thani is a branch of the ancient Tamim tribe of central Arabia. Originally they were nomadic Bedu, but the region's sparse vegetation led them to settle in the Peninsula's coastal areas around Zubara, where they fished and dived for pearls. The first Al-Thani emir, Sheikh Mohammed bin Thani, established his capital at Al-Bida in the mid-19th century, thereby laying the foundations of modern Doha.

Sheikh Mohammed strengthened his position against other local tribes by signing a treaty with the British in 1867. In 1872 the second Al-Thani emir, Jasim, signed a treaty with the Turks allowing them to build a garrison in Doha (Doha Fort). The Turks were expelled under the third Al-Thani emir, Sheikh Abdullah (the emir who lived in the palace that now houses the National Museum), after Turkey entered WWI on the opposite side to Britain. Thereafter, the British guaranteed Qatar's protection in exchange for a promise that the ruler would not deal with other foreign powers without British permission – an agreement that endured until independence was proclaimed on 1 September 1971.

Rags to Oil Riches

Qatar's history from WWI to the end of the 20th century reads rather like a fairy tale. Life in Qatar, even before the collapse of the pearl market in the 1930s, was marked by widespread poverty, malnutrition and disease. The arrival of oil prospectors and the establishment in 1935 of Petroleum Development Qatar, a forerunner of today's state-run Qatar General Petroleum Corporation (QGPC), signalled the beginning of a brave new world, even though WWII delayed production of oil for another 10 years.

Although not huge in comparative terms, the oil revenue instantly turned the tiny, impoverished population into one of the richest per capita countries in the world. Qatar's first school opened in 1952 and a full-scale hospital followed in 1959, marking the beginning of long-term investment in the country's modernisation. Most of these improvements occurred under the leadership not of Sheikh Abdullah's son Ali, nor his grandson Ahmed, but under that of his nephew Khalifa bin Hamad al-Thani, who, over a period of 15 years, ran many of the country's ministries, including foreign affairs, oil and the police.

On 22 February 1972 Khalifa ousted his politically apathetic kinsmen in a palace coup. Astutely, one of his first gestures was to crack down on the extravagance of the royal household. Celebrating the stability that his reign and increasing oil prices brought to Qatar, Sheikh Khalifa invested in Qatar, particularly in terms of developing an all-encompassing welfare state that provides free education and healthcare, job opportunities in the public sector and generous pensions for Qatari nationals.

People & Society

The National Psyche

Watching 4WDs racing over the sand dunes, attached to trailers holding sand buggies and skis, it's clear that this is a very rich country. Back in the 1970s it wasn't uncommon to see a brand-new Mercedes-Benz, with 22-carat gold badge and no number plate, squealing through the streets, having just been handed over to a potential customer on approval. Such enormous wealth delivered to the young, who had little or no recollection of the hardships of life before the riches of oil, came at a price calculable in terms of the arrogance of the nouveau riche; their unwillingness to work; a military staffed by officers but no privates; and jobs half started but not seen through.

Times have changed, however. The evident wealth of modern Doha is built now not on money alone but on education and the growing confidence of Qatari professionals. Not all of Doha is as glittering as the new West Bay developments may indicate and behind the flush of wealth is a realisation that sustainability of the country's achievements depends on commitment and effort. This growing work ethic among Qatari nationals is evidenced by their involvement in the new industries, in the health and education sectors and at grass roots level in the shopping malls, resorts and sports facilities. This represents a much more robust legacy for the country's future than petrodollars alone.

Lifestyle

Despite its significant neighbour, Saudi Arabia, with which it shares a religion (the Wahhabi sect of Islam) as well as a border, Qatar has managed to steer a remarkably independent course, seeking ties with Iran, for example, and even more contentiously with Israel in the 1990s.

Qataris aim to be equally as independent in society: while observant of a conservative form of Islam, Qataris are not afraid of extending hospitality to those of a different mind; while it is still unusual to see Qataris drinking alcohol, there is a tolerance of visitors who do; and while men and women are discreetly dressed, there's no harassment of the disrespectful tourist. Wahhabism does not preclude women working outside the home or driving but it does forbid any activity that may incite illicit relationships between men and women. In Qatar, unlike in Saudi Arabia, driving and working are not considered areas of likely temptation. Most significant is Qatar's press, which has enjoyed complete freedom of expression since 1995, resulting in one of the most exceptional media phenomena of modern times – Al-Jazeera Independent Satellite TV Channel.

Family life, at the heart of most Arab societies, is equally so in Qatar. Despite a high divorce rate, the country manages to reflect the espousal of Western materialism while paradoxically retaining something of the Bedouin simplicity of life: the day can stop for tea with a stranger; the emergency exit on a plane is spread with prayer carpet; and a business dinner may be rejected in favour of kebabs with friends.

Multiculturalism

An arriving visitor will be stamped into the country by a Qatari, but thereafter they could be forgiven for thinking they had stepped into another country – or at least pockets of many. There are car-hire attendants from Pakistan, shopkeepers from India, nightclub entertainers from the Philippines, and Brits turning pink in the afternoon sun during a day off from the oil and gas industries. Forming only a quarter of the population of their own country, Qatari men are recognisable in the multiethnic crowd by their impeccable white *thobe* (floor-length shirt-dress), *gutra* (white headdress) and long, black-tasselled *agal* (head rope); women by their narrow-eyed *yashmak* (veil).

The broadmindedness of an otherwise conservative nation stems not only from interaction with the thousands of immigrant workers who have helped build the country, but also from the fact that so many Qataris have travelled or studied abroad. Alas, that broadmindedness doesn't always translate into fair treatment of the immigrant population, many of whom continue to be treated as second-class citizens.

Arts

Although the rapid modernisation of Qatar has encouraged a certain Westernisation of culture, some distinctive elements of traditional cultural expression remain, particularly in terms of music and dance, as evident during Eid al-Adha and Eid al-Fitr or social occasions, such as weddings. With its Bedouin inheritance, only a specialist is likely to pick up the nuances that distinguish Qatar's music or dance from that of other Gulf States, but numerous events throughout the country make Qatar one of the easier places to encounter these art forms.

Contact Qatar Tourism Authority (www. experienceqatar.com) or check local 'What's On' listings in the *Gulf Times,* the *Peninsula* or the *Qatar Tribune* to see what's happening where.

For contemporary arts and crafts, spare an hour to browse round the new galleries in Souq Waqif. Interest in orchestral music is enjoying a revival with the **Qatar Philharmonic Orchestra** (qatarphilharmonicorchestra.org), sponsored by the charitable Qatar

BONDING BEADS

Sit in a coffeehouse in Qatar, be present at a business meeting or watch a party of *sheesha* (water pipe used to smoke tobacco) smokers and you will notice that they are bonded by a common activity: they are twirling a set of beads between thumb and forefinger, or flicking the entire set of 33, 66 or 99 beads around the wrist. At a party or wedding, they may even be whirling them overhead like a rattle.

These are not any old beads: they could be pearl or jade; bought in the local souq, or collected bead by bead and at great cost from around the world. Qataris favour amber beads, however, and a trip to a specialist *misbah* (prayer bead) shop in Souq Waqif will gladden the eye with strands of yellow, gold and treacle-coloured amber.

Men have carried *misbah,* traditionally threaded by women, since the early days of Islam to help in the contemplation of God. A user usually rolls each bead while reciting the names or attributes of Allah.

While many continue to use the beads for religious purposes, prayer beads in Qatar have become a social item and if you really want to be in with the in-crowd, then you'll acquire this necessary accessory. Let them sit in the pocket ready to be whipped out when the haggling gets tough or, like the 'How are you?' that can be repeated 10 times or more in the course of an evening's engagement, bring them out when a pause threatens conversation. If you let them function like a piece of intuited discourse, as well as talisman and storyteller, comforter and companion, you'll find you are holding the ultimate symbol of male bonding.

Foundation and playing at venues like Katara and Aspire around town.

Poetry & Dance

On National Day (3 September), you may be lucky to see a troupe of male dancers performing Al-Ardha in a display of patriotic affection. It's hard to know whether to call the performance a dance with words or a poem in motion, as during Al-Ardha, a poet chants celebrations of horsemanship and valour while threading a path between two opposing lines of dancers, each of whom echoes a verse of the poem while fluttering his sword in the air.

Another fascinating spectacle sometimes seen on National Day is Al-Qulta. Witnessing this kind of spontaneous poetry making is remarkable for those who understand Arabic, as two facing poets improvise with great skill on a given topic. Even without knowing what is being said, the occasion is exciting as the poets are accompanied not by instruments but by syncopated *tasfiq* (the slapping of palm to palm), while the audience gets carried away with the rhythm of the poetry.

There is a long association between the Gulf countries and those of the east coast of Africa, and an interchange of culture is an inevitable bonus of trade. One dance that reflects East Africa's more relaxed integration of the sexes is Al-Lewa, performed by a mixture of men and women for pleasure.

At weddings it is a traditional mark of respect for young women, who are often daringly dressed in the absence of men in low-fronted, backless ball gowns, to dance for the bride. Today, the music is often imported from Egypt and is a sort of pan-Arabic pop, performed by men hidden behind a screen. If lucky enough to be invited to a wedding, the visitor (strictly women only) may be treated to Al-Khammary, performed by a group of masked women, or to Al-Sameri, a thrilling spectacle in which the dancers gyrate their loosened hair in time with the accelerating beat.

Crafts

The traditional Bedouin skill of weaving for carpets, tents, rugs and curtains was practised by modern Qataris until only about two decades ago, when machinery and cheap imports shut down the industry. Carpet wool, however, is still often prepared in the traditional way. The wool is washed and soaked in lemon juice and a crystalline mixture to remove impurities and oil, boiled for about 10 hours, dried in the sun and then dyed (often with imported dyes from India and other Gulf States). Goat hair is still used to make tents (particularly the black tents with white stripes, which are now seen more readily in the garden of a wealthy villa than in the interior). Camel hair, plaited using two hands, one foot and a strangely shaped piece of wood, is used for ropes and bags. A form of basket weaving, called *al-safaf* (using palm leaves and cane) is still practised in the villages.

Jewellery making is a craft that continues to thrive: while the traditional Bedouin pieces of silver and stone are now difficult to find, expert local goldsmiths and jewellers engage in centuries-old practices of sword decoration and bridal ornamentation. The *burda* (traditional Qatari cloak) is still worn in Qatar and the cuffs and sleeves are decorated by hand, using thin gold and silver threads.

Environment

The Land

One would expect the area of a country to be finite. Not so in Qatar, where extensive reclamation programs keep adding a square kilometre or two to the total. The Qatar peninsula is generally given as 11,586 sq km, about 160km long and 55km to 80km wide, and includes 700km of shallow coastline. It includes one or two islands, but not the neighbouring Hawar Islands, which were a bone of contention until the oil-rich islands were awarded to Bahrain. While Qatar is mostly flat, the oil-drilling area of Jebel Dukhan reaches a height of 75m.

The sand dunes to the south of the country, especially around the inland sea at Khor al-Adaid, are particularly appealing. Much of the interior, however, is marked by gravel-covered plains. This kind of desert may look completely featureless but it's worth a closer look: rain water collects in *duhlans* (crevices), giving rise intermittently to exquisite little flowering plants. Roses even bloom in the desert, though not of the floral kind: below the *sabkha* (salt flats that lie below sea level), gypsum forms into rosettes, some measuring 8in to 10in across. Stone mushrooms and yardangs, weathered out of the limestone escarpment near Bir Zekreet, offer a geography lesson in desert landscape. Anyone with an interest in sharks' teeth, shale or any other aspect of Qatari wildlife can contact **Qatar's Natural History Group** (www.qnhg.org), which runs regular field trips and slide shows.

Wildlife

A passion for hunting, traditionally with falcon or saluki (a Bedouin hunting dog), has marked Qatar's relationship with birds (particularly the tasty bustard) and mammals, with the double consequence that there is little wildlife left. The Qataris are the first to admit this and are most eager to remedy the situation. Gazelle, oryx (Qatar's national animal) and Arabian ibex are all locally extinct, but ambitious breeding programs aim to reintroduce the animals into the wild. A herd of oryx can be seen, by permit only or while on a tour, at a private reserve near Al-Shahaniya. There are also protected areas, north of Al-Khor, for the endangered green turtle, which nests on the shore.

Altogether easier to spot, a rich and diverse number of birds (waders, ospreys, cormorants, curlews, flamingos, larks and hawks) frequent the coastal marshes and the offshore islands. A golf course may seem an unlikely birding venue, but the lush oasis of Doha Golf Club occasionally attracts the glorious golden oriole and crested crane. The mangrove plantations north of Al-Khor are another good place to get the binoculars out.

A dusting of rain or dew in the colder months and a dried-up wadi (river bed) can be transformed into a hub of activity: the trumpets of Lycium shawii and the orchid-like Indigofera intricata are two recently classified plant species that have surprised botanists.

Environmental Issues

Qatar is now 2m higher than it was 400 years ago thanks to 'geological uplift', a phenomenon where movements in the earth's crust push the bedrock up. As a result, the underground water table sinks, or at least becomes more difficult to access. In Qatar, uplift has resulted in increasing aridity and sparseness of vegetation. This, combined with encroaching areas of sand and *sabkha*, has given environmentalists much to be concerned about.

FLOTSAM & GYPSUM

Look up at the door lintels or window frames of any old house or mosque in Qatar and chances are it will be decorated with a filigree of white plaster – only it isn't plaster, it's gypsum, otherwise known as calcium sulphate. Found in abundance locally, and sometimes combined with chippings of driftwood washed up on the beach, it was used to clad the exterior of houses, forts, mosques and wind towers, as an improvement on mud. Able to withstand extreme changes in temperature and humidity, this durable material lent itself to moulding and carving. Some of the abstract plant designs and geometric patterns that can be seen on important buildings across the Gulf illustrate how working with gypsum has evolved into a complex craft.

Qatar's mangrove wetlands, which provide a breeding ground for waders and crustaceans such as shrimps, are threatened by the multiple hazards of grazing camels, oil seepages and land reclamation. Various projects are afoot to protect this important coastal habitat, including the replanting of mangroves north of Al-Khor, but there are no official nature reserves as yet. Several privately owned projects, such as Al Wabra Preserve (www.qatarvisitor.com and search for 'Al Wabra'), help protect endangered species.

SURVIVAL GUIDE

ⓘ Directory A-Z

ACCOMMODATION

Qatar's main sights are all within day trip distance of the capital. As a result, most visitors stay in the large selection of hotels available in Doha and neighbouring West Bay and West Bay Lagoon. The following notes may be helpful in determining what type of accommodation to book:

➡ Qatar has accommodation to fit most pockets, although travellers will find it difficult to find single/double rooms for less than QR350/450 per night. Doha has a good, modern hostel, costing QR240 per night with linen provided: check www.hihostels.com/dba/hostels for details.

SLEEPING PRICE RANGES

The following price ranges refer to a double room with bathroom and AC in high season (November to March). Taxes are included in the price. Listings are arranged by price and then by author preference within a price category.

$ less than QR500 (US$140)

$$ QR500–1000 (US$140–US$280)

$$$ more than QR1000 (US$280)

➜ Many of the cheaper hotels near Souq Waqif are in areas condemned for redevelopment in the near future, but they will relocate to the area behind the National Museum.

➜ Midrange accommodation usually implies a carpet, minibar, satellite TV and view of something other than an internal stairwell.

➜ Qatar has some of the world's best top-end accommodation, including resorts. Most offer weekend (Friday-Saturday) specials and other deals in association with selected airlines.

➜ 'Wild camping' is possible in some parts of the country but you will need to be self-sufficient and preferably have a 4WD to gain access to beaches or sand dunes. Basic camping equipment is available from Carrefour in City Centre-Doha.

ACTIVITIES

Beaches

The coast of Qatar is almost a continuous line of sandy beaches with pockets of limestone pavement. As pretty as it looks, the sea is very shallow, making it almost impossible to swim. There are some good beaches, however, at the top resorts in Doha, at the Sealine Beach Resort (p226) near Mesaieed and Al-Ghariya Resort (p228). The nearest public-access beach close to Doha is at Katara (p218). None of the wild beaches have facilities, and shade is a problem in the summer.

Sand Sports

The sand is beginning to attract people to Qatar in the same way that the snow draws the crowds elsewhere, with sand skiing, quad-bike racing and sand-dune driving all becoming popular sports, though largely for those with their own equipment. The Sealine Beach Resort (p226), south of Mesaieed, is the best place for these activities, offering quad bikes and helpful assistance if you get stuck in the dunes. For 4WD trips into the sand dunes, contact any tour agency or pitch up at the Sealine.

Spectator Sports

Qatar is the sporting capital of the region. For details on any of the sporting fixtures hosted in Doha, visit **Qatar Marhaba** (www.qatarmarhaba. com) and search for sports. Most events – including Qatar ExxonMobil Tennis Open, Sail the Gulf Regatta, the Emir's Sword horse race, Moto GP and Emir's Cup camel race – are clustered into the first half of the year.

BOOKS

➜ *Qatar,* by David Chadock, revised in 2006, is the definitive illustrated reference to Qatar.

➜ *Arabian Time Machine: Self-Portrait of an Oil State*, by Helga Graham (if you can find a copy), is an interesting collection of interviews with Qataris about their lives and traditions, before and after the oil boom.

➜ *Qatari Women Past and Present*, by Abeer Abu Said, explains the changing and traditional roles of women in Qatar.

➜ *Qatar – Enchantment of the World*, by Byron Augustin, gives a recent overall view of life in Qatar.

CUSTOMS REGULATIONS

Doha airport has a large **duty-free shop** (www. qatardutyfree.net). No alcohol, narcotics or pork-related products may be brought in through customs – and no pornographic magazines from back home. Goods originating from Israel may also pose problems if you are stopped by customs.

EMBASSIES & CONSULATES

Most embassies are in the 'Diplomatic Area', north of the Sheraton Doha Hotel & Resort, and few have specific road addresses. All are open from 8am to 2pm Sunday to Thursday, but telephone first.

Bahraini (☑ 44 839 360; doha.mission@mofa. gov.bh)

French (☑ 44 021 777; www.ambafrance-qa. org; Al-Corniche, West Bay Diplomatic Area)

German (☑ 44 082 300; www.doha.diplo.de; Al-Jezira al-Arabiyya St)

Kuwaiti (☑ 44 832 111; kweqatar@kuwaitembassy.com.qa; Diplomatic St, West Bay Diplomatic Area)

Omani (☑ 44 931 910; omanembassy.doha@ yahoo.com; C Ring Rd)

Saudi Arabian (☑ 44 832 030; fax 44 832 720; Diplomatic St, West Bay Diplomatic Area)

UAE (☑ 44 838 880; emarat@qatar.net.qa) Off Al-Khor St.

UK (☑ 44 962 000; www.ukinqatar.fco.gov.uk; Al-Istiqlal St)

USA (☑ 44 884 101; www.qatar.usembassy. gov; 22 February St)

Yemeni (☑ 44 432 720, Fax 44 429 400; Al-Jazeera St) Located near Al-Sadd Plaza.

FOOD & DRINK

For information about Qatar's cuisine, see p210 and the Flavours of Arabia chapter (p459).

In a country that adheres to the rigorous Wahhabi sect of Islam, which enjoins strict codes of conduct, it may come as some surprise to discover that alcohol is available in many top-end hotel bars. A cynic might point to the increasing number of international sporting and commercial events being held in the country, for which the availability of a bar is a major consideration. But whether permitted for pragmatic reasons or through tolerance, alcohol should be consumed discreetly and public displays of drunkenness should be avoided at all costs.

INTERNET ACCESS

Internet facilities are available at all top-end hotels, and there is an increasing number of internet cafes around the capital. The main ISP is **Internet Qatar** (☑125; www.qtel.com.qa), part of Qtel. Prepaid dial-up cards can be purchased from supermarkets and are valid for six months. Free wireless internet access is offered at many hotels, some cafes and public parks in Doha.

Qtel Hotspot broadband offers high-speed internet access at selected locations (including Souq Waqif) with the use of a pre-paid hotspot card. See www.qtelhotspot.net.qa for details.

LEGAL MATTERS

Breaking the law can have severe consequences. For more information, see the Expats chapter (p33) and consult your embassy.

MONEY

The currency of Qatar is the Qatari riyal (QR). One riyal is divided into 100 dirhams. Coins are worth 25 or 50 dirhams, and notes come in one, five, 10, 50, 100 and 500 denominations. The Qatari riyal is fully convertible.

ATMs & Credit Cards

All major credit and debit cards are accepted in large shops. Visa (Plus & Electron), MasterCard and Cirrus are accepted at ATMs at HSBC, the Qatar National Bank and the Commercial Bank of Qatar, which also accepts American Express (Amex) and Diners Club cards.

Moneychangers

Currencies from Bahrain, Saudi Arabia and the UAE are easy to buy and sell at banks and moneychangers. Travellers cheques can be changed at all major banks and the larger moneychangers. Moneychangers can be found around the Gold Souq area of central Doha. There is little difference in exchange rates between banks and moneychangers.

Tipping & Bargaining

A service charge is usually added to restaurant (and top-end hotel) bills. Local custom does not require that you leave a tip and, although it is certainly appreciated, there is a danger of escalating the habit to the detriment of the workers involved (some establishments reduce wages in anticipation of tips that may or may not be forthcoming). It is therefore recommended that local custom is followed, unless exceptional service or assistance warrants an exceptional gesture.

Bargaining is expected in the souqs and, although Western-style shopping centres have fixed prices, it's still worth asking for a discount in boutiques and smaller shops.

OPENING HOURS

Qataris love their 'siesta', and Doha resembles a ghost town in the early afternoon. These opening hours prevail throughout Qatar.

Banks 7.30am to 1pm Sunday to Thursday.

Government offices 7am to 2pm Sunday to Thursday.

Internet cafes 7am to midnight.

Post offices 7am to 8pm Sunday to Thursday, 8am to 11am and 5pm to 8pm Saturday.

Restaurants 11.30am to 1.30pm and 5.30pm to midnight Saturday to Thursday, 5pm to midnight Friday.

Shopping centres 10am to 10pm Saturday to Thursday, 4pm to midnight Friday.

Shops 8.30am to 12.30pm and 4pm to 9pm Saturday to Thursday, 4.30pm to 9pm Friday.

PHOTOGRAPHY

Shops selling memory cards and batteries are plentiful in Doha. All studios can print digital photos from a memory card. They can also transfer photos to a CD from a memory card or film. Many photographic shops also arrange passport photos. Remember to respect local sensibilities by asking before photographing people.

POST

There is a general post office in northern Doha and another in central Doha. For a full list of postal rates, see www.qpost.com.qa.

ⓘ QATAR – IS IT SAFE?

Many Western visitors have been deterred from coming to the Gulf on account of the hostilities in the Middle East and unrest in neighbouring Bahrain. Qatar, however, is one of the safest and most politically stable countries to visit, and experiences minimal crime.

The poor quality of driving is the only danger worth pointing out, especially as intolerant local drivers are not very cautious about pedestrians.

For those hiring a 4WD, beware the pockets of soft sand and *sabkha* around the coast and in the interior that are not always apparent until it's too late. Drivers should always stick to tracks when going off-road and make sure they have all the necessary equipment (water, tow rope, jack, spare tyre etc) for an emergency, as passing cars are sometimes few and far between, especially in the interior.

PUBLIC HOLIDAYS

In addition to the main Islamic holidays listed in the Arabian Peninsula directory, Qatar observes the following public holidays:

Accession Day 27 June
National Day 3 September

TELEPHONE

The country code for Qatar is 974. There are no specific area or city codes. The international access code (to call abroad from Qatar) is 0.

All communications services are provided by **Qtel** (www.qtel.com.qa). Local calls are free, except from the blue-and-white Qtel phone booths which charge a nominal fee. Phonecards (which come in denominations of QR10, QR30 and QR50) are available in bookshops and supermarkets around Doha and can be used for direct international dialling.

The cost of an International Direct Dial call is cheaper between 7pm and 7am, all day Friday and on holidays. At peak times international calls cost around just QR2 per minute.

Directory enquiries can be contacted on ☑180. Call ☑150 for international inquiries.

Mobile Phones

Qtel operates a prepaid GSM mobile phone service called Hala Plus. Cards in a variety of denominations are widely available in shops.

TRAVELLERS WITH DISABILITIES

Little provision has been made in Qatar for travellers with disabilities, although the new resorts have tried to make accommodation wheelchair accessible. The corniche area of Doha and the new malls are easily accessed, but many of the other sights and souqs are not. No provision is made for the visually or hearing impaired.

VISAS

➡ All nationalities need a visa to enter Qatar
➡ Around 33 nationalities can obtain a two-week, single-entry visa on arrival.
➡ Visit the government website (www.moi.gov.qa) and search the 'Visitor Gateway' section to be sure of the latest information.
➡ To avoid being turned back from a lengthy queue, fill out the application card (in piles on top of the visa counter) before you reach the visa counter.
➡ Payment is by credit card only.
➡ You can buy an eCash card from QNB at the arrivals hall at Qatar International Airport which acts as a credit card for the prepaid sum.
➡ Multi-entry tourist and business visas are applied for through a Qatari embassy or consulate. Three passport-sized photos, an application form filled out in triplicate and a letter from the hosting company is required. These visas are issued within 24 hours.
➡ Visa extensions valid for two weeks can be obtained through your hotel or a travel agent.
➡ Charges for overstaying are high.

WOMEN TRAVELLERS

Qatar is a safe place for women to travel and women can move about freely, without any of the restrictions that are often experienced in other parts of the region. Harassment of women is not looked upon kindly by officials. Dressing conservatively (especially covering shoulders and knees) is not only respectful of local sensibilities but brings less unwanted stares.

ⓘ Getting There & Away

AIR

Doha International Airport (☑44 656 666; www.dohaairport.com) is 2.5km from the city centre.

The national carrier **Qatar Airways** (☑44 496 666; www.qatarairways.com; Al-Matar St) has daily direct services from London to Doha, and several direct flights a week from Paris, Munich, Jakarta, Kuala Lumpur and from most cities in the Middle East. Qatar is also serviced by several major airlines: British Airways flies direct from London to Doha daily, KLM flies direct from Amsterdam, while Emirates flies to Doha from most major hubs via Dubai. There is no airport departure tax.

Airlines Flying to/from Qatar

British Airways (BA; ☑ 44 321 434; www.
ba.com) Heathrow Airport, London

EgyptAir (MS; ☑ 44 356 020; www.egyptair.
com.eg) Cairo

Emirates (EK; ☑ 44 384 477; www.emirates.
com) Dubai

Etihad Airways (☑ 44 366 657; www.etihadair-
ways.com; ☎) Abu Dhabi

Gulf Air (☑ 44 998 022; www.gulfairco.com)
Manama

Kuwait Air (KT; ☑ 44 435 340; www.kuwait-
airways.com) Kuwait City

Oman Air (WY; ☑ 44 321 373; www.omanair.
aero) Muscat

Saudi Arabian Airlines (SV; ☑ 44 440 121;
www.saudiairlines.com) Jeddah

LAND
Border Crossings

Residents of Qatar, Saudi Arabia and the UAE
can drive across the Qatar-Saudi border, providing they have insurance for both countries. Bear
in mind that if you want to travel *from* Qatar,
you must have a Saudi visa (or transit visa) in
advance.

Bus

From Doha, **Saudi Arabian Public Transport
Co** (Saptco; www.saptco.com.sa) has daily
buses (from QR 50 to QR150 depending on
destination) to Dammam with onward connections to Amman (Jordan) Manama (approximately five hours); Abu Dhabi (six hours) and
Dubai (seven hours); and Kuwait (approximately
10 hours). All routes can be booked online.
Departures are from the central bus station
in Doha. You must have a valid transit visa for
Saudi Arabia in advance, and an onward ticket
and visa for your next destination beyond Saudi
Arabia's borders.

ⓘ Getting Around

BUS

The public bus system operates from the central
Al Ghanim Bus Station (p225) with air-conditioned bus services to Al-Khor, Al-Wakara and
Masaieed among other destinations. Prices cost
from QR3 to QR9.

CAR & MOTORCYCLE

If you're driving around Doha, you'll discover
that roundabouts are very common, treated
like camel-race tracks and often redundant in
practice. Finding the right way out of Doha can
also be difficult: if you're heading south towards
Al-Wakrah or Mesaieed, take the airport road
(Al-Matar St); the main road to all points north is
22 February St (north from Al-Rayyan Rd); and
to the west, continue along Al-Rayyan Rd. Some
other notes:

➡ Driving in Qatar is on the right-hand side.

➡ Numerous petrol stations are located around
Doha but there are few along the highways.

➡ Authorities are strict with anyone caught
speeding, not wearing a seat belt or not carrying a driving licence: heavy on-the-spot fines
are handed out freely.

➡ Don't even think about drink driving.

Hire

➡ A visitor can rent a car with a driving licence
from home – but only within seven days of
arriving in Qatar (although expats resident in
other GCC countries can drive for up to three
months).

➡ After seven days, a temporary driving licence
must be obtained, issued by the Traffic Licence

PRACTICALITIES

➡ **Magazines** *Marhaba, Qatar's Premier Information Guide,* published quarterly, is an
excellent source of information regarding events in Qatar, and includes some interesting
feature articles on Qatari life and culture. It costs QR20. *Time Out Doha* gives the most
comprehensive listings for dining and entertainment.

➡ **Newspapers** Qatar's English-language newspapers, the *Gulf Times* and *The
Peninsula,* are published daily, except Friday. International newspapers and magazines
are available one or two days after publication at major bookshops in Doha.

➡ **Radio** Programs in English are broadcast on 97.5FM and 102.6FM each afternoon
from 1.15pm until 4pm. The BBC is available on 107.4FM.

➡ **TV** Channel 2 on Qatar TV (QTV) broadcasts programs in English and international
satellite channels are available at the majority of hotels. The renowned Al-Jazeera
Satellite Channel is broadcast in English and Arabic from Doha: it has become one of the
most watched and most respected Arabic news channels in the Arab world.

➡ **Smoking** Widespread but top-end hotels reserve rooms for non-smokers.

➡ **Weights & Measures** Qatar uses the metric system.

FRIENDSHIP CAUSEWAY

Relations between Qatar and its neighbour, Bahrain, have not always been the best. Shared royal family has been a bone of contention for one thing and it was only relatively recently the two countries stopped haggling over ownership of the Hawar Islands. Driven by a growing sense of community within the Gulf region, however, and with a shared mission to attract higher volumes of tourists, the two countries have at last put their differences aside. As if consolidating the friendlier relations, work is scheduled to begin on a 40km road link between Qatar and Bahrain. It will take over four years to complete and will involve multiple bridges supported on reclaimed land, similar to King Fahd Causeway that links Bahrain to Saudi Arabia. When complete, it will form the longest fixed link across water in the world.

Office. It lasts for the duration of your visa and rental agencies can arrange this for you.

→ The minimum rental period for all car-hire agencies is 24 hours and drivers must be at least 21 years old.

→ Major agencies charge about QR140/750 per day/week for the smallest car.

→ The cost of a 4WD can be very high (around QR500/2800 per day/week); an ordinary car is perfectly suitable for reaching all the places mentioned by Lonely Planet with the exception of Khor al-Adaid.

→ A 4WD is essential, however, for those wanting to explore the interior in greater depth or wishing to camp on a remote beach.

Al-Muftah Rent-A-Car (☑ 44 634 433; www.rentacardoha.com; Doha International Airport; ⊙24hr) With over 40 years of experience in Doha, this is a reliable and cheaper local alternative to the major car hire companies.

Avis (☑ 44 667 744; www.avisqatar.com)

Budget (☑ 44 310 411; www.budgetqatar.com)

Europcar (☑ 44 621 188; www.europcar.com)

LOCAL TRANSPORT
Taxi

The turquoise taxis belonging to Mowasalat-Karwa offer a good service, charging QR4 and QR1.800 for each subsequent kilometre.

The easiest way to catch a taxi is to ask your hotel to arrange one, although technically you can wave one down from the side of the road. To visit most sights outside Doha, it's better to hire a car or arrange transport with a tour company as it usually works out considerably cheaper and it saves long waits for return transport.

Saudi Arabia
المملكة العربية السعودية

Best Places for Culture

➡ Madain Saleh (p259)
➡ National Museum (p243)
➡ Dir'aiyah (p250)
➡ Old Jeddah (p253)
➡ Camel Market & Races (p250)

Best Places for Nature

➡ Asir National Park (p264)
➡ Al-Soudah (p264)
➡ Diving at Yanbu (p256)
➡ Farasan Islands (p265)
➡ Red Sands (p250)

Why Go?

The birthplace and spiritual home of Islam, Saudi Arabia is as rich in attractions as it is in stirring symbolism. It is also one of the most difficult places on earth to visit.

For those who do get in, rock-hewn Madain Saleh is Arabia's greatest treasure. Other wonders abound, from the echoes of TE Lawrence along the Hejaz Railway to the mud-brick ruins of Dir'aiyah, Jeddah, gateway to the holy cities of Mecca and Medina, has an enchanting old city made of coral, while the Red Sea coast has world-class diving. Elsewhere, this is a land of astonishing natural beauty, particularly the plunging landscapes of the Asir Mountains in the Kingdom's southwest.

Best of all, there are few places left that can be said to represent the last frontier of tourism. Whether you're an expat or a pilgrim, Saudi Arabia is one of them.

When to Go

Saudi Arabia

Nov–Mar Cooler temperatures make daytime weather bearable and nights surprisingly chilly.

Apr–Oct Temperatures above 40°C, high humidity along the coast; Ramadan; April sandstorms.

Year-round Red Sea diving has excellent visibility all year, but in summer morning dives are best.

AT A GLANCE

⇒ **Currency**: Saudi riyal (SR)

⇒ **Money**: ATMs widespread, credit cards widely accepted

⇒ **Visas**: Only business visas (no tourist visas)

⇒ **Mobile Phones**: GSM phone network widespread

Fast Facts

⇒ **Official name** Kingdom of Saudi Arabia

⇒ **Capital** Riyadh

⇒ **Area** 2,149,690 sq km

⇒ **Population** 26.5 million

⇒ **Country code** ☑966

Exchange Rates

Australia	A$1	SR3.9
Bahrain	BD1	SR9.9
Euro zone	€1	SR4.9
Kuwait	KD1	SR13.1
Oman	OR$1	SR9.7
Qatar	QR1	SR1.03
UAE	Dh1	SR1.02
UK	£1	SR5.7
USA	US$1	SR3
Yemen	YR100	SR1.74

Resources

⇒ **Lonely Planet** (www.lonelyplanet.com/saudiarabia) Includes the Thorn Tree bulletin board.

⇒ **Saudi Arabian Information Resources** (www.saudinf.com) Includes helpful addresses.

SAUDI ARABIA

Daily Costs

Saudi Arabia isn't a budget destination. Eating well for SR50 to SR75 per day is rarely a problem, but few budget hotels accept Westerners – expect to pay at least SR500 for a double in a decent midrange hotel. It is, of course, easy to pay much more than this for both food and accommodation; a more realistic midrange budget, once you factor in transport, is around SR1000 per day.

ITINERARIES

One Week

Begin in Riyadh, with a couple of days exploring the modern architecture, **Masmak Fortress**, **National Museum** and the nearby **camel races**. On the third day, factor in an afternoon at **Dir'aiyah** and camp in the Red Sands. Fly to Al-Ula and spend a day amid the wonderful Nabataean ruins of **Madain Saleh**, with extra time for one or two stops along the **Hejaz Railway**. Fly down to **Jeddah**, Saudi Arabia's most beguiling city, and lose yourself in the souqs and coral houses of Old Jeddah and a stroll along the corniche.

Two Weeks

With an extra week, allow for a couple of days' diving around **Yanbu**, then head for the hills (especially in summer) of pretty **Taif**; make it a weekend if you want to catch the camel races. Fly or drive to Abha and use it as a base for exploring the **Asir Mountains**, especially Jebel Soudah and the hanging village of **Habalah**. Other options to round out your second week include diving in the Red Sea from the **Farasan Islands** or, if the security situation permits, a foray to wonderful **Najran** in the Kindgom's far southwest.

Essential Food & Drink

⇒ **Mezze** Truly one of the joys of Arab cooking and similar in conception to Spanish tapas, with infinite possibilities.

⇒ **Fuul** Mashed fava beans served with olive oil and often eaten for breakfast.

⇒ **Shwarma** Ubiquitous kebab- or souvlaki-style pita sandwich stuffed with meat.

⇒ **Baby camel** Among the tenderest of Saudi meats, it's a particular specialty of Jeddah and the Hejaz.

⇒ **Red Sea seafood** Fresh and varied and at its best when slow-cooked over coals or baked in the oven; try *samak mashwi* (fish basted in a date puree and barbecued over hot coals).

⇒ **Khouzi** A Bedouin dish of lamb stuffed with rice, nuts, onions, sultanas, spices, eggs and a whole chicken.

RIYADH

الرياض

📍 01 / POP 4.7 MILLION

Once a mudbrick waystation along desert trading routes, Riyadh is now one of the wealthiest cities in the world. The country's political, financial and administrative capital is also a city with a fascinating subtext. Nowhere are the contradictions of modern Saudi more evident than in Riyadh. Seen from afar, soaring, sparkling, stunning modern towers rise above the dusty desert and shiny 4WDs throng modern highways. Up close, Riyadh is conservative, cautious and sober (certainly compared to Jeddah). This sometimes jarring, always intriguing mix is combined with fine hotels and restaurants and some excellent sights.

◉ Sights

National Museum
MUSEUM

(King Abdul Aziz Museum; Map p246; 📞 ext 1290 402 9500; www.nationalmuseum.org.sa; King Saud Rd; adult/child/student SR10/free/free; ⊙ men & schools 9am-noon Sun, Mon, Wed, Thu & 3.30-9.30pm Tue, women & schools 9am-noon Tue, families 3.30-9.30pm Sun, Mon & Wed-Fri) This state-of-the-art museum is one of the finest in the Middle East. Encased within modernist architecture, its two floors contain eight well-designed and informative galleries covering Arabian history, culture and art. The galleries beautifully display evocative rock carvings, engaging models and a full-scale reconstruction of a Nabataean tomb from Madain Saleh. Films (in English via headphones) shown on 180° screens complement the exhibits, as do virtual visits to sites and other excellent interactive displays.

Masmak Fortress
HISTORIC SITE, MUSEUM

(Qasr al-Masmak; 📞 411 0091; Imam Turki ibn Abdullah St; ⊙ men 8am-noon & 4-9pm Sat, Mon & Wed, women & families 8am-noon & 4-9pm Sun & Tue, 9am-noon Thu) **FREE** This squat fortification was built around 1865 and was the site of Ibn Saud's daring 1902 raid, during which a spear was hurled at the main entrance door with such force that the head is still lodged in the doorway. The information panels and short, chest-thumping films on the storming of the fortress and the 'reunification' of Saudi Arabia are reverential towards the Al-Sauds, but worth watching nonetheless. Highlights among the exhibits include maps and a fascinating range of photographs of Saudi dating from 1912 to 1937 in galleries converted from diwans (living rooms).

Al-Faisaliah Tower
NOTABLE BUILDING

(Map p246; 📞 273 3000; www.rosewoodhotels.com; King Fahd Rd, off Olaya St; admission SR45, viewing platform adult/family SR40/50; ⊙ 10am-midnight, viewing platform 10am-11.30pm Sat-Thu, noon-11.30pm Fri) Designed by British architect Norman Foster and built in 2000 by the Bin Laden construction company, Al-Faisaliah Tower was the first of the startling new structures to rise above Riyadh's skyline. It's most famous for its enormous glass globe (24m in diameter and made of 655 glass panels) near the summit.

Its 44 floors contain a five-star deluxe hotel and four exclusive restaurants, offices, apartments, the Sky shopping mall (p248) and a fabulous **viewing platform** (Globe Experience). The tower's needlepoint pinnacle (with a crescent on the tip) sits 267m above the ground.

Kingdom Tower
NOTABLE BUILDING

(Map p246; King Fahd Rd) Riyadh's landmark tower is a stunning piece of modern architecture – it's particularly conspicuous at night when the upper sweep is lit with constantly changing coloured lights.

Rising 302m high, its most distinctive feature is the steel-and-glass 300 ton bridge connecting the two towers. High-speed elevators fly you (at 180km/h) to the 99th floor **Sky Bridge** (Map p246; 📞 201 1888; adult/child SR25/12.50; ⊙ 10am-midnight) from where the views are breathtaking (you're allowed to take photos from up here). Avoid weekends and evenings after 6pm when it can get very crowded.

✪ Festivals & Events

Jenadriyah National Festival
CULTURAL FESTIVAL

Saudi Arabia's largest cultural festival runs over two weeks in late February or early March at a special site about 45km northeast of central Riyadh. Commencing with the King's Cup (an epic camel race with up

Saudi Arabia Highlights

1 Marvel at **Madain Saleh** (p259), the 'other Petra', with its evocative tombs in a stunning desert setting.

2 Dive the dazzling depths of Saudi's Red Sea and spot sharks, sea turtles and stunning coral reefs at **Yanbu** (p256).

3 Meander among the old merchants' houses, ancient markets and myriad museums of **Old Jeddah** (p253) and enjoy delicious coffee and conversation along the **corniche** (p253).

4 Wander the mud-brick ruins of **Dir'aiyah** (p250), a Unesco site and birthplace of modern Saudi Arabia.

5 Listen for the ghost of TE Lawrence along the **Hejaz Railway** (p261).

6 Escape the summer heat like a Gulf Arab and head for the hills of **Taif** (p256).

7 Enjoy the clear mountain air and exceptional scenery around **Jebel Soudah** (p264).

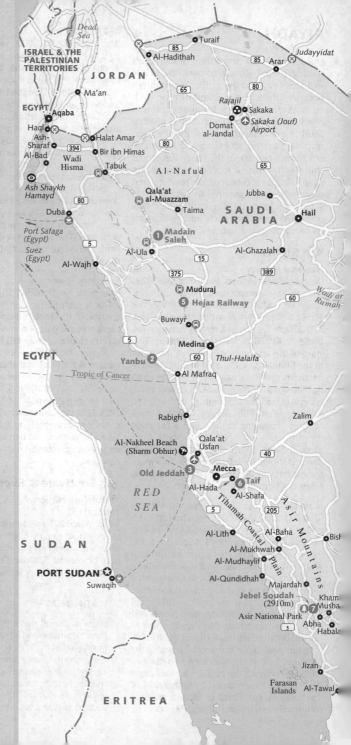

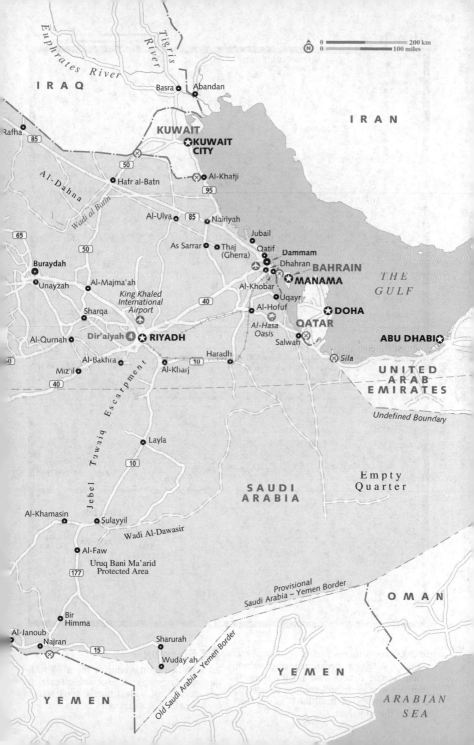

Riyadh

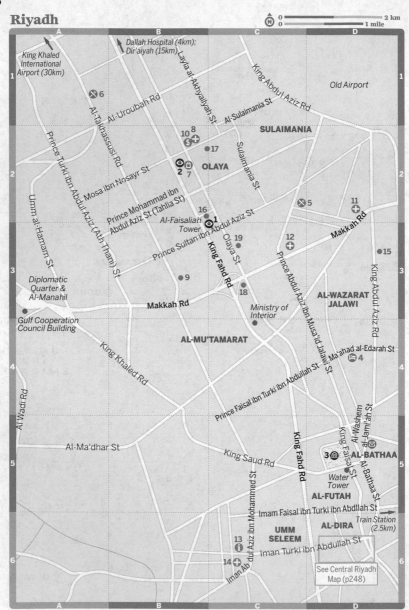

N   0 ─────────── 2 km
    0 ─────────── 1 mile

King Khaled International Airport (30km)

Dallah Hospital (4km); Dir'aiyah (15km)

Old Airport

Al-Takhassusi Rd

Al-Urubah Rd

Layla al-Akhyaliyah St

King Abdul Aziz Rd

Al-Sulaimania St

SULAIMANIA

Prince Turki ibn Abdul Aziz (Ath Thani) St

Mosa ibn Nosayr St

Umm al-Hamam St

Prince Mohammad ibn Abdul Aziz St (Tahlia St)

OLAYA

Sulaimania St

Al-Faisaliah Tower

Prince Sultan ibn Abdul Aziz St

Olaya St

Olaya Aziz St

King Fahd Rd

Prince Abdul Aziz ibn Musa'id Jalawi St

Makkah Rd

King Abdul Aziz Rd

Diplomatic Quarter & Al-Manahil

Makkah Rd

Ministry of Interior

AL-WAZARAT JALAWI

Gulf Cooperation Council Building

King Khaled Rd

AL-MU'TAMARAT

Ma'ahad al-Edarah St

Prince Faisal ibn Turki ibn Abdullah St

Al-Wadi Rd

Al-Ma'dhar St

King Saud Rd

King Fahd Rd

Al-Washem

King Faisal St

Al-Jami'ah St

Al-Bathaa St

AL-BATHAA

Water Tower

AL-FUTAH

Iman Abdul Aziz ibn Mohammed St

Imam Faisal ibn Turki ibn Abdllah St

Train Station (2.5km)

UMM SELEEM

AL-DIRA

Iman Turki ibn Abdullah St

Iman Abdul Aziz ibn Mohammed St

See Central Riyadh Map (p248)

to 2000 participants racing across a 19km track), the festival program includes traditional songs, dances and poetry competitions, as well as demonstrations of falconry and exhibitions of traditional crafts from around the Kingdom.

🛏 Sleeping

Riyadh's hotels fill up during the week with business travellers. Things are quieter at weekends. Most budget hotels won't accept bookings from non-Arabs.

Riyadh

Al-Khozama Hotel HOTEL $$
(Map p246; ☎465 4650; www.rosewoodhotels.com; Al-Faisaliah Tower, Olaya St; d/ste from SR480/1120; @☒) Though the rooms aren't large, they are comfortable, well-furnished and squarely aimed at the modern business traveller. With a lively lobby, a good patisserie, a coffeehouse, and three reputable restaurants offering a good variety and quality of cuisine including Al-Nakheel (Arabic) and Da Pino (Italian), it's a popular choice.

Riyadh Palace Hotel HOTEL $$
(Map p246; ☎405 4444; www.riyadhpalacehotel.com; off Al-Bathaa St, Ministries Area; s/d from SR 700/800 ste SR1500-3000; P@☒) The décor here is a little tired, but this is actually not a bad place to stay. The rooms are well-sized, the staff very friendly and there is no restriction on foreign women dining in the main restaurant.

★ Al-Faisaliah Hotel LUXURY HOTEL $$$
(Map p246; ☎273 2000; www.rosewoodhotels.com; Al-Faisaliah Tower, Olaya St; s/d/ste from SR1280/1620/2025; P@☒) All the details of a fabulous modern hotel are present at Al-Faisaliah, including fresh orchids and chocolates delivered daily to your room and your own butler 24 hours a day. Il Terrazzo restaurant enjoys a fine reputation and the hotel is hugely popular with Riyadh's demimonde for celebrating weddings and birthdays.

Four Seasons Hotel LUXURY HOTEL $$$
(Map p246; ☎211 5000; www.fourseasons.com; 15-24th fl, Kingdom Tower, King Fahd Rd; r/ste from SR1680/3100; @☒) Located in the Kingdom Tower, the hotel's biggest drawcard is the breathtaking views. Or the insane level of luxury – this temple to modernist design is probably Riyadh's finest hotel.

✗ Eating

All of the following have family sections unless indicated.

There are a mass of cheap eats and *shwarma* stands along Prince Mohammad ibn Abdul Aziz St (Tahlia St). Choose the busiest. There are supermarkets around Olaya St including Euromarche and Al-Azizyyah Supermarket.

Mama Noura MIDDLE EASTERN $
(Map p246; ☎470 8881; Prince Abdul Aziz ibn Mosa'ad Jalawi St; kebabs SR13-20; ⊙6am-3.30am) Large, bright and clean, this Turkish place remains perennially popular among Riyadhis, who come for the succulent *shwarma* (sandwich/plate SR4/12) or famous felafel (SR4 to SR15). There is no family section, but take-away is possible.

★ Najd Village MIDDLE EASTERN $$
(Map p246; ☎464 6530; Al-Takhassusi Rd; mains SR10-30; ⊙12.30pm-3.30am) Serving Saudi food in a Saudi setting (designed like a central-region village), this place is almost unique in the Kingdom. It's the perfect place

SAUDI ARABIA RIYADH

Central Riyadh

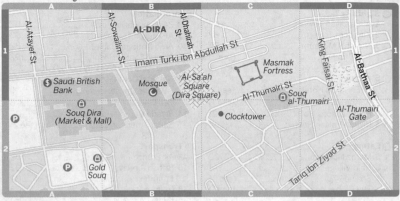

to sample *kasba* (meat with rice), or the Najd region speciality, *hashi* (baby camel). The set menu (SR100; minimum five people) includes 14 different mains, coffee, dates and even *bachoor* (incense). Prices are reasonable and it's much loved by locals.

Spazio 77   INTERNATIONAL **$$$**
(Map p246; ☑211 1888; www.spazio77.com; Kingdom Tower; pasta SR77-89, mains SR94-246; ☺10am-1am Sat-Thu, 1pm-1am Fri) Located in the nook of the 'necklace' of the Kingdom Tower, Spazio 77 is a combination brasserie, coffeehouse, sushi bar, cigar bar and, of all things, an oxygen bar. Michelin-starred French chef Alain Soliveres oversees the kitchen but there's a family-friendly Friday buffet.

The Globe   INTERNATIONAL **$$$**
(Map p246; ☑273 3000; www.rosewoodhotels.com; Al-Faisaliah Tower; 3-/4-/5-course set menus from SR290/380/425; ☺noon-2.30pm, 8pm-12.30am) The Globe is one of five restaurants in Al-Faisaliah Tower and one of the most romantic spots in town. Cosy, dimly lit and with spectacular views, this is one of the best restaurants in Riyadh. The food is as elegant as the setting.

🛍 Shopping

In a country where there are few public diversions, shopping has become a national sport.

With more designer outlets than you can shake a Gold Amex card at, **Kingdom Tower** (☑211 2222; Al-Mamlaka Mall; ☺9am-noon & 4-11pm Sat-Thu, 4-11pm Fri) even has a floor for women only (Ladies Kingdom) and the **Sky Shopping Mall** (Map p246; ☑273 0000;

☺10am-11.30pm Sat-Thu, noon-11.30pm Fri) in **Al-Faisaliah Tower** (☺9.30am-noon & 4-10.30pm Sat-Tue, families only 10am-11.30pm Wed-Thu & 4-10.30pm Fri) is also well known and popular.

Souq al-Thumairi   HANDICRAFTS
(Al-Thumairi St; ☺9am-noon & 4-9pm Sat-Thu, 4-9pm Fri) For authentic handicrafts, head to Souq al-Thumairi immediately south of the Masmak Fortress in the Al-Dira area. The shops in the small lanes offer everything from carpets to coffee pots and silver daggers to silver jewellery.

Jarir Bookstore   BOOKS
(Map p246; ☑462 6000; www.jarirbookstore.com; Olaya St; ☺9am-2pm & 4-11pm Sat-Thu, 4-11pm Fri) The excellent Jarir Bookstore has extensive selections in Arabic and English. This branch is the most accessible.

ℹ Orientation

Riyadh sprawls over 960 dusty sq kms. Most of its street signs are in Arabic only. Al-Bathaa is the central, older portion of town. Most of what you'll require in Riyadh lies north of here, especially in Olaya and Sulaimania, the main business and shopping areas.

The main north-south thoroughfares are Olaya St and King Fahd Rd, while Makkah Rd is the main east-west artery.

ℹ Information

EMERGENCY
Ambulance (☑997)
Fire (☑998)
Police (☑999)
Traffic Accidents (☑993)

INTERNET ACCESS

There are loads of internet cafes across Riyadh and the restrictions on foreign women using them seem to have relaxed. Most hotels and chain coffee shops offer free wi-fi.

MEDICAL SERVICES

24-Hour Pharmacy (Map p246; Mosa ibn Nosayr St) In Al-Akariya Centre.

Dallah Hospital (454 5277; cnr King Fahd & Al-Imam Saud ibn Abdul Aziz ibn Mohammad Rds) This hospital northeast of Riyadh accepts emergency cases on a walk-in basis.

MONEY

Banks and money changers can be found throughout Riyadh, including on Olaya St and Al-Bathaa St.

TRAVEL AGENCIES

Al-Tayyar (Map p246; 9200 12333; www.altayyargroup.com; Al-Takhassusi Rd; 9am-1.30pm & 4.30-8pm Sat-Thu) The largest travel company in the Kingdom and one of the most reputable, Al-Tayyar can organise car hire, air tickets, accommodation and tours.

ⓘ Getting There & Away

King Khaled International Airport (p280) lies 25km north of the city centre. Look out for the royal terminal. All domestic air services are operated by the main carrier, **Saudi Arabian Airlines** (9200 22222; www.saudiairlines.com; Olaya St, Saudia; 8am-10pm Sat-Wed).

Al-Aziziyah Bus Station (213 2318) lies 17km south of the city centre.

ⓘ Getting Around

TO/FROM THE AIRPORT

Buses (SR15, every two hours) run from 8am to 10pm daily between Al-Aziziyah **Saptco Bus Station** (213 3219) and the airport, via the main bus stop in Al Bathaa.

A taxi from the airport to the city centre costs SR80 and from the city centre to the airport SR60 – confirm the price before setting off.

TAXI

Riyadh's white taxis charge SR10 for a journey of 1km to 2km, but always negotiate the price first.

WORTH A TRIP

JUBBA

Northwest of Riyadh, the Najd plateau is hemmed in by the Hejaz Mountains to the west with sand deserts surrounding the other three sides. Crossing the plateau, the drive between Riyadh and Madain Saleh is, for the most part, a long, lonely stretch of road. Fortunately, close to the midpoint is one of Saudi Arabia's more intriguing sites: Jubba.

Jubba is rightly famed for its impressive petroglyphs (rock carvings) of prehistoric animals and is arguably the premier pre-Islamic site in Saudi. The finest carvings date from around 5500 BC, when much of this area was an inland lake and local inhabitants carved game animals drawn to the waters. Elegant rock-cut ibex and oryx abound and there are also significant inscriptions in Thamudic (a pre-Arabic alphabet) dating to 1000 BC. In 1879 intrepid British explorer Lady Anne Blunt described Jubba as 'one of the most curious places in the world, and to my mind, one of the most beautiful'.

The huge site covers 39 sq km and among the enigmatic stone circles are crude carvings of camels and other domesticated animals dating from AD 300. The closest carvings to Jubba are 3km away.

A permit is necessary to visit the site. You can either obtain it from Riyadh, the **Hail Museum** (533 1684; 9am-noon) FREE or from the custodian of the keys and local guide, the energetic and entrepreneurial **Ateeq Naif al-Shamari** (057 494 877). To find him, follow the signs to Naif's Palace of Heritage, which is just off the main street. The museum – along with the palace – is a family heirloom and the result of a lifetime's collection of antiques and artefacts. Mr Ateeq doesn't speak English.

The town of Hail has the nearest habitable accommodation with the simple but adequate **Al-Jabalain Hotel** (532 0402; King Abdul Aziz Rd; s/d SR250/300) and **Hotel Sahari Hail** (532 6441; fax 532 4390; King Khaled St; r SR110). Also in Hail, **Lebanese House Restaurant** (532 6736; King Khaled St; mezze SR5, mains SR5-20; 1pm-1am) is good for a meal.

Saptco (531 0101) has buses to Hail from Riyadh (SR120, eight hours, three daily), Al-Ula (SR80, five hours, one daily), Jubba (SR25, one hour, two daily) and Jeddah (SR130, 12 hours, one daily nonstop).

SAUDI ARABIA RIYADH

DESTINATION	AIR	BUS	TRAIN
Jeddah	17 daily flights from SR280	12 daily buses, SR150	None
Dammam	seven daily from SR150	24 daily, SR80	five daily, from SR80
Al-Ula	Mon & Sat from SR280	two daily, SR190	None
Taif	three daily, SR250	over 10 daily, SR125	None

AROUND RIYADH

Camel Market & Races

Riyadh's popular **camel market** (Souq al-Jamal; ◔ sunrise-sunset) [FREE] is one of the largest in the Arabian Peninsula. Spread out north of the Dammam road 30km from the city centre (take the Thumamah exit), this is a fascinating place to wander. Late afternoon is when the traders really find their voices. If you want to put in a bid, you'll need a good SR5000 to SR10,000.

At 4pm on some Thursdays, camel races take place at the camel race track along the extension of Al-Uroubah St in the Thumamah district, 10.5km from Riyadh.

Dir'aiyah
الدرعية

The ancestral home of the Al-Saud family and the birthplace of the Saudi-Wahhabi union, the historic site **Old Dir'aiyah** (☏486 0274; ◔8am-4.30pm Sat-Thu, 4pm-5.30pm Fri winter, 8am-5.30pm Sat-Thu, 4pm-5.30pm Fri summer) [FREE] makes a welcome escape from the frenzy of Riyadh.

This is one of the most evocative places in the Kingdom and its Unesco-supervised reconstruction saw it gain World Heritage status in 2010. The visitors centre is excellent, with fantastic black-and-white photographs of the old town, and yet it is almost always deserted; most of the town was abandoned during the 20th century. Note that parts of the site are treacherous under foot.

ℹ Getting There & Away

There's no public transport to Dir'aiyah, which lies 25km northwest of Al-Bathaa. A one-way taxi costs SR50 or expect to pay at least SR150 for a return taxi, including waiting time.

If you're driving, take King Fahd Rd north and follow the signs off to the west after passing Dallah Hospital. The road then turns north again – follow the brown signs marked 'Old Dir'aiyah'.

Sand Dunes

There are numerous stretches of sand dunes just off the Riyadh–Mecca Hwy.

The **Red Sands**, just west of the turn-off to Duruma around 40km west of Riyadh, are probably the most evocative as they boast a backdrop of the cliffs of the Jebel Tuwaiq Escarpment – a great sight at sunset. To see them properly, you'll need a 4WD.

HEJAZ
الحجاز

Meaning 'barrier', the region derives its name from the great escarpment that runs along Hejaz, separating it from the great plateaux of the interior. Historically, Hejaz has always seen itself as separate from the rest of the Kingdom. Outward looking and cosmopolitan, the Hejazi are fiercely proud of their heritage – a few even mutter about independence. Explore the Red Sea coastline and make time for languid Jeddah.

Jeddah
جدة

02 / POP 3.2 MILLION

Converging point for pilgrims and traders for centuries, Jeddah, the country's commercial capital, is the most easygoing city in the Kingdom, not to mention its most beguiling. The Al-Balad district, the heart of Old Jeddah, is a nostalgic testament to the bygone days of old Jeddah, with beautiful coral architecture casting some welcome shade over the bustling souqs beneath.

But the attractions aren't just above ground; Jeddah also offers fantastic diving. See p274 for details.

◉ Sights & Activities

Al-Tayibat City Museum for International Civilisation   MUSEUM

(Map p252; ☏693 0049; Rayhanat al-Jazirah St; student/adult SR25/35; ◔8am-noon & 5-9pm Sat-

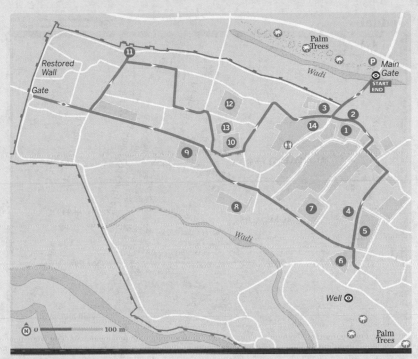

Walking Tour
Dir'aiyah

START MAIN GATE CARPARK
END VISITORS CENTRE
LENGTH 2KM, ONE TO TWO HOURS

As you climb up from the car park, the ❶ **Palace of Salwa** – once a four-storey complex of palaces, residential and administrative buildings and the home of Mohammed ibn Abd al-Wahhab – towers above the ❷ **visitors centre** on your left. Directly opposite, the ❸ **Al-Saud Mosque** was once connected to the palace by a bridge.

The main path continues south, then east, then south again to the ❹ **Palace of Fahd** and ❺ **Palace of Abdullah bin Saud**. Further south are the somewhat nondescript ruins of the ❻ **Palace of Thunayyan Bin Saud**, behind which are good views out over the palm groves.

Returning to the main path, walk west for around 250m, passing the ruined ❼ **Palace of Mishaari** on the right and the newly restored ❽ **Al-Turaif Bath**, with its decoratively painted doors. After a further 100m to the west and northwest, respectively, you'll find the restored ❾ **Palace of Nasser** and the ❿ **Palace of Saad bin Saud**, which has turrets, wall and door decorations. This is how much of Dir'aiyah must have once looked.

The main lane continues west before entering an open area where few houses remain. You can continue on to the restored sections of the wall (which once ran for 15km around the perimeter of Dir'aiyah) or branch off to the north to the ⓫ **Tower of Faisal**. A different path twists back to the Palace of Saad bin Saud, passing en route the ruined ⓬ **Palace of Fahran bin Saud** and the ⓭ **Saad bin Saud Mosque**.

Circle the Palace of Saad bin Saud from where a path heads north and then east back to the entry gate, passing some of the best-preserved ⓮ **houses** along the way.

Jeddah

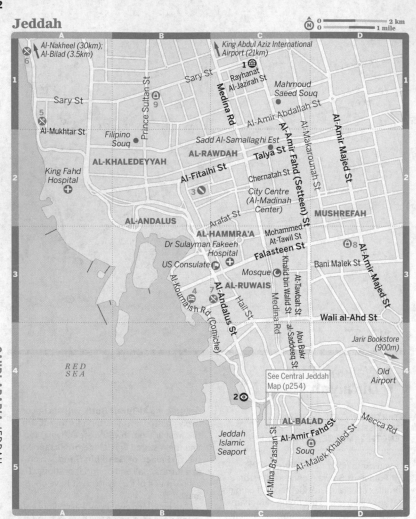

Al-Nakheel (30km);
Al-Bilad (3.5km)

King Abdul Aziz International
Airport (21km)

Sary St

Sary St

Al-Mukhtar St

Filipino
Souq

Prince Sultan St

Medina Rd

Rayhanat
Al-Jazirah St

Mahmoud
Saeed Souq

Al-Amir Abdallah St

King Fahd
Hospital

AL-KHALEDEYYAH

Sadd Al-Samallaghi Est

AL-RAWDAH

Al-Fitaihi St

Talya St

Al-Amir Fahd (Setteen) St

Al-Makarounah St

Al-Amir Majed St

Chernatah St

City Centre
(Al-Madinah
Center)

MUSHREFAH

AL-ANDALUS

Arafat St

AL-HAMMRA'A

Dr Sulayman Fakeeh
Hospital

Mohammed
At-Tawil St

Falasteen St

US Consulate

Mosque

Khalid bin Wald St

Bani Malek St

Al-Kournaish Rd (Corniche)

AL-RUWAIS

Hall St

Al-Andalus St

Medina Rd

At-Tawbah St
al-Saddeeq St

Wali al-Ahd St

Al-Amir Majed St

RED
SEA

See Central Jeddah
Map (p254)

Abu Bakr
al-Saddeeq St

Jarir Bookstore
(900m)

Old
Airport

Jeddah
Islamic
Seaport

Al-Mina Ba'ashan St

AL-BALAD

Al-Amir Fahd St

Souq

Al-Malek Khaled St

Mecca Rd

Thu) The four-floor collection here ranges from exquisite Islamic manuscripts and old coins to stunning furniture and pottery. Exhibits are accompanied by good captions and information panels, as well as some dioramas. Note that the museum can't open for fewer than 10 people; try to form a group or telephone to join one.

Shallaby Museum of Traditional Handicrafts & Hejazi Heritage MUSEUM
(☏ 697 7442; Al-Balad; ◷ 10am-1pm & 6-11pm Sat-Thu) FREE Shallaby Musem has a good collection of coins, silver antiques and traditional Bedouin clothes.

Fish Market MARKET
(Map p252; west of Al-Kournaish Rd; ◷ 5am-9pm) FREE The colourful and frenetic fish market in Al-Balad has at least 50 species of fish on display ranging from hammerhead sharks to grouper, parrot fish and squid. Don't miss the daily sale of the morning's catch (from 5am to 9am) when the action really gets going. Note that as the market's situated close to the coast guard and port, photos are not permitted.

Jeddah

Old Jeddah (Al-Balad)

Souq al-Alawi
SOUQ

(Map p254; ⊙8am-1pm & 5-9pm Sat-Wed) This souq runs off Al-Dahab St and is the most extensive in the Kingdom. The market stalls cut into the heart of the old city and buzz with the activity of traders and pilgrims. The atmosphere is especially cosmopolitan during the hajj season. Be here at sunset when the call to prayer fills the lanes – this is Arabia at its best.

Old Coral Houses
NOTABLE BUILDINGS

Jeddah's old coral houses are in a sorry state. Unique among the sea of dilapidation is the restored **Naseef House** (Map p254; ⓘ647 2280; admission SR25; ⊙5-9pm), which belonged to one of Jeddah's most powerful trading families. It's set back from Souq al-Alawi. Look out for the wide ramps installed by King Abdul Aziz in place of staircases so that camel-mounted messengers could ride all the way to the upper terrace in order to deliver messages.

Shorbatly House (Map p254; Maydan al-Bayal) also boasts some lovely *mashrabiyya* (balconies with perforated screens to allow the air to circulate and inhabitants to look out without being seen). Though once restored during the 1980s, it has since been allowed to deteriorate. It is officially closed to visitors, but the staff at Naseef House may be able to arrange access.

Corniche

Do as Saudi Arabians do and take a walk along the 35km-long **corniche** (Al-Kournaish Rd). On a warm night you'll get a real sense of Jeddah – students sit stooped over books, while families share picnics and men gather to gossip and cut commercial deals.

Look out for the famous sculptures that line the wide pedestrian areas for 30km north from the port. Among the highlights are four bronzes by British sculptor Henry Moore, as well as work by Spaniard Joan Miró, Finnish artist Eila Hiltunen and Frenchman César Baldaccini.

🛏 Sleeping

Most of Jeddah's midrange hotels are in Al-Balad. Jeddah's budget hotels rarely accept bookings from Westerners.

Al-Bilad Hotel
HOTEL $$

(ⓘ694 4777; www.albiladhotel.net; North Corniche; s/d SR520/650, bungalow SR950; @ ⓦ) Situated halfway between the airport and downtown, the Bilad is much loved for its 'escape the crowds' feel and cosy atmosphere. Facilities include a bakery, a lovely covered verandah (with air-con in summer) and landscaped gardens with sea glimpses and birdsong.

Red Sea Palace Hotel
HOTEL $$

(Map p254; ⓘ642 8555; www.redseapalace.com; King Abdul Aziz St; d/ste SR600/1100; ⓦ) Large, comfortable rooms, albeit with slightly tired decor, at reasonable prices makes this a viable alternative to the luxurious options elsewhere in town. The hotel has two restaurants.

Intercontinental Hotel
LUXURY HOTEL $$$

(Map p252; ⓘ661 1800; www.intercontinental.com; Corniche; r from SR1125; @ ⓢ ⓦ) The chic Inter-Continental boasts three main drawcards: a waterside location with a private beach, good facilities (including decent restaurants) and attention to detail – right down to complimentary underwater cameras and playing cards for the kids. And of course the rooms are suitably luxurious.

Qasr Al-Sharq
LUXURY HOTEL $$$

(ⓘ659 9999; www.qasralsharqjeddah.com; North Corniche; s/d SR1900/2050; Ⓟ @ ⓢ ⓦ) Decorated by the same designer who worked on Dubai's famous Burj al-Arab, the self-described seven-star Al-Sharq prides itself on luxury. The dazzling decor includes no less than 60kg of gold leaf, silk curtains and a 12m chandelier; rooms all have a 42-inch plasma TV (with obligatory gold panelling) and 24-hour butler service. Beautiful, but in an insane supermodel sort of a way.

SAUDI ARABIA JEDDAH

Central Jeddah

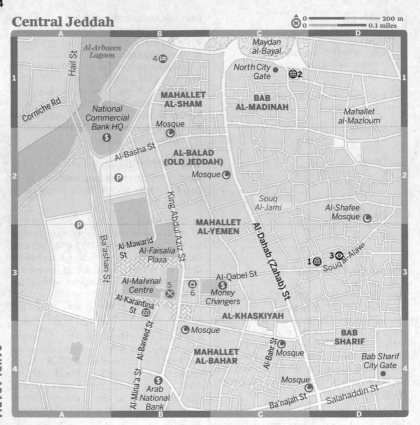

Central Jeddah

✕ Eating

Look at www.jeddahfood.com for up-to-date reviews of Jeddah's restaurant scene.

Al-Mahmal Centre
FAST FOOD $

(Map p254; King Abdul Aziz St; ⊙ Sat-Thurs 8am-11.30pm, Fri 1-11.30 pm) For a table with a view, the 7th floor of the Al-Mahmal Centre has several small restaurants serving Turkish, Lebanese and Filipino fast food.

★ Yildizlar
TURKISH, LEBANESE $$

(Map p252; ✆ 653 1150; www.yildizlar.net; Al-Andalus St; mains SR30-75; ⊙ 1pm-1am) Lavish in both decor and dining, the Yildizlar is a local institution serving a splendid mix of Turkish and Lebanese. Dishes range from boneless pigeon with truffles (SR75) to caviar (SR165 to SR185), fabulous fish dishes (SR65 to SR180) and gorgeous grills (SR30 to SR60). It can get busy and more than a hint noisy.

Al-Nakheel Restaurant
MIDDLE EASTERN $$

(Map p252; ✆ 606 6644; Al-Mukhtar St; mains SR30-50; ⊙ 9am-3am) Styled like a traditional tent (with open sides to let in the sea breezes) this is the place to come for a taste of Jeddah. It's wildly popular – Jeddah's women come to let their hair down. The food is great, with fish and seafood a speciality.

Green Island   SEAFOOD $$

(Map p252; ☑694 1234; North Corniche; mains SR45-110; ☺5pm-1.30am) Spread across the water in the form of little chalets-on-stilts – with glass floor panels that reveal the fish and the water beneath – this is the place to come if you're after a final splurge or a romantic revival. The menu is a fusion of Lebanese, Indian and Continental cuisines with seafood dominating most dishes. The **cafe** (☑694 0999; North Corniche; mains SR15-30; ☺8am-2am Sat-Thu, 1pm-2am Fri) is also excellent.

🛍 Shopping

Jarir Bookstore   BOOKS

(www.jarirbookstore.com; ☺9am-2pm & 4.30-11pm Sat-Thu, 4.30-11pm Fri) There are branches of this bookstore on **Falasteen St** (Map p252; ☑673 2727), **Sary St** (Map p252; ☑682 7666) and **Jamea Plaza** (☑687 2743).

Khayyam Al-Rabie Est   FOOD

(Map p254; ☑647 6596; off Al-Qabel St; ☺9am-2pm & 4.30-11pm Sat-Thu, 4.30-11pm Fri) For dates, nuts and nibbles, head straight for the famous Khayyam Al-Rabie Est which, with its fairy lights and floor to ceiling rows of goodies (including more than 50 varieties of dates in all shapes, shades, colours and textures), is like an Aladdin's cave for the sweet-toothed.

ℹ Information

EMERGENCY

Ambulance (☑997)
Fire (☑998)
Police (☑999)
Traffic Accidents (☑993)

MEDICAL SERVICES

Dr Sulayman Fakeeh Hospital (☑660 3000, 665 5000; Falasteen St) Has a good accident and emergency department.

MONEY

Head for the row of **money changers** (Al-Qabel St, Al-Balad; ☺9am-1.30pm & 4.30pm-10pm), who offer good rates and don't charge commission.

TRAVEL AGENCIES

Sadd Al-Samallaghi Est (☑668 5054; www.samallaghi.com; Talya St) This one-stop shop arranges flights around the Peninsula, day trips around Jeddah, longer excursions to Madain Saleh, car rental, diving, desert safaris and boat trips. It's one of Saudi Arabia's best operators.
Al Shitaiwi Travel & Tourism (☑02-679 4022; www.alshitaiwitours.com) Runs tours and can arrange flights and car rental.

ℹ Getting There & Away

AIR

Jeddah's **King Abdul Aziz International Airport** (☑688 5526, 684 1707; Medina Rd) is 17km north of the city centre. **Saudi Arabian Airlines** (Saudia; ☑632 3333; King Abdul Aziz St) departs from the south terminal. Foreign airlines use the north terminal.

Daily domestic departures include Abha (SR190), Dammam (SR390), Hail (SR250), Medina (SR140), Riyadh (SR280), Taif (SR110) and Yanbu (SR110). For Al-Ula you'll need to fly via Riyadh.

BUS

See the table below for bus travel information. For Al-Ula (SR125) some services travel via Medina. If you're a non-Muslim, inform the ticket vendor when you buy your ticket. The driver of your bus should drop you outside the haram boundaries and another bus should come and pick you up from there.

ℹ Getting Around

A taxi from the town centre to the south/north airport terminals costs SR45/55 (add SR15 to SR25 in the high season). A short hop in town costs around SR15.

SAUDI ARABIA JEDDAH

BUSES

Buses for the following destinations depart daily from the Saptco Bus Station.

DESTINATION	LENGTH	FREQUENCY	COST
Abha	nine hours	every two hours	SR120
Dammam	14 to 15 hours	every two hours	SR265
Jizan	nine hours	every hour	SR120
Riyadh	12 hours	every two hours	SR150
Taif	three hours	every hour	SR40
Yanbu	five hours	every two to three hours	SR75

Taif الطائف

☑ 02 / POP 987,900

Taif in summer can seem like a breath of fresh air, and compared to humid Jeddah it truly is. At 1700m above sea level, its gentle, temperate climate is its biggest attraction, and in summer Taif becomes the Kingdom's unofficial capital. With wide, tree-lined streets, traditional architecture, a lively souq and beautiful surrounding scenery, it's not hard to see why even the king relocates here.

Taif is known for the cultivation of roses and fruit – honey-sweet figs, grapes, prickly pear and pomegranates. Over 3000 gardens are said to grace Taif and its surrounds.

◉ Sights

Shubra Palace MUSEUM, HISTORIC BUILDING
(☑ 732 1033; Shubra St; ☺ 8am-2pm Sat-Wed Sep-May, 8am-noon & 5-7pm Jun-Aug) FREE The city's museum is in a beautiful early 20th-century house that is the most stunning vestige of old Taif, with latticework windows and balconies and interior Italian marble from Carrara. King Abdul Aziz used to stay here and it was later the residence of King Faisal.

Al-Kady Rose Factory NOTABLE BUILDING
(☑ 733 4133; off As-Salamah St; ☺ 9.30am-2.30pm Sat-Thu) FREE The largest rose factory in Taif, the 120-year-old Al-Kady Rose Factory is well worth a visit, particularly at harvest time (May to July) when it's open 24 hours. Rose water (SR12 per bottle), used to scent clothes, baths, cooking and drinks, is sold here.

Souq SOUQ
(☺ 9am-2pm & 4.30-11pm Sat-Thu) Taif's souq is one of the largest in the Kingdom and is worth a wander, particularly on a summer's evening when the people of Taif takes to its streets.

Beit Kaki HISTORIC BUILDING
(As-Salamah St; ☺ 8am-2pm Sat-Wed Sep-May, 8am-noon & 5-7pm Jun-Aug) FREE Built in 1943 as a summer residence for one of Mecca's most important merchant families, Beit Kaki is one of Taif's finest buildings. The intricately carved balconies and window and door frames have all been sympathetically restored and the building is now a small museum.

🛏 Sleeping

Taif is a popular summer retreat (May to September) and advance reservations are advised.

Safari Hotel HOTEL $
(☑ 734 6660; Musala St; low/high season s SR100/140, d SR125/175) The best budget choice; all rooms have balconies. Ask for a 'mosque-side' view, although be prepared for an early wake-up call if you do.

Al-Barraq Hotel HOTEL $
(☑ 650 3366; fax 651 1322; Shehar St; low/high season s SR185/250, d SR300/350) Al-Barraq is popular among the diplomatic expat community and it's easy to see why – rooms are spacious, comfy and the luxurious lobby, laden with marble and chandeliers, offers old-world glamour. There are also two restaurants, a health club and jacuzzi.

InterContinental Hotel LUXURY HOTEL $$
(☑ 750 5050; www.intercontinental.com; Hawiyah St; r/ste from SR594/1080; @ ☒) Around 10km from Taif's airport, the refurbished InterContinental offers great facilities and services.

✕ Eating

As-Shafa MIDDLE EASTERN $
(☑ 733 0332; just off Shubra St; mains from SR1.50; ☺ noon-1am) Behind the Saudia office, As-Shafa serves delicious Saudi/Turkmenistan dishes, including *manti* (like ravioli; two pieces SR1.50); it's much admired locally.

Ahlan Wa Sahlan TURKISH $
(☑ 732 7324; www.ahlanwasahlanrest.com; Shubra St; sandwiches from SR7, mains SR20-26; ☺ 7am-noon & 1pm-1am) Light, bright and clean, the Ahlan has a great pick-and-point counter containing fresh Turkish dishes that change daily, including vegie and seafood options.

ⓘ Getting There & Away

Taif airport (☑ 685 5527) is 25km north of the town. There are daily flights to/from Riyadh (SR250) and Dammam (SR400). There are also bus services to Riyadh (SR125, nine hours, 10 daily), Jeddah (SR40, three hours, 20 daily) and Abha (SR120, eight hours, three daily).

ⓘ Getting Around

Taxis charge SR15 for short journeys around town (including to/from the bus station) and SR45 to the airport. From the airport, they charge SR75.

Yanbu ينبع

☑ 04 / POP 250,000

With its port, refineries and petrochemical plants, this is hardly the Kingdom's most attractive spot. But it's a different story beneath the surface (of the sea, that is), as Yanbu is one of Saudi's premier diving locations.

🏃 Activities

Dream Divers
DIVING

(☑420 9584; www.dreamdiver.net; King Abdul Aziz St; per person per day for 2 dives incl tanks, weight belt & lunch box SR300; ⊙9am-noon & 2-10pm) Dream Divers has the best reputation of the various dive centres in Yanbu. If you're without equipment, BCDs and regulators can be hired for US$40 each, a mask and snorkel for US$25. PADI scuba-diving courses are also offered, including a seven-day open water course: per person all inclusive SR1850. Bring your own boots, fins and wetsuit.

🛏 Sleeping & Eating

Danat Hotel
HOTEL $

(☑391 2222; danat_hotel@yahoo.com; King Abdul Aziz St; s/d SR180/215) Decorated in browns and creams like a giant crème caramel, the rooms are nevertheless comfortable, clean, and conveniently situated two doors down from Dream Divers.

Arac Yanbu Resort
RESORT $$$

(☑328 0000; www.arac.com.sa; Prince Abdul Majeed Rd; chalets incl service charge for 1/2/3 people weekday SR700/1000/1400, weekend SR1100/1400/1900) The Arac is 17km from town and 10km from the airport and boasts great facilities in a good location. These include a private beach where women can swim – albeit in trousers and T-shirt – and a whole host of watersports, a cafe and restaurant. The comfortable two-storey chalets are built on the waterfront.

Iskenderun Restaurant
TURKISH $

(☑322 8465; King Abdul Aziz St; mains from SR12; ⊙1pm-2am) Canary-coloured, cheap and cheerful, Iskenderun is Yanbu's favourite eating establishment. Try the speciality: the *shwarma iskender* served with a special, secret sauce. Mezze, pide (Turkish pizza), fish fillets and fresh fruit juices are also served.

ℹ Getting There & Away

The airport lies 10km northeast of the town centre. **Saudia** (☑322 6666; King Abdul Aziz St) has twice daily flights to Jeddah (SR110) and Riyadh (from SR360). Coming by car, Yanbu lies 230km (around 2½ hours) from Jeddah.

CAMEL CHAOS

Each weekend (Thursday and Friday), every two weeks during July and August, the town of Taif departs for the races. Open to all, the camels come from far and wide including from other Peninsula countries. It's a spectacular sight. Located 10km outside Taif, the four races run from 3pm to 5.30pm and attract from between 25 to 100 participants in a single race! No wonder: first prize is SR150,000 in cash, 10 cars and 100 bags of wheat.

MADAIN SALEH & THE NORTH
مدائن صالح و الشمال

Madain Saleh is without doubt the most impressive site in Saudi Arabia and should be on every visitor's must-see list.

Al-Ula
العلا

☑04

Al-Ula – gateway to Madain Saleh – is a small town lying in the heart of exceptionally beautiful country, with palm groves running down the centre of the wadi (valley or river bed) and forbidding red sandstone cliffs rising up on two sides.

As well as extraordinary Nabataean tombs in the vicinity, there are the delightful ruins of Old Al-Ula – one of the best examples of traditional architecture in modern Saudi.

◉ Sights

Al-Ula Museum of Archaeology & Ethnography
MUSEUM

(☑884 1536; Main St; ⊙8am-2.30pm Sat-Wed) **FREE** This small museum is attractively designed with some intriguing and informative displays on the history, culture, flora and fauna of the area, as well as on Madain Saleh and Nabataean culture.

Old Al-Ula
HISTORIC SITE

Old Al-Ula is one of the most picturesque old towns in Arabia. The mudbrick town stands on the reputed site of the biblical city of Dedan, mentioned in Isaiah (21:13) as home base of Arab caravans, and in Ezekiel (27:20-21) as trading partner of the Phoenician city of Tyre. The buildings that you'll see mostly date back a few hundred years, although bricks from much earlier settlements have been used in their construction.

Medieval Al-Ula was walled, with two gates protecting 800 families, and was occupied until the late 1970s. Throughout the atmospheric ruins there are superb house doors made from tamarisk. Rising up from the centre of the old town are the remnants of the fortress Umm Nasir. The palm trees and maze of low mudbrick walls, directly across the road from the old town, were once farms whose owners lived in the old town.

Jebel Khuraibah
MOUNTAIN

Situated northeast of town is the impressive site of Jebel Khuraibah – three peaks and a fortress that once formed part of the capital of the ancient Kingdom of Lihyan. Rock-cut tombs squat at the foot of the peaks, with the names of their owners inscribed in the Lihyanite and Dedanite scripts above the openings. The most impressive one is the 'Lion Tomb' – so-called for the two lions carved on either side of the entrance. At Khuraibah is a huge headless sandstone figure, while climbing to the top of the central peak reveals stone walls, stairs and walls, linking all three crags together into a ruined fortress city.

Umm al-Daraj
HISTORIC SITE

At the northwestern end of the town, some kilometres north of Old Al-Ula, Umm al-Daraj (Mother of Steps) is worth a detour. Climbing up the hill reveals a former Lihyanite sacrificial altar and some beautiful Lihyanite inscriptions; ancient petroglyphs – depicting people and camels – graffiti the site.

From the top of the steps there are stunning views out over the wadi. You'll need a guide to find Umm al-Daraj, but try to get there for sunset – it's well worth the climb.

☞ Tours

Arac Hotel Al-Ula
GUIDED TOUR

(☑884 4444; www.aracresort-alula.com) The Arac Hotel Al-Ula can organise day tours to Madain Saleh for groups using local guides. If you're travelling on your own, they may take you but you would need to pay the entire group rate (around SR750 including guide and vehicle). Other options include guided excursions by 4WD into the desert. Lunch boxes can be prepared on request.

Hamid M Al-Sulaiman
GUIDED TOUR

(☑055-435 3684) A local tour guide – and the author of a splendid coffee-table book on Madain Saleh – is Hamid M Al-Sulaiman. With intimate knowledge of the area, he offers 4WD tours of all the local sites, including up Al-Harra (a mountain from which there are good views), the Hejaz Railway and camel excursions, as well as a few not offered by the hotels. Though his English is limited, he is reliable, keen to please and good company.

🛏 Sleeping & Eating

★ Arac Hotel Al-Ula
HOTEL $$

(☑884 4444; www.aracresort-alula.com; Madain Saleh Rd; s/d/ste from SR360/440/1600; ᴘ🅿🛜🏊) The only hotel close to Madain Saleh, the three-star Arac Hotel offers attractive, well-sized rooms 7km from Al-Ula on the main road to Madain Saleh; if you're not part of a group you'll need your own vehicle. The restaurant serves up good buffets during high season as well as a la carte offerings at other times, while the large, inviting swimming pool is open to both men and women at different times. The staff are especially friendly, the gardens make a nice contrast to the arid surrounds and the hotel can arrange a site permit for Madain Saleh.

Al-Ula Matam Buchary
MIDDLE EASTERN $

(☑884 1124; Khaled Bin Walid St; mains SR5-13; ⊙1pm-1.30am Sat-Thu) Of Al-Ula's small selection of restaurants, Al-Ula Matam Buchary, which lies 100m south of Saptco, has the best reputation. It's signposted in Arabic only and there's no family section, but it does do takeaway. Try the flavoursome barbecue half-chicken (SR10).

➊ Getting There & Around

There are direct flights to Al-Ula from Riyadh (SR280) on Wednesday and Friday. From elsewhere in the Kingdom you'll need to fly via Riyadh.

Saptco (☑884 1344) runs buses to Al-Ula from Jeddah (SR125) and Riyadh (SR190).

Around Al-Ula

A wonderful natural rock formation, **Elephant Rock** (Sakharat al-Fil) towers above the sands in a landscape of red rocky monoliths. Also known as Mammoth Rock, it lies 11km northeast of Al-Ula, just off the road to Hail, some 7km from the Arac Hotel Al-Ula.

Madain Saleh مدائن صالح

If you can only visit one place in Saudi Arabia, make it Madain Saleh. This crossroads of ancient civilisations, pilgrims, explorers, trade caravans and armies finds its most remarkable expression in the elaborate stone-carved tombs of the Nabataeans. Although the tombs are less spectacular than the misnamed 'Treasury' at better-known Petra in Jordan, the setting of sweeping sand and remarkable rock formations is unique and unsurpassed.

⊙ Sights

Extraordinary **Madain Saleh** (⊘9am-6pm Sat-Thu, 2-6pm Fri) FREE is home to 131 tombs. The enigmatic tombs combine elements of Greco-Roman architecture with Nabataean and Babylonian imagery. Recent excavations have revealed the foundations of unprepossessing houses and a market area for traders and caravans.

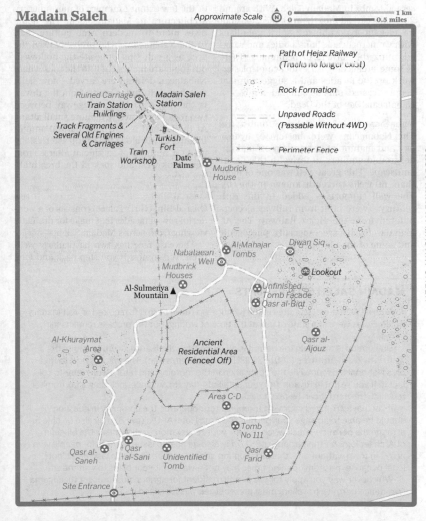

Madain Saleh

Approximate Scale ⊕N 0 — 1 km / 0 — 0.5 miles

Legend:
- ⊢–⊦–⊦ Path of Hejaz Railway (Tracks no longer exist)
- Rock Formation
- — — Unpaved Roads (Passable Without 4WD)
- –×–×– Perimeter Fence

Map labels:
- Ruined Carriage
- Train Station Buildings
- Madain Saleh Station
- Track Fragments & Several Old Engines & Carriages
- Turkish Fort
- Train Workshop
- Date Palms
- Mudbrick House
- Al-Mahajar Tombs
- Diwan Siq
- Nabataean Well
- Lookout
- Mudbrick Houses
- Al-Sulmenya Mountain
- Unfinished Tomb Facade
- Qasr al-Bint
- Al-Khuraymat Area
- Ancient Residential Area (Fenced Off)
- Qasr al-Ajouz
- Area C-D
- Tomb No 111
- Qasr al-Saneh
- Qasr al-Sani
- Unidentified Tomb
- Qasr Farid
- Site Entrance

SAUDI ARABIA MADAIN SALEH

Qasr al-Saneh RUIN

Qasr al-Saneh is an appropriate place to start a tour of Madain Saleh, as it reveals many of the essential elements of Nabataean funerary architecture: a relatively unadorned facade; the two five-step motifs at the top; a simple interior burial chamber with shelves for corpses; and inscriptions above the doorway. Built around AD 50, Qasr al-Saneh was in use for just 50 years before the Nabataean kings were overwhelmed by Rome.

Al-Khuraymat RUIN

This area of tombs, about 750m north of Qasr al-Saneh, has some of the best preserved tombs in Madain Saleh. With around 20 tombs carved into the rock face, look out for elegant gynosphinxes: spirit guardians with women's heads, lions' bodies and wings adorning the corners of pediments. There is some archaeological evidence of plasterwork on the facades and a suggestion that people feasted outside familial tombs – a Nabataean 'Day of the Dead'.

Nabataean Well & Al-Mahajar Tombs RUIN

The Nabataeans were masters of hydrology and manipulated rain run-off and underground aquifers to thrive in this desert landscape. This great well was one of more than 60 wells currently known in the city. The wall supports – added in the 20th century – were built from railway sleepers pilfered from the Hejaz Railway. The Al-Mahajar tombs are especially photogenic and some of the oldest.

Hejaz Railway Station HISTORIC BUILDING

At the northern edge of the site is the Madain Saleh Station of the Hejaz Railway. The site has been comprehensively restored and therefore lacks the lonely and decrepit charm of the stations elsewhere. The complex, built in 1907, consists of 16 buildings, which include a large workshop – with a restored WWI-era engine – shells of train carriages and a rebuilt Turkish fort that served as a resting place for pilgrims travelling to Mecca.

Diwan RUIN

The diwan (meeting room), carved into a hillside to shield it from the wind, is one of the few extant examples of non-funerary architecture in Madain Saleh. The name owes more to modern Arab culture than to the Nabataeans, who probably used the area as a cult site. Opposite the hollowed-out room are niches cut into the rock where Nabataean deities were carved – now sadly weathered. Running south from the diwan is the Siq, a narrow passageway between two rock faces lined with more small altars. At the far end is a striking natural amphitheatre. Climb along the southeastern slope up to a number of sacrificial altars. From here, look west and soak in the breathtaking views.

Qasr al-Bint RUIN

Qasr al-Bint (Girl's Palace) consists of a wonderful row of facades that make for dramatic viewing from across Madain Saleh.

The east face has two particularly well-preserved tombs. If you step back and look

---

MADAIN SALEH SITE PERMITS

As with all archaeological sites in the Kingdom, a (free) permit is required to visit Madain Saleh. Rules were in a state of flux at the time of writing, but the process remains fairly simple.

One option is to obtain the permit in advance from the **Saudi Commission for Tourism & Antiquities** (☎ 01-880 8855; www.scta.gov.sa/en). The office is next to Riyadh's National Museum. File the application in the morning and return a day later to collect it. If you're not in Riyadh, fax your details 14 days in advance, including a fax number to which the permit can be faxed back.

If you have arranged your visit through a tour operator, the company in question should be able to arrange your permit. The Arac Hotel Al-Ula (p258) may also be able to arrange the permit – check when making your reservation – while the Al-Ula Museum of Archaeology & Ethnography (p257) *may* also be able to issue permits for people who arrive in town without one; this latter option should only be seen as a last resort, not least because museum opening times may not always suit your plans to visit the site.

Whichever way you apply for the permit, resident foreigners must present their *iqama* (residence permit); travellers must present their passport and visa.

THE HEJAZ RAILWAY

The Hejaz Railway, with its echoes of TE Lawrence and the Arab Revolt, cuts across northwestern Arabia with abandoned and evocative stations, substations and garrison forts.

The official idea of the railway was to make it easier for pilgrims to reach Medina and Mecca, cutting the journey time from Damascus from six weeks to just four days. In addition to the tracks and station buildings, forts were also built every 25km for garrisons of Turkish soldiers whose role was to protect the railway from bandits. The line opened in 1908, stretching over 1000 miles through largely desert terrain; the planned extension to Mecca was never built.

During the First World War, the Ottomans sided with Germany (who had helped build the railway). Sherif Hussein, the Hashemite ruler of the Hejaz, made an alliance with the British to drive out the Turks. Harnessing the hostility of the local Bedouin, TE Lawrence helped to orchestrate the Arab Revolt, attacking trains and sabotaging the tracks. The Turkish garrison in Medina was soon cut off from the remainder of the Ottoman forces whose empire was crumbling. The railway became unviable and ceased to run after 1918.

Many of the stations and substations remain, and they're well worth visiting. There are at least 19 substations between Medina and Madain Saleh with many alongside the Medina-Al-Ula road. North of Madain Saleh, there are a further 13 substations.

up near the northern end of the west face, you'll distinguish a tomb that was abandoned in the early stages of construction and would, if completed, have been the largest in Madain Saleh – only the step facade was cut.

Qasr Farid
RUIN

Qasr Farid in the south is the largest tomb of Madain Saleh and perhaps the most stunning. Carved from a free-standing rock monolith, its location gives it a rare beauty, especially just before sunset. Try to arrive for sunset, when the enigmatic tomb passes through shades of pink and gold until darkness falls: breathtaking.

ⓘ Information

You need a permit to visit Madain Saleh. These are available from the hotel in Al-Ula or tour operators – you'll need to fax them your details a week in advance.

Video cameras are not allowed inside the site; be aware that surveillance is carried out. Bring your passport and visa – you will need to present them at the gate along with the permit.

ⓘ Getting There & Away

The road from Al-Ula (23km) is easy to find. The site entrance is marked off the road with a blue 'Antiquities' sign.

ASIR
عسير

'Asir' means 'difficult' in Arabic, after the legendary difficulties involved in crossing the Asir Mountains by camel. It is this remoteness that has helped preserve the distinctive cultural heritage of the Asir region.

With much closer historical ties to Yemen than the rest of Arabia, Asir is home to beautiful – albeit fast-disappearing – stone, slate and mudbrick architecture nestled among towering mountains of rare beauty, forests barely a hundred kilometres from the Empty Quarter, and valleys that drop steeply to the Red Sea coastal plain.

On the coast, look out for traditional conical huts showing the African influence from across the sea. In the mountains, and easier to spot, are ubiquitous Arabian baboons now living an easy life on leftovers thrown to them by passing Saudi tourists.

As always in southwestern Saudi Arabia, check the security situation before travelling to the Asir region.

Abha
أبها

☑07 / POP 202,000

Abha, perched 2200m above sea level, is a real shock to the senses after the rest of Saudi, not to mention an excellent base for exploring the southwest. Not only is it palpably cooler, but the neat green lawns, marigolds, mountains and mist also make

Abha

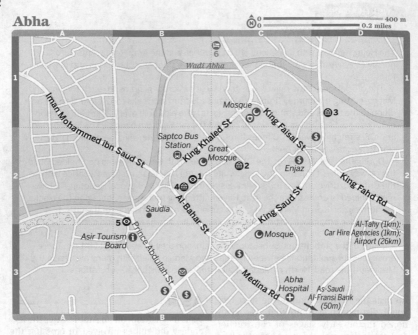

Abha

Sights

1	Old Abha	B2
2	Shada Palace	C2
3	Traditional House	D1
4	Traditional House	B2
5	Tuesday Market	B2

Sleeping

6	Al-Masif Hotel	C1

a startling impression. For Saudis the cold, mist and rain are a novelty and they flock here – along with Gulf Arabs – to escape the relentless heat and humidity of summer.

Sights

Shada Palace HISTORIC BUILDING
(off King Khaled St; 9am-2pm Sat-Thu winter, 9am-6pm Sat-Thu summer) FREE Built in 1927 for a local Saudi governor, this palace is one of the few traditional buildings left in Abha. Its squat, mud-walled tower provides an interesting counterpoint to the modern architecture that now surrounds it.

Tuesday Market SOUQ
(off King Khaled St; 6.30am-1pm & 4pm-6.30pm Sat-Thu, 8am-10.30am & 4pm-6.30pm Fri) Abha's

Tuesday market is worth a visit. Although open daily, Tuesday is the busiest day. The market sells locally made handicrafts such as coloured basket ware, traditional leather baby carriers and clay ovens. There's also a gold souq and a gloriously scented herb, spice and incense souq. Look out also for the women's kaftans embroidered with traditional Asiri patterns. Prices start at SR150.

Asir National Park Abha Visitors Centre VISITOR CENTRE
(4pm-11pm last week Jun-1st week Sep) The national park's (p264) visitors centre contains some interesting and informative panels on the park, a scale model and an upstairs viewing platform. The auditorium runs a 20-minute film about the park's construction.

Old Abha HISTORIC SITE
There's sadly not much of Old Abha left, but the few good examples of traditional architecture are well worth seeking out. Some of the best-preserved houses lie southwest of the Grand Mosque on the same square as the Town Hall, so you'll need to ask the police guarding the building for permission to take photographs. There's another well-preserved facade about 100m north of the intersection between King Faisal and King Fahd Sts.

⚡ Activities

In summer, French-monitored paragliding from Al-Soudah (SR275) and rock climbing (grades from 3a to 7b) at Habalah (including all equipment SR200) are possible. Mountain bikes can also be hired.

🛏 Sleeping

In the high season (June to August), you'll usually need to book up to two months in advance, especially for weekends; note that prices can more than double.

Al-Masif Hotel   HOTEL $

(☎228 7000; almasifhotel@hotmail.com; King Faisal St; low season s/d SR145/210, high season s/d SR190/250, 2-/3-bed apt SR500/600) Though the decor's mostly brown and the bathrooms have seen better days, the Al-Masif is peaceful, centrally located and friendly. The hotel's newly refurbished apartments are very comfortable.

★ Abha Palace Hotel   HOTEL $$

(☎229 4444; www.abhapalace.com.sa; Nahran Rd; s/d from SR625/775; @☀) Located 1.5km southwest of the town centre, Abha Palace is starting to look a little tired but it's still our pick for the best place in town. Facilities are splendid and include a ladies health club and pool, while travellers report friendly service.

InterContinental Hotel   HOTEL $$$

(☎224 7777; www.intercontinental.com; high season s/d SR900/1100; @☀) Perched 10,000ft above sea level, atop the escarpment in Al-Soudah, and originally designed as a palace for a Saudi prince, the InterContinental is luxurious but starting to show signs of age. The hotel is only open from June to September. It's about 10km west of town.

🍴 Eating

Along King Saud St there is a string of small Yemeni restaurants that serve delicious and filling *fuul* (SR7) or omelettes (SR5) for breakfast, as well as succulent *shwarma* sandwiches (SR6) and half roasted chickens (SR15).

Al-Tahy   MIDDLE EASTERN $

(☎228 331; Prince Sultan St; mains from SR10; ⏱1pm-1am) One of very few restaurants in Abha with a family section, the Al-Tahy is much-beloved by locals for its fresh and excellent mezze and meals such as stuffed aubergine and chicken tajine. The restaurant is 1.25km from the town centre.

Green Mountain Restaurant   MIDDLE EASTERN $$

(☎229 1519; Green Mountain; mains SR25-35; ⏱8am-midnight) Lit up at night with green lights, this large restaurant (situated at the top of the hill known as Green Mountain) is hard to miss. Take in the spectacular views

SAUDI ARABIA ABHA

WHO WERE THE NABATAEANS?

There are many theories about where the Nabataeans came from, although most scholars agree that they were early Bedouins who lived a nomadic life before settling as farmers in the area in the 6th century BC. They developed a specialised knowledge of desert water resources (using water channels known as *qanats*) as well as the intricacies of the lucrative trade caravan routes. These two skills would form the foundations of the Nabataean empire.

The Nabataean merchant families grew incredibly wealthy from 200 BC, organising caravans of frankincense and feeding the insatiable markets of the ancient world. Nabataean wealth, which had derived initially from plundering trade caravans, shifted to exacting tolls (up to 25% of the commodities' value) upon these same caravans as a means of securing Nabataean protection and guiding the caravans to water. The Nabataean capital was at Petra (Jordan) and Madain Saleh was their second city.

Through a mixture of shrewd diplomacy and military force, the Nabataeans kept at bay the Seleucids, Egyptians, Persians and later, for a time, the Romans. The Nabataeans never really possessed an 'empire' in the common military and administrative sense of the word. Instead, from about 200 BC they had established a 'zone of influence' that stretched to Syria and Rome and south into the Hadramaut. But it was all undone when the Romans cleverly cut out the middlemen by building fleets on the Red Sea and importing frankincense directly. An impoverished Nabataean Kingdom staggered on for a few years but was formally absorbed as a province of the Roman Empire in AD 106.

WORTH A TRIP

NAJRAN

Although currently off-limits to foreign visitors due to instability close to the Yemeni border, the oasis at Najran is one of Saudi Arabia's hidden treasures; we include it here in case the situation changes during the life of this book. Najran is known for its traditional markets, towering mudbrick, fortress-like homes known as *qasr* strung out along the wadi, the fine archaeological site of Al-Ukhdud, and an exceptional mudbrick fort.

over coffee and cake at a table outside, or do as the locals do and suck on a *sheesha* (water pipe). Meals and snacks are also available although neither the food (or prices) are anything special.

ℹ️ Information

There are various banks with ATMs in the centre. To change money, try **Enjaz** (☎ 229 0271; King Saud St; ⊙ 9am-noon & 5-8pm Sat-Wed, 5-8pm Fri).

The **Asir Tourism Board** (☎ 231 1506; off King Khaled St) can organise English-speaking guides, as well as trips to the brightly painted, traditional houses of the area – the mudbrick villages of Alianfa or Rejal Al-Maa.

ℹ️ Getting There & Away

AIR

Saudia (☎ 223 7777; King Khaled St; ⊙ 9am-6pm Sat-Thu) has several daily departures to Jeddah (SR190), Riyadh (SR280) and Dammam (SR390).

BUS

Abha's main **Saptco Bus Station** (☎ 226 3929; King Khaled St) sits diagonally opposite the Great Mosque. There are departures to Jeddah (SR120, nine hours, every two hours), Taif (SR120, eight hours, three daily) and Jizan (SR45, four hours, three daily). For Riyadh, take the free bus to Khamis Mushayt (45 minutes, every 10 minutes) and change.

ℹ️ Getting Around

The airport is 26km from town and signposted from the Abha–Khamis Mushayt road. There are no taxis in Abha so you'll have to make arrangements with your hotel – most will collect you or drop you at the bus station or airport. Car-hire agencies can be found at the airport and in town.

During the summer season cable cars link the top of Green Mountain with the Asir National Park Abha visitors centre and the New Abha hotel (one-way/return SR35/70).

Around Abha

Asir National Park

This **national park** (⊙ summer) **FREE** was Saudi Arabia's first and contains some of the Kingdom's most spectacular scenery, with mountains reaching nearly 3000m before plunging down to the coast. The park encompasses some 450,000 hectares stretching from the Red Sea, across the mountains and east into the desert. The park's territory is not contiguous, with pockets of land (separated by towns, villages and farmlands) fenced off for protection.

Al-Soudah

Al-Soudah, or 'the black one', so named for the black clouds that so often surround it, is jaw-droppingly beautiful. Located close to the summit of the Kingdom's highest peak, **Jebel Soudah** (2910m), about 22km west of Abha, this is the place to come for precipitous cliffs, deep valleys and mountain-tops disappearing behind the clouds.

There's no better way to enjoy the views than taking the **As-Sawdah Cable Car** (☎ 229 1111; return ticket SR80; ⊙ 9am-9pm Apr-Sep, winter by special request). It's well signposted from Abha. It drops down off the escarpment to the traditional mudbrick village of **Rejal Al-Maa**, with wonderful views to accompany you all the way, including stone villages, terraced fields, juniper forests off in the distance and even the occasional defensive watchtower.

Habalah

The old village of Habalah sits precariously halfway down a cliff face about 63km southeast from Abha. To reach the village, you can take the **cable car** (☎ 253 1919; adult/child return SR60/40; ⊙ 9am-9pm Jun-Aug, public holidays & weekends Sep-May). Though it's only a short ride (600m, 3½ minutes), the views en route are impressive.

Habalah is a place apart. The name means 'rope valley' or 'the ropes', a reference to the fact that this village, built of stone hewn from the rock at the foot of sheer 300m cliffs, was once accessible only by rope ladders (habal). The village was settled about 350 years ago by members of the Khatani tribe who sought the most inaccessible location as a means of protection from the Ottomans.

Despite seeming to cling to the precipice, the village was almost self-sufficient, sustained by terraced farms where they grew coffee, fruit and vegetables as well as raising sheep, chickens and goats. If you look carefully along the rim of the cliff above the village you can still see the iron posts to which ropes were tied to lower people, goods and frightened livestock to the village. Remarkably, it was inhabited until about 1980.

Sadly, little remains of the old village and some of the last villagers were forcibly removed with the completion of the cable car. And in its place is a hideous, concrete tourist complex whose only aim is to milk money during the high season.

A via ferrata (climbing route with the aid of fixed cables) has been established up the rock face from Habalah.

Farasan Islands   جزر فرسان

[07]

The Farasan Islands form part of an archipelago about 40km off the coast of Jizan. Farasan, the main island, makes a great break from the mainland for one big reason – fabulous diving. The area is bursting with marine life and diving is superb in the shallow, plankton-rich waters. The islands also have some of the few remaining coastal mangroves and endangered dugongs in the Red Sea. Galloping around on land is a herd of 500 Arabian gazelle and the recent success in attracting divers to the island has resulted in slightly more environmental protection above water as well as below.

The town of Farasan has several traditional houses built from coral with intricately decorated and carved doorways. These were the homes of former merchants and pearl dealers. A small Turkish fort sits on the edge of town.

Given the current instability in Saudi regions close to the Yemeni border, check the prevailing security situation before planning a visit here.

Farasan Coral Resort ([✓]316 0000; www.coralhotels.com.sa; Janaba Corniche; s/d low season SR440/575, s/d high season SR600/750; [@]) offers comfortable rooms, a private beach (where women can swim), a restaurant, children's play area, ferry booking service and boat trips (SR275 per hour per boat for up to six people).

Access to Farasan Island is from the mainland town of Jizan with two (free) daily ferries at 7am and 3pm in both directions; the crossing takes one hour and 20 minutes. The Seaport Authority ([✓]for ferries from Farasan 316 3446, for ferries from Jizan 317 2864; Jizan Port; [✓]6am-6pm) issues tickets for the two ferries and if you're coming with a car, it's best to reserve two days in advance.

EASTERN PROVINCE
المنطقة الشرقية

The Eastern Province is the centre of Saudi Arabia's oil industry and, as such, you're more likely to live and work here than visit.

DON'T MISS

HIGHLIGHTS OF THE EAST

→ **Al Hofuf** (also known as Al-Hasa and Al-Ahsa) is believed to form the largest oasis in the world with over three million palm trees that produce more than half a million tons of dates a year. It's a two-hour drive from Dammam or 4½ hours from Riyadh.

→ The **Aramco Exhibit** ([✓]03-874 7400; www.saudiaramco.com; Ott Dallah Rd; [✓]7am-6.30pm Sat-Wed, 9am-noon & 3-6.30pm Thu, 3-6.30pm Fri) **FREE** in Dhahran is one of the best museums in the country with interactive exhibits and fascinating displays on the oil industry

→ **Al-Khobar Restaurants** The newest, most liberal and most attractive of the three cities that make up Greater Dhahran, Al-Khobar has fabulous restaurants, including seafood-rich **Al-Sanbok** (www.sanbok.com; Khobar Corniche South; [✓]noon-3pm & 6-11.30pm).

→ The Bedouin market at **Nairiyah**, about 250km north of Dammam, is worth a visit if you're here on a Thursday. For foreigners not interested in sheep, goats or camels, the attraction has long been the Bedouin weavings (mostly rugs).

The province boasts the longest history of Westerners living and working in Saudi Arabia, and the sprawling satellite towns of Dammam, Al-Khobar and Dhahran are prosperous and relatively liberal.

UNDERSTAND SAUDI ARABIA

Saudi Arabia Today

Since the terrorist attacks on New York and Washington on 11 September 2001 and the discovery that 15 of the 19 accused hijackers were Saudi, the world's attention has focused on Saudi Arabia. In 2003 and 2004, a series of widely reported Al-Qaeda terrorist attacks targeted Westerners in Riyadh, Al-Khobar and Yanbu. As a result, the Saudi authorities have been very keen to be seen to combat terrorism, even as they speak publicly in support of widespread resentment on the Arab street towards Western policies and Western cultural incursions. And for as long as security issues (in the form of international terrorism) and economic issues (in the form of flowing oil) ally with Washington, Saudi Arabia will remain a vital strategic partner to the West. Such are the contradictions of modern Saudi Arabia.

In August 2009, fighting and cross-border raids by Shiite Houthi Yemenis threatened to draw Saudi Arabia into a regional war. Further, the so-called 'Arab Spring', which brought regime change across North Africa, civil war to Syria and, perhaps most seriously, significant unrest in neighbouring Bahrain, was potentially another serious challenge for the Al-Sauds. The usual mixture of repression and promises of reform has kept the instability at bay, at least for now, but the Al-Sauds remain on their guard.

Amidst these wider geopolitical dramas, regional, tribal and sectarian allegiances also stoke local discontent and the traditionally quiescent Saudi media has been sidestepped by local uptake of satellite TV, which reports on the jockeying for power among the royal family, their financial and social scandals and an increasingly restless Saudi youth.

The Saudi economy's dependence on oil exports (around 90% of export revenues) remains a serious concern to the government, particularly as most estimates suggest that the Kingdom has less than a century left before the pumps run dry. King Abdullah's educational reforms are aimed at diversifying the economy and addressing the Kingdom's stubbornly high unemployment rate. Of all the current reforms underway in the Kingdom, it is this overhaul of education that offers the best hope of preparing for an uncertain future.

THE RECAPTURE OF RIYADH

Saudi Arabia almost never happened. In the later years of the 19th century, the Al-Sauds were in retreat from Ottoman armies eager to reassert their hegemony over Arabia. In 1893, the Al-Rashids (a powerful rival tribe from Hail who were allied to the Ottomans) seized Riyadh. However, with Ottoman power on the wane, and Al-Rashid eyes on expansion elsewhere in Arabia, the Al-Rashids failed to notice the clandestine approach from the south of Ibn Saud and a handful of his followers who had spent 50 days in the sands of the Empty Quarter, all the while covering their tracks. Masmak Fortress stood on the outskirts of old Riyadh and, on 15 January 1902, the raid was launched, the Rashidi governor of Riyadh was killed and Riyadh fell almost immediately to the Al-Sauds. It has been unchallenged as the Al-Saud stronghold ever since.

History

Ancient Arabia

The myriad kingdoms and empires that grew from the desert sands of Arabia all had one commonality (at least prior to Mohammed) in frankincense. Ancient gods were placated with holy smoke and the peoples of Arabia got very rich providing frankincense to the eager worshippers of ancient Egypt, Persia and Rome.

One of the most intriguing groups of these trading states were the Nabataens (p263): Bedouin clans who gathered at the extraordinary rock-hewn twin cities of Madain Saleh and Petra (in Jordan).

The phenomenal explosion of Islamic-inspired armies out of Arabia shattered the weary Byzantine and Sassanid Empires; but following the Prophet Mohammed's death in AD 632, Arabia slumped into torpor again and was economically insignificant to both the sophisticated Umayyad and Abbasid caliphates. Arabia was only saved from total irrelevance by the utmost spiritual significance of the holy cities of Mecca and Medina.

Trade caravans still crossed the desert, linking the cities and small towns of the Hejaz and the interior with the great cities of the wider Islamic world, but in 1517 the powerful Turkish Ottomans, under Salim I, invaded Arabia and took control of the two holy cities: a most unwelcome development in the Peninsula.

Wahhabi Islam & the Al-Sauds

In 1703 a seemingly insignificant man was born in the insignificant oasis village of Al-Uyaynah in the Wadi Hanifa of central Arabia. Yet this man – Mohammed ibn Abd al-Wahhab – would ultimately transform the lives of all the inhabitants of the Arabian Peninsula. After a period of itinerant religious scholarship, Al-Wahhab returned to Al-Uyaynah and preached his message calling for the purification of Islam and a return to the original values proclaimed by the Prophet Mohammed.

Al-Wahhab's reformist agenda was initially successful and he converted the local sheik to his message. But the severe punishments Al-Wahhab meted out to those he accused of sorcery, adultery and other crimes unnerved the local authorities and he was banished into exile. Al-Wahhab sought refuge in Dir'aiyah, 65km from Al-Uyaynah, where he was granted protection by Mohammed ibn al-Saud, the local emir. Al-Wahhab provided religious legitimacy to the Al-Sauds who in turn provided political protection for Al-Wahhab. Together they built a power base that relied on the formidable combination of politics and religion.

With growing anger throughout Arabia that the holy cities of Mecca and Medina were under Ottoman control, the Saudi-Wahhabi emirate expanded rapidly. Upon his death, Al-Saud was succeeded by his son Abdul Aziz, who captured Dir'aiyah's rival city in central Arabia – Riyadh – in 1765. In 1792 Al-Wahhab died but the inexorable expansion of the Saudi-Wahhabi emirate continued.

In 1803 the Saudi-Wahhabi army finally marched on the holy cities of the Hejaz and defeated Sherif Hussain of Mecca. The Saudi-Wahhabi emirate was recognised by the Mecca authorities, whereupon this first Saudi empire stretched from Al-Hasa in the east, to Hejaz in the west and to Najran in the south.

The Birth of Saudi Arabia

It didn't last long. The Ottoman Sultan Mahmoud II ordered his over-powerful Viceroy of Egypt, Mohammed Ali, to retake Hejaz in the sultan's name. Supported by many Arabian tribes who resented domination by the Saudi-Wahhabis, Mohammed Ali's armies successfully captured Mecca and Medina in 1811 and conquered the Saudi-Wahhabi stronghold of Dir'aiyah on 11 September 1818. Mohammed Ali topped off his triumph by executing Abdullah ibn al-Saud (Abdul Aziz's successor).

Although the Al-Sauds would wrest back control of Riyadh for long periods, they spent the rest of the 19th century fighting the Ottomans, rival tribes and themselves to no apparent gain. The decisive battle for the future of modern Arabia came in 1902, when a 21-year-old Abdul Aziz ibn Abdul Rahman ibn al-Saud (Ibn Saud) and his small band of followers successfully stormed Riyadh under cover of night and daringly captured the fortress.

With deft diplomacy and the momentum of a successful military campaign, Ibn Saud orchestrated a conference at which Arabia's Islamic clergy condemned Sherif Hussain (ruler of Mecca) as a mere puppet of 'The Turk'. Sherif Hussain promptly responded by proclaiming himself the King of the Arabs. In 1925 the Saudi-Wahhabis took Mecca and Medina; the following year Ibn Saud proclaimed himself king of the Hejaz and sultan of Najd, and on 22 September 1932, Ibn Saud announced the formation of the Kingdom of Saudi Arabia.

The Power of Oil

In 1933 Saudi Arabia signed its first oil concession. Four years later, the Arabian American Oil Company (Aramco) discovered commercial quantities of oil near Riyadh and around Dammam in the east. In 1943 President Roosevelt established the Kingdom's political importance by grandly stating that the Kingdom was 'vital for the defence of the USA'.

In 1964, King Faisal began to provide his citizens with a stake in the economic benefits of oil. He introduced a free health service for all Saudi citizens and began a building boom that has transformed Saudi Arabia from an impoverished desert kingdom into a nation of modern infrastructure.

In response to the USA's unconditional support for Israel, Saudi Arabia imposed an oil embargo in 1974, a move that quadrupled world oil prices and reminded the world of the country's importance in an economy wholly dependent upon oil.

A Kingdom of Contradictions

On 25 March 1975 King Faisal was assassinated by a nephew and the throne formally passed to Faisal's brother Khaled. Real power, however, lay with another of Faisal's brothers, Fahd.

In November 1979 the Great Mosque of Mecca was overrun by 250 fanatical followers of Juhaiman ibn Saif al-Otai, a militant Wahhabi leader, who claimed that the Mahdi (Islamic Messiah) would appear in the mosque that very day. During two bloody weeks of fighting, 129 people were killed.

CREATIVE CRUISING

If you think it might be difficult to survive a city with the most restricted entertainment scene in the world, spare a thought for young Saudis. In a country where cinema is banned, singles are kept strictly separated from the opposite sex and nightclubs are nonexistent, young Saudis have resorted to novel means of making contact.

The least subtle of these are the *shebab* (teenage boys) with little else to do but 'impress' other drivers with their speed. Cars cruise up and down outside girls' schools and the *shebab* sometimes throw their phone numbers from the window in the hope of receiving a call on their mobile.

A similar charade takes place in the shopping malls (particularly the Al-Faisaliah and Kingdom Towers). Called 'numbering', it's the Saudi version of a casual encounter. Blue Tooth technology has facilitated things still further by allowing total strangers to text each other without even knowing each other's numbers.

In 1980, riots broke out in the towns of the Qatif Oasis (the heartland of the Kingdom's 300,000 Shiites). The riots were brutally repressed.

On 14 June 1982 the figurehead King Khaled died aged 69. Fahd became king and set about reinforcing the twin pillars of modern Al-Saud rule. He made a priority of proving himself a moderate and reliable friend of the West, while in 1986 proclaiming himself the 'Custodian of the Two Holy Mosques'.

The First Iraq War

When Iraq invaded Kuwait in August 1990, Saudi Arabia's decision to allow foreign military forces to operate from Saudi soil would prove one of the catalysts for propelling Osama bin Laden, a Saudi, and his Al-Qaeda movement onto the world stage.

In 1991 a petition calling for reforms and greater openness was sent to King Fahd by liberal intellectuals. It was quickly followed by a contrary petition by conservative Islamic scholars – a struggle within Saudi politics that continues to this day.

After a great deal of fanfare, the feeble Consultative Council (Majlis ash-Shoura) was opened on 20 August 1993. When Fahd died in August 2005, his half-brother Abdullah ascended to the throne and Prince Sultan bin Abdulaziz al-Saud became crown prince.

People & Society

Saudi society is still strictly segregated between the public (male) and private (female) domain. Family and Islam form the twin pillars of Saudi society and family members leave home once married.

Population

Around 80% of Saudi Arabia's population is concentrated in urban areas – with more than one-third of the population living in the megacities sprawling around Riyadh, Jeddah and Mecca. But overall population density is low: there are 13 people per square kilometre and the truly desert regions have less than one person per square kilometre.

Saudi's population is very young (almost 49% of the population is under 25 years old), with an annual population growth rate of 1.5% – meaning the population doubles around every 30 years. Saudi authorities are confronted with the dilemma of providing for a disaffected, young, Islamicised population with not enough jobs to go around. King Abdullah is said to be a keen student of history and very conscious of the circumstances of the Shah of Iran's downfall in 1979.

The Bedu

The Bedu (Bedouin) represent 15% of the Saudi population and although they're looked down upon by many city-dwelling Saudis the Bedu remain the bedrock of Saudi society. The traits historically associated with the Bedu are legendary and include: a refusal to surrender to outside authority; a fierce loyalty to one's family and tribe; the primacy of courage and honour; the purity of language and dialect as preserved in poetry and desert legends; a belief in the desert codes of hospitality, blood feuds and mutual obligations; the tradition of *razzia* or raiding against travellers or other tribes.

Some 1.8 million Bedu still claim to live a semi-nomadic lifestyle in Saudi Arabia, living for at least part of the year in movable encampments of black goat-hair tents, following grazing fields for their livestock and sources of water.

The Lives of Women

Despite the opening of the country's first co-educational university in 2009, education remains officially strictly segregated. The education system is strongly criticised by educated Saudis for its reliance on rote learning and heavy emphasis on Wahhabi Islam to the exclusion of much else. Official school curriculums are under review and many are expectant of significant change in line with the rest of King Abdullah's reforms.

A woman's life in Saudi is more controlled than anywhere else in the industrialised world, particularly with regard to freedom of movement. Women are officially forbidden to drive within Saudi's cities – although this only became a formal law in 1990, following protests by 47 women deploring restrictions to their day-to-day lives. There have been petitions handed to King Abdullah requesting a woman's right to drive and he has publicly stated that 'things will change'. Yet Saudi and foreign women drive freely within the oil company compounds of Aramco and have done so for years. The whole protracted dance is consistent with

PREPARING FOR PRAYER

In Saudi Arabia, *everything* closes during *salat* (prayer time). Strictly enforced, it can last for up to 30 minutes. If you're already inside a restaurant and eating, you'll usually be allowed to finish your meal (with the curtains drawn and door locked), but note that most places won't let you in unless they think you can finish in time. In shops, banks and other places, you will usually be asked to leave to avoid problems with the *mutawwa* (religious police). Business also stops temporarily in offices.

Prayer times vary throughout the Kingdom and from day to day, and there are at least four during business hours. A list of prayer times appears daily on page two or three of *Arab News*.

King Abdullah's canny process of incremental reform.

Officially Saudi women may not travel abroad without the permission of their husbands or fathers, but this too is under pressure, with prominent Saudi women challenging cultural restrictions in the media and on the internet. Saudi Arabia has signed the UN Convention to Eliminate Discrimination Against Women.

Girls officially enjoy the same right to attend a segregated school and university as boys and later to work as teachers, doctors, nurses, social workers, business managers and journalists. Visible Saudi and Arab journalists on the satellite news channels beamed daily from the Gulf into Saudi homes are altering both private and public perceptions of a woman's role. Many Saudis (including women) also claim women in Saudi Arabia live free from the fear of public sexual violence.

Multiculturalism

Modern Saudi Arabia is a paradox; it's one of the most insular societies on earth, yet only half of the population are actual Saudis. Official figures place the number of foreign expatriates living and working in the Kingdom at 5.5 million or more. However, this is widely suspected as being a gross understatement and certainly the large cities can feel distinctly Asian rather than Arab.

Westerners often work in high-skilled and technical jobs for which Saudis do not yet have qualifications or experience – something King Abdullah's educational reforms are aimed at resolving. Non-Western expats (primarily Pakistanis, Bangladeshis, Indians and Filipinos) perform mostly unskilled labour such as taxi driving, construction work and domestic help, which many Saudis believe is beneath them. However, there is a substantial and growing cadre of medical professionals and information technology specialists from the Indian subcontinent who have altered Saudi perceptions. Many of these workers complain of ill-treatment, exploitation and abuse, although Saudi law in theory protects its legal immigrants. There is also a substantial headache for the Saudi authorities in the shape of *umrah* and hajj pilgrims from poor Islamic countries staying on in the Kingdom to work illegally. The local media often attributes crime to illegal immigrants, stoking traditional prejudices about non-Arabs and reinforcing conservative views that Saudi is an otherwise crime-free country.

Religion

Islam is not just the religion of Saudi citizens, it's the religion of Saudi society and the Saudi state, and is all-encompassing.

Officially, all Saudis are Muslim; 15% are Shiites who live particularly in the eastern provinces. The practice of other religions is strictly forbidden in Saudi Arabia. Non-Muslims cannot even be buried within the borders of the Kingdom.

Wahhabi Islam

Islamic orthodoxy in Saudi Arabia is Wahhabi Islam (an offshoot of Hanbali or the 'literalist' school of Islamic interpretation). It's named after Mohammed ibn Abd al-

BOOKS ABOUT SAUDI ARABIA

Some of the following titles are available from any branch of Jarir Bookstore. Those that aren't are probably banned inside the Kingdom, for obvious reasons.

➡ Wilfred Thesiger, *Arabian Sands*: if you only read one book about about the early explorers, make it this one.

➡ Charles M Doughty, *Travels in Arabia Deserta*: a rival to Thesiger's meditations on the Bedouin and their desert home.

➡ Marcel Kurpershoek, *Arabia of the Bedouin*: a nuanced account of a Dutch diplomat's search for the magic of poetry among Bedouin nomads.

➡ Ionis Thompson, *Desert Treks from Riyadh*: excellent for excursions around the capital.

➡ Kathy Cuddihy, *An A–Z of Places and Things Saudi*: contains everything from the *abeyya* and Islamic banking to an overview of key places around the kingdom.

➡ Sandra Mackey, *The Saudis: Inside the Desert Kingdom*: a searing expat account from the early 1980s.

➡ John R Bradley, *Saudi Arabia Exposed*: another insider account from a respected journalist.

➡ Robert Lacey *Inside The Kingdom*: gripping and succinct analysis and probably the best (and most frightening) overview available of the Kingdom today.

➡ Saddeka Arebi, *Women and Words in Saudi Arabia*: fascinating insight into the world of Saudi women.

➡ Rajaa Alsanea, *Girls of Riyadh*: sensational first novel that lifts the lid on the lives of young Saudi women.

Of the coffee-table books, *Kingdom of Saudi Arabia*, published by the Supreme Commission of Tourism, makes a great pictorial souvenir. Other glossy tomes include *The Traditional Architecture of Saudi Arabia*, by Geoffrey King, and the beautifully produced *Travellers in Arabia – British Explorers in Saudi Arabia*, edited by Eid al Yahya, which includes maps and evocative photographs.

Wahhab, who preached his 'new' message in the 18th century – essentially a call to return to the Arab purity of Islam and a rejection of Sufism, Turkish and especially Persian influences on Islamic thought and practice.

At the heart of the Wahhabi doctrine is a denunciation of all forms of mediation between Allah and believers, and a puritanical reassertion of *tawhid* (the oneness of God). Under the Wahhabis, only the Quran, the Sunnah (the words and deeds of Mohammed) and the Hadith (Mohammed's sayings) are acceptable sources of Islamic knowledge. Under Wahhabi doctrine, communal prayers are a religious duty and rulings on personal matters are interpreted according to Sharia'a.

One of the primary undercurrents in modern Saudi Arabia is the battle over who can be considered the true inheritors of the Wahhabi legacy. Famously, Al Qaeda believes that it is they, not the Al-Sauds, who are the real guardians of Wahhabism.

Religion in Public Life

Wahhabi Islam is a dominating factor in daily life for many, if not most, Saudis, yet this has not led to rejections of technology, the mass media, or a lack of awareness about the outside world and social currents swirling beyond the Kingdom's borders.

The ubiquitous satellite dish is seen on buildings throughout the country (including the holy city of Medina) and foreign news channels are easily captured with the right receiver. Even the once feeble local media has been shaken up by this incursion into Saudi living rooms.

King Abdullah himself was forced to intervene in October 2009 when a female Saudi journalist was ordered by Saudi courts to be flogged for organising a TV program on which a Saudi man described his active sex life. The broadcasting Lebanese channel had its licence revoked and offices in Riyadh and Jeddah closed, but it seems that very few Saudis actually turned the TV off. This almost two-faced attitude towards Western culture has been tempered by the growth of explicitly Arab language mass media like Al-Jazeera, often based in the Gulf States or Lebanon.

These Arab media organisations make it considerably harder for conservative factions within Saudi to simply condemn TV as un-Islamic and this has also contributed to the massive growth in the numbers of

Saudis online. Internet censors are playing catch-up with an increasingly sophisticated Saudi youth who channel their internet via third party servers based in the Gulf and avoid official censorship. This exposure is fundamentally transforming Saudi culture but in ways that are hard to measure.

Arts

Literature

Bedouin poetry and storytelling are part of a rich oral tradition with desert and Islamic legends, often in poetic form, at their heart. However, little has been committed to written form and even less translated into English.

Novelists who chronicle the impact of oil money and modernisation on a deeply traditional desert kingdom include Hamza Bogary, Ahmed Abodehman and Abdelrahman Munif; the latter's citizenship was revoked and his books, thinly veiled parables of Saudi Arabia, banned in the Kingdom. The impact of rapid modernisation upon Bedouin society is beautifully portrayed in his novel *Cities of Salt*. Hamid al-Damanhuri's *Thaman al-Tadhiyah* (The Price of Sacrifice) and *Wa-Marrat al-Ayyam* (And the Days Went By) are two novels available in English.

Although almost a decade ago, one 2005 firestorm of literary controversy still resonates. *Girls of Riyadh* was the first novel by a young Saudi woman, Rajaa Alsanea, describing the intertwining lives of four young Saudi women, friends since school days. The book garnered surprising praise from Arab intellectuals, while eliciting howls of disapproval from Saudi conservatives, scandalised by its frankness.

Architecture

Saudi Arabia boasts a fine palette of traditional stone and mudbrick architecture – Al-Ula and the abandoned city of Dir'aiyah are probably the best examples. Mud-fortress architecture finds its most enchanting expression in Najran in southwestern Arabia. Elsewhere, so much has already disappeared beneath the modernising steamroller, or is deteriorating fast. However, restoration projects backed by members of the royal family are successfully preserving some interesting architec-

THE RETURN OF THE ARABIAN ORYX

Just two hundred years ago, the Arabian oryx (Oryx leucoryx), with its distinctive white coat and curved horns, roamed across much of the Arabian Peninsula, with the greatest concentrations present in the Nafud Desert in northern Arabia and the Rub al-Khali (Empty Quarter) in the south. Their range may even have extended into what is now Iraq and Syria. Hunting devastated the population which retreated deeper into the desert, pursued by automatic weapons and motorized vehicles. Wiped out in the northern Nafud in the 1950s, the last wild oryx was killed in the Dhofar foothills of Oman in 1972.

But all was not lost and it wasn't long before an ambitious program of reintroducing Arabian oryx to their former territories was launched. A captive breeding program had begun in the early 1960s when four wild oryx (three males and a female) were caught in south-eastern Saudi Arabia. In 1964, nine Arabian oryx (gifts from Gulf sheikhs) were taken to Phoenix Zoo in the United States of America. By 1977, the 'World Oryx Herd' in America had grown to almost 100. Between 1978 and 1992, members of the herd were transported back to the Middle East,including 55 oryx to Saudi Arabia. Smaller populations were transported to Jordan, Israel, the United Arab Emirates and Oman.

In Saudi Arabia, Arabian oryx from the breeding program of the National Wildlife Research Center (NWRC; www.nwrc.gov.sa) in Taif were released into the fenced Mahazat as-Sayd protected area (2,244 sq km). Since 1995, 149 oryx have been released into the 'Uruq Bani Ma'arid protected area in the northwestern part of the Rub' al-Khali near Sulayyil. Their territory now measures 12,000 sq km and, despite the challenges of poaching and drought, the remaining herd (estimated over 500 animals) is the only viable population of Arabian oryx in the wild.

ture. A growing awareness of Saudi culture and history beyond Islam is being fostered by King Abdullah and 60 new museums are scheduled to open across the Kingdom during the next decade, mostly in restored traditional buildings.

The Red Sea littoral is famous for its coral homes. The best examples are in Jeddah where merchants built stunning homes from Red Sea coral with lattice-work wooden balconies.

The most startling expressions of contemporary Saudi architecture are found in Riyadh with the Kingdom and Al-Faisaliah Towers. However, they could soon be overshadowed by another Kingdom Tower (Burj al-Mamlakah) which is to be built in Jeddah. Slated for completion in 2018, the new skyscraper is set to be the world's tallest building and the first to reach 1km high.

Environment

The Land

Saudi Arabia takes up 80% of the Arabian Peninsula. Over 95% of Saudi Arabia is desert or semi-desert, and the country is home to some of the largest desert areas in the world, including Al-Nafud (Nafud Desert) in the north and the Empty Quarter in the south.

Just 1.67% of Saudi territory is considered to be suitable for agriculture and less than 2% of the land is covered by forest.

Wildlife

Illegal hunting is still a major problem in Saudi Arabia and, during your travels, the animal you are most likely to come across is the Arabian *hamadrya* (baboon), which proliferates along the mountain roads of southwestern Saudi Arabia.

The waters of Saudi's Red Sea are teeming with wildlife, and include five species of marine turtle. Whales and dolphins are also present in the Red Sea and the Gulf.

For more information on the Kingdom's wildlife, contact the National Commission for Wildlife Conservation & Development (NCWCD; Map p246; ☎ 01-441 8447; ⊙ 7.30am-2.30pm Sat-Wed).

ENDANGERED SPECIES

According to the International Union for the Conservation of Nature (IUCN), the list of endangered mammals in Saudi Arabia includes the dugong, Arabian oryx, Arabian leopard and Nubian ibex. Captive breeding and reintroduction programs are at the forefront of the government's work to arrest the slide.

Endangered bird species include the Arabian bustard (found on the Tihamah coastal plain). The ostrich and houbara bustard are currently being bred in captivity and the latter has been successfully reintroduced into the wild.

National Parks

Saudi authorities now run 15 wildlife reserves (or 'himma') amounting to over 500,000 hectares of the country; these are part of a wider plan to include more than 100 protected wildlife and ecological bio-zones.

Travellers wishing to visit any reserve must apply for permission from the National Commission for Wildlife Conservation & Development (p272). Some of the best places to see wildlife are at the 'Uruq Bani Ma'arid Protected Area (www.arabian-oryx.gov.sa/en/ubm) in the Empty Quarter, and the Farasan Islands.

Environmental Issues

Saudi Arabia's environmental problems are legion and include desertification, pollution, deforestation, lack of local education and awareness, and critical depletion of underground water.

Illegal hunting – even of endangered species – is a particular problem. Once a Bedouin survival strategy, many Saudis enjoy the sport and the Kingdom is still a popular hunting destination for wealthy Gulf Arabs.

The dramatic expansion of Saudi's population, as well as overgrazing by domestic herd animals, has led to a decline in numbers of wild ungulate species and ensured that a range of wildlife species are now highly endangered.

On the positive side, captive breeding programs and the subsequent reintroduction of species formerly extinct in the wild – most famously the Arabian oryx – are among the most successful in the world.

The Kingdom's water shortages are especially worrying for the ruling family. Expensive seawater desalination plants are all over the country, but the depletion of underground aquifers continues at an alarming rate.

SURVIVAL GUIDE

ℹ Directory A–Z

ACCOMMODATION
Camping
Camping is permitted anywhere in the Kingdom (bar security-sensitive areas) and Saudis love to camp. At the handful of camping grounds, such as Asir National Park, there are no facilities but the sites are free.

Hotels
Quoted room rates include private bathroom, unless stated otherwise, and exclude the 15% service charge that is added to your bill by all five- and some four-star hotels and restaurants.

In the high season – during the hajj (particularly in Jeddah), at the end of Ramadan, during school holidays and in summer (June to August) – prices in Abha, Taif and other mountain regions can increase anywhere between 50% and 150%.

Saudi Arabia has a generous selection of top-range hotels and the government is keen to get Westerners on business trips to stay in them. Most offer the usual five-star facilities including business centres, internet access, swimming pools and fitness centres. Hotels quote rack rates, but offer corporate discounts to tour operators, embassies and companies with whom they have prior agreements and it's always worth checking online for cheaper deals. If you're travelling for business ask your company to fax the hotel with your dates to ensure a discount.

SLEEPING PRICE RANGES

Throughout this chapter, the order of accommodation listings is according to price, from the cheapest to the most expensive. Each place to stay is accompanied by one of the following symbols. The price relates to a double room with private bathroom; unless otherwise stated, room prices do not include taxes or breakfast.

$ less than SR400
$$ SR400–1000
$$$ more than SR1000

Note that many hotels offer weekend packages, which offer special rates – if you're planning a whole weekend somewhere, enquire.

During hajj season, the end of Ramadan and school holidays, reserve well in advance.

ACTIVITIES
4WD Excursions

There are ample opportunities to leave tarmac roads behind and explore Arabia's desert interior. Among the most rewarding are the sand seas of the Empty Quarter, following the Hejaz Railway, and excursions into the Al-Nafud desert.

Locally produced guides to off-road excursions within the Kingdom can be found in any branch of the Jarir Bookstore, while most of the country's travel agencies can arrange guided expeditions.

Beaches

Saudi's beaches can disappoint. Many are built on, litter strewn and very crowded at weekends. They're almost all men-only. The best bet is to head for the five-star coastal hotels, which often have their own private beach where women also can swim (usually covered up by a T-shirt and trousers).

Diving

Saudi Arabia is a fabulous diving destination. Indeed, those who do know it rank it among the best diving countries in the world. Its relative obscurity is its greatest advantage – its reefs remain mercifully empty of divers and boats.

Note that women (local and foreign) are permitted to dive, although conservative behaviour is still sometimes expected, such as wearing loose clothing over your wetsuit until just before you get into the water.

Even in winter, the water temperatures rarely drop too low (at the southern sites from 24°C to 26°C) though wetsuits of between 5mm to 6mm are advised in winter and 3mm to 4mm in summer. Saudi's greatest advantage is its visibility, which ranges from good to astonishing (up to 35m to 40m is not uncommon). In general, there are few currents to contend with.

More experienced divers prefer to boat-dive, particularly around Al-Lith, Yanbu and the Farasan Islands, where the diving can be spectacular.

Diving Operators

Dream Divers (p257) has a great reputation locally and abroad and has offices in **Jeddah** (☎ 02-234 0473; www.dreamdiver.net; Corniche Rd, Dream Marina, South Obhur, Jeddah), Yanbu and Al-Lith. Also recommended is **Desert Sea Divers** (☎ 02-656 1807; www.desertseadivers.com; Al-Kournaish St, Jeddah). Both operators can arrange visas for diving holidays and both offer a live-aboard diving boat.

Red Sea Divers (Map p252; ☎ 660 6368; www.redseadivers.com; Al-Kournaish St, Jeddah) is a UK-based dive company with a representative in Jeddah. It can arrange most types of diving.

Equipment can be hired per day (regulators and BCDs SR20 to SR30) although it's becoming easier to buy in Saudi. Jeddah has a decompression chamber.

Where to Dive

Jeddah
➙ There are more than 50 dive sites and a number of wrecks (accessible even to inexperienced divers) reached by day boats operated by local dive clubs.
➙ A colourful selection of hard and soft corals.
➙ Offering a good variety of smaller reef fish, including Anthea, sergeant major, large-sized trevally jack, kingfish and Spanish mackerel.
➙ During the season there are yellow fin, rays, moray eels and turtles.

Yanbu
➙ Lies 230km north of Jeddah.
➙ Boasts outstanding visibility (34m to 40m average).
➙ Hammerheads found at deeper depths (from around 40m).
➙ Wide variety of fish including Napoleon wrasse, blue-spotted rays, moray eels and turtles.

Al-Lith
➙ Lies 180km south of Jeddah.
➙ Giant bumphead parrot fish are a major draw.

PRACTICALITIES

➙ DVD Systems: Like much of Europe and the Middle East, Saudi Arabia belongs to DVD Region 2

➙ Electricity: both 110VAC and 220VAC; European two-pin plugs are the norm, but three-pronged British plugs are also present

➙ Weights & Measures: Saudi Arabia uses the metric system

➙ Discount Cards: Although there is no official discounting policy for holders of student cards, some official sites will offer discounts if you ask for them and upon presentation of official student accreditation (international or local).

➙ Smoking is banned in most public spaces, including restaurants, coffee shops and shopping malls.

➡ Sharks (grey, white-tip and black-tip mainly) seen all year, others (hammerhead chiefly) during winter.

➡ Large variety of hard and soft corals as well as coloured sponges and sea whips.

➡ Currently, the only accommodation is at **Ahlam Marina & Resort** (☎ 07-733 4112; cabins per night SR300), with a restaurant and a fishing and dive shop.

➡ Other attractions include caverns, caves and islands used as nesting sites by leatherback and green turtles, and excellent birdlife (including sooty gulls, blue legged boobys, white-eyed gulls, little bitterns, crab plovers, goliath herons, night herons, pelicans, flamingos, ospreys and sooty falcon).

Farasan Islands

➡ Lies 40km off Jizan, 722km from Jeddah.

➡ Though visibility is not always perfect, waters around the Farasan Islands can offer the most spectacular diving of all – the nutrients and plankton attract large pelagic species including whales, whale sharks and mantas and on the drop-offs, many hammerheads.

CHILDREN

Saudi Arabia has numerous amusement parks for children – just about every medium-sized town has one. They're usually family-only affairs and cost SR15/8 per adult/child.

CUSTOMS REGULATIONS

Despite all warnings, some travellers continue to try to enter Saudi with alcohol. If you are caught with any amount, you will be returned home on the next flight. If you're deemed to be in possession of a quantity that exceeds 'personal consumption' punishments are severe (including the death penalty if convicted of smuggling).

DVDs, videos or suspect-looking books are passed to the Ministry of Information officials for inspection. Unfamiliar or suspect-looking items may be confiscated for further inspection for up to 48 hours. Receipts are issued for later collection once items have been inspected and passed. Laptops and computer media are not checked unless officials are suspicious.

EMBASSIES & CONSULATES

All of the following are in Riyadh's diplomatic quarter in the west of Riyadh. They generally open from 9am to 4pm Saturday to Wednesday.

Australian (☎ 01-488 7788; www.saudiarabia. embassy.gov.au)

Bahraini (☎ 01-488 0044; www.mofa.gov.bh/ riyadh/Home.aspx)

Canadian (☎ 01-488 2288; www.canadainternational.gc.ca/saudi_arabia-arabie_saoudite)

French (☎ 01-434 4100; www.ambafrance-sa. org)

EATING PRICE RANGES

Throughout this chapter, the following price ranges refer to a standard main course. Unless otherwise stated, service charges and taxes are included in the price:

$ less than SR30
$$ SR30–120
$$$ more than SR120

German (☎ 01-277 6919; www.riad.diplo.de)

Irish (☎ 01-488 2300; www.embassyofireland. org.sa)

Jordanian (☎ 01-488 0039; www.jordanembassyksa.gov.jo)

Kuwaiti (☎ 01-488 3500)

New Zealand (☎ 01-488 7988; www.nzembassy.com/saudi-arabia)

Omani (☎ 01-482 3120)

Qatari (☎ 01-483 5544)

UAE (☎ 01-488 1227; www.uae-embassy.ae/ Embassies/sa)

UK (☎ 01-488 0077; ukinsaudiarabia.fco.gov. uk)

USA (☎ 01-488 3800; riyadh.usembassy.gov)

FOOD

For information about Saudi Arabia's cuisine, see p242 and the Flavours of Arabia chapter (p459).

INTERNET ACCESS

Internet cafes are present in larger Saudi towns and are men-only domains outside of Jeddah and Riyadh. Connections are generally adequate and cost SR3 to SR10 per hour.

Most four-star and all five-star hotels and many coffeehouses now offer wireless access if you have your own device.

The internet is strictly policed, with over 6000 sites currently blocked. Most are pornographic, but they also include sites discussing politics, health, women's rights and education. For a full list of internet topics prohibited by the Saudi authorities, visit www.al-bab.com/media/docs/ saudi.html.

LEGAL MATTERS

Saudi Arabia imposes strict Sharia'a (Islamic law), under which extremely harsh punishments are imposed. For more information, see the Expats chapter (p33) and consult your embassy.

If you're involved in a traffic accident call 999 (it doesn't have to be an emergency), don't move your car (even by 1m) and don't leave the scene until the police arrive.

SAUDI ARABIA DIRECTORY A–Z

BANNED SUBSTANCES

The following items are banned in Saudi Arabia. If you try to bring any of them into the country, penalties range from confiscation for minor offences up to imprisonment or deportation for more serious offences.

➡ Alcohol

➡ Artwork or items bearing religious symbols

➡ Many books, DVDs and videos

➡ Firearms and explosives

➡ Illegal drugs or medication without a doctor's prescription

➡ Politically sensitive material, material overly critical of the government or royal family; this may include seemingly innocent newspaper articles

➡ Pork products

➡ Pornography or any publications containing pictorial representations of people (particularly women) in a less than conservative state of dress

➡ Symbols or books of other religions (including the Bible)

Try to get the name of the other driver and registration and insurance numbers of the vehicle. To claim insurance a police report is obligatory. Sometimes Saudis in a hurry offer to pay for minor damages on the spot, but you should insist on a police report as garages are not allowed to carry out repairs without one.

MAPS

The best maps of Saudi Arabia are Farsi Maps. They're available at branches of the Jarir Bookstore throughout the Kingdom (SR22 each). The series includes many general maps of most regions and excellent city maps for Riyadh, Jeddah, Al-Ahsa (Al-Hofuf), Abha, Taif, Mecca and Medina among other locations.

MEDIA

All forms of media (other than satellite TV) are controlled by the government, although that grip has definitely loosened in recent years thanks to the advent of satellite news channels beamed into people's homes from elsewhere in the region and further afield.

Newspapers & Magazines

The English-language dailies *Arab News* (www. arabnews.com) and the *Saudi Gazette* (www. saudigazette.com.sa; SR5 each) are surprisingly frank, although they steer clear of any criticism of the royal family or Islam.

International newspapers (the *Guardian*, the *Times*, *International Herald Tribune* and *Le Monde*) and magazines (*Time* and *Newsweek*) are available from any branch of Jarir Bookstore, usually within three days of publication. Don't expect your foreign newspaper to include all of its pages – censors routinely extract articles about Saudi Arabia and any photographs considered vaguely risqué or controversial.

Radio

Jeddah Radio (96.2FM) broadcasts in English and French, while the **BBC World Service** (www. bbc.co.uk/worldservice/) is available online and on short-wave frequency (11.760khz or 15.575khz).

TV

Satellite TV is widely available. NBC2 (www.nbc-2.com) broadcasts films in English 24 hours, and Saudi Arabia TV Channel 2 (www.sauditv2.tv) broadcasts in English (everything from Australian soap operas to *Islam Q&A*).

MONEY
Credit Cards

Many establishments accept credit cards, including most medium- to large-sized hotels, restaurants, airline offices and shops. Surprisingly some tour operators don't – check first.

Currency

The unit of currency is the Saudi riyal (SR) and one riyal (SR1) is divided into 100 halalas. Coins come in 25 and 50 halala denominations. Notes come in SR1, SR5, SR10, SR20, SR50, SR100, SR200 and SR500 denominations. The Saudi riyal is a hard currency and there are no restrictions on its import or export.

Exchanging Money

Banks and ATMs that accept international cards are ubiquitous throughout Saudi. For exchanging cash, you'll get a much better rate at a money exchange bureaux. All major hard currencies are exchanged and commission is not usually charged, but check this first. Exchange desks at hotels offer poor rates.

OPENING HOURS

Opening hours vary according to the season and province. In general:

Banks 8.30am to noon and 4.30pm to 8pm Saturday to Wednesday. At airports, banks are open 24 hours.

Offices 7.30am to 2.30pm or 3.30pm Saturday to Wednesday

Post offices 7.30am to 10pm Saturday to Wednesday, 4.30pm to 10pm Friday

Restaurants 7am to 10.30am, noon to 3pm and 6pm or 7pm to midnight (to 1am or 2am at weekends)

Shopping centres 9am or 10am to midnight Saturday to Thursday

Shops & souqs 8am or 9am to 1pm or 2pm and 4.30pm or 5pm to 9pm, Saturday to Wednesday

Note that during prayer times – five times a day – *everything* shuts.

In Saudi, the weekend is Thursday and Friday.

PHOTOGRAPHY

Photography in certain areas is still off-limits due to security concerns – government buildings, embassies, airports, seaports, desalination or electricity plants, oil rigs, royal palaces and police stations or anything vaguely connected with the military or security services. Don't photograph people without their permission, and never photograph women (even in a general street scene).

Filming is still prohibited at some archaeological sites; if you get caught, your camera may be confiscated. If you're coming to Saudi with a tour operator, it can organise a video permit for you, as well as a letter to customs (stating that you'll arrive with a camera).

Memory cards and batteries can easily be found in Riyadh and Jeddah.

POST

The queues at Saudi post offices can be long, especially in the main city branches at weekends and in the evenings.

Any internationally addressed parcel must first be taken to the post office unwrapped so that Saudi customs can inspect it. If a parcel includes DVDs they may be viewed by customs before you can mail them.

Most Saudis use their company mailboxes instead of a private box. If you're living in Saudi, you should follow suit or get a box at your local post office.

Public Holidays

No holidays other than **Eid al-Fitr** (dates vary), **Eid al-Adha** (dates vary) and **National Day** (23 September) are observed in the Kingdom.

SAFE TRAVEL
Dos & Don'ts

Conservative dress is the rule of thumb in Saudi Arabia. Shorts in public are a big no-no (except at the private beaches operated by some top-end hotels and expat compounds).

Unmarried couples shouldn't travel together and if they do they may be stopped and investigated.

Alcohol is strictly illegal in Saudi Arabia.

You should carry your passport with you at all times. While travelling on business carry a letter of introduction (and many copies) from your company.

Mutawwa

Formally known as the Committee for the Propagation of Virtue and the Prevention of Vice, the *mutawwa* (religious police) have an infamous reputation as moral vigilantes out to enforce strict Islamic orthodoxy.

Operating independently of other branches of the security services, the *mutawwa* are at their most authoritative (and hence not to be argued with) when accompanied by uniformed police.

They became less visible (and less welcome) in cities like Jeddah and Al-Khobar following a horrific fire at a Mecca Girls School in 2002. The *mutawwa* pushed schoolgirls back into the burning building because they weren't dressed 'correctly'. Fifteen people died.

Ramadan

For Muslims, public observance of the fast is mandatory. For non-Muslims, smoking, eating or drinking in public could result in arrest.

Road Safety

Saudi Arabia has one of the highest incidents of road fatalities in the world. Some of the worst hazards are:

➡ The coastal road that links Jeddah to Jizan (Road No 55), which has the highest fatality rate in the Kingdom.

➡ Camels wandering onto unfenced roads, particularly at night.

➡ Buses and taxis suddenly veering across the road to pick up or drop off passengers.

➡ Pick-up trucks suddenly pulling out at junctions or after petrol stations.

MINDING THE MUTAWWA

The *mutawwa* (religious police) are a source of both fear and fascination for many travellers, but if you dress and behave appropriately, you have little to fear. Indeed, some *mutawwa* are known to give *hawajas* (Westerners) a wide berth.

The *mutawwa* are conspicuous for their *thobes* (men's shirt-dress), which are worn above their ankles, and for wearing *gutras* (white head cloths) without *agals* (head ropes), since God alone is entitled to wear 'crowns'.

The places you're most likely to encounter *mutawwa* are, in descending order: Al-Ula, Jizan, Abha, Hail, Al-Hofuf, Riyadh, Taif and Najran.

SAUDI ARABIA DIRECTORY A–Z

ℹ️ VISA RULES

When planning your Saudi visa, remember to keep the following in mind:

➡ A Saudi sponsor is necessary for any visit to the Kingdom, be it for business or tourism, and they are legally responsible for the conduct and behaviour of visitors whilst in the Kingdom.

➡ Passports must be valid for a minimum of six months.

➡ When applying for a visa, women under 30 years old must be accompanied by either their brother or husband, who must also arrive in and leave Saudi at the same time.

➡ Men and women are only allowed to travel together and are granted a visa to do so if they are (a) married (with an official marriage licence) or (b) form part of a group.

➡ It's not permitted for an unmarried couple to travel alone together in Saudi Arabia and doing so runs the risk of arrest.

➡ Vehicles driving outside of towns at night with one or no lights on.

➡ Vehicles trying to overtake on corners. Saudi drivers expect you (and sometimes oncoming traffic too) to pull over so that they can pass.

Sexual Harassment

Hollywood movies and hardcore porn channels (now widely available in the Kingdom) have greatly coloured the Saudi perception of Western women. Stares, leers and obscene comments are sometimes reported by Western women travellers.

It's rarely more than this, however, and the social disgrace that comes from having touched a woman in public is one of your most effective weapons. If your harasser persists, report him to the police or security men that can be found on most streets and malls in the Kingdom.

Remember also – the more conservatively you dress, the more conservatively you will be treated, particularly with regards to wearing a headscarf.

Terrorism

Since the attacks on Western targets in 2003 and 2004, security has been dramatically tightened around residential compounds and embassies.

Nevertheless, security incidents still occur in the Kingdom, including an attempted suicide bombing of a government minister in Jeddah in August 2009. The biggest current security concern remains Islamist acts of terror against government installations and public gatherings. While there may be little cause for undue alarm, it pays to remain vigilant at all times.

In recent years, fighting along the Yemeni border has had the potential to escalate and travel in southern Asir, Narjan and the Empty Quarter is sometimes restricted by the Saudi authorities. Expect lots of security checkpoints in these regions. While in Saudi Arabia, you should also register with your embassy, and keep a close eye on warnings issued by them in the form of emails or text messages.

TELEPHONE

The mobile-phone network run by STC operates on the GSM system.

At the time of writing mobile networks were offering myriad rapidly changing deals, usually to attract migrant workers wanting to call home. The major networks included:

➡ STC (www.stc.com.sa)

➡ Zain (www.zain.com)

➡ Mobily (www.mobily.com.sa)

For directory assistance, call 📞 905 (domestic) or 📞 900 (international).

VISAS

Saudi bureaucracy is at its most opaque when applying for a visa but one thing is clear: independent travel to Saudi Arabia does not currently exist.

Top of the restricted list of travellers into Saudi Arabia remains citizens of Israel, but also includes people of Jewish faith from other countries. All visitors to Saudi must declare their religion – those declaring 'Jewish' or 'none' will usually be refused a visa.

Any evidence of travel to and from Israel will result in refusal of entry into Saudi. Saudi immigration officials are fully aware of the land crossings into both Jordan and Egypt from Israel. Entry stamps from either Egypt or Jordan's land border crossings with Israel – Rafah (Egypt), Allenby Bridge and Aqaba (Jordan) – will usually result in a Saudi visa not being issued in the first place, or if the visa does magically appear, then the unfortunate traveller will probably end up being turned back at Saudi immigration. If you have evidence of travel to Israel in your passport and intend to travel to Saudi Arabia in the future use a brand new passport for your Saudi visa application.

For a full list of possible visa types, see www.saudiembassy.net/services.

Hajj & Umrah Visas

For hajj visas there's a quota system of one visa for every 1000 Muslims in a country's population. The system of administration varies from country to country but typically involves an application processed by a Saudi-authorised hajj and *umrah* travel agency. Every Saudi embassy has a list of authorised hajj and *umrah* travel agencies for that particular country.

Umrah (any pilgrimage to Mecca that is not hajj) visas are granted to any Muslim requesting one (in theory) although if you are not from a Muslim majority country or don't have an obviously Muslim name, you'll be asked to provide an official document that lists Islam as your religion. Converts to Islam must provide a certificate from the mosque where they went through their conversion ceremony.

Umrah and hajj visas are free, but are valid only for travel to Jeddah, Mecca, Medina and the connecting roads.

There has been a recent crackdown on hajj and *umrah* visa holders illegally staying on to work in the Kingdom and security roadblocks for checking visa permits are common throughout the Hejaz region.

Residence (Work) Visas

Residence (work) visas are arranged via a Saudi employer who is also an individual's visa sponsor. There are annual job category quotas in place for residence (work) visas and individuals are regularly assigned a different visa category from the job actually being performed. For example, a nurse may receive an engineer's visa, or vice versa, as the various annual job quotas are filled. The restrictions on length of stay, multiple entries in and out of Saudi Arabia will often vary and the restrictions particular to each visa must be carefully confirmed before arrival in the Kingdom.

Visa categories can and do provide a major source of headaches for expat workers to Saudi Arabia, especially in relation to the nature of the stay offered to accompanying family members. The visa restrictions and length of stay in Saudi Arabia granted to each family member will often differ depending on gender and age. These details should not be assumed to be the same for younger children, teenagers or spouses and should be carefully checked before arrival in the Kingdom.

Note that residence visas are usually issued using a lunar calendar and this often leads to additional confusion. Visa exit dates should be double checked and reconfirmed on arrival in Saudi Arabia.

Tourist Visas

At the time of writing there are no tourist visas being issued. A brief period in which tourist visas were issued by authorised Saudi travel agents to groups of at least four individuals ended in 2010. Although there is always talk of a new visa regime on the horizon, there appears little likelihood of the scheme being reinstated during the lifespan of this book. If the scheme does return, expect the requirement that all itineraries must be approved, and visas issued by an authorised Saudi travel agency.

Transit Visas

Transit visas are required for those passing through the Kingdom for periods longer than 18 hours. In practice, these visas rarely apply for Western visitors – you're expected to show why your travel arrangements prevented you from passing through the Kingdom more rapidly, something which may be difficult given current airline schedulings. Transit visas are issued free of charge.

Transit visas used to be issued for independent car travel across Saudi Arabia but these were suspended following the murder of four French travellers in 2007.

Business Visas

Business visas are arranged via an employer and a sponsoring Saudi partner for a specific business purpose.

The Saudi sponsor (either an individual or company) then applies to the Saudi Chamber of Commerce and Industry for approval. If approval is granted, an invitation letter will be sent to you, or directly to the Saudi embassy in your home country.

Note that you must make your visa application in your country of nationality or permanent residency.

Depending on the Saudi embassy where you are applying for a visa (always phone ahead to double-check requirements), typically you will require a letter from your employer or company outlining the nature of your business in Saudi Arabia and a letter of support from your local chamber of commerce.

Armed with this paperwork and confirmation from your Saudi sponsor, your business visa is usually granted without difficulty by the embassy and often on the same day if you visit in person. An application by post usually takes a week to 10 days to be returned.

Note that in theory a single businesswoman is not allowed to check into a hotel without the presence of her Saudi sponsor or a male representative of her Saudi sponsor. In the larger cities such as Riyadh and Jeddah this rule is not usually applied, but in smaller towns and more conservative regions of the Kingdom this rule may be upheld by hotel check-in staff. Be prepared.

WOMEN TRAVELLERS

Saudi Arabia is rightly considered one of the most difficult countries in the world for Western women to travel. The strict segregation of the sexes and the prohibition on female drivers leads to obvious limitations on freedom of movement. However, women are also accorded (officially) great respect and are typically urged to the front of queues, served first at banks, check-in desks and ticket offices.

Saudi men's attitudes towards women do vary from the big cities to the smaller rural towns and many urban educated Saudi men will make a point of shaking hands with Western women, especially in social or business settings. Take your cue from those around you and remember that in traditional Saudi eyes it never hurts (them at least) for you to be too covered up.

Restrictions

Access to almost all internet cafes, and most mid- and budget-range hotels is impossible, as is access to many restaurants. Most towns and villages have at least one restaurant with a 'family section' where women, whether accompanied or not, must sit – those that do not provide takeaways. Museums and some sights have special family-only hours, and banks have 'Ladies' branches'.

What to Wear

Women must by law wear an *abeyya* (full-length black robe). Though a headscarf is not compulsory, you should always have one at hand as the *mutawwa* may insist that you wear it.

❶ Getting There & Away

ENTERING SAUDI ARABIA

Immigration is much quicker than it used to be (except during hajj and Ramadan when you can expect long queues). All bags including hand luggage are x-rayed but usually only opened when further investigation is warranted. Don't forget to fill in immigration cards.

Note that departure security is vigorous and time consuming. You're advised to arrive early – 1½ hours before departures for domestic flights, three hours before international flights. If you're travelling with Saudi Arabian Airlines (Saudia), save time by obtaining your boarding pass up to 24 hours in advance.

If you're arriving by land, procedures are similar, although expect long delays if you're bringing your own car into the Kingdom.

AIR

The national carrier is **Saudi Arabian Airlines** (Saudia; ☎ 01-488 4444; www.saudiairlines.com), which flies to dozens of destinations across the Middle East, Europe, Asia and the USA. It has a respectable safety record and is

usually on time and comfortable. Saudia usually offers a free domestic flight with an international ticket.

There are four airports handling international traffic in Saudi Arabia:

King Abdul Aziz International Airport (☎02-684 2227) In Jeddah.

King Fahd International Airport (☎03-883 5151; www.kfia.com.sa) In Dammam.

King Khaled International Airport (☎01-221 1000; www.riyadh-airport.com) In Riyadh.

Medina International Airport (☎04-842 0000) In Medina.

Airlines Flying to/from Saudi Arabia

Air Arabia (www.airarabia.com)

Air France (www.airfrance.com)

British Airways (www.british-airways.com)

EgyptAir (www.egyptair.com.eg)

Emirates (www.emirates.com)

Etihad Airways (www.etihadairways.com)

Gulf Air (www.gulfair.com)

Iran Air (www.iranair.com)

Kuwait Airways (www.kuwait-airways.com)

Lufthansa (www.lufthansa.com)

Middle East Airlines (www.mea.com.lb)

Oman Air (www.oman-air.com)

Qatar Airways (www.qatarairways.com)

Royal Jordanian Airlines (www.rj.com)

Yemenia (www.yemenia.com)

LAND
Border Crossings

At the time of research there were problems with a number of Saudi border crossings – the land borders with Iraq, Jordan and Yemen were closed to non-Arab travellers. Check with your embassy for the latest information.

Make sure you have visas for the countries you wish to enter. And never agree to carry either passengers (if you're driving) or baggage through borders.

Car & Motorcycle

To avoid traffic queues at busy times (such as during holidays) travel early or late in the day. All open borders operate 24 hours. If you're driving someone else's car, make sure you carry a letter granting permission from the owner.

❶ Getting Around

AIR

Most domestic air routes in Saudi Arabia are still best served by Saudi Arabian Airlines (p280) but the national carrier also has a low-cost domestic rival in the form of **Nas** (www.flynas.com).

The competition has increased already with frequent flights between major towns. Unlike international tickets (which travel agents can sell at discounted prices) domestic Saudia tickets cost the same price whether bought from an agency or direct from Saudia.

Domestic tickets can be bought from abroad. Tickets can be changed as often as you like (though SR20 is sometimes charged) and you can get refunds (minus an administration charge of SR20) even on missed flights. Putting yourself on the waiting list is well worthwhile as there are so many no-shows.

Checking in 1½ hours prior to departure is advised for domestic flights. Note that Medina airport lies outside the haram (forbidden) area so it can be used by tourists.

Bookings by telephone can also be made if you're flying within 24 hours (you can pick the ticket up at the airport). For information on flight schedules and information, call 9200 22222.

BUS

All domestic bus services are operated by the **Saudi Arabian Public Transport Company** (Saptco; ☑ 800-124 9999; www.saptco.com.sa). The company is professionally run and has a good safety record with well-maintained buses.

The buses are comfortable, air-conditioned and clean. Standing passengers are not allowed, talking to the driver is prohibited and smoking is strictly prohibited. Saptco also guarantees that if a bus breaks down, a repair vehicle is sent within two hours, a replacement within four.

All buses have on-board toilets, and make rest stops every few hours. For general information, fare prices and timetables, dial 800 124 9999

toll-free, with recorded messages in Arabic and English.

Unaccompanied foreign women can travel on domestic buses with their *iqama* (residence permit) if an expat, or with a passport and visa if a tourist. The front seats are generally unofficially reserved for 'families' including sole women, and the back half for men. The same applies on international buses, however women under 30 years old must be accompanied by their brother or husband, as per visa requirements.

Check in half an hour before domestic departures, one hour before international departures (although passengers with hand luggage can arrive 10 minutes before). If the bus is full, you join the waiting list and board the bus five minutes before departure if there are any no-shows.

Note that during hajj, services are reduced across the country as buses are seconded for the pilgrims.

Classes

There are no classes, except on one service: the Saptco VIP Express service that runs between Riyadh and Al-Khobar (SR90, five hours).

Costs

Bus fares cost approximately half of the equivalent airfare. Return tickets are 25% cheaper than two one-way fares. Online booking is now available.

Reservations

When purchasing your ticket, you'll need to show your passport (visitors) or *iqama* (expats). Dur-

BUS

Saptco (☑ 800 124 9999; www.saptco.com.sa) offers the best international bus services and other companies from surrounding countries also cover the same routes for similar prices. Saptco prices are kept low by the government. Departures are primarily from Riyadh, Jeddah and Dammam. There are currently no buses to Iraq, while you'll need to change in Dubai if travelling to Oman.

FROM	TO	PRICE (SR)	DURATION (HRS)	FREQUENCY
Riyadh	Amman	200	22	three weekly
Riyadh	Kuwait	210	eight	three weekly
Riyadh	Bahrain	120	six	three daily
Riyadh	Dubai	140	12	daily
Jeddah	Amman	200	18	daily
Jeddah	Sana'a	175	24	three weekly
Dammam	Bahrain	60	60	five daily
Dammam	Doha	220	220	daily
Dammam	Kuwait	120	120	four weekly
Dammam	Abu Dhabi	125	125	daily
Dammam	Dubai	125	10	daily

ing hajj season, Ramadan or in summer, booking at least a week in advance is advisable.

Tickets can be bought up to three months in advance for domestic journeys, six months for international. If tickets are cancelled or unused, you can get a refund (less 10%) for a one-way ticket (or unused return) or 30% for a return ticket if it hasn't expired (within three/ six months for domestic/international destinations).

Tickets are best bought from Saptco itself.

CAR & MOTORCYCLE

Despite its impressive public transport system, Saudi Arabia remains a country that glorifies the private car (the shiny 4WD is king). Roads are generally sealed and well maintained.

Motorcycles are rare and generally considered a vehicle of the rural poor.

Driving Licence

If you'll only be in the country for less than three months and want to rent a car, you should always have your International Driving Permit (IDP) available to show.

If you're going to be in the Kingdom for more than three months, you'll need to get a local driving licence, which is arranged by your employer. You'll also have to do a driving test and purchase insurance.

Fuel

It seems miraculous to a Westerner, but it's still only around 60 halalas per litre for unleaded petrol. All petrol stations charge the same (by law). Petrol stations are ubiquitous throughout the country.

Hire

International and local car-hire agencies can be found in the larger towns in the Kingdom, as well as at international airports. Local companies tend to be significantly cheaper, but always check that *full* insurance is included. Prices usually stay the same throughout the year.

Rates for the smallest cars at international agencies generally start at SR120 per day (including full insurance) and can start from SR600 for 4WDs. For rental of a month or more, prices drop significantly. Be sure to negotiate.

There's usually an additional charge of around SR0.75 to SR2 per kilometre, although most agencies offer the first 150km free. Women travellers (who are not permitted by law to drive) will need a driver – around SR125 per eight-hour day plus SR30 per extra hour.

Insurance

If you are travelling with a car from another GCC country, insurance and the Collision-Damage Waiver (CDW) are mandatory. With car hire it's usually included in the price but it pays to check very carefully.

Road Rules

The main rules include:
- ➡ Driving on the right side of the road.
- ➡ Leaving the scene of an accident is a serious offence and can result in fines of over SR1000, imprisonment and deportation.
- ➡ Not carrying a valid driving licence can result in a night in jail and a hefty fine.
- ➡ Right turns are allowed at red lights unless specifically forbidden.
- ➡ The speed limit in towns is 60km/h, 70km/h or 80km/h.
- ➡ The speed limit on open highways is 120km/h (but can drop to 90km/h or 100km/h).

LOCAL TRANSPORT

Taxi

Taxis are found in most of the larger towns and are known as 'limousines' locally; they can be hailed anywhere. Note that it's much cheaper to negotiate the fare first (as locals do) rather than use the meter.

TRAIN

Saudi Arabia currently has only one stretch of train track in the entire country, between Riyadh and Dammam via Al-Hofuf.

Plans are afoot to link Jeddah, Mecca and Medina by high-speed link to assist with hajj pilgrimage. If this rail expansion occurs, further extensions to Aqaba in Jordan and on to Egypt have also been discussed by Saudi officials. However, this would be a number of years away – if it happens at all.

Ambitious future rail plans also include a 'North–South Line' linking Riyadh with Hazm, 'The Land-bridge' linking Jeddah and Riyadh and a 'West Coast Line'.

Note that schedules change often; check the website for the latest information (www.saudirailways.org). Maximum luggage allowance is between 20kg and 40kg depending on the class of ticket (per excess kilo SR1 to SR2); luggage is loaded onto a separate carriage.

The gate closes five minutes before departure, but you should get there one hour before departure for police checks and luggage x-rays.

Classes

There are three classes: 2nd, 1st and VIP class. The main difference between them is leg room (plus TV and a meal in the splendidly named 'Rehab' VIP class). All classes have access to the train restaurant.

Women can travel unaccompanied (with ID) and sit in any class. In 2nd there's a separate carriage and in VIP and 1st there are special designated areas.

Costs

You'll need a passport or *iqama* (residence permit) to travel. Travelling by train in 2nd class is still slightly cheaper than the equivalent bus fare and there are discounts for passengers with special needs and Saudi students.

Reservations

Reservations (☑ 92 000 8886) can be made a minimum of 24 hours before departure and a maximum of 90 days in advance, and from any station to any station.

Tickets can be changed three hours before departure (although you forfeit 10% of the total cost). Check all tickets are correct after purchase and note that there is no refund if you miss your train.

During school holidays, Ramadan and hajj, book well in advance. At weekends (Thursday and Friday), book three to four days in advance.

United Arab Emirates
اتحاد الإمارات العربية

Includes ➡

Best Places for Culture

➡ Sheikh Zayed Grand Mosque (p328)

➡ Sharjah Heritage Museum (p311)

➡ Sheikh Mohammed Centre for Cultural Understanding (p295)

➡ Deira Souqs (p291)

➡ Sharjah Museum of Islamic Civilisation (p314)

Best Places for Nature

➡ Liwa Oasis (p336)

➡ Sir Bani Yas Island (p338)

➡ Al Ain Zoo (p340)

➡ East Coast Diving (p350)

➡ Umm Al Quwain Lagoon (p319)

Why Go?

For most people, the United Arab Emirates (UAE) means just one place: Dubai, the sci-fi-esque city of iconic skyscrapers, palm-shaped islands, city-sized malls, indoor ski slopes and palatial beach resorts. But guess what? Beyond the glitter awaits a diverse mosaic of six more emirates, each with its own character and allure.

An hour's drive south, oil-rich Abu Dhabi, the country's capital, is quickly gaining a reputation as a hub of culture, sport and leisure. Beyond its borders looms the vast Al Gharbia desert, whose magical silence is interrupted only by the whisper of shifting dunes rolling towards Saudi Arabia.

North of Dubai, Sharjah has the country's best museums, while tiny Ajman and Umm Al Quwain provide glimpses of life in the pre-oil days, and Ras Al Khaimah is busy building up its tourism infrastructure. For the best swimming and diving, head to the emirate of Fujairah and frolic in the clear waters of the Gulf of Oman.

When to Go?

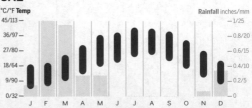

High Season (Nov–Mar)
Moderate temps, higher room rates, major festivals, good camping.

Shoulder Season (Mar–May & Oct)
Hot days, balmy nights, good for beach vacations, desert camping.

Low Season (Jun–Sep) Hot and humid, steep hotel discounts, best time for diving.

Daily Costs

The sky's the limit when it comes to spending money in the UAE, but you can keep expenses down, for example by eschewing the glitzy five-star for a solid midrange hotel where standard doubles can be had for Dh400 to Dh600. A glass of beer or wine is about Dh25 or Dh40, respectively, but if you stick to water, you can get a nice three-course meal for around Dh50, and a shwarma to go costs just Dh4. Museums are free or cheap but expect to pay Dh150 and up for guided tours and admissions to waterparks and other big attractions.

ITINERARIES

Two Days

If you're in the UAE just on a short layover, base yourself in the Downtown Dubai area. Spend day one checking off the iconic sights on a **Big Bus Tour**, then head up to the **Burj Khalifa** at sunset (book way ahead), take a spin around **Dubai Mall** and have dinner in **Souk Al Bahar** with a view of the **Dubai Fountain**. The next day, take a cab to Sharjah for a glimpse into the past in the **Heritage Area**, stocking up on souvenirs at the **Central Souq** and enjoying dinner in bubbly **Al Qasba**.

One Week

Spend two days in futuristic Dubai and one in retro Sharjah before heading south to Abu Dhabi to marvel at the **Sheikh Zayed Grand Mosque**, zoom around **Ferrari World** and learn about the new Culture District on **Saadiyat Island**. For total contrast, dip into the desert next to face a huge dune, magical silence and plenty of camels, preferably on an overnight trip. Wrap up with a day in Al Ain and its fabulous **zoo** and Unesco-recognised heritage sites.

Essential Food & Drink

Strangely, restaurants serving authentic Emirati food are scarce. If you do get a chance, try these typical dishes, and don't miss out on the succulent local dates!

➤ **Balaleet** Vermicelli blends with sugar syrup, saffron, rosewater and sauteed onions in this rich breakfast staple.

➤ **Fareed** Mutton-flavoured broth with bread; popular at Ramadan.

➤ **Hareis** Ground wheat and lamb slow-cooked until creamy (bit like porridge); sometimes called the 'national dish'.

➤ **Khuzi** Stuffed whole roasted lamb on a bed of spiced rice.

➤ **Madrooba** Salt-cured fish (*maleh*) or chicken mixed with raw bread dough until thick.

➤ **Makbus** A casserole of spice-laced rice and meat (usually lamb) or fish garnished with nuts, raisins and fried onions.

AT A GLANCE

➤ **Currency** UAE dirham (Dh)

➤ **Mobile phones** GSM network is widespread

➤ **Money** ATMs are common in urban areas

➤ **Visas** Available on arrival for 34 nationalities

Fast Facts

➤ **Capital** Abu Dhabi

➤ **Country code** ⌨ 971

➤ **Language** Arabic

➤ **Official name** United Arab Emirates

➤ **Population** 7.9 million

Exchange Rates

Australia	A$1	Dh3.18
Bahrain	BD1	Dh9.74
Euro zone	€1	Dh4.77
Kuwait	KD1	Dh12.88
Oman	OR1	Dh9.57
Qatar	QR1	Dh1
Saudi Arabia	SR1	Dh0.97
UK	UK£1	Dh5.62
USA	US$1	QR3.64
Yemen	YR100	Dh1.71

For current exchange rates see www.xe.com.

Resources

➤ **Lonely Planet** (www.lonelyplanet.com/uae)

➤ **UAE Ministry of Information & Culture** (www.uaeinteract.com)

➤ **UAE Government** (www.government.ae)

➤ **Time Out** (www.timeoutdubai.com)

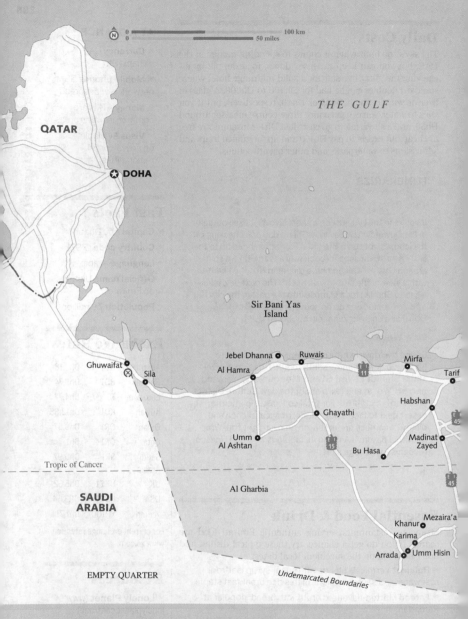

THE GULF

QATAR

✪ DOHA

Sir Bani Yas
Island

Jebel Dhanna ⊙   Ruwais ⊙   Mirfa ⊙
                                                          Tarif ⊙
Ghuwaifat ⊙   Al Hamra ⊙
          Sila ⊗
                                              Habshan ⊙
                        ⊙ Ghayathi
                                              Madinat ⊙
          Umm ⊙   Zayed
          Al Ashtan   Bu Hasa ⊙

Tropic of Cancer -

SAUDI
ARABIA   Al Gharbia

                                         Mezaira'a ⊙
                                   Khanur ⊙
                                   Karima ⊙
                          Arrada ⊙ ⊙ Umm Hisin

EMPTY QUARTER   Undemarcated Boundaries

United Arab Emirates Highlights

1 Shop til you drop at the **Dubai Mall** (p306), then soar to the top of the **Burj Khalifa** (p291) and finish up with cocktails at the iconic **Burj Al Arab** (p295) hotel.

2 Count the domes and minarets of the **Sheikh Zayed Grand Mosque** (p328) and get some kicks at **Ferrari World Abu Dhabi** (p329).

3 Catch a glimpse of the pre-oil days in Sharjah's atmospheric **Heritage Area** (p311)

4 Lose yourself in the labyrinth of Al Ain's shady **date-palm oases** (p343)

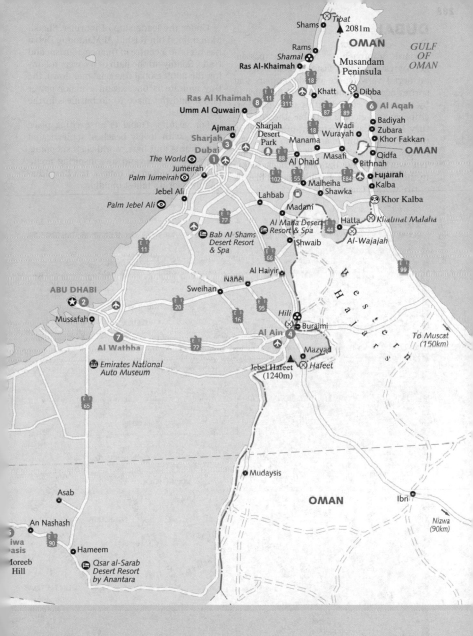

Tibat
Shams
2081m
Rams
OMAN
Shamal
GULF OF OMAN
Ras Al-Khaimah
Musandam Peninsula
18
Khatt
Dibba
11
E 311
8
Ras Al Khaimah
87
89
6 **Al Aqah**
Umm Al Quwain
Badiyah
Wadi
Zubara
Ajman
Sharjah Desert Park
Wurayah
Khor Fakkan
18
3
Manama
Masafi
Qidfa
OMAN
Dubai
Bithnah
1
Al Dhaid
The World
88
E84
Jumeirah
102
55
Fujairah
Palm Jumeirah
Malheiha
Kalba
Jebel Ali
Lahbab
Shawka
Khor Kalba
Palm Jebel Ali
Madam
Halla
Khalmat Malaha
E 77
Al Maha Desert Resort & Spa
44
Bab Al Shams Desert Resort & Spa
E 11
Al-Wajajah
Shwaib
E 99
66
Al Haiyir
Western
Nahel
Sweihan
E 20
95
Hili
E 16
Buraimi
ABU DHABI
2
Al Ain
4
Hajar
Mussafah
E 72
Mazyad
To Muscat (150km)
7
Al Wathba
Emirates National Auto Museum
Jebel Hafeet (1240m)
Hafeet
E 65

Asab
Mudaysis
An Nashash
OMAN
Ibri
iwa asis
90
Nizwa (90km)
Aoreeb Hill
Hameem
Qsar al-Sarab Desert Resort by Anantara

5 Wonder at the spectacle of sand dunes shimmering in shades from apricot to cinnamon in the **Liwa Oasis** (p336)

6 Come face to face with turtles and sharks in the fertile waters off **Al Aqah** (p348)

7 See the 'ships of the desert' run like mad around a

camel race track, for instance at **Al-Wathba** (p354)

8 Wander among the ghostly ruins of the ancient fishing village of **Jazirat Al Hamra** (p321) in Ras Al Khaimah

DUBAI

دبي

♩ 04 / POP 2.1 MILLION

Aboard approaching airplanes, passengers wrestle against fastened seat belts for an aerial view: space-age skyscrapers that sprout across an endless desert hemmed in by a coastline etched with palm-shaped archipelagos. Welcome to Dubai, the 21st-century Middle Eastern Shangri-la powered by unflinching ambition and can-do spirit. The motto: if you can think of it, it shall be done. The world's tallest building? Check. Skiing in the desert? Check. Islands shaped like the entire world? Check.

Under the leadership of its ruler, Sheikh Mohammed bin Rashid Al Maktoum, Dubai has become a centre of finance, tourism and trade. Solidly on the path of recovery following the 2009 global financial meltdown, the tiny emirate is once again a major power player and *the* place to do business in the Middle East.

For visitors, Dubai is an exciting place to visit, with lovely beaches, sophisticated restaurants and bars, world-class shopping, ultra-luxe hotels, and awe-inspiring architecture, including, of course, the Burj Khalifa, the world's tallest building.

Dubai

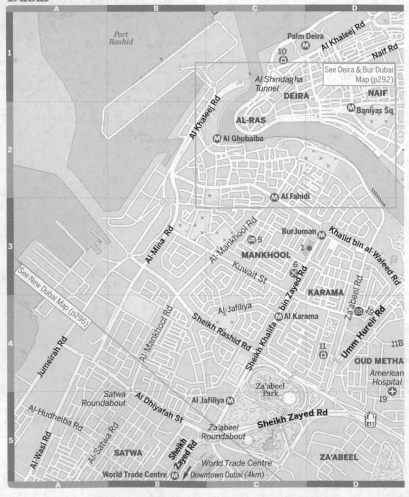

Dubai

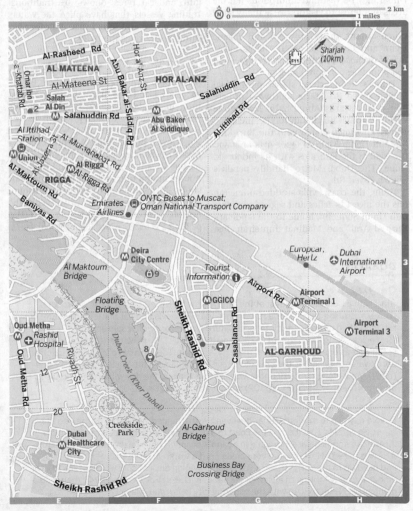

But there's more to the emirate than 21st-century glitz and glam. Despite appearances, Dubai's culture is solidly rooted in Islam and generations of Bedouin heritage. Glimpses of the past are rare but can still be had along the creek, in the souqs of Deira and the historic Al Fahidi Neighbourhood. A few hours spent here will open up your eyes to another Dubai, a Dubai before it became an experiment in a new kind of urbanism. It's this juxtaposition of the traditional past and the high-tech present that makes it such an intriguing and compelling place to visit.

Sights

Dubai may be vast and amorphous but the areas of interest to visitors are actually fairly well defined. Not far from Dubai international airport, dusty, crowded and chaotic Deira and Bur Dubai are the city's oldest neighbourhoods, teeming with mosques and souqs and best explored on foot.

Dubai's main artery, skyscraper-flanked Sheikh Zayed Rd, starts southwest of here and runs towards Abu Dhabi, linking the various iconic neighbourhoods, including shiny Downtown Dubai with the Burj Khalifa and Dubai Mall, Al Quoz arts area and the Mall of the Emirates with its indoor ski slope. The Dubai Metro handily parallels Sheikh Zayed Rd.

Along the coast, villa-studded Jumeirah has the nicest beaches and segues smoothly into Umm Suqueim, home to the landmark Burj Al Arab and Madinat Jumeirah. Just beyond are the ritzy resorts and residential towers of Dubai Marina with the artificially created Palm Jumeirah lying just offshore.

Deira & Bur Dubai

Straddling the creek, Deira and Bur Dubai offer an eye-opening peek into the city's past. Bur Dubai's neatly restored historical quarter is wonderful for late-afternoon strolls while, a quick *abra* (water taxi) ride away, dazzlingly multicultural Deira is most famous for its cacophonous souqs and the colourful dhow wharfage. Loaded with everything from air-conditioners to chewing gum and car tyres, dhows are traditional trading vessels that have plied the waters between here and Iran, India and other far-flung locales since the 1830s.

Al Fahidi Historical Neighbourhood
HISTORIC QUARTER
(Map p292; btwn Al Fahidi St & Dubai Creek, Bur Dubai; M Al Fahidi) FREE Traffic fades to a quiet hum in the labyrinthine lanes of Dubai's heritage quarter (formerly known as the Bastakia Quarter), teeming with restored wind-tower houses built a century ago by Persian pearl and textile merchants. Today, no one lives here any longer and buildings house cultural offices, small museums, craft shops and galleries. Feel free to peek behind open doors and pop into courtyards like the one of Al Serkal Cultural Foundation (Map p292; 353 5922; 10am-8pm Sat-Thu) FREE.

DUBAI IN...

One Day
Start with a Cultural Breakfast at the Sheikh Mohammed Centre for Cultural Understanding (p295) for a rare chance to meet locals and eat home-cooked Emirati food, then delve further into local culture and history with a spin around Al Fahidi Historical Neighbourhood (p290) and the nearby Dubai Museum (p291). Process your impressions during lunch at the leafy Arabian Tea House (p302), then catch an *abra* (water taxi) across the creek to forage for bargains in the bustling Deira Souqs (p291). Walk along the busy dhow wharves and wrap up the day with a dinner cruise aboard Al Mansour Dhow (p302) and a nightcap at QDs (p305).

Two Days
Devote day two to modern Dubai, beginning with a guided visit of the Jumeirah Mosque (p294). Cab it down the coast to explore the modern but charming Madinat Jumeirah souqs before indulging in a canalside lunch while gazing at the iconic Burj Al Arab (p295). Next up, give your credit card a workout at the Dubai Mall (p306) and head up to the Burj Khalifa (p291) observation deck at sunset (book ahead). For dinner, pick any table with a view of the dancing Dubai Fountain (p294), then grab a nightcap at Neos (p305) with the glittering city below you. Magic!

Excellent pit stops include XVA Cafe (p301) and the Arabian Tea House (p302) next to the well-regarded **Majlis Gallery** (Map p292; ☑ 353 6233; www.themajlisgallery.com; Al Fahidi St; ☺ 10am-6pm Sat-Thu).

There's also a short original section of old Dubai's **city wall** from around 1800.

The compact area is easily explored on an aimless wander but for a more in-depth experience it's well worth joining a guided walking tour run by the Sheikh Mohammed Centre for Cultural Understanding (p295) at 10am on Sunday and Thursday (Dh50, reservations advised).

Dubai Museum
MUSEUM
(Map p292; ☑ 353 1862; Al Fahidi St; adult/child Dh3/1; ☺ 8.30am-8.30pm Sat-Thu, 2.30-8.30pm Fri; Ⓜ Al Fahidi) Housed in the 1787 Al Fahidi fort, the one-time seat of government and residence of Dubai's rulers is now a low-key museum that explores Dubai's history, culture and traditions. Beyond a slick multimedia presentation charting Dubai's exponential growth from tiny trading post to megalopolis, endearing freeze-frame dioramas recreate scenes from old Dubai, including a souq, a school and a Bedouin desert camp. Geared more towards adults is the archaeology section which presents locally unearthed vessels, tools, weapons and other artefacts in artfully lit glass cases.

Shindagha Heritage Area
HISTORIC SITE
(Map p292; Al Shindagha Rd; Ⓜ Al Ghubaiba) The Shindagha waterfront, in the crook of the creek, is one of the most historic areas in Dubai, with origins in the 1860s. It gained in importance when the ruling family relocated here in the late 19th century. Many of the historic structures have been rebuilt and now house small museums. A paved walkway with a few cafes parallels the waterfront and is popular with strollers and joggers. The nicest time to visit is around sunset.

Sheikh Saeed al-Maktoum House
MUSEUM
(Map p292; ☑ 393 7139; Al Shindagha Rd; adult/child Dh2/1; ☺ 8am-8.30pm Sat-Thu, 3-9.30pm Fri; Ⓜ Al Ghubaiba) The crown jewel along the Shindagha Heritage Area is the Sheikh Saeed al-Maktoum House, a grand courtyard building that was the official residence from 1912 until 1958 of Sheikh Saeed, the great-grandfather of Dubai's present ruler, Sheikh Mohammed. It was built in 1896 and, aside from being an architectural marvel, it now contains a museum of pre-oil times, with fantastic photographs of undeveloped Dubai in the 1940s and '50s as well as coins, stamps and documents dating back to 1791.

Deira Souqs
MARKET
(Sikkat al-Khail St; Ⓜ Al-Ras) Steps from the Deira Old Souq *abra* station, the guttural singsong of Arabic bounces around the lanes of the small, covered **Spice Souq** (Map p292; Btwn Baniyas Rd, Al-Sabkha Rd & Al-Abra St) as vendors work hard on you to unload aromatic frankincense, dried lemons, chillies, exotic herbs and spices. A stroll away, on and around Sikkat al Khail St, awaits the enormous **Gold Souq** (Map p292; Sikkat al-Khail St, btwn Souq Deira & Old Baladiya Sts) whose stores overflow with every kind of jewellery imaginable – tasteful diamond earrings to over-the-top golden Indian wedding necklaces. Bonus: the people-watching. You'll see everyone from touts hawking knock-off watches to hard-working Afghan guys dragging heavy carts of goods, to African women in colourful kaftans.

Wrap up a souq tour in the 'fragrant' but fabulous **Fish Market** (Map p288; off Al Khaleej Rd) where you'll observe vendors and customers haggling wildly over shrimp the size of bananas, metre-long kingfish and other wriggling wares. The **fruit and vegetable souq** next door isn't nearly as exciting but great for stocking up on bargain-priced produce. Note that the current fish market was scheduled to reopen in a brand-new facility opposite Dubai Hospital, some 2¼km further east on Al Khaleej Rd, in 2014.

◉ Downtown Dubai

Burj Khalifa is the crowning glory of Dubai's new vibrant and urban centre that is also home to key tourist sites and prestigious five-star hotels, restaurants and bars.

★ Burj Khalifa
NOTABLE BUILDING
(Map p296; ☑ toll free 800-2884 3867; www.at thetop.ae; 1 Emaar Blvd, entry ground fl, Dubai Mall, Downtown Dubai; reserved admission adult/child under 13 Dh100/75, instant admission Dh400; ☺ 10am-10pm Sun-Wed, to midnight Thu, 9am-midnight Fri-Sat; Ⓜ Burj Khalifa/Dubai Mall) Call it impressive or preposterous, there's no denying that the elegantly tapered Burj Khalifa is a groundbreaking feat of architecture and engineering: the world's newest tallest building pierces the sky at 828m. It opened on 4 January, 2010, only six years after excavations began. Up to 13,000 workers toiled day and night, at times putting up a new

Deira & Bur Dubai

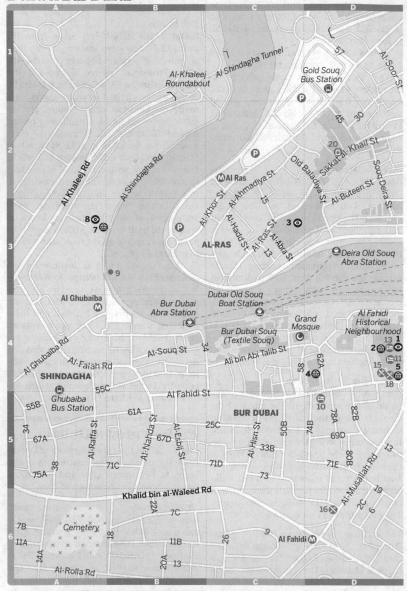

floor in as little as three days. Inside this self-proclaimed 'vertical city' is a mix of offices and apartments and the sleek **Armani Hotel** (Map p296; www.armanihotels.com).

For visitors, the main attraction is the observation platform **At the Top** on the 124th floor. If the haze isn't too dense, you can easily pinpoint such sites as The World, the Burj Al Arab and the high-rises of Sheikh Zayed Rd. Getting there takes you past various multimedia exhibits to a double-deck lift that travels at 10m per second for an entire

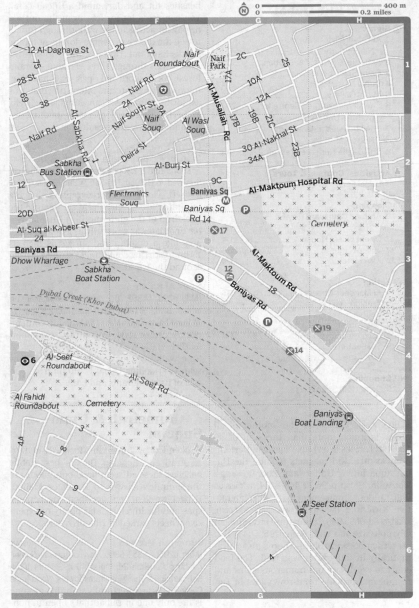

minute to reach level 124 at 442m. There's a terrace to step out on and telescopes (Dh25 for five minutes) for close-ups.

Admission is by timed ticket. To get the timeslot of your choice, prebook online at least a week in advance. Lines are shortest on Monday and Tuesday. Budget about 90 minutes for a visit.

Dubai Mall   MALL
(Map p296; www.thedubaimall.com; Emaar Blvd; ⊙10am-10pm Sun-Wed, to midnight Thu-Sat;

Deira & Bur Dubai

Ⓜ Burj Khalifa/Dubai Mall) The 'mother of all malls' is much more than the sum of its 1200 stores: it's a veritable family entertainment centre. Kid magnets include the Dubai Aquarium & Underwater Zoo, the **Sega Republic** (Map p296; ☎448 8484; admission Dh10) indoor amusement park, the interactive **KidZania** (Map p296; www.kidzania.com; adult/child Dh95/140) miniature city and an Olympic-size **ice rink** (Map p296; ☎437 1111; per session incl skates Dh50). There's also a dramatically lit four-storey waterfall. The food court is excellent, and numerous cafes and restaurants provide front-row views of Dubai Fountain.

Dubai Aquarium & Underwater Zoo   AQUARIUM

(Map p296; ☎448 5200; www.thedubaiaquarium.com; Dubai Mall ; tunnel & zoo Dh55; ◷10am-10pm Sun-Wed, to midnight Thu-Sat; Ⓜ Burj Khalifa/Dubai Mall) Dubai Mall's most mesmerising sight is this gargantuan aquarium where 33,000

beasties flit and dart amid artificial coral. You can see a lot for free from the outside or pay for access to the walk-through tunnel to see the dark cave where dozens of toothy sharks hang out. Upstairs, the **Underwater Zoo** travels through three eco-zones – rainforest, rocky shore and open sea – introducing you to such rare and interesting denizens as air-breathing African lungfish, cheeky archerfish that catch insects by shooting water and otherworldly sea dragons.

Dubai Fountain   FOUNTAIN

(Map p296; Burj Khalifa Lake, off Emaar Blvd; ◷shows 1pm & 1.30pm, then every 30min 6-11pm Sun-Wed, to 11.30pm Thu-Sat; Ⓜ Burj Khalifa/Dubai Mall) FREE These choreographed dancing fountains are spectacularly set against the backdrop of the glittering Burj Khalifa. Water undulates as gracefully as a belly dancer, arcs like a dolphin and surges as high as 150m to stirring soundtracks gathered from around the world.

Souk Al Bahar   SOUQ

(Map p296; ☎362 7012; www.soukalbahar.ae; off Emaar Blvd; ◷10am-10pm Sat-Thu, 2-10pm Fri; Ⓜ Burj Khalifa/Dubai Mall) Designed in contemporary Arabic style, this attractive complex features natural-s
tone walkways, high arches and front-row seats overlooking Dubai Fountain from several of its restaurants and bars.

◉ Jumeirah & Umm Suqeim

Bookended by Jumeirah Mosque and Burj Al Arab and hugging Dubai's best public beaches, these adjacent neighbourhoods are the emirate's answer to Bondi or Malibu. Expect excellent boutique shopping, copious spas and health clubs, and plenty of expensive wheels parked in villa driveways.

Jumeirah Mosque   MOSQUE

(Map p296; ☎353 6666; www.cultures.ae/jumeirah.htm; Jumeirah Rd; tours Dh10; ◷tours 10am Sat, Sun, Tue & Thu; Ⓜ Emirates Towers, World Trade Centre) This architecturally stunning mosque is the only one in Dubai that's open to non-Muslims, and only during guided tours offered through the Sheikh Mohammed Centre for Cultural Understanding (p295). An introduction to Islamic religion and culture is followed by a Q&A session. *Abayas* (cloaks), scarfs and *dishdashas* (men's shirt-dresses) may be borrowed by those deemed not dressed modestly enough. No need to pre-book; cameras allowed.

Burj Al Arab
ARCHITECTURE, HOTEL

(Map p296; ☑ 301 7777; www.burj-al-arab.com; off Jumeirah Rd, Umm Suqeim; Ⓜ Mall of the Emirates) An architectural icon and symbol of modern Dubai, this sail-shaped hotel sits on an artificial island and is well worth a visit if only to gawk at an interior that's every bit as gaudy as the exterior is gorgeous. The lobby is ringed by pillars sheathed in gold leaf and tall enough to fit the Statue of Liberty. If you're not staying, you need a bar or restaurant reservation to get past lobby security. For maximum bang for the dirham, go for sunset drinks at Sky Bar (Map p296; ☑ 04 399 1111; Hilton Dubai Jumeirah, The Walk at JBR; minimum tab Dh250; ⊙ 6.15pm-2.30am). Check the website for details, dress codes and reservations.

Madinat Jumeirah
NEIGHBOURHOOD

(Map p296; Al Sufouh Rd, Umm Suqeim; Ⓜ Mall of the Emirates) There's plenty to do at Madinat Jumeirah, a fanciful hotel, shopping and entertainment complex with the Burj Al Arab in the background. Explore the Arabian-style architecture, get lost in the labyrinth of the souvenir-saturated souq or take an *abra* ride (Dh75 for 20 minutes) through the Venetian-style canals to a romantic waterfront restaurant. Sure, there's an undeniable 'Disney does Arabia' artifice about the whole place, but it's all done tastefully and is, not surprisingly, one of Dubai's most popular spots.

◉ Dubai Marina & Palm Jumeirah

In Dubai Marina you not only find bobbing yachts but also the phalanx of buttercream-yellow residential towers known as the Jumeirah Beach Residence (aka JBR) flanking a popular pedestrian walkway. Jutting into the Gulf is the Palm Jumeirah, home to luxury villas and resorts and anchored by the garish Atlantis – The Palm, which is served by a monorail.

The Walk at JBR
NEIGHBOURHOOD

(Map p296; Dubai Marina, along Jumeirah Beach Residence; ⊙ 10am-10pm Sat-Thu, 3.30-10pm Fri; Ⓜ Jumeirah Lakes Towers) In this city of air-conditioned malls, this attractive outdoor shopping and dining promenade was an immediate hit when it first opened in 2008.

Join locals and expats in strolling the 1.7km stretch, watching the world on parade from a pavement cafe, browsing the fashionable boutiques or ogling the shiny Ferraris, Maseratis and other fancy cars cruising by (Thursday and Friday nights).

Lost Chambers
AQUARIUM

(Map p296; ☑ 426 0000; Atlantis – The Palm, Palm Jumeirah; adult/child Dh100/70; ⊙ 10am-11pm; monorail Aquaventure) This fantastical labyrinth of underwater halls, passageways and fish tanks recreates the legend of the lost city of Atlantis. Some 65,000 exotic marine creatures inhabit 20 aquariums, where rays flutter and jellyfish dance, moray eels lurk, and pretty but poisonous lionfish float. The centrepiece is the massive Ambassador Lagoon.

🏃 Activities

Wild Wadi Water Park
WATER PARK

(Map p296; ☑ 348 4444; www.wildwadi.com; Jumeirah Rd, next to Jumeirah Beach Hotel; admission over/under 110cm Dh220/175; ⊙ 10am-6pm Nov-Feb, to 7pm Mar-May, Sep & Oct, to 8pm Jun Aug; Ⓜ Mall of the Emirates) When the kids grow weary of the beach, you'll score big time by taking them to Wild Wadi. Over a dozen ingeniously interconnected rides follow a vague theme about Arabian adventurer

---

OPEN DOORS, OPEN MINDS

Such is the enlightened motto of the **Sheikh Mohammed Centre for Cultural Understanding** (Map p292; ☑ 353 6666; www.cultures.ae; Al Mussalah Rd, eastern edge of Al Fahidi Historical Neighbourhood; centre free, breakfast/lunch Dh60/70; ⊙ 8am-6pm Sun-Thu, 9am-1pm Sun; Ⓜ Al Fahidi), a unique institution founded by Sheikh Mohammed in 1995 to build bridges between cultures and help visitors and expats understand the traditions and customs of the UAE. Aside from guided tours of the Al Fahidi Historical Neighbourhood and Jumeirah Mosque, the centre also hosts a hugely popular **Cultural Breakfast** (admission Dh60; ⊙ 10am Mon & Wed) and a **Cultural Lunch** (admission Dh70; ⊙ 1pm Sun & Thu) where you get a chance to meet, ask questions of and exchange ideas with nationals while tasting delicious homemade Emirati food. Book ahead.

New Dubai

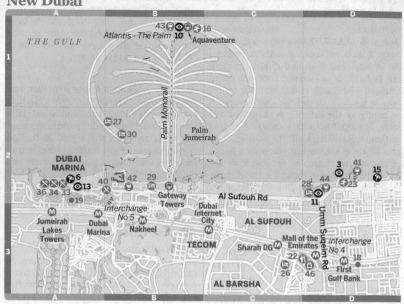

UNITED ARAB EMIRATES DUBAI

New Dubai

Juha and his friend Sinbad the Sailor who get shipwrecked together. There are plenty of gentle rides for tots, plus a big-wave pool, a white-water rapids 'river' and the 32m-high Jumeirah Sceirah slide where you can reach speeds of 80km/h. Kids must be at least 110cm tall for some of the more wicked rides. Note that from April to October, the park is open for women and children only on Thursday evening.

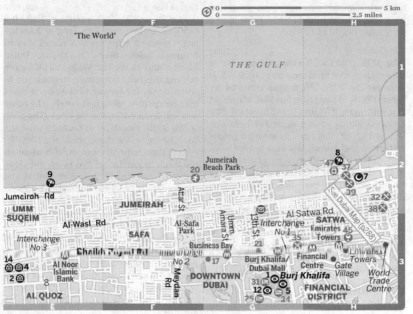

Aquaventure   WATER PARK

(Map p296; ☑426 0000; www.atlantisthepalm.
com; Atlantis – The Palm, Palm Jumeirah; over/un-
der 120cm Dh225/180; ⊙10am-sunset; monorail
Aquaventure) Adrenaline rushes are guaranteed at this water park at the Atlantis hotel.
The centrepiece is the 27.5m-high Ziggurat
(great views!), the launch pad for seven
slides, including the most wicked of them
all: Leap of Faith, a near-vertical plunge into

a shark-infested lagoon, albeit protected by a transparent tunnel. Some rides have a minimum height of 120cm.

Ski Dubai   SKIING
(Map p296; ☑ 409 4000; www.skidxb.com; Mall of the Emirates; adult/child snow park Dh100/50, ski slope per 2hr Dh180/150, penguin encounter per person Dh175; ☺ 10am-11pm Sun-Wed, to midnight Thu, 9am-midnight Fri, 9am-11pm Sat; Ⓜ Mall of the Emirates) Skiing in the desert? Where else but in Dubai? The city's most incongruous attraction, Ski Dubai, is a faux winter wonderland built right into the gargantuan Mall of the Emirates. It comes complete with ice sculptures and live penguins, a tiny sledding hill, five ski runs (the longest being 400m) and a Freestyle Zone with jumps and rails.

The chemical-free snow, generated by snow guns at night, is surprisingly velvety. Admission includes all gear except gloves and hats, for hygiene reasons; these are available for sale (gloves from Dh10, hats Dh30).

🖝 Tours

Big Bus Company   BUS TOUR
(☑ 389 1600; www.bigbustours.com; 24hr ticket adult/child Dh220/100, 48hr Dh295/130) The 'hop on, hop off' city tours aboard open-topped double-decker buses are a good way for Dubai first-timers to get their bearings. Buses run on two interlinking routes, making 21 stops at malls, beaches and landmarks and also include such extras as a souq walking tour and a dhow cruise. Tickets are sold online, on the bus, at kiosks in malls and at hotels. There's also a two-hour Night Tour (adult/child Dh125/75) leaving Dubai Mall at 7.30pm.

Wonder Bus Tours   BUS TOUR
(Map p288; ☑ 359 5656; www.wonderbusdubai.net; BurJuman mall, Bur Dubai; adult/child Dh130/85; Ⓜ BurJuman) Offers a combined city and creek tour aboard an amphibious bus with live commentary and twice daily departures from BurJuman mall.

easytour   BUS TOUR
(Map p288; ☑ 331 1399; http://easytour.ae; BurJuman mall, Bur Dubai; adult/child Dh140/70; ☺ 9am & 2.30pm; Ⓜ BurJuman) This four-hour tour in an open-top bus includes live narration, free soft drinks, a walking tour of Dubai Mall and admission to Dubai Museum. Departs twice daily from BurJuman mall. A two-hour Night Tours departs at 8pm (adult/child Dh100/60).

Dubai Ferry   BOAT TOUR
(Map p296; ☑ 800 9090; www.rta.ae; adult/child Dh50/25; ☺ 11am, 5pm, 7pm, 9pm; Ⓜ Dubai Marina) One-hour trips on two routes aboard futuristic-looking boats. One departs Dubai Marina and skirts The Walk at JBR before circling the Palm Jumeirah, treating you to stunning skyline views and close-up peeks of luxe beachfront villas and hotels. The other sets sail from Al Ghubaiba dock (Map p292; ☑ 800 9090; www.rta.ae; Al Ghubaiba water station, Shindagha Waterfront; adult/child Dh50/25; ☺ tours 11am, 5pm, 7pm, 9pm; Ⓜ Al Ghubaiba) on the creek in Bur Dubai and takes you along the coast past the QE2 in Port Rashid and the Jumeirah beaches. Ten-passenger minimum.

✯✯ Festivals & Events

Dubai Shopping Festival   SHOPPING
(www.mydsf.com) From mid-January to mid-February hordes of global bargain-hunters descend upon Dubai and the city is abuzz with concerts, fireworks and other special events. Repeats in July as 'Dubai Summer Surprises'.

Art Dubai   ART
(www.artdubai.ae) Art is booming in Dubai, as reflected in the growing number of artist studios and galleries. This late-March art show at Madinat Jumeirah is a prestigious showcase for the latest talents and trends in creative expression in the region.

Dubai World Cup   HORSE RACE
(www.dubaiworldcup.com) In late March/early April Dubai's racing season culminates in the world's richest horse race but, with no betting allowed, attention turns to the loony fashion-free-for-all of the attendees.

Dubai International Film Festival   FILM
(DIFF; www.dubaifilmfest.com) December sees this noncompetitive cine-showcase of the latest international indie flicks and new releases from around the Arab world and the Indian subcontinent.

🛏 Sleeping

When picking a place to stay in Dubai, identify what type of experience you're most keen to have, then base yourself in the area that best reflects your expectations in order to minimise time spent on the road. In other words, if you want to centre your explorations on Dubai Creek, the souqs and heritage areas, stay in Deira or Bur Dubai. For an immersion in Dubai's cutting-edge urbanity, find a place near Downtown Dubai. And if the beach beckons, head to Jumeirah or Dubai Marina.

Deira & Bur Dubai

Dubai Youth Hostel　　　　　HOSTEL **$**
(Map p288; ☑ 298 8151/61; www.uaeyha.com; 39 Al-Nahda Rd, btwn Lulu Hypermarket & Al-Bustan Centre, Al Qusais; dm/s/d/tr incl breakfast HI members Dh90/170/200/270, nonmembers Dh100/190/230/300; ⊙reception 24hr; @☒; ⓂStadium) Dubai's only hostel is north of the airport, far from most Dubai attractions but only a short walk from a metro station. It has a great range of facilities, including a pool, tennis court, coffee shop and laundry. Private rooms in the newer wing (Hostel A) come with TV, refrigerator and bathrooms, but amenities in the four-bed dorms in the older wings (Hostels B and C) are minimal.

Riviera Hotel　　　　　　　HOTEL **$$**
(Map p292; ☑ 222 2131; www.rivierahotel dubai. com; Baniyas Rd; r from Dh600; @☎; ⓂUnion) The Riviera's updated rooms are a delight with their soothing colour scheme, plush carpeting and classy slate grey and cream bathrooms. Those in front are noisier but have creek views. No alcohol.

★XVA Hotel　　　　BOUTIQUE HOTEL **$$**
(Map p292; ☑ 353 5383; www.xvahotel.com; off Al Fahidi St, Bur Dubai; d incl breakfast Dh600-800; ☎; ⓂAl Fahidi) This classy oasis around three courtyards gives you the feeling of staying in an authentic Arabian guesthouse. Each of the seven rooms was designed by a different artist and sports Arabesque flourishes, traditional furniture and rich colours. Amenities include a fridge and water cooker but no TV.

Arabian Courtyard Hotel & Spa　　HOTEL **$$**
(Map p292; ☑ 351 9111; www.arabiancourtyard.com; Al Fahidi St; r from Dh650; @☒; ⓂAl Fahidi) This gracefully aging hotel is an excellent launch pad for city explorers and a good-value pick in a central location. The Arabian theme extends from the turbaned lobby staff to the design flourishes in 173, mostly decent-sized, rooms. Get a top-floor one for views of the creek. Best of the six-pack of restaurants is Mumtaz Mahal for delightful Indian fare and nightly entertainment.

Golden Sands
Hotel Apartments　　HOTEL, APARTMENT **$$**
(Map p288; ☑ 355 5553; www.goldensandsdubai. com; off Al-Mankhool Rd; studio apt from Dh325; @☎☒; ⓂBurJuman) Golden Sands gets kudos for being a pioneer of the hotel apartment concept in Dubai and remains one of the best-value stays. The 750 studios, one- and two-bedroom apartments are spread over 12 standalone buildings behind the BurJuman mall. There are numerous other hotel apartments in the same area as well.

Orient Guest House　　BOUTIQUE HOTEL **$$**
(Map p292; ☑ 351 9111; www.orientguesthouse. com; off Al Fahidi St; d Dh600-650; ☎; ⓂAl Fahidi) Tucked into the historic Al Fahidi quarter, this boutique hotel captures the feeling of old Dubai. Rooms face a central courtyard, keeping light and heat at bay, and feature traditional wooden furniture and delicate chandeliers. The bathrooms are tiny and the pillows thin, but the charming service and romantic vibe more than compensate.

Downtown Dubai

Al Manzil Hotel　　　　　　HOTEL **$$**
(Map p296; ☑ 428 5888, www.almanzilhotel.ae; Emaar Blvd; r from Dh900; @☎☒; ⓂBurj Khalifa/Dubai Mall) Arabesque meets mid-century modern at Al Manzil, where rooms whip vanilla, chocolate and orange hues into a sophisticated style sorbet. The open-plan rooms may not be for the ultramodest, but the giant rainfall showerheads and free-standing tub are tempting nonetheless.

Address Downtown Dubai　　LUXURY HOTEL **$$$**
(Map p296; ☑ 436 8888; www.theaddress.com; Emaar Blvd; r from Dh1400; @☎☒; ⓂBurj Khalifa/Dubai Mall) The Address embodies all Dubai has to offer: beauty, style, glamour, sexiness and ambition. The oversized rooms are dressed in rich woods and tactile fabrics and endowed with killer views and the latest communication devices. And if that's not enough, the 24-hour gym and five-tiered infinity pool beckon.

Palace – The Old Town　　LUXURY HOTEL **$$$**
(Map p296; ☑ 428 7888; www.thepalace-dubai. com; Emaar Blvd, Old Town Island; r from Dh1500; @☎☒; ⓂBurj Khalifa/Dubai Mall) City explorers with a romantic streak will be utterly enchanted by this luxe blend of old-world class and Arabic aesthetics. Retire to chic and understated rooms styled in soothing earth tones, and wave goodnight to Burj Khalifa,

the world's tallest tower, from your balcony overlooking Dubai Fountain.

Jumeirah & Umm Suqeim

This section also includes a couple of lower-priced properties inland, near the Mall of the Emirates.

Centro Barsha　　　　　　　HOTEL **$$**
(Map p296; ☑704 0000; www.rotana.com; Al Barsha; d from Dh500; @ 🛜 🏊; Ⓜ Sharaf) An easy 10-minute walk from the Mall of the Emirates, this basic but good-value hotel has snug, contemporary rooms hued in soft yellows, creams and browns and outfitted with features like desks, flatscreen TVs and abstract art. There's a comfy cocktail bar, a

AL QUOZ – DUBAI'S GALLERY QUARTER

Abu Dhabi may try to hog the UAE culture mantle, but it's brash Dubai that is increasingly becoming key to keeping tabs on what hot in Middle Eastern art. Fueling the boom is the Art Dubai (p298) art fair, international galleries and a growing local art scene. The most cutting-edge galleries are in Al Quoz, a dusty and chaotic industrial area south of Sheikh Zayed Rd between Downtown Dubai and the Mall of the Emirates. Most are tucked away in nondescript buildings and dusty warehouses with a major hub being the **Alserkal Avenue** (Map p296; www.alserkalavenue.com; 8th Avenue; Ⓜ First Gulf Bank) complex. Roughly 20 galleries have taken advantage of the high-ceilinged warehouses and turned them into pristine, white-walled art spaces, and there are plans to double the compound by 2014. Here's a short list of our Al Quoz favourites.

➜ **Gallery Isabelle van den Eynde** (Map p296; ☑323 5052; www.ivde.net; Alserkal Avenue, Unit 17; ☺10am-7pm Sat-Thu) This innovative gallery has lifted some of the Middle East's most promising talent from obscurity into the spotlight. The distorted photography of Iranian-born Ramin Haerizadeh and Cairo-based Lara Baladi's mythology-laced installations, videos and collages are among the works that have attracted collectors and the curious since the space opened in 2005.

➜ **Green Art Gallery** (Map p296; ☑346 9305; www.gagallery.com; Alserkal Avenue, Unit 28, 8th & 17th Sts; ☺10am-7pm Sat-Thu) This gallery dates back to 1995 and has since been a key player in the promotion of local artists in the region. Typical exhibitions include a solo show of works by renowned Turkish photographer Nazif Topcuoglu, and a seven-channel video installation entitled Balloons on the Sea by Turkish artist Hale Tenger, which was voted one of the best international shows of 2011 by leading contemporary art magazine *Artforum*.

➜ **Carbon 12** (Map p296; ☑340 6016; carbon12dubai.com; Alserkal Avenue, Unit D37, 8th & 17th Sts; ☺11.30am-7pm Sat-Thu) This edgy gallery represents paintings, sculpture, photograph and media created by hand-picked, newly discovered talent as well as internationally established artists. The clear lines and minimalist vibe of the white-cube space offers a perfect setting for both large-scale and smaller pieces.

➜ **Third Line** (Map p296; ☑341 1367; www.thethirdline.com; Al Quoz, near 6th & Marabea St; ☺11am-7pm Sat-Thu) Run by a couple of talented young curators (Sunny Rahbar and Claudia Cellini), this is one of the city's most exciting spaces for contemporary Middle Eastern art. Artists represented often transcend the rules of traditional styles to create new forms, including emerging Emiratis and already-famous names like Iranian artist Farhad Moshiri, and controversial Iraqi artist Hayv Kahraman with her depictions of honour killings, gender and war.

➜ **Courtyard** (Map p296; ☑347 5050; www.courtyard-uae.com; 6a St) This cultural complex wraps around its eponymous courtyard, flanked by an eccentric hodgepodge of buildings that makes it look like a miniature movie-studio backdrop: here an Arab fort, there a Moorish facade or an Egyptian tomb. It's the brainchild of Iranian expat artist Dariush Zandi, who also runs the bi-level gallery Total Arts at The Courtyard, specialising in Middle Eastern art. Other spaces are occupied by a cafe, artists' studios and various creative businesses.

couple of acceptable restaurants and a fitness centre, plus a rooftop pool.

★ **One&Only Royal Mirage** RESORT $$$
(Map p296; ☑ 399 9999; http://royalmirage.oneandonlyresorts.com; Al Sufouh Rd; r from Dh2600; @ 🛜 🛋; M Nakheel) A class act all around, the Royal Mirage consists of three parts: the Moorish-style Palace, the Arabian Court, and the Residence & Spa, with its majestic spa and hammam (bathhouse). All rooms face the sea and are tastefully furnished and supremely comfortable. Spend your days meandering the palm-lined gardens, relaxing by the giant pool, or strolling along the 1km private beach. The bars and restaurants are among Dubai's best. Minimum stays may apply during peak months.

Mina A'Salam, Madinat Jumeirah RESORT $$$
(Map p296; ☑ 366 8888; www.jumeirah.com; Al Sufouh Rd, Umm Suqeim; r from Dh2500; @ 🛜 🛋; M Mall of the Emirates) Huge, amenity-laden rooms with balconies overlooking the romantic jumble that is Madinat Jumeirah or the striking Burj Al Arab. Guests have the entire run of the place and adjacent sister property Al Qasr, including the pools, the private beach and the kids club. Rates include free admission to Wild Wadi Waterpark (p295).

🏨 Dubai Marina & Palm Jumeirah

★ **Jumeirah Zabeel Saray** LUXURY HOTEL $$$
(Map p296; ☑ 453 0000; www.jumeirah.com; West Crescent, Palm Jumeirah; r from Dh2500; @ 🛜 🛋; M Nakheel) Wits its domed ceiling, golden pillars, and jewel-like lamps, Zabeel Saray's lobby could easily be over-the-top, yet miraculously comes off classy and kitsch-free. Inspired by Ottoman palaces, the exotic decor transfers in more subtle ways to the rooms, where everything is calculated to take the edge off travel. Open up the balcony door to let in the ocean breezes and admire the sparkling Dubai skyline. The Talise Spa, too, is a supreme relaxation station, complete with a Turkish hammam and a saltwater lap pool. A great selection of restaurants, including the vaunted Al Nafoorah (p304), makes for content tummies. The hotel is a 20-minute (Dh30) cab ride away from the metro station.

One&Only The Palm BOUTIQUE HOTEL $$$
(Map p296; ☑ 440 1010; www.oneandonlyresorts.com; West Crescent, Palm Jumeirah; r from Dh3690; 🛜 🛋) The impressive skyline of New Dubai looms just across the water, yet this romantic and mega-posh boutique resort is about as far away from the hubbub as you can get without leaving the city. Exuding the private feel of an elegant estate, One&Only The Palm has rambling gardens, a vast pool and Moorish-influenced rooms daubed in cheerful turquoise and purple. Naturally, rooms are outfitted with all requisite 21st-century tech touches. When you're ready to get back to the 'real world', there's a free boat shuttle to the sister property One&Only Royal Mirage on the mainland from the private marina.

🍴 Eating

Deira & Bur Dubai

Bur Dubai has some classy cafes with heritage flair, while Deira's ethnic street scene is unsurpassed. Snag a pavement table beneath flickering neon, soak up the local colour and fill up for under Dh20.

XVA Café CAFE $
(Map p292; ☑ 353 5383; www.xvahotel.com/cafe; off Al Fahidi St, Al Fahidi Historical Neighbourhood; mains Dh20-35; ⏱ 9am-7pm Sat-Thu year-round, also 10am-5pm Fri Nov-Apr; 🍽; M Al Fahidi) Escape Dubai's bustle at this artsy courtyard cafe where the menu eschews meat in favour of such offerings as eggplant burger, tuna salad and *morjardara* (rice topped with sautéed veggies and yogurt). The mint-lemonade is perfect on a hot day. Gordon Ramsay is said to be a fan.

Baithal Ravi PAKISTANI $
(Map p292; Al-Mussalah St; mains Dh15-40; ⏱ 24hr; M Al Fahidi) The full complement of classic subcontinental Indian fare packs comfort and complexity in this bi-level restaurant handily located next to Al Fahidi metro station. The creamy chicken *handi* (pot) gets top marks.

Local House ARABIC $$
(Map p292; ☑ 354 0705; www.localhousedubai.com; Al Fahidi St; mains Dh30-55; ⏱ 11am-11pm; M Al Fahidi) Lovely courtyard in a traditional house with camel burger on the menu.

LOCAL KNOWLEDGE

DIPPING WITHOUT DIRHAMS

If you're not staying at a beachfront five-star hotel but want to swim in the Gulf, head to one of these public beaches:

➡ **Jumeirah Open Beach** (Map p296; next to Dubai Marine Beach Resort & Spa; Ⓜ Trade Centre) `FREE` – with kiosks, toilets and showers.

➡ **Jumeirah Beach Park** (Map p296; ✆ 349 2555; Jumeirah Beach Rd; per person/car Dh5/20; ⊙ 7am-11pm Sun-Wed, to 11.30pm Thu & Fri; Ⓜ Business Bay) – well-kept, with lifeguards, grassed picnic areas, barbecues, changing rooms and playgrounds.

➡ **Kite Beach** (Map p296; 3km north of the Burj al-Arab; Ⓜ Noor Islamic Bank) `FREE` – past Umm Suqeim Hospital, pristine but facility-free.

➡ **Umm Suqeim** (Map p296; btwn Jumeirah Beach Hotel & Kite Beach; Ⓜ First Gulf Bank) `FREE` – fabulous views of the Burj Al Arab, showers, changing rooms and a separate section for surfers.

➡ **Jumeirah Beach Residence Open Beach** (Map p296; Jumeirah Beach Residence; Ⓜ Dubai Marina) `FREE` – No facilities.

Arabian Tea House
CAFE **$$**
(Map p292; ✆ 353 5071; www.arabianteahouse.com; Al Fahidi St, Al Fahidi Historical Neighbourhood; mains Dh30-45; ⊙ 8am-10pm; Ⓜ Al Fahidi) A grand old tree and shaded cabanas provide cool respite at this charismatic cafe in the courtyard of an old Dubai house. The food is respectable cafe fare – salads, sandwiches, pasta, quiches – but it's the leafy, sun-dappled garden that makes this place so special. For a local treat, try the Arabic breakfast.

Al Mansour Dhow
INTERNATIONAL **$$$**
(Map p292; ✆ 222 7171; www.radissonblu.com/hotel-dubaideiracreek; Baniyas Rd, outside Radisson Blu Hotel; 2hr dinner cruise Dh195; ⊙ 8pm; Ⓜ Union) Don't expect culinary flights of fancy from the international buffet, but the romance factor of floating along the glittering creek on an old wooden dhow decorated with bands of twinkling lights should make up for any gustatorial lack of inspiration. After filling up, recline with a *sheesha* in the upper-deck lounge.

Shabestan
IRANIAN **$$$**
(Map p292; ✆ 222 7171; Baniyas Rd, Radisson Blu Hotel, Deira; mains Dh90-155; ⊙ 12.30-3.15pm & 7.30-11.15pm; Ⓜ Union, Baniyas Square) Reservations are essential at Dubai's top Persian outpost with creek views. Nibble on hot, fresh bread and homemade yoghurt while anticipating such flavour bombs as smoky *mizra ghasemi* (eggplant dip), tangy *fesenjan-ba morgh* (roast chicken in a pomegranate sauce) and vermicelli ice cream with saffron and rose water.

✗ Downtown Dubai

Expect to pay top dirham for first-rate culinary indulgences at five-star hotel restaurants or head to the Dubai Mall food court for a quick budget bite.

Baker & Spice
INTERNATIONAL **$$**
(Map p296; ✆ 425 2240; http://bakerandspice.com; Souq Al Bahar; mains Dh45-145; ⊙ 8am-11pm; 🖥; Ⓜ Burj Khalifa/Dubai Mall) This is one of the best healthy-eating options in town, no matter whether you're keen on fresh croissants, crisp salads or grilled fish or chicken. There are new menu choices daily, and many dishes are homemade using local and, where possible, organic ingredients.

More
INTERNATIONAL **$$**
(Map p296; ✆ 339 8934; www.morecafe.biz; Dubai Mall, ground fl, near Dubai Fountain; mains Dh30-70; ⊙ 8am-11.30pm Sun-Thu, to midnight Fri & Sat; 🖥; Ⓜ Burj Khalifa/Dubai Mall) This jazzy, industrial-flavoured space draws a congenial mix of locals, expats and tourists. The menu hopscotches around the world, from Thai curries and Italian pastas to Dutch pancakes and fist-sized burgers. There are five more branches, including one at the Mall of the Emirates.

Na3Na3
MIDDLE EASTERN **$$**
(Map p296; ✆ 438 8888; www.theaddress.com; Emaar Blvd, Address Dubai Mall; lunch/dinner Dh120/140; ⊙ 6.30am-1am; Ⓜ Burj Khalifa/Dubai Mall) If you're new to Middle Eastern food, the bountiful and beautifully displayed buffet in this airy restaurant would be a good

place to start a culinary investigation. Resist the temptation to fill up on the delicious mezze (appetisers) so you can try some of the hot dishes and fresh breads streaming from the open kitchen. The curious name, by the way, means 'mint' in Arabic and is pronounced 'nana'.

Hoi An
VIETNAMESE $$$

(Map p296; ☑ 405 2703; www.shangri-la.com; Sheikh Zayed Rd, Shangri-La Hotel; mains Dh110-160; ⊗ 7pm-midnight; M Financial Centre) Teak latticework, plantation shutters and lazily rotating ceiling fans evoke a sensuous Colonial-era vibe at this upmarket French-Vietnamese restaurant where the flavours are lively and bright. Start with the crispy crab rolls, move on to lotus leaf-wrapped sea bass or mud crab with sweet Thai basil and wrap up with chocolate fondant with raspberries.

✕ Jumeirah & Umm Suqeim

Jumeirah restaurants draw wealthy locals and tourists. Those at Madinat Jumeirah generally have good-quality food and are the most scenic, if pricey. For local flavour and superb ethnic eats, head inland to Satwa.

★ Ravi
PAKISTANI $

(Map p296; ☑ 331 5353; Al Satwa Rd, Satwa; mains Dh15-25; ⊗ 24hr; M World Trade Centre) Everyone from cabbies to five-star chefs flock to this legendary Pakistani eatery where you dine like a prince and pay like a pauper. Loosen that belt for heaping helpings of kick-ass curries, succulent grilled meats, perky dal and fresh naan.

Al Mallah
LEBANESE $

(Map p296; ☑ 398 4723; Al Diyafah St, Satwa; dishes from Dh5; ⊗ 6am-4am Sat-Thu, noon-4am Fri; M World Trade Centre) Serving some of the most delicious *shwarmas* around, along with excellent Lebanese food, this busy eatery with shaded outdoor seating is a great choice for a quick snack.

Saladicious
CAFE $$

(Map p296; ☑ 345 5822; www.saladicious.com; Al-Hudheiba Rd; mains Dh25-60; ⊗ 830am-11.30pm; M World Trade Centre) They've got salads, sure, and creative ones at that, but there are so many more tastebud temptations on the menu of this upbeat cafe, from robust risottos to velvety soups and perky pastas. Every-

RAS AL KHOR WILDLIFE

Fight in the middle of to...
life Sanctuary (☑ 6...
4pm Sat-Thu) FREE...
...n winter, but...
of salt flats...
the san...
The...
bi...

UNITED ARAB E...

304

...ES DUBAI

Noodle...
(Map...
Souk Madinat Jumeirah, Al Sufouh Rd; mains Dh45-60; ⊗ noon-midnight; M Mall of the Emirates) At this reliable, always-packed, pan-Asian joint everyone sits at long wooden communal tables and orders by ticking dishes on a tear-off menu pad. There's enough variety – from curry laksa to pad thai to roast duck – to please disparate tastes. Beer and wine available. There are five other locations, including at Dubai Mall and BurJuman Mall.

The Meat Co
STEAKHOUSE $$$

(Map p296; ☑ 368 6040; www.themeat.com; Madinat Jumeirah; burgers Dh55-135, mains Dh150-500; ⊗ noon-11.30pm; M Mall of the Emirates) This canalside carnivore favourite – with Burj Al Arab as a backdrop no less – takes its meat seriously with super-aged Angus and melt-in-your-mouth Wagyu, all perfectly prepared just the way you like it. Even the burgers are gourmet affairs, especially the rib meat pattie with garlicky portobello mushrooms.

✕ Dubai Marina & Palm Jumeirah

Plenty of high-end eating in the hotels plus reasonably priced fare with sidewalk seating along The Walk at JBR.

Bombay by the Bay
INDIAN $$

(Map p296; ☑ 429 7979; The Walk at JBR, near Rimal Tower 5; mains Dh22-58; ⊗ noon-3pm & 6-11.15pm; M Jumeirah Lakes Towers) This breezy upstairs restaurant offers a festival of flavours from around the subcontinent. Try to get a table on the balcony for views of The Walk and the sea.

wn, about 5km south of Downtown Dubai, **Ras Al Khor Wild-**
06 6822; www.wildlife.ae; cnr Oud Metha Rd & Ras Al Khor St; ⊙9am-
is an amazing nature preserve. Pretty pink flamingos steal the show
fact avid birdwatchers can spot more than 250 species in this pastiche
intertidal mudflats, mangroves and lagoons. At the mouth of Dubai Creek,
tuary is also an important stop over on the East African–West Asian Flyway.
are three hides (platforms) with fantastically sharp binoculars for close-ups of the
ds without disturbing them. The flamingo roost is off the junction of Al Wasl and Oud
Metha Rds.

MIRATES DUBAI

Köşebaşi
TURKISH $$

(Map p296; ☑439 3788; www.kosebasi.com; The Walk at JBR; mains Dh23-55; Ⓜ Jumeirah Lakes Towers) Dishes at this Istanbul-based chain of Turkish grill restaurants sparkle with flavour and authenticity. Menu stars include Toros Salata, an inspired variation of tabbouleh dressed in pomegranate sauce, the handground lamb kebab and the *lahmacun*, a spicy stuffed Turkish pizza.

BiCE
ITALIAN $$$

(Map p296; ☑399 1111; The Walk at JBR, Hilton Dubai Jumeirah; pastas Dh80-210, mains Dh150-220; ⊙noon-3pm & 7pm-midnight; Ⓜ Jumeirah Lakes Towers) This top Italian is often fully packed so book ahead. Head chef Cosimo embraces the honesty of the Italian table by letting just a few top-quality ingredients shine. Beef carpaccio, veal Milanese, homemade pasta, wild-mushroom risotto, linguini with seafood...there are few menu surprises but no one is complaining. The tiramisu is reputedly the best in town.

Toro Toro
SOUTH AMERICAN $$$

(Map p296; ☑399 8888; Al Sufouh Rd, Grosvenor Tower Two; small plates Dh60-115; ⊙7pm-2am Sat-Wed, to 3am Thu & Fri; Ⓜ Dubai Marina) The decor packs as much pizazz as the food at this popular restaurant helmed by star chef Richard Sandoval who mines pan-Latin richness in such dishes as *pollo estofado* (braised chicken) and *achiote* barbecue salmon. Everything comes on small plates, perfect for grazing and sharing. A sweeping menu of cocktails, cachaca and *copas* (wine) keep the bar hopping until the wee hours.

AL Nafoorah
LEBANESE $$$

(Map p296; ☑453 0444; www.jumeirah.com; Jumeirah Zabeel Saray, West Crescent, Palm Jumeirah; mains Dh70-160; ⊙12.30-3pm & 7pm-2am Sun-Thu, all day Fri & Sat) With its floor-to-ceiling archways, dark-wood carvings and elegantly set tables, Al Nafoorah is poised to take you on a culinary magic carpet ride. Nibble on a three-tier platter of olives, pickles, nuts and carrots while perusing the huge menu, perhaps settling on a selection of mezze (with great hummus) followed by a classic mixed grill or seafood platter.

101 Lounge & Bar
MEDITERRANEAN $$$

(Map p296; ☑440 1030; thepalm.oneandonlyresorts.com; West Crescent, Palm Jumeirah, One&Only The Palm; mains Dh80-240, tapas selection of 3/6/9 Dh90/160/220; ⊙11am-1am) With a phalanx of Dubai's high-rises dramatically unfolding across the water, it may be hard to concentrate on the food at this buzzy pavilion hovering above the private marina of the ultra-swish One&Only The Palm resort. Come for nibbles and cocktails in the bar or go for the full dinner experience (seafood ravioli, roast cod fish, mixed seafood grill) while a resident DJ plays chill tunes in the background.

Self-Catering

There are several major supermarket chains with branches throughout town. **Carrefour** (Map p288; ☑295 1600; Baniyas Rd, Deira City Centre; ⊙9am-midnight Sat-Wed, to 1am Thu & Fri) has the biggest selection but the quality tends to be better (and prices higher) at **Spinneys** (Map p288; ☑351 1777; www.spinneys-dubai.com; Trade Centre Rd; ⊙24hr; Ⓜ Al Karama). Both stock many products from the UK, North America and Australia and are predictably popular with Western expats; they even have separate 'pork rooms' that are off-limits to Muslims. **Choithram** (Map p292; ☑223 2488; www.choithrams.com; Al Nasser Sq, Dubai Tower; ⊙24hr; Ⓜ Baniyas Sq) is cheaper and caters more to the Indian and Pakistani communities. Many markets are open until midnight; some never close.

🍸 Drinking & Nightlife

Rooftop Bar
BAR

(Map p296; ✆399 9999; Al Sufouh Rd, Arabian Court, One&Only Royal Mirage, Umm Suqeim; ⏲5pm-1am; Ⓜ Nakheel) The fabric-draped nooks, cushioned banquettes, Moroccan lanterns and Oriental carpets make this candle-lit outdoor bar one of Dubai's most sublime spots. Come at sunset to watch the sky change colours, or after dinner when it gets buzzy.

Rooftop at Madinat
BAR

(Map p296; ✆366 6730; Al Sufouh Rd, Souq Madinat Jumeirah; ⏲7am-2am Sun-Wed, to 3am Thu & Fri; Ⓜ Mall of the Emirates) Not to be confused with the lounge at the Royal Mirage, this alfresco party pen above the Trilogy club has killer views of the Burj Al Arab, cosy day beds for lounging and some of the finest DJ nights in town.

QDs
BAR, CLUB

(Map p288; ✆295 6000; Dubai Creek Golf & Yacht Club, Deira; ⏲6pm-2am; Ⓜ GGICO) Watch the ballet of illuminated dhows floating by while sipping cosmos or puffing on a *shee-sha* pipe at this creekside lounge. Oriental carpets and cushions set an inviting mood on the raised centre ring.

Neos
BAR

(Map p296; ✆436 8927; Address Downtown Dubai, Emaar Blvd; ⏲6pm-2am; Ⓜ Burj Khalifa/Dubai Mall) It takes two lifts to get up to this highest bar in town, a glamour vixen where you can mix with the posh set 63 floors above Dubai Fountain.

Irish Village
PUB

(Map p288; ✆282 4750; www.irishvillage.ae; 31 St, Al Garhoud; ⏲11am-1.30am; Ⓜ GGICO) Better known as 'the IV', this always-buzzy pub with its faux Irish main street facade is popular with expats for its pondside 'beer garden'. No happy hour, but there's Guinness and Kilkenny on tap. Not far from the airport, next to Dubai Tennis Stadium and the Aviation Club.

Bahri Bar
COCKTAIL BAR

(Map p296; ✆04-366 6730; Al Sufouh Rd, Mina A'Salam Hotel, Madinat Jumeirah; ⏲4pm-2am Sat-Wed, to 3am Thu & Fri; Ⓜ Mall of the Emirates) Cocktails with a mesmerising view of the Burj Al Arab are the main draw at this polished grown-up bar. Come early to score a comfy sofa on the carpet-covered verandah. Live band after 9.30pm.

360°
BAR, CLUB

(Map p296; ✆406 8769; Jumeirah Rd, Jumeirah Beach Hotel, Umm Suqeim; ⏲6pm-2am Tue-Thu, 4pm-2am Fri & Sat; Ⓜ Mall of the Emirates) Capping a long pier, 360° has been through a makeover but still delivers the same magical views of the Burj Al Arab. On weekends there's a guest list and the place is crawling with shiny happy hotties, but other nights are mellower.

★Trilogy
CLUB

(Map p296; Al Sufouh Rd, Souk Madinat Jumeirah; ⏲9pm-late; Ⓜ Mall of the Emirates) With three floors of Moroccan-inspired decor and a sumptuous gold-and-silver colour scheme, this is high-octane dance spot for illustrious party people, including the occasional celeb. It's right by the entrance to Souk Madinat.

Barasti Bar
BAR, CLUB

(Map p296; ✆399 3333; Al Sufouh Rd, Le Meridien Mina Seyahi Beach Resort, Dubai Marina; ⏲11am-2am; Ⓜ Nakheel) Seaside Barasti is the top spot for laid-back sundowners on a hot afternoon. No need to dress up – you can head straight here after a day at the beach. Not a place for quiet time; on weekends there can be up to 3000 revellers.

Nasimi Beach
CLUB

(Map p296; ✆426 2626; Atlantis, The Palm Jumeirah; ⏲9am-1am, to 2am Fri; monorail Aquaventure) The Atlantis' spin on Barasti draws a more upmarket crowd to its fantastic beachside setting. Spend the day lounging on a beach bed, then hit the dancefloor after sunset. Friday nights are buzziest, when international DJs hit the decks.

Zinc
CLUB

(Map p296; ✆331 1111; Sheikh Zayed Rd, Crowne Plaza Hotel, Downtown Dubai; ⏲7pm-3am; Ⓜ Financial Centre) This reliable stand-by has a killer sound system and plays R&B, popular tunes and house for a crowd that just likes to have fun without the pretence, including lots of cabin crew.

☆ Entertainment

Jambase
LIVE MUSIC

(Map p296; ✆366 6730; Al Sufouh Rd, Souq Madinat Jumeirah, Jumeirah; ⏲7pm-2am Tue-Sat; Ⓜ Mall of the Emirates) If you enjoy dining, drinking and dancing without changing location, this moody basement supper club (mains Dh110-210) should fit the bill. The ambience gets increasingly energetic as blood-alcohol levels rise and the band moves

DUBAI FOR CHILDREN

Many hotels have kids clubs and activities but there's also plenty of diversions around town. Both tots and teens can keep cool on the rides and slides at **Wild Wadi Water Park** (p295) or **Aquaventure** (p297), on the slopes at **Ski Dubai** (p298) or the **Dubai Ice Rink** (p294) at Dubai Mall. For fish encounters, head to **Lost Chambers** (p295) at the Atlantis – The Palm or the **Dubai Aquarium & Underwater Zoo** (p294) in Dubai Mall. Just about every mall also has an indoor amusement park such as **Magic Planet** at Mall of the Emirates and **Sega Republic** (p294) at Dubai Mall. Little kids may enjoy playing grown-ups at **KidZania** (p294), also at Dubai Mall. **Peekaboo** (www.peekaboo.ae) has creches and play centres for children aged zero to seven at several shopping malls. A good online resource is www.uae4kidz.biz.

Formula and nappies (diapers) are widely available at supermarkets and pharmacies. Children under five travel for free on public transport.

on from mellow jazz to soul, R&B, Motown and other high-energy sounds.

Dubai Community Theatre & Arts Centre
THEATRE
(DUCTAC; Map p296; ☑ 341 4777; www.ductac.org; Sheikh Zayed Rd, Mall of the Emirates; Ⓜ Mall of the Emirates) This nonprofit venue puts on crowd-pleasing quality theatre, dance, movie screenings, art shows and concerts. Much support is given to Emirati talent.

Madinat Theatre
THEATRE
(Map p296; ☑ 366 6546; www.madinattheatre.com; Al Sufouh Rd, Souq Madinat Jumeirah ; Ⓜ Mall of the Emirates) This handsome 442-seat theatre feeds the cravings of Dubai's culture crowd with eclectic programming ranging from drama to comedy and musicals.

Vox Mall of the Emirates
CINEMA
(Map p296; ☑ 341 4222; www.voxcinemas.com; Sheikh Zayed Rd, Mall of the Emirates, Al Barsha; tickets Dh35, 3D films Dh50; Ⓜ Mall of the Emirates) Blockbuster-heavy multiplex also has private screening rooms with extra-comfy chairs and food and drink service.

Reel Cinemas
CINEMA
(Map p296; ☑ 449 1988; 2nd fl, Dubai Mall, Downtown Dubai; tickets Dh35, 3D films Dh45, Platinum Movie Suite Dh130; Ⓜ Burj Khalifa/Dubai Mall) Pre-assigned seats, THX sound and a staggering 22 screens – including the superluxe Platinum Movies Suites, 3D screening rooms and the Picturehouse arthouse cinema – make Reel one of the top flick magnets in town.

Meydan Racecourse
HORSE RACING
(☑ 327 0077; www.meydan.ae/racecourse.asp; 5km southwest of Sheikh Zayed Rd; general admission free; prices vary for entry into premium seating sections; ☺ Nov-Mar; Ⓜ Business Bay) The horses are fun but there's also great people-watching on race day at this state-of-the-art stadium south of Downtown Dubai. General admission is free and the dress code is casual. Check the website for the racing schedule. Doors open at 5pm, races start at 6.30pm, usually on Thursdays, sometimes on Saturdays. The season culminates in late March with the elite Dubai World Cup, the world's richest horse race (US$10 million in total prize money).

🔒 Shopping

Dubai has just about perfected the art of the mall, which is the de facto, air-conditioned 'town commons', the place to go with the family and friends to chat, eat, shop and take in some entertainment. For local colour, head to the souqs in Deira and Bur Dubai, which can be a font for souvenirs, as is tourist-geared Souq Madinat Jumeirah. Jumeirah Beach Rd (near the Jumeirah Mosque) has some indie boutiques with designer labels, while Karama is famous for offering knock-off versions of the same.

Dubai Mall
MALL
(Map p296; ☑ 362 7500; Emaar Blvd , Downtown Dubai; ☺ 10am-10pm Sun-Wed, to midnight Thu-Sat; 🛜; Ⓜ Burj Khalifa/Dubai Mall) Elegant if somewhat confusingly laid out, the world's largest mall has some 1200 outlets, a walk-through aquarium and an Olympic-sized ice rink (p294).

Mall of the Emirates
MALL
(Map p296; ☑ 409 9000; www.malloftheemirates.com; Sheikh Zayed Rd, Al Barsha; ☺ 10am-10pm Sun-Wed, to midnight Thu-Sat; Ⓜ Mall of the Emirates) Massive mall with 520 stores, a 14-screen multiplex cinema (p306), the Magic Planet family entertainment centre,

a community theatre (p306) and Ski Dubai (p298).

Deira City Centre   MALL

(Map p288; ✆ 295 1010; www.deiracitycentre.com; Baniyas Rd; ⊙10am-10pm Sun-Wed, to midnight Thu-Sat; Ⓜ City Centre) Older, low-key mall with 370 shops is especially good for high-street fashions and electronics; also has a Carrefour supermarket, a Magic Planet family entertainment area and an 11-screen multiplex.

BurJuman   MALL

(Map p288; ✆ 352 0222; www.burjuman.com; Sheikh Khalifa Bin Zayed St, Bur Dubai; ⊙10am-10pm Sat-Wed. to midnight Thu & Fri; ⏾; Ⓜ BurJu-man) Midsize mall with high-end labels and an easy-to-navigate floorplan, also a tourist office booth.

Souq Madinat Jumeirah   SHOPPING CENTRE

(Map p296; ✆ 366 8888; www.jumeirah.com; Madinat Jumeirah, Al Sufouh Rd; Ⓜ Mall of the Emirates) More a themed shopping mall than a traditional Arabian market, this souq is a bit of a tourist trap, with prices that are considerably higher than they are in real souqs. Still, it's an attractive spot for a wander.

Karama Shopping Strip   SHOPPING CENTRE

(Map p288; 18B St, off Sheikh Rashid Rd, Bur Dubai; Ⓜ Al Karama) The place to come for knock-off designer sunglasses, clothing and handbags. Great prices on pashminas, but check the quality. Also souvenirs and imported handicrafts. Haggling should get you at least 30% off the asking price.

Bateel   FOOD

(Map p288; www.bateel.com; BurJuman Mall; Ⓜ BurJuman Centre) Bateel's scrumptious date chocolates and truffles are made from 120 varieties using European chocolate-making techniques. Staff are happy to give you a sample before you buy. There are other branches in most malls, including Dubai Mall, Deira City Centre and Souk Al Bahar.

Ajmal   BEAUTY

(Map p288; www.ajmalperfume.com; Deira City Centre; Ⓜ Deira City Centre) Ajmal stocks exotic Arabian essential oils and perfumes poured into exquisitely beautiful bottles, which make truly divine souvenirs. Other branches can be found all over the city, including at Mall of the Emirates, Dubai Mall and BurJuman.

S*uce   FASHION

(Map p296; ✆ 344 7270; http://shopatsauce.com; Village Mall, Jumeirah Beach Rd; ⊙10am-10pm Sat-Thu, 4-10pm Fri; Ⓜ Emirates Towers) Dubai's indie fashion pioneer, S*uce (pronounced 'sauce') keeps the style brigade looking sharp in top-tier denim, flirty frocks, sassy accessories, sexy sandals and deluxe tees by established and up-and-coming designers, some of them local. Other branches in Dubai Mall and Dubai Marina Mall.

ℹ Information

EMERGENCY

Ambulance (✆ 999, 998)

Fire (✆ 997)

Police (✆ 999)

Tourist Security Department (✆ 800 4438)

MEDICAL SERVICES

Pharmacies Hotline (✆ 223 2323) Pharmacies are generally open from 9am to 10pm but some are open 24/7. Call the hotline for details.

American Hospital (✆ 336 7777, emergency 309 6877; Oud Metha Rd, Bur Dubai; ⊙ walk-in clinic 10am-5pm) Private hospital with 24/7 ER and walk-in clinic (no appointment needed).

Dubai Hospital (✆ 219 5000; near Abu Baker Al Siddiq Rd & Al Khaleej Rd, Deira) One of the region's best government hospitals with 24/7 ER.

Rashid Hospital (✆ 337 4000; off Oud Metha Rd, Bur Dubai) Main hospital for emergencies, near Al Maktoum Bridge.

MONEY

ATMs are plentiful throughout the city. Reliable currency exchanges include **Al-Rostamani** (http://alrostamanigroup.ae) and **UAE Exchange** (✆ 229 7373; www.uaeexchange.com) with multiple branches around town, including major malls and the airport.

POST OFFICE

Central Post Office (✆ 337 1500; Za'abeel Rd, Karama; ⊙ 8am-8pm Sat-Thu, 5-9pm Fri) In Karama, between Zabeel and Umm Hurair Rds.

Jumeirah Post Office (✆ 04-344 2706; Al-Wasl Rd, near 13 St, Jumeirah; ⊙ 8am-8pm Sat-Thu, 5-9pm Fri)

TOURIST INFORMATION

Tourist Information (✆ 223 0000; www.definitelydubai.com) There are 24-hour information kiosks in Terminal 1 and 3 at Dubai International Airport as well as booths at **Deira City Centre**, **BurJuman**, **Wafi Mall**, **Ibn Battuta** and **Mercato Mall**, although the latter are frequently unstaffed.

ℹ Getting There & Away

AIR
Dubai International Airport (☎ 224 5555, flight enquiries 224 5777; www.dubaiairport. com) Busy air hub with three terminals and a famed duty-free selection. Terminal 3 is used exclusively by Emirates Airlines. Terminals are linked by shuttle buses operating 24/7 at 10-minute intervals.

BUS
The Roads and Transport Authority (p360) operates local buses within Dubai as well as inter-emirate routes. Buses are air-conditioned and dirt-cheap but can get crowded. Maps and timetables are available at the stations as well as online.

The two main stations are **Al Ittihad** (cnr Omar ibn al-Khattab & Al-Rigga Rds), next the Union metro station in Deira, and **Al Ghubaiba** (Al Ghubaiba Rd, Bur Dubai), opposite the Carrefour supermarket, in Bur Dubai.

Departures from Al Ittihad include:

DESTINATION	FARE (DH)	TIME (HR)	FREQUENCY
Ajman	7	1-1½	every 20 mins
Fujairah	25	25	every 45 mins
Ras Al Khaimah	20	25	every 45 mins
Sharjah	5	35	every 10 mins
Umm Al Quwain	10	45	every 45 mins

Note that only the Sharjah and Ajman services return passengers to Dubai. From the other towns, you have to return by local taxi or bus. Routes are generally served between 6am and 11pm.

Buses to Al Ain and Abu Dhabi leave from Al Ghubaiba station. There's also a 24-hour service to Sharjah with departures every 30 minutes between midnight and 6am.

Departures from Al Ghubaiba include:

DESTINATION	FARE (DH)	TIME (HR)	FREQUENCY
Abu Dhabi	25	2hr	every 20 mins
Al Ain	20	2hr	every 40 mins
Sharjah	7	40-50mins	every 20 mins

The Roads and Transport Authority (p360) also operates hourly buses to Hatta (Dh7, 2¼ hours) leaving from **Al Sabkha** (cnr Al-Sabkha St & Deira St, Deira) station in the heart of the Deira souqs.

CAR
Dubai has scores of car-rental agencies, from major global companies to no-name local businesses. The former may charge slightly more but you get peace of mind knowing that you can get full insurance and that they'll get you out of a fix if you need assistance.

Avis (☎ airport 224 5219, head office 04-295 7121; www.avis.com)

Budget (☎ airport 224 5192, head office 282 2727; www.budget-uae.com)

Europcar (☎ airport 224 5240, head office 339 4433; www.europcar-dubai.com)

Hertz (☎ 206 0206; www.hertzuae.com)

TAXI
Taxis to Sharjah and the other northern emirates incur a Dh20 surcharge. Shared taxi leave from Al Ghubaiba bus station and cost Dh20 to Sharjah and Dh50 to Abu Dhabi. Engaged cabs to Abu Dhabi range from Dh250 to Dh350, depending on distance and company. To order a taxi call the Dubai Taxi Corporation (p310).

ℹ Getting Around

Negotiating most of Dubai by foot, even combined with public transport, is highly challenging, not only because of the heat, but also due to the lack of pavements, traffic lights and pedestrian crossings. Most visitors get around town by taxi. The Dubai Metro is also an excellent mode of transport with two lines and sparkling-clean trains. Although bus lines offer good coverage, they are slow and have baffling timetables.

TO/FROM THE AIRPORT
Dubai Metro

The Red Line stops at Terminals 1 and 3. Luggage is limited to two pieces, one not exceeding 81cm by 58cm by 30cm and the other not exceeding 55cm by 38cm by 20cm. Getting caught with alcohol aboard (even if purchased at the airport duty-free shop) entails a Dh200 fine.

Taxi

Airport taxis have a starting meter of Dh20 and a per-kilometre charge of Dh1.71 (Dh25 plus Dh1.86 per kilometre for vans and 'ladies taxis', see p310). Sample fares:

DESTINATION	COST (DH)	TIME (MIN)
Deira Gold Souq	50	25
Bur Dubai	50	25
Downtown Dubai	60	25
Jumeirah, Umm Suqeim	80	35
Dubai Marina	90	45

Bus

Buses leave from Terminal 1 but they're comparatively slow and cumbersome. There is no luggage limit.

Useful lines include bus 4 to the **Gold Souq Bus Station** (off Al-Khor St, near Gold Souq, Deira) in Deira, and bus 42 which skirts the Mankhool hotel apartment area en route to Ghubaiba bus station (p308) in Bur Dubai. Both run every 30 minutes from around 5.30am to 11pm.

PUBLIC TRANSPORT

Dubai's local public transport is also operated by the RTA and consists of the Dubai Metro, buses, water buses and *abras* (water taxis).

Abra

Abras are motorised traditional wooden boats linking **Bur Dubai** and **Deira** across the creek on two routes:

Route 1 Bur Dubai Abra Station to **Deira Old Souq Abra Station**; daily between 5am and midnight.

Route 2 Dubai Old Souq Abra Station to Sabkha Abra Station around the clock.

Abras leave when full (around 20 passengers), which rarely takes more than a few minutes. The fare is Dh1 and you pay the driver halfway across the creek. Chartering your own *abra* costs Dh120 per hour.

Bus

RTA (p360) operates a clean, comfortable and air-conditioned bus network. The front of each bus is reserved for women and families. For information and trip planning call RTA or check the website.

From Saturday to Thursday, most routes operate at 15- to 20-minute intervals between 6am and 11.30pm. Friday service is less frequent and may start later and finish earlier. Night buses operate at 30-minute intervals in the interim.

Dubai Metro

Dubai Metro was inaugurated in 2010 and operates on two lines:

Red Line Links Rashidiya near Dubai International Airport to Jebel Ali past Dubai Marina, mostly paralleling Sheikh Zayed Rd

Green Line Links Al Qusais with Dubai Healthcare City

➡ Lines intersect at Union Square in Deira and at BurJuman Station in Bur Dubai. Trains are met by cabs and feeder buses to take you to your final destination.

➡ Trains run roughly every 10 minutes from 6am to 11pm Saturday to Thursday and 2pm to midnight on Friday.

➡ Each train consists of five cars. The front car is divided into a women-only section and a

'gold class' section where a double fare buys carpeted floor and leather seats.

➡ Mobile-phone service is available throughout as is wi-fi access for Dh10 per hour when paying with a credit card (less if you buy a prepaid scratch card).

Palm Monorail

The **Palm Monorail** (www.palm-monorail.com; one-way/return Dh15/25; ☺10am-10pm) is a driverless tram that runs along the trunk of the Palm Jumeirah between the Gateway station and the Atlantis Hotel in 10 minutes. It will eventually be linked to the Dubai Metro. It's a fun ride but taxis are no more expensive, even if you're travelling alone.

Water Buses

Air-conditioned water buses travel on two routes along the creek and in the Dubai Marina at 15-minute intervals. Tickets are Dh2 per trip. Nol cards are valid.

Route B1 Ghubaiba to Al Seef via Dubai Old Souq, Sabkha and Baniyas stations (7am-10pm Sat-Thu, 10am-midnight Fri)

Route BM1 The Walk at JBR to Dubai Marina Mall (10am-midnight Thu, noon-midnight Fri, noon-10pm Sat, 10am-10pm Sun-Wed)

ⓘ BUS & METRO FARES & TICKETS

The RTA network is divided into four zones with fares depending on through how many zones you've travelled.

Before you hop aboard a bus, train or water bus, you must purchase a rechargeable Nol Card from vending machines or ticket offices in all stations. Short-term visitors should get the Red Card, which costs Dh2 and may be recharged by up to 10 journeys. Fares range from Dh2 and Dh6.50 per trip up to a daily maximum of Dh14.

If you intend to make more than 10 trips get a Silver Card for Dh20 (including Dh14 of credit). Trips cost between Dh1.80 to Dh5.80 up to a daily maximum of Dh14.

The Gold Card costs double and gives you access to the gold-class carriage.

The correct fare is automatically deducted from your card when you swipe it upon entering and exiting a metro train or a bus.

Children under age five and shorter than 90cm travel free.

TAXI

Taxis (☑208 0808; www.dtc.dubai.ae) are metered, quite inexpensive and the fastest and most comfortable way to get around, except during rush-hour traffic. Flag one down in the street or order it by phone.

➤ Daytime flag fall is Dh3 (Dh6 with advance booking, Dh10 during peak times) plus Dh1.60 per kilometre (Dh3.50 from 10pm to 6am or Dh7 when booked), including all tolls. The minimum fare is Dh10.

➤ Trips to Sharjah and the other northern emirates incur a Dh20 surcharge.

➤ Tip about 10%. Always carry small bills since most cabbies can't or won't give change.

➤ There's rarely a problem with women riding alone, even at night, although you can also request a woman driver (ask for a 'ladies taxi') when booking. Eight-seaters (family vans) and special-needs taxis are also available.

➤ Many hotels operate a limo service, which may cost as much as double. Confirm the fare in advance and if you don't like it, ask the concierge to call you a regular cab.

➤ Rather than asking to be taken to a street address, mention the nearest landmark (eg a hotel, mall, roundabout, major building). If your cabbie is lost, ask him or her to radio his office for directions.

AROUND DUBAI

If you're tired of big-city mayhem and crave a little peace and quiet, these luxe desert resorts will show you a calmer, unhurried side of the emirate.

Al Maha Desert Resort & Spa

It may only be 65km southeast of Dubai (on the Dubai to Al Ain Rd), but **Al Maha** (☑832 9900; www.al-maha.com; ste from Dh2900; 🗟🗷) 🐾 feels like an entirely different universe. Gone is the traffic, the skyscrapers and the go-go attitude. At this remote desert eco-resort it's all about getting back to some elemental discoveries about yourself and where you fit into nature's grand design.

Part of the Dubai Desert Conservation Reserve (DDCR), Al Maha is one of the most exclusive hotels in the Emirates and named for the endangered Arabian oryx, which are bred as part of DDCR's conservation program. The resort's 42 luxurious suites are all standalone, canvas-roofed bungalows with private plunge pools. Each one has its own patio with stunning vistas of the beautiful desert landscape and peach-coloured dunes, punctuated by mountains and grazing white oryx and gazelles.

Rates include two daily activities such as a desert wildlife drive or a camel trek. Private vehicles, visitors and children under 12 years of age are not allowed, and taking meals at your suite rather than in the dining room is a popular choice. Save 30% by reserving a month or more in advance.

Bab Al Shams Desert Resort & Spa

Resembling an Arabian fort and effortlessly blending into the desertscape, Bab Al Shams (☑381 3231; www.meydanhotels.com; r incl breakfast from Dh1150; @ 🗟 🗷) is a tonic for tourists seeking to indulge their *The Thousand and One Nights* fantasies. Its labyrinthine layout displays both Arabic and Moorish influences; rooms are gorgeous, spacious and evocatively earthy, with pillars, lanterns, paintings of desert landscapes and prettily patterned Bedouin-style pillows.

While this is the perfect place to curl up with a book or meditate in the dunes, the stimuli-deprived will find plenty to do. A wonderful infinity pool beckons, as does the luscious Satori Spa and an archery range. Children under 12 years of age can let off steam in Sinbad's Club. Offsite activities include desert tours and horse and camel rides. Bab al-Shams is about 40 minutes south of Dubai.

Hatta حتا

Cradled by the craggy Hajar Mountains, Hatta, an enclave of Dubai emirate, is a popular weekend getaway. Its main attraction is its cool, humidity-free climate and magnificent mountain scenery. While it makes a good base for off-road trips, Hatta itself is a wonderful place to relax.

◉ Sights

Hatta Heritage Village　　　　　MUSEUM
(☑852 1374; ⊗8am-8.30pm Sat-Thu, 2.30-8.30pm Fri) **FREE** This sprawling village recreates the Hatta of yore. It is housed in the ruler's restored historic fort with *majlis* (meeting room), a traditional courtyard house and various *barasti* (palm-leaf) buildings. Displays on weaponry, local music, palm-tree

products, handicrafts, weaving, traditional dress and old village society illustrate the past. There are nice views from a restored defensive tower from 1880 whose doors are about 2.5m above the ground – guards had to use ropes to climb up there.

To get there, turn south at the main roundabout and drive for about 3km, then turn left at the sign. It's about a 1.5km walk from the Hatta bus terminal.

Hatta Rock Pools   OUTDOORS

Hatta's other main attraction is this series of pools and waterfalls carved out of the rocky bed of a wadi (river bed). Access was closed during our visit as the government was constructing a road and upgrading facilities. Check locally if the area has reopened.

🛏 Sleeping & Eating

Hatta Fort Hotel   HOTEL $$$

(☏809 9333; www.jaresortshotels.com; Main roundabout; d from Dh1100; 🅿🛜🏊) The only lodging option in town, Hatta Fort Hotel is popular with expats at weekends and exudes a 1960s country-club feel thanks to its manicured lawns and expansive grounds. The 48 spacious and classy chalets brim with Arabic design flourishes amid stone walls and wood-beamed ceilings. All have a private patio or balcony with dreamy mountain views.

Café Gazebo does breakfast, lunch and snacks until 7pm (Dh25 to Dh60), while the fine-dining restaurant Jeema (mains Dh60 to Dh130) opens for dinner and sometimes has live entertainment.

ℹ Getting There & Away

Hatta is about 125km east of Dubai. Bus E16 shuttles hourly between Dubai's Al Sabkha station and Hatta's new bus terminal, about 2.5km south of the main roundabout (Dh7, 2¼ hours). The first bus from Hatta leaves at 5.35am, the last at 9.30pm. Buses from Dubai run between 6am and 10pm.

The 125km drive from Dubai via Hwy E44 is punctuated by roaming camels, rippling sand dunes and the occasional oasis, all set against a backdrop of the mighty mountains. Stretches of road pass through Oman and although there are no immigration or customs formalities, you may be asked for your passport at soldier-staffed road blocks. This is largely an effort to stop illegal immigration. If you're driving a rental car, make sure you're allowed to take it to Hatta and that you have insurance cover in Oman. You can avoid all this by taking the slightly longer northerly route via Hwy E102.

NORTHERN EMIRATES

Sharjah   الشارقة

⌖ 06 / POP 990,000

Sharjah doesn't dazzle with glitz but with culture and got the Unesco nod back in 1998 when it was declared Arab Capital of Culture; and deservedly so. Once you have penetrated the traffic-clogged outskirts of town, the historic old town is easy to navigate on foot. Plan on setting aside several hours to explore the Heritage and Arts Areas, as well as the souqs and excellent museums.

Aside from the main city of Sharjah, the enclaves of Dibba Al Hisn, Khor Fakkan and Kalba on the eastern coast also belong to the emirate.

One caveat: Sharjah takes its decency laws very seriously, so do dress modestly. That means no exposed knees, backs or bellies – and that goes for both men and women. It's also the only emirate that is 'dry' (ie no alcohol is available anywhere).

⊙ Sights

Many of Sharjah's top sights are scattered around the partly walled in Heritage Area FREE and the adjacent Arts Area, just off the Corniche. Both are part of an ambitious long-term redevelopment project called Heart of Sharjah, which aims to restore the historic buildings and turn them into hotels, museums, shops and restaurants while preserving the feel of the pre-oil days. It is scheduled for completion in 2025. See www.shurooq.gov.ae for details or visit the information office in the *majlis* (meeting room) of the Bait Al Naboodah building.

★Sharjah Heritage Museum   MUSEUM

(☏06-568 0006; www.sharjahmuseums.ae; Heritage Area, off Corniche; adult/child Dh5/free; ⊙8am-8pm Sat-Thu, 4-8pm Fri) This creatively curated museum goes a long way towards demystifying local culture and traditions for Western minds. Each of the five galleries zeros in on different aspects of local life, from living in the desert to religious values, birth and burial rituals to holiday celebrations, marriage and wedding ceremonies, and folk medicine. An abundance of quality original objects and excellent English panelling make a visit here a satisfying and educational experience.

Sharjah

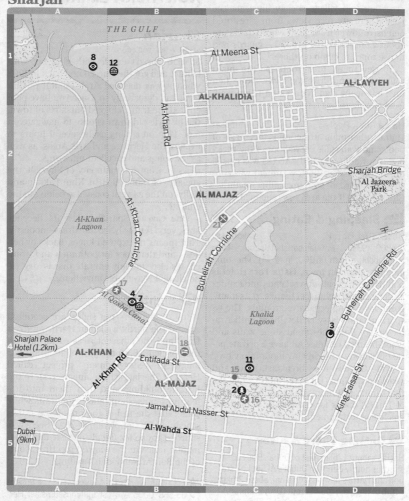

Bait Al Naboodah HISTORIC SITE
(☑06-568 1738; www.sharjahmuseums.ae; Heritage Area, off Corniche; adult/child Dh5/free; ☺8am-8pm Sat-Thu, 4-8pm Fri) This 1845 house, a former pearl trader's home with a grand entranceway, elaborately carved decorations and an ample courtyard, is a fine example of early Emirati architecture and daily living. Head upstairs for close-ups of the pretty porch.

Souq Al Arsah MARKET
(Courtyard Souq; Heritage Area, off Corniche; ☺9am-9pm Sat-Thu, 4-8pm Fri) One of the oldest souqs in the UAE (which in this case

means about 50 years), Souq Al Arsah once crawled with traders from Persia and India and local Bedu stocking up on supplies, their camels fastened to posts outside. Despite a thorough facelift, it's still an atmospheric place, even though vendors now vie for tourist dirham with pashminas, *dhallahs* (coffee pots), herbs and spices, old *khanjars* (daggers) and traditional jewellery in air-conditioned comfort.

Sharjah Art Museum MUSEUM
(☑06-568 8222; www.sharjahmuseums.ae; Arts Area, off Corniche; ☺8am-8pm Sat-Thu, 4-8pm

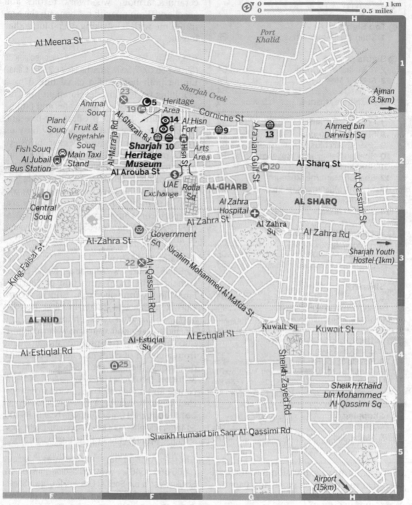

Fri) **FREE** Just east of the Heritage Area, the Arts Area is anchored by one of the region's largest and most impressive art museums and the organiser of the Sharjah Biennal. Its galleries are a great place to keep tabs on Arab contemporary art, including works by Biennial winners and such established artists as UAE painter Abdul Qader Al Raes. Watercolours of historic Sharjah by Ali Darwish also get a lot of wall space, as do paintings by 18th- and 19th-century European Orientalists. A highlight here are the dozen lithographs by Scottish artist David Robert. Curators keep things dynamic by mounting monthly changing exhibits, and there's a nice cafe to boot.

Many of the surrounding historic buildings contain galleries, workshops and studios, including one for disabled artists.

Sharjah Calligraphy Museum MUSEUM
(☏ 06-569 4561; www.sharjahmuseums.ae; Heritage Area, off Corniche; adult/child Dh5/free) Even if you don't understand the meaning of the beautiful calligraphy on display in this handsome gallery, you'll probably still admire its high aesthetic value and the variety

Sharjah

of styles, forms of expression and materials used (canvas, ceramics, wood and paper).

Sharjah Museum of Islamic Civilisation
MUSEUM

(☏06-565 5455; www.islamicmuseum.ae; cnr Corniche & Arabian Gulf St; adult/child Dh5/free; ☉8am-8pm Sat-Thu, 4-8pm Fri) Pretty much everything you always wanted to know about Islam is addressed in this well-curated museum in a converted souq right on the waterfront. The ground-floor galleries zero in on different aspects of the Islamic faith, such as the Five Pillars of Islam, including the ritual and importance of hajj. Other rooms trace Arab scientific accomplishments, especially in mathematics and astronomy, while the upper floor navigates through 1400 years of Islamic art and artefacts with manuscripts,

ceramics, armour, woodwork, textiles and jewellery. Wrap up with tea beneath the central dome with its striking deep-blue zodiac mosaic.

Al Qasba
NEIGHBOURHOOD

(☏06-556 0777; www.alqasba.ae; Al Qasba Canal) Lining both banks of a canal linked by a twinkling bridge, this development presents a lively mix of restaurants, cafes and family-friendly fun. The strip offers car-free and carefree strolling and is especially busy on Friday night and Saturday. For birds-eye views of the city, take a spin on the landmark **Eye of the Emirates** (☏06-556 0777; Al Qasba; adult/child Dh30/15; ☉4pm-midnight Sun-Wed, 3pm-1am Thu & Fri, seasonal variations possible), a 60m-high Ferris wheel. There's also a superb contemporary art gallery, the **Maraya Art Centre** (☏06-556 6555; www.maraya.ae; Al Qasba; ☉10am-10pm Sat-Thu, 4-10pm Fri).

Al Majaz Waterfront
PARK

(☏06-552 1552; www.almajaz.ae; Khalid Lagoon Corniche) The main attraction of Sharjah's latest family fun zone is the **Sharjah Fountain** (☉half-hourly 7.30pm-midnight Mon-Sat) **FREE** which, after dark, choreographs music, light, laser and spurting water columns into impressive five-minute shows. Aside from a clutch of cafes and fast-food outlets, diversions include the 18-hole **Al Majaz Minigolf** (adult/child Dh25/15; ☉4pm-midnight) course and a jogging track made from recycled tyres. Romantic types can charter an **abra** (adult/child Dh15/10, private boat Dh80-100; ☉4pm-midnight Apr-Oct, 2.45pm-midnight Nov-Mar) for watery views of the city panorama.

Sharjah Archaeological Museum
MUSEUM

(☏06-566 5466; www.archaeologymuseum.ae; Sheikh Rashid bin Saqr Al Qassimi Rd, btwn Sheikh Zayed St & Cultural Sq; adult/child Dh5/free; ☉8am-8pm Sat-Thu, 4-8pm Fri) Dig deep into Sharjah's past at this elegant museum which does a fine job of displaying and interpreting locally unearthed artefacts from the Stone Age to AD 600. Walk among re-created tombs and houses and admire ancient tools, 3500-year-old bronze spearheads, dainty shell necklaces, well-preserved Iron Age pottery and Roman gold coins. A taxi here from the city centre should cost about Dh10.

Sharjah Aquarium
AQUARIUM

(☏06-528 5288; www.sharjahaquarium.ae; far west end of Al Meena St; adult/child incl Maritime Museum Dh20/10; ☉8am-8pm Mon-Thu, 4-9pm Fri, 8am-9pm Sat) Enter an 'abandoned dhow' for close-ups of maritime creatures from the UAE's west and east coast without getting your feet wet. Moray eels lurk, blacktip reef sharks prowl, eagle rays flop and jellyfish dance around tanks that re-create Dibba Rock, mangroves, Shark Island's coral reefs and other local watery habitats. We like the touchscreens, but a few more labels wouldn't hurt.

Sharjah Maritime Museum　　MUSEUM
(☑ 06-522 2002; far west end of Al Meena St; adult/child Dh8/4; ☺ 8am-8pm Sat-Thu, 4-8pm Fri) For a salty introduction to the UAE, visit this charming museum that displays enough traditional dhows, exhibits on pearling and fishing equipment to keep your imagination afloat for a half hour or so.

✦✦ Festivals & Events

Sharjah Biennial　　ART
(www.sharjahbiennial.org) Held every two years between March and May (next in 2015), this is one of the most important art events in the Arab world.

Sharjah International Book Fair　　BOOKS
(www.sharjahbookfair.com) Since 1981, this major regional book fair, held in November, presents the latest tomes in Arabic, English and other languages.

🛏 Sleeping

Sharjah Heritage Hostel　　HOSTEL $
(☑ 06-569 7707; www.uaeyha.com; off Corniche St, behind Al Zahra'a (Blue) Mosque; dm per person Dh65; ☺ reception noon-midnight) In a superb and quiet location on the edge of the Heritage Area, this new hostel occupies a beautifully restored historic courtyard building. Carved wooden doors lead to eight clean, well-kept dorms with five or six single beds, air-con and a small refrigerator. Take bus 14 to Al Rolla Sq stop.

Sharjah Youth Hostel　　HOSTEL $
(☑ 06-522 5070; www.uaeyha.com; 262 Al Merkab St, Al Sharqan; dm Dh50; P) On a noisy street, this functional hostel has all sorts of different room configurations, including spacious air-con dorms sleeping up to five in side-by-side single beds (linen provided) as well as private twins and family rooms, some with attached bathroom. Kudos to the guest kitchen (there's a supermarket a five-minute walk away), deductions for the location some 4km east of the city centre. Bus 14

AL NOOR MOSQUE VISITS

One of the most beautiful of Sharjah's 600 mosques, **Al Noor** (Corniche, east Khalid Lagoon) has gorgeous architecture and a dream setting overlooking the Khalid Lagoon. It is the only one in the emirate that is open to non-Muslims for free guided tours operated by the nonprofit **Sharjah Centre for Cultural Communication** (☑ 06-548 2211; www.sjhculture.com; ☺ 10am Mon) **FREE**. Tours last about one hour and conclude with a question-and-answer session. Dress modestly, of course, and do bring a camera and curiosity.

stops about 1km away at Al Sharq St, and a public beach is not much further.

Sharjah Rotana Hotel　　HOTEL $
(☑ 06-563 7777; www.rotana.com; Al Arouba St; d from Dh300; P 🛜 ⛱) This good-value city hotel puts you within a whisker of key museums and souqs. Rooms are decked out in elegant, muted tones; snag one on the upper floors for sweeping views (and less street noise). Free shuttles to malls, Deira and a private beach.

Golden Tulip Sharjah　　HOTEL $$
(☑ 06-519 7777; www.goldentulipsharjah.com; Buheirah Corniche; r/ste from Dh600/900; P 🛜 ⛱) With a killer location mere steps from Al Qasba and Al Majaz Waterfront, the Golden Tulip has newly done-up rooms and suites, many with kitchenettes. It's within the glass-fronted Al Fardan Centre mall and has a pool and separate work-out facilities for men and women.

Coral Beach Resort　　RESORT $$
(☑ 06-522 9999; www.coral-international.com; Al Muntazah St; r from Dh600; P 🛜 ⛱) On the border with Ajman, this resort hits the mark with all sorts of travellers. Kids love the pools (one with slides) and Kids Club; active types can hit the gym or the tennis court; and couples can relax in the hammam or over a romantic seaside dinner. Most rooms have ocean views, but the private beach is small and can get crowded. Wi-fi (public areas only) is Dh150 (!) per day.

Sharjah Palace Hotel　　HOTEL $$
(06-593 9333; www.sharjahpalacehotel.com; Al Taawun St; d from Dh800; P 🛜 ⛱) This new-

ℹ HOP-ON HOP-OFF TOURS

Since November 2012, red double-decker sightseeing buses (www.viator.com; adult/child Dh85/45; ☉9am-8pm Sat-Wed, 9am-10pm Thu & Fri) have been braving Sharjah's traffic to deliver tourists to 15 of the city's sightseeing hotspots, including the Heritage Area and Al Majaz Waterfront, on a hop-on hop-off basis. Tickets are valid for 24 hours and taped commentary comes in English, German, Russian and Arabic.

comer towering over Al Mamzar Lagoon welcomes you with a Bedouin tent in the lobby. Rooms feature classic furniture and natural hues paired with a busy carpet pattern. Bonus points for the free wi-fi throughout.

✖ Eating

Bangkok Town   THAI $$
(☏06-556 8282; cnr Al Qasba & 9th Sts, behind Grand Buhaira Cinema; mains Dh30-70; ☉lunch & dinner) The food here is as tantalising as ever at this old-school parlour where you dine in snug, linen-bedecked booths or beneath thatched roofs. The menu is especially strong when it comes to fish and seafood (there's even a live tilapia tank) but all the classics are accounted for as well.

★ Shababeek   LEBANESE $$
(☏06-554 0444; www.shababeek.ae; Block B, Qanat Al Qasba; mezze Dh18-26, mains Dh35-65; ☉noon-11.30pm) With its deep-purple walls, black furniture and Arabic design flourishes, this chic Lebanese restaurant channels Dubai swish but without the attitude – or the alcohol. Portions are not huge but flavours are delicately paired and the selection way beyond the usual hummus, tabbouleh and kebabs.

Sammach   SEAFOOD $$
(☏06-528 0095; Sharjah Aquarium; mains Dh50-75; ☉noon-11pm) Tucked below the Sharjah Aquarium, this top-notch 'fishy' contender delivers the catch of day to your waterfront table with full-on views of Sharjah's high-rise forest. Pick from the menu or ask the chef to prepare a piece of fish or crustacean just the way you like it.

Royale Spice Restaurant   INTERNATIONAL $$
(☏tollfree 800 777 423; www.royalespice.com; behind Al Diwan Al Amiri; mains Dh30-80) A wonderfully retro vibe rules at this sprawling restaurant where the menu hopscotches from India to China and the Middle East without losing a step. If you're not tempted by the creamy curries and flaky naan, perhaps the shredded duck or whole fried pompret will make your tummy happy.

Sadaf   IRANIAN $$
(☏06-569 3344; www.sadaffood.com; Al-Mareija St; mains Dh40-80; ☉lunch & dinner) The Sharjah branch of this popular mini-chain enjoys cult status among locals for its excellent authentic Iranian cuisine. The spicy, moist kebabs are particularly good and the *zereshk polo meat* (rice with red barberries and chicken or meat) is another star pick. There are plenty of other dining optiona on this street.

Casa Samak   SEAFOOD $$$
(☏06-522 9999; Corniche Rd, Coral Beach Resort; mains Dh80-115; ☉noon-4pm & 7-11pm) The Gulf views impress as much as the food at this beachfront fish-and-seafood shrine that's always packed to the gills thanks to dock-fresh ingredients and flawlessly crafted plates. For non-pescaterians there's now a barbecue buffet as well.

🔒 Shopping

Central Souq   MARKET
(Blue Souq; near Al Ittihad Sq, east Khalid Lagoon; ☉9am-1.30pm & 4.30-10.30 Sat-Thu, 4-11pm Fri) The beautiful Central Souq occupies two structures designed in an appealing, if flashy, Arabic style. The ground floor has mostly modern jewellery, watches and designer clothing, while the little stores upstairs sell pashminas, rugs and curios from such far-flung places as Afghanistan and Rajasthan. If possible, visit in the evenings – only tourists shop here during the day.

Mega Mall   MALL
(www.megamall.ae; ☉10am-11pm Sat-Thu, 2-11pm Fri) With 150 shops it's small by Dubai standards but comes with a multiplex cinema and an indoor theme park complete with roller coaster and haunted house. The supermarket is open 24 hours.

ℹ Information

Al Zahra Hospital (☎06-516 8902; www.
alzahra.com; Al Zahra Sq, Al-Ghuair) Central
clinic with 24/7 ER.

Central Post Office (☎06-572 2219; Government Sq, Al Soor; ⊙8am-8pm Sat-Thu, 4-8pm
Fri)

**Sharjah Commerce & Tourism Development
Authority** (☎06-556 6777; www.sharjah-
welcome.com)

ℹ Getting There & Away

AIR

Sharjah International Airport (☎06-558 1111;
www.shj-airport.gov.ae) is 15km east of the
central city and has significantly increased its
capacity since becoming the hub of Air Arabia
(p359), the region's first budget airline.

CAR

From Dubai, take Sheikh Rashid Rd across
Garhoud Bridge and continue into Sharjah on Al
Ittihad Rd. The drive should take between 30 and
60 minutes, depending on traffic and where in
Dubai you started from.

TAXI

The **main taxi stand** is next to the bus station,
but taxis can actually be flagged down anywhere
in town. Trips to Dubai come with a Dh20 surcharge. Expect to pay about Dh50 to Dubai International Airport, Dh90 to Dubai Mall, Dh200 to
Fujairah or Al Ain and Dh300 to Abu Dhabi.

If possible avoid travelling between Dubai and
Sharjah during peak rush hour (weekdays 7am
to 10am, 1pm to 2pm and 5pm to 9pm) as roads
can get frustratingly clogged.

ℹ Getting Around

TO/FROM THE AIRPORT

Bus 14 (Dh4) and express buses 88 and 99
(Dh5) all travel to the Sharjah city centre. A taxi
ride costs about Dh45, including a Dh20 airport
surcharge. Bus 111 goes to Al Rashidiya station
of the Dubai Metro.

BUS

Buses are operated by **Mowasalat** (☎600
522 282; www.mowasalat.ae) and travel on
nine routes between 5.30am and 11.30pm at
intervals ranging from 10 to 30 minutes. Regular
tickets cost Dh4, express routes are Dh5. Bus 14
is the handiest.

Sharjah's central Al Jubail bus station is next
to the fish and vegetable souq and within walking
distance of the Central Souq.

Sharjah Transport Authority (p360) runs bus
services to other emirates from the bays on the
western end of the station. Dubai-based RTA
(p360) buses leave from the other end of the
station. Sample fares include:

DESTINATION	FARE (DH)	TIME (HR)	FREQUENCY
Abu Dhabi	30	3hr	every 45 mins
Ajman	5	½	every 20min
Al Ain	30	2hr	every 45 mins
Dubai	7	1	every 10mins
Fujairah	25	2½	every 75mins
Ras Al Khaimah	25	2	every 15mins
Umm Al Quwain	15	1	every 15 mins

TAXI

Taxis (☎600 545 455; www.stc.gov.ae) can
be either flagged or booked. The flagfall is Dh3
(Dh4 from 11pm to 6am), plus Dh1 per 650
metres. The average taxi ride within town costs
between Dh10 and Dh15. There's a Dh20 extra
charge for rides originating at the airport and
for trips to Dubai.

Sharjah Desert Park

The main attraction of this **desert park**
(☎06 531 1999; adult/child Dh15/5; ⊙ 9am-6pm
Sun-Mon & Wed-Thu, 2-6pm Fri, 11am-6pm Sat)
about 26km east of central Sharjah is the
Arabia's Wildlife Centre (www.breedingcen-
tresharjah.com), an indoor zoo showcasing the
diversity of local critters. Venomous vipers,
flamingos, wildcats, mongooses, hyenas,
wolves and the splendid Arabian leopard all
make appearances.

For a more hands-on experience, take
the kids to the **Children's Farm** (☎531 1127;
⊙closed noon-4pm), where they can meet,
pet and feed goats, camels and ducks, and
ride ponies and camels. For additional background, visit the **Sharjah Natural History
& Botanical Museum** (☎531 1411).

The park grounds also include a cafe
and picnic facilities. To get there from central Sharjah, follow Al Dhaid Hwy (E88) for
about 26km, past the Sharjah Airport.

Ajman عجمان

📍 06 / POP 262,000

North of Sharjah, Ajman is the smallest of the seven emirates. Although still comparatively laid back, it too has been swept up in a wave of development in recent years. Additions include the big Ajman City Centre mall, fine hotels and the Emirates City residential area.

For visitors, the main attraction is the pretty, palm-lined, white-sand beach. Strolling along the Corniche, where locals like to barbecue and picnic in cooler weather, is a pleasant way to while away some time.

👁 Sights

Ajman Museum MUSEUM
(☑ 06-742 3824; Central Square; adult/child Dh5/2; ⏰ 9am-1pm & 4-7pm Sat-Thu, 4-7pm Fri) This late 18th-century fort served as the ruler's residence until 1970 and also saw a stint as the

police station. Now a museum, it illustrates aspects of Ajman's past with an assortment of photographs, weapons, tools and archaeological artefacts.

🛏 Sleeping

Ramada Hotel & Suites HOTEL **$**
(☑ 06-740 4666; www.ramadaajman.com; Sheikh Khalifa bin Zayed Rd; r from Dh350; 🅿🛜🏊) If you're suffering from culture shock, this island of Western comforts might feel as welcome as a hug from an old friend. It's close to Ajman City Centre mall but about 2.5km from the beach, although there's free shuttle service several times daily.

Kempinski Hotel Ajman HOTEL **$$$**
(☑ 06-745 5555; www.kempinski-ajman.com; Corniche (Arabian Gulf St); r from Dh1100; 🅿🛜🏊) Away from the action on the northern Corniche, this hotel is on a pretty beach with soft, white sand, sea shells and palm trees. It's a lovely place to kick back for a couple of

Ajman

THE GULF

days. Rooms flaunt the gamut of amenities and even the smallest are pretty spacious.

✗ Eating & Drinking

India House   INDIAN $

(☑06-744 2497; Sheikh Humaid bin Abdul Al Aziz St; meals Dh4-20; ☺7.30am-3.30pm & 5.30pm-midnight; ☑) Specialising in authentic Indian vegetarian dishes, this spotless cafeteria is especially popular with expats for its extensive menu featuring value-priced thalis, biryanis, tandoor dishes, kebabs and curries from all parts of the subcontinent. Next to Choithrams supermarket.

Hai Tao   CHINESE $$$

(☑06-714 5555; Corniche, Kempinski Hotel Ajman; mains Dh50-100; ☺6.30-11.30pm Wed-Mon) One of four stellar restaurants at the Kempinski, Hai Tao is decorated in traditional Chinese style (complete with wooden rickshaw and golden-roofed pagoda) and serves up superb Szechwan and Cantonese dishes, including an exceptional roast duck.

Outside Inn   PUB

(☑06-742 4387; Corniche) Ponder life while counting the waves and nursing a brewski at this British pub – and expat fave – next to the Holiday Beach Club.

❶ Getting There & Away

BUS

Ajman has no local bus service. Dubai-based RTA buses travel from Al Ittihad bus station (p308) in Deira (Dubai) to Ajman (Dh7, 50 minutes). Bus 112 makes the trip (Dh5, 30 minutes) several times hourly from Sharjah's Al Jubail station (p317) but does not pick up passengers on the way back.

TAXI

Shared taxis to Deira (Dh15) and Sharjah (Dh10) leave from the **stand** (Sheikh Humaid bin Abdul

---

Al Aziz St) just past the intersection with Al Karama and Al Ittihad Sts. Taxis to Ras Al Khaimah (Dh25) and Umm Al Quwain (Dh15) leave from the taxi stand near Ajman City Centre mall. You'll need to agree on the fare beforehand. Metered taxis to Dubai range from Dh35 to Deira and Dh85 to Jumeirah.

Umm Al Quwain   أم القيوين

☑06 / POP 56,000

Umm Al Quwain, a tiny emirate wrapped around an island-dotted lagoon, is in many ways the 'anti-Dubai'. Small, sleepy, rather quaint and without a single international mega-resort, its retro-feel stands in sharp contrast to the glamour-emirate to the south. Steer your way here if you're after a taste of the UAE as it was in its pre-oil days.

The old town, business district and a few hotels are at the northern tip of a long and narrow peninsula accessed by the busy, strip mall-lined King Faisal Rd. Other attractions are along Hwy E11 heading north.

◉ Sights & Activities

Umm Al Quwain Museum   MUSEUM

(☑06 765 0888; Al Lubna Rd; adult/child Dh4/free; ☺8am-2pm Sat-Thu & 5-8pm daily, women only Tue) This beautifully restored 1768 fort served as the local rulers' residence and seat of government until 1969. Highlights include the fine *majlis* (meeting room), old Bedouin jewellery, fancy weapons and such prized archaeological finds as two statues of headless falcons.

Lagoon Boat Trips   OUTDOORS

(☑06-765 0000; Flamingo Beach Resort; per hr Dh190; ☺8am-4pm) The emirate's mangrove-lined islands are home to lots of birds, including graceful flamingos and the largest Socotra cormorant colony in the UAE. The Flamingo Beach Resort can arrange for boat trips to the islands. The hourly rate is good for up to 15 people.

Crab Hunting   OUTDOORS

(☑06-765 0000; www.flamingoresort.ae; Flamingo Beach Resort; adult/child Dh190/110; ☺6pm) The Flamingo Beach Resort also organises crab hunting trips to the lagoon's mangroves. Rates include the boat ride, equipment, instruction and a dinner buffet at the resort where everyone's catch is cooked up on the spot.

Umm Al Quwain

UNITED ARAB EMIRATES UMM AL QUWAIN

Umm Al Quwain

◎ Sights
1 Umm Al Quwain Museum.....................B1

◉ Activities, Courses & Tours
   Crab Hunting.................................(see 2)
   Lagoon Boat Trips.......................(see 2)

◷ Sleeping
2 Flamingo Beach Resort........................B1

◉ Eating
   Dhow Buffet...................................(see 2)
3 Lulu Centre...A3

Dreamland Aqua Park   WATER PARK
(☑ 06-768 1888; www.dreamlanduae.com; Hwy E11; adult/child under 1.2m Dh135/85; ⊙ 10am-6pm) Packed with old-school charm, the UAE's first water park is well maintained and has some wicked slides, including some for smaller kids, and even a pool bar serving cold beers and cocktails at reasonable prices. It's on Hwy E11, some 10km north of the turn-off for the Umm Al Quwain peninsula.

◷ Sleeping

Dreamland Aqua Park   CAMP, CABIN $
(☑ 06-768 1888; www.dreamlanduae.com; Hwy E11; tents adult/child Dh385/300, cabins Dh450/350;

P ⊛) Be the first one on the slides in the morning when you camp out in simple wooden cabins or in a tent right on the grounds of the waterpark. Rates include camping gear as well as meat for throwing on your own barbecue at dinner, plus a belly-dancing show, breakfast and lunch.

Umm Al Quwain Beach Hotel   RESORT $$
(☑ 06-766 6647; www.uaqbeachotel.com; Beach Rd, off King Faisal Rd; d from Dh750; P ⊛ ⊛) Stresses melt pronto beneath a *barasti* umbrella on this resort's lovely Gulf-fronting sandy beach. Lodging is in nicely furnished one- to three-bedroom villas, all overlooking the water, and there's a welcoming Lebanese restaurant with *sheesha*. The resort is on the peninsula; look for the turn-off on the west side of King Faisal Rd just north of the Clocktower roundabout (near KFC).

Barracuda Beach Resort   RESORT $$
(☑ 06-768 1555; www.barracuda.ae; Hwy E11; r/ste from Dh750/950; P ⊛ ⊛) Renowned for its off-licence liquor store, this whitewashed Mediterranean-style resort has simple yet spacious tiled-floor studios and suites with balconies and lagoon views. No beach, though, despite the name.

Flamingo Beach Resort   RESORT $$
(☑ 06-765 0000; www.flamingoresort.ae; Corniche Rd; d/ste Dh550/850; P ⊛ ⊛) With large but dated rooms, the Flamingo has seen better days, although the well-kept grounds, lagoon-facing sandy beach and friendly staff make up somewhat for any style shortcomings. Another bonus: easy access to mangrove explorations and crab hunting.

✖ Eating

The best source for self-caterers is the giant **Lulu Centre** (☑ 06-766 6331; King Faisal Rd; ⊙ 8am-11.30pm), near Al Kuwait roundabout.

Al Ayaam   LEBANESE $
(☑ 06-766 6969; King Faisal Rd, across from KFC; mezze Dh8-15, mains Dh15-40; ⊙ 9am-3.30pm & 6pm-1am) This unassuming eatery makes some of the best Lebanese in town and at very reasonable prices to boot.

Dhow Buffet   INTERNATIONAL $$
(☑ 06-765 0000; Flamingo Beach Resort; buffet Dh75; ⊙ dinner) Pick your favourites from the lavish buffet set up in a retired dhow, then lug your loot to a table in the sand or on the lawn for dining beneath the starry sky.

Aquarius
INTERNATIONAL **$$**

(🎵 06-768 1555; www.barracuda.ae; Barracuda Beach Resort; mains Dh30-100; ⏱ 8am-11pm) Match your mood to the food at this casual waterfront eatery, whose offerings run the gamut from burgers to chicken tikka and fish 'n' chips.

🛈 Getting There & Away

BUS

Coming from Sharjah catch bus 115 (Dh15, hourly) at Al Jubail bus station (p317). From Dubai, bus E601 leaves from from Al Ittihad bus station (p308) in Deira (Dh10, every 45 minutes). Buses stop at UAQ's Union roundabout, where they are met by taxis. Both lines continue on to Ras Al Khaimah via Hwy E11 but don't pick up on the way back to Sharjah.

CAR

Umm Al Quwain is about 40km north of Dubai via Hwy E11. For the old town, turn off onto King Faisal Rd, just past the junction with the E55.

TAXI

Cab rides to Dubai start at Dh120; for Sharjah budget Dh50, Ajman Dh40 and Ras Al Khaimah Dh60.

🛈 Getting Around

The only way to get around Umm Al Quwain is by taxis, which are cheap and plentiful; just flag one down. Most rides cost between Dh5 and Dh10.

Ras Al Khaimah   رأس الخيمة

🎵 07 / POP 241,000

Surrounded by the hazy Hajar Mountains, Ras Al Khaimah (or simply 'RAK') is the UAE's northernmost emirate. Outdoor enthusiasts love it here, thanks to diverse scenery, ranging from sandy beaches to sprawling oases, hot springs to sun-baked desert, all backed by the fierce mountains.

Growth has been exponential in RAK in recent years, resulting in a free-trade zone, luxury beachfront resorts, high-end residential area, and new leisure facilities such as the Iceland Waterpark. Most of the development is based in an area called **Jazirat Al Hamra**, some 15km south of RAK City. Still further south, new resorts are due to open up soon on the artificial offshore **Al Marjan** island cluster, right on the emirate's border with Umm Al Quwain.

In **RAK City** itself, a newish landmark is the pearly white and multidomed Sheikh Zayed Mosque, which overlooks Al Qawasim

Corniche, a paved promenade with kiosks, benches and restaurants fronting the creek.

RAK is also the gateway to the spectacular Musandam Peninsula, an enclave of Oman.

⊙ Sights

National Museum of Ras Al Khaimah
MUSEUM

(🎵 07-233 3411; off Al Hisn Rd; adult/child Dh3/2; ⏱ 10am-5pm Wed-Mon Sep-May, 8am-noon & 4-7pm Wed-Mon Jun-Aug) For a glimpse into the local past, take a spin around this thoughtfully curated exhibit in an 18th-century fort that, until 1964, served as the residence of the Qawasim rulers. Aside from the usual ethnological assortment, there's some nifty artefacts dug up in Julfar, an important port town from the 13th to the 18th centuries. Gems include intricately patterned Iron Age softstone vessels and 18th-century terracotta urns.

RAK Pearls Museum
MUSEUM

(🎵 050-198 0480; http://www.rakpearls.com/peral-museum; Al Qawasim Corniche; adult/child Dh15/10; ⏱ 10am-6pm Sat-Thu) This snazzy new museum imaginatively chronicles the importance of pearls in the regional culture and economy. Learn about the harsh life of pearl divers, checking out such gear as tortoiseshell nose clips. Upstairs, be dazzled by a showcase of shiny beauties, including the 'Miracle of Arabia', which measures 12mm in diametre and proudly snuggles on red velvet.

Jazirat Al Hamra Fishing Village
NEIGHBOURHOOD

(off Hwy E11, Jazirat Al Hamra; ⏱ 24h) **FREE** For an authentic glimpse of the pre-oil era, poke around this deliciously spooky ghost town, one of the oldest and best preserved coastal villages in the UAE. First settled in the 14th century, its people subsisted mostly on fishing and pearling until they suddenly picked up and left in 1968. A stroll among this cluster of coral stone houses, wind towers, mosques, schools and shops is at its most atmospheric at sundown. Get off Hwy E11 opposite Majan Printing. When the paved road curves left, turn right onto a graded dirt road and head towards the minarets.

🏃 Activities

There's fantastic trekking and rock climbing in the Hajar Mountains. Contact Dubai-based **Arabia Outdoors** (🎵 055-955 6209; www.arabiaoutdoors.com) or Absolute Adventure (p349) in Dibba for options.

Ras Al Khaimah

Ras Al Khaimah

⊙ Sights
1 National Museum of Ras Al
  Khaimah...B2
2 RAK Pearls Museum............................A3

🛏 Sleeping
3 Hotel Ras Al Khaimah.........................A4

✕ Eating
4 Al Sahari...A2
  Pesto Restaurant.........................(see 2)
5 Pure Veg Restaurant..........................D1

🍷 Drinking & Nightlife
6 RAK Popular Café...............................C2
7 Tree Top Bar.......................................D2

☆ Entertainment
8 Grand Manar.......................................C3

Iceland Water Park   WATER PARK
(☎07-206 7888, tollfree 800-969 725; www.ice-
landwaterpark.com; Jazirat Al Hamra, Hwy E11; adult
Dh150, child under 120/80cm Dh100/free; ☺10am-
6pm Sun-Wed, to 7pm Thu-Sat, women only 8pm-
midnight Fri) Penguins rule this 'arctic' water
park, challenging you to five rides down
Polar Mountain, including a death-defying,
near-vertical plunge down 40m-high Mount
Attack. Most rides have a 1.2m height minimum. Food and drinks, including alcohol,
are available. Packed on weekends.

👉 Tours

Bedouin Oasis   GUIDED TOUR
(☎055-710 9165; www.arabianincentive.com;
adult/child Dh340; ☺7-10pm) It's a bit cliched,
but dinner in a recreated Bedouin desert
camp, lit by candles and lanterns, is nevertheless a memorable experience. Rates include soft drinks, henna, camel rides, belly
dancing and sheesha.

🛏 Sleeping

Hotel Ras Al Khaimah　　HOTEL $
(☎ 07-236 2999; near cnr Khuzam St & Al Qawasim Corniche; d from Dh250; P 🛜 ☒) If money is an issue, this reliable hilltop stand-by won't break the bank. Furnishings and decor may not be of the latest vintage, but facilities include an outdoor pool and a 24-hour restaurant with good Lebanese fare. No alcohol.

★ Banyan Tree Al Wadi　　RESORT $$$
(☎ 07-206 7777; www.banyantree.com; Al Maz raa; from Dh2000; P 🛜 ☒) This desert resort offers the ultimate in luxury with its generously spaced out canopied villas amid rolling sand dunes. All boast a private plunge pool and Arabesque design touches throughout. It's surrounded by a nature preserve where you may encounter gazelles, camels and oryxes on guided walks or safaris. The resort is also home to a falconry mews and tours are offered daily (Dh230) at 8am and 4pm, giving you a chance to learn more about these majestic birds. It's about 14km south of New RAK (7km south of Hwy E311).

Guests also have access to the private beach of sister property **Banyan Tree Ras Al Khaimah Beach** (contact details as above), an equally romantic and exclusive peninsula retreat in New RAK.

Cove Rotana Resort　　RESORT $$$
(☎ 07-206 6000; www.rotana.com; Al Hamra Rd, off Hwy E11; r from Dh950; P 🛜 ☒) About 8km south of central RAK, this rambling full-service resort resembles a higgledy-piggledy Arab village wrapped around a lagoon and borders 600m of magnificent white sandy beach. Avoid the 'classic room' category if you want a watery view.

Hilton Ras Al Khaimah Resort & Spa　　RESORT $$$
(☎ 07-228 8844; www.3hilton.com; Al Maareedh St; r from Dh1150; 🛜 ☒) With 475 large and luxe rooms, 1.5km of private beach and six pools along with 13 restaurants and plenty of sports activities, this resort is like a town unto itself. Highlights include unwinding in the hammam and romantic sunset drinks in the Dhow Beach Bar.

🍴 Eating

Cafe La Luna　　ITALIAN $
(☎ 07-243 4600; www.laluna.ae; Al Hamra Yacht Club & Marina, Jazirat Al Hamra; mains Dh25-50; ⊙ 9am-11pm Sat-Wed, to midnight Thu-Fri) Snag an outside table and enjoy your pizza and pasta with a view of the bobbing yachts of Al Hamra Marina. This upbeat nosh spot also serves excellent coffees and a small breakfast selection (croissants, omelettes). The access road is off Hwy E11, opposite Majan Printing.

OFF THE BEATEN TRACK

SHAMAL

Atop a craggy mountain above the village of Shamal, some 5km northeast of RAK City, are the ruins of one of the UAE's oldest archaeological sites, a mystery-shrouded fort called **Sheba's Palace**. Nope, *the* legendary Queen of Sheba who ruled around 1000 BC never actually slept here. She couldn't have since the palace was only built some time between the 13th and 16th centuries AD, during the Julfar period, possibly as the ruler's summer retreat. Today, little of what must have been quite an impressive compound survives, merely a few stone walls and a badly ruined barrel-shaped building. The views from up here, though – stretching from sea to village to mountain – are superb.

Few tourists ever make it up here, since it takes a bit of an effort to find this unmarked site. From RAK City, follow Al Rams Rd (Hwy E18) about 4km north and turn right at the brown sign pointing to Shamal Folk Arts and Theatre Society (Saqr Heritage Village). Follow this road for 1.5km past the Heritage Village to a roundabout, turn right and continue 2.3km to the modern mock-fort of the People Heritage Revival Association. Turn left, go through Shamal village, turning left at the T-junction, and continue for another 750m until you see a gravel lot on your right with stone steps leading up a mountain. It's about a 15-minute climb to the top, the last stretch on gravel and stone. Dead goat encounters possible.

A taxi from RAK City should cost Dh100 to take you there, wait 30 minutes and return. Agree on the fare before you leave.

CROSSING INTO THE MUSANDAM PENINSULA

RAK is the jumping-off point for the magnificent Musandam Peninsula, an Omani enclave, via the Shams/Tibat border post about 35km north of RAK City. Beyond the border await a dramatic coastal drive and the town of Khasab, where you can catch dhow cruises and go snorkelling with dolphins.

If you are from one of the countries eligible to get an on-the-spot tourist visa for the UAE (see p359), you won't need to obtain a separate visa for Oman. Everyone else must pay a Dh35 exit fee at the UAE border post in Shams and OR5 (Dh50) upon entering Tibat.

If you're driving, bring a copy of the car registration and proof of insurance valid in Oman or obtain Omani insurance at the border (Dh100). If you're renting, make sure that you're permitted to take the car outside of the UAE.

Al Sahari   MIDDLE EASTERN $
(☑ 07-233 3966; Sheikh Mohammad bin Salem St; sandwiches Dh2-10, mains Dh20-45; ☺ noon-midnight) Locals are fond of this tidy dining room with blue walls, linen table cloths and copious mezze, kebabs, fried fish and shrimp and fresh juices. Women and families sit on the left, men on the right. The attached cafeteria serves Arabic breakfast and sandwiches.

Pure Veg Restaurant   INDIAN $
(☑ 07-227 3266; Al Muntasir Rd/120th St, opp Al Manama Hypermarket; mains Dh8-17; ☺ 7.30am-2pm & 5pm-midnight; ☑) Meat is a no-no at this clean and convivial eatery whose extensive menu hopscotches around India, featuring delicious dosas, tasty tandooris and fragrant curries.

Pesto Restaurant   ITALIAN $$
(☑ 07-226 4030; Al Qawasim Corniche; mains Dh40-105; ☺ noon-midnight) Chef Guiseppe Randazzo pairs punctilious craftsmanship with a passion for classic recipes passed down through generations of his Italian family. Tuck into flavour-packed porcini ravioli or pistachio-encrusted rack of lamb while taking in views of the creek, then en-

joy a post-prandial *sheesha* on the upstairs terrace.

Passage to Asia   ASIAN $$$
(☑ 07-228 8844; www.3hilton.com; Hilton Ras Al Khaimach Resort & Spa; nigiri Dh45-75, mains Dh65-130; ☺ 6.30-11.30pm) The menu at this elegant restaurant combines two of Asia's most popular cuisines: Japanese and Thai. Kudos for the lovely setting amid tropical flowers and the wonderfully attentive service. It's right next to the **Pura Vida** (☑ 07-228 8844; Al Maareedh St; mains Dh105-220, churrasco Dh205; ☺ dinner) Brazilian restaurant, in case you're more in the mood for meat.

🍷 Drinking & Entertainment

Tree Top Bar   BAR
(Al Jazah Rd, Doubletree Hotel; ☺ noon-1am) Enjoy alfresco drinks and mellow tunes with the city and creek glistening below from the rooftop terrace of this central hotel. Snacks available.

Club Acacia   NIGHTCLUB
(☑ 243 4421; www.acaciahotelrak.com; Acacia Hotel, Jazirat Al Hamra; ☺ 10pm-3am) Cut some rug on the dance floor of this stylish disco at the Acacia Hotel or come for karaoke, darts and snooker.

RAK Popular Café   CAFE
(☑ 07-228 8334; Hotel Rd; ☺ 4pm-1am) Local guys love the traditional *barasti* coffeehouse overlooking the lagoon where they play backgammon, drink coffee and puff on a *sheesha* well into the night.

Grand Manar   CINEMA
(☑ 07-227 8888; www.grandcinemas.com; Manar Mall; tickets Dh35) Megaplex with English-language blockbusters.

ℹ Getting There & Away

AIR

The grandly named but tiny **Ras Al Khaimah International airport** (☑ 07-244 8111; www.rakairport.com) is about 18km south of RAK City via Hwy E18. The main carrier is RAK Airways (p359), which has flights to destinations in Southeast Asia, Saudi Arabia and Qatar.

BUS

Buses leave from Hwy E11 opposite the Cove Rotana Resort between 7am and 8pm. Arriving buses are met by taxis for onward travel. Buses leave hourly from 7.30am to 9pm and fares are Dh10 to Umm Al Quwain, Dh15 to Ajman and Dh25 to Sharjah and Dubai.

CAR & MOTORCYCLE

RAK is linked to the other emirates via the slow coastal Hwy E11, called Sheikh Mohammad bin Salem St within city limits, and the much faster Hwy E311. Hwy E18 goes north to the Musandam Peninsula and south to the airport and the hot springs at Khatt.

TAXI

A seat in a shared taxi is Dh10 to Umm Al Quwain, Dh15 to Ajman, Dh20 to Sharjah and Dh25 to Dubai. The main taxi stand is on Hwy E11 opposite the Cove Rotana Resort.

ℹ️ Getting Around

Taxis (☑ 800 1700) can be flagged down or booked by phone. Flagfall is Dh3 plus Dh1 for every 650m.

Khatt Hot Springs

Hot springs in the desert? Who needs it? Well, if your bones ache or your muscles are sore, the 40°C mineralised water gushing forth from the natural hot springs at the **Harmony Ayurveda Centre** (☑ 07-244 8141; Khatt; admission Dh50; ⊙ 7am-9pm) apparently does wonders in limbering you up. Relax in gender-segregated pebble-floored pools or choose from the huge spa menu (honey and sesame body polish anyone?). Admission is free if you're staying at the **Golden Tulip Khatt Springs Hotel & Spa** (☑ 07-244 8777; www.goldentulipkhattsprings.com; Khatt; d Dh800-900; 🅿 🛜 🏊), a castle-shaped behemoth on a hilltop above the springs, which also has its own relaxation options (pool, sauna, steam room, ice grotto). Rooms are good-sized and will treat you to date palm–dotted valley views; service could be sharper.

Khatt is about 25km southeast of RAK City. Follow Hwy E18 past the airport, then look for signs.

ABU DHABI أبو ظبي

☑ 02 / POP 1.63 MILLION

Abu Dhabi has invested heavily in culture, education and environmental innovation in recent years. Slowly, almost stealthily, the largest – and wealthiest – emirate is emerging from the shadow of Dubai, its glamorous northern neighbour. In other words, if you haven't visited for a while, you'll be in for a surprise.

On Saadiyat Island, a gaggle of starchitects is designing an entire cultural district that will include branches of the Louvre and the Guggenheim. Near the airport, construction of Masdar, the world's first carbon-neutral city, is progressing nicely. Elsewhere in town, futuristic skyscrapers are forever changing the skyline, most notably the disc-shaped HQ and the Gate Tower, a glass-and-steel behemoth that's deliberately leaning 18 degrees (14 degrees more than the Tower of Pisa!). Already completed is the glorious Sheikh Zayed Grand Mosque, whose snowy white marble domes hover above the city like a mirage. Near the airport, Yas Island is a sparkling new tourist development headlined by the Ferrari World Abu Dhabi theme park and the spectacular Yas Hotel, which literally has a Formula 1 racetrack roaring through it.

Abu Dhabi is by far the largest emirate, comprising almost 87% of the country's total area. Looking at the city today, it's hard to imagine that only decades ago, it was little more than a fishing village with a fort, a few coral buildings and a smattering of *barasti* huts. To get a sense of the past, head to the enigmatic desert, peppered with oases such as Al Ain and Liwa. While the emirate may have become rich from what lies beneath, a strong connection to the desert and the sea is something that remains more important than petrodollars.

⊙ Sights

Abu Dhabi's sights are scattered across town with clusters in the city centre and on Yas Island. Sheikh Zayed Grand Mosque is between the two areas, near Al Maqta Bridge.

Abu Dhabi Corniche   STREET
One of the most pleasant developments in recent years is the expansion and extension of the waterfront Corniche, with its white sandy beaches and wide Mediterranean-style promenade. You can rent a sunbed and beach umbrella here; Fridays are busiest.

Sheesha cafes are spread across the grassy verge next to the Corniche and are great for soaking up some local ambience. A great way to get around is by bicycle. **Funride** (☑ 556 6113; www.funridesports.com; adult/child per hr Dh30/20) has rentals at the **Hilton** (W Corniche Rd), the **Sheraton** (E Corniche Rd) and the **Chamber of Commerce**, all on or near the Corniche.

Emirates Palace   LANDMARK
(☑ 02-690 9000; www.emiratespalace.com; W Corniche Rd) You don't have to check in to check

Abu Dhabi

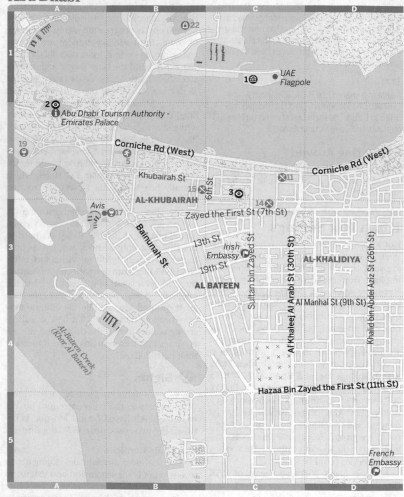

out this over-the-top glam hotel. It was built at the cost of a cool Dh11 billion, which explains the mindboggling use of marble, gold and crystal (1002 Swarovski chandeliers!) throughout as well as the ATM that dispenses solid gold bars. With nearly 400 rooms and suites, 114 domes and a 1.3km private beach it is as intriguingly colossal as it is swish.

Enjoy classic English afternoon tea (Dh225) or, at the very least, have a good wander around the lobby, perhaps ogling ancient art from China, Egypt, Africa, Greece and Rome on display at the world-renowned **Barakat Gallery** (690 8950; www.barakatgalleryuae.com). Also stop by the **Saadiyat Island Cultural District Exhibition** (10am-10pm) FREE, which provides an overview of the museum cluster taking shape off the shore of Abu Dhabi.

Abu Dhabi Heritage Village MUSEUM
(02-681 4455; near Marina Mall, Breakwater; 9am-5pm Sat-Thu, 3.30-9pm Fri) FREE This fortress-like compound lets you catch a glimpse of life in the pre-oil days, with an ersatz souq, mosque, *barasti* house and Bedouin encampment complete with goat-

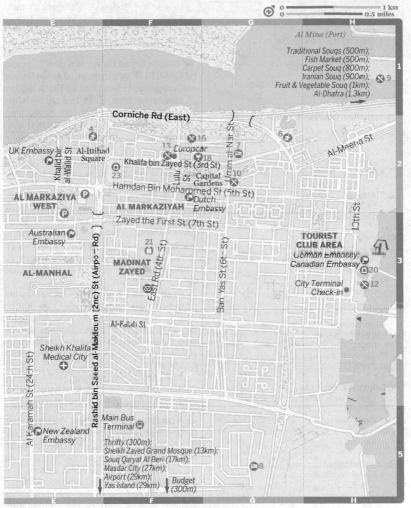

Al Mina (Port)

Traditional Souqs (500m);
Fish Market (500m);
Carpet Souq (800m);
Iranian Souq (900m);
Fruit & Vegetable Souq (1km);
Al-Dhafra (1.3km)

Corniche Rd (East)

UK Embassy   Al-Ittihad
Square

Khalifa bin Zayed St (3rd St)

Capital
Gardens

Hamdan Bin Mohammed St (5th St)

Dutch
Embassy

AL MARKAZIYA
WEST

AL MARKAZIYAH

Zayed the First St (7th St)

Australian
Embassy

TOURIST
CLUB AREA

German Embassy;
Canadian Embassy

MADINAT
ZAYED

AL-MANHAL

City Terminal
Check-in

Al-Falah St

Sheikh Khalifa
Medical City

Main Bus
Terminal

New Zealand
Embassy

Thrifty (300m);
Sheikh Zayed Grand Mosque (13km);
Souq Qaryat Al Beri (17km);
Masdar City (27km);
Airport (29km);
Yas Island (29km)   Budget
(300m)

hair tents. Watch craftsmen at work and study displays of Bedouin jewellery, traditional clothing, cooking utensils, camel harnesses and equipment used by pearl divers and merchants.

Traditional Souqs   MARKET

(Al Mina Port area) One of the few authentic places left in Abu Dhabi is the souq area in Al Mina. A highlight is the **fish market**, where you can buy the fish straight off the boat and even have it cooked at one of the stalls on the market's edge. More haggling goes on across the street in the **fruit and vegetable souq** and south of here in the **Carpet Souq** and **Iranian Souq**, which sells household goods, earthenware, plants and crafts.

Women's Handicraft Centre   ARTS CENTRE

(☎02-447 6645; south end of Al Karamah/24th St; admission Dh5; ☺7am-3pm Sun-Thu) Anyone interested in traditional Emirati handicrafts should swing by this government-run centre where local women are engaged in textile weaving, embroidering, basket-making, silver-threading and all sorts of other time-honoured crafts requiring remarkable dex-

Abu Dhabi

terity. It's all a great way to showcase and preserve the country's folk-art heritage.

Take off your shoes before entering the various workshops and ask permission first before snapping away. All items are for sale in a small shop. For a souvenir that lasts about two weeks, get your hands swathed in an artistic henna tattoo.

To get here, follow Al Karamah St until it deadends at the General Women's Union. The crafts centre is behind the main union building (ask the guard for directions).

★ **Sheikh Zayed Grand Mosque** MOSQUE
(☑ 02-441 6444; www.szgmc.ae; off Airport Rd, near Al Maqta Bridge; ☺ 9am-10pm Sat-Thu, 4.30-10pm Fri, closed prayer times) **FREE** This snowy white mosque – conceived by Sheikh Zayed himself – can accommodate up to 40,000 worshippers and is architecturally impressive inside and out. More than 80 marble domes dance on its roofline, which is held aloft by over 1000 pillars and punctuated by four 107m-high minarets.

Taking design cues from Morocco, Turkey and even India's Taj Mahal, the interior is a made-to-impress mix of marble, gold, semi-precious stones, crystals and ceramics. Walk on the world's largest Persian carpet (which took 2000 craftsmen two years to complete) with seven massive gold-plated crystal chandeliers dangling above you.

You're free to walk around except during prayer times or join a free 45- to 60-minute guided tour (in English). See the website for the latest prayer and tour timings and be sure to wear long, loose fitting, ankle-length trousers or skirts; women must also wear a headscarf.

Approaching the mosque, you'll pass by Sheikh Zayed's mausoleum where attendants recite the Quran 24/7 (no photos).

Abu Dhabi Falcon Hospital WILDLIFE RESERVE
(☑ 02-575 5155; www.falconhospital.com; Al Raha; 2-/3-hr tour adult Dh170/220, child Dh60/80; ☺ tours 10am & 2pm Sun-Thu) Falcons have an almost mythical status in Arab culture. The largest falcon hospital in the world with 'patients' arriving from all over the region, this veterinary clinic also provides fascinating guided tours. Visit the falcon museum, the examination room an d the free-flight aviary before having a live raptor sit right on your arm (bring that camera!). The three-hour tour includes a falcon pedicure and lunch.

Reservations are mandatory and tickets are available online. The hospital is about 6km southeast of Abu Dhabi airport. Coming from central Abu Dhabi, follow Airport Rd (E20) to Sweihan Rd in the direction of Falah City; about 3km past the junction with Hwy E11, turn right after the water tank (before exit 30A) and follow the signs to the hospital.

Activities

Yas Island, offshore from the airport, is revving up to reel in the testosterone crowd. Since 2009, the world's racing elite has descended in November for the Formula 1 race on the 5.5km Yas Marina Circuit, which features 21 wicked turns and straightways leading to top speeds above 300km/h. Uniquely, it runs straight through the futuristic Yas Viceroy Hotel.

Ferrari World Abu Dhabi   THEME PARK
(☑ 02-496 8001; www.ferrariworldabudhabi.com; Yas Island; adult/child under 1.3m Dh225/185, VIP pass Dh325/265; ⊙ 11am-8pm Tue-Sun, seasonal variations) If you want bragging rights to having 'done' Formula Rossa, the world's fastest rollercoaster (top speed 240km/h), visit this temple of torque and celebration of all things Ferrari in a spectacular building on Yas Island. Tamer diversions include a flume ride through a V12 engine, a motion-simulator that lets you ride shotgun with a racecar champion, and an imaginative 4D adventure. There's also a somewhat saner rollercoaster that has you 'race' a Ferrari F430 Spider around the track. Between thrills, check out the car exhibitions or live shows.

Yas Waterworld   WATER PARK
(www.yaswaterworld.com; Yas Island; adult/child Dh225/185, with Fast Pass Dh325/265; ⊙ 10am-6pm Nov-Feb, to 7pm Mar-May, Sep & Oct, to 8pm Jun-Aug) The UAE's newest and grandest water park will get you wet on 43 rides, slides and other liquid attractions as you follow a little Emirati girl named Dana on her quest for a magical pearl. With four thrill levels, there are rides for nervous nellies and adrenaline junkies alike. Top draws include the Bandit Bomber rollercoaster with water and laser effects; a hair-raising looping slide called Liwa Loop; and Dawwama, a wild tornado ride through a 20m-high funnel.

Yas Central   CAR RACING
(www.yasmarinacircuit.com; Yas Island; tours Dh120, driver/passenger rides from Dh1500/825; ⊙ 9am-11pm, tours 10am-noon & 2-4pm) Yas Central is the gateway to the racing world. Here you can go behind the scenes of this state-of-the-art venue on guided tours to see the support pit garages, the media centre and the Paddock area. If you want to hit the track yourself, a variety of driver and passenger experiences are available. Check the website for details.

🚌 Tours

Big Bus Tours   BUS TOURS
(☑ toll-free 800 244 287; www.bigbustours.com; adult/child Dh200/100) This hop-on hop-off service loops past all major sights, including the Sheikh Zayed Grand Mosque, the Emirates Palace Hotel and Ferrari World Abu Dhabi. Tickets are available online or at stops.

⭐ Festivals & Events

Abu Dhabi Film Festival   FILM
(www.abudhabifilmfestival.ae) Stars, starlets, directors, critics and cinephiles descend upon Abu Dhabi in October.

ABU DHABI IN...

One Day
Kick off the day with a tour of the stunning **Sheikh Zayed Grand Mosque** (p328), then head into town for lunch, perhaps at Zyara Cafe (p331), followed by a postprandial stroll along the **Abu Dhabi Corniche** (p325). Pop into the **Central Souq** (p327), then cab it over to the **Abu Dhabi Heritage Village** (p326) for a sense of society in the pre-oil days. Admire the out-of-this-world opulence of **Emirates Palace** (p325) next and maybe even stay for cocktails or dinner.

Two Days
In the morning, find out what it takes to turn a desert island into a futuristic Cultural District at the Saadiyat Story, a free exhibit on **Saadiyat Island** (p326). Next up, hop two islands further to have your eyeballs pressed into their sockets aboard the world's fastest roller coaster at **Ferrari World Abu Dhabi** (p329). Several hours later stagger over to the **Viceroy Abu Dhabi** (p330) hotel to marvel at the eccentric design and the fact that a Formula One racetrack runs right through it. Wrap up the day with a spin around the **Souq Qaryat Al-Beri** (p333) and dinner at one of its fine restaurants.

ⓘ YAS EXPRESS

A great way to get around Yas Island is aboard the free **Yas Express**, a shuttle bus that links Yas Viceroy Hotel, Yas Central, Ferrari World Abu Dhabi, Yas Waterworld and hotels at Yas Plaza every 40 minutes between 9am and 9pm.

Abu Dhabi Grand Prix　　　CAR RACE
(www.yasmarinacircuit.ae) The Formula 1 racing elite tests its mettle on this wicked 5.5km-long track on Yas Island in early November.

🛏 Sleeping

Abu Dhabi doesn't have a youth hostel, and budget accommodation is practically non-existent, although most hotels listed here offer steep discounts when business is slow (including summer, Ramadan, and non-European holiday times).

Traders Qaryat Al-Beri　　　HOTEL **$$**
(☑ 02-510 8880; www.tradershotel.com; Qaryat Al-Beri, Bain Al-Jessrain; r from Dh550; 🅿 🛜 ⛉) The cutting-edge cool lobby welcomes you with upbeat pop-art flair and bright colours, but rooms are more subdued, while modern and spacious. A private beach and pool beckon when the sun's up, while at dinnertime some of the city's best restaurants are just a stroll away.

The Village – One to One Hotel　　　HOTEL **$$**
(☑ 02-495 2000; www.onetoonehotels.com; off Salam/8th St; r from Dh545; 🅿 🛜 ⛉) Close to the city centre, this sassy lifestyle hotel scores points with trendy, design-minded travellers. The 127 rooms are spread over 18 buildings, each with its own rooftop pool, giving the place a boutique feel despite its size. Facilities include an excellent gym, a lounge-bar and several eateries.

Aloft Abu Dhabi　　　HOTEL **$$**
(☑ 02-654 5000; www.aloftabudhabi.com; Abu Dhabi National Exhibition Centre; d from Dh450; 🅿 🛜 ⛉) The loft-like rooms, rooftop pool and jazzy ambience should radiate enough urban poshness to appeal to the style patrol. Rooms sport such zeitgeist-compatible touches as free wi-fi, big flatscreen TVs, iPod docking stations and walk-in showers, while the popular rooftop bar Relax@12 (p332) has killer views and cocktails. It's in the ADNEC exhibition centre not far from the Sheikh Zayed Grand Mosque.

Centro Yas Island　　　HOTEL **$$**
(☑ 02-656 4444; www.rotana.com/centroyasisland; Golf Plaza, Yas Island; r from Dh500; 🅿 🅿 🛜 ⛉) The first outpost of Rotana's hip spin-off is sitting pretty on Yas Island and packs a lot of style and comfort into its compact rooms. Rates include access to the gym at the adjacent Yas Island Rotana.

Le Royal Méridien Abu Dhabi　　　HOTEL **$$**
(☑ 02-674 2020; www.leroyalmeridienabudhabi. com; Sheikh Khalifa St; d from Dh700; 🛜 ⛉) An urge to splurge would be well directed towards this luxe abode that's a favourite with international glitterati and politicos. Rooms are super-plush with big beds you won't want to leave and all the expected creature comforts, from luscious towels and bathrobes to fancy-brand toiletries. The views of the Corniche are spectacular and there are lots of great bars and restaurants on-site.

Eastern Mangroves Hotel & Spa　　　LUXURY HOTEL **$$$**
(☑ 02-656 1000; http://abu-dhabi.anantara.com; Eastern Ring Rd, Salam St; d from Dh1000; @ 🛜 ⛉) The moment you step into the lobby with its display of dates, *mashrabiya* patterns and oud player, you know that Arabian hospitality is taken very seriously at this luxe abode overlooking a lush bed of mangroves (kayak tours available). And so is spaciousness and luxury, especially in the soothingly furnished rooms with teal and orange colour accents. Work up an appetite in the infinity pool or state-of-the-art gym before grazing on sushi, Asian, Arabic and Italian fare prepared in the show kitchen of the Impressions restaurant. Sheikh sightings distinctly possible.

Yas Viceroy Abu Dhabi　　　HOTEL **$$$**
(☑ 02-656 0000; www.viceroyhotelsandresorts. com; Yas Island; from Dh725; @ 🛜 ⛉) The most visually dramatic addition to Abu Dhabi's hotelscape sits in pole position on Yas Island, not far from the Ferrari World Abu Dhabi theme park. The avant-garde, steel-and-glass structure with its organically shaped 'flyer saucer' roof is especially dramatic when illuminated at night. Rooms are considerably more down-to-earth and sport the gamut of tech toys and creature comforts.

✖ Eating

Automatic Restaurant   LEBANESE **$**
(☑ 02-676 9677; cnr Hamdan & 6th Sts; sandwiches Dh4-7, mains Dh18-65; ☻11am-1am) Stick to the standards at this local chain where the shwarma is as succulent as the hummus is creamy and the kebabs have just the right crispy tan.

Café Du Roi   FRENCH **$**
(☑ 02-681 5096; Corniche Rd West, Al Khalidiya; mains Dh15-35; ☻7am-midnight; ☎) With superb coffee and delicious pastries, croissants and sandwiches, plus seven choices of fluffy filled omelettes, this French-style cafe is the perfect spot for some leisurely lingering. Also at Abu Dhabi Mall.

★ Zyara Cafe   MIDDLE EASTERN **$$**
(☑ 02-627 5007; Al Jazeera Tower, Corniche St; mains Dh40-100; ☻8am-midnight) The panoramic windows offer primo Corniche views at this convivial and artily furnished cafe where everyone from families to friends gathers to combat hunger pangs. Everything on the menu is made in-house, including the refreshing mint lemonade and the creamy blueberry cheesecake. If possible, avoid the lunchtime crush.

Hanoi Cafe   VIETNAMESE **$$**
(☑ 02-626 1112; www.hanoi-cafe.com; Khalifa St; mains Dh30-50; ☻10am-11pm) The minimalist decor provides little distraction for the richly flavoured and healthily prepared *pho* (noodle) soups, crispy spring rolls and mains ranging from caramelised ginger chicken to tiger prawns in tamarind sauce. Not superauthentic, perhaps, but tasty for sure.

Jones the Grocer   INTERNATIONAL **$$**
(☑ 02-639 5883; www.jonesthegrocer.com; Pearl Plaza lower, ground fl, 32nd St; mains Dh50-60; ☻8am-11pm Sun-Thu, 9am-11pm Fri & Sat) Catering to an urban-chic clientele, this local outpost of the Australian chain has open kitchens overlooking the dining area decked out in stainless steel and earthy wood colours. Talking points include a chilled cheese room with samples to taste, and an eclectic menu with plenty of organic goodies. It's next to the Oryx Hotel.

La Brioche Cafe   FRENCH **$$**
(☑ 02-626 9300; www.labriocheuae.com; Khalifa St; mains Dh22-70) A slice of Paris in the UAE, this minichain charmer makes heaping salads, bulging sandwiches and some of the best bread, croissants and pastries (baked fresh and local) in town. Service is swift and smiley.

Finz   SEAFOOD **$$**
(☑ 02-697 9011; Beach Rotana Hotel & Towers, Abu Dhabi Mall, Tourist Club Area; mains Dh60-100; ☻12.30-3.30pm & 7-11.30pm) Amble down the jetty to snag a table at this wooden A-frame with terraces above the azure sea, then order a cocktail and prepare for some of the finest seafood around. Whether grilled, wok cooked, baked or prepared in the tandoor oven, the results are invariably delicious.

Mezlai   EMIRATI **$$$**
(☑ 02-690 7999; www.kempinski.com; Emirates Palace, 1st fl; mains Dh110-205; ☻1pm-10.30pm) Meaning 'old door lock', swank Mezlai delivers a rare chance to sample high-end Emirati food prepared from locally sourced organic produce and meats. Home-grown favourites include hammour *mafrook* (a whitefish spread served with fresh bread) and lamb *medfoun* (slow-cooked, banana leaf-wrapped lamb shoulder). Pair it with a side of camel milk–mashed potatoes.

ABU DHABI'S 'SILICON VALLEY' OF CLEAN-TECH

A most ambitious development is taking shape next to Abu Dhabi airport: **Masdar City** (☑ toll-free 800 627 327; www.masdar.ae; btwn Hwys E10 & E20, just west of airport; ☻8.30am-4.30pm Sun-Thu), the world's first carbon-neutral, zero-waste city powered entirely by renewable energy. Nope, it's not the latest Hollywood fantasy but a real US$22 billion project to be completed by 2016. The firm of British starchitect Lord Norman Foster is providing the blueprint for what will essentially be a living laboratory for around 50,000 people. Some of the world's brightest minds have gathered here to find new, clean and sustainable ways to build the cities of the future.

Masdar City is open to the public and can be explored on foot or using one of the podlike, driverless PRT (Personal Rapid Transit) vehicles. For a thorough background, download the free *Exploring Masdar City* booklet and a map from www.masdarconnect.com.

BACCHANALIAN BOATING

The Abu Dhabi Corniche and skyline form a magical backdrop for a leisurely dinner aboard a traditional dhow. Based next to the Fish Market at the port, **Al Dhafra** (☏02-673 2266; www.aldhafra.net; dinner Dh250; ☺cruise 8.30-10.30pm) runs two-hour dinner cruises with a fixed three-course Arabic meal, including nonalcoholic beverages. Sit in air-conditioned comfort downstairs or alfresco on the *majlis*-style upper deck.

Bord Eau   FRENCH $$$

(☏02-509 8888; www.shangri-la.com; Shangri-La Hotel, Qaryat Al-Beri; mains Dh90-150, five-course blind tasting menu with wine Dh500; ☺7-11.30pm) To put it plainly, Bord Eau is a restaurant out of a foodie's daydream. The classic yet updated French fare (onion soup, foie gras, chateaubriand, etc) is flawlessly executed with flavours that are calibrated to perfection. The ambience is formal without being stuffy. Good for a special occasion or serious date night. Find it between the bridges.

Marco Pierre White
Steakhouse & Grill   STEAKHOUSE $$$

(☏02-654 3333; Fairmont Bab Al Bhar; mains Dh200-250; ☺7pm-1am) Meat lovers will be in heaven at this swish nosh spot dreamed up by British celebrity chef Marco Pierre White. The dining room gets theatrical flourish from a dramatic 'flame wall' but fortunately the culinary pyrotechnics are kept in check in the kitchen. The emphasis is squarely on quality cuts, prepared both in classic English style and innovative grilled variations.

Self-Catering

Big, central supermarkets with convenient opening hours include **Carrefour** (☏681 7100; www.carrefouruae.com; Marina Mall; ☺9am-midnight Sat-Wed, to 1am Thu), which has lots of products from Europe. North American expats tend to prefer **Spinneys** (☏681 2897; www.spinneys-dubai.com; cnr 5th & 6th Sts, Khalidiya; ☺9.30am-8.30pm Sat-Thu, 3.30-8.30pm Fri). A popular local chain is **Abu Dhabi Coop** (☏645 9777; www.abudhabicoop.com/english; Abu Dhabi Mall; ☺8am-midnight). All have additional branches around town (see the websites for locations).

Drinking & Nightlife

Relax@12   BAR

(☏02-654 5183; www.relaxat12.com; Khaleej Al Arabi St, near Adnec, Aloft Abu Dhabi; ☺5pm-2am) This stylish rooftop bar indeed puts you in a mood for relaxing with mellow sounds, comfy seating and an extensive drinks menu that won't eviscerate your wallet. Sushi and tapas are available to help you stay stable and dancing in the attached **Club So-Hi** (Mondays to Fridays).

Ray's Bar   BAR

(www.jumeirah.com; Jumeirah Etihad Towers, Corniche West; ☺5pm-3am) The highest bar in town floats on the 62nd floor of this ultra-deluxe hotel and lets you appreciate just how massive the landmark Emirates Palace down below really is. From Wednesday to Friday, DJs deliver deep house while discerning sippers gather for civilised conversation.

Belgian Beer Cafe   BAR

(☏02-666 6888; www.belgianbeercafe.com; Intercontinental Hotel, Bainouna St, Khor Al Bateen; ☺5pm-1am) Join the local expat crowd and enjoy a wide choice of imported draughts and bottled beers. And don't forget that excellent accompaniment – a plate of perfectly fried fries with the obligatory mayo on the side.

Cristal   BAR

(☏02-614 6000; Khalifa St, Millennium Hotel; ☺noon-2.30am) Dressed in polished mahogany and illuminated by candlelight and a fireplace, dapper Cristal is a haven for the testosterone-fuelled crowd. Whiskey and cigars are de rigueur for men, while the ladies sip on French champagne. For sophistication on the cheap, come during happy hour (5pm to 8pm).

Eight   BAR, CLUB

(☏02-558 1988; www.eightabudhabi.com; Shangri-La Hotel, Souq Qaryat Al-Beri) Popular with cabin crews, this libation station at the Shangri-La delivers a potent cocktail of style. At night, it morphs into a hot-stepping club that on occasion gets some really hot DJs from the international circuit to hit the turntables. Great views.

Hemingways   BAR

(☏02-681 1900; Hilton Abu Dhabi; ☺noon-1am) A cantina popular with long-term expats, Hemingways is where you can watch the game on the big screen over beer and a bowl of nachos or other Latin munchies. Live band Mondays to Saturdays, Ladies' Night Tuesdays and Sunday Quiz Night keep the punters coming back.

Allure by Cipriani CLUB
(☎02-657 5400; www.nightcluballure.com; Yas Island Yacht Club) Drink in the mesmerising views of the curvy Viceroy Yas Island and the Formula 1 track from the terrace, then retire to the sensuously glam interior of this platinum crowd weekend hotspot. Resident DJs keep toes tapping with R&B and chart hits.

Sax CLUB
(☎02-674 2020; Royal Meridien Abu Dhabi; ☺7pm-3.30am) In the early evening Sax lures chatty jet-setters huddled in intense tête-à-têtes, then cranks up the superb sound system to pack the dance floor with a glam-tastic, international crowd. Different promotions – Ladies' Night, Cabin Crew Night, Lebanese Weekend – keep things dynamic.

☆ Entertainment

The latest Hollywood blockbusters play at the multiplex cinemas **Grand Abu Dhabi** (☎02-645 8988; www.grandcinemas.com; Tourist Club/10th St; tickets Dh35) and the superluxe **Vox Cinemas** (☎02-681 8464; www.voxcinemas.com; Marina Mall; tickets from Dh47).

Jazz Bar LIVE MUSIC
(☎02-681 1900; Corniche Rd West, Hilton Abu Dhabi; ☺7pm-2am Sun-Fri) Cool cats flock to this sophisticated supper club that serves contemporary fusion cuisine (mains Dh50-200) in a modern art deco–inspired setting against the backdrop of a live band.

🔒 Shopping

Souq at Central Market SOUQ
(☎02-810 7810; www.centralmarket.ae/souk; Khalifa St; ☺10am-10pm Sun-Thu, to 11pm Fri & Sat) Norman Foster's reinterpretation of the traditional souq is a stylish composition of warm lattice woodwork, stained glass, walkways and balconies on the site of Abu Dhabi's historic central market. Ironically, it's the location that is the souq's biggest handicap, lost as it is within a forest of ho-hum office high-rises. As of this writing, many storefronts remained empty and few shoppers were browsing the high-end stores.

Souq Qaryat Al-Beri SOUQ
(☎02-558 1670; next to Shangri-La Hotel, btwn Maqta & Mussafah Bridges) This 21st-century take on the classic souq gets thumbs up for

its appealing Arabian architecture and waterfront location. There are some nice restaurants, retail and souvenir shops and *abra* rides through faux canals.

Marina Mall MALL
(☎02-681 2310; www.marinamall.ae; Breakwater; ☺10am-10pm Sat-Wed, to 11pm Thu, 2-11pm Fri) For locals, the main draw of this big mall on the Breakwater seems to be Ikea, but fortunately there are over 400 other stores in case you don't need yet another Billy bookcase. Entertainment options include a multiplex cinema, tiny ice-skating rink and **Fun City** (☎02-681 5526; Marina Mall, Breakwater; ☺10am-11pm Sat-Wed, to midnight Thu, 2pm-midnight Fri), a huge activity centre for children that includes a (relatively tame) rollercoaster and dodgem cars.

Abu Dhabi Mall MALL
(☎02 645 4858; www.abudhabi-mall.com; 10th St; ☺10am-10pm Sat-Wed, to 11pm Thu, 4-10pm Fri) This elegant mall has 200 high-street and designer stores, the Grand Cinemas (p333) multiplex, a big food court, a children's entertainment area and a huge supermarket.

Madinat Zayed Gold Centre MALL
(☎02-633 3311; www.madinatzayed-mall.com; 4th St; ☺9am-11pm) If you're in the market for stuff that glitters, browse around the 70 jewellery stores in what is also a regular mall.

ABU DHABI FOR CHILDREN

Keep tempers cool by taking the kids to the brand-new **Yas Waterworld** (p329), a state-of-the-art water park. A huge indoor amusement park with a jungle theme, **Fun City** (p333) will keep tots entertained with bumper cars, a roller coaster, carousels and arcade games. If you prefer the outdoors, take them to the beaches along the Corniche or to **Khalidiya Garden** (Khaleej al-Arabi/30th & Sheikh Zayed the First/7th Sts, Al-Khalidiya; admission 3-10pm Sun-Thu & 11am-11pm Fri Dh1, other times free; ☺6am-midnight), which has large grassy areas perfect for picnics, as well as inflatable slides, trampolines and pony rides. Older kids might also enjoy a visit to the **Falcon Hospital** (p328) or a desert safari, while teenaged speed freaks will love you for treating them to **Ferrari World Abu Dhabi** (p329).

ℹ Orientation

The city of Abu Dhabi occupies an island connected to the mainland by three bridges: Sheikh Zayed Bridge, which links Hwy E10 (Abu Dhabi–Dubai Rd) with Al Salam (8th) St; Al Maqta Bridge, which connects Hwy E22 (Abu Dhabi–Al Ain Rd) and Hwy E20 (Airport Rd) with Rashid Bin Saeed Al Maktoum (2nd) St; and Musaffah Bridge which links Hwys E20 and E22 with Al Khaleej Al Arabi (30th) St.

All main roads run through the Abu Dhabi city centre and culminate at the Corniche. Planned along a classic grid system, the central city would be easy to navigate if only streets didn't have multiple names as well as numbers. Roads paralleling the Corniche have uneven numbers (Corniche Rd being 1st St); those running vertically have even numbers (hence Al Salam St is also known as 8th St).

The airport is about 30km east of the Corniche, close to Yas Island, which is accessed by Hwy E12 (Sheikh Khalifa Hwy), which continues to Saadiyat Island and eventually links up with the Corniche via Sheikh Khalifa Bridge.

ℹ Information

Abu Dhabi Tourism Authority (ADTA; ☑ toll-free 800 555; www.visitabudhabi.ae) Has information desks in the airport arrivals hall, at **Emirates Palace** (W Corniche Rd) and in Al Maqta Fort (next to Al Maqta Bridge).

Central Post Office (☑ 02-610 7211; 4th St; ⊙ 7.30am-9pm Sat-Thu, 5-9pm Fri)

Police (☑ emergencies 999, tourist police 699 9999)

Sheikh Khalifa Medical City (☑ 02-610 2000; Al Bateen St) 24-hour emergency room. For locations of 24-hour pharmacies, call ☑ 777 929.

ℹ Getting There & Away

AIR

Abu Dhabi International Airport (☑ 02-505 5555, automated flight information ☑ 02-575 7500; www.abudhabiairport.ae) is about 30km

---

ABU DHABI – TAKING ON THE ART WORLD

Art lovers take note: one of the world's most ambitious cultural construction projects is taking shape on Saadiyat Island off the coast of Abu Dhabi. When all is said and built, the new **Cultural District** will consist of four museums and a performing arts centre, making it (what else?) the largest cluster of art repositories in the world.

Construction has been fraught with delays but finally picked up again in early 2013 when the first construction contract was awarded. Three of the five buildings are now projected to be open by 2017. Other plans for the island include homes for around 150,000 people alongside five-star hotels, resorts, golf courses and a shopping mall.

Created by five Pritzker Prize–winning architects (the Pritzker Prize is the 'Oscar' of architecture), each structure seems more daring than the next, with the **Louvre Abu Dhabi** perhaps being the most anticipated. Designed by Jean Nouvel, its most distinctive feature is a perforated white dome that appears to hover above the water. Galleries will exhibit artwork drawn from several museums, including the Paris Louvre and the Centre Georges Pompidou.

Also on the drawing board is Lord Norman Foster's **Zayed National Museum**, which honours the UAE's 'founding father'. Foster translated Sheikh Zayed's love of falconry into an avant-garde structure with jutting steel-and-glass galleries inspired by flight and feathers. Each 'feather' will contain a gallery highlighting different historical and cultural aspects of the country.

The **Guggenheim Abu Dhabi** promises to be a similarly exciting building: a cacophonous composition of geometrical shapes – cuboids to cones, cylinders to prisms – designed by Frank Gehry. It will showcase international contemporary art.

Envisioned for a second phase is a spaceshiplike **Performing Arts Centre** by Iraqi-British Zaha Hadid as well as Tadao Ando's comparatively austere **Maritime Museum**.

For a preview and a sense of the ambition of the project, visit the Saadiyat, a high-tech exhibit that combines substance with slick sales presentation techniques. It's in the **Manarat Al Saadiyat** (www.saadiyat.ae; Saadiyat Island; ⊙ 10am-8pm) **FREE** exhibition centre, right on the island. Coming from central Abu Dhabi, take Sheikh Khalifa Bridge to Sheikh Khalifa Hwy (E12) and follow the signs. From Dubai, follow Hwy E11 to the Saadiyat Island exit and from there to Hwy E12. There's also a smaller exhibit at the Emirates Palace (p325).

east of the city centre. It has three terminals, including Etihad's exclusive base, Terminal 3. Free wi-fi throughout.

CAR

Abu Dhabi is 150km south of Dubai via Sheikh Zayed Rd (Hwy E11). All the international car-rental agencies have branches at the airport and within the city.

Avis (02-621 5400; www.avis.com; Baynunah St, Intercontinental Hotel)

Budget (02-633 4200; www.budget.com; nr 4th & 13th Sts)

Europcar (02-626 1441; www.europcarabudhabi.com; Khalifa St, opp National Bank of Abu Dhabi)

Thrifty (02-445 5011; www.thriftyuae.com; nr Delma/13th & Maktoum/2nd Sts)

TAXI

Shared taxis leave from next to the main bus terminal. Expect to pay Dh20 for shared rides to Dubai or Al Ain. Engaged (private) **taxis** (600 535 353; www.transad.ae) cost between Dh250 and Dh300 to either and can be booked in advance.

ⓘ Getting Around

TO/FROM THE AIRPORT

Air-conditioned bus A1 picks up from outside the arrivals area of all terminals at intervals ranging from 30 to 60 minutes around the clock (1¼ hours, Dh3) and travels via the central bus station all the way into town as far as the Tourist Club Area.

Etihad passengers can use free shuttle buses to and from Dubai, Al Ain and Sharjah (show your boarding pass).

Taxis cost Dh70 to Dh80 for the half hour trip to the city centre.

If you're leaving on Etihad, Gulf, Cathay Pacific, Air Berlin and a few other airlines, you may be able to check your luggage and pick up a boarding pass between four and 24 hours before departure at four remote check-in locations: **City Terminal** (02-644 8434) near Abu Dhabi Mall, Adnec, Park Rotana and Crowne Plaza on Yas Island.

BUS

Abu Dhabi Bus Services (8005 5555; www.ojra.ae) currently operates nine public bus routes around the clock. Useful route include bus 32, 44 and 54, which all go from the city centre out to the Sheikh Zayed Grand Mosque. Bus 5 links the Marina Mall with the port and Tourist Club Area via the central business district.

Rides cost Dh2; put the coin in the fare box by the driver. For multiple trips, consider the Ojra Day Pass (Dh3), sold at such bus stops at Marina Mall, Abu Dhabi Mall and Al Whada Mall. For more routes and other details, call or check the website.

The **central bus terminal** (cnr 4th & 11th Sts) is about 4km south of the Corniche. RTA (p360) buses to Dubai leave every 30 minutes from 5.30am to 10.30pm (Dh25, two hours).

The Abu Dhabi Department of Transportation (p360) operates numerous services within the emirate. Destinations include:

DESTINATION	FARE (DH)	TIME (HR)	FREQUENCY
Al Ain (X90)	25	1¾	half-hourly
Madinat Zayed (X60)	25	2½	hourly
Mezaira'a (X60)	30	3	hourly
Jebel Dhanna (X87)	35	4½	daily

TAXI

Taxis are metered and charge Dh3.50 at flagfall plus Dh1.60 per kilometre. Between 10pm and 6am rates climb to Dh4 and Dh1.69, respectively, and a Dh10 minimum fare comes into effect.

AL GHARBIA الغربية

The desert is a land of contradictions: vast yet intimate, barren yet beautiful, searing yet restorative. In short, it's a special, spiritual, almost mystical place that's often so whisper-quiet it feels as though someone has pushed the mute button. So if you really want to get away from it all, steer your pony south and west of Abu Dhabi into the Al Gharbia region, which is all desert, all the time. There are two main areas, the Liwa Oasis and Sir Bani Yas Island on the far western coast.

Madinat Zayed مدينة زايد

En route to the Liwa desert, you'll likely pass through Madinat Zayed, the largest town in the Al Gharbia region. Along the main commercial strip, you'll find ATMs, internet cafes, a hospital, a petrol station, Al Dhafra Co-op supermarket and the brand-new City Mall.

Every December or January, thousands of long-legged, humped beauties descend upon town to take part in **Al Dhafra Camel**

Festival (www.aldhafrafestival.com), which centres on a camel beauty contest along with heritage activities, auctions, crafts and merriment of all sort.

Madinat Zayed also has its own **camel race track** just south of town, with races usually taking place on Fridays between October and March. Overlooking the track is the spanking new **Tilal Liwa Hotel** (☑02-894 6111; www.tilal-liwa.hotel-rn.com; Million St, Madinat Zayed; r from Dh430; 🅿🛜🏊), a modern and comfortable fort-style retreat where you can count the colours of the desert through a giant arch spanning across the infinity pool.

Still further south, en route to Liwa, you'll drive past the **Shams solar plant**, which will eventually be one of the largest of its kind in the world. Phase one should have gone live by the time you're reading this; it is capable of supplying energy for 20,000 homes.

Madinat Zayed is about 180km southwest of Abu Dhabi via Hwy E11 west and E45 south. From here, it's another 45km to Mezaira'a, the main town in the Liwa desert. Bus X60 from Abu Dhabi stops here en route to Mezaira'a (Dh25, hourly).

Liwa ليوا

Approximately 250km south of Abu Dhabi, the Liwa Desert is a 150km arc of villages and farms hugging the edge of Saudi Arabia's Empty Quarter (Rub'al-Khali), which truly lives up to its name: only the odd roaming camel or small verdant oasis magnifies just how spectacular this endless landscape of undulating sand dunes, shimmering in shades of gold, apricot and cinnamon, really is.

This is the Arabia described by explorer Sir Wilfred Thesiger, but it's also the birthplace of the Maktoum and Al Nahyan families, now the rulers of Dubai and Abu Dhabi respectively. Once you visit, you'll understand why the Liwa has a special place in the hearts of nationals who come here to get back to their roots, relax and just take in the arid splendour of this glorious landscape.

The commercial heart of the oasis is Mezaira'a, with activity centred on the junction of Hwy E43 from Madinat Zayed and Hwy E90, the main road through the Liwa. Here you'll find a gas station, an ATM, a supermarket and a hospital.

◎ Sights & Activities

The Liwa is best visited in your own vehicle, as the joy of travelling here is to be able to drive through the villages and stop spontaneously to photograph a lone camel, a proud fort or a spectacular 'desert rose' (flower-like crystallised gypsum).

Along the main road (Hwy E90), the most spectacular stretch is between Hameem and Mezaira'a. The dunes here are like shifting mountain ranges of sand, with green farms providing an occasional and unexpected patchwork effect.

The landscape west of Mezaira'a, towards Karima, is flatter and more open. An oddity here is the **Khanur Fish Farm**, where you can buy fresh tilapia, carp and other fish and grill it up at your campsite later on. The turn-off for Khanur is about 20km west of Mezaira'a. Ask locally for directions to the farm.

For the most sublime views of sand dunes, though, veer off the main highway just past central Mezaira'a and follow the signs to Mo-

---

EMIRATES NATIONAL AUTO MUSEUM

A hangar-size ode to the automobile, the **Emirates National Auto Museum** (www.enam.ae; Hwy E65; ⊙9am-1pm & 2-6pm, may vary) **FREE** is one of those rather kooky roadside attractions that one does not really expect to find in these parts. Some 45km south of Abu Dhabi, on the lonely Hwy E65 towards the Liwa Oasis, the pyramid-shaped structure holds about 250 vehicles – from concept cars to American classics – the oldest being a steam-powered Mercedes from 1885. It's the private collection of Sheikh Hamad bin Hamdan Al Nahyan, aka the 'Rainbow Sheikh' (in 1983 the sheikh bought seven Mercedes 500 SEL, one for each day of the week, painted in the colours of the rainbow).

Alas, opening hours are erratic at best, but even if no attendant is present, you can still marvel at some strange vehicles on display in front of the building: a monster truck, an eight-bedroom motor home (complete with balcony), and the 'earth on wheels' in the form of the Globe Trailer.

reeb Hill (or *Tal Mireb* – the signs will say both). Soaring almost 300m high, this is one of the world's tallest dunes and the only real 'sight' in the Liwa as such. To get to the dune (whose name translates as 'scary mountain'), turn left at the second roundabout, about 5km west of central Mezaira'a, and keep right when you reach the Liwa Resthouse. Continue along this well-signposted, paved road for about 20 minutes. The dune is where the road ends – you can't miss it!

⚡ Festivals & Events

Liwa International Festival　　　SPORTS
(www.admc.ae) The large flat area at the base of Moreeb Hill is the staging ground of the Liwa International Festival, usually held in January, and featuring car and bike races alongside shooting competitions, falconry, camel racing, hot-air balloon rides and other events.

Liwa Date Festival　　　FOOD
(www.liwadatesfestival.ae) In July, the quest for the best date is on at the Liwa Date Festival, which also features cooking competitions, a souq and a kids' tent.

🛏 Sleeping & Eating

Camping is hugely popular in the Liwa, although there were no designated camp sites at the time of research. If you do decide to camp, make sure to take out all your trash. Discarded rubbish, especially anything made of plastic, is highly dangerous when ingested by camels and other local wildlife. If you don't have camping gear, you can get fully kitted out by **Liwa Oasis Picnic** (📞050-812 0288) in an industrial area off the road to Moreeb Hill.

The best place to stock up on food and water is **Al Dhafra Hypermarket** (🕐8am–9pm) at the end of a commercial strip on the road to Madinat Zayed, next to the 24-hour petrol station. The market also has an ATM.

Liwa Resthouse　　　GUESTHOUSE **$**
(📞02-882 2075; fax 02-882 9311; Mezaira'a; d from Dh200; 🅿) This government-run resthouse is frill-free and functional but run by friendly folk. Faded furnishings, including an ancient TV and a fridge, characterise the big rooms. A cafeteria serves three meals a day. To get here, head west of Mezaira'a and pass through the unmarked gate at the second roundabout, just past the local police office. Cash only.

Liwa Hotel　　　HOTEL **$$**
(📞02-882 2000; www.liwahotel.net; Mezaira'a; r from Dh500; 🅿🛜❄) This hilltop contender set amid gardens offers dust-free respite after a day in the desert. Enjoy sunset drinks on your balcony facing a palace of the late Sheikh Zayed's (itself on a green sand dune!). There's an all-day coffeeshop for light meals and a restaurant (mains Dh40 to Dh85) serving international standards – don't expect any culinary flights of fancy. Alcohol available.

★Qsar Al Sarab　　　RESORT **$$$**
(📞02-886 2088; http://qsarsalsarab.anantara.com; 1 Qsar Al Sarab Rd, near Hameem; r from Dh1500, villa from Dh3400; 🅿🛜❄) Modelled on an actual Al Ain fort, this discreet retreat perfectly captures the desert vibe and blends seamlessly into its surroundings. Qsar Al Sarab's earth-toned rooms are decorated with original Bedouin artefacts as is the resort throughout – and come with balconies looking out over sweeping sand dunes and grazing oryx and gazelles. True, there's nothing at all around here, but with three restaurants, two bars, a relaxing spa, a library, a huge tree-form swimming pool with canopied daybeds and various outdoor activities available, you're at no risk of getting bored.

ℹ Getting There & Around

BUS
Bus X60 travels to Mezaira'a from Abu Dhabi's central bus station via Madinat Zayed (Dh30, 3½ hours). From Mezaira'a, local bus 640 travels west along Hwy 90 as far as Arrada Farms, while No 650 goes east to Hammeem Farms. There is no public transport to Moreeb Hill.

CAR
All the main roads are fit for 2WD vehicles, but you'll need a 4WD to go off-road.

Coming from Abu Dhabi, head west on Hwy E11 and turn south either on Hwy E65 to Hameem or on E45 to go via Madinat Zayed. The total trip is 250km either way. There are petrol stations on Hwy E65 at the Emirates National Auto Museum (p336), in Tarif on Hwy E11 and in Madinat Zayed. In the Liwa, you'll find gas in Hameem, in Mezaira'a, near the Khanur turnoff and in Umm Hisin.

From Jebel Dhanna/Ruwais, the long and lonely Hwy E15 also goes to the Liwa; gas is available in Ghayathi.

Abu Dhabi to Sila

Linking Abu Dhabi with Sila on the border with Saudi Arabia is Hwy E11, a mind-numbing, 350km-long, dual-carriage highway. The road is flanked by palm trees and fences beyond which lie the emirate's rich oil and gas fields. The main reason to travel along here is to get to Sir Bani Yas Island.

A good spot to break the journey after a couple of hours is in Mirfa, a low-key, sleepy fishing village with a nice sandy beach. The town comes to life in April during the 10-day Al Gharbia Watersports Festival (www.algharbiafestivals.com), which sees kite-surfing, sailing and swimming competitions along with dhow and dragon boat racing. If you want to stay, steer towards the falcon-shaped Mirfa Hotel (☏ 02-883 3030; www.mirfahotel.com; r from Dh500; P 🛜 🗗), which has big, if dated, rooms and a nice pool.

If you had any doubt as to the oil wealth of the UAE, it'll evaporate when you see Ruwais, an industrial town about an hour past Mirfa that exists only to service the massive refineries set up along there. Needless to say, there's little reason to stop.

Not far from Ruwais is Jebel Dhanna, the jumping off point for Sir Bani Yas Island. It has absolutely gorgeous white sandy beaches and shallow azure water perfect for the kiddies to splash around. An unexpected high-end treat is the five-star Danat Resort Jebel Dhanna (☏ 02-801 2222; www.danatho-

---

tels.com; r from Dh800; P @ 🛜 🗗), where you can hang in hammocks, relax by the pool, hit the tennis courts or rent a kayak. There's a cafe, a buffet restaurant, fine Italian fare at Zaitoun (pizza & pasta Dh60-100, mains Dh90-200), a bar and a club that's popular with expat workers from Ruwais.

Workers are also the main clientele of the adjacent Dhafra Beach Hotel (☏ 02-801 2000; www.danathotels.com; Jebel Dhanna; r from Dh450; P 🛜 🗗), which does little to hide its three-decade pedigree. Staying here gives you full access to the Danat, though.

As remote as it is, there are buses going out here from Abu Dhabi's central bus station. Bus X87 makes the trip all the way to the ferry terminal in Jebel Dhanna in 4½ hours (Dh35, daily). Bus X70 heads straight to Mirfa (Dh25, daily) and also meets the X87 in Tarif.

If you're driving, note that despite being surrounded by oil fields, there's a dearth of petrol stations, so take every opportunity to refuel – Hwy E11 is not a good place to run out of gas.

Sir Bani Yas Island
جزيرة صير بني ياس

A great way to shake off the stresses nibbling at your psyche is by taking a trip to Sir Bani Yas Island and contemplating life surrounded by a luxurious resort, thousands of free-roaming animals and the calm azure waters of the Gulf.

This 87 sq km desert island was originally Sheikh Zayed's private retreat. It was his love of animals that inspired him to turn it into a nature reserve and to bring many native species back from the brink of extinction. Today, 60% of the island is the protected home of 25 indigenous and introduced animal species, including sand gazelles, Barbary sheep, ostriches and even giraffes and cheetahs. Rarities include the Indian blackbuck, an antelope that can reach speeds of up to 90km/h, and several species of oryx, including the Arabian oryx, one of the world's most endangered animals.

Abu Dhabi's royal family still maintains two palaces in the island's south but if they forgot your invitation, you can still visit through the only resort, the fancy Desert Island Resort & Spa. The resort can also arrange day trips, although only a limited number of spots are available and then usually only on weekdays. Check details with

---

FUN FACTS ABOUT CAMELS

Camels...

➡ can reach a top speed of 40km/h

➡ are pregnant for 13 to 15 months

➡ can go up to 15 days without drinking

➡ soak up water like a sponge when thirsty, guzzling up to 100L in 10 minutes

➡ don't store water in their humps

➡ have a life expectancy of 50 to 60 years

➡ have a three-part stomach

➡ in Arabia are one-humped dromedaries

➡ can travel 160km without drinking

➡ move both legs on one side of the body at the same time

the property directly. Note that you cannot visit the island without a reservation for the resort or at least a tour.

🏃 Activities

Nature & Wildlife Drive
DRIVING TOUR

(adult/child Dh150/75; ⊙6.30am-4pm) Island activities range from mountain biking to snorkelling, kayaking to guided walks, but if you only do one thing while on the island, make it a Nature & Wildlife Drive. The drive is a two-hour animal-spotting safari aboard a Jeep (or minibus on busy days) around the island's savannah-like interior. Guides are very knowledgeable about the local fauna and flora and will often go out of their way to find critters for you to look at. Try to get an early morning or late afternoon tour when the animals are at their most active.

Sir Bani Yas Stables
HORSE RIDING

(rides Dh250-500) For an intimate nature encounter, book a horseback ride at the state-of the art Sir Bani Yas Stables. Guides will match the horse to your level of experience and kit you out with shoes, chaps and a helmet before taking you on a ride along the beach or through the bush.

Anantara Spa
SPA

(massages Dh650-800) A great relaxation station is the lush Anantara Spa, where you can choose from an extensive massage and treatment menu to work out the kinks and turn you into a glowing lump of tranquility. Options include a jet lag massage, a mother-to-be massage and an emerald gemstone massage.

🛏 Sleeping & Eating

At the ultra-deluxe **Desert Islands Resort & Spa** (⌨02-801 5400; http://desertislands.anantara.com; r from Dh1600; @ 🤖 🎽) you'll sleep sweetly in elegantly exotic, oversized rooms hued in calming browns, beiges and dark reds. There's tasteful regional art throughout and private balconies overlooking the flower-filled garden, free-form infinity pool and the shimmering sea. Deep-pocket types in need of extra privacy can rent their own pool villa.

If the tummy grumbles, you have several options. In the daytime, there's **Al Shams** (mains Dh40-70; ⊙9am-midnight), which overlooks the pool and serves fresh salads, pasta, fish and chips and other snacks and light meals. At dinnertime, pick your way around the international buffet at The Palm or indulge in a seafood dinner at the beachfront **Samak** (mains Dh60-150; ⊙7.30-10.30pm) restaurant with its open-fire grill and dedicated 'salt guru'. With advance notice, you can even hire a chef to prepare a meal just for you for a private dinner in an extra special location. Alcohol is served throughout.

In 2013, Desert Islands will open two more outposts on the island. On the west side, in the middle of the savannah, animal sightings from your African-themed chalet at **Al Sahel Lodge** (r from Dh1950 incl breakfast; 🤖 🎽) complex are pretty much guaranteed. Each of the 30 villas has open-beam cathedral ceilings, four-poster beds and a colour scheme that perfectly matches the surroundings.

Al Yamm Lodge (r from Dh1950 incl breakfast; 🤖 🎽) is another villa cluster on the eastern shore, this time with a breezy Mediterranean flair. Wriggle your toes in the soft white sand from your private porch and count the flamingos flapping over the open sea. Bonus points for the stylish freestanding oval tubs.

ℹ Getting There & Away

AIR

Rotana Jet (www.rotanajet.com) flies to Sir Bani Yas from Abu Dhabi's Al Bateen Executive Airport on Tuesdays, Thursday and Saturdays; the round trip is Dh400. There's also seaplane charter service operated by **Seawings** (www.seawings.ae) leaving from the Jebel Ali Marina and Seaplane Base in Dubai on Thursday and Saturday.

BOAT

From the Jebel Dhanna ferry jetty, boats make the 20-minute trip to the island every two hours between 10am and 10pm. A minivan will take you to the resort in another 20 minutes.

BUS

Bus X87 makes it out to the ferry jetty from Abu Dhabi's central bus station daily (Dh35, 4½ hours).

CAR

The Jebel Dhanna ferry jetty is about a 250km drive west of Abu Dhabi and 350km southwest of Dubai via Hwy E11. Past Ruwais, follow the signs to the jetty.

If you want someone else to do the driving, ask the resort to arrange a limo service, which starts at Dh650 from Abu Dhabi and Dh1000 from Dubai.

EAST OF ABU DHABI

Al Ain
العين

🖉 03 / POP 614,000

With markets, forts, museums and a famous date-palm oasis, Al Ain is a breath of fresh air after the frantic pace of Dubai and even Abu Dhabi, both about a two-hour drive away. On the border with Oman, the birthplace of Sheikh Zayed has greatly benefited from his patronage and passion for greening the desert, even garnering the moniker 'Garden City'. But the desert is never far away: simply drive the winding road up Jebel Hafeet for sweeping views of the arid splendour that is the Empty Quarter. Al Ain itself is an increasingly dynamic place with a couple of excellent museums, an archaeological park, a superb zoo and a relative abundance of greenery.

Al Ain rubs up against the town of Buraimi across the Omani border. Those who are not citizens of the Gulf Cooperation Council (GCC) must use the **Hili border crossing** in northern Al Ain and take a short taxi ride to the centre from there. GCC citizens can use the more central **Al Mudeef crossing**.

◉ Sights

Al Ain is quite tough to navigate thanks to its many roundabouts. Brown signs directing visitors to the major tourist attractions are helpful, but a few more wouldn't hurt.

Sheikh Zayed Palace Museum MUSEUM
(🖉 03-751 7755; www.adach.ae; cnr Al Ain & Sultan bin Zayed First Sts; ◷ 8.30am-7.30pm Sat-Thu, 3-7.30pm Fri) FREE This nicely restored, rambling palace on the edge of Al Ain Oasis was Sheikh Zayed's residence from 1937 until 1966. It is a beautiful cinnamon-coloured building set around several courtyards amid beds of cacti, magnolia trees and lofty palms. You can step inside the *majlis* where the ruler received visitors, see his wife's curtained, canopied bed and snap a photo of the Land Rover he used to visit the desert Bedu.

★ Al Ain Zoo ZOO
(🖉 03-782 8188; www.awpr.ae; off Zayed Al Awwal & Nahyan Al Awwal Sts; adult/child Dh15/5; ◷ 9am-8pm Oct-May, 4-10pm Jun-Sep) The region's largest and most acclaimed zoo, founded by Sheikh Zayed in 1968, has spacious enclosures inhabited by both indigenous and exotic species. Observe grazing Arabian oryx, big-horned Barbary sheep, lazy crocodiles, tigers and lions and dozens of other species, some of them born at the zoo, which has a well-respected conservation and breeding program. Special treats for tots include the Elezba petting zoo, bird shows and giraffe feedings.

The foot-weary can hire golf-cart-style shuttles to take them around the nicely landscaped grounds with hop-on and hop-off options at the main enclosures. There's also a reasonably priced cafeteria and lots of nice picnic spots.

Al-Jahili Fort HISTORIC SITE
(🖉 784 3996; Hazah St, 9am-5pm Sat, Sun & Tue-Thu, 3-5pm Fri) FREE Beautifully restored, this massive fort was built in 1890 by Sheikh Zayed I (1836–1909) as a summer residence. His grandson, UAE founding father Sheikh Zayed, may have been born here in this building in 1918. Today it houses a visitor information centre and small exhibits on Zayed I and on British explorer, writer and photographer Sir Wilfred Thesiger.

Al Ain National Museum MUSEUM
(🖉 03-764 1595; www.adach.ae; Zayed bin Sultan St; adult/child Dh3/free; ◷ 8.30am-7.30pm Sat-Thu, 3-7.30pm Fri) This charmingly old-fashioned museum is perfect for boning up on the ancient past of the Al Ain region. Highlights include ancient weapons, jewellery, pottery, coins and other objects excavated from tombs at nearby Hili and Umm an-Nar, which date to the 3rd millennium BC.

The ethnography galleries zero in on various aspects of the daily life of the Bedu and settled people, including education, marriage and farming. There's some beautiful silver jewellery, traditional costumes and a harrowing display of simple surgical instruments with lots of sharp points and hooks – ouch!

Al Ain Camel Market MARKET
(Zayed Bin Sultan St, behind Bawadi Mall; ◷ 7am-sunset) FREE It's dusty, noisy, pungent and chaotic, but never mind: Al Ain's famous camel market is a wonderful immersion in traditional Arabic culture so rare in the UAE today. All sorts of camels are holed up in pens, from wobbly-legged babies that might grow up to be racers to imposing studs kept for breeding. The intense haggling is fun to watch. Some traders may offer to give you a tour (for money) but you're totally free to walk around on your own. If you want to take photographs, ask first and perhaps

Al Ain & Buraimi

offer a small tip. Trading takes place in the morning, but it's usually possible to see the corralled animals all day long.

The market is about 7km south of central Al Ain, near the Meyzad border crossing to Oman. Buses 900, 950, 960 and 980 stop at nearby Bawadi Mall.

Activities

Wadi Adventure WATER PARK
(☎03-781 8422; www.wadiadventure.ae; near Hazza bin Sultan & Jebel Al Hafeet St; adult/child Dh100/50; ☻10am-10pm Tue-Sun) Unleash your inner daredevil at this new adventure water park at the foot of Jebel Hafeet. 'Hang ten' on over 3m-high waves, hop aboard a kayak or raft to brave gushing whitewater, or hit the vertigo-inducing high-ropes course. General park admission buys access to the pools, lounge areas and restaurant only. An all-day kayaking pass, a 55-minute surf ses-

sion and a 90-minute rafting trip cost Dh100 each. Women only Tuesday after 5pm. Bus 970 stops nearby.

Al Ain & Buraimi

SUBLIME SAND DUNES

Avoid dull drives on drab roads by taking the following routes through stunning desert scenery.

Liwa: Abu Dhabi to Hameem (mostly Hwy E65) Take pleasure in the peach-and-cinnamon dunes dotted with date-palm oases. Take the road to Hameem instead of the main route via Madinat Zayed; the turn-off is about 20km out of Abu Dhabi on the Musaffah to Tarif road.

Liwa: Liwa Resthouse to Moreeb Hill (Tal Mireb) Marvel at these enormous apricot-coloured dunes on the edge of the Empty Quarter – the largest you'll see in the UAE.

Mahafiz: Sharjah to Kalba Rd (Hwy E102) Count the camels, if you can! See how they blend into the sands along route S116 as it winds east past camel farms to Kalba on the Gulf of Oman.

Al Ain: Dubai to Al Ain Rd (Hwy E66) Be amazed by the big tangerine dunes on the approach to Al Ain around Shabat. To truly appreciate them you'll have to pull over to get a look through the roadside greenery.

Shwaib: Al Ain to Hatta Rd (Hwy E55) Graceful gazelles leap through desert shrubs on the big red dunes in the grounds of a sheikh's palace at Shwaib. From Al Ain, head north on E66 towards Dubai for about 50km, then cut right to Shwaib; drive down into the town to see rugged mountains on your right and gazelles on your left.

🛏 Sleeping

Al Ain Faida   HOTEL $
(☑ 03-701 4444; www.onetoonehotels.com; Al Wagan Rd; d from Dh350) Long in the tooth for a long time, this historic villa resort set around its own lake was getting a major makeover during our visit and should have emerged as a boutique hotel with family appeal by the time you're reading this.

Danat Al Ain Resort   RESORT $$
(☑ 03-704 6000; www.danathotels.com; cnr Khalid bin Sultan (147th) & Al Salam Sts; r from Dh700; P 🗺 🛰) With three pools, a big playground, a 24-hour gym, tennis and squash courts, all plunged within lush landscaped grounds, the Danat is a top pick for families and active types. Rooms are plus-sized and feature balconies; suites have their own full kitchens. The restaurants are among the best in town, and three bars provide night-time entertainment.

Al Ain Rotana Hotel   HOTEL $$
(☑ 03-754 5111; www.rotana.com; Zayed bin Sultan St; d from Dh675; P 🗺 🛰) This central hotel with its soaring atrium lobby is a top choice and has plush, spacious rooms in various sizes, all sporting the full range of mod cons. Surrender to slothdom by the sparkling pool, or work up an appetite on the squash court or in the well-equipped gym before a sumptuous dinner at the always-reliable Trader Vic's.

Hilton Al Ain   HOTEL $$
(☑ 03-768 6666; www.hilton.com; Khalid bin Sultan (147th) St; d from Dh740; @ 🗺 🛰) Though showing its age in parts, this popular hotel has large, comfortable rooms with balconies. Waist-watchers can work off the carbs in the big gym, the tennis court or in the lap pool; families, meanwhile, give the place a thumbs up for the kiddie activities and separate family pool with a long water slide and pirate boat.

🍴 Eating

Cafeteria Al Mallah   LEBANESE $
(☑ 03-766 9655; Khalifa St; sandwiches Dh4-9, mains Dh23-55; ⏱ 11am-3pm & 5pm-midnight) This simple, spotless eatery serves reliable Lebanese staples, including succulent chicken *shwarmas* and a kick-ass hummus with pine nuts.

Hut Cafe   CAFE $
(☑ 03-751 6526; Khalifa St; dishes Dh14-26; ⏱ 8am-1am; 🛰) Near Pizza Hut, this country-French-style cafe appeals to a mostly local crowd with retro charm, friendly service, newspapers and free wi-fi. A calm spot on busy Khalifa, it's popular for cooked breakfasts, cakes and sandwiches.

⭐ Luce   ITALIAN $$
(☑ 03-704 6000; www.danathotels.com; Danat Al Ain Resort; mains Dh70-110; ⏱ 6-11.30pm; 🛰) One of the best restaurants in town, this Ital-

ian charmer casts its net wide by dividing its menu into 'classic' and 'trendy' dishes, accounting for everything from pizza to *scaloppine*. The three-course dinner with wine for Dh140 is a steal. On Saturday, the spacious, marble-floored room turns into a jumping nightclub after the last fork's been put down.

Paco's   TEX-MEX $$

(☑ 03-768 6666; Khalid bin Sultan (147th) St, Hilton Al Ain; mains Dh35-95; ⊗ noon-1am Sat-Wed, to 2am Thu & Fri) It's always fiesta time at this boozy Tex-Mex cantina where you can gobble up the burritos, burgers or prime rib while following the latest ManU vs Chelsea match on the big-screen. A live band jumps into action after 9.30pm Tuesday to Saturday.

Al Diwan Restaurant   INTERNATIONAL $$

(☑ 03-764 4445; Khalifa St; mains Dh30-70; ⊗ 8am-2am) Lebanese *shish tawooq* (marinated chicken grilled on skewers), pizza margarita, Mexican steak, Iranian yoghurt chicken – this big, bright eatery with floor-to-ceiling windows certainly covers all the bases. Judging by what's on the plates of diners, though, the grilled meats are the main reason the place retains its local-fave status.

Trader Vic's   FRENCH POLYNESIAN $$$

(☑ 03-754 5111; www.rotana.com; Zayed bin Sultan St, Al Ain Rotana Hotel; mains Dh60-120; ⊗ 12.30-3.30pm & 7.30-11.30pm) Sip exotic rum concoctions while taking in the trippy tiki decor and anticipating platters of crispy duck, jumbo prawns or sesame chicken. Many dishes are prepared in a superhot Chinese oven in the centre of the restaurant. A live band gets your toes tapping at dinnertime.

❶ Information

Tourist Office (www.visitabudhabi.ae; Al Jahili Fort; ⊗ 9am-5pm Tue-Thu, Sat & Sun, 3-5pm Fri)

❶ Getting There & Away

AIR

Served by only eight airlines, you're unlikely to arrive at **Al Ain International Airport** (☑ 03-785 5555; www.airport.ae/al-ain-international-airport.html), about 13km northwest of the city centre. If you do, a taxi into downtown costs Dh40, a ride on a local bus 960 costs Dh5. Bus 490 links Al Ain with Abu Dhabi International Airport (p334) (Dh25, three hours) every three hours.

BUS

Al Ain's **bus station** (off Zayed bin Sultan St) is behind the souqs. Express bus X90 shuttles back and forth to Abu Dhabi every 30 minutes between 4.30am and midnight (Dh15, 1½ hours). Buses to Dubai (Dh20) depart every 40 minutes from 5.40am to 11.40pm and to Sharjah (Dh25) every 45 minutes between 7am and 10pm.

AL AIN'S WORLD HERITAGE SITES

In June 2011, four sites in Al Ain became the first in the UAE to be inscribed on Unesco's World Heritage List thanks to their archaeological, cultural and historical significance. Aside from the locations described below, the honour includes the ancient dome-shaped tombs at the foot of Mt Jebel Hafeet, which are not yet open for visitors.

Al Ain Oasis (☑ 763 0155; www.adach.ae; off Zayed bin Sultan St) **FREE** A marked route leads through this 3000-acre date palm oasis, an atmospheric labyrinth of shaded walkways and cultivated plots irrigated by a traditional *falaj* (underground system of tunnels). There are nearly 150,000 date palms here, along with mango, almond, banana and fig trees. Look for the ruins of an ancient fortress and a mosque as well as date storage containers.

Hili Archaeological Park (www.adach.ae; Hili,; ⊗ 10am-1pm, families only 4-11pm) **FREE** This nicely landscaped park is the largest Bronze Age complex in the UAE, dating back some 4000 years. Use the knowledge you've gained at Al Ain National Museum to make better sense of the archaeological remains, including the foundations of a tower and mudbrick buildings as well as the restored circular Grand Tomb with its decorative carvings. It's about 10km north of central Al Ain, en route to Dubai, and served by bus 900.

Bida Bint Saud A 40m-high rock dominates this isolated site, about 15km north of central Al Ain, with communal tombs at its top and smaller circular tombs, some dating back 3000 years, at its base. To get there, follow Mohammed bin Khalifa St to Hwy E95 to the village of Bida Bint Saud.

Oman's bus company **ONTC** (☎ +968 2449 0046; www.ontcoman.com) runs buses between Buraimi and the Ruwi station in Muscat (OR4.20, five hours) via Sohar. These leave Buraimi at 7am, 1pm and 7pm from Saara Al Jadeda, near Bank Muscat.

CAR

From Dubai, it's 150km south to Al Ain via Hwy E66. Coming from Abu Dhabi, head east on Hwy E22 for about 160km. Europcar, Avis and Hertz are among car rental agencies with branches in Al Ain.

TAXI

Al Ain's long-distance taxi station is next to the bus station. Taxis to Dubai or Abu Dhabi are about Dh200. Seats in a shared taxi go for Dh20 to Dubai and Dh25 to Abu Dhabi.

❶ Getting Around

Al Ain's public buses run roughly every 30 minutes from 6am to midnight at Dh2 per trip. Check www.ojra.ae for routes and schedules.

Taxis are metered; most in-town rides cost between Dh10 and Dh20.

Jebel Hafeet   جبل حفيت

This jagged 1240m-high limestone mountain rears out of the plain south of Al Ain. From its base, a 12km-long paved road corkscrews to the top, past evocatively eroded formations and shrubs eking out a living between the rocks. There are several pull-outs for picture-taking before the road culminates at a huge parking lot with a snack bar. Enjoy the cool air while taking in the sublime vistas of the oasis city hemmed in by the ochre sands. On your way back, stop for a cold drink or a meal at the **Mercure Grand Hotel** (☎ 03-783 8888; www.mercure. com; r Dh400; @ ☎).

The road up Jebel Hafeet starts about 16km south of central Al Ain via Khalifa bin Zayed Al Awwal St (122nd St); follow the brown signs.

EAST COAST

Facing the Gulf of Oman, the UAE's eastern coast belongs almost entirely to the emirate of Fujairah, interrupted only by the three small Sharjah enclaves of Dibba Al-Hisn, Khor Fakkan and Kalba. Tourism is concentrated north of the town of Khor Fakkan, where the Hajar Mountains dip down to

long, white-sand beaches with excellent swimming and diving.

South of Khor Fakkan, industry replaces idyll thanks to massive container ports and a new oil export terminal just outside Fujairah. Nearly two million barrels of oil from fields in the UAE's western desert arrive here daily via a 370km-long pipeline.

Several archaeological sites, some dating back 4000 years, provide evidence of the coast's long and turbulent history. The legacy of the Portuguese, who swarmed the area in the 16th century to control the spice trade, survives in a handful of forts.

Fujairah City   الفجيرة

☎ 09 / POP 189,000

The biggest town on the East Coast, Fujairah City is the eponymous emirate's business and commercial hub. Office buildings line its main strip, Hamad bin Abdullah Rd, while its northern waterfront is hemmed in by vast fields of circular oil storage containers. Still, the town is worth stopping in if only to get a sense of Fujairah's past at the restored fort and the adjacent museum. Local residents are also proud of several new developments: the massive, gleaming white Sheikh Zayed Mosque, the emirates' first big shopping mall, and the new (and much faster) Sheikh Khalifa Hwy to Dubai.

◉ Sights

Fujairah Museum   MUSEUM
(☎ 09-222 9085; cnr Al-Nakheel & Al-Salam Rds; adult/child Dh5/free; ⊗ 8am-6pm Sat-Thu, 2.30-6pm Fri) Archaeological finds from nearby digs conducted at Bidya, Bithnah and Qidfa – including vessels, arrowheads and carnelian beads – reveal that the area has been settled for at least 3500 years. Other halls are crammed with ethno items like weapons, costumes and Bedouin jewellery. Although the significance of many objects is undisputable to the lay visitor, a few more captions and explanations would make a visit here more meaningful.

Fujairah Fort   HISTORIC SITE
(near cnr Al-Nakheel & Al-Salam Rds) **FREE** Draped over a rocky outcrop, overlooking Fujairah's old village and date-palm oasis, this beautifully restored fort looks splendid, especially when floodlit at night. Built from mud, gravel, wood and gypsum in the 16th century, it's a clever composition of circular

Fujairah

Fujairah

Sights
1 Fujairah Fort.................................C1
2 Fujairah Museum..........................C2
3 Sheikh Zayed Mosque....................B2

Sleeping
4 Hilton Fujairah Resort.....................D1

Eating
5 Al Meshwar.................................B3
Delhi Darbar........................(see 7)
6 Sadat.......................................D2
7 Saffrons....................................C3
8 Taj Mahal..................................C3

Drinking & Nightlife
9 Breezes Beach Bar.........................D1
Fez Night Club.....................(see 4)

Shopping
10 Central Souq...............................D3

and square towers that aided in its defence. Although officially closed, there are caretakers on site who might unlock the heavy wooden doors for a closer look at the as yet empty – interior.

Parts of the historic village surrounding the fort have also been reconstructed and you're free to walk around the expansive grounds and go inside the buildings.

Sheikh Zayed Mosque MOSQUE
(cnr of Al-Ittihad & Al-Salam Sts) By the time you're reading this, Fujairah's grand new mosque, honoring Sheikh Zayed, should have started welcoming worshippers. Said to be the size of three football fields and festooned with six 100m-high minarets, the white granite and marble edifice can accommodate up to 28,000 worshippers, including 2500 women in a basement prayer hall. It won't be open to non-Muslims, but the impressive exterior alone warrants a look.

Al Hayl Fort HISTORIC SITE
(Al Hayl; ⊘ closed Fri) FREE Built around 1830, this is one of the best preserved forts in the country, tucked deep into the jagged Hajar Mountains, yet easily reached without a 4WD. There's usually a caretaker to show you around (tip appreciated). It's about

13km southwest of Fujairah via the signposted road off E89, opposite the City Centre mall. Best when the sun is low.

Sleeping

Fujairah Youth Hostel HOSTEL $
(☑ 09-222 2347; www.uaeyha.com; 203 Al-Faseel Area, White City, next to Abu Jandal School; dm HI

MASAFI MARKET

The road from Dubai towards the eastern coast is strangely desolate, a dune landscape punctuated only by power poles. A minor roadside attraction is the **Friday Market** (Masafi; ⏰ 8am-10pm daily) in Masafi, a strip of nearly identical stalls that's actually open daily. Rugs, pottery, household goods and knick-knacks are for sale, but it's actually best for stocking up on local produce.

member/nonmember Dh50/65; ⏰ reception 9am-11pm) In a residential area close to small shops and the so-so beach, this fairly well-kept hostel has 48 beds in gender-segregated dorms with air-con. Bathrooms are shared. If there's space, families and couples can rent a dorm for themselves (Dh180). The town centre is about 3km south.

Hilton Fujairah Resort RESORT **$$**
(☎ 09-222 2411; www.hilton.com; Al-Faseel Rd, at Coffeepot Roundabout; r incl breakfast from Dh700; P ♠ ⛱) Small, easygoing and well-managed, this is a Hilton for people who don't like Hiltons and your best in-town beachfront choice. Spread your towel on a narrow sandy strip bookended by rock jetties, while your little ones let off steam in the kids' club and playground. Standard rooms are just that – get a suite for extra comforts.

✗ Eating

★ **Saffrons** INDIAN **$**
(☎ 09-222 7752; Hamad bin Abdullah Rd; mains Dh9-18; ⏰ 8am-3pm & 6-11.30pm) Curries are like second to naan (pardon the pun) at this cafeteria-style South Indian nosh spot. Everything tastes genuine, fresh and inflected with an authentic medley of spices. Make sure your bill includes an order of something cooked in the tandoor (clay oven).

Delhi Darbar PAKISTANI **$**
(☎ 09-222 6459; Hamad bin Abdullah Rd; most mains Dh10-15; ⏰ 7.30am-1.30am) Skip the Chinese selections and pick from the richly flavoured masalas at this simple eatery that also offers a large selection of mutton dishes.

Taj Mahal INDIAN **$$**
(☎ 09-222 5225; Hamad bin Abdullah Rd; mains Dh15-45; ⏰ noon-3pm & 6-11pm) Locals love the Taj, with its rustic Raj interior decor and extensive North Indian menu – everything from tandoori chicken to mutton rogan josh to prawn curry . Skip the Chinese offerings.

Sadaf IRANIAN **$$**
(☎ 09-223 3400; www.sadaffood.com; Corniche Rd; mains Dh40-80; ⏰ noon-3pm & 7pm-midnight) A branch of the popular Sadaf franchise, this fairly formal Iranian eatery serves up deliciously moist, grilled kebabs and delicately spiced Iranian rice amid hilariously retro-kitsch decor.

Al Meshwar LEBANESE **$$**
(☎ 09-222 1113; Hamad bin Abdullah Rd; mezze Dh13-28, mains Dh22-75; ⏰ 9am-1am; ♠) In a *Flintstones*-inspired building, this is a hugely popular nosh spot although the food can be uneven. Stick with simple stuff – hummus, grilled meats, *sambousek* (meat pies) – and you should be fine. Cosy *sheesha* lounge downstairs, more formal family restaurant upstairs.

🍷 Drinking & Nightlife

Breezes Beach Bar BAR
(☎ 09-222 2411; www.hilton.com; Al-Faseel Rd, nr Coffeepot Roundabout, Hilton Fujairah Resort; dishes Dh50-75; ⏰ 11am-midnight) This waterfront bar at the Hilton is great for sunset cocktails, *sheesha* and light meals (burgers, salads, pasta, Dh50 to Dh75).

Fez Night Club NIGHT CLUB
(www.hilton.com; Al-Faseel Rd, nr Coffeepot Roundabout; ⏰ 9pm-3am) If you want to keep partying, head to the jaunty Fez, also at the Hilton, for a round of pool or darts, or a spin on the dance floor when the band starts up.

🛍 Shopping

Central Souq MARKET
(⏰ 8am-9pm) At the bottom of the main strip, Hamad bin Abdullah Rd, locals shop for meat, fish, produce, dates and spices at the traditional Central Souq, set up in a no-nonsense market hall.

Fujairah City Centre MALL
(www.fujairahcitycenter.com; ⏰ 10am-10pm Sun-Wed, to midnight Thu & Fri) Fujiarah's new pride and joy is the emirate's first big modern mall, Fujairah City Centre, on the outskirts of town just before the junction of E89 and Sheikh Khalifa Hwy to Dubai.

ℹ Getting There & Away

BUS

Hourly bus 700 runs to Dubai's Al Ittihad station (p308) in Deira from the **stop** next to the old Plaza Cinema (Dh25, two hours). The last bus leaves at 9.45pm. Buses are met by taxis for onward travel.

CAR

Locals rejoiced when the opening of the scenic Sheikh Khalifa Hwy (Hwy E84) through the Hajar Mountains in December 2011 cut the trip between Fujairah and Dubai to under an hour. Coming from Dubai, head north on E311 or E611, then east on E102 (Sharjah–Kalba Hwy) and turn onto the Hwy E84 about 2km east of the Maleha overpass.

TAXI

Taxis (✆09-223 3533) to Dubai or Sharjah cost about Dh130 to Dh160. Budget about 40Dh to Dh50 to Al Aqah or Badiyah and Dh70 to Dh80 Dibba. Most rides within Fujairah cost no more than Dh10.

Khor Fakkan   خورفكان

About 25km north of Fujairah, Khor Fakkan is dominated by its super-busy container port. At times, an entire armada of ships can be seen on the horizon, queuing to dock, unload or refuel. Still, Khor Fakkan is not without charm, especially along the family-friendly **Corniche**, which is flanked by palm trees, gardens, kiosks, and playgrounds. Several kilometres long, it links the port and the **fish market** (⊗7am-noon Sat-Thu & 4-10.30pm daily) at the southern end with the storied **Oceanic Hotel** (closed for renovation at press time) at the opposite end. Khor Fakkan also has a clean and simple **youth hostel** (✆09-237 0886; www.uaeyha.com; 78 Sheikh Khalid bin Mohammed Al Qassimi St, behind

Al Safeer Centre; dm HI members/nonmembers Dh50/60; ⊗reception hours 9am-11pm) in an old white villa on the busy main road next to Al Kansa Mosque.

For excellent Indian food, try **Taj Khorfakkan Restaurant** (✆09-237 0040; www.grouptajmahal.com; Al-Tufail bin Malik St, off Corniche Rd; mains Dh22-45; ⊗noon-midnight) opposite Al Safeer Centre. There's also **Iranian Pars Restaurant** (✆09-238 7787; cnr Corniche Rd & Sheikh Khalid bin Mohammed al-Qassimi St; mains Dh30-45; ⊗11am-midnight), which gets local thumbs up for its Iranian fare, including super-tasty chelo kebab.

Since Khor Fakkan is an enclave of the Sharjah emirate, it's 'dry' as a bone.

Badiyah   بادية

Badiyah (also spelt Bidyah and Bidiya), 8km north of Khor Fakkan, is famous for its teensy **mosque** (Dibba Rd, Hwy E99; ⊗7am-10pm) FREE. The modest structure, adorned with four three-tiered domes and resting on a single internal pillar, dates back to AD 1446 and may well be the oldest mosque in the UAE.

The interior has a lovely contemplative feel, enlivened only by colourful prayer mats. A sign says that non-Muslims are not allowed to enter, but you're free to catch a peek provided you're modestly dressed and take off your shoes; women must also cover their hair.

The mosque is built into a low hillside along the coastal road just north of Badiyah village and guarded by two ruined **watchtowers**. It's well worth walking up here for superb 360-degree views of the Hajar Mountains, the Gulf and a date-palm plantation.

On the northern outskirts of Badiyah, fruit and veg vendors set up shop daily along the road.

LOCAL KNOWLEDGE

BULL BUTTING

On Fridays, Fujairah hosts the ancient sport of bull butting in a muddy patch off the Corniche, just south of the 'Hand Roundabout' (just look for the huge fleet of parked SUVs). Dozens of animals tethered to posts await their turn, snorting derisively and kicking up dirt while, in the arena, two bulls lock horns and pit their strength against each other as hundreds of locals cheer them on. The goal is for one bull to butt the other out of a circle, which usually takes only a couple of minutes.

It's all a mad, disorganised spectacle introduced centuries ago by the Portuguese. Today, the tradition is upheld by two local clubs who host fights on alternate Fridays. The animals don't get killed, but they do occasionally get injured, usually around the ears and the neck.

Al Aqah العقة

Al Aqah is known for having the eastern coast's best beaches, flanked by high-end hotels. This is prime **snorkelling and diving** territory, and even beginners can have a satisfying experience thanks to **Snoopy Island**, named by some clever soul who thought the shape of this rocky outcrop about 100m offshore resembled the *Peanuts* cartoon character sleeping atop his doghouse. The 2008/09 red tide killed off much of the coral, but the waters here still teem with all sorts of colourful critters, including – if you're lucky – green sea turtles and (harmless) black-tip reef sharks. The best time to hit the water is in the morning, as the tide may cloud the water around midday, and afternoon winds may make it choppy. Also watch out for jellyfish.

🛏 Sleeping & Eating

**Le Méridien Al Aqah
Beach Resort**   RESORT **$$**
(📞09-244 9000; www.lemeridien-alaqah.com; Dibba Rd, Hwy E99; from d Dh850; 🅿🛜🏊) This glass-and-concrete behemoth competes with the mountains for height and does a fine job of delivering all the trappings of a beach vacation. Pass the days lazing poolside, hitting the spa or exploring an offshore wreck, then retreat to big, balconied rooms overlooking the lush gardens and private beach. Kids get

---

BIRDING IN KALBA

About 15km south of Fujairah City on the Omani border, the town of Kalba is famous for its creek (Khor Kalba), a pastiche of mangroves, tidal creeks and sandy beaches, which are key breeding grounds of many rare bird species, including the white-collared kingfisher and the Sykes's warbler. The area is also a wintering spot of the Indian pond heron.

In 2012, Khor Kalba was closed to the public while undergoing rehabilitation as part of the Sharjah government's effort of developing Kalba into an ecotourism destination. With strong binocs, you might still be able to spot the birds from the partly opened bridge overlooking the creek and mangroves. Check www.uaebirding.com or www.shurooq.gov.ae for updates.

---

their kicks in the Penguin Club, older ones can make friends in the Teens Club.

Among the nine bar and eateries, the elegant **Swaad** (mains Dh80-130; ⏱7-10.30pm) beckons with stellar Indian dinners, while **Sapore** (mains Dh55-195; ⏱noon-3.30pm & 7-10.30pm) is a romantic Italian eatery. For cocktails with a view head up to **Astros** (⏱6pm-1am) on the 20th floor, or stay beachside for snacks and *sheesha* at **Gonu** (⏱noon-5pm & 7pm-midnight), which also serves delicious grilled fish and seafood.

Sandy Beach Hotel & Resort   RESORT **$$**
(📲09-244 5555; www.sandybm.com; off E99, Al Aqah; d from Dh550, ocean view d Dh800, 1-/2-bedroom cabin Dh700/920; 🅿🛜🏊) Opposite Snoopy Island, this simple, family-oriented resort oozes retro charm, especially if you're staying in one of the cabins dotted around the flowery gardens. Each has its own barbecue grill, so you can wrap up a day of snorkeling off the lovely white-sand beach with a home-cooked meal rather than a mediocre one at the restaurant. For more comfort but less character, book an apartment in the modern wing. The PADI dive centre rents equipment and organises boat trips.

Dibba دبا

Dibba was put on the map of history in 633 as the site of a key rebellion fought after the death of Mohammed, which resulted in the trouncing of non-Muslims and the firm establishment of Islam. Bones found in a cemetery just outside Dibba are believed to belong to some of the rebels.

Today the town is unique in that its territory is shared by two emirates and the Sultanate of Oman. The most commercial part is the southernmost, **Dibba Al-Fujairah**, where ATMs, supermarkets and cafeterias line the main highway, Sheikh Zayed bin Sultan Rd (E89).

North of here, **Dibba Al Hisn**, an enclave of the emirate of Sharjah, has changed almost beyond recognition in recent years. New developments include a row of government buildings along Al Fareed St, while along the waterfront, Al Hisn Island, a fun zone of restaurants, parks and playgrounds, is taking shape.

For now the most interesting part is **Dibba Al Baya**, across the border in Oman, which is a launch pad for exploring the ruggedly beautiful Musandam Peninsula. Local

WORTH A TRIP

WADI WURAYAH وادي الوريعة

Tucked into the Hajar Mountains and famous for its waterfall, Wadi Wurayah (Wurayah Canyon) was designated the UAE's first protected mountain area by the World Wildlife Fund in 2009. The harsh habitat harbours many endemic animal species, including threatened ones such as the Arabian tahr, the mountain gazelle and the caracal lynx.

To get there, head inland near Zubara on a paved road that corkscrews for about 14km through the harsh rocky landscape, deadending at a viewpoint overlooking the wadi. It's a steep hike down into the canyon where there is a small pool and a waterfall hemmed in by (sigh!) graffiti-festooned rocks.

With a 4WD and a GPS it's possible to make the bone-rattling drive to the waterfall, but this is no trip for the inexperienced. Get advice locally before setting out.

operator **Sheesa Beach** (☑ in Oman +968 2 683 6551; www.sheesabeach.com; Dibba Bayal, Oman; ⊙ 8am-5pm), on the waterfront about 3km north of the Corniche border crossing, organises dhow cruises and dive trips, while **Absolute Adventure** (☑ 04-345 9900; www. adventure.ae; day trips from Dh350; ⊙ Oct-Apr) specialises in trekking, mountain biking and kayaking tours.

At press time, travellers eligible for a free UAE tourist visa did not require an Omani visa to cross into Musandam (bring your passport), but UAE authorities had tightened requirements for UAE residents. Look into the current situation before heading out (eg by calling a hotel or tour operator).

🛏 Sleeping

There's camping along Dibba beach as well as in the dunes north of the Golden Tulip Hotel on the Omani side. Nearby, Absolute Adventure rents a simple beachfront house with bunk beds to groups of up to six people for Dh1250 to Dh1950 per day, including breakfast.

Royal Beach Hotel   HOTEL **$$**
(☑ 09-244 9444; www.royalbeach.ae; 8km south of Dibba; r incl breakfast weekday/weekend Dh640/975; @ ☒) This friendly, low-key indie resort sits on a splendid stretch of golden sand facing Dibba Rock, a popular dive and snorkelling site thanks to its shallow coral gardens. On-site Freestyle Divers (p350) rents gear and also does dive trips and PADI courses. All rooms have a private terrace facing a manicured lawn and the private beach strewn with *barasti* umbrellas. The hotel does not sell alcohol but there's a handy off-licence hole-in-the-wall (open noon to 2am) nearby. Ask around... Otherwise, the nearest place to get a buzz is the scruffy Holiday Beach Hotel next door.

Radisson Blu Resort, Fujairah   RESORT **$$**
(☑ 244 9700; www.radissonblu.com/resort-fujairah; 6km south of Dibba; d incl breakfast from Dh800; P @ ☒) With its modest entrance hidden at the end of a long, narrow driveway, the Radisson may not be the kind of place that wows you at first glance. But beyond the generic lobby you'll find yourself in an immaculately kept, well-run, full-service property with multiple pools, several good restaurants and smiley staff. Even standard rooms are large and all have sea-facing balconies.

UNDERSTAND UNITED ARAB EMIRATES

History

Early History

The earliest significant settlements in the UAE date back to the Bronze Age. In the 3rd millennium BC, a culture known as Umm Al Nar arose near modern Abu Dhabi. Its influence extended well into the interior and down the coast to today's Oman. There were also settlements at Badiyah (near Fujairah) and at Rams (near Ras Al Khaimah) during the same period.

The Persians and, to a lesser extent, the Greeks, were the next major cultural influences in the area. The Persian Sassanid empire held sway until the arrival of Islam in AD 636, and Christianity made a brief appearance in the form of the Nestorian Church, which had a monastery on Sir Bani Yas Island, west of Abu Dhabi, in the 5th century.

During the Middle Ages, the Kingdom of Hormuz controlled much of the area, including the entrance to the Gulf, as well as

DIVING THE EAST COAST

Practically every major resort along the eastern coast has a PADI-accredited dive centre that rents snorkeling gear, does diving certification and organises dive and snorkelling trips, including to the Musandam Peninsula. Rates vary slightly but expect to pay from Dh350 for a two-dive trip including full equipment. Snorkelling gear rents for around Dh100 per day.

Al-Boom Diving (✆09-204 4925; www.alboomdiving.com; Le Meridien Al Aqah Beach Resort; ⏰8am-6pm)

Divers Down (✆09-237 0299; www.diversdown-uae.com; Miramar Al Aqah Beach Resort; ⏰8am-5pm)

Freestyle Divers (✆09-244 5756; www.freestyledivers.com; Royal Beach Hotel, opposite Dibba Rock; ⏰9am-5pm)

Sandy Beach Diving Centre (✆09-244 5555; www.sandybm.com; Sandy Beach Hotel & Resort, opposite Snoopy Island, Al Aqah; ⏰8am-6pm)

Scuba 2000 (✆09-238 8477; www.scuba-2000.com; Al Badiyah Beach, 1km north of Badiyah mosque; ⏰9am-7pm) Local owner, caters mostly for experienced divers and also provides simple lodging for Dh200 (nondivers Dh250).

most of the regional trade. The Portuguese arrived in 1498 and by 1515 they occupied Julfar (near Ras Al Khaimah). They built a customs house and taxed the Gulf's flourishing trade with India and the Far East, but ended up staying only until 1633.

British Rule

The rise of British naval power in the Gulf in the mid-18th century coincided with the consolidation of two tribal factions along the coast of the lower Gulf: the Qawasim and the Bani Yas, the ancestors of the rulers of four of the seven emirates that today make up the UAE.

The Qawasim, whose descendants now rule Sharjah and Ras Al Khaimah, were a seafaring clan based in Ras Al Khaimah whose influence extended at times to the Persian side of the Gulf. This brought them into conflict with the British, who had forged an alliance with the Al Busaid tribe, the ancestors of today's rulers of Oman, to prevent the French from taking over their all-important sea routes to India.

The Qawasim felt that Al Busaid had betrayed the region and launched attacks on British ships to show that they weren't going to be as compliant. As a result, the British dubbed the area the 'Pirate Coast' and launched raids against the Qawasim in 1805, 1809 and 1811. In 1820 a British fleet destroyed or captured every Qawasim ship it could find, imposed a peace treaty on nine

Arab sheikhdoms in the area and installed a garrison.

This was the forerunner of another treaty, the 1835 Maritime Truce, which greatly increased British influence in the region. In 1853 the treaty was modified yet again and renamed the Treaty of Peace in Perpetuity. It was at this time that the region became known as the Trucial States. In subsequent decades, the sheikhs of each tribal confederation signed agreements with the British under which they accepted formal British protection.

Throughout this period, the main power among the Bedouin tribes of the interior was the Bani Yas tribal confederation, made up of the ancestors of the ruling families of modern Abu Dhabi and Dubai. The Bani Yas were originally based in Liwa, an oasis deep in the desert, but moved their base to Abu Dhabi in 1793. In the early 19th century, the Bani Yas divided into two main branches when Dubai split from Abu Dhabi.

Black Gold

Until the discovery of oil the region remained a backwater, with the sheikhdoms nothing more than tiny enclaves of fishers, pearl divers and Bedu. Rivalries between the various rulers occasionally erupted into conflict, which the British tried to thwart. During this time the British also protected the federation from being annexed by Saudi Arabia.

After the collapse of the world pearl market in the early 20th century, the Gulf coast sank into poverty. However, the sheikhs of Abu Dhabi, Dubai and Sharjah had already discussed oil exploration in the area, with Abu Dhabi's Sheikh Shakhbut granting the first of several oil concessions in 1939 to the Anglo-Iraqi company Petroleum Concessions Limited. The first cargo of crude left Abu Dhabi in 1962 and Dubai, which even back then had been busy cementing its reputation as the region's trading hub, exported its first barrel in 1969.

The Road to Unification

In 1951, the British set up the Trucial States Council (the forerunner to today's Supreme Council) with the initial goal being to form a federation including Bahrain, Qatar and the Trucial States. With the British hinting at an exit from the Gulf in 1971, Abu Dhabi's ruler Sheikh Zayed set about negotiating with the other sheikhdoms in the Trucial States to create one nation: the United Arab Emirates was born on 2 December 1971. Six emirates signed up immediately, Ras Al Khaimah joined the following year and Bahrain and Qatar remained independent. The UAE's first president was Sheikh Zayed, its 'founding father', who held the position he held until his death in 2004. Still greatly revered by his people, he also commanded huge respect across the Middle East. After his death, power passed peacefully to his son Sheikh Khalifa bin Zayed Al Nahyan, who's still got the job today.

Today, the UAE remains the region's only federation and is in no danger of breaking up. In fact, if anything, the financial bailouts by oil-rich Abu Dhabi of Dubai during the 2009 economic crisis tightened the bond and demonstrated the emirates' commitment to – and interdependence on – each other.

Government & Politics

The UAE is composed of seven emirates: Abu Dhabi, Dubai, Sharjah, Ras Al Khaimah, Ajman, Umm Al Quwain and Fujairah. 'Emirate' comes from the word 'emir' (ruler). In practice, the seven hereditary emirs of the UAE are called sheikhs. Though there is a federal government led by one of the sheikhs (the president), each ruler is completely sovereign within his emirate.

The seven rulers of the emirates form the Supreme Council, the highest body in the land, which ratifies federal laws and sets general policy. There is also a Council of Ministers, or cabinet, headed by the prime minister who appoints ministers from all the emirates. Naturally, the more populous and wealthier emirates like Abu Dhabi and Dubai have greater representation.

The cabinet and Supreme Council are advised, but can't be overruled, by a parliamentary body called the Federation National Council (FNC). Half of its 40 members are elected by the 6689 members of the Electoral College (selected by the ruler of each emirate); the other 20 are directly appointed by rulers. There are eight representatives each from Abu Dhabi and Dubai, six from Sharjah and Ras Al Khaimah and four from Ajman, Umm Al Quwain and Fujairah. Nine FNC members are women.

Economy

The UAE has the world's seventh-largest oil reserves (after Saudi Arabia, Venezuela, Canada, Iran, Iraq and Kuwait), but the vast majority of it is concentrated in the emirate of Abu Dhabi. It is thought that at current levels of production, oil and gas will run out in about a century and, sensibly, the government has been working hard at diversifying the country's economy. Tourism, trade, transport, finance and real estate have brought down the portion of GDP derived from oil and gas to about 25%. In Dubai, which has very little oil of its own, only 5% of the economy is oil-based.

The fiscal crisis of 2008 hit Dubai especially hard. After real estate prices plummeted as much as 50%, the emirate was unable to meet its debt commitments but markets stabilised after Abu Dhabi rode to the rescue with a US$10 billion loan. Still, the country's GDP suffered a contraction of 2.7% in 2009 but has been rebounding since, first slowly by 1.4% in 2010, then 4% in 2011 and still achieving a respectable 2.3% in 2012. Contributing to the recovery were high oil prices along with increased government investment in job creation and infrastructure.

The free trade zones have also been significant factors in the rebound. Companies are enticed here by the promise of full foreign ownership, full repatriation of capital and profits, no corporate tax for 15 years, no currency restrictions, and no personal income tax. One of the largest is the Jebel Ali Free Zone in Dubai, which is home to 5500 companies from 120 countries.

People & Society

The UAE population is one of the most diverse, multicultural and male (three quarters of the population) in the world. In stark contrast to neighbouring Saudi Arabia and nearby Iran, it is, overall, a tolerant and easygoing society. Most religions are tolerated (Judaism being the most blatant exception) and places of worship have been built for Christians, Hindus and Sikhs. Notwithstanding, traditional culture and social life are firmly rooted in Islam, and day-to-day activities, relationships, diet and dress are very much dictated by religion.

Emirati Lifestyle

Don't be surprised if you hear expats make crude generalisations about Emiratis (called 'nationals' or 'locals' in everyday speech). You may be told they're all millionaires and live in mansions, or that they refuse to work in ordinary jobs, or that all the men have four wives. Such stereotypes simply reinforce prejudices and demonstrate the lack of understanding between cultures within the UAE.

Not all Emiratis are wealthy. While the traditional tribal leaders, or sheikhs, are often the wealthiest UAE nationals, many have made their fortune through good investments, often dating back to the 1970s. All Emiratis have access to free healthcare and education as well as a marriage fund (although the budgets don't often meet the expenses of elaborate Emirati weddings).

The upper and middle classes of Emirati society generally have expansive villas in which men and women still live apart, and male family members entertain guests in the *majlis* (meeting room). In all classes of Emirati society, extended families living together is the norm, with the woman moving in with the husband's family after marriage, although some young couples are now choosing to buy their own apartments for a little more privacy than the traditional arrangement allows.

Women & Marriage

Gender roles are changing, with more and more Emirati women wanting to establish careers before marriage. Women make up 75% of the student body at universities and 30% of the workforce. Successful Emirati women serving as role models include Foreign Trade Minister, Sheikha Lubna Khalid Al Qasimi, who was ranked among the world's 100 most powerful women by Forbes.

Living with such a large proportion of expats, and an increasing number of Western cultural influences, has led to both growing conservatism and liberalisation. This is especially noticeable among young Emirati women: while some dress in Western fashion (usually those with foreign mothers), most 'cover up' with an *abeyya* (a full-length black robe) and *shayla* (headscarf) out of choice when in the presence of men who are not relatives. What is worn underneath is a personal choice; look closely and you'll often catch glimpses of silk stockings in high-heels poking out from beneath those modest frocks. Also note the great variety in robes and scarfs; some are made by Gucci or Prada and are embroidered or festooned with Swarovski crystals.

One aspect of Emirati society that's difficult for most Western visitors to understand is the fact that most marriages are still arranged, often to a cousin or other blood relative. However, it's now common for the couple-to-be to get to know each other a bit before exchanging wedding vows. Both can refuse to marry if they feel the person is not right for them. A woman may also divorce her husband, although this rarely happens.

The UAE Marriage Fund, set up by the federal government in 1994 to facilitate marriages between UAE nationals, provides grants to pay for the exorbitant costs of the wedding and dowry, and promotes mass weddings to enable nationals to save for a down payment on a house.

Business & the Workplace

Most Emiratis work in the public sector, as the short hours, good pay, benefits and early pensions are hard for people to refuse. The UAE government is actively pursuing a policy of 'Emiratisation', which involves encouraging Emiratis to work in the private sector, and encouraging employers to hire them. In the long term, the government hopes to be much less dependent on financing an inflated public sector and on relying on an imported labour force, which account for about 80% of the population. While professional expats hail mostly from Western countries, especially the UK, blue-collar and service workers come mostly from Bangladesh, India, Pakistan, Nepal, China and the Philippines and, increasingly, from Africa as well.

One aspect of Emirati business society that hasn't changed in centuries is the notion of *wasta* (clout and influence). Basically, if you have the right networks (which generally means being born into one of the major families) you can get things done – whether it be clinching a massive business deal with the government or getting the best parking place at work.

Arts

Owing to its Bedouin heritage, the most popular art forms in the UAE are traditional dance, music and poetry, although of late other forms of artistic expression have seen a surge in popularity. Sizeable art communities have sprouted in Dubai and Sharjah alongside world-class galleries and such international art festivals as Art Dubai, Abu Dhabi Art and the Sharjah Biennial. Abu Dhabi, in fact, is especially ambitious when it comes to positioning itself as an art world leader by building outposts of the Louvre and the Guggenheim on Saadiyat Island (p334).

The UAE also hosts two annual film festivals: the Abu Dhabi Film Festival (p329) in October and the Dubai International Film Festival (p298) in December.

Poetry

In Bedouin culture a facility with poetry and language is greatly prized. Traditionally, a poet who could eloquently praise his own people while pointing out the failures of other tribes was considered a great asset. Modern UAE poets of note include Sultan

THE UAE DEMYSTIFIED

You can't buy alcohol? Partially true. When arriving by air, you can, as a non-Muslim visitor over 18, buy certain quantities of booze in the airport duty-free shop. With the exception of 'dry' Sharjah, where alcohol and even *sheesha* smoking (using a waterpipe) is banned, you can also purchase alcohol in licensed bars and clubs that are generally attached to four- and five-star hotels for on-site consumption. Expat residents can acquire an alcohol licence, which entitles them to a fixed monthly limit of alcohol available from alcohol stores. The only store where you can officially buy alcohol without a licence is at the Barracuda Beach Resort in Umm Al Quwain. There are also a couple of unlicensed (ie illegal) hole-in-walls, which we can't really tell you much about...

There's no pork? Pork is available for non-Muslims in a special room at some supermarkets (such as Spinneys and Carrefour). In many hotel restaurants, pork is a menu item and is usually clearly labelled as such. However the 'beef bacon' and 'turkey ham' that are commonly available are nothing more than a reminder of how tasty the real thing is...unless you're a vegetarian, of course.

Do women have to 'cover up'? All locals ask is that people dress respectfully, with clothes that are not too revealing – especially outside of Dubai (Sharjah in particular). Emiratis will judge you on how you dress: men in shorts and women in tube tops will not earn much respect.

Homosexuals are banned? Simply being homosexual is not illegal as such, but homosexual acts are – as is any sex outside marriage.

What about those guys holding hands? Simply a sign of friendship. It's OK for married couples to hold hands as well, but serious public displays of affection by couples (married or not) are frowned upon, and fines and jail terms can result. Really.

If you're HIV-positive you'll be kicked out? Yes. As a worker coming to live in Dubai you will be tested for HIV as well as other things such as diabetes. If you are proven to be HIV-positive, you'll be deported.

Dubai is the capital? No! Abu Dhabi is. Both are emirates (like states) and both are the capitals of their respective state, but Abu Dhabi is the seat of UAE power. It just looks like Dubai is the capital, but Abu Dhabi's too busy counting the oil revenue to care...much.

CAMEL RACING

Camel racing is not only a popular spectator sport but is deeply rooted in the Emirati soul and originally practised only at weddings and special events. These days it's big business with races held on modern, custom-built 6km- to 10km-long tracks between October and early April.

Pure-bred camels begin daily training sessions when they're about two years old. The local Mahaliyat breed, Omaniyat camels from Oman, Sudaniyat from Sudan and interbred Muhajanat are the most common breeds used in competition. Over 100 animals participate in a typical race, each outfitted with 'robo-jockeys' since the use of child jockeys was outlawed in 2005. Owners race alongside the camels in SUVs on a separate track, giving commands by remote.

There's no fixed racing schedule, although two- or three-hour meets usually take place starting around 7am on Friday, sometimes with a second race around 2.30pm. Training sessions can sometimes be observed at other times. For exact times, check the local newspapers or call the numbers below. Admission is free. Here's a rundown of the main tracks where you can see these great desert athletes go nose to nose:

Al-Wathba (☎ 050-614 7007, 583 9200) Abu Dhabi – about 45km east of town via the E22 towards Al Ain; take exit 47, turn right to Al-Wathba Palace and right again to the track.

Al Marmoum (☎ 055-676 0006; www.dcrc.ae; off Hwy E66; ☼ usually 7am-10pm Wed-Fri Oct-Apr) Dubai – about 40km south of town en route to Al Ain, near Al Lisaili; go past the Dubai Outlet Mall and the Sevens rugby stadium and turn right at exit 37.

Al Sawan (nr Digdagga; ☼ usually 6.30am-9.30am Fri & Sat Nov-Mar) Ras Al Khaimah – about 15km southeast of RAK City via E18. Drive towards RAK airport as far as Digdagga, turn off opposite the big World Discount Store (just before the free-standing minaret) and drive for about 5km.

al-Owais (1925–2000) and Dr Ahmed al-Madani (1931–95).

Nabati (vernacular poetry) is especially popular and has traditionally been in spoken form. These days, sheikhs such as Sheikh Mohammed bin Rashid al-Maktoum, Dubai's ruler, are respected poets in this tradition.

There are scores of well-known male poets in the UAE who still use the forms of classical Arab poetry, though they often experiment with combining it with other styles. There are also some well-known female poets, most of whom write in the modern *tafila* (prose) styles. Important names are Rua Salem and her sister Sarah Hareb as well as Sheikha Maisoon al-Oasimi.

Music & Dance

Emiratis have always acknowledged the importance of music in daily life. Songs were traditionally composed to accompany different tasks, from hauling water to diving for pearls. The Arabic music you're most likely to hear on the radio, though, is *khaleeji*, the traditional Gulf style of pop music. Alongside this, an underground rock and metal music scene is increasingly taking shape, with a few Dubai bands worth noting, including Kicksound (alternative rock), Vin Sinners (rock), Coat of Arms (metal), Jay Wud (rock) and Xceed (rock).

The UAE's contact with East and North African cultures through trade, both seafaring and by camel caravan, has brought many musical and dance influences to the country. One of the most popular dances is the *ayyalah*, a typical Bedouin dance performed throughout the Gulf. The UAE has its own variation, performed to a simple drumbeat, with anywhere between 25 and 200 men standing with their arms linked in two rows facing each other. They wave walking sticks or swords in front of themselves and sway back and forth, the two rows taking it in turn to sing. It's a war dance and the words expound the virtues of courage and bravery in battle.

Environment

Environmental awareness is increasing at the macro level in the UAE, due in no small part to the efforts of the late Sheikh Zayed, who was posthumously named a 'Champion of the Earth' by the UN Environment Programme (UNEP) in 2005. With his efforts in wildlife preservation, such as Sir Bani Yas Island, which operates a breeding program for endangered Arabian wildlife species, as well as the ban on hunting with guns decades ago, Sheikh Zayed foresaw the acute threats to the endangered native species of the region.

In Dubai, the Dubai Desert Conservation Reserve (DDCR) comprises 225 sq km (5% of the area of the Dubai emirate) and integrates both a national park and the superluxe Al-Maha Desert Resort & Spa. One of DDCR's most notable achievements is the successful breeding of the endangered scimitar-horned oryx. Migrating birds and flamingos are the darlings of the Ras Al Khor Wildlife Sanctuary, at the head of Dubai Creek within view of Burj Khalifa and the high-rises on Sheikh Zayed Rd. Sharjah has a successful breeding centre at the Sharjah Desert Park, as does Al Ain Zoo, which is being expanded into a wildlife park with a heavy focus on sustainability.

In terms of going green at the micro level, much work needs to be done in the UAE. Water and energy wastage (nearly all water comes from desalination plants) and littering are major issues. However, recycling bins are increasingly popping up at such places as malls and bus and metro stations. Meanwhile, public-transport systems are proliferating. Dubai Metro inaugurated in 2009 and other emirates, such as Sharjah, have recently introduced public bus networks. Meanwhile, in Abu Dhabi, the most ambitious environmental project is taking shape: when completed, Masdar City (p331) will be the world's first carbon-neutral community.

For more information, check the website of the UAE's leading environmental organisation, the nonprofit, nongovernmental **Emirates Environmental Group** (www.eeg-uae.org).

SURVIVAL GUIDE

ⓘ Directory A–Z

ACCOMMODATION

The UAE has the gamut of places to unpack your suitcase, from ultraposh beach resorts to romantic boutique hotels and buttoned-up business properties, furnished hotel apartments with kitchens to basic hostels and inns where bathrooms may be shared. Those in the midrange usually represent the best value for money.

Camping

Although the UAE has no official campgrounds, pitching a tent on a beach or in the desert is very popular with locals and expats and is a free and safe way to spend the night. Be prepared to pack everything in (and out), don't litter and bring a shovel to bury your 'business'. For camping destinations consult locally published specialist guides widely available in bookstores everywhere.

Hostels

There are five hostels affiliated with Hostelling International in the UAE: one each in Dubai, Khor Fakkan and Fujairah and two in Sharjah. All are open to men and women, although solo women are a rare sight. Facilities are basic and shared and smoking and alcohol prohibited. Accommodation is in dorms or family rooms, which may be available to small groups and couples depending on availability and the manager's mood.

Cost

Since rates fluctuate wildly – depending on such factors as demand, location, season, day of the week and major events or holidays – prices provided by Lonely Planet should only be regarded as guidelines. Prices are official rack rates provided by the hotels but better rates can usually be obtained through the hotel websites or online booking engines. Predictably, rates are highest between November and March and lowest in July and August.

CHILDREN

It's easy to travel through the UAE with children. Many top-end hotels and some midrange ones have kids clubs, pools and playgrounds. There are plenty of beaches, parks, playground and activity centres (many in shopping malls) to keep kids amused; many restaurants have children's menus and high chairs.

Formula is readily available in pharmacies, and disposable nappies at grocery stores and super-

---

SLEEPING PRICE RANGES

The prices in this chapter are for an air-conditioned standard double room with private bathroom in peak season (November to March). Unless otherwise stated breakfast is included in the price.

$ less than Dh400

$$ Dh400–Dh1000

$$$ more than Dh1000

markets. High chairs are available in restaurants and babysitting facilities are available in some midrange and all top-end hotels, as well as at some shopping malls.

CUSTOMS REGULATIONS

UAE airports have duty-free shops in the arrivals and departure areas. At the time of going to print, visitors over 18 arriving at Dubai International Airport were allowed to bring in the following duty-free:

➡ 4L of wine or spirits or two cartons of beer at 24 cans each (non-Muslims only)

➡ 400 cigarettes and 50 cigars and 500g of loose tobacco

➡ Gifts up to the value of Dh3000

Note that these regulations change frequently and suddenly. There may be slight variations if you're arriving at another UAE airport.

You are generally not allowed to bring in:

➡ Alcohol if you cross into the UAE by land

➡ Materials (eg books) that insult Islam

➡ Firearms, pork, pornography and Israeli products.

EMBASSIES & CONSULATES

All embassies listed below are in Abu Dhabi, but most countries also maintain consular office in Dubai. Call or check the respective website for details.

Australian (☏02-401 7500; www.uae.embassy.gov.au; Sheikh Zayed the First/7th St, 8th fl, Al Muhairy Centre, Abu Dhabi)

Canadian (☏02-694 0300; www.canadainternational.gc.ca; Towers at the Trade Centre, Abu Dhabi Mall, West Tower, 9th & 10th fl)

Dutch (☏02-695 8000; http://uae.nlembassy.org; Hamdan St, 6th fl, Al Masoud Tower, Abu Dhabi)

French (☏02-813 1000; www.ambafrance-eau.org; cnr Delma/13th & Nahyan/26th Sts, Abu Dhabi)

German (☏02-596 7700; www.abu-dhabi.diplo.de; Towers at the Trade Center, West Tower, 14th fl, Abu Dhabi Mall)

Irish (☏02-495 8200; www.embassyofireland.ae; 19th St, off 32nd St, Khalifa Al Suwaidi Development)

New Zealand (☏02-441 1222; www.nzembassy.com/united-arab-emirates; Villa 226/2, Al Karamah/24th St, btwn 11th & 13th Sts)

UK (☏02-610 1100; http://ukinuae.fco.gov.uk/en/; Khalid bin Al Walid/22nd St)

US (☏emergencies only 02-414 2200; http://abudhabi.usembassy.gov; off Airport Rd, btwn 29th & 33rd Sts , Embassy District, nr Abu Dhabi National Exhibition Centre)

FOOD & DRINK

Filling your tummy in the UAE is an extraordinarily multicultural experience with a virtual UN of ethnic cuisines to choose from. Lebanese, Indian and Iranian fare are the most common, but you'll basically find anything from British fish and chips to German sauerkraut and South African *boerewors* (sausage). For typical cuisine found throughout the country, see p285 and the Flavours of Arabia chapter (p459).

By law, alcohol may only be sold in restaurants and bars in hotels or in members-only clubs, such as golf clubs, which often admit paying nonmembers. Because of the 30% tax on alcohol in the country, prices are high. Expect to pay around Dh25 for a bottle of beer, from Dh40 for a glass of wine and from Dh50 for a cocktail. The only 'dry' (meaning alcohol is not permitted) emirate is Sharjah.

GAY & LESBIAN TRAVELLERS

Homosexual acts are illegal under UAE law and can incur a jail term. You will see men walking hand in hand, but that's a sign of friendship and no indication of sexual orientation.

Although no bars, clubs or cafes would dare identify themselves as gay-friendly for fear of being raided and shut down, there are venues throughout Dubai and Abu Dhabi that attract a sizeable gay and lesbian crowd.

Gay- and lesbian-interest websites cannot be accessed from inside the UAE.

For more on the subject, pick up copies of *Gay Travels in the Muslim World* by Michael Luongo and *Unspeakable Love* by Brian Whitaker.

INTERNET ACCESS

Getting online in the UAE should not be a problem. Nearly every hotel has in-room internet access, either broadband or wireless, although rates can be extortionate. A growing number of restaurants, cafes and shopping malls offer their own wireless services, usually free with purchase.

Skype and other Voice over Internet Protocol (VoIP) software continues to be banned in the UAE, although rumours of an impending lift have been making the rounds. If the programs are

---

EATING PRICE RANGES

The following price ranges refer to an average main course. Prices may or may not include VAT and a service charge, as this varies by emirate. Details are almost always spelled out (in fine print) in restaurant menus.

$ less than Dh30

$$ Dh30–Dh90

$$$ more than Dh90

already installed on your smartphone or computer before you arrive, you should be able to use them with no problem.

LEGAL MATTERS

Drugs are simply a bad, bad idea. The minimum penalty for possession of even trace amounts is four years in prison, and the death penalty is still on the books for importing or dealing in drugs (although it's not been enforced in ages). Even if you are in a room where there are drugs, but are not partaking, you could be in as much trouble as those who are. The secret police are pervasive, and they include officers of many nationalities.

There are also import restrictions for prescription medications that are legal in most countries, such as diazepam (Valium), dextromethorphan (Robitussin), fluoxetine (Prozac) and anything containing codeine. Check with the UAE embassy in your home country for the latest list. If medication you need is on it, ask what kind of papers you need (eg original prescription, letter from your doctor) in order to bring such medication into the UAE legally.

Other common infractions that may incur a fine, jail time or even deportation include drinking alcohol in an unlicensed public place; buying alcohol without a local licence; writing bad cheques; unmarried cohabitation; and public eating, drinking and smoking during daylight hours in Ramadan. Another big no-no is sexual or indecent public behaviour.

If arrested, you have the right to a phone call, which you should make as soon as possible (ie before you are detained in a police cell or prison pending investigation). Call your embassy or consulate first so they can get in touch with your family and possibly recommend a lawyer.

For more information on legal matters, see the Expats chapter and consult your embassy.

MONEY

The UAE dirham (Dh) is fully convertible and pegged to the US dollar. One dirham is divided into 100 fils. Notes come in denominations of five, 10, 20, 50, 100, 200, 500 and 1000. Coins are Dh1, 50 fils, 25 fils, 10 fils and 5 fils.

Currency exchange offices such as UAE Exchange, Al Rostamani or Travelex sometimes offer better rates than banks. Not all change travellers cheques, but currencies of neighbouring countries are all easily exchanged.

There are globally linked ATMs all over the country, at banks, shopping malls, some supermarkets and big hotels. Major credit cards are widely accepted; debit cards less so, although they're usually no problem at bigger retail outlets.

In each emirate, a different level of municipal and service tax is charged against hotel and

---

PRACTICALITIES

➡ **News & Magazines** Widely read English-language dailies are The National, Gulf News, Gulf Today and Khaleej Times. Content is government-controlled. Time Out produces the most popular weekly listings magazine, with separate editions for Dubai and Abu Dhabi. What's On is a less insightful monthly. International magazines and newspapers are readily available.

➡ **Radio** Popular stations include BBC Worldwide (87.9) and Dubai Eye (103.8) for news and talk; Dubai FM (92), Channel 4 FM (104.8) and Emirates Radio 1 (104.1) and 2 (99.3) for music.

➡ **TV** There are several English-language TV channels, including Abu Dhabi's Channel 48 and Dubai One, and scores of English-language satellite channels.

---

restaurant bills. This is somewhere between 5% and 20%. If a price is quoted 'net', this means that it includes all taxes and service charges.

OPENING HOURS

Hours listed here are guidelines only and may vary slightly by individual business. The UAE weekend is on Friday and Saturday. Hours are limited during Ramadam and in summer.

Banks 8am to 1pm (some until 3pm) Sunday to Thursday, 8am to noon Saturday

Government offices 7.30am to 2pm (or 3pm) Sunday to Thursday

Restaurants noon to 3pm and 7.30pm to 11pm or midnight

Shopping malls 10am to 10pm Sunday to Wednesday, 10am to midnight Thursday and Friday

Souqs 9am to 1.30pm and 4.30pm to 9pm or 10pm (often later in Dubai and Abu Dhabi), closed Friday morning

Supermarkets 9am to midnight daily, some open 24 hours

PHOTOGRAPHY

Memory cards, batteries and other accessories for digital cameras are available in major supermarkets, at shopping malls and in electronics stores. Taking video or photographs of airports, government offices, military and industrial installations may result in arrest and/or prosecution. Also ask permission before photographing people, especially Muslim women.

POST

Your hotel should be able to send mail for you, but otherwise stamps are available at local post offices operated by **Emirates Post** (☎ 600 599 999; www.emiratespost.com) and found in every city and town. A letter to Europe costs Dh4.75, while a postcard costs Dh3 and a 1kg parcel costs Dh95.50. Rates to the US or Canada are almost identical: Dh5.50 for letters, Dh3 for postcards and Dh97 for the 1kg parcel. Mail generally takes about a week to 10 days to Europe or the USA and eight to 15 days to Australia.

PUBLIC HOLIDAYS

As well as the major Islamic holidays (p486), the UAE observes the following public holidays:

New Year's Day 1 January

Accession Day (of HH Sheikh Zayed) 6 August

National Day 2 December

A mourning period of up to one week usually follows the death of a royal family member, a government minister or a head of a neighbouring state. Government offices, some businesses and state-run tourist attractions (such as museums) are closed on these days. Events may be cancelled.

SAFE TRAVEL

The UAE has a low incidence of crime and even pickpocketing and bag snatching are rare. One very real danger is bad driving. Courtesy on the road simply does not exist. People will cut in front of you, turn without indicating and race each other on highways.

Out of the cities, remember the left lane is for passing only – block them at your own risk as speeds of up to 200km/h are not unusual. Some drivers also have a tendency to zoom into roundabouts at frightening speeds and try to exit them from inside lanes. Pedestrian crossings are no guarantee that drivers will stop or even slow down.

If you have an accident, even a small one, you must call the police (☎ 999) and wait at the scene. If it's a minor accident, move your car to the side of the road. You cannot file an insurance claim without a police report.

If you are swimming at an unpatrolled (ie public) beach, be very careful. Despite the small surf, there may be dangerous rip tides and drowings are not uncommon.

Do not buy counterfeit and pirated goods, even if they are widely available. Not only are these goods illegal in the many countries, purchasing them is a violation of local law.

TELEPHONE

The UAE has an efficient communications system that connects callers with anywhere in the world, even from the most remote areas. There are two mobile networks: Etisalat and Du.

Both are government-owned and there's little difference between the two, although Etisalat's network is slightly bigger.

In April 2013, Etisalat unblocked Skype (it was previously blocked in the UAE), making it possible to download the software within the UAE and to use all of its features.

Local calls (within the same area code) are free.

Mobile Phones

The UAE's mobile-phone network uses the GSM 900 MHz and 1800 MHz standard, the same as Europe, Asia and Australia. Mobile numbers begin with either 050 (Etisalat) or 055 (Du).

If you don't have a worldwide roaming service but do have an unlocked phone, consider buying a prepaid SIM card, eg at Dubai Duty Free, any Etisalat office or licensed mobile-phone shops. The excellent-value Ahlan Visitor's Mobile Package lasts 90 days, costs Dh60 and includes Dh25 of credit.

Recharge cards in denominations of Dh25, Dh50, Dh100, Dh200 and Dh500 are sold at grocery stores, supermarkets and petrol stations.

Phone Codes

If dialling a UAE number from another country, dial the country code ☎ 971, followed by the area code (minus the zero) and the subscriber number. To phone another country from the UAE, dial ☎ 00 followed by the country code. For directory enquiries call ☎ 181, for international directory assistance call ☎ 151.

When making calls within the UAE, dial the seven-digit local number if already in the city and using a landline. If dialling a number in another city – or using a mobile phone – dial the two-digit area code provided throughout this book first.

Phonecards

Coin phones have been almost completely superseded by card phones. Phonecards are available in various denominations from grocery stores, supermarkets and petrol stations.

TOILETS

The best advice is to go when you can. Public toilets in shopping centres, museums, restaurants and hotels are Western-style and are generally clean and well maintained.

Those in souqs and bus stations are usually only for men. Outside the cities you might have to contend with hole-in-the-ground loos at the back of restaurants or petrol stations, although these are increasingly rare.

You'll always find a hose and nozzle next to the toilet, which is used to rinse yourself before using the toilet paper.

VISAS

Entry requirements to the UAE are in constant flux, so all information below can only serve as a guideline. Always obtain the latest requirements from the UAE embassy in your home country.

At the time of writing, citizens of the UK, France, Italy, Germany, the Netherlands, Belgium, Luxembourg, Switzerland, Austria, Sweden, Norway, Denmark, Portugal, Ireland, Greece, Finland, Spain, Monaco, Vatican, Iceland, Andorra, San Marino, Liechtenstein, United States, Australia, New Zealand, Japan, Brunei, Singapore, Malaysia, South Korea and Hong Kong are granted a free 30-day tourist visa upon arrival in the UAE.

Everyone else must have a visit visa arranged through a sponsor – such as your UAE hotel or tour operator – prior to arrival in the UAE. The nonrenewable visas cost Dh210 and are valid for 30 days.

Visas can be extended for a further 30 days at a cost Dh500 at an immigration office in the emirate in which you arrived.

If you're transiting via the UAE and are a citizen of a country eligible for an automatic 30-day tourist visa, you do not need to pre-arrange a transit visa. Other nationalities need to get the airline or a local hotel to organise a 96-hour visa. The official fee is Dh165.

Gulf Cooperation Council (GCC) citizens only need a valid passport to enter the UAE and stay indefinitely.

WOMEN TRAVELLERS

Many women imagine that travel to the UAE will be much more difficult than it actually is. No, you don't have to wear a burka, headscarf or veil. Yes, you can drive a car. No, you won't be constantly harrassed.

In fact, the UAE is one of safest Middle Eastern destinations for women travellers. It's fine to take cabs, stay alone in most hotels and walk around on your own in most areas. Having said that, this does not mean that some of the problems that accompany travel just about anywhere in the world will not arise in the UAE as well, such as unwanted male attention and lewd stares, especially on public beaches. Try not to be intimidated and appear self-confident.

Even though you'll see plenty of Western women wearing skimpy clothing in public, you should not assume that it's acceptable to do so. While most are too polite to actually say anything, Emiratis find this disrespectful. When it comes to beach parties and nightclubs almost anything goes, but take a taxi there and back.

Although prostitution does not officially exist, authorities do little to suppress the small army of 'working women' catering to both expats and Emiratis in clubs, bars and backstreets. In terms of dress, they're often indistinguishable from other women, which is confusing to men and can open up the possibility of non-working women being solicited erroneously.

ⓘ Getting There & Away

ENTERING THE UAE

If you're a citizen of a country eligible to collect a free visit or transit visa upon arrival, simply proceed straight to the immigration desk or border post and get your passport stamped. If you are entering on a sponsored visa you'll need to go to the clearly marked visa collection counter at the airport when you arrive. Also see the section on visas on p359.

Passports

All passports must be valid for at least six months from the date of arrival. It is generally not possible to enter with an Israeli passport, but anyone entering the UAE with an Israeli stamp in a non-Israeli passport should have no problem.

AIR
Airports & Airlines

Dubai International (p308) and Abu Dhabi International (p334) are the UAE's main airports. A growing number of flights, especially charters, also land at Sharjah International Airport (p317). Ras Al Khaimah, Al Ain and Fujairah also have small airports but few, if any, passenger flights. Departure tax is included in the ticket price.

Emirates Airlines (www.emirates.com) Dubai-based, extensive route network, excellent service and high safety record.

Etihad Airways (www.etihadairways.com) Based in Abu Dhabi with the same credentials as Emirates Airlines.

Air Arabia (☎ 06-508 8888; www.airarabia. com) Sharjah-based low-cost carrier flying to North African, Middle Eastern, Asian and select European destinations, including Amsterdam, London and Barcelona.

FlyDubai (☎ 04-231 1000; www.flydubai.com) Discount carrier with around 50 destinations, mostly within the Middle East, India and Central Asia.

RAK Airways (☎ 07-207 5000; www.rakairways.com) Flights to Egypt, Qatar, Pakistan, Nepal, India and Bangladesh.

LAND
Border Crossings

The UAE shares borders with Oman and Saudi Arabia, but only GCC citizens are permitted to cross into Saudi at the Ghuwaifat/Sila border post in the far west of the UAE.

Non-GCC citizens headed for mainland Oman may use the Hili checkpoint in Al Ain, the Hatta checkpoint east of Dubai and the tiny coastal Khatmat Malaha crossing south of Fujairah.

If you're headed for Khasab on the Musandam Peninsula, use the Shams/Tibat checkpoint north of Ras Al Khaimah. There's another border crossing to the Musandam in Dibba on the east coast but military checkpoints make it impossible to drive to Khasab from there.

Unless you have a free UAE tourist visa, there's a Dh35 fee when leaving the UAE and a Dh50/OR5 fee at the Omani entry point (cash only).

Bus

Oman National Transport Company (ONTC; www.ontocoman.com) runs comfortable express buses with televisions and toilets on board between Muscat (Oman) and Dubai . Express bus 204 travels via the coastal Khatmat Malaha crossing and Fujeirah in seven hours (OR5.5 or Dh53). Express bus 201 goes via Hatta in 5½ or six hours for the same fare.

In Dubai, buses leave from a **bus stop** (28A St, near 11D St; Ⓜ Al Rigga) in Deira, just northwest of the airport, near the Caravan restaurant. Tickets are sold in the Al Manhal shop.

Car & Motorcycle

If you intend to drive into the UAE, bring your passport, visa (if any), drivers licence, car registration and proof of adequate insurance coverage. Make sure you have enough gas since petrol stations are few and far between.

ℹ Getting Around

AIR

Abu Dhabi-based **Rotana Jet** (☑ 02-444 0002; www.rotanajet.com; one-way from Dh200) has daily connections between Abu Dhabi and Al Ain, twice daily flights to Fujairah and thrice-weekly flights to Sir Bani Yas Island.

BUS & MINIBUS

A growing fleet of public buses makes interemirate travel increasingly convenient. A list of the main bus companies follows. For specific route information, see the Getting There & Away sections in this chapter.

Roads and Transport Authority (RTA; ☑ toll-free 800 9090; www.rta.ae) Based in Dubai, service to Sharjah, Al Ain, Abu Dhabi and Ras Al Khaima from several bus stations in Bur Dubai and Deira.

Sharjah Transport Authority (☑ 7000 6 7000; www.stc.gov.ae) Destinations include Dubai, Ajman, Ras Al Khaimah, Masafi, Fujairah, Khor Fakkan, Abu Dhabi, Al Ain.

Abu Dhabi Department of Transportation (☑ toll-free 800 55555; www.dot.abudhabi. ae) Service within the emirate, eg to Al Ain, Mezaira'a (for the Liwa desert) and Jebel Dhanna (for Sir Bani Yas Island).

CAR

Having your own wheels is a great way to see the UAE, allowing you to get off the major highways and to stop as you please. Well-maintained multilane highways link the cities, often lit along their entire length. For off-road driving, you need a 4WD. If you have a breakdown call the **Arabian Automobile Association** (☑ 800 4900; www. aaauae.com).

Hire

To hire a car, you'll need a credit card and a valid driver's licence. International drivers licences are not usually compulsory, although it won't hurt to have one.

Daily rates start at about Dh175 for a small manual car such as a Toyota Yaris, including comprehensive insurance and unlimited miles.

Expect surcharges for airport rentals, additional drivers, one-way hire and drivers under 25. Most companies have child and infant safety seats for a fee, but these must be reserved well in advance.

Local agencies may be cheaper but the major international ones have the advantage of larger fleets and better emergency backup.

For longer rentals, prebooked and prepaid packages, arranged in your home country, may work out cheaper than on-the-spot-rentals. Check for deals with the online travel agencies, travel agents or brokers such as **Auto Europe** (www.autoeurope.com) or **Holiday Autos** (www. holidayautos.com).

If you plan on taking the car to Oman, bring written permission from the car rental company in case you're asked for it at the border. You'll also need car insurance that's valid in Oman. Omani insurance is available at most border crossings.

PUBLIC TRANSPORT

Dubai, Abu Dhabi and Sharjah are the only emirates with public bus services. Dubai also has the high-tech Dubai Metro, which links some of the major attractions and malls and is an inexpensive, efficient way to get across town. See the Getting Around sections in this chapter for details.

TAXIS

Taxis are cheap, metered and ubiquitous and – given the dearth of public transportation in some emirates – often the only way of getting around.

Most drivers can also be hired by the hour. In that case, rates should be negotiated unless fixed fees are set in place. In Dubai, for instance, the fee for six hours is Dh300, for 12 hours it's Dh500.

Most cabs can also be engaged for long-distance travel to other emirates, in which case you should negotiate the fee at the beginning of the trip.

Few drivers are fluent English speakers and many are more familiar with landmarks than streets names. It helps if you mention parks, shopping malls or hotel names when giving directions for your desired destination. Tip about 10% for good service.

Shared Taxis

For inter-emirate travel, shared taxis are an alternative for some travellers. Although fares tend to be similar, they leave when full, which may be more frequently than scheduled bus service. They do get cramped, so people in need of much personal space will likely not feel so comfortable. Women solo travellers may feel especially uncomfortable. You can get these taxis engaged (ie privately, not shared) if you are willing to pay for all of the seats.

The following companies are all well established and licensed by the Department of Tourism & Commerce Marketing (DTCM). They offer a wide choice of tours, ranging from city excursions of Dubai, Al Ain and Abu Dhabi to more active trips, such as trekking in the Hajar Mountains or overnight desert safaris. Check the websites for details and prices. Note that some tours only depart with a minimum number of passengers. If you have a choice, Arabian Adventures has a particularly good reputation and repeatedly receives positive feedback from tourists.

Alpha Tours (☑ 04-294 9888; www.alpha-toursdubai.com)

Arabian Adventures (Map p296; ☑ 04-303 4888; www.arabian-adventures.com; Sun-downer adult/child Dh330/295)

Desert Rangers (Map p296; ☑ 04-357 2200; www.desertrangers.com; adult/child Dh300/210)

Hormuz Tourism (Map p288; ☑ 04-228 0663; www.hormuztourism.com)

Knight Tours (Map p296; ☑ 04-343 7725; www.knighttours.co.ae; Al-Wadi Bldg, Sheikh Zayed Rd)

Orient Tours (Map p288; ☑ 04 282 8238; www.orienttours.ae)

Yemen   يمن

Best Places for Culture

➡ Old Sana'a (p367)

➡ Wadi Hadramawt (p394)

➡ Haraz Mountains (p374)

➡ Tihama (p379)

➡ Ma'rib (p388)

Best Places for Nature

➡ Socotra (p391)

➡ Haraz Mountains (p374)

➡ Jabal Bura (p381)

➡ Kamaran Island (p380)

Why Go?

Yemen is, in many ways, the birthplace of all our lives. In days past, the sons of Noah knew it as the land of milk and honey, Gilgamesh came here to search for the secret of eternal life, wise men gathered frankincense and myrrh from its mountains and, most famously, a woman known simply as Sheba said Yemen was her home.

Yet since the book of mythology was closed, Yemen has remained largely locked away in a forgotten corner. This is a huge oversight, because Yemen is a deeply romantic and utterly unique place in which to travel.

However, there is a problem: travel here has never come easily, nor in complete safety; but today Yemen dances on the brink of catastrophe and you should assess the security situation carefully before taking the plunge. But if the security situation allows then the rewards of travelling here are enormous.

When to Go

Yemen

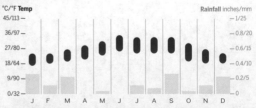

Sep–Dec The monsoon rains are ending, the mountains are green and the hiking superb

Nov–Feb This is the time to hit the Tihama Red Sea coastal regions or the eastern deserts.

Jun–Sep Gale force monsoon winds can make visiting Socotra island a bit of a pain

Daily Costs

Basic living costs in Yemen are low. A simple meal in a cheap local cafe can be had for US$2 to US$3 or double that at a posher restaurant. Budget hotels are US$10 to US$15; mid-range hotels average US$20 to US$40. Bus travel is cheap.

What sends the cost of living right up is the fact that at present, due to the unstable security situation, you can only travel in Yemen as part of an organised tour for which you're looking at a minimum of US$100 per day – often more.

IS YEMEN SAFE?

The first question on the mind of every visitor to Yemen is almost certainly: 'is it safe?'. The simple answer, as of April 2013, is No. Since the political demonstrations of 2010 Yemen has been virtually at war with itself. At one point much of the country was completely out of central government hands and there was heavy fighting throughout Yemen including in the capital, Sana'a. Today things are better, but far from perfect. A degree of security has returned to Sana'a, parts of the nearby mountain areas, the island of Socotra and one or two other areas, and the first brave tourists are starting to return. However, in early 2013 Yemen was still considered highly dangerous and Lonely Planet does not recommend travelling there given the unstable security situation. For more information, see p404.

On the Ground Research

Due to the highly dangerous security situation throughout Yemen we were unable to conduct on-the-ground research anywhere in the country. This chapter is a combination of information dating back to 2010, and remotely researched information obtained via the telephone and internet in 2012. For Sana'a, around Sana'a and parts of the Haraz Mountains, on the ground research was conducted by a Yemeni tour company.

Itineraries

Travel itineraries in Yemen are greatly influenced by the current security situation. A few years ago most of the country was open to foreign tourists. Today, hardly anywhere is (although things are starting to improve again). At the time of writing the following was the only realistic itinerary and even that was liable to be shut down at short notice.

Start in the old city of Sana'a allowing a catlike curiosity to lead you through alleyways, up back streets and into interesting corners. Then climb into the Haraz Mountains to explore by foot the numerous villages and breathtaking scenery here in the trekking heartland. Returning to Sana'a fly to the island of Socotra for some birdwatching, beach time and more hiking.

At A Glance

→ **Currency** Yemeni riyal (YR)

→ **Mobile Phones** Widespread phone network; foreign phones sometimes blocked.

→ **Money** ATM's accept Visa cards in bigger towns. Also bring US dollars cash.

→ **Visas** Only issued to people on an organised tour. Not available on arrival.

Fast Facts

→ **Capital** Sana'a
→ **Country code** ⌐967
→ **Language** Arabic
→ **Official name** Republic of Yemen
→ **Population** 23 million

Exchange Rates

Australia	A$1	YR 224
Bahrain	BD1	YR569
Euro zone	€1	YR280
Kuwait	KD1	YR754
Oman	OR1	YR558
Qatar	QR10	YR590
Saudi Arabia	SR10	YR572
UAE	Dh10	YR584
UK	UK£1	YR 328
USA	US$1	YR 214

Resources

→ **Lonely Planet** (www.lonelyplanet.com/yemen) Tips and information.

→ **Yemen Times** (www.yementimes.com) News.

→ **British Government Travel Advice** (www.fco.gov.uk) Travel warnings issued by the British government.

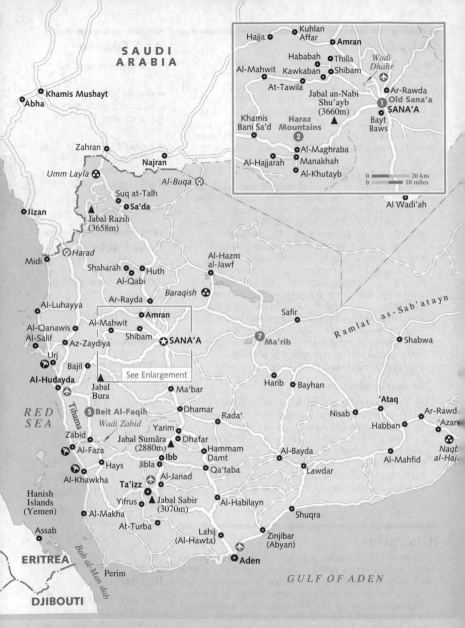

Yemen Highlights

1 Sigh over Sana'a's cake-icing-like houses in **Old Sana'a** (p367) and saunter through ancient alleyways created by the son of Noah and a mischievous bird.

2 Weave a trail through a tapestry of fortresses and fields in the **Haraz Mountains** (p374).

3 Wander the sandcastle cities of weird and wonderful

Wadi Hadramawt (p394) (only if it's safe) where giants once roamed and scorpions line the entrance to Hell.

4 Act like a medieval knight and search for dragons and

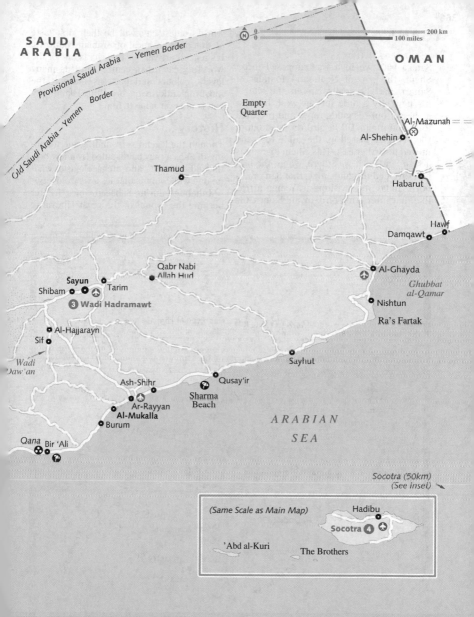

SAUDI ARABIA

OMAN

200 km
100 miles

Provisional Saudi Arabia – Yemen Border

Old Saudi Arabia – Yemen Border

Empty Quarter

Al-Mazunah

Al-Shehin

Habarut

Hawf

Damqawt

Thamud

Al-Ghayda

Ghubbat al-Qamar

Qabr Nabi Allah Hud

Nishtun

Sayun

Ra's Fartak

Shibam

Tarim

3 Wadi Hadramawt

Al-Hajjarayn

Sif

Sayhut

Wadi Daw'an

Ash-Shihr

Qusay'ir

Sharma Beach

Ar-Rayyan

Al-Mukalla

ARABIAN

Burum

SEA

Qana

Bir 'Ali

Socotra (50km)
(See inset)

(Same Scale as Main Map)

Hadibu

Socotra **4**

'Abd al-Kuri

The Brothers

the secret of eternal life in stupendous **Socotra** (p391).

5 Bargain for a camel or two and be swallowed up by the colour and chaos of **Beit Al-Faqih** (p382), Yemen's

largest weekly market, in the fascinating Tihama region.

6 Sit back with friends, relax and enjoy an afternoon **qat** session – the key to Yemeni social life (p402).

7 If it's safe, venture back through time in **Ma'rib** (p388), to the sandy streets of the Queen of Sheba's capital.

SANA'A صنعاء

🎵 01 / POP 1.7 MILLION

Sana'a isn't where it was supposed to be. Shem, the son of Noah and founder of Sana'a, had originally chosen the site of his new city a little further west, but just as he set out his guide ropes and prepared for some major DIY a bird dropped out of the heavens, picked up the guide rope and moved it further east. This, Shem knew, was a sign, and so it was there, where the bird had dropped the guide rope, that Sana'a was born. Today most visitors to Yemen arrive, like that interfering bird, by air. Sana'a, the

world's oldest city, will be their first taste of this most mystical of Arabian countries. It's a good arrival, for this city is one of the world's great urban centres, and its many layers, colours and patterns make it the most romantic, living, breathing Islamic city you could ever hope to find.

History

Though the legend surrounding the founding of Sana'a may be disputed by a few boring old scientists and archaeologists, what no one will doubt is that it's a very old city.

Inhabited during Sabaean times, it later became the capital of the great Himyarite

Sana'a

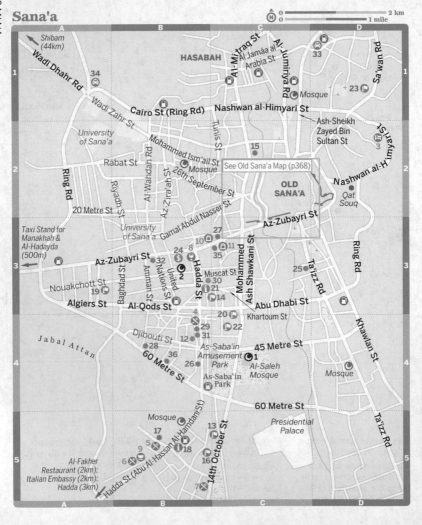

dynasty in the early 6th century AD. It also served as a power base for two foreign powers: the Abyssinians and the Persians. In the 7th century AD Islam arrived, altering forever the face of the city, as early mosques and minarets rose up to replace the old churches. The city was later expanded under the Ottomans.

After the civil war in the 1960s, Sana'a experienced a period of rapid growth, doubling in size every four years. Historically, politically and economically, it was the obvious choice for the capital of the reunited Yemen in 1990. Today Sana'a is the fastest-growing capital city in the world and this is creating a predictable range of social problems.

Sights & Activities

Art Galleries & Centres

Sana'a has a respectable arts scene and several galleries are scattered about the old town. The best are the **Gallery Al-Bab** (Map p368; inside the gates of Bab al-Yaman) FREE, **National Art Centre** (Map p368) FREE and the **Sheba Art Gallery** (Map p368) FREE.

Old Sana'a

It would be fair to say that the Unesco-protected old city of Sana'a is one of the most beautiful cities anywhere on earth and

nothing is likely to prepare you for the moment you first pass through the gates of the Bab al-Yaman. Most people spend days wandering without aim through this enormous work of art and that's certainly the best way to absorb this magnificent city.

At the heart of it all is the **Souq al-Milh** (Map p368; NE of Bab al-Yaman). Though the name indicates that the sole product is salt, this is something of a misnomer. Everything from mobile phones to sacks of sultanas is available here. It's almost impossible to point to individual buildings, souqs or sights, but the qat market, in the centre of the old town, is frenetically busy around lunchtime. The spice souq is every oriental fantasy brought to life and the small cellars where blinkered camels walk round and round in circles crushing sesame seeds to make oil is a glimpse into a bygone age. For many the abiding memory of the city is likely to be of the topsy-turvy, cake-icing-like houses and the dreamy mosques. Walking the streets of old Sana'a as the evening prayer call rings out across the rooftops is a deeply romantic and exotic experience and something you're never likely to forget.

Finally, a compulsory activity for tourist and local alike is to climb to the top of one of the tower houses and relish the ravishing

YEMEN SANA'A

views over the city as the sun sinks below the surrounding mountains.

Mosques & Gardens

All but one of the mosques in Sana'a are open only to Muslims, but you can often get a fleeting glimpse inside a mosque through a doorway, and the majestic minarets are there for all to enjoy. Of the many mosques other than Al-Saleh and the Great Mosque, ones to look out for include the small but elegant **Qubbat al-Bakiriyah Mosque**, built by the Ottomans and renovated in the 19th century; the 17th-century **Qubbat Talha Mosque**, with its unusual minaret; the de-

crepit mid-16th-century **Al-'Aqil Mosque** to the north of Souq al-Milh; and the **Salah ad-Din Mosque**, due east of Al-'Aqil Mosque, built in the 17th century.

Finally, the city may not look like a lush and green place, but while exploring old Sana'a keep an eye peeled for the hidden communal vegetable gardens that once made the city self-sufficient.

Al-Saleh Mosque
MOSQUE

(Map p366; Mohammed Ash Shawkani St;) FREE In order to ensure that nobody ever forgets his 33-year reign ex-President Ali Abdullah Saleh inaugurated the enormous Al-Saleh Mosque

Old Sana'a

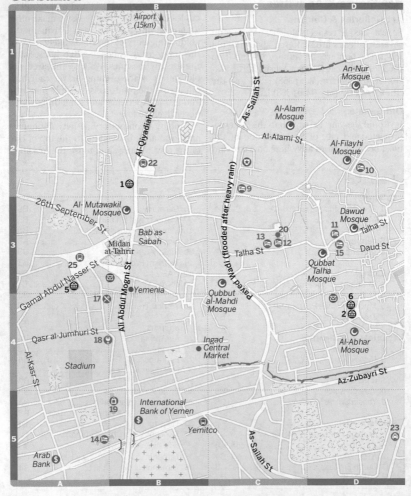

in 2008. Costing around US$60 million to build and holding around 40,000 worshippers it's the biggest mosque in Yemen and the only one in Sana'a open to non-Muslims. Opposite As-Saba'in Park, the mosque is undoubtedly overwhelming, (its minarets are so big they have aeroplane warning lights mounted on them!) if a little tacky. Despite some mumbling about how the money could have been better spent on hospitals and schools, most Yemenis are quite proud of the mosque. It's open to non-Muslims from dawn to dusk daily outside of prayer times – dress appropriately and take a travel permit

with you as it's not unknown for the guards to ask to see one.

Great Mosque
MOSQUE

(Al-Jamaa al-Kabir; Map p368) **FREE** Of the 50 mosques still standing in the old city, the Great Mosque north of Bab al-Yaman, is the most significant. For centuries it served as an important Islamic school and centre of learning, and attached to it is a library containing the largest and most famous collection of manuscripts in Yemen.

Old Sana'a

Qat Souqs

As well as the atmospheric old town qat souq, there's a bigger one further east, near the ring road, and another, the Ingad Central Market, just to the west of the dry wadi (now a road) that runs through the western fringe of the old city.

Museums

⭐**National Museum**   MUSEUM
(Map p368; ☏ 271696; Ali Abdul Mogni St; admission YR1000; ⊘ 8.30am-12.30pm & 4-8pm Sat-Wed, 8.30am-12.30pm Thu) Claiming to be the largest museum on the Arabian Peninsula, the National Museum is certainly one of the best. The ground and 1st floors contain a breathtaking collection of statues, figurines and other artefacts from the pre-Islamic kingdoms of Saba and Hadramawt. The 2nd floor concentrates on the medieval Islamic period while the top floor features a slightly less rewarding mishmash of stuffed lions and re-creations of the souqs of Sana'a.

Military Museum   MUSEUM
(Map p368; ☏ 276635; Gamal Abdul Nasser St; admission YR300; ⊘ 9am-12.30pm & 3-8pm Sat-Wed, 3-7pm Thu & Fri) The ground floor contains Sabaean overflow from the National Museum, which means this military museum is more interesting than it sounds. After that the displays revert to the standard death and guns of military museums the world over, though this one also includes some graphic photos of executions during the Imanic era.

Dar al Hayas a Sanania   MUSEUM
(Map p368; admission YR200; ⊘ 8am-6pm) This renovated old tower house is the newest museum in the city. It reveals something of the life and times of a traditional Sana'a home. The opening hours are very erratic but as the owner lives there you only need knock on the door if it's closed to be allowed in.

Tours

City tours of Sana'a (for around US$50 to US$60) are offered by local travel operators.

🛏 Sleeping

The old city might be cramped, noisy and sometimes uncomfortable, but without any doubt its immense character and colour means that it's the best place to stay. Unless you're a businessperson requiring form and functionality, then it's very hard to know why you would opt for the soulless streets and hotels of the ugly new town.

🛏 Old City

All of the following are converted tower houses marketed as 'palace hotels', though none were ever anything of the sort. Prior to the current problems in Yemen there were a couple of other tourist hotels in Sana'a including the **Sanaä Nights Tourist Hotel** (Map p368; Talha St), the **Taj Talha Hotel** (Map p368; Talha St; @) and the **Golden Daar Hotel** (Map p368; Talha St; 🛜). If the security situation continues to improve then the owners of these hope to re-open.

Arabia Felix Tourist Hotel   HISTORIC HOTEL $$
(Map p368; ☏ 287330; www.dynertia.net/arabiafelixhotel.com; As-Sailah St; s/d/tr incl breakfast €24/25.30/33; 🛜) This hotel's best asset is its small but attractive garden. Rooms are small and simple. Some include a bathroom and some don't, but the price is the same!

⭐**Dawood Hotel**   HISTORIC HOTEL $$
(Map p368; ☏ 287270; www.dawoodhotel.com; Talha St; s/d without bathroom US$30/45, s/d US$50/60, ste US$120; @🛜) Despite some price hikes over the past couple of years the Dawood continues to offer the best value for money in town. It's a lovingly restored tower house with sparkling clean rooms full of delightful textiles, Arabian cushion seats and bundles of real and not-so-real antiques. The beds are soft and comfortable, the views memorable and the sunny courtyard overlooks communal vegetable gardens. The best thing though is the warm and friendly staff that come a-knocking each evening with frankincense for your room. Try and get one of the better rooms on the upper floors. Breakfast included.

★ **Burj Al Salam Hotel** HISTORIC HOTEL **$$$**
(Map p368; ☎ 483333; www.burjalsalam.com; s/d/ ste from US$70/90/140; @⚡) Burj Al Salam is a smart four-star hotel that's lost in the heart of old Sana'a. The small standard rooms are perfectly presented with heavy wooden furniture, stone floors and large windows, while the suites are big enough to get thoroughly lost in. The biggest attraction might be the arresting rooftop views and the luxurious *mafraj* (literally 'room with a view').

🛏 New City

Say'un Hotel HOTEL **$$**
(Map p368; ☎ 274838; sayunhotel@y.net.ye; Ali Abdul Mogni St; s/d YR4000/6000) The scrappy reception and stairway leads you to fear the worst, but the rooms are actually much cleaner and better than you might expect. The hotel is good for couples on a budget, but staff are not at all used to foreigners. There are a couple of other similar hotels nearby although they are even less sure of what to do with foreigners.

Mövenpick HOTEL **$$$**
(Map p368; ☎ 546666; www.movenpick-hotels. com; Berlin St; s/d from US$135/155; P@⚡☒)

This monster on the hill, which is doing its utmost to ruin the Sana'a skyline, is also undeniably the best hotel in the city. It hardly needs saying that the rooms and facilities are of the highest calibre, but the best features are a pool that's practically the size of a small ocean and the huge, impressive views. There is heavy security at the entrance gate.

🍴 Eating

Not surprisingly, Sana'a has the best range of restaurants in the country, including a few serving international dishes. In the evening the old city is something of a non event when it comes to filling your belly and, unless you're happy to eat in your hotel, you'll need to catch a taxi out to the new town in order to get a decent meal.

Of the hotel restaurants in the old town the standout is the restaurant inside the Arabia Felix Tourist Hotel, which has an international menu featuring curries, pasta, seafood and Yemeni staples for around YR600.

★ **Houmald Salta** YEMENI **$**
(Map p368; Souq al-Milh; meals YR400-600; ☺noon-3pm) Next to the qat market in the heart of the old city. This restaurant is

YEMEN SANA'A

A CITY CAUGHT IN TIME

Sana'a is so perfectly preserved that it is said you can walk a square kilometre in any direction without encountering a single new building. The old city is particularly famous for its 'tower houses'. Reaching up to six or eight storeys, they have been called 'the world's first skyscrapers'; Sana'a contains no fewer than 14,000 of them.

Tower houses tend to follow a set design: on the ground floor are the stables and storerooms; on the 1st floor the rooms used for entertaining; the 2nd floor is usually reserved for the women and children; and on the 3rd and 4th floors are the bedrooms, bathrooms and kitchen. At the very top of the house is the *manzar* (attic), which contains the *mafraj* (literally 'room with a view'). Serving often as windows in the *mafraj* are moon-shaped, stained-glass windows known as *qamariyas*. Today much qat-chewing takes place here.

The ground and 1st floors of the building are generally constructed of stone, and the upper levels of mud brick. Outside, the facade is whitewashed with lime (which protects the mud from rainwater) and decorated with geometrically patterned lines. The stone foundations of some houses are thought to date back at least a thousand years (the oldest building in the city was constructed a staggering two thousand years ago).

The original plan and pattern of the Sana'a tower house is said to have come from the legendary Palace of Ghumdan, a 2nd-century masterpiece whose lights could be seen in Madinah, 1000km to the north, and which was said to have been as close to heaven as you could come on earth. The Great Mosque is thought to have been partially constructed with materials from this palace.

The fighting of 2011 largely spared the old city and very little damage has been reported.

regarded as having the best *salta* (a kind of stew and the traditional lunch dish of the highlands) in Sana'a and is a pre-qat-session institution. Buy the accompanying sheets of bread from the women standing around outdoors. There are several similar places nearby.

Palestine Restaurant
YEMENI $

(Map p368; off Midan at-Tahrir; meals from YR600) Attracting hordes of local workers for lunch and residents of the neighbourhood for dinner this is the best of several cheap and cheerful restaurants in the very heart of the city. The chefs whip up a mean chicken and rice.

★ Al-Shaibani Modern Restaurant
YEMENI $$

(Map p366; ☎266375; Hadda St; meals YR600-1000) This is the restaurant that all the other restaurants in Yemen want to take after. All the Yemeni staples here are done to perfection, but it's the oven-baked fish that rules the roost.

Zeyna Food
ETHIOPIAN $$

(Map p366; 14th October St; meals YR500-800; ☺noon-3pm) Run more as a hobby than a business by an Ethiopian woman, this incredibly popular lunchtime restaurant gives you the opportunity to try Ethiopia's national dish, *injira* (sourdough flatbread) and *wat* (spicy, curry like dish), a decidedly acquired taste! There's also a small range of Italian dishes for those not into acquired tastes.

Mysore Palace Restaurant
INDIAN $$$

(Map p366; ☎426359; off Hadda St; mains YR500-1000; ☺11.30am-3.30pm & 6.30-11pm) You know this is a real deal Indian restaurant by the fact that the vast majority of the customers are expat Indians. Its spicy variety makes for a delicious change after a repetitive Yemeni diet.

Al-Fakher Restaurant
YEMENI $$$

(☎427999; Hadda St; mains YR800-2500) The Yemeni food served at this upmarket restaurant seems to have almost nothing in common with all that fatty meat and stringy chicken that's been masquerading as Yemeni food elsewhere in the country. Put simply the food here is divine and if the *Tihama Hanid lamb* (lamb wrapped in banana skins and slow cooked in a beehive oven) doesn't make you drool then nothing will. Don't pass up a dessert of *fatat maoz* (a stunning mix of banana, honey and custard).

El-Deewan Restaurant
LEBANESE $$$

(Map p366; ☎425528; off Hadda St; mains YR900-1800) One of Sana'a's top restaurants, this is where well-to-do Sana'a folk go for a splurge. The Lebanese food is without peer in Yemen and as well as eating inside you have the option of tucking in outside in the shady garden.

 ## Drinking

Various Turkish-style coffeehouses can be found around Bab al-Yaman, including the **coffeehouse** next to the wall, immediately to the left of the gate as you enter the old city (look out for the awning). For a more sophisticated and cosmopolitan coffee check out one of the new coffeeshops starting to spring up in the city. Probably the best known such place is **News@Cafe** (Map p366; ☎424170; off Hadda St) where you can get a serious caffeine fix whilst partaking in an Ethiopian coffee ceremony. It's popular with the city's Ethiopian and Western expat communities and, maybe more interestingly, a tiny community of middle-class Yemeni women who are happy to talk openly to strangers.

Excellent fruit-juice stalls are dotted around town; the best is **Al-Asdeqa** (Map p368; Qasr al-Jumhuri St; juices around YR80), or the three superb, unnamed, **juice stalls** that stand on the corners of Hadda St and Az-Zubayri St. As well as doing every juice imaginable these three make some of the best *arayesi* (p402) in the country.

Shopping

Popular souvenirs include the *jambiya* (tribesman's ceremonial dagger) and traditional jewellery.

Yemeni honey is well known – and justly so. Honey shops are found throughout the capital, though it's not cheap: around YR3000 to YR4000 for 500g, YR6000 to YR8000 for 1kg. Beautiful honeycombs (packaged in sealed metal discs) cost YR2000 to YR8000 (depending on quality).

Rows of shops selling gold and silver jewellery can be found on Gamal Abdul Nasser St. Also well worth a look (or a sniff) are the perfume and spice shops. **Yahsob Spice** (Map p366; Az-Zubayri St) and **Yassin Spices** (Map p366; Az-Zubayri St) both have good collections of the latter.

There are very few bookshops selling English-language publications. Your best bet is the bookshop of the **Sheba Hotel** (Map p368; Ali Abdul Mogni St).

ℹ Orientation

The old walled city was originally composed of separate parts – east and west – divided by present-day Ali Abdul Mogni St, one of the principal thoroughfares in the city. At the crux of the division and still functioning as the administrative heart of the city is Midan at Tahrir, where the post office, telecoms and internet cafes can also be found. The heart of the old city is Bab al-Yaman and the souqs leading off it. Many of the travel agencies, Yemenia offices, upmarket shops and better restaurants can be found among the bright lights of Az-Zubayri and Hadda Sts. Sana'a's street names are confusing. Many streets have had different names at different periods, some have different names for different sections and few actually have street signs anyway. Unless you've grown up there, trying to navigate the wonderfully winding streets of the old city is almost impossible.

ℹ Information

EMERGENCY

The following emergency numbers apply throughout Yemen:

Fire Brigade (☎179)
Police (☎199)
Tourist Police (☎01-226663; As-Sailah St)

INTERNET ACCESS

Internet cafes are mushrooming all over the city centre. Also most mid-range and top-end hotels in the city have wi-fi or normal internet for guest use. Names and hours change like a chameleon changes colour and because of this we haven't named any particular internet cafes. If your hotel doesn't have internet ask them for the nearest internet cafe.

MEDICAL SERVICES

For minor problems, pharmacies (where English is spoken) provide a good over-the-counter service. The **Saudi-German Hospital** (☎313333; http://san.sghgroup.com.sa; North Sixty St) is considered to be the best by expats.

MONEY

Many of the main bank branches in Sana'a now have ATMs (although they often break down), which accept international cards. There's a freestanding ATM provided by the Yemen Commercial Bank on Midan at-Tahrir. There are several ATMs at the airport. Foreign-exchange offices are found along Az-Zubayri St.

SEX & THE HIVE

Yemen may not seem like the land of milk and honey, but since ancient times it has been famous for its honey, which you'll frequently be told is the best in the world. The top-quality honey comes from the Wadi Daw'an in the far east of the country, where nomadic beekeepers transport wooden hives around in search of 'ilb (Christ's thorn tree) flowers for the bees to feed on. Honey in Yemen is appreciated for more than just its taste and is often used by tribes in order to seal a deal as well as in traditional medical practices. When mixed with myrrh, it provides relief from constipation and with carrot seeds supposedly becomes the perfect aphrodisiac!

Arab Bank (☎276585; Az-Zubayri St) Has an ATM.
Yemen Commercial Bank (Map p366; ☎218600; fax 209566; Az-Zubayri St) The most reliable ATM.

POST

Tahrir Post Office (☎271180; Midan at-Tahrir; ◷8am-2pm & 3-8pm)

TOURIST INFORMATION

Sana'a is still awaiting a much-needed tourist office. Tourist information centres were supposed to have opened at both the airport and in the city centre years ago, but for the moment you'll continue to find nothing but a veil of secrecy. The best place for information and maps is at one of the local travel agencies.

Ministry of Tourism (Map p366; ☎570820; off Hadda St) The Ministry of Tourism building was completely destroyed in the recent fighting in Sana'a. It's currently located at the southern end of the city but the location may change again.

Tourism Promotion Board (Map p366; ☎570820; www.yementourism.com; off Khartoum St) Staff here can smile and hand out a few leaflets but not much else.

ℹ Getting There & Away

AIR

The national carrier, **Yemenia** (Map p366; ☎toll free countrywide number 8001000; www.yemenia.com; 60 Metre St), has various offices around town, but the main one is on 60 Metre St. It offers one-way flights to Aden (US$104), Al-Hudayda (US$82), Ar-Rayyan (Mukalla;

US$140), Sayun (US$140), Socotra (US$80) and Ta'izz (US$82).

Private 'internet' airline Felix Airways (p380) has flights to Aden (US$90), Al-Ghayda (US$105), Al-Hudayda (US$74), Al-Mukalla (US$119), Sayun (US$119), Socotra (US$185) and Ta'izz (US$74). As well as being able to buy direct online, most travel agencies also sell flight tickets with Felix.

BUS

Currently tourists are not allowed to travel by bus anywhere in Yemen. The following is included in case the situation changes. The bus company **Yemitco** (☑ 269875; Az-Zubayri St) runs a service to Al-Hudayda (YR1300, five hours, three daily), Aden (YR1800, six hours, at least six daily) and Ta'izz (YR1500, five hours, hourly from 6am).

One of many private operators, **Madne Buses** (Map p368; ☑ 773629284; Bab al-Yaman) has daily services to Al-Hudayda (YR1000) and Ta'izz (YR1100) whilst the **General Land Transport Company** (Map p368; ☑ 480431; Bab al-Yaman) has good buses going to Aden (YR1800) and Ta'izz (YR1300).

TAXI

As with buses, tourists are not currently allowed to travel by taxi anywhere in Yemen. The following is included in case the situation changes.

Shared taxis usually leave from spots on the outskirts of the city on the road leading to their destinations. To reach these departure points, take a minibus from Bab al-Yaman (YR50).

Shared taxis run west to Manakhah (YR1200, 2½ hours, many daily), and Al-Hudayda (YR2500, 4½ hours, six daily). They also run north to Amran (YR500, one hour, several daily), Hajja (YR1200, two hours, six per day); and south to Ta'izz (YR2500, five hours, lots throughout the day), and Aden (YR3000, eight hours, lots throughout the day).

ⓘ Getting Around

TO/FROM THE AIRPORT

For all intents and purposes there are no buses running between the airport and city centre. You can get there by bus but it involves several changes and a bit of walking. Save yourself a lot of sweat and frustration by taking a contract taxi (private hire) which charges YR4000 between the old town and the airport.

PUBLIC TRANSPORT

Minibuses (which operate from 6am to 1am) run all around town and are quick and cheap (around YR50). Nippier still are motorbike taxis, which charge YR250 to YR350 for hops around town.

TAXI

Meters are not normally used, so fares should be negotiated in advance. Short hops around town cost YR50 in a shared taxi, YR300 (tourists will be asked YR400 to YR500) in a contract taxi. A cross-town journey will cost around YR2500.

AROUND SANA'A

Wadi Dhahr وادي ظهر

The most popular afternoon excursion from Sana'a is to the palace of **Dar al-Hajar** (admission YR1000; ☺ 8am-1pm & 2-6pm) in the fertile Wadi Dhahr. Constructed as a summer residence for Imam Yahya in the 1920s, the palace has become something of a symbol of Yemen, and it's not hard to see why – it erupts forth off its rock table like a giant red-and-white toadstool.

Inside, you will find that few of the rooms are furnished, but for most the main attractions are the great rooftop views and the stunning stained-glass windows throwing flecks of multicoloured light across the floor. Don't miss the ancient subterranean wells that go right through the rock (one is apparently 275m deep).

The surrounding countryside, with its pretty little villages, is a fun place to explore on foot.

THE HARAZ MOUNTAINS AND AROUND جبال حراز

Rising abruptly off the steamy Red Sea coastal plains the sheer-sided Haraz Mountains have, for centuries, acted as a cultural fortress protecting the Yemeni heartland from interfering foreigners. Today the suspicion of outsiders is largely a thing of the past, but what hasn't changed one jot is the grandeur of the mountains and the beauty of their tapestry of terraced fields and fortified villages, all huddled together on the most unlikely of crags. At the time of going to print the Haraz Mountains had just re-opened to tourism. This is prime trekking territory and now things are calming down it will hopefully once again be possible to spend days, or even weeks, weaving along the mule trails that link up the different villages.

Shibam شبام

Not to be confused with the town of the same name in eastern Yemen, this ancient village lies 2300m above sea level, at the foot of Jebel Kawkaban (2800m). Shibam is an ancient settlement and during the 1st century AD it even served as capital of a small, and short-lived, state. It served as the capital again for the local Yafurid dynasty in the 9th century, when its grand mosque – one of the oldest in Yemen – was built.

⊙ Sights

Non-Muslims are, as normal in Yemen, forbidden from entering the mosque, but even so its exterior walls and solid minaret are pleasing to the eye. Other eye candy is the old town gate and the bustling little souq, which is the site of a very colourful Friday market (☉6.30am-1pm). Attracting people from all around, it's well worth a visit if you're in the area.

If you're wondering about the little 'caves' hollowed into the mountainside, they're old tombs – an ancient local tradition. Jebel Kawkaban is also known for its birdlife, particularly raptors.

⌂ Sleeping & Eating

Hameda Hotel HOTEL $
(☑450480; r per person with breakfast & dinner YR3000) The current dearth of visitors to Yemen shows in the fact that the clean, foreigner-friendly rooms complete with gorgeous window carvings, ant-sized bathrooms and soft, comfortable beds, lie sadly empty most of the time. A good breakfast and dinner is thrown in with the bargain-basement price.

★ Hameda Tourist Hotel & Restaurant YEMENI $$$
(☑450480; lunch YR1500) Make sure you only had a small breakfast before coming to gorge on the lunchtime feast served up here. So much food, of such good quality, is dished up that you'll leave looking like you're eight months pregnant. The restaurant sits about 200m south of the taxi stop and is run by the same family as the Hameda Hotel. It's best to reserve in advance.

ⓘ Getting There & Away

Shared taxis run to Al-Mahwit (YR800, 1½ hours, three to four daily), At-Tawila (YR350, 40 minutes, 10 daily), Kawkaban (YR150, 15 minutes, lots daily), Sana'a (YR500, 50 minutes, four to five daily) and Thilla (YR100, 15 minutes, 10 daily).

Kawkaban كوكبان

Perched dramatically on the top of Jebel Kawkaban and lording it over Shibam, some 350 vertical metres below, is the remarkable village and fortified citadel of Kawkaban. During the 15th century, it served as a capital to the Bani Sharaf Al-Deen dynasty and was once renowned for its school of music. In times of conflict the citizens of Shibam would scurry up here to join their brothers and, thanks to some huge grain silos and water cisterns (which can still be seen today), everyone was able to continue going about their life largely unperturbed by any siege. In fact, it wasn't until the civil war of the 1960s and the coming of air power that Kawkaban was finally conquered.

⌁ Activities

The main activity in Kawkaban is hiking. The manager of the Hotel Jabal Kawkaban is a good source of information and can also act as a guide or else supply another reliable one. There are no set trekking routes with nicely signed way-markers or any other facilities for foreign walkers, and for all except the hour-long hike down the mountain to Shibam, you will need a guide. It's best to explain to your guide how long and difficult you would like to make your hike and let him suggest something suitable. One highly recommended route is the three- to four hour hike to the lookout point at Bakour. Longer hikes, over several days, can also be organised and camping equipment supplied. Should you need them, donkeys can also be hired. In general the countryside around Kawkaban consists primarily of gentle plateaus interspersed with soaring peaks and the hiking is fairly easy, though this also means that the scenery doesn't match places such as Manakhah. If the mere thought of a hiking boot makes you puffed out, content yourself with a leisurely stroll through the village to check out both the cisterns and the eagle-eye view off the edge of the escarpment down to Shibam.

⌂ Sleeping & Eating

Hotel Jabal Kawkaban HOTEL $
(☑451427; r per person incl breakfast & dinner YR2000) Simple dorm-style rooms full of soft

cushions and a warm welcome await. The manager is something of a one-man tourist office.

Kawkaban Hotel HOTEL $
(☎450154; fax 450855; s/d incl breakfast YR2000/2700) It's real luck of the draw here as to whether you get one of the dark and dastardly cell-like rooms or one of the spacious and comfortable double rooms. Either way the price remains fixed. Lunch costs an additional YR1000 and dinner YR800 each.

Hotel Al-Taj Tourism HOTEL $
(Planet's Tower Hotel; ☎450170; r incl breakfast, lunch & dinner YR3000) Slightly tatty rooms come with larger than average bathrooms, a strangely forlorn atmosphere and a lobster and typewriter on the wall!

ⓘ Getting There & Away
From near the Grand Mosque in Shibam, there is a steep footpath leading 2.5km up to Kawkaban.

Shared taxis use the circuitous 7km road to Shibam (YR150). For taxis further afield, go to Shibam first.

Thilla (Thula) ثلا

Set against a great pillar of rock mounted by a fortress, the chameleon-camouflaged town of Thilla, about 9km north of Shibam, was once an important theological centre. Today it's known more for its lovely architecture than books of learning. An impressive stone wall surrounds the town, making for a memorable arrival through one of its seven gates.

⊙ Sights
Thilla is one of those classic Yemeni mountain towns that appears almost organic, so perfectly does it meld into its setting. There are few formal attractions, but a walk through the dusty streets is highly enjoyable. Look out for the 25 mosques and tombs that dot the town, including the Great Mosque (Al-Jami'a al-Kabir Mosque), with its distinctive stone minaret. Many of the houses have thrown a little razzamatazz into their largely grey-brown exteriors by adding brilliantly whitewashed stone window frames and heavy, carved wooden doors. The little souq also brings some colour to the village.

Husn Thilla FORT
(admission YR500; ⊙sunrise-sunset) From town, an old and beautifully constructed stone staircase leads up to Husn Thilla. The fort remained unconquered by the Ottomans, and though the exterior is impressive, the interior is sadly devoid of life. There are memorable views, and inside the fort walls are tombs, cisterns and granaries. It's about a 45-minute uphill (very much uphill!) walk from the village.

🛏 Sleeping & Eating

Dar Al-Salam Hotel HOTEL $$
(☎07665575; www.alsalamhotels.com; s/d US$40/70; P🐾) Not exactly blending in harmoniously with the small village it dwarfs, this new four-star hotel will at least please those who can't live without room service and internet connection.

ⓘ Getting There & Away
Thilla is an easy half-day hike from Shibam.

Shared taxis run to Sana'a (YR300, about one hour, five to six daily) and Shibam (YR100, 20 minutes, lots daily).

Hababah حبابه

Although similar in style and architecture to Thilla (and lying 10km away), Hababah has a special feature: a large, oval water cistern, where people still come to collect water, drive their animals to drink or even have a swim (it's not a good idea for foreigners to join in). With the old tower houses reflected in the still water, it makes for an extremely picturesque scene. There are no facilities for sleeping or eating.

Shared/contract taxis run to Shibam and Thilla (YR100/300, 15 minutes, 10 daily).

At-Tawila طويلة

About halfway between Shibam and Al-Mahwit is the village of At-Tawila. The village, and its tumbling terraced fields, is stunningly located at the base of a series of rock needles, around which the afternoon mist and clouds play games of hide and seek. If you have the time, it's well worth stopping off for a walk along one of the many trails that lead up behind the village. Should you want to stay the night then the Hotel Rest-Alhana (☎07-456369; r per person incl breakfast & dinner YR3000) in At-Tawila has a couple of rooms with pretty wall carvings and communal bathrooms. It's on the main road through town, but the sign is in Arabic only.

Al-Mahwit المحويت

The bustling market town of Al-Mahwit is the largest of the mountain towns to the west of the capital and, like Manakhah to the south, it makes a superb trekking base. Al-Mahwit lies in the centre of some of the most fertile country in Yemen and the road from Sana'a takes you past numerous fruit, coffee, tobacco and qat fields.

Like At-Tawila, Al-Mahwit was once an important coffee-collecting centre, as well as an administrative town during the 16th-century Ottoman rule.

◉ Sights & Activities

The **old town**, perched on a hilltop, marks the site of the Ottoman regional capital and is worth a walk, as is the town's **souq**. There is good **hiking** potential in the attractive surrounding countryside. A stunning but easy three- to four-hour walk begins from the hamlet of Bait Gawza a few kilometres out of town and worms its way along the edge of a sheer ledge back to Al-Mahwit via the villages of Kadha and Almasia.

Nobody, especially hikers, should miss out on the early morning pilgrimage to **Ar-Riady**, a viewpoint just to the northwest of town where the mountains cascade downwards for what seems like hundreds upon hundreds of metres and your tummy starts spinning in a vertigo-inspired twizzle. As the morning heats up you can watch the dancing clouds surge up out of the Red Sea plains and swallow up the villages precariously perched on ledges and rock needles below you.

🛏 Sleeping & Eating

In the past a popular hotel with foreigners was the **Al-Majed Tourist Hotel** (s/d YR2000/3000), on the main dirt road leading off the main surfaced road.

Manakhah مناخة

♩ 01

The largest commercial centre in the high mountains, Manakhah might be a nondescript town, but it's the centre of Yemeni trekking. From here everything from gentle hour-long rambles to serious multiday expeditions fan out across the highlands.

◉ Sights & Activities

Hikes lasting from one hour to a week or more are possible. Trekking is a year-round activity, but during the summer monsoon period it can be uncomfortably hot, not to mention a little damp. In the past the hotels were able to provide guides and equipment for any kind of hike. As tourism begins to pick up and the hotels re-open it's likely this will begin again.

As with other Yemeni trekking centres the lack of organised, way-marked trails means that it's much better to let a local guide suggest a route suitable for your experience and available time. The standard half-day hike is a downhill one from Al-Khutayb back to Manakhah.

Away from blisters and bivvy bags, attractions in Manakhah include the lively morning market (at its most raucous on Tuesday and Sunday), which draws all manner of characters from the surrounding villages.

🛏 Sleeping & Eating

Manakhah used to have some of the most enjoyable guesthouses in Yemen, but at the time of research the total lack of foreign tourists meant that all had closed down. If security continues to improve and tourists return then it's almost certain that both the superb **Al-Hijjarah Tourist Hotel & Restaurant** and the **Manakha Tourist Hotel** (Manakhah Askari Hotel) will re-open.

Around Manakhah

Al-Khutayb (Al-Hoteib) الحطيب

Lying 6km south of Manakhah and perched on a solitary hilltop is the pilgrimage site of Al-Khutayb (Al-Hoteib). Dedicated to a 12th-century preacher revered by followers of the Ismaili sect, the shrine attracts pilgrims from as far afield as India, and in fact the complex has a slightly Indian look to it. Ask a Yemeni about this place and they will no doubt gleefully regale you with stories about all the immoral activities that take place here - very little of which is probably true! You can walk around the area, though the shrine is fenced off to non-Muslims.

Al-Hajjarah الهجرة

Stunningly situated on a mountain precipice 5km west of Manakhah, and a little higher up the mountain, is the spectacular 11th-century village of Al-Hajjarah. The Ottomans found its strategic position useful when defending the roads from the coast to Sana'a. Nowadays this setting and its century-old stone and whitewashed tower houses (some up to eight storeys) have caught the eye of visitors with mountain-walking in mind.

⊙ Sights & Activities

Until recently, the Al-Ba'aha quarter was inhabited by Jews. Above this is the old Muslim quarter, with its huge entrance gate. Look out for the painstakingly constructed terraces, which permit the villagers to eke out an impossible living from the very steep slopes of the mountain.

Like Manakhah, Al-Hajjarah is an excellent trekking base and as tourism picks up it's again hoped that trekking will recommence here.

🛏 Sleeping & Eating

Al-Hajjarah's only hotel, the excellent Husn al-Hajjara Tourism Hotel & Restaurant was closed at the time of research. It is likely to re-open as tourism picks up again.

NORTHERN YEMEN

The rough-and-ready north has always been Yemen's hardest and proudest region and even today its fierce tribes are regarded with trepidation and respect by the rest of the country. Parts of this area seem to be always engaged in some kind of dispute, and armed conflict between tribes and the central government is common. At the time of writing the entire region was out of bounds to foreign tourists and we have been unable to conduct on-ground research in Sa'da and Shaharah since 2007 and in the rest of the region since late 2009.

In the province of Sa'da a violent uprising has dragged on since 2004 between government forces and a group of Zaydi fighters called the Al-Houthis. The group is led by Abdul Malik al-Houthi who claims they're fighting discrimination of their minority Shia community whilst the Yemeni government claim they are trying to overthrow the government and install Shia religious rule. After several false ceasefires the government launched a full-scale offensive against the rebels in August 2009. The conflict quickly became international after clashes erupted between the Houthis and Saudi forces. At one point the Houthis had even managed to occupy several villages in Saudi Arabia. The Yemeni government also accuses Iran of backing the rebels, while the Houthis make counter-accusations that Al-Qaeda has joined Sunni tribal fighters in aiding the government forces against them and, ironically, that the US were launching aerial bombardments against them (the US responded by saying they were attacking Al-Qaeda elements). Finally, if there weren't already enough players in the mix, a number of tribal groups opposed to the Houthis joined the fight on the side of the government. A ceasefire in early 2010 didn't stop the fighting completely but it certainly helped reduce it. However, when the wider Yemeni revolution began in 2011 the Houthis quickly aligned themselves with the protesters and by March of that year they had taken control of Sa'da city as well as much of the province; and by the middle of 2011 they also controlled much of neighbouring Al-Jawf province; by the end of the year they had advanced into Amran and Hajjah governorates; and by the end of 2012 the Houthis were even in control of parts of Sana'a governorate. Today, they have essentially carved out a state within a state.

The upshot of all this fighting has of course been the widespread creation of internally displaced people (the UN estimates that around 366,000 people have been made homeless by the conflict so far), hundreds of civilian deaths and the breakdown of normal government services in the north. Both Unicef and Islamic Relief Worldwide accuse the Houthis of using child soldiers. The current chaos in Yemen, and extreme danger for outsiders in north Yemen means that very few journalists have had access to the Sa'da region for a number of years and obtaining accurate information on what has been happening there is very difficult.

Amran ﻋﻤﺮﺍﻥ

🗐 07

First impressions of ancient Amran, situated on an old trading route 52km northwest of Sana'a, aren't good. The town appears to be a rash of half-completed modern developments and seems to offer little reason to stop, but once past this you'll discover a fruity and flavoursome old quarter with something of a wild west feel to it. The town is also known for the quality of its leatherwork.

⊙ Sights

The quiet **old town** is in remarkably good shape and the locals do a sterling job of keeping the streets clean. If you've been in Yemen for sometime, you probably won't think much of Amran, but if you're new to the game, you'll think its proud adobe houses and masses of excitable children quite enchanting. The highlights of a visit are walking along the city walls, which virtually surround the old quarter, and inspecting the eastern **entrance gate**. Look out for the **ancient stone inscriptions** around the entrance to the town as well as on some of the house facades. The souq in the new town is a riotous affair.

Hajja حجة

☑ 07 / POP 53,887

Modern Hajja can't be described as attractive, but the journey there – which takes you over, around and along crest after crest of magnificent mountain – certainly is.

Shaharah شهارة

Fortified mountain villages are two-a-penny in Yemen, but Shaharah is the pick of the crop. The village lies at 2600m and overlooks mountainous bulging swells to the south and shimmering hot plains to the north. The climb up from these plains to the village takes you through some of the most jaw-dropping scenery in the country.

Sa'da صعدة

☑ 07 / POP 51,900

Ancient Sa'da was once a city of major importance on the trade routes north to Damascus, as well as one of Arabia's original, and most devoted, Islamic cities. It remains to this day the most conservative and traditional town in Yemen. Sa'da (and its region) is known for its particular style of adobe architecture, which gives the houses the impression of having a coat of mud tiles. The Great Mosque (Al-Hadi Mosque), which dates to the 9th century, is considered one of the oldest in Yemen. The town also has some impressive fortifications, including a remarkable 16th-century adobe wall and its original gates.

TIHAMA (RED SEA COAST)

The flat and featureless Tihama is the chalk next to highland Yemen's mountainous cheese. The contrasts are more than

YEMEN HAJJA

BOYS WITH TOYS

The abundance of weapons in private Yemeni hands is legendary, with estimates of 60 million weapons in the hands of 24 million citizens. The most visible form of gun is the Kalashnikov, but you can also take your pick from a wide assortment of pistols, rifles, hand grenades, large jeep-mounted weaponry, surface-to-air missiles and even anti-aircraft guns. While the trade in such heavy weapons is a little more discreet, the sale of machine guns, grenades and pistols has always been very open and obvious. Before the current unrest the government had made some headway in cracking down on gun ownership and gun-markets; although only in areas where they had full control. In the tribal areas the ownership and trade in guns remained virtually unchanged. What progress had been made had almost certainly suffered a huge setback thanks to the recent turmoil and the government's near total lack of control over large areas of the nation.

For the average Yemeni, with their strong tribal background, guns are an essential of daily life. Blood feuds between tribal groups can continue for years and at times reach levels of almost all-out warfare. These ethnic vendettas result in around 2000 deaths per year. With the never-ending instability in Yemen and the larger region, it's no surprise that gun-running is big business here and Yemeni firepower has been found throughout eastern Africa and the Middle East. The Yemeni/Saudi border has always been a fairly porous and loosely defined affair, and with the tribes holding more power than the central government, in this region smuggling has long been a mainstay of the economy. Though there is no way of knowing where many of these weapons end up, most observers agree that Al-Qaeda groups both in Yemen and elsewhere do take advantage of this easy weapons supply.

just geographical. With Africa being only a stone's throw away, the flamboyant influence of that continent seems to be present everywhere. The clothing is so bright that sunglasses are needed to look at it, the solid stone houses of the mountains have turned into African-style mud-and-thatch huts, the weekly markets are even more animated and the overall attitude is much more liberal. All in all, the final package is a fascinating contrast to the rest of the country – just don't attempt to explore it during summer, when it becomes so hot that even the camels start dreaming about being polar bears.

Throughout the worst of the troubles in 2011 the whole of the Tihama was, like virtually everywhere in the country, closed to foreign tourists. At the time of writing the southern Tihama (from Kamaran Island to Al-Makha) had just re-opened to tourists though for the moment very few foreigners have ventured back. North of Kamaran Island the security situation remains something of a question mark and travel permits were not being issued. We were unable to conduct on-ground research for the Tihama for this edition and the information contained here either dates from late 2009/early 2010 or has been researched remotely via telephone and the internet.

Al-Hudayda الحديده

☑ 03 / POP 410,000

With its wide and clean streets, parks full of shady, snooze-enticing benches, pleasant pavement cafes and a pedestrian-friendly seaside corniche, Al-Hudayda, capital of Tihama, is one of Yemen's most European-flavoured cities and is an immensely popular spot for holidaying Yemenis. All this makes it an excellent base for further explorations of the Tihama.

◉ Sights & Activities

The Al-Hudayda **fish market** (⊘ 6am-noon), 2km southeast of the centre of town, is a slippery and smelly must-see that's frenetic, cocky and fun. Come early in the morning to watch the day's catch being unloaded in front of a hectic, seagull-like mob of buyers and sellers. The daily trawl nets everything from plump prawns and glistening groupers to huge hammerhead sharks. In fact, Al-Hudayda is one of the biggest shark fishing ports in the world and the local shark population is being utterly deci-

mated. The majority of sharks are caught just for their fins which supply the shark fin soup market in China. The traditional dhow boats are also very photogenic. The old and, it must be said, decrepit Turkish quarter is another possible sight, as are the nearby **souqs**.

Maybe the best way to pass an afternoon in Al-Hudayda is to do as the locals do: buy an ice cream and stroll along the **seafront corniche** (look out for Ottoman and Southeast Asian-influenced buildings) or laze about with a book in one of the town's parks.

One kilometre south of the fish market is the main **town beach**. It's certainly not a place for a foreign tourist to go for a swim, but its muddy sands are packed with holidaying Yemeni families eating ice creams, taking camels rides and bobbing about in the waves in inflatable rings – the women whilst fully veiled.

🛏 Sleeping

There's plenty of accommodation in Al-Hudayda, but none of it really represents value for money. Be warned that in the past Al-Hudayda got very busy during Yemeni holidays and all hotels tripled their prices. At such times unless you've reserved in advance then you've almost no chance of finding a bed.

In the past some of the better places to stay were the budget **Hotel Darcum** (Sana'a St), which offered great value, the equally good mid-range **Dream Hotel** (off Sana'a St) and the newer mid-range **Rotana Star Tourist Hotel** (off the Corniche).

✕ Eating

As with all large Yemeni towns there are plenty of places to eat including the central **Al-Sindbad Broast & Restaurant** and the **Shardi Al-Morgan Restaurant** which was renowned far and wide for its prawn dishes.

ℹ Getting There & Away

The national carrier **Yemenia** (☑ 201474; www.yemenia.com.ye) has one-way flights to Sana'a (US$82), **Felix Airways** (☑ 565656; www.felixairways.com; Airport Rd) covers the same route for a little less (US$74).

Kamaran Island جزيرة كمران

Tantalising the adventurous with thoughts of pristine reefs and ancient tales of pirates, smugglers and buried treasure is a string of

Al-Hudayda

desert islands floating in the limpid waters of the steamy Red Sea. However, due to the fact that the pirates and smugglers, if not the buried treasure, are still out there, most of these islands, including the jewel in the crown, the Hanish Islands, have long been out of bounds to tourists.

All is not lost though; Kamaran Island, sitting a kilometre or so off the coast, offers would-be sea dogs a chance to live the life of a castaway.

Kamaran Island offers excellent diving as well as a range of organised activities, but don't come expecting balmy tropical beaches. Utterly barren and blasted by unceasing winds, this is a real desert island in every sense of the word.

The only formal place to stay, **Kamaran Island Resort** (☑ 733711742; www.kamaran.net; r per person with all meals US$65), at the northern end of the island, has a shabby collection of Tihama style traditional huts with filthy common bathrooms and decent seafood meals (nonguests pay an unfathomably expensive US$20 per meal). The resort rents out diving equipment and boats as well as snorkelling gear.

Other entertainment includes exploring Kamaran towns' weathered and partially

Al-Hudayda

🛏 Sleeping
1 Dream Hotel	B2
2 Hotel Darcum	B2
3 Rotana Star Tourist Hotel	A3

🍴 Eating
4 Al-Sindbad Broast & Restaurant	A1

🚍 Transport
5 Yemenia	B2

collapsed coral buildings and end-of-the-world atmosphere.

Getting to Kamaran is half the fun. From Al-Hudayda travel up through unremittingly desolate scenery to the bleak, wind-battered town of **Al-Salif** which is truly the town the Gods forgot. The port for Kamaran, which sits just to the south of the main fishing port, consists of a fallen-over hut and a tea shop. Boats depart to Kamaran village every hour or so.

Jabal Bura   جبل برع

Butting outward and upward into the pancake flat Tihama, Jabal Bura (2271m) is where the Haraz Mountains give a final mighty push toward the Red Sea and the result is little short of spectacular.

Calling Jabal Bura a single mountain is misleading; instead it's a massif comprising several peaks and valleys. The attractions for visitors are two fold; the lush, forested area around the Wadi Rayjaf forms the **Jabal Bura Protected Area** (⊙6am-6pm), which is the closest mainland Yemen comes to a national park. For Arabia the wadi is shockingly green with water flowing down it year round, ponds full of croaking frogs and a real life genuine forest of trees (remember those?). Plenty of exciting birdlife calls the wadi home as do zillions of gaudy-winged butterflies and troops of hamadryas baboons. Signed walking trails of various lengths lead off from the road, but come early in the morning or late in the day if you want to see any wildlife. You'll need your own transport to access this part of the mountains.

The second drawcard for visitors is the **trekking** and stupendous views found much higher up the mountain slopes. Trekking around these parts is still very much in its infancy and most people organise their trek through a Sana'a tour company. The best base for trekking always used to be **Al-Memkab village**. Pick-ups run here from Bajil a couple of times a day. The road up the mountain to Al-Memkab is such a terrifying swirl of switchbacks that it has been known to reduce people to tears! On reaching the village, and wiping away tears of fear, you'll be greeted by a view that's so extraordinary it'll probably reduce you back to tears.

Beit al-Faqih   بيت الفقيه

For much of the week Beit al-Faqih lies as dormant and quiet as a winter seed, but come past early on a Friday morning and you'll think spring has sprung in the most outrageous manner possible. This is because each Friday every villager, trader and farmer from miles around turns up to be a part of the biggest, brightest and boldest weekly **market** in Yemen. For the average rural Yemeni, daily life revolves around a series of weekly markets – they're places to stock up on supplies, catch up on gossip, seal a deal and have a bit of fun. This is especially true in Tihama, which has taken the system of nomadic weekly markets to heart. As a sight

it's spectacular and as an experience unforgettable. A morning here spent bartering over spices, clay pots and even goats and camels will certainly be a highlight of any Yemeni adventure.

The famous market was first established in the early 18th century, when it served as a coffee exchange, attracting merchants and traders from India, Morocco, Egypt, Iran, Constantinople and Europe. After the deals were signed and sealed, the coffee beans were packed up and shipped around the world from the nearby ports of Al-Hudayda or Al-Makha. With the collapse of the coffee trade, Beit al-Faqih sought to diversify – today coffee makes up only a tiny fraction of the items on sale. Instead, it's the day-to-day needs of the Tihama villager that form the bulk of the trade.

The market kicks into gear just after dawn every Friday morning and by lunchtime everyone's heading back home for the week. Try to arrive as early as possible (if only to beat the heat) and give yourself at least two hours to explore properly. Should you be unlucky enough to pass through on a different day of the week, you could stop off to watch the town's famous **weavers** at work (from 7am to 1pm and 4pm to 6pm daily, except Friday). There are no recommended hotels in town, so it's best to stay overnight at Al-Hudayda (62km to the north).

Zabid   زبيد

Zabid is Yemen's third Unesco World Heritage Site, but unlike its fellow club members, Old Sana'a and Shibam, who like to flaunt their beauty for all to see, Zabid likes to keep its secrets well hidden.

The countryside around Zabid has been inhabited since virtually the dawn of humanity, with Zabid itself built around AD 819 on the orders of Mohammed ibn' Abdullah ibn Ziyad, the local Abbasid governor. Not content with founding a city, he also established the first in Zabid's long and distinguished line of madrassas (Quranic schools). The city soon became known – both inside and outside of Yemen – as a centre of Islamic and scientific learning, and between the 13th and 15th centuries, when it also served as the capital of Yemen, Zabid played host to over 5000 students in more than 200 colleges.

The last 500 years have been less kind on Zabid and the town has gradually faded in importance. Don't feel sorry, though, because this is just karma paying Zabid back for the pain it has caused school children the world over: it was a scholar from Zabid who was responsible for that school days torture called algebra!

The walled town was declared a World Heritage Site in 1993 and, in 2000, with over 40% of the old city houses replaced with new structures, Zabid was registered on the organisation's 'Danger List', requiring urgent funds for restoration.

Finally, as if algebra and Unesco recognition wasn't enough, Zabid has another dubious claim to fame. It's reputedly the hottest town on earth.

◉ Sights & Activities

The dazzling whitewashed, low-rise town is a shy place and keeps most of its best features tucked away out of view. Without a bit of local help, a visitor will probably leave with staid impressions, having seen little but a series of plain exterior walls. Fortunately, help is at hand in the form of a friendly and generous local population. Walk the sweltering streets and an invitation for tea in somebody's house is almost a given. As soon as this happens, the hidden world of Zabid opens up before you. Plain on the exterior, the interior of the walls, which face onto small courtyards, are nothing short of carved and sculpted works of art in a hundred different patterns and geometrical designs.

Built around the central souqs, the residential areas of the city were originally divided into different quarters for the different professional classes – merchants, artisans, dignitaries and scholars. The city retains some of its low defensive wall (at the peak of its glory Zabid had four concentric walls) and also some of the original gates, including **Bab as-Siham**, **Bab ash-Shabariq** and **Bab an-Nakhl**. Various ornate buildings, such as the **Nasr Palace**, testify to the town's former prestige and wealth.

Zabid boasts 86 mosques and madrassas (a considerable decline from the 230 it's once supposed to have had), including the **Al-Asha'ir Mosque**, which was built during Mohammed's lifetime in AD 629, and the **Al-Jami'a Mosque** (Friday Mosque), which dates to the 16th century. Look out, also, for the white, 13th-century **Al-Iskandar Mosque** in the **citadel** on the edge of town. Unusually in Yemen, it's often possible for non-Muslims to quietly enter some of the mosques with a guide.

Formerly the citadel's granary, the restored **Zabid Granary Museum** (☺ sunrise-sunset) now serves to 'explain the history of Zabid' and exhibits the finds of the archaeological mission working here since 1983. The six sections are themed (mainly historically) and contain a wide range of artefacts, from cannon balls and fragments of fine pottery to Ottoman pipes and lovely Islamic woodcarvings. At the time of writing, we had no information on whether or not the museum was still open.

Al-Makha   المخا

♪ 04

Ask most people what mocha means and they'll instantly reply 'coffee' or 'Starbucks'. So it's somewhat ironic that Al-Makha, the original coffee port, is one of the few towns on the planet without a branch of Starbucks or its ilk. In fact, Al-Makha doesn't have a lot of anything these days – except flies and heat.

The history of Al-Makha stretches way back to the days before Islam (and Starbucks), but its heyday was during the 17th century when it became the world's foremost coffee-exporting centre. Back then, Al-Makha had a population of some 20,000 people. Nowadays it's a forlorn and wind-blown town of a few hundred hardy souls who make their bread and butter through fishing and smuggling. Africa is only a hop and a skip away and the chaos in Somalia as well as Yemen provides an endless source of income for the unscrupulous. Alcohol, weapons, drugs, consumer goods and, most disturbingly, people all enter and leave Yemen through this narrow back door.

◉ Sights & Activities

Reminders of past glories are few and far between. The most impressive building is the **Masjid ash-Shadhil**, a blazing white 15th-century mosque. Nearby is an old **minaret** and a few piles of rubble that were once **merchant villas**. The newer part of town has a **qat market**, a **beach** with a few garishly painted boats and a large morning-only **fish market** and a weighing room, whose floors are ankle-deep in thick, black squid ink.

SOUTHERN YEMEN

Yemen's south is the richest and most developed region of the country. It's also the greenest and most fertile and has long been considered the breadbasket of Arabia. There is a huge amount of historical, cultural and geographic variety in this area. In the far south is the run-down, sweltering port of Aden, the former British colony and old capital of the south. Further north, and in complete contrast, are the lush and cool highland towns of Ibb, Jibla and Ta'izz, where rain falls year-round. Until recently this was the safest and easiest part of the country in which to travel, particularly for those reliant on public transport. During research for this book, this whole region remained off limits to travellers following the unrest of 2011, but as we went to press word started coming through that although Aden, a town with deep problems, remains closed to tourists, Ta'izz, Ibb and Jibla were reportedly about to re-open.

We have been unable to conduct on-the-ground research in Southern Yemen since late 2009/early 2010 and information contained here is a combination of that period, and remote updates conducted by phone and internet.

Ibb   إب

☑ 03 / POP 213,000

Situated 194km south of Sana'a, Ibb boasts a strategic position on a high hill in the western foothills of the Ba'adan Mountains. Settled since early Islamic times, the town grew into an important administrative centre during the time of the Ottomans. Today it's largely, and unjustifiably, ignored by most travellers. This is a shame because its chaotic market area and pretty old town are a pure delight to explore, and when combined with nearby Jibla, Ibb makes for a perfect overnight pause on the journey between Sana'a and Ta'izz.

Ibb and its governate enjoy one of the highest rainfall levels in Yemen, which has given rise to the nickname 'the green province'.

◉ Sights & Activities

The large and boisterous central **market** area in Ibb is a noisy clash of colours, sounds and smells that feels more Indian than Yemeni. It's one of the most enjoyable markets in the country. Immediately behind the market is the whitewashed old quarter, which, aside from around the qat market, is a much more staid but no less rewarding place to explore. The stone houses, designed in a style unique to Ibb, are typically four to five storeys high, with facades decorated with geometrical friezes and circular *qamiriya* (usually moon-shaped, stained-glass windows).

In the middle of the old town, **Al-Jalaliya Mosque** dates to the time of the Ottomans. The **fortress** perched on the hill nearby is, sadly, closed, but you can get good views of the town from **Jabal Rabi**, around 700m from the town centre.

🛏 Sleeping

There are a couple of basic hotels in the market area. They're all as cheap as chips, but much less appetising. It's much better to stay out on the road to Al-Udayn, on the edge of town, where there are a bunch of cleaner, quieter and far superior hotels. The **Al-Riyad Hotel** (Al-Udayn St) was always a popular one out here with foreign tourists.

THE PECULIAR INCIDENT OF THE GOAT & THE BERRY

Most of us need our early-morning caffeine kick to get going, but have you ever wondered who discovered coffee? Well, according to the Yemenis, it wasn't a person at all but rather a humble goat. It's said that a shepherd was out in the Yemeni hills with his goats when he noticed that one of them, having eaten some peculiar berries, started behaving strangely. Mystified by this sight, the old man took a bite himself and within moments felt 20 years younger. Astonished by this discovery, he raced back to his village and spread the news. One of the people he told was a poet who accompanied the shepherd back into the mountains to try them for himself. After swallowing a few of the berries, the poet felt so enlightened that he immediately composed a poem in praise of this odd shrub. It was this poem that spread the fame of coffee around the world. And the goat we all have to celebrate for our morning rituals? Rumour has it that in thanks he was eaten for lunch the next day.

JIBLA جبله

Situated 8km southwest of Ibb, Jibla is stunningly placed at the summit of a hill. The town served as the capital for much of highland Yemen under the Sulayhid dynasty in the 11th and 12th centuries, and was particularly prosperous under the benevolent and impossibly long-named Sayyida al-Hurra Arwa bint Ahmad as-Sulayhi. Fortunately this mouthful was quickly reduced to plain old Queen Arwa, but by the time of her death at the age of 92, she had proved she was anything but plain. By building numerous schools, roads, bridges and mosques, her policies of investing the kingdom's treasury in projects for the good of the average person mean that she's still remembered fondly today as a 'Little Sheba'.

It was thanks to this investment in education that the town gained a reputation as a centre for Islamic learning, and even today the annexe next to the Queen Arwa Mosque (admission by donation) serves as a madrassa. The crumbling Dar as-Sultana Palace is worth checking out though due to the dangerous state of the semi-collapsed building you cannot enter. If it's still open the Queen Arwa Museum contained some lovely annotated manuscripts belonging to the queen and her father. Finally, Jibla has attained local fame for its excellent qat market.

Ta'izz تعز

✈ 04 / POP 467,000

Ibn Battuta, the great 14th century Arab traveller, once described Ta'izz as 'one of the largest and most beautiful cities'. It's still large – Yemen's third-largest city – but for beauty you need to look a little harder. The city has suffered heavily from unplanned urban growth, which has left it without any real central soul. It played a major role in the increasingly violent protests of 2010–11. These reached a bloody peak in late May when Salih's soldiers opened fire on demonstrators and killed between 28 and 64 people. After that demonstrations became increasingly violent with protesters, tribal fighters and defected soldiers all using weapons against Saleh loyalists. By 7 June 2011 the opposition had largely taken control of the city.

◎ Sights & Activities

Bab al-Kabir is the main entrance to the old town, but only parts of the original 13m-high wall remain, including two of its gates – Bab al-Musa and Bab al-Kabir. Well worth a wander particularly in the early evening are the bright and brash souqs spread around Bab al-Kabir. Look out for the local cow's cheese (little white disks laid out in rows) and the sacks of delicious dried dates. Beyond the souqs and mosques, the old-town architecture is unlikely to do much for you. Back in the newer streets there's a large and very lively fruit souq off Gamal Abdul Nasser St. Ta'izz is a good place to buy textiles and jambiyas. Look out also for the famous women merchants of Ta'izz, who traditionally do the buying and selling.

The National Museum (26th September St), which wasn't really a museum at all, but more the petrified palace of Imam Ahmed, was closed for renovations back in 2010. We have been unable to confirm if it has reopened. if it has then don't miss it, because it's an absolute treat that reveals something of the life and times of its previous and slightly peculiar owner.

It's not exactly a tourist attraction but the university, next to the museum, always has groups of students (men and women) hanging around and eager to make friends with foreigners.

🛏 Sleeping

You wouldn't describe the accommodation scene in Ta'izz as very memorable. In the past popular places to stay were the Asia Hotel (At-Tahrir St), Royal Ta'izz Tourism Hotel (Gamal Abdul Nasser St), Al-Shreef Tourist Hotel & Suites (At-Tahrir St) and the upmarket Al-Saeed Hotel Ta'izz (✈ 200311; www.al-saeed-hotel-taiz.com; s/d from US$139/158; 🛜🖥).

🍴 Eating

There are lots of places to eat in Ta'izz. In the past, two of the better places were the Leyali Al-Arab (Arabian Nights Restaurant; Asayfarah St) and the Al-Shibani Restaurant (Gamal Abdul Nasser St).

Ta'izz

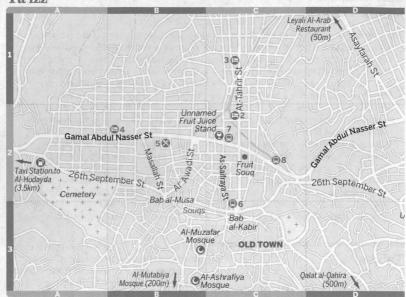

Leyali Al-Arab
Restaurant
(50m)

Asayfarah St

3

At-Tahrir St

2

Unnamed
Fruit Juice
Stand

7

4

Gamal Abdul Nasser St

5

Masallah St

Al-Awlaqi St

As-Saifraya St

Fruit
Souq

8

Gamal Abdul Nasser St

Taxi Station to
Al-Hudayda
(3.5km)

26th September St

Cemetery

Bab al-Musa
Souqs

26th September St

Al-Muzafar
Mosque

6

Bab
al-Kabir

OLD TOWN

Al-Mutabiya
Mosque (200m)

Al-Ashrafiya
Mosque

Qalat al-Qahira
(500m)

ℹ Getting There & Away

The national carrier **Yemenia** (☑ 217126; www.
yemenia.com; Gamal Abdul Nasser St) has one-
way flights to Sana'a (US$82). **Felix Airways**
(☑ 565656; www.felixairways.com) has flights
to Sana'a (US$74).

Aden   عدن

☑ 02 / POP 590,000

History

According to legend, Noah's Ark was built
and launched in the area, and Cain and Abel
hung out for a while. Inscriptions dating to
the 6th century BC are the first concrete
mentions of the town, but it's clear that it
has long served as an ancient trading centre.
Since the 10th century Aden has also been
one of Yemen's largest towns, and by the
13th century its inhabitants numbered some
80,000 people.

Initially serving as the capital of a series
of local dynasties, Aden was later taken over
by the Ottomans, followed by the British in
1839. After the opening of the Suez Canal in
the middle of the 19th century, its strategic
importance grew, and it soon numbered

among the largest ports in the world and as
one of the stars of the British Empire.

Aden served as the capital of the PDRY
from 1967 until reunification, when it was
declared a free-trade zone. Although badly
damaged in the 1994 War of Unity, it made
a brief recovery of sorts with the government pouring money into developing and
modernising the port. Just as things began
to look shipshape, disaster again struck
when terrorist groups aligned to Al-Qaeda
attacked the US warship the *USS Cole* and
effectively scared away most international
shipping.

Even before the 2011 revolution an increasing number of southern secessionists,
complaining of discrimination at the hands
of a northern dominated government, wanted Aden to become capital of an independent south Yemen. Since 2009 this has led to
increasing violence in the city, and, by the
height of the chaos in 2011, Aden was a divided city with neighbourhood militias setting up road blocks and numerous gun and
bomb attacks taking place. Fighting between
government forces, tribal groups, Al-Qaeda
in the Arabian Peninsula and secessionists
throughout the south and east of the country created tens of thousands of homeless
people; with around 100,000 internally dis-

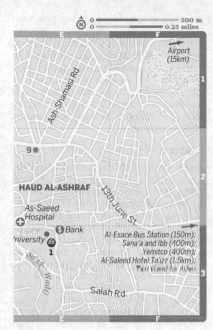

placed people descending on Aden. Many of these people have moved into schools and other public buildings and brought many public services in the city to a near stand still. By late 2012 there was the first glimmer of hope that things were finally starting to calm down again, as the government pushed back the Islamic militants who had taken control of large parts of south Yemen.

Sights & Activities

We have been unable to confirm opening hours, prices etc for either of the following. Descriptions are based on research conducted in 2010.

National Museum for Antiquities MUSEUM (off Al-Aidrus St; Sat-Thu) The excellent National Museum for Antiquities has wonderful exhibits from the ancient Kingdoms of Yemen including marble and gypsum statues of humans that look like zombies brought back from the dead. Other highlights include exhibits from the early Islamic period.

Upstairs on the 1st floor is the **Ethnographical Museum**, which has a musty and poorly displayed collection of traditional dress from across the country. Another highlight is the museum building itself.

Aden Tanks RUINS (end of Sayla St) Believed to date from the 1st century, Aden Tanks were designed not just to collect precious water for the city, but also to remove water in times of flash flooding. A series of ingenious steps, arches and conduits channels the rainwater into a set of beautifully built cisterns. The 13 cisterns (all that remain of the original 53 tanks) have a total capacity of 20 million gallons. Developed by successive dynasties, the tanks eventually fell into disuse, until uncovered in the mid-19th century by the British, who, despite their best efforts and modern technology, never did manage to get them to work again.

Sleeping

Aden used to have a number of decent places. We have been unable to update any for this edition but prior to 2011 good places to get some sleep were the **Ala'mer Hotel** (www.alamer-hotel.com; Al-Midan St;) and the upmarket **Gold Mohur Hotel** (Gold Mohur Bay;).

Eating

There are lots of places to eat in Aden. In the past, two of the better places were the **Reem Tourist Restaurant** (Ghandhi St) and the **Al-Ryan Tourism Restaurant**.

Getting There & Away

Yemenia (253969; yemenia.com.au; Queen Arwa Rd) has flights to Sana'a (US$104). **Felix Airways** (565656; www.felixairways.com) has flights to Sana'a (US$100), Al-Mukalla (US$102), Socotra (US$173) and Sayun (US$102).

EASTERN YEMEN

Eastern Yemen is one of the few places left in Arabia where the desert world of Thesiger still clings on, albeit with increasing precariousness. Home of nomadic Bedouin tribal people, ruined cities of legend and startling oases, this massive chunk of apricot dunes and bleak stonescapes is for many the most romantic corner of Yemen.

Ma'rib   مأرب

🎵 06

It's hard to imagine that this rotting desert town was ever a seat of power, but it was from these very same streets that a woman of intense beauty once came forward and changed the story of Arabia. Bilqis, guardian of the frankincense trade routes, lover of Solomon, mother of the throne of Abyssinia, daughter of the devil and known to the world simply as the Queen of Sheba is rumoured to have based her capital here. The Quran relates other, equally fantastical stories of Ma'rib, famously describing it as a paradise on the left bank and a paradise on the right bank. By all accounts this was a true description – the city, built on taxes from the incense trade, was impossibly wealthy and, thanks to its famous dam, very fertile. It's said that a person could walk for four days in any direction and not leave the shade of the palm groves and orange trees.

Even in good times tribal tensions run high in Ma'rib and the town could never be described as safe. Many tourists have been kidnapped in and around Ma'rib over the years and the area is a hotbed of militant activity. As such Ma'rib has been closed to tourists for a number of years and we have been unable to conduct on-the-ground research here since 2007. In the unlikely event that the town reopens to tourism during the lifetime of this book we urge you to exercise extreme caution.

History

Ma'rib has been inhabited almost since the dawn of time and is one of the world's oldest towns. It is, of course, famous above all else for being the supposed home of the Queen of Sheba, though whether or not she really did grace the streets of Ma'rib is unknown. What cannot be doubted is that the Sabaean capital quickly became the most important staging post on the frankincense trade route, and it was during this period that the dam was constructed. The good times couldn't last, though, and with the bursting of the dam the people of Ma'rib scattered across the deserts of Arabia, and the town virtually ceased to exist. Some say that it was the dispersal of the peoples of Ma'rib after this event that led to the birth of the Arab peoples. It wasn't really until the modern age and the discovery of oil that the fortunes of Ma'rib started to revive – a point that has been made most clear with the construction of a new dam and the greening of the desert.

The last few years haven't been all plain sailing, though; Ma'rib is consistently one of the most troubled places in Yemen. Since 2011 the central government have had almost no control over Ma'rib and Islamic militants have filled the power vacuum.

THE GREAT DAM & THE IRON RAT

Ma'rib's great dam was enormous, measuring 720m long, 60m wide and about 35m high. It was capable of irrigating about 70 sq km of desert and sustaining a population of between 30,000 and 50,000 people.

The ingenuity of the dam lies not just in the choice of its site (where water collects at the base of a number of valleys), but also in its brilliant and complex construction. Aside from the dam there was a complex and sophisticated series of drains and channels surrounding it.

However, the dam was eventually destroyed by a rat with iron teeth chewing away the base of the dam (apparently the rat made its way down from Syria by jumping from hump to hump along a huge camel caravan). One silver lining to this cataclysmic event was that with the destruction of the dam the people of Ma'rib were turned into nomads who set off to conquer and colonise every corner of Arabia, and if some medieval texts are to be believed, they even got as far as Tibet.

WHO DOES SHE THINK SHE IS?

The most beautiful and alluring woman ever to live had hairy legs and the cloven foot of the devil. Her fame has lasted 3000 years, yet nobody remembers her name. She's a player in the ancient legends of Judaism, Christianity and Islam, yet no one knows where she lived. She's the most famous daughter of Yemen, mother of the throne of Ethiopia and the original Jerusalem pilgrim. Even today, she remains a household name, and any girl seen to be getting above herself can expect to be compared to her. She is, of course, the Queen of Sheba, but she may never even have existed.

Legend holds that the Queen of Sheba's first public appearance was when she paid a visit to the court of King Solomon in 10th-century BC Jerusalem. The reasons and results of her visit vary depending on whether you are using Jewish, Christian, Islamic or Ethiopian accounts, but the general consensus is that it was rumours of Solomon's wealth and wisdom that drew her to his court. The best-known story in the West is the Ethiopian tradition that recounts how Solomon became enraptured with her beauty and devised a plan to have his wicked way with her. He agreed to let her stay in his palace only on the condition that she touched nothing of his. Shocked that he should consider her capable of such a thing, she agreed. That evening the king laid on a feast of spicy and salty foods, and after all had eaten well, Sheba and Solomon retired to separate beds in his sleeping quarters. In the night Sheba awoke thirsty from all the salty food she had consumed and reached across for a glass of water. The moment she put the glass to her lips Solomon awoke and triumphantly claimed that she had broken her vow. 'But it's only water,' she cried. To which Solomon replied, 'And nothing on earth is more precious than water.'

Ethiopian tradition holds that the child that resulted from the deceitful night of passion that followed was Menelik I, from whom the entire royal line of Ethiopia claim direct descent. Though all the ancient sources agree that a meeting took place between the two rulers, things become a little murky after that point. The Bible doesn't even give Solomon's mysterious visitor a name, Jewish legend kindly gives Sheba hairy legs and a cloven foot, and Quranic accounts say that Solomon heard rumours of a kingdom ruled by a queen whose subjects worshipped the sun. He commanded a jinn (spirit) to bring her to him, and when Bilqis, as she is known in the Arab world, arrived at Solomon's crystal palace, she immediately accepted the Abrahamic tradition of worshipping one god alone.

Finding out whether Sheba existed and where her capital was located has not proved easy. The strongest claims have come from Ethiopia, which believes that Aksum (Axum) was her capital, and Yemen, which says it was Ma'rib (others claim she came from northwest Arabia or Nigeria). Both cities were important trade and cultural centres and it's likely that both were, if not ruled by the same monarch, then closely tied through trade. So far neither has any evidence to suggest that the Queen of Sheba ever existed. Whatever the truth, the legend persists and every Yemeni will swear that Ma'rib was the home of the most beautiful cloven-footed woman to have ever lived.

⊙ Sights

Great Ma'rib Dam RUIN

Lying 8km southwest of town is the extraordinary Great Ma'rib Dam, justly Yemen's most famous monument. The dam is believed to date to at least the 8th century BC. It was periodically repaired; the last recorded time that major works were carried out was in the 6th century AD, after which it probably fell into disuse. Sadly, much of the remaining walls have been used to build the new town. Only two sluice gates (look out for the Sabaean inscriptions) remain. The vast stones, used for the dam's foundations, were covered in a kind of 'waterproofing' consisting of clay and plastered with stones and gravel on the sides. At the tip of the dam, two gaps in the wall channelled the water into the irrigation canals.

'Arsh Bilqis RUIN

Lying on the Safir road, the ancient and enigmatic 'Arsh-Bilquis (Bilqis Palace/Bilqis Throne/Temple of the Moon) is the site of the famous five-and-a-half columns often seen in tourist brochures. Although linked to the legend of the Queen of Sheba, archaeologists now believe that the temple predates the queen, and is actually around 4000 years old and was dedicated to the moon.

The temple consists of a square with an open courtyard, at the centre of which lies the old sacred well. Twelve steps lead from the open area to the hall, and there's a row of fixed marble seats on the western side and a plinth on which a 6m statue of the Sabaean Holy Oxen once stood.

Mahram Bilqis   RUINS
The kidney-shaped Mahram Bilquis (Temple of Bilqis/Awwam Temple) is believed to date from at least 800 BC and was dedicated to the sun god. Measuring 94m by 82m, it's the largest of all the Sabaean temples. Remains include a 9m-high wall, a hall with columns and a row of eight, 12m-high columns.

Old Ma'rib   OLD TOWN
Rising like a spectre from the surrounding landscape is the eerie silhouette of Old Ma'rib. Originally built long before the 1st millennium BC and sitting on foundations that are vastly more ancient, it suffered much damage from bombs during the 1962 civil war, but for the layperson it's the most romantic of the archaeological sites. A number of years ago the last family finally moved out and with their departure one of the oldest inhabited towns on earth effectively ceased to exist.

Shabwa   شبوا

Shabwa, the political, economic and religious capital of the ancient kingdom of Hadramawt, situated on the bank of Wadi Arma, has been described as 'a city forever beyond the hills', an appropriate description

for a place that has remained fantastically remote right up until today.

The town, which is thought to have been founded sometime between 1500 and 1200 BC, was an important collection point for the camel caravans traversing the desert. Traditionally, the caravans were obliged to pay the high priest of Shabwa one-tenth of the total value of their load. As a result, the city grew rich – rich enough to turn the surrounding desert into a 4800-hectare garden of trees, fields and flowers.

Much of Shabwa awaits further excavation, but for the moment there are the remains of the old city walls, the ruins of an ancient temple, various storerooms and what is said to be the royal palace to the east of the site.

Al-Mukalla   المكلا
☑ 05 / POP 182,500

◉ Sights & Activities
Al-Mukalla's old town and corniche are interesting. The former is reminiscent of Zanzibar and India, and has an exotic (but incredibly dirty) feel to it. It's not at all like an inland Yemeni town. The corniche has a more European flavour and used to make a great place for an evening walk. The Mukalla Museum (Corniche), occupying part of the elegant former Sultan's Palace, contains displays relating to the sultan and to the town's history.

◉ Sleeping
Al-Mukalla used to be a popular holiday destination with both Yemenis and Saudis wanting to dip their toes in the sea. Today, most hotels probably stand empty or have closed down. In the past popular places to stay with western tourists were the cheap Al-Salama Hotel (☑ 305210; Al-Mukalla St), the mid-range Ryboon City Hotel (☑ 303606; Fouah St; @) and the very pleasant top-end Al-Bustan Hotel (☑ 318770; www.albustan-mukalla.com; @ ✉).

◉ Getting There & Around
Yemenia (☑ 303444; www.yemenia.com.au; Al-Ghar al-Amar St) has flights to Sana'a (US$140). Felix Airways (☑ 565656; www.felixairways.com) has flights to Sana'a (US$119), Socotra (US$118) and Aden (US$102).

The airport (based at Ar-Rayyan) lies 40km from Al-Mukalla.

Socotra

سقطرى

♫ 05 / POP 160,000

The secret of eternal life shouldn't be something that's easy to stumble across and by cleverly hiding it out on Socotra the gods have certainly taken that thought to heart. At 3650 sq km Socotra is easily the largest Yemeni island and traditionally one of the most inaccessible. Lying 510km southeast of the mainland, the island has developed in near total isolation from the rest of the world. Rumoured to have once been a refuge for dragons and the Phoenix, it continues to provide a refuge for all manner of extraordinary fauna and flora, much of which is found nowhere else. Because of the number of its endemic plants and creatures, it's been described as the 'Galapagos of the Indian Ocean'. While this is a little optimistic, there is no denying that Socotra is a unique and otherworldly island. It's the kind of place where people speak a language unknown to anyone else, where the knowledge of how to make fire by rubbing sticks together is still common and where the elderly recall days when money didn't exist.

⊙ Sights & Activities

Explore the ramble of half-built streets in Hadibu, as well as the botanical gardens 2km east of town, which contain examples of all the island's most important native flora.

Tourism is still a fairly new concept to the island, but in a very short space of time an admirable range of tours and activities has become available. There's little to see or do in Hadibu, so try to organise everything in advance to avoid wasting time there. With no real organised public transport and, outside Hadibu, no hotels or restaurants, it would be very hard to explore Socotra in a truly independent manner. Therefore, virtually everyone uses the services of either a local or Sana'a-based agency.

For most people the island highlights are the exhilarating hiking, divine beaches and the extraordinary flora and fauna. The best beach by far is the deserted bridal-white sands and blissful blues of **Detwah Lagoon** at **Qalansiyah** in the west of the island. There's a small and well-run **campsite** here with pre-erected tents for YR1000. Not far behind on the beach is **Homhil**, in the east of the island, where fresh and salt waters mingle beneath mountainous dunes.

Diving & Snorkelling

The diving (equipment/guide/boat US$60/50/50) in Socotra is world class, with the attraction being fish rather than coral. Some of these fish grow very big indeed and include curious schools of dolphins, comical turtles (both in the summer only) and lots of very large and decidedly less-friendly sharks! Most of the dive sites in Socotra are virtually unexplored. A recommended dive operator is the **Socotra Diving Centre** (☎ 777007588).

There's also excellent snorkelling (YR500 equipment rental), with the Dihamri Marine Protected Area, around 15km from Hadibu, and the Roosh Marine Protected Area, around 30km from Hadibu, being the best places for peering under the waves.

Socotra

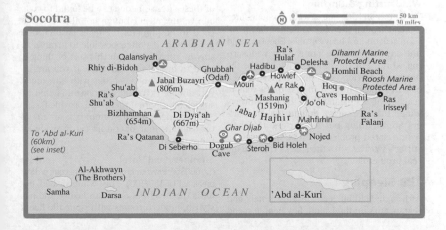

Hiking

There's great hiking potential, with the green hills and granite outcrops of the 1500m Hajhir Mountains providing dragons, cave dwellers and views. Unless you're planning a long trans island hike, you'll need a vehicle to reach some of the best walking areas. It's compulsory to take two guides – one from a Hadibu tour agency (YR5000) to act as a translator and one local guide to act as a, well, guide (YR5000). There are two standard high-mountain walks each taking a minimum of four hours excluding stops. In general experienced hikers will find the walking fairly easy.

For a different kind of hike, camel trekking (camel per day YR8000, guide per day YR5000) in the foothills can be organised. This is a fantastic adventure that involves staying with nomadic families and trekking for up to a week. Serious naturalists and botanists will appreciate the knowledge of a guide and any of the tour agencies should be able to line you up with someone experienced.

Caving

Caving is a new activity for which Socotra (and the Dhofar Mountains around Hawf) has immense potential. The island is thought to boast one of the world's largest cave systems, though they remain almost entirely unexplored to date. The Dogub Cave on the south coast has huge stalagmites and stalactites, and is one that everyone can enjoy, while the immense Hoq Caves will require a guide to lead you 3km underground deep into the bowels of the island – keep your eyes peeled for dragons.

Windsurfing & Surfing

With day-in day-out strong to gale-force winds through the May to September monsoon season and heavy swells, Socotra could one day be a massive name in the windsurfing world. For the moment it's just for the hardcore. Surfers will also find some excellent breaks hidden in the more remote reaches of the island, but the same heavy winds that are such a delight for windsurfers are anything but for surfers. However, wind-related problems will be the least of a surfer's worries – it's the sharks that are the real problem!

🛏 Sleeping

Although Hadibu has the only hotels and restaurants on the island, few people spend

more than a night here at the beginning and end of their trip. Prior to 2011 there were several places to stay in Hadibu, including **Socotra Holiday Hotel** (r from YR3500), **Taj Socotra Hotel** (☑660627; tw YR3500) and **Socotra Tourist Hotel** (☑660725; r YR3500). We were unable to contact any of them, and prices listed are from 2010. We were, however, able to update Summer Land Hotel's prices remotely.

Camping is not permitted everywhere (so check first). Some good, established spots include **Wadi Dae'rho** near the freshwater pool, **Nojed** on the south coast, **Homhil** and **Dihamri** in the east and **Detwah Lagoon** in the west. Facilities vary in all of these 'campsites' ranging from a toilet and some pre-erected tents and huts (Dihamri and Detwah Lagoon) to nothing at all. At most of these sites someone can be found to cook an evening meal (though not always, so it's good to be prepared). Pitches cost YR1000 per person. It's often possible to arrange to stay in villages, though this sort of thing is hard to organise in advance. If you are invited to do so, be generous with how much you donate (YR2000 per person should be sufficient – more if meals are provided).

If you need to hire camping gear, any of the island's tour operators can provide all the standards.

Summer Land Hotel   HOTEL $$$
(☑660350; www.summerlandsocotra.com; s/d incl breakfast US$60/100) This whitewashed hotel is the height of Socotran luxury and has stylish, modern rooms with stone tile floors

and oh-so-comfortable beds, but with cold-water-only showers it's mega overpriced (although hot water is apparently on the way). The staff know the island well and can sort you out with tours, car hire and camping equipment.

Eating

There are few eating options in Hadibu and none at all outside the town. **Taj Socotra Restaurant** (meals YR700-1000), below the hotel of the same name, is every local's favourite eating establishment.

Shopping

Socotra Women's Association Shop CRAFT (⊙7am-11am & 3-5pm Sat-Thu) Situated on Hadibu's main road, this small but interesting shop – which sells locally made handicrafts, incense and even small packets of 'dragon's blood' – was closed throughout much of 2011–12, but the word is that it's about to re-open. Money raised goes towards local women's projects.

ℹ Information

All of the services below are found in the capital, Hadibu. Two excellent publications on Socotra are *Soqotra – the Birds & Plants* and *The Lost World of Socotra*, by Richard Boggs. The former

is available in Hadibu the latter in Sana'a or abroad.

Dragons Blood Tree Agency (☑660136; www.socotraislandadventure.com) One of the best regarded of the island's handful of tour companies.

El Ahmed Tourism Agency (☑0777210276; www.atsi-socotra.com; Main Rd)

National Bank of Yemen (☑660192; ⊙7.30am-2pm Sat-Thu) Changes US dollars and euros (cash only).

Soqotra Eco-Tourism Society/Visitors Information Service (☑660253) The official HQ for the Soqotra Eco-Tourism Society, which was set up in early 2003 with the aim of promoting and developing tourism and infrastructure projects on the island in a sustainable manner for the benefit of all. It has some maps and brochures. Ring before visiting, as its opening hours are erratic. There's a branch office at the airport, which opens (sometimes) for flight arrivals. It also organises good tours of the island.

ℹ Getting There & Away

The national carrier **Yemenia** (☑660123; www.yemenia.com; ⊙7am-noon & 3.30-5.30pm) flies from Socotra to Sana'a (US$234). **Felix Airways** (☑565656; www.felixairways.com) has flights to Sana'a (US$184), Aden (US$173) and Al-Mukalla (US$118). It's essential to book well in advance.

AN ARABIAN EDEN

The remote Socotran archipelago has been described as an Arabian Garden of Eden and is known for its high number of endemic plants and animals. There are around 850 plant species, of which approximately 230 to 260 species are found nowhere else on earth. The Hajhir Mountains and the limestone plateaus contain the richest variety of endemic plants. The most famous of these is the stumpy Dragon's Blood Tree, whose red sap was for years sold as dragon's blood and used as a cosmetic and for medical reasons. Another favourite is the Cucumber Tree, the only cucumber plant to grow in tree form. In total, 52 of Socotra's endemic plants are included on the International Union for Conservation of Nature (IUCN) Red List of Threatened Species.

The fauna also includes a large proportion of endemics. Only seven types of terrestrial mammals call the island home and most of these were introduced. Two, a bat and a shrew, are considered endemic. Officially a phoenix hasn't been seen for donkey's years, but even so the bird life is spectacular and consists of 140 species, 11 of which are endemic. These are the Socotra buzzard, Socotra scops owl, Socotra pipit, Socotra golden-winged grosbeak, Socotra white-eye, Socotra warbler, Socotra bunting, Socotra sunbird, Socotra starling, Socotra cisticola and the Socotra sparrow. New birds are still being discovered on a yearly basis. The most visible bird on the island, though, is the Egyptian vulture. For an excellent twitching trip report on Socotra, including a rundown on the island's best birding sights, see www.worldtwitch.com/socotra_yemen_birding_des.htm. There are 26 reptile species, 23 of which are endemic and while most are small lizards or little harmless snakes, we swear we caught a quick glimpse of a fire-breathing dragon flying past one evening.

ⓘ Getting Around

One of the biggest construction projects in recent years (well, OK, recent centuries) has been the construction of an island ring road, as well as linking trans island roads. Despite this there is currently only a very limited public transport network which comprises the odd minibus travelling between Hadibu and Qalansiyah, so you will need to rent a jeep (US$75-100), which can be done through any of the island's tour agencies.

WADI HADRAMAWT
وادي حضرموت

🔊 06 / POP 1.09 MILLION

Hemmed in by so much sun-blasted desert, the vast Wadi Hadramawt, a dry river valley lined with lush oases, is like another world. In an instant, sterility is replaced by fertility and ochre browns give way to disco greens. It's the sort of place where stories can grow tall, and magic and mystery seem to permeate the very air. It was originally populated by a race of giants called 'Ad, who, according to legend, were given wealth unlike anyone else. But instead of thanking God for his generosity, they wasted their time worshipping idols, building fabulous cities

and generally running about living life like it was meant to be fun. In retaliation for this behaviour God sent violent winds, tremendous sandstorms and, according to some sources, a plague of dog-sized ants who tore the 'Adites apart limb by limb. With a past like this, it's hardly surprising to learn that this magic kingdom has skyscrapers built of mud, camels that turn into rocks and honey that tastes of liquid gold.

Shibam
شبام

As you get closer the heat haze lifts and you realise that what you are looking at is not really a group of fossilised giraffes rearing up out of the palms, but something even more improbable. It's Shibam, a 2500-year-old city of seven- and eight-storey tower blocks built entirely out of mud and faith.

History

Shibam is thought to date from the 4th century BC, but was built on the ruins of an even older city. It was later settled by citizens of old Shabwa after their city was destroyed. Later the town grew to boast the most important market in the region, and served for centuries (right up to the 16th century) as

Wadi Hadramawt

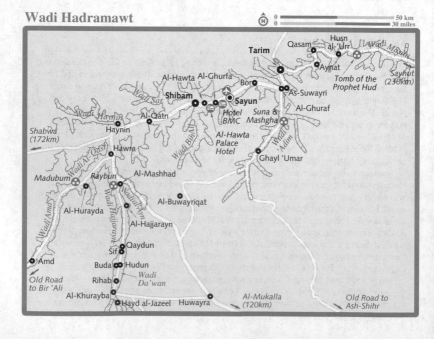

an important capital for local dynasties. The current structure of the city is around 500 years old. In 1982 the town was declared a Unesco World Heritage Site.

◉ Sights & Activities

Old Town   HISTORIC SITE
(⊘7am-6.30pm) Although old Shibam covers a very small area, it manages to pack over 500 dwellings into this confined space. The exterior of the buildings tends to be dull and featureless, but keep an eye open for the magnificent decorative doors and windows.

Shibam is a silent and reserved place and in the mid-afternoon heat, when everyone else is safely tucked away indoors, it can feel a little like a museum or a library. It's worth taking a late-evening stroll along the **city walls**, which date from the 17th century, and out into the fields of date palms. Other worthy sites include the **Sultan's Palace**, built in AD 1220, and the various **mosques** (none of which are open to non-Muslims), including the **Sheikh ar-Rashid Mosque** (also known as the Al-Jami or Great Mosque), which dates from the 10th century. Next door to this mosque is the tiny **Minbar Museum** which contains a stunningly restored medieval minbar (pulpit) from next door's mosque. At the **souq** next to the mosque, look out for the frankincense that has been sold here for centuries.

A bit of a tourist tradition used to be to climb the rocky hill above the 'suburb' of Sahil Shibam, opposite the town, to watch the sun fall behind the city.

⏢ Sleeping & Eating

Currently all the tourist class hotels in and around Shibam are closed. If tourism starts up again they will surely re-open. There were two main hotels: the very pleasant **Shibam Motel** and the **Al-Hawta Palace Hotel** (@☎), which was probably the nicest hotel in all of Yemen.

Sayun   سيون

☎ 05 / POP 49,100
Sayun has a distinguished history. From the earliest days, it was developed by the local Hadramawt clans and dynasties, and since the 15th century has been the wadi's capital. Today, despite being the heart and soul of Hadramawt, dusty Sayun is a town with a

---

SECURITY – EASTERN YEMEN

Unfortunately, during the political crisis of 2011–12 large parts of this region fell out of central government control and into the hands of Al-Qaeda affiliated groups. Throughout 2012 the new Yemeni government, backed by what are assumed to be US drone strikes as well as US intelligence information, has been fighting back and much lost ground has been regained. For the traveller though the entire area is completely closed due to the extreme danger of visiting. Sadly, it's unlikely the situation will improve much during the lifetime of this book.

---

slow beat set against a background of hills and palm trees.

◉ Sights

Sayun is home to a number of interesting mosques and tombs, such as the Al-Habshi Tomb, opposite the cemetery, and the 16th-century Al-Haddad Mosque, south of the cemetery. Non-Muslims cannot enter any of them, however.

Sultan's Palace   MUSEUM
(☎402285, Central Sq) Originally built as a 19th-century defensive fort, the Sultan's Palace was converted into a residential palace by the Sultan Al-Katheri in the 1920s. The sultan wasn't a subtle man and his house, containing a mere 90 rooms, towers over Sayun like an exaggerated wedding cake. So proud was the sultan of his new home that it's said he beheaded the main architect in order to prevent him building a copy anywhere else. It now houses one of the best museums in the country.

⏢ Sleeping

In the past the most popular hotels with western tourists were the budget **Rayboon Hotel** (☎406921), the midrange **Hotel BMC** (☎428040; fax 428042; Al-Ghorfah St; @☎) and the quite plush **Samah Seyun Hotel** (☎403623; @☎).

ⓘ Getting There & Away

The national carrier **Yemenia** (☎402550; www.yemenia.com) flies to Sana'a for US$140. **Felix Airways** (☎565656; www.felixairways.com) has flights to Sana'a (US$119) and Aden (US$102).

Tarim تريم

🎵 05

Situated 35km northeast of Sayun, the ramshackle town of Tarim has served as the seat of kings since ancient times, and was Wadi Hadramawt's capital before Sayun. It used to be famous as a centre of Islamic learning, as testified to by its library, and at one time had a mosque for every day of the year. During the past century many of the people of Tarim have set off to seek their fortunes abroad, and those who have succeeded have often returned to build sumptuous 'palaces' in and around the city.

Today it feels as if Tarim's day is done – a few more years and it will have melted back into the desert dust from which it sprung.

◉ Sights

Tarim is famous for the quantity and quality of its mud-brick 'palaces', many of which were constructed by Yemenis returning to their homeland after making their fortunes in the Far East.

Al-Kaf Palace HISTORIC BUILDING

('Ish Shaa Palace; 🎵417500) As-Sayed Omar bin Sheikh al-Kaf built the Al-Kaf Palace, Tarim's most flamboyant, apparently using a book of different architectural styles as a template, in a kind of 'pick-your-own' project! The result is an unlikely mishmash of styles – art nouveau, art deco, baroque, Southeast Asian and Hadrami. Back in its day, it must have been beautiful, but now it's a crumbling relic and a visit here is a little sad as you think about the marvellous lifestyle that this building once represented.

Al-Ahgaf Manuscript Library HISTORIC BUILDING

(🎵41522; admission free) Housed in the back of the Great Mosque (or Masjid al-Jami), Al-Ahgaf Manuscript Library is the second-largest library in the country and contains over 5000 manuscripts, though most are hidden from prying eyes. Some of the more beautifully illustrated manuscripts are on display in glass cabinets. All captions are in Arabic.

Al-Muhdar Mosque MOSQUE

The large and dazzling-white Al-Muhdar Mosque, built in 1915, is the symbol of Tarim and until the construction of the new Al-Saleh Mosque in Sana'a it boasted the tallest minaret in Yemen; it soars nearly 40m into the air.

Wadi Daw'an وادي دوعن

🎵 06

It is hard to imagine how anywhere in the Yemeni desert could be more spectacular and mysterious than the Wadi Hadramawt, but sitting quietly on the sidelines, there is one such place. The Wadi Daw'an might only be small, but it packs one hell of a punch – everything you thought breathtaking about the Wadi Hadramawt is here in force, but unlike the camouflaged mud villages of the main wadi, these villages come in a lush patchwork of shades and colours.

Some of the wadi's most attractive villages, in a north to south direction, include

---

OF PETRIFIED CAMELS & TORTURED SOULS

Travel half a day east of Sayun, to the Wadi Masilah, and you will come across an extraordinary sight: a small town of prim and proper houses set at the foot of a tomb. This is the tomb of the Prophet Hud, and this is no ordinary town. The great-great-grandson of Noah, Hud was a giant of a man, the size of a palm tree according to some. He was sent by God to make the 'Adites – the race of giants who were the original inhabitants of Hadramawt – change their immoral and lax ways. This wasn't well received by the 'Adites. They chased Hud and his snow-white camel up to the far end of the wadi, where he eluded his pursuers by riding straight into the cliff face which parted for him and all of his camel but its hump, which was instantly turned to stone.

It's said that Hud is the father of all south Arabians and his tomb, where the camel's hump can still be seen, is the location of an annual three-day pilgrimage. Aside from these three days, though, the tomb and its surrounding town is utterly deserted and lifeless, haunted, it's said, only by ghosts.

Not far away is rumoured to be the mysterious Well of Barhut, a bottomless well whose walls are lined with scorpions and snakes. It's said to be the place where fallen angels and the souls of infidels end their days.

Al-Mashhad, which, with the 15th-century Tomb of Hasan ibn Hasan, is a local pilgrimage site and a near-deserted village. Next down the line, and clambering up the side of a cliff, is maybe the most impressive village of them all, Al-Hajjarayn, which is also among the oldest villages in the region. One of the biggest villages in the wadi is Sif, whose pastel-fringed houses sprawl across the wadi bed, and whose old quarter sits proudly atop a knuckle of rock.

Al-Khurayba is the final village in the wadi and is famous for its massive acid-trip 'palace' of rainbow-coloured squares. It was built by a Saudi businessman with roots in the area, who is also responsible for a wave of new schools, clinics and roadworks.

The valley is currently unsafe for westerners to visit and is closed to tourists.

UNDERSTAND YEMEN

Yemen Today

For a couple of years following Yemen's 2006 presidential elections, the country appeared to be on the rise and was the most stable it had been in years. However, the good times weren't to last and things started to spiral out of control. In Sa'da province, in the far north of the country, a bloody uprising that had rumbled on since 2004 between the army and the Houthis, a Zaydi rebel group, flared up again and since then a stop-start civil war has engulfed the far north of Yemen. For more on the Houthi rebellion and the Sa'da War, see p378.

As if conflict in the north wasn't bad enough trouble was also brewing in the south where secessionists started calling for independence of the former South Yemen due to claims of discrimination and the unfair distrubtion of the oil wealth. Anti-Sana'a protests started to turn increasingly violent and a number of unarmed protesters were killed by government security services.

As these two events were threatening to tear the country apart Al-Qaeda's influence started to grow, unemployment rise and levels of corruption grow. The seeds had been sown for major social unrest and it was now just a case of waiting for something to spark the fire.

The Arab Spring & the End of an Era

When the Arab Spring protests erupted across the wider region in late 2010 and early 2011 it didn't take long for the people of Yemen to come out onto the streets to call for change. Initially the protests were calling for action against high unemployment, dreadful economic conditions and high levels of corruption, as well as against the government's proposals to modify the constitution of Yemen. It didn't take long though for protesters to start demanding the resignation of President Saleh.

The first really big demonstration took place in Sana'a on 27 January 2011 when an estimated 16,000 people took to the streets. Within three weeks tens of thousands of Yemenis were protesting in the streets of towns right across the country. By the start of March the protests were becoming more violent and on 18th March, 52 protestors were killed in Sana'a after government security agents fired on the protestors. This led to an increasing flow of government ministers and military leaders defecting to join the protesters.

By April a Gulf Cooperation Council-brokered plan allowing Saleh to cede power in exchange for immunity was put forward. Three times Saleh agreed to sign only to back down at the last moment. All the while the protests became more and more violent and the government started to lose complete control of much of the country. When, towards the end of May, Saleh refused to sign the deal for the third time, Sheikh Sadiq al-Ahmar, the head of the Hashid tribal federation, one of the most powerful tribes in the country, declared his support for the opposition and brought his armed supporters to Sana'a. Almost immediately fighting erupted between them and loyalist security forces with the result that Sana'a was turned into a battle ground as gunfire and heavy artillery rocked the city. Things culminated on 3 June when Saleh was seriously injured in an attack (it remains unclear whether this was a bomb blast or a shell) on a mosque he was praying in. The next day he was flown to Saudi Arabia for medical treatment and Yemenis celebrated the fall of Saleh. Or so they thought.

Saleh's vice-president, Abd al-Rab Mansur al-Hadi, was made acting president, but from his hospital bed Saleh kept indicating that he would return to Yemen. For three months Yemen was trapped in a kind of limbo; the protests continued unabated and, taking advantage of the chaos, Al-Qaeda in the Arabian Peninsula started taking control of huge swathes of the east and south of the country. Everyone was predicting the end of Yemen as a functioning state. Finally, in September 2011, Saleh suddenly re-appeared in Yemen, but his time was up and on the 23rd November he finally signed a Saudi brokered agreement to resign.

History

Sabaeans & Himyarites

Aside from legend, a shroud of mystery still envelops the early origins of southern Arabia. The area now known as Yemen came to light during the 1st millennium BC, when a sweet-smelling substance called frankincense first hit the world's markets. Carefully controlling the production and trade of this highly lucrative commodity were the Sabaeans, initially based in eastern Yemen.

Over the ensuing centuries, the Sabaean Empire expanded and came to dominate almost all the rest of modern-day Yemen. The temples and Great Dam at Ma'rib date from this period.

As Sabaean power waned, new powers and empires began to rise in its wake. The greatest of these was the Himyar empire. Initially based in the central highlands, the Himyarites' power grew, and by the late 3rd century AD they had seized control of nearly all the remaining country.

Foreign Powers & the Coming of Islam

Over the succeeding centuries Yemen was invaded many times by hungry regional powers looking for expansion.

Among the powers that passed through its portals – but never managed to fully contain the country – were the Ptolemaic dynasties, the Abyssinians and the Persians (from modern-day Egypt, Ethiopia and Iran respectively). Today, Yemenis are still proud of the fact that no foreign power has ever managed to conquer the country completely.

In the early 7th century AD there came a new invasion. It was to prove far more significant than any that had come before: it was the arrival of Islam.

Initially most Yemenis converted to Sunnism, but over the next few centuries individual Shiite sects, such as the Zaydis, were born. During this time, various mini-states grew, ruled by such dynasties as the Sulayhids and Rasulids.

Ottoman & British Occupation

From the 15th century onwards foreign powers, including the Egyptians and Portuguese, vied again for control of the Red Sea coast. But it was the Ottomans (from modern-day Turkey) who made the greatest impact. Occupying parts of Yemen from 1535 to 1638, and again from 1872 to 1918, they ignored, or failed to capture, the remote inland areas ruled by local imams (prayer leaders). During the 17th century the Qassimi dynasty ruled over much of this region, but its power declined with the demise of coffee trading, upon which it had relied.

In the middle of the 19th century a new power rocked up. From 1839 to 1967 the British occupied and controlled parts of southern Yemen, including the port of Aden, which was declared a British protectorate. Strategically valuable to Britain's maritime ambitions, the port soon grew into a major staging post.

Meanwhile in the north, after WWI and the defeat of Germany (with whom the Ottomans were allied), a new royal Zaydi dynasty, the Hamid al-Din, rose up to take the place of the former occupiers.

Civil War

Until 1962 central and northern Yemen had been ruled by a series of local imams. However, on the death of the influential imam Ahmad, a dispute over succession broke out, embroiling the whole region in a war that dragged on for the next eight years.

On the one side, army officers supported by Egypt proclaimed the Yemen Arab Republic (YAR), while on the other, the royalists based in the north, and backed by Britain and Saudi Arabia, were loyal to Ahmad's son and successor. The YAR forces eventually won.

Following the National Liberation Front's victories in the guerrilla campaign against the British, the colonialists were forced to withdraw from southern Yemen in 1967. Three years later the People's Democratic Republic of Yemen (PDRY) was born. It became the first and only Marxist state in the Arab world.

In the north of the country, meanwhile, Field Marshall Ali Abdullah Saleh had instituted a progressive rule of the YAR with his General People's Congress (GPC). Conflicts between tribes were contained, and the constitution vowed to respect both Islamic principles and Western values, such as personal freedom and private property.

In the PDRY, however, there was turmoil. Power struggles within the Yemen Socialist Party (YSP) had led to rising tension. Finally, in Aden in January 1986, a two-week civil war broke out. The situation was aggravated by the collapse of the Soviet Union, previously the major benefactor of the PDRY. As a result, the south was thrown into a state of bankruptcy.

Additionally, border disagreements between the two states had led to short conflicts in 1972, 1978 and 1979. Yet, despite the political differences, most Yemenis hated having a divided country.

Reunification

On 22 May 1990 a reunified Republic of Yemen was declared and in 1991 Yemen made regional history. The country became the very first multi-party parliamentary democracy on the Arabian Peninsula. Saleh took the position of president and Ali Salim al-Bidh (the leader of YSP, the ruling party of the former PDRY) became vice-president.

Things didn't get off to a good start for the new nation. During the 1990-91 Gulf War, Yemen appeared to side with Iraq (by choosing not to support UN economic sanctions against the country), and in doing so managed to alienate not only the US and its allies, but also its Gulf neighbours, in particular Saudi Arabia and Kuwait. This led to the expulsion of over one million Yemeni emigrant workers from Saudi Arabia and devastated the economy.

On the home front things also began to sour and the YSP and its members started to feel increasingly marginalised by the GPC and its coalition partner Islah.

Eventually tensions came to a head, and in 1994 civil war again broke out between the north and the south. Bidh's attempts to secede from the north were quashed, and he fled the country.

The country was reunified shortly afterwards and the GPC again swept to power in elections held in 1997.

In September 1999 the country held its first-ever presidential election, and Saleh was re-elected as the country's president.

September 11 & Beyond

Following the attacks of 11 September 2001, Yemen was viewed with suspicion by the US. With its remote, unruly and little-policed interior, Yemen was suspected of providing – even unwittingly – a refuge for Al-Qaeda members and supporters, as well as supplying a bolt-hole for militant Islamists. A number of incidents encouraged this perception. In October 2000 the US warship the *USS Cole* was bombed in Aden harbour, killing 17 US servicemen. Following this the French supertanker, the *Limburg*, was bombed in 2002. In an effort to avoid further isolation, the Yemeni government was very quick to sign up to the USA's 'War on Terror'.

In the 2006 presidential elections, Saleh was re-elected by a large margin in elections that international monitors declared largely free and fair. The general consensus among the populace, however, was that after so many years under his rule it was a case of better the devil you know.

Government & Politics

Yemen's first constitution came into force in 1991. Under this system, the president is head of the executive and is elected every seven years; the last presidential election was held in September 2006, the next one was due in 2013. However, the protests of 2010–2012 and the fall of Saleh led to special elections being held in February 2012 (further elections will be held in 2014). The president also selects the prime minister, who in turn chooses the cabinet. The main legislative body is the Yemeni parliament, which counts 301 members. Parliamentary elections are held every six years (the next parliamentary election is due to be held in 2013).

There are more than 40 active political parties, but the main two are: the ruling General Peoples Congress and the JMP, which is an alliance of five opposition parties including the largest, Islah, the main Islamic party in the country. Yemen's legal system is based on Sharia'a (Islamic law).

Economy

Yemen is the poorest country in the Arabian Peninsula. The economy did grow at a rate of between 3.3% and 7.7% between 2000 and 2010, but as the state itself collapsed so did the economy. In 2011 the economy shrank to -10.5% and it remains in a shambles. Oil is Yemen's economic mainstay and prior to 2010 accounted for around 70% of government revenue. Nevertheless, compared to other peninsula countries, Yemen's oil wealth is modest, and the country's oil supplies are forecast to completely run dry by 2017. Another thorn in the side of economic growth is corruption. In 2012 Transparency International ranked Yemen 156 out of a list of 174 countries in its Corruption Perceptions Index (with number one being the least corrupt).

The country is highly, and increasingly, dependent on foreign aid and development money.

People & Society

The National Psyche

The notion of nationality is almost completely lost on a Yemeni. First and foremost is clan, and men with city jobs may still hurry homewards if their tribe or tribal land comes under threat. Second comes the family. Finally, at the bottom of the chain, comes nationality. Pervading all is Islam, a firm fixture and focus in most Yemenis' lives.

Lifestyle

According to UN figures, the average Yemeni is poor (47% of the population lives below the poverty line of US$2 per day and 17.5% on less than US$1.25 per day), illiterate (just 63.9% are literate; divided into 81.2% of men and 46.8% of women) and hard-pressed to find a job.

Yemeni society is very traditional, conservative and steeped in superstition. With 3 doctors per 10,000 people, many Yemenis still rely on traditional medicine for medical treatment and healing. Keep an eye out for people bearing scars on their head or neck, where bad spirits have been expunged by 'cupping'.

Women are more 'liberated' than they look. Many work and drive, but on average still have more than four babies each.

Population

With 24 million inhabitants Yemen has one of the largest populations on the Arabian Peninsula, and one of the highest growth rates (2.57% annually) in the world. The country's population has increased tenfold in 30 years and Sana'a is the fastest growing capital in the world. It is a very young country, with nearly half its population (42.5%) under 15 years old. Yemen is also still a firmly rural society, with 68% of its population living in the countryside.

Along the Tihama, the population is more closely linked to the African mainland. In the interior, the lighter skin of the Semitic 'Arabs' is visible. Bedouin tribes inhabit parts of the desert region to the east.

TRIBAL POWER

Yemen's tribes still wield a lot of power, sometimes more than the government, and for most Yemenis tribal loyalty comes before national loyalty. Groups of tribes form bigger federations. There are three such federations in the northern part of Yemen – the Hashids, Bakils and Zaraniqs – and no government can be formed without an equal representation of these groups. In the southern part of the country, where the government of the former PDRY did its utmost to erode the powers of the tribes, the tribal structure is weaker, though since reunification a certain amount of 'retribalisation' has taken place.

In the mountainous central regions and the Tihama each tribe has a fairly rigidly defined 'territory', which is still passionately defended from other tribes. This rule doesn't apply to the nomadic Bedouin of the desert regions. Conflict between the tribes is common in many areas. If a person kills someone from an opposing tribe, his entire tribe will be held liable. In this way blood feuds between tribes can continue for years.

Every tribe is led by an elected sheikh, whose job it is to resolve conflicts or, if that is not possible, to raise a tribal army and lead the battle.

Religion

Islam is Yemen's state religion. Most Muslims are Sunnis, many of whom follow the Shafa'i sect. Of the Shiites, most follow the Zaydi sects and are based primarily in the far north. In some parts of Yemen (Hadramawt in particular) many pre-Islamic beliefs have been incorporated into daily life.

The majority of the Jewish population emigrated to Israel in the 1950s. Emigration has continued, and now only one or two families are estimated to remain in Yemen (largely in the north, in and round Ar-Rayda and Sa'da). In early 2007 the last of the remaining Jewish families were told by Islamic fundamentalists to leave immediately or be killed – most were subsequently airlifted to Israel.

The influence of Saudi inspired Wahhabi Islam is growing in Yemen and with it the country seems to be becoming ever more conservative.

Arts

For the traveller, Yemen's arts can most easily be appreciated in the varied architecture of its towns and villages, and in its museums. Beautiful examples of ancient art can be found in the latter, as well as more contemporary examples of artisanship. In the larger towns, galleries showcase modern works.

Literature

Poetry – originally oral literature – has been an important art form in Yemen since pre-Islamic times. The most famous Yemeni poet by far is Al Baradouni. Novelists include author of *The Hostage*, Za'id Mutee' Dammaj, one of the very few writers who has been translated into English.

Music

Yemen's music varies greatly from region to region and reflects the different influences of the areas. Tihama music, with its frenetic beat, for example, resembles East African music. The best known Yemeni singer is Abu Baker Salem Balfaqih.

Among the most popular instruments are the oud (or lute), played by virtuosos such as Ayoub Taresh, the *semsemiya* (a kind of five-stringed lyre) and the *mizmar* (reed or

pan pipes). Look out also for the *doshan,* a kind of minstrel, paid today to entertain at celebrations such as weddings. Yemeni pop music hasn't exactly conquered the world but one interesting name to watch out for is Hagag AJ; a Yemeni-American rapper who fuses English and Arabic lyrics.

For a time (under the Imam Yahya in the 1940s), music was banned in Yemen.

Dance

Like music, dance forms an important part of Yemeni social traditions. The best known is the *jambiya* 'dance', in which men perform a series of steps and hops in small groups brandishing their *jambiya* (dagger). Technically, this isn't actually a dance but a bond between tribal members, and each region has its own variation. Women and men always dance separately in public.

Architecture

Like Yemen's music, its architecture varies from region to region. Building design depends on available materials (such as mud, reeds or stone), the local climate (seen by thick and high walls to counter the heat or cold) and the region's historical links with other regions or powers (such as Africa, Southeast Asia or the Ottomans).

As Yemen endured a war on average every seven years throughout the 20th century and a similar rate of violence for centuries prior to that, many rural homes are perched on the highest hilltop, sometimes surrounded by walls and towers for added defence.

Water has long played an important part in Yemen, and some of the country's oldest architecture also represents extraordinary civil-engineering feats, such as the Great Ma'rib Dam.

Food & Drink

Yemeni food is simple but good. Breakfast usually consists of little more than a cup of *shai* (sweet tea) accompanied by fuul (a kind of paste made from beans, tomatoes, onions and chilli) or what is, in our opinion, the world's finest scrambled eggs! Lunch is the main meal of the day and Yemenis tuck in eagerly. A hunk of mutton is the favoured fare, or beef, goat or chicken. Dishes are often served with a thin but delicious broth, such as *shurba wasabi* (lamb soup), a small salad and a huge sheet of flat bread (over 40 mouth-watering kinds of bread exist in Yemen).

The dish of choice in the highlands is *salta,* a piping-hot stew containing meat broth, lentils, beans, fenugreek (giving it its distinctive aroma) and coriander or other spices. Add some meat and you get *fahsah.* For dinner, *fasouliya* (beans) or fuul often suffices. Other regional favourites include *Hanid lamb* from the Tihama which is lamb wrapped in banana leaves (or more likely just tinfoil) and slow cooked in a beehive oven. *Borma* is a soup made of lamb meat and *kidba* is an Ethiopian-style seasoned fried liver. For dessert tuck into some delicious *arayesi* (a traditional wedding dessert

EATING THE FLOWERS OF PARADISE

The first thing every new arrival in Yemen will notice are the bulging cheeks of the qat chewer. Qat, khat, chat or miraa are the leaves of the shrub *Catha edulis*. Originally from Ethiopia, the qat plant has spread across parts of East Africa and into Yemen where the afternoon qat-chewing session has become almost the pivotal point of many Yemeni lives.

Classed by the World Health Organization (WHO) as a drug of abuse that can produce mild to moderate psychical dependence, it has been banned in most Arab and Western countries, including Saudi Arabia where possession is a serious offence, the US and almost all European nations except for the UK where it's currently legal.

Chewing qat is an important social activity in Yemen and around 80% of the male population are thought to be regular chewers. Women also chew but to a lesser degree (45%) and much more discreetly, as do an increasing number of young children. Qat plays an important part in the Yemeni economy, both good and bad. For farmers the profit on qat is five times that of crops, and these profits have done something to slow down the drift to urban areas. On the negative side, 17% of the average family's income is spent on qat and, with each chewer often spending four hours every afternoon chewing, over 14.6 million working hours are lost daily in Yemen.

Environmentally the consequences of qat are bad news. The total amount of land given over to qat has grown from 8000 hectares in 1970 to 103,000 in 2000. Qat is also a thirsty plant and 40% of all the water used in Yemen goes on watering it.

The effects of qat have long been debated – most Yemenis will insist that it gives an unbeatable high, makes you more talkative (at least until the come down when the chewer becomes withdrawn and quiet), suppresses hunger, prevents tiredness and increases sexual performance. Others will tell you that it gives no noticeable high, makes you lethargic, slightly depressed, constipated and reduces sex drive!

If you're going to chew qat, you need to make sure the setting is perfect in order to enjoy the experience. Ask for the sweetest qat you can get (most Yemenis regard this as poor quality, but first-time chewers find even this very bitter) and get a good group of people together to chew with, because qat is, above all else, a social drug. Take yourself off to a quiet and comfortable spot (ideally a *mafraj:* literally 'room with a view') sit back, relax and enjoy the conversation while popping leaves individually into your mouth where you literally just store them in one cheek and gently chew them. All going well you'll be a qat 'addict' by the end of the day, but remember when it comes to the end of the qat session you should spit the gooey mess out – only Ethiopians swallow.

that's basically a thick mash of fruit topped with nuts and jelly).

Meat is a luxury for the well-off, so there's usually a good selection of vegetarian options available. Apart from fuul, plates of boiled or fried vegetables, rice or a salad are also offered.

On the coast fresh fish – often cooked in a traditional clay oven – provides a treat not to be missed. Lebanese starters have made it onto many posher menus and fast-food joints serving burgers and kebabs are increasingly common in bigger towns. Meals in Yemen are rushed affairs with little time devoted to lingering conversations.

Fresh fruit juices are filling, healthy and delicious, but are likely to contain tap water at cheaper stalls. *Shai* is normally hot, black and sweet, and often spiced with mint or cardamom. For some reason the *shai* served in hotels is usually dreadful. Yemeni coffee is not what you'd expect from the original home of *mokha*. It's a cloudy, amber and very weak brew called *qishr* which is made from coffee husks and infused with cloves or other spices. If it's the caffeine buzz you're after, ask for *bunn* or buy a jar of instant coffee from any grocery store and just ask for hot water to mix it with. Various saccharine soft drinks are widely available, as is bottled mineral water.

SURVIVAL GUIDE

ℹ Directory A–Z

ACCOMMODATION
Camping

Aside from a couple of sites in Socotra there are no established campsites in Yemen, but it's possible to pitch a tent in most rural places (except obvious restricted areas, such as near military bases). Camping equipment can be rented from the Sana'a-based travel agencies.

Hotels

Although rock-bottom places can be unearthed in all of Yemen's towns (for YR800 to YR1200), they're not recommended. The filthy dormitory rooms have rope beds with no mattresses and, if you're lucky, rotten blankets. Qat chewers and itinerant merchants (invariably male) are the main clientele, so foreign men will have raised an eyebrow at them and foreign women will simply be turned away.

Similar but cleaner and more accustomed to travellers of both sexes are the budget hotels, which offer singles/doubles with shared

or sometimes private bathrooms for around YR2000/3000. Some of these are converted traditional tower houses, which offer simple but attractive and cosy dormitory-style accommodation aimed squarely at foreign tourists. In the smaller towns and villages where few eating options exist, these traditional tower houses may also offer half-board for a few hundred riyals.

In all of the larger towns and in many of the smaller ones, there's usually at least a couple of midrange options where singles/doubles with bathroom cost from YR3500/6000. Cheap but clean, and occasionally well loved, they offer great value.

In the capital and one or two of the larger towns, there are a few top-end options, where rooms cost from US$60 to just over US$150.

All the rooms listed by Lonely Planet come with private bathroom (and often a TV) unless otherwise stated. In highland Yemen air-con in hotels is rare as the altitude makes it unnecessary. In coastal and desert regions air-con tends to be pretty much universal even in the cheaper places.

BOOKS

➡ *Arabia Felix – An Exploration of the Archaeological History of Yemen*, by Alessandro de Maigret – for anyone hooked on Yemen's ancient history, this book is considered the definitive introduction to the subject. Hard to find.

➡ *A History of Yemen*, by Paul Dresch – another superb historical account of Yemen's past.

➡ *Yemen – Travels in Dictionary Land*, by Tim Mackintosh-Smith – this award-winning book is a modern classic: it's a witty, erudite but very wordy account of contemporary life and is probably the first book you should read on Yemen. It was published in America as *Yemen: The Unknown Arabia*.

➡ *Motoring with Mohammed*, by Eric Hansen – tells of action-packed and amusing travels around Yemen in the late 1980s.

➡ *Eating the Flowers of Paradise*, by Kevin Rushby – a brilliant and, at times, hair-raising exploration of the world of qat in both Yemen and Ethiopia.

➡ *The Zanzibar Chest*, by former war correspondent Aidan Hartley – focuses primarily on the battles of Africa, but includes many forays

GOVERNMENT WEBSITES

➡ **Australian Department of Foreign Affairs** (www.smartraveller.gov.au)

➡ **French government** (www.diplomatie.gouv.fr/fr)

➡ **UK Foreign Office** (http://www.fco.gov.uk/en/travel-and-living-abroad/travel-advice-by-country/)

➡ **US Department of State** (www.travel.state.gov)

into Yemen and is one of the most powerful books you are ever likely to read.

➡ *Sheba*, by Nicholas Clapp – an interesting and easy-to-read account of Clapp's search for the origins of the myth.

➡ *The Southern Gates of Arabia*, by Freya Stark – a travel classic written by English woman Stark who journeyed through the Hadramawt in the early 1900s.

➡ *Yemen – Land and People*, by Sarah Searight – a good textual and pictorial overview of the country.

➡ *Yemen: Jewel of Arabia*, by Charles and Patricia Aithie – this glossy coffee-table book whets the appetite before a trip and serves as a good souvenir after one.

➡ *Salmon Fishing in the Yemen*, by Paul Torday – this best-selling novel was for many people the one and only time they've ever heard of the country. It's a light-hearted read with some good descriptions of Yemen's mountains.

➡ *Socotra: A Natural History of the Islands and Their People*, by Catherine Cheung – if you're interested in the natural history of Socotra this is the one for you.

➡ *The Last Refuge: Yemen, Al-Qaeda and the Battle for Arabia*, by Gregory D Johnsen – a fascinating and well researched account of the terror group in Yemen.

➡ *Yemen: Dancing on the Heads of Snakes*, by Victoria Clark – a brilliant run-down on modern Yemeni politics and tribal culture.

DANGERS & ANNOYANCES

Travelling anywhere in Yemen (except Socotra) has become a much more dicey prospect than it was just a few years ago and most western governments warn against ALL travel to Yemen (and note that by ignoring these warnings you may well be making your travel insurance invalid). On the plus side petty crime, even in the big cities, is almost non-existent.

Mines

During the 1994 War of Unity, unknown quantities of land mines were planted. After a sustained anti mining campaign, many have been cleared, but mines remain, particularly around the old North/South Yemen border. During their retreat from parts of Abyan province, Al-Qaeda in the Arabian Peninsula planted numerous landmines. So far at least 3000 have been removed from around Zinibar and Jaar. It's almost certain that further mines were laid during the recent unrest. As well as Abyan, the most likely areas for this to have occurred are Sa'da province, Shabwa, Hadramawt and Ma'rib, but the simple truth is that for the moment no-one really knows.

Terrorism

Yemen is the home of Al-Qaeda in the Arabian Peninsula. According to the US government this is the most active and dangerous branch of Al-Qaeda. The group, which had previouly been confined to remote regions that were largely out of bounds for foreigners, used the recent chaos and the collapse of the government to expand their territory massively. In fact at one point they were basically in control of more of the country than the government and their influence extended almost to the doors of Aden and to within less than 100km of Sana'a. By early 2013 they had lost a lot of ground to a resurgent Yemeni army but they remain highly dangerous and a major threat to the stability of the nation. Al-Qaeda has vowed to kill all 'infidels' (that means you!) in Yemen and you should keep a sharp eye out for any suspicious behaviour. It's also a good idea to be careful in any hotels frequented by tourists – and anywhere that expatriates gather. In general expatriates working for international corporations are at a higher risk than casual tourists, but only because they have a more set pattern of movement. Recent Al-Qaeda attacks in Yemen include shootings, bombings and kidnapping (for more on this see below).

Those arrested in the past for connection with terrorism have almost always turned out to be foreign Arabs living in Yemen illegally. Again this is now changing and more Yemenis are now working with Al-Qaeda. The Yemeni government though, has been at pains to express its absolute condemnation of terrorism, and the majority of Yemeni people their disgust and horror of it.

The following are just a few of the more notable recent attacks on foreign tourists or expatriates. In 2007 seven Spanish tourists were killed in an attack in Ma'rib; in January 2008 two Belgians were shot and killed in Hadramawt; and in 2009 a suicide attack left four South Koreans dead in Shibam, Hadramawt. In June 2009 a group of nine expatriates of mixed nationalities were kidnapped near Sa'da, in 2008 there were two attacks on the US embassy in Sana'a resulting in 17 deaths and an attack on the Italian embassy. In July 2011 a British national was killed in a bomb attack in Aden. In 2012 an American teacher was killed in Ta'izz.

Although this list makes it appear that fewer foreigners have been involved in terrorist attacks in the past couple of years, bear in mind that this is because there are now very, very few foreigners remaining in Yemen. In contrast hundreds of Yemenis have died in terror attacks since 2010.

To sum up, at the time of going to print, anywhere the government allows you to travel should be considered fairly safe (but the situation can change fast: attacks can occur anywhere at anytime and you could well be the first target in an area considered safe). Anywhere else in the country should be considered as very dangerous. Do not try any heroics. Socotra island has escaped the violence and can be considered safe; though even here you should still keep your wits about you. Whatever you do remember that the security situation is very fluid – check and check again with embassies, tour companies and on the Thorn Tree forum on the Lonely Planet website.

Kidnappings

Heavily armed tribes have long taken to kidnapping foreign tourists and expatriates in order to publicise their grievances with the government. Normally the victims have been well treated and released unharmed after a few days when the government agrees to the kidnappers' terms (normally for a new road, school or for fellow tribal members to be released from prison). At one point the spate of kidnappings became so common that a speaker in the Yemeni parliament described being kidnapped as 'a great adventure for the tourist'. Today, this is no longer the case. Now kidnapped foreigners are routinely 'sold' to Al-Qaeda and few are heard from again. The rate of kidnap of foreigners also seems to be accelerating and is occurring throughout the country including in the middle of Sana'a in broad daylight (as was demonstrated by the kidnapping in December 2012 of three foreigners studying at a langauge school in Sana'a).

For expats working in Yemen, in order to lower the risk of kidnap you should not stick to a daily routine; you should change your route to work and do not frequent the same restaurants and other public spaces on a regular basis. Tourists are at a lower risk of kidnap in Sana'a but only because they don't have a set pattern. Outside Sana'a everyone is at equal risk.

EMBASSIES & CONSULATES

With the current situation in Yemen it's a very good idea to register with your embassy in Sana'a and enquire about any current security concerns. For those countries without diplomatic representation in Yemen (such as Australia, Canada and Ireland), you can register (via email or online) at your embassy in Riyadh.

Most embassies and consulates open between around 9am and 1pm from Saturday to Wednesday.

Dutch (☑ 01-421800; http://yemen.nlembassy.org; off 14th October St)

French (Map p366; ☑ 01-268888; www.ambafrance-ye.org; off Khartoum St)

German (Map p366; ☑ 01-413174; www.sanaa.diplo.de; off Hadda St)

Italian (☑ 01 432587; www.ambsanaa.esteri.it/Ambasciata_Sanaa; Hadda St)

Omani (Map p366; ☑ 01-208874; Al-Hoboob Corp St)

Saudi Arabian (Map p366; ☑ 01-240856; http://embassies.mofa.gov.sa/sites/yemen/AR/Pages/default.aspx; Al-Qods St)

UAE (Map p366; ☑ 01-248777; Circular Lane)

UK (☑ 01-302480; http://ukinyemen.fco.gov.uk; Thaher Himyari St (Nashwan al Himyari St) East Ring Rd)

USA (Map p366; ☑ 01-755 2000; http://yemen.usembassy.gov; Sa'wan St)

FOOD

For information about Yemen's cuisine see the Food & Drink section (p402) and the Flavours of Arabia chapter (p459).

LEGAL MATTERS

Breaking the law can have severe consequences. For more information, see the Expats chapter (p33) and consult your embassy.

MONEY

The unit of currency is the Yemeni riyal (YR), divided into 100 fils. Banknotes come in denominations of YR10 (rare), YR20, YR50, YR100, YR200, YR500 and YR1000. Each note is translated into English on one side. Only YR5 and YR10 coins remain, and though both sides of these coins are in Arabic only, they are of different sizes (the YR10 coin is the larger). Many people won't accept ripped or damaged banknotes.

Some midrange hotels, all top-end hotels and most travel agencies quote in US dollars or, increasingly, in euros. Where appropriate Lonely Planet also quotes in these currencies,

---

EATING PRICE RANGES

The following price ranges refer to a standard main course. Unless otherwise stated tax is included in the price.

$ less than YR650
$$ YR650–900
$$$ more than YR900

AL-QAEDA & YEMEN

Nothing stirs excitement in media circles like Al-Qaeda, and so when, on Christmas Day 2009, an Al-Qaeda group based in Yemen attempted to blow up an airliner over Detroit in the US, the world's media went into a frenzy and descended en masse on Yemen.

This was far from the first time that Yemen and Al-Qaeda have been mentioned in the same sentence. In 2000 an Al-Qaeda cell blew up the *USS Cole* in Aden harbour and killed 17 US service personnel. Since then Al-Qaeda-attributed attacks have been a frequent occurrence in Yemen and have included suicide attacks against foreign tourists and attacks on Western embassies and Yemeni government and security personnel. One of their bloodiest attacks came in May 2012 when a suicide bomber killed nearly 100 Yemeni soldiers in Sana'a.

But it was the attempted aeroplane bombing that really shone the spotlight on Yemen as this was the first time this group had attempted to launch a direct attack on the US. So, who is this group and what is it doing in Yemen? Known as Al-Qaeda in the Arabian Peninsula (AQAP), the group was formed in January 2009 as the result of a merger of Al-Qaeda in Saudi Arabia with that of its Yemeni branch. It's thought to be led by Nasir Wuhaishi, a Saudi who was one of 23 Al-Qaeda members who escaped from a Sana'a prison in 2006. In August 2011 Wuhaishi was rumoured killed in a battle with Yemeni troops in the south of the country. However this was denied by AQAP and in December 2011 Wuhaishi released a statement on a jihad website. Several other high-profile members of the group are former Guantanamo Bay detainees. Experts think that AQAP is one of the best funded and most stable of all the Al-Qaeda groups and the one that poses the greatest threat to the West.

Prior to the 2011 protests the group was largely confined to remote corners of Shabwa, Ma'rib, Abyan and Hadramawt were they found shelter with the tribes. However, the recent power vacuums in Yemen gave AQAP the opportunity they needed to expand their influence. Using the alias of Ansar al-Sharia the group essentially took total control of the province of Abyan (just east of Aden) and greatly expanded their presence in many other parts of the country. By mid-2012 the Yemeni army was engaged in heavy fighting with the group and by the end of the year had pushed AQAP/Ansar al-Sharia out of the regional capital of Zinjibar and other towns. However, at the time of writing the group still hold territory elsewhere including Rada close to Sana'a and large parts of Ma'rib, Shabwa, Hadramawt and Abyan.

The US, through the use of unmanned drones, military training for the Yemeni army and the use of special forces, are thought to be heavily involved in the fight against AQAP in Yemen and drone attacks on suspected militants are now a common occurrance (the US never confirms the use of drones). In September 2011 the US scored a notable sucess with the killing of Anwar al-Aulaqi, an American-Yemeni thought to be a talent recruiter, motivator and publicist for AQAP, in a drone strike in southeast Yemen. The drone strikes though are also thought to have led to the death of a large number of women, children and other innocents (including a government mediator) and these have done much to increase tribal anger against the Yemeni and US governments and increase support of Al-Qaeda.

but payment is always acceptable in the Yemeni riyals equivalent.

ATMs & Credit Cards

Most of the bigger bank branches in the large towns have ATMs that accept foreign cards. Most will only allow you to withdraw the equivalent of US$200 per transaction up to a daily limit of US$600. Problems with foreign cards are very common and you shouldn't rely solely on them. There are several ATMs at Sana'a airport.

Credit cards (Visa commonly, MasterCard sometimes and Amex rarely) are accepted for payment by airlines, some tour operators and some top-end hotels, but you'll incur a steep 5% to 10% surcharge.

Cash

Cash is by far the simplest form of carrying your money and, as there is little petty theft, carrying around big bundles of money is not a huge worry. US dollars and euros are the currencies of choice.

Banks offer slightly lower rates for cash than foreign-exchange offices, but are more likely to change travellers cheques. There's no black market, so there's no advantage to changing money on the street.

Moneychangers

Numerous (and well-signposted) foreign-exchange offices are found in the cities and larger towns. They offer shorter queues than the banks, faster service, longer opening hours (usually 9am to 9pm, except Friday) and almost always offer a better rate of exchange (at least for cash). Check out a few first, as rates can vary slightly between offices. Commission is seldom charged, but check in advance.

Travellers Cheques

As in many countries travellers cheques can be difficult to change outside the largest towns (and increasingly even in them). Also, changing them generally incurs a 3% to 5% commission or more.

OPENING HOURS

Business hours in Yemen vary. Outside the central highlands, where the climate is hotter, there is often an extended midday break (but businesses open earlier and close later). Some businesses close at 1pm regardless and re-open around 6pm. It's best to try and get stuff done in the morning though before 'qat time' kicks in...

Banks 8am to noon Saturday to Thursday, open only until 11am on Thursday

Government offices 8am to 3pm, although in practice many close by 1pm or 1.30pm

Post offices 8.30am to 1pm and 3.30pm to 7pm Saturday to Thursday. Usually open for an hour from 7pm to 8pm on Friday

Restaurants 7am to 11pm, although they may open earlier and close later in larger towns

Shops & private businesses 9am to noon and 4pm to 8pm Saturday to Thursday. Some open on Friday as well.

Telecom & internet centres 7am to 11pm

Yemenia 8am to 1pm or 2pm and 5pm to 7pm or 8pm Saturday to Wednesday, 9am to noon Friday

PUBLIC HOLIDAYS

In addition to the main Islamic holidays, Yemen observes the following holidays:

May/Labour Day 1 May

National/Unity Day 22 May

September Revolutionary/Anniversary Day 26 September

October Revolutionary/Anniversary Day 14 October

Evacuation/Independence Day 30 November

VISAS

Everyone, except citizens of the Gulf Cooperation Council (GCC) countries, requires a visa to enter Yemen. Visas are not available on arrival. Visas must be obtained from an embassy or consulate beforehand and they will only be issued to people on an organised tour with a recognised Yemeni (or foreign) tour company. This essentially means independent travel around Yemen is no longer possible (with the exception of Sana'a and Socotra; although even here you will still need to employ the services of a tour company in some form or other in order to obtain a visa). If there is no embassy in your home country, you can obtain a visa from an embassy/consulate in a neighbouring country (neighbouring your country or neighbouring Yemen). Note that Israelis or travellers to Israel (with an Israeli stamp in their passport) will be denied a visa/entry to Yemen.

If you're staying more than two weeks you must register at any police station (although try to do it in Sana'a) within the first two weeks of your stay. It's a fairly painless procedure that costs YR1000 although at the time of research the rule was brand new and not everyone knew about it. If you don't register you will be fined YR5000 on leaving Yemen. With the situation as it is in Yemen at the moment, it would also be a very good idea to register with your home embassy on arrival in Sana'a.

Take note also of the travel-permit restrictions.

Travel Permits & Closed Areas

Due to civil war and tribal tension, as well as problems with kidnapping and terrorism, certain areas are completely out of bounds to foreign visitors – everywhere else except Sana'a and Socotra require a travel permit and the services of a tour company.

Currently, the only areas open to foreign tourists on an organised tour are: Sana'a and environs, the Haraz Mountains (including Shibam, Kawkaban, Thilla, Hababah, Al-Mahwit and Manakhah and around), parts of the Tihama Red Sea coastal areas and, further south, Ta'izz, Ibb and Jibla as well as the island of Socotra. However, most Yemeni tour companies are only willing to take tourists to Sana'a and Socotra as they still deem the risk of visiting other parts of the country too high.

Note that the situation changes very fast – often on a day-to-day basis and there is often confusion as to where is, and is not, open. The tourist police and tour companies in Sana'a are the best people to ask for up-to-date information and the Yemen branch on Lonely Planet's Thorn Tree forum (www.lonelyplanet.com) also has plenty of to-the-minute information.

Travel permits, which are free, can be obtained from the Tourist Police (p373) in Sana'a (your tour company will generally arrange these for you). Although officially open 24 hours, if you do go and get permits on your own, you're best advised to come to the office between 8am to 6pm Saturday to Thursday, when you're more likely to get somewhere! To gain a permit from the tourist police, you'll need the following:

➡ passport and photocopy of passport (including personal and visa details)

➡ itinerary (showing where you're travelling to, when and for how long)

➡ means of transport, eg air, car hire (including the name of the car-hire company or travel agency)

➡ names of everyone in your group

➡ details of your return journey home (date of departure, flight etc).

Take wads of photocopies of the permit (around seven or eight per day of travel), as you'll have to dish them out at the checkpoints across the country.

If you significantly change your itinerary, you should inform the tourist police and/or the travel agency within 24 hours. Alternatively, obtain another permit from the nearest major police station. If it's just a minor change, you won't have any problems.

Note that if you are only flying around Yemen (and not using overland transport), you do not need travel permits.

You should not attempt to visit closed areas. Fortunately, the police turn back the occasional foolhardy visitor long before they can put themselves and other people into serious danger, by trying to visit a closed area.

Police Escorts

At the time of writing, it was compulsory to take a police escort everywhere in Yemen except Sana'a and Socotra (including while just walking around any towns). Again, your tour company will organise this.

WOMEN TRAVELLERS

Yemen's attitude towards and treatment of foreign (and local) women is more relaxed than its neighbour, Saudi Arabia, although things do seem to be becoming more conservative. Female tourists can drive rented or private vehicles, and do not have to wear head coverings although in all areas head covering is advised, if only as a gesture of respect (some readers have reported stone-throwing, spitting and glares from local women and children when not dressed 'appropriately'). Conservative dress is expected. Female toilets can be hard to find, but many restaurants have 'family rooms' with toilet facilities.

🛈 Getting There & Away

AIR

Most international traffic arrives and departs from **Sana'a International Airport** (http://sanaa.airport-authority.com). Not many airlines outside the Middle East now serve Yemen. A few airlines, particularly from Middle Eastern countries, also use Aden. Since 2010 both these airports have been subjected to last minute closures for security reasons.

Yemen's national carrier, **Yemenia** (Map p366; ☑ 8001000; www.yemenia.com; Hadda St, Sana'a), flies to dozens of destinations across the Middle East, Europe (including Paris and Rome), Africa and Asia. Yemenia has a reasonable safety record (see www.airsafe.com for details), although in 2009 one of its planes crashed en route to the Comoros Islands, resulting in the deaths of 152 people. Yemenia flights sometimes experience delays or cancellations (particularly during Ramadan and the hajj pilgrimage), so reconfirmation is essential. In late January 2010 the British government banned all direct flights between Yemen and the UK. Any traveller arriving in their home country or a third country from Yemen can now expect to be subjected to significant security checks.

Airlines Flying to/from Yemen

EgyptAir (MS; Map p366; ☑ 01-273452; www.egyptair.com; Az-Zubayri St) Hub: Cairo.

Emirates (EK; Map p366; ☑ 01-444442; www.emirates.com; 60 Metre St) Hub: Dubai.

Ethiopian Airlines (ET; Map p366; ☑ 01-427993; www.ethiopianairlines.com; Beirut St, off Hadda St) Hub: Addis Ababa.

Gulf Air (GF; Map p366; ☑ 01-40922; www.gulfair.com; Hadda St) Hub: Bahrain.

Qatar Airways (QR; Map p366; ☑ 01-506030; www.qatarairways.com; Hadda St) Hub: Doha.

Royal Jordanian Airlines (RJ; Map p366; ☑ 01-446064; www.rja.com.jo; Hadda St) Hub: Amman.

Saudi Arabian Airlines (SV; Map p366; ☑ 01-402992; www.saudiairlines.com; Az-Zubayri St) Hub: Jeddah.

LAND
Border Crossings

At the time of research all land border crossings are closed to foreign tourists. In the event of this changing in the lifetime of this book, there are buses from Al-Mukalla and Sayun to Oman.

SEA

Although cargo boats sometimes connect Yemen (the ports of Aden, Al-Mukalla and Al-Hudayda principally) to ports on the Peninsula, as well as to Egypt, Eritrea and Sudan, there are currently no regular services or timetables, and finding a vessel willing to take a foreigner is likely to prove almost impossible at the moment. One option that was being used by tourists prior to 2010 was to hitch a ride on a *sambuq* (boat) between Al-Makha and Djibouti. From Djibouti you can journey on into the highlands of Ethiopia or the lowlands of Somaliland. At the current time though it's unlikely you will be allowed to do this.

TOURS

Currently the only way to visit Yemen is with a tour agency. However, few tour operators outside the country offer tours to Yemen. Fortunately, there are a number of good local companies based in Sana'a that can help organise your trip.

The standard rate among travel agencies in Sana'a is US$70-100 per vehicle per day. This is for a large 4WD and also includes the driver's fee, his food and accommodation, petrol and 230km to 250km free mileage per day. The rate increases to US$150 per day for longer trips (ie more than 250km or about six hours' driving). Good discounts can usually be negotiated for longer trips.

Guides (costing from around US$40 to US$50 per day, including food and accommodation) speaking English, French, Italian, Spanish, German or Russian can also usually be organised.

Arabian Horizons Travel & Tourism (Map p366; ☏01-506010; www.arabianhorizons.com; Hadda St) Branches in Aden, as well as in the USA and Canada.

ATG (Formerly YATA; Map p366; ☏01-441260; www.atg-yemen.com; just off Hadda St) Offers all the standard tours and specialises in diving.

FTI Yemen (Map p366; ☏01-253210; www.ftiyemen.com; Al Qiada St) A slick professional outfit that can arrange almost any kind of tour almost anywhere in Yemen. It has its own boat for diving trips in the Red Sea.

Marib Travel & Tourism (Map p366; ☏01-426832, 01-426831; www.marib-tours.com; Beirut St, off Hadda St) Probably the most helpful tour company in Sana'a, this friendly and well-regarded outfit values customer service and really goes out of its way to try and help. It can organise standard tours throughout the country as well as specialist trips, including diving, mountain hiking and travel for senior citizens. Highly recommended.

Radfan Agency Tours (Map p368; ☏01-272231; http://visityementours.weebly.com; Talha St) Friendly, long established agency.

Yemen Trek Tours (Map p366; ☏01-516957; www.yementrek.com; Ta'izz Rd) These guys are good and we receive lots of positive feedback from happy punters. Trekking and camel tours are its speciality. The owner also speaks fluent French.

ⓘ Getting Around

AIR

The national carrier is **Yemenia** (☏8001000; www.yemenia.com; ☺ usually 8am-1.30pm & 4-7pm Sat-Thu).

It's considerably cheaper to buy Yemenia tickets in Yemen through a Yemenia office rather than through a travel agency. For the cheapest fares, book flights well in advance. Yemenia offices can be found in all of Yemen's main towns, and accept Yemeni riyals, US dollars, euros and usually Amex, MasterCard and Visa credit cards.

Yemenia flights are prone to both delays and cancellations. Always reconfirm flights.

A private, alternative airline is Felix Airways (p380). The cheapest tickets are those bought online but foreigners can only travel on the more expensive H fare. It has a route network that roughly matches Yemenia, but it seems to be more reliable and a bit cheaper.

BUS

At the current moment foreign tourists are not allowed to travel by bus across Yemen. If this changes then buses travel to almost all the larger towns (sometimes several a day), and services are pretty punctual and safe.

The longest-established bus company is **Yemitco** (Yemen International Transport Company; ☏800/000; www.yemitco.com; ☺5am-8pm, in the south 9am-1pm & 3-8pm Sat-Thu, 4-8pm Fri), which offers comfortable seats in air-conditioned buses. In the last couple of years it seems to be losing out to a multitude of newer companies and now generally only runs a reliable service in the most-populated central areas.

LONG-DISTANCE TAXIS
Shared Taxi

Connecting all the main towns and villages, and operating very much like buses, are the shared taxis (known as *bijou*). Although rarely more comfortable than buses, they tend to be faster, and leave at more convenient times and more frequently. However, they only leave when full, so you can be in for a long wait. When travelling to more remote places, try and catch the first departure. As with the buses, foreigners are not currently permited to use these.

LOCAL TRANSPORT
Bus

Minibuses (which run from 6am to around midnight) ply the streets of all the major towns. They're cheap, but unless you know exactly where they're heading, taxis are an easier, faster and certainly more comfortable option.

Taxi

In a shared taxi, short hops around town cost YR50 and for a cross-town contract taxi (private hire) you'll need to negotiate, but Yemeni taxi drivers are generally more honest than most of the world's cabbies!

Motorcycle Taxi

If you want to beat the traffic in the larger towns, you can always hop on the back of a motorbike taxi.

Understand Oman, UAE & Arabian Peninsula

Oman, UAE & Arabian Peninsula Today

With the exception of Yemen, the Arabian Peninsula is enjoying what is termed in Oman as a 'Renaissance' – a rebirth of former confidence and strength, marked by investment in culture, education, health care and infrastructure, and a gentle relaxation of the strictly autocratic regimes of the mid-20th century. Guided by the Islamic faith, each country of the Peninsula is feeling towards a modern society, sharing many of the aims of the Western world while endeavouring to maintain an Arab identity.

Best on Film

Lawrence of Arabia (1962) David Lean's classic desert epic.
A Dangerous Man: Lawrence after Arabia (1991) Starring Ralph Fiennes in an unofficial sequel to *Lawrence of Arabia*.
Lessons of Darkness (1992) Herzog's exploration of apocalypse in Kuwait's oil fields after the Gulf War.
The Kingdom (2007) Action film examining Saudi Arabia's relationship with the USA.

Best in Print

Seven Pillars of Wisdom (TE Lawrence; 1935) Superb evocation of the desert during the Arab Campaign 1915–18.
Arabian Sands (Wilfred Thesiger; 1959) Captures the Bedouin way of life before it is lost forever.
Orientalism (Edward Said; 1978) The book that redefined the Western love affair with the Middle East.
Arabia Through the Looking Glass (Jonathan Raban; 1980) Perceptive descriptions of the Gulf states, challenging stereotypes.
Nine Parts of Desire: The Hidden World of Islamic Women (Geraldine Brooks; 1994) Revealing account by Australian journalist living under the veil.

Rapid Change

It is hard to think of another region where the pace of change has been so phenomenal. Grandparents across Arabia remember when a trip to the capital meant a long journey by donkey, when education was reserved for the well-connected and when housing was hot and inadequate. Infant mortality rates were high, life expectancy low.

Within the space of 50 years, the Peninsula has changed beyond recognition. Icons of the region's success are visible from the superhighways of Saudi Arabia to the soaring towers of Gulf cities. This rapid growth is of course largely due to the discovery of oil, but it is also due to a willingness to embrace modernity and the complex technologies it involves. Computer competence, e-governance, and a mobile-phone culture are commonplace across the region.

Urbanisation

Rapid change comes at a cost. While there's pride in recent achievements, there are frustrations too. There's resentment, for example, towards Arabia's ever-growing expatriate population who helped build the region's infrastructure but who are now reluctant to leave.

Industry has drawn people away from their villages and disrupted the time-honoured patterns of rural life. Those on the fringe of encroaching urbanisation find the traditions they valued are undermined, leaving little recognisable of a Bedouin heritage. For those remaining in remote areas, there is disappointment at the perceived exclusion from the benefits bestowed on an urban life.

The Arab Spring

Frustration with the process of modernisation and the perceived threat of encroaching ideologies inevitably leads to political repercussions – a situation that Al-Qaeda and other fundamentalist groups have been quick to exploit.

In 2011, with Libya, Tunisia, Egypt and Syria in turmoil, the Arabian Peninsula witnessed its own Arab Spring. Mostly propelled by students who felt sympathy with the democratic aspirations of their North African counterparts, there were minor protests in Oman, more pronounced problems in Bahrain and an ousting of the president in Yemen. But while it is convenient to lump the unrest into the collective term 'Arab Spring', the reasons for the uprisings in each of those countries were primarily local in nature, informed by domestic concerns such as religious sectarianism, unemployment and a minimum wage.

Relationship with the West

Besides, evidently democracy is not the only way of effecting good governance. Oman, as reported in the UK *Guardian* for example, was named as the 'most improved country in the world over the past 40 years' by the UN Development Fund. According to many commentators (not least former US Secretary of State Hilary Clinton who praised the 'remarkable gains' made under Oman's absolute monarch, Sultan Qaboos), the countries of the Peninsula, with their prosperous, well-fed, well-educated, well-housed and mostly peaceful populations, have been well served by what is commonly termed 'benign dictatorship'. Interestingly, this is a subject now taught in some business schools as part of the project management process. In some ways, the emerging countries of the Peninsula are just that: a project in progress in which, over the past half century, a strong leader with a clear vision and an unquestioned mandate to govern has been behind the countries' phenomenal growth and modernisation. In an article in the *Financial Times* in 2011, distinguished journalist Robert Kaplan describes how the legitimacy of Arabian dictatorship is built on a social contract that allows for autocratic decisions to be made in the public good for the advancement of society – a legitimacy 'built on royal tradition' that aligns with the historical experience of the countries concerned.

It has not gone without comment in the media of the region that the only multiparty democracy in the region, Yemen, is the least developed in terms of infrastructure, education and health care. Many local commentators predict that its descent into virtual civil war will be hard to resolve without unconditional leadership acceptable to all tribal factions.

Attitudes towards democracy partially inform the region's relationship with the West. For strict Muslims, as conversations with local *mutuwa* (religious police) reveal, democracy is often seen as the politics of the West, synonymous with liberal standards and moral permissiveness. Some younger Arabs see democracy as the pathway to free speech but, as the Arab Spring in Oman demonstrated, there is limited understanding about the attendant responsibilities that temper democratic freedom. But time will tell.

POPULATION: **65.4 MILLION**

LITERACY RATE: **85%**

UNEMPLOYMENT RATE: **9%**

LAND AREA: **3,097,988 SQ KM**

LAND MASS: **WORLD'S LARGEST PENINSULA**

UNIQUE FEATURE: **ENCOMPASSES WORLD'S LARGEST SAND DESERT**

if the Arabian Peninsula were 100 people

70 would identify as indigenous Arab
17 would identify as Sub-continental
8 would identify as other Arab
3 would identify as Eastern expatriate
2 would identify as Western expatriate

belief systems
(% of population)

Muslim   Christian   Other

population per sq km

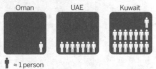

Oman   UAE   Kuwait

≈ 1 person

Unesco World Heritage Sites

Qala'at al-Bahrain (Bahrain) Dilmun heritage and coastal fort.

Bahla Fort (Oman) Newly completed restoration project ongoing for two decades.

Land of Frankincense (Oman) Dhofar's ancient trading ports and caravan routes connected with the precious sap.

Bat and Al-Ayn (Oman) Pre-Islamic burial sites.

Aflaj (Oman) Ancient irrigation system.

Madain Saleh (Saudi Arabia) Nabataean outpost in the middle of a sandstone desert.

Dir'aiyah (Saudi Arabia) Ancient ruins on the outskirts of Riyadh.

Al-Ain (UAE) Cultural sites associated with the famous oasis.

Shibam (Yemen) Old walled city.

Zabid (Yemen) Ancient walled city.

Socotra (Yemen) Home to endemic species.

Best to Avoid

Left hand Use the right hand when eating with locals, shaking hands and passing gifts.

Feet Tuck the offending soles under you when sitting on the floor.

Shoes Remove them before entering a mosque or someone's home.

Too much flesh Cover shoulders and knees in all public places.

Now that a flavour of democracy is enjoyed in greater representation on national assemblies, for example, perhaps the old social contract built on traditional authority rather than on public opinion will, as Kaplan predicts, simply 'peter out as...society advances'.

Current Challenges

In foreign politics, the insurgency in Yemen, an Al-Qaeda stronghold, threatens to provoke Saudi into conflict, as competing ideologies battle for a foothold in the only impoverished corner of the Peninsula. In domestic politics, the Arab Spring uprisings still grumble on in Bahrain and Kuwait and people have become less tolerant if change does not favour their vision of the future.

In the economy, all countries across the region are scared, not so much that oil reserves have reached their peak, but that new methods of extraction are reconfiguring the market. This has placed a much greater emphasis on diversification, building up industries such as trade and commerce, benefited by the Peninsula's location as a hub between East and West. Tourism is another area of prime emphasis, albeit hampered by security concerns in neighbouring countries such as Egypt, Iraq and Syria.

One of the biggest challenges is the process of swapping to an indigenous workforce. It takes time for the benefits of a modernised education system to produce home-grown expertise and there is resistance from some immigrant communities to train their local replacements. Without progress in the human resource development of the region, however, there is concern that a two-tier society will inevitably lead to further resentment and instability.

Balancing the Future

Peninsula Arabs have encountered the shock of the new, anger at the passing of valued traditions, and the rejection of external pressures, and the familiar cycle has concluded with a general acceptance of modernisation. The process will only be complete, however, when each country finds a way in which to honour its heritage and give a greater sense of inclusion to its citizens. The establishment of *majlis ashura* (public representation) in public policy is a good start and the inclusion of women as they join the ranks of government ministers (except in Saudi) is also viewed favourably. Propelled ahead of male colleagues by a proven propensity for education and with less commitment to *wusta* (nepotism), Arabia's women are seen as the change agents of the future.

There is one anchor in this fomenting region that has attracted academics, enthralled creative minds, enriched Western study of mathematics, medicine and literature for centuries, and that is Islam. TE Lawrence summed up the spiritual core of the Peninsula thus: 'It is the old, old civilisation, which has refined itself clear of household gods and half the trappings which ours hastens to assume.' It will be interesting to see to what extent that spiritual core can withstand the conflicting pressures of a global, internet age.

History

Sixty years ago the countries of the Arabian Peninsula were a collection of impoverished, disparate states, more easily defined by tribe than by nation. Any sense of the former glory days of incense routes and East African empires was lost in the sands of time. So how did the region suddenly reinvent itself as a major economic powerhouse with a strong sense of regional identity? This chapter answers that question by looking at the region's inheritance of trading excellence and social coherence.

Tropical Roots (66,000,000–10,000 BC)

Stand in the middle of Wadi Fanja on the outskirts of Muscat and you may just uncover more than the toads and grasshoppers of today's arid vista. This was where archaeologists discovered a herbivorous dinosaur, not unlike Zalmoxes or Rhabdodon dinosaurs from France and Romania. What is interesting about this discovery is that it shows that the climate of eastern Arabia, some 66 million years ago, was far more verdant than it is today, with savannah-like grasslands and abundant rainfall. Crocodiles also inhabited places like Wadi Fanja, suggesting that permanent rivers helped to cut the deeply incised mountain ranges of today's Peninsula.

Homo erectus was attracted to the rich hunting and gathering grounds of southern Arabia more than a million years ago. Homo sapiens arrived on the scene around 100,000 BC and began more organised settlement. Visitors to museums across the region, particularly the National Museum in Bahrain and Bait al-Baranda in Muscat, will see charcoal burners and spearheads, dating from 10,000 BC, as evidence of the earliest forms of social cohesion.

Born to Trade (10,000 BC–AD 500)

Visit any souq across the Peninsula, or attend any meeting between doctor and patient, teacher and pupil, and you will realise instantly that rules and regulations are fluid, negotiable entities to be haggled over, argued about and artfully manipulated. Perhaps this is because trade runs through the blood of Peninsula peoples, shaping modern daily interac-

Travel to the museums of Pakistan and the Mediterranean and you'll be sure to find the small round seals that were the hallmark of Dilmun traders. These seals represented their personal signatures and their wide distribution is evidence of the extent of their trading influence, far beyond the Arabian Peninsula.

TIMELINE	c 66,000,000 BC	c 100,000 BC	6000–3200 BC
	Unlike the deserts of modern Arabia, the Peninsula is covered in savannah-like grasslands, rainfall is abundant and permanent rivers are home to crocodiles and herbivorous dinosaurs.	Homo sapiens live a hunter-gatherer life across the Peninsula, burning fires and rearing their own livestock. They form the first organised communities in the region.	Loose groups of Stone Age and Bronze Age individuals occupy the Peninsula, setting up intricate trade routes between Arabia and Mesopotamia (Iraq) and the Indus Valley.

tions as it has shaped each country's ancient heritage. Not surprisingly, then, trade informed the very earliest aspects of the region's history.

Copper was where it all began. It was mined in Majan (the ancient name of Oman) and traded through the mighty Dilmun Empire. It's easy to simplify the lives of the ancients, but the early seafaring traders of Dilmun were no barbarians: they spent their mineral wealth on fine glass; ate too many dates and suffered bad teeth; took the time to thread beads of carnelian to hang round their beloveds' necks; enjoyed complex legends; and expressed their interest in life through their administrations of death – much like their contemporaries in Egypt.

The Peninsula's early wealth wasn't founded on ore alone, however. It was due in large part to a tree, and a particularly ugly one at that. Frankincense, the aromatic resin of the Boswellia sacra tree, was the chief export and economic mainstay of the region. Grown in southern Arabia and carried by caravan across the great deserts of the interior along time-worn trading routes, it helped fund the mighty Nabataean civilisation that controlled much of northwestern Arabia from 200 to 100 BC. Its sacred sap sustained entire empires across the Peninsula, found its way into the inner sanctum of temples in Egypt, Jerusalem and Rome, is recorded in the Bible and the Quran, and is used to this day in many of the world's most sacred ceremonies. According to Pliny, writing in the 1st century AD, it was thanks to the frankincense trade that the people of southern Arabia became the richest people on Earth.

Visit Madain Saleh in Saudi Arabia today – where the Nabataeans carved spectacular tombs into the desert cliffs, similar to those of their capital Petra (Jordan) – and it's easy to understand that frankincense was no ordinary trade: it touched the soul. Indeed, for over 5000 years frankincense (which to this day is used in religious ritual and all special ceremonies of an Arabian home) made southern Arabia not just one of the richest regions of the ancient world, but also a land presumed to be touched by magic.

Tradition dictates that the tree is a gift from Allah, and is thus not to be propagated, bought or sold, only harvested if it happens to be within your plot of land. Needless to say, that hasn't stopped people from trying. In an attempt to protect their precious resources, the Jibbali, descendants of the ancient people of Ad, honed the art of misinformation. Flying red serpents and toxic mists were just some of the mythical tribulations rumoured to protect groves from evil eye and thieving hand. Gathering the aromatic gum was similarly fraught with danger. The collectors were often slaves or those banished to the area as punishment. They fell sick from deadly infections indigenous to the area and life beyond the monsoon catchment was a wickedly harsh affair.

The Queen of Sheba is fabled to have laid frankincense at the feet of King Solomon and the three wise men took it to Jerusalem. According to Pliny, only 3000 families had the right of harvesting frankincense – but with exclusions: men were forbidden to cut trees after contact with women.

c 3000 BC	3000–2000 BC	323 BC	c 200 BC–AD 100
Dilmun, the first great civilisation in the Peninsula, is founded off the coast of Bahrain; it extends from Failaka Island (near present-day Kuwait) towards the hills of Oman.	In Oman, tombs at Bat and Gaylah are erected along mountain ridges by the Hafit and the Umm an Nar cultures – people belonging to the low-lying territories of the Gulf.	Alexander the Great, attracted to Arabia's wealth, dies leaving his plan to mount an expedition to the region unfulfilled. His admiral, Nearchus, establishes an important trading colony on Failaka Island.	The Nabataean Empire controls northwestern Arabia and grows rich by taxing frankincense caravans travelling between southern Arabia and Damascus. Much of the Gulf comes under the influence of Persian dynasties.

The Incense Route

The trade was centred on Sumhuram, which the Greeks called Moscha and which is now known as Khor Rouri. Today the ruins of this once-great port are a short drive from Salalah, the capital of Dhofar and the second-largest city in modern Oman. Looking out to sea on a wet and windy day in July, when the grazing camels and flamingos shelter in the upper reaches of the lagoon and leave the violent shore to the ghost crabs, it's little wonder that easier ports would eventually be found for readier cargo, and Khor Rouri left to slip back to nature.

The Birth and Growth of Islam (AD 570–1498)

Given that today one out of every four people are Muslim, there can be no greater moment of historical importance on the Arabian Peninsula than the birth of the Prophet Mohammed in the year AD 570.

As one of the world's most influential spiritual leaders, it is easy to focus on Mohammed's teachings and forget his historical context, but in many ways the limited descriptions of his childhood give a good indication of life in the desert at that time. As his father died before he was born, Mohammed became the poor ward of his grandfather. Although his family were settled Arabs, he was given to a Bedouin foster mother, as

Staying in religious schools to avoid expensive hostelries, 14th-century Muslim pilgrim Ibn Battuta set the standard for budget travelling. Intending to perform hajj at the age of 20, his 'gap year' lasted 24 years. He clocked up an impressive 120,000km in Arabia and Asia, far out-travelling his contemporary, Marco Polo.

c 300	570	610	622–632
Central and western Arabia develop into a patchwork of independent city-states, sustained either by the frankincense trade or by farming, while the Gulf is subsumed into the Sassanian empire from Persia.	The Ma'rib dam, upon which the livelihoods of 50,000 people depend, bursts its banks, scattering the people of Adz in the Peninsula's most significant migration. Prophet Mohammed is born.	Mohammed receives his first revelation. Considered by Muslims as the word of God, the Quran subsequently lays the foundations of a new, monotheistic religion that condemns the worship of idols.	Mohammed and his followers flee Mecca for Medina in 622, marking the beginning of the first Islamic state. The new religion spreads across the Peninsula, despite Mohammed's death in 632.

was the custom at the time, to be raised in the desert. Perhaps it was this experience that gave him a sense of moderation and the preciousness of resources. In the desert, too, there were no intermediaries, no priests and no prescribed places of worship – nothing separating the people from the things that they believed in.

Mohammed went on caravans and became a trusted trader before returning to Mecca, which at that time was a large and prosperous city that profited from being the centre of pilgrimage. Mecca was the home of the Kaaba, a sanctuary founded by Abraham but occupied by the images and idols of many other tribes and nations.

The worship of the one-true god and the condemnation of idols was at the heart of Mohammed's teaching and inevitably the Meccans took fright, forcing Mohammed to flee to Medina in 622. Mohammed's mighty legacy, however, transcended his personal history and the new religion of Islam quickly spread across the Peninsula and to the world beyond. Ironically, as the Islamic empire expanded, so the fortunes of Arabia waned, but to this day the Peninsula holds a special place in history as the birthplace of one of the world's great monotheistic religions.

The Europeans Arrive (1498–1650)

There is something satisfying about standing under the Tomb of Bibi Miriam in Qalhat, Oman, knowing that two of the world's great medieval travellers, Marco Polo and Ibn Battuta, stood there too. Their travels prefigured a revival in Western trading interests in Arabia and it wasn't long before the pilgrim caravans of Mecca were once again transporting spices and drugs from the Orient to Europe via the ports of Istanbul and Venice.

Meanwhile, a great Omani seafarer, Ahmed bin Majid, helped Vasco da Gama navigate the Cape of Good Hope in 1498 and, in good faith, told him of his own wondrous country on the Straits of Hormuz. The Portuguese quickly understood the strategic significance of their 'discovery' and by 1507 Portugal had annexed the Yemeni island of Suqutra (Socotra), occupied Oman and colonised Bahrain. Travel along the coast of the Gulf today and Portuguese forts appear with regularity: cut inland, and there's no trace of them. The Portuguese were only interested in protecting their trade routes and made no impact on the interior of these countries at all – a suitable metaphor for the negligible cultural exchange that took place. When they were eventually ousted by the mid-17th century, they left not much more than a legacy of military architecture – and the Maria Theresa dollar.

British 'Protection' (1650–1914)

'One great distinguishing feature of Muscat,' wrote the English diplomat James Silk Buckingham in 1816, 'is the respect and civility shown by all

---

Books:
Early
History

Arabia & the Arabs: From the Bronze Age to the Coming of Islam (Robert Hoyland)

Frankincense & Myrrh (Nigel Groom)

Famed 19th-century traveller Richard Burton learnt Arabic and entered Mecca disguised as a hajja (pilgrim). Nicknamed 'Ruffian Dick' by his contemporaries for his waywardness, he was obliged in his *Personal Narrative of a Pilgrimage to Al-Madinah and Meccah* to make his 'love of adventure minister to the advance of geographical science'.

632–850	850–1300	1498	1507
The Muslim capital moves to Damascus, heading an empire from Spain to India. Mecca and Medina lose their earlier political importance but grow as the spiritual homes of Islam.	Arabia's old trade routes collapse and the Peninsula declines in wealth and importance. Petty sheikhdoms bicker over limited resources, under the control of Tartar moguls, Persians and Ottoman Turks	In a generous but ominous gesture, a celebrated sailor from Oman, Ahmed bin Majid, helps Vasco da Gama navigate the Cape of Good Hope, leading a decade later to occupation.	Portugal annexes the Yemeni island of Suqutra (Socotra). It uses this vantage point to complete an occupation of Oman and goes on to colonise Bahrain.

classes of its inhabitants to Europeans'. It is an interesting comment because it appears to show that the intimate British involvement with Oman and the 'Trucial States', (the countries along the southern rim of the Gulf) over the next two centuries was founded on mutual benefit rather than solely on colonisation and exploitation. On the one hand, the various treaties and 'exclusive agreements' that Britain signed with the sultan and emirs of the region kept the French at bay and thereby safeguarded British trading routes with India. On the other hand, the British helped maintain the claims to sovereignty of the emerging Gulf emirates against marauding Turkish and Persian interests and from the powerful ambitions of the eventual founder of Saudi Arabia, Ibn Saud.

During WWI, British interests in the Gulf were threatened by the Ottomans. The sultan, siding with the Germans, declared jihad (holy war), calling on Muslims everywhere to rise up against the Allied powers of

HISTORY BRITISH 'PROTECTION' (650–1914)

THE FRANKINCENSE TREE

Drive along the road from Salalah to the Yemeni border, and you may be forgiven for missing one of the most important aspects of the Arabian Peninsula's history. Sprouting from the limestone rock as if mindless of the lack of nutrition, leafless and (for much of the year) pretty much lifeless, *Boswellia sacra* must be one of the least spectacular 'monuments' on a traveller's itinerary. Indeed, with its peeling bark and stumped branches, the frankincense tree looks more like something out of *The Day of the Triffids* than a tree that established the early fortunes of the region.

What makes the tree so special, of course, is its aromatic sap, known as 'lubban' in Arabic or 'frankincense' in English. The sap oozes in white- or amber-coloured beads from incisions made in the bark and is left to harden in the sun. Frankincense has a natural oil content, allowing it to burn well, and the vapour is released by dropping a bead of the sap onto hot embers.

To this day, the pungent aroma is used locally with great enthusiasm, wafted at the entrance of a house to ward away evil spirits or to perfume garments. It has other traditional uses too. The sap has medicinal qualities and was used in just about every prescription dispensed by the Greeks and the Romans. It is still used in parts of the Peninsula to treat a wide range of illnesses, including coughs and psychotic disorders, believed to be the result of witchcraft. Internationally, frankincense remains a part of many (particularly Christian) religious rites and is included as an ingredient in exotic perfumes.

Although the frankincense tree grows in Wadi Hadramawt in Yemen as well as in northern Somalia, the specimens of Dhofar in southern Oman have been famed since ancient times for producing the finest-quality sap. The tree favours the unique weather system of this corner of southern Arabia, just beyond the moisture-laden winds of the *khareef* (summer season) but near enough to enjoy their cooling influence. As such it is notoriously difficult to root elsewhere.

1902	1912	1916	1932
In 1902 Abdul Aziz bin Abdul Rahman al-Saud, known as Ibn Saud, begins a series of conquests which eventually leads to the formation of the state of Saudi Arabia.	The Saudis pose a serious threat to the Gulf sheikhdoms. British protection saves Kuwait, Qatar and the UAE from being subsumed into Saudi Arabia.	Hussein leads an Arab revolt against the Ottomans in anticipation of being crowned 'King of the Arabs'. The British sign the Balfour Declaration instead, favouring the establishment of Israel.	Ibn Saud combines the two crowns of Hejaz and Najd, renaming his country the 'Kingdom of Saudi Arabia'. In the same year, oil is struck in commercial quantities in Bahrain.

Britain, France and Russia. In response, the British persuaded Hussein bin Ali, the Grand Sherif of Mecca, to lead an Arab revolt against the Ottomans in exchange for a promise to make him 'King of the Arabs' once the conflict was over. To the famous disgust of British army officer TE Lawrence, the British negotiated with the French on the carving up of the Ottoman Empire and assisted the Zionist movement instead.

Despite this monumental sell-out, visit any corner of the Arabian Peninsula today and you are bound to meet a pink-faced Brit, basking in the desert sun. Equally, talk to leaders across the region and chances are they were educated in part in the UK. The special relationship between the British and the Arabs of the Peninsula has endured the trials and tribulations of history, and is one of the positive legacies of 19th-century colonialism.

The American journalist Lydell Hart made 'El-Lawrence' into a media superhero. The *Sunday Times* of June 1968 hailed Lawrence as a 'Prince of Mecca, riding across Arabia'. Hollywood did the rest.

The Pearling Industry (1914–1930)

One of the mixed pleasures of visiting a Gulf jewellery shop is to hold a natural pearl in the palm of one's hand and see reflected in its gorgeous lustre the not so illustrious history of the region.

Although pearls have come to be associated with Bahrain, they were harvested throughout the Gulf – many cities, including Salalah, Doha and until recently Manama, have famous modern monuments commemorating the lost industry. Each region gave rise to a specific type of pearl. Pteria shells, or winged oysters, were extensively collected for their bluish mother-of-pearl off the coast of Ras al-Khaimah. The large shells known in the trade as 'Bombay Shells' were found in Omani waters and chiefly exported to London for pearl inlay and decorative cutlery. With an annual export of 2000 tonnes, worth UK£750,000, the most common pearl oyster of the Gulf was Pinctada radiata, collected off the coasts of Kuwait, Bahrain and the UAE.

The pearling season began each year in late May. Fishermen remained at sea, through the blistering summer, without interruption until mid-October. Supplies were ferried out by dhow.

Given the volume of the trade, it is not surprising that it supported the local economies of much of the Gulf. Trading in pearls has existed since the 3rd millennium BC but it was only in the 19th century, with the collapse of other trade routes in the region, that pearls assumed their economic value. In the 1920s, with what seemed like an insatiable international appetite for pearls, the trade reached its apex.

Pearling was brutally hard work. Workers were divided into divers (who descended for the shells with a weight between their feet) and pullers (who would hoist the divers back up again by rope). Neither were paid wages. Instead, they would receive a share of the total profits for the season. A puller's share was half to two-thirds of a diver's. Boat owners would usually advance money to their workers at the beginning of the season. But the divers were often unable to pay back these loans

1948	1960	1961–71	1973
The 'Gulf rupee' replaces the Indian rupee as the common currency of all Gulf States, reflecting a shift away from the jurisdiction of the British Raj after India's independence.	The Middle East produces 25% of the non-Communist world's oil. The 1960s bring the winds of change and hand-in-hand with independence comes a sense of national and regional identity.	In 1961 Kuwait gains independence from Britain. In late 1971 Bahrain and Qatar follow suit followed by the sheikhdoms of the lower Gulf which combine to form the United Arab Emirates.	The Gulf States embargo of oil to the West – the 'oil weapon' – is first used to powerful effect during the Arab-Israeli War to protest against the West's support for Israel.

LAWRENCE OF ARABIA

If there is one name in Arab history that most Western people will recognise, it's surely that of TE Lawrence, better known as Lawrence of Arabia – the same Lawrence, in fact, who wrote to his sceptical biographer that 'history isn't made up of the truth anyhow, so why worry'. This is an interesting question when it comes to the history of the Arabian Peninsula as there appears to be no definitive version of events. The story assumes a different shape – particularly since the beginning of the 20th century – according to whose account you read.

Lawrence's own account of Arabian history, so eloquently described in *The Seven Pillars of Wisdom,* is a case in point. You might imagine, from what he writes, that Lawrence and General Allenby, the senior British Officer responsible for the Arab Campaign, single-handedly brought the modern Arabian Peninsula into being during the Arab Revolt from 1915 to 1918: 'On my plan, by my effort,' he states triumphantly on the taking of Aqaba.

But where are the Arabs in Lawrence's account? What did they make of the pale-skinned, blue-eyed eccentric? Read Suleiman Mousa's account of the campaign in *TE Lawrence: An Arab View* and you barely recognise the same moment in history: while Lawrence is busy taking credit for little skirmishes, larger battles led by the Arabs are only briefly mentioned; Lawrence arrives triumphant in cities where Arab leaders Feisal and Auda have been waiting for days. Far from the great white hunter, he is remembered in many Arab accounts as a sickly individual with boils who, like a spoof in a Western, mistakenly shot his own camel. But then such is history from an *Arab* perspective.

We'll never know whether Lawrence was centre-stage or sideshow. What the example illustrates, however, is the caution with which you need to approach the history of the Peninsula. In the early 21st century, this must surely sound familiar to anyone following current events in the region in local and Western media. It's tempting to agree with Lawrence that history can at times be more about fiction than fact.

and got further into debt each year. As a result they were often bound to a particular boat owner for life. If a diver died, his sons were obliged to work off his debts. It was not unusual to see quite elderly men still working as divers.

Suddenly, around 1930, the unthinkable happened. The Japanese invented a method of culturing pearls. This, combined with the Great Depression, caused the bottom to drop out of the international pearl market. The Peninsula's great pearling industry petered out almost overnight; although the collapse brought great hardship to the Gulf in the decades before the discovery of oil, few had the heart to regret it.

1981	1990	1991	2006
In May, Saudi Arabia, Kuwait, Bahrain, Qatar, the UAE and Oman form the Gulf Cooperation Council (GCC) to increase economic cooperation and in response to the perceived threat from Iran.	In August, Iraq invades Kuwait and annexes the state. King Fahd of Saudi Arabia appeals to the US for help and the US and Allied forces launch Operation Desert Storm.	Yemen makes regional history by becoming the first multiparty democracy on the Arabian Peninsula after the reunification of the country in the previous year.	The Asian Games are hosted in Doha – a coup for Qatar and the region as a whole. Oman pulls out of the proposed single currency, a setback for greater GCC integration.

Impact of Oil and Modernisation (1930–2010)

Books: Modern Regional History

Inside Al Qaeda: Global Network of Terror (Rohan Gunaratna)

A History of the Middle East (Peter Mansfield)

Among the Gulf's Arab rulers, interest in diversifying the economy to include oil was spurred on by the collapse, around 1930, of the pearling industry, which for centuries had been the mainstay of the Gulf's economy.

Early in the 20th century, a rare resource was discovered on the Peninsula that was to change the face of the region forever. It is upon this resource that the super-modern cities of the Gulf have been crafted out of the sea on reclaimed land, and upon which the nations of Arabia have been pulled by the sandal-straps into the 21st century.

Within a few years almost every ruler in the Gulf had given some kind of oil concession in an attempt to bolster their finances. The region's nascent industry was suspended temporarily during WWII but resumed soon after, increasing output to rival that of Iran, the world's biggest producer by 1960.

In the 1960s and '70s the new wealth, and the threat of cutting off oil supplies to Europe and the US, gave Middle Eastern countries an international influence they hadn't enjoyed for centuries. After each embargo, a surge in oil prices increased both their wealth and their power, triggering the first wave of an enormous building boom in the Gulf that has continued almost unabated for half a century. Western expatriates flocked to the region, providing engineering and financial expertise while hundreds of thousands of Asian expats were brought in as manual labour. This change in demographics has left a legacy which continues to have profound effects on the indigenous populations: on the one hand it has resulted in tolerant, multicultural societies and greatly enhanced infrastructure; on the other hand, it has led to an outnumbering in some countries of the indigenous Arab population and a difficulty in all countries (bar Yemen) of ensuring work opportunities for locals.

When the bottom fell out of the oil market in 1985, to varying degrees all Gulf countries had trouble keeping up their building programs while maintaining the generous welfare states that their people had come to expect. This crisis, together with ongoing fears about reaching peak production, and the shock factor of the global economic downturn that began in 2008, have had hidden benefits, however, forcing each country of the Gulf Cooperation Council (GCC) to diversify its economy.

But the days of black gold are not over yet. Exploration continues across the region together with investment in research into ever more sophisticated ways of extraction such as fracking. Despite the new hunt for renewable energies such as solar, wind, wave and waste-to-energy power, it's unlikely that any of these green technologies will replace oil in the collective memory of the region. Oil, after all, has given Arabia back its place in the world.

2007	2008	2009	2011
The building boom across the Peninsula reaches its peak as multibillion dollar projects, just about unthinkable elsewhere in the world, reach fruition in all countries of the Peninsula except Yemen.	The global recession starts to bite in the Arabian Peninsula with catastrophic effect in Dubai by 2009. Qatar and Oman remain relatively unscathed.	An escalation of civil war in Yemen makes regional headlines as the bombing of so-called Yemeni rebels on Saudi Arabian territory threatens to destabilise an otherwise peaceful Peninsula.	The Arab Spring erupts, leaving Bahrain in particular in turmoil. Peninsula governments crack down on corruption and review their policies to quell the restiveness of local populations.

The Culture

'The manners of mankind,' wrote the 18th-century British traveller Lady Wortley Montagu, 'do not differ so widely as our voyage writers would make us believe'. Her account of Arabs in the 18th century, however, was a disappointment to her contemporaries who had hoped to read about wild Islamic fundamentalists and dusky-eyed maidens. It is easy to focus on the elements of difference between cultures, but the more one travels in Arab lands, it's the similarities that prove more persuasive.

People

The Western stereotype of the male Peninsula inhabitant has changed over the last century. Where once he was characterised as gaunt, austere in habit and fierce of temper, he's now portrayed as rich and extravagant; invariably overweight; an owner of camels, multiple wives, many children and several cars – in that order – and robed in sheet and teacloth. Male youths are portrayed as wiry and neurotic, wearing Semtex vests. Women only feature in relation to the *hijab* (veil) debate and in cartoons they appear as indefinable black shapes.

These stereotypes are thankfully being exposed for what they are by the growing multiculturalism of many Western communities and the greater exposure to Arab 'customs and manners' through the media. Nonetheless, it's worth investigating to what extent any of these stereotypes retain a grain of truth.

Guests are usually seen to the door, or even to the end of the corridor or garden. Traditionally this represents the safe passage of guests across your tribal territory. If you have Arab visitors, make sure you do the same!

Lifestyle

Drive through the suburbs of Peninsula cities and you'll see domed villas with spangled concrete that glistens in the sun. Walk through the gold souqs and you'll see women with Gucci handbags, buying diamonds and pearls. Park outside the Ritz-Carlton in Manama or the Burj al-Arab in Dubai and you'll be embarrassed to be driving a Toyota Echo. Undoubtedly, huge private fortunes have been made in the oil rush and building expansion.

But that isn't the whole picture. Universal education and the mass media have increased expectations, and people who were content with one floor now want two. Cement and steel prices have doubled in a decade and the burgeoning Arab 'middle class' frets over securing loans to finish the house. If shopping before pay day is anything to go by, most families are left with little at the end of the month.

The rest of the picture is completed by stepping out of the city altogether. Lives in mountain villages, in desert oases, on the dunes or in coastal fishing villages may seem to have been little impacted by city incomes, but then you spot the satellite dish attached to the *barasti* (palm frond) walls; the electricity poles marching up the wadis; the communally owned truck that has allowed settlement to replace nomadic existence. Water, electricity, roads, education and healthcare: this is the real wealth of the region today and it is remarkably evenly spread given the challenges of geography and topography.

Health & Life Expectancy

A more modern lifestyle, be it in the city or the interior, has brought changes to the health of many Peninsula people. Not all those changes are for the better.

Local epidemiologists identify that the disproportionately high incidence of diabetes in the region has grown out of the continuation of a traditional diet (where dates and sweetmeats like *halwa* play an inextricable role in matters of hospitality), combined with an increase in popularity of a newly imported fast-food culture, high in sugar and salt content. Add to this considerably less exercise in the newly urbanised lives of many Peninsula Arabs and it's easy to see the severe challenge faced by healthcare systems across the region (with the possible exception of Yemen).

But it's not all doom and gloom! Wander the terraces of southern Arabia 20 years ago, and you'd see women bent double in the fields, baked by the sun, arthritic in the mud, or weighed down with herbage, trudging back to their homes, pausing to stack stones in the crumbling terrace walls. For many of the Peninsula inhabitants, it's pointless being nostalgic about the demise of hard manual labour, even if a modern lifestyle comes at the price of 'modern' diseases such as hypertension.

The statistics regarding diabetes in Arabia are alarming: five of the 10 countries with the world's highest rates of diabetes are in the Peninsula, namely the United Arab Emirates, Qatar, Bahrain, Kuwait and Saudi Arabia.

Population & Ethnic Diversity

In the Gulf, names are all important. Names tell a lot about who is from where, and each country is acutely mindful of such distinctions: 'with a name like that, he must be a Baluchi (not real Emirati); he speaks Swahili so he must be Zanzibari (not real Omani); he's from the coast (not real Yemeni)'. And so it goes on until you wonder if there's any such thing as a 'real anybody'. Such gossiping about ethnicity makes you realise that Arab allegiances are linked to tribe before nation.

Centuries of trading and pilgrimage have resulted in an extraordinarily mixed population and only a few pockets of people, such as the Jibbalis of southern Oman – the descendents of the ancient people of Ad – or Jews in the northern parts of Yemen, can claim ethnic 'purity'.

Oddly, for the visitor, it is not always Arabs you'll notice much anyway. The indigenous population of the entire Peninsula numbers less than 50 million out of a total population of 78 million. In Saudi and Oman non-nationals account for 10% and 15% respectively of the population but this figure rises to 25% in Yemen, 55% in Bahrain, 66% in Kuwait, 80% in Qatar and 81% in UAE.

The large presence of other nationals on the Peninsula came about after the discovery of oil. Hundreds of thousands of expatriate workers were brought in to help develop the region's industries, and provide skills and knowledge in creating a modern infrastructure. Although none of these nationals were originally permitted citizenship, many have stayed a lifetime and set up businesses under local sponsorship, changing the demographics of the entire Peninsula.

The issue now is how to reduce the dependence on expat labour and train the local population to fill their place: inevitably, few expats willingly train locals to take over their jobs. Equally, in some of the wealthier Gulf countries, there is a reluctance from locals to take on manual labour and a distaste for jobs in the service industry.

For a seminal read on the subject of Western perceptions of the Arabic Orient, Edward Said's *Orientalism* is the definitive text. In this compelling deconstruction of Western stereotypes regarding Arabia, Said famously defines the West's contrary relationship with the Middle East as one of 'otherness'.

Bedouin Roots

It's easy to underestimate the Bedouin heritage of Arab society if your visit is concentrated on the big cities of the Gulf. Yet even here there are weekend escapes to the desert (in Oman), a new falcon souq (in Doha), and tents set up outside the house (in Kuwait). These are all indicative of a strong attachment to an ancient culture that runs through all the countries of the Peninsula.

The attitude towards the camel is an interesting case in point. The donkey played just as important a role in transportation in the mountains of the Peninsula, but no one breeds donkeys for fun. Camels, on the other hand, are as prevalent as ever and in some corners of Arabia (such as Dhofar) are proliferating at such a speed (due to their leisurely modern lifestyle), they are threatening the fragile ecology of their habitat. Of course, racing has something to do with the obsession with camel ownership, but the animal is more deeply involved in the Arab psyche than mere racing. Camels evoke ancient nomadic lifestyles, the symbol of community through hardship and endurance – the inheritance, in short, of Bedouin roots.

The term 'Bedu' (Bedouin in singular and adjectival form) refers not so much to an ethnic group as to a lifestyle. Accounting for their appeal to Western imaginations in the 18th century, the Danish explorer Niebuhr claimed that man is 'fond even of the very shadow of that liberty, independence, and simplicity which he has lost by refinement'. City Arabs today, stressed by familiar modern anxieties regarding wealth and how to keep it, are similarly wistful about a bygone era, even if they are more likely to be the descendants of townspeople and seafarers.

> **Encounter the Bedu in…**
>
> Sharqiya Sands, Oman
> ....
> Khor al-Adaid, Qatar
> ....
> Interior, Kuwait
> ....
> Rub al-Khali, Saudi Arabia, Oman & UAE

Marriage & the Role of Women

Islam allows men to have four wives, but only if a man can treat each equally. In reality, there are few Peninsula Arabs who can afford the luxury of two houses, two sets of gold, two extended families of in-laws – let alone four. Nor, with the greater demands of the modern workplace, can many aspire to satisfying more than one partner in equal share – though only wives will let you in on this secret.

And it's not just about expense either. While law permits a man four wives, even two centuries ago no 'man of quality' would make use of this and no 'woman of rank' would suffer it. In fact, Peninsula women are far more empowered than might be supposed, and they don't like sharing their husband and his income any more than Western women. If the

---

THE MODERN BEDOUIN

Most Bedu have modernised their existence with 4WD trucks (it's not unusual to find the camel travelling by truck these days), fodder from town (limiting the need to keep moving), and purified water from bowsers. Some have mobile phones and satellite TV, and most listen to the radio. Many no longer move at all. Bedouin customs, dating from the earliest days of Islam, remain pretty much unchanged, however – especially their legendary hospitality towards strangers.

Living arrangements tend to stay the same too with tents generally divided into a haram (forbidden area) for women and an area reserved for the men. The men's section also serves as the public part of the house, where guests are treated to coffee and dates, or meals. It's here that all the news and gossip – a crucial part of successful survival in a hostile environment – is passed along the grapevine.

The Bedouin family is a close-knit unit. The women do most of the domestic work, including fetching water (sometimes requiring walks of many kilometres), baking bread and weaving. They are also often the first to help pull, dig and drive a tourist's stuck 4WD out of the soft sand. The men are traditionally the providers in times of peace, and fierce warriors in times of war. Though most Bedu are more peaceful these days, warring still goes on in northern parts of Yemen and border incursions are not unusual in the Empty Quarter.

EXPAT PECKING ORDER

Though officially treated equally, there's clearly a pecking order among the Peninsula's expats. At the top of the order are the Westerners. For the hundreds of thousands of Western expats, life is a tax-free merry-go-round, usually with rent and annual airfare home included in generous packages. The life, at least in the big Gulf cities, includes sun, sea, sand and a good social life in a lifestyle few could afford back home.

Next come the middle-income workers from other Middle Eastern countries. Their first and foremost preoccupation is to save money. Typically these expats stay just long enough to stockpile enough dollars to build a house back home and send their children to college. In some countries, such as Egypt, Jordan and Yemen, remittances from nationals working abroad constitute the backbone of the economy.

Languishing at the bottom are the labourers from India, Pakistan and Bangladesh. While a minority (around 5% to 10%) enjoy a standard of living similar to the Western and Peninsula communities, the majority are manual labourers. Conditions for migrant workers in the Gulf states have been condemned by Human Rights organisations such as Amnesty International and Human Rights Watch. For male migrant workers, conditions include digging roads in 45°C heat or working on building sites that lack safety provisions. Women employed as domestic servants are often required to work long hours for wages much lower than those paid to nationals of the Gulf states. Despite these conditions, a single labourer may be able to support his entire extended family in his home country from his monthly pay packet. Some Asians remain on the Peninsula for up to 20 years, only seeing their families for two months once every two years. Recognising the problem of hardship among many members of the Asian expat community, GCC labour ministers are due to meet in 2013 to discuss a standardised employment contract designed to protect migrant workers' rights.

wife doesn't like something, she can and often does make the man's life a misery and, as controller of the household, often co-opts the children into her camp. Divorce is easily enacted and is becoming less of a taboo, especially in Oman and the Gulf countries, because women will put up with less these days. Modern Peninsula women are educated, usually far harder working at college than men and therefore often more successful in the workplace. They are entitled to earn and keep their own income (unlike the man who surrenders his salary to the household) and as such have an independence unthinkable by their grandmothers.

Or was it ever thus? 'The Europeans are mistaken in thinking the state of marriage so different among the Mussulmans from what it is with Christian nations,' wrote Niebuhr in the 18th century. 'Arabian women enjoy a great deal of liberty, and often a great deal of power, in their families'.

It's hard to imagine women letting go of their tight-knit sisterhood, but now that they also want a slice of the man's traditional role too, something's got to give. It is partly recognition of this fact that has led to such heated internal debate among Arab women across the region. On the one hand, discussion in Saudi Arabia focuses on fundamental women's rights – to vote, to drive, to travel unescorted by male relatives, to represent and be represented in a public forum. On the other hand, in UAE and Oman (where equality of education has led to an equality of expectation), it focuses on issues familiar to a Western context such as breaking through the glass ceiling, how to train in traditionally male-oriented disciplines like engineering but still be able to pick and choose over shift hours or working on site.

With more women graduating from some of the top universities across the region than men, inevitably questions are being asked about primary carers in the family and the psychological fall-out on men whose

Rural Peninsula families comprise an average of six children. Children were traditionally seen as a resource, not an expense – another pair of hands to work the land or provide support in old age. For many they are now seen as a status symbol of both wealth and fertility.

once unquestioned authority is being undermined by poor performance relative to their female counterparts.

Family Size & Welfare

The family, guided by Muslim principles, is still at the centre of the Arab way of life. The family is an extended unit often comprising whole villages, united around a common tribal name. Avoiding actions that may bring shame to the family is of paramount importance. Saving face is therefore more than a reluctance to admit a mistake – it's an expression of unwillingness to make a family vulnerable to criticism. Equally, promotion or success is not calculated in individual terms, but in the benefits it bestows on the family. Of course, everyone knows someone who can help in the collective good, and accruing *wusta* (influence) is a Peninsula pastime.

The efforts of one generation are reflected in the provision of education and opportunity for the next. This comes at a cost and few Arabs these days can afford the large families of up to 12 children of a decade ago; indeed the average is now around 3.3 children.

The governments of each country have made generous provision for families across the region – in terms of free education and healthcare – but the resources won't last forever and the younger generation are beginning to see that they have to work hard to secure the same opportunities for their children.

Travel & Pilgrimage

When tax is minimal and petrol cheaper than bottled water, owning a car or two isn't the extravagance one might imagine. The car is a status symbol but it's also a symbol of travel. Arabs love to travel – to fam-

Nine Parts of Desire, by Geraldine Brooks, is an objective and well-balanced investigation into the lives of women under Islam, covering various countries of the Middle East and exposing some of the many myths regarding the treatment of women in the Arab world.

THE CULTURE PEOPLE

PENINSULA LIVES

Ahmed is a fisherman near Shwaymiya in Oman. He gets up before dawn, performs his ablutions and walks to the mosque for dawn prayers. By the time he returns, his sons have dragged the boat to the water's edge. His wife has prepared something light to break the night's fast and will have rice waiting on their return from sea; his daughters are out collecting firewood. A flotilla of 10 or 20 boats tears up the calm waters on the age-old hunt for tuna. Half asleep in the middle of the afternoon, the day's work accomplished, the catch drying in the sun or dispatched to town in the freezer truck, his family arranged around him in various states of slumber and repose, Ahmed asks why anybody else would want another life: 'I have my children, my wife and my fishing. What more could a man wish for?' What indeed? But they do wish for more, and that's why two of his seven sons are now enrolled in the military, and his eldest daughter is hoping to train in Salalah to become a nurse.

Fatima is married to Faisal, an administrator in the Wildlife Commission in Riyadh. Fatima remembers the days when her father took her brothers on hunting parties looking for houbara bustards (near-endangered large birds prized for their meat). She never imagined she'd marry someone involved in their protection. She's not quite sure what all the fuss is about but the steady income helps pay for the education of their two children. She was adamant about that: both daughters were to have the best. One is studying pharmacy and the other is good with figures and will make an able accountant. She could do with some help with the family accounts – especially with the investments she's made. She recently bought a part share in a truck for one of the construction companies. It's already returning a profit. She dons her *abeyya* (full-leng black robe) and sinks into the street outside, glad to be anonymous – she'll have to sort out the feud with the neighbours soon because Faisal is clearly never going to muscle up to that task!

ily members at the weekend, foreign countries for honeymoons, and of course to Mecca for hajj or *umrah* (literally 'little pilgrimage').

Dress & Fashion

The very thought of calling the quintessentially cool and elegant dress of the Arabs 'sheet and teacloth' would appall most inhabitants of the Peninsula. Men take huge pride in their costume, which, in its simplicity and uniformity, is intended to transcend wealth and origin.

A loose headscarf, known as *gutra*, is worn by many Peninsula males: in the Gulf States it is of white cloth, while in western Kuwait and Saudi Arabia it is checked. The black head rope used to secure the *gutra* is called *agal*. It's said to originate in the rope the Bedu used to tie up their camels at night. The Omanis and Yemenis usually wear a turban, wrapped deftly about a cap. In Oman these are pastel-hued and decorated with intricate and brightly coloured embroidery.

Most Peninsula men also wear the floor-length 'shirt-dress', which in Saudi Arabia, Bahrain and Qatar is known as a *thobe*, and in Kuwait, the UAE and Oman as a *dishdasha*. Most are white, and some have collars and cuffs, while others are edged with tassels and white-thread embroidery at the neck. On ceremonial occasions, the dress is completed with a finely wrought belt and ceremonial dagger, and a silk outer garment. In Yemen and cold areas in the winter, men wear tailored jackets.

Women's dress is more varied. It often comprises a colourful long dress or an embroidered tunic with trousers and heavily decorated ankle cuffs. In the cities, modern dress is common. Over the top, women usually wear a black gown known as an *abeyya*. This can either be worn loose and cover the head as well (as in Saudi Arabia) or it can be worn as a fashion item, tailored to the body and spangled with diamantes (as in Oman). In Yemen, the women's outer costume comprises a startling layer of coloured cotton cloth.

All Arab women cover their hair but they don't all wear the burka (veil) – in Oman and the UAE, they mostly do not cover the face. Veils can be of a thin gauze completely covering the face; a cloth which covers the face but not the eyes; or a mask concealing the nose, cheeks and part of the mouth – in Sana'a, women wear striking red-and-white tie-dye cloth to cover the face and in the sands in Oman, a gold-coloured peaked mask is favoured.

Why the Low Crime Rate?

Strict codes of moral conduct expounded by Islam

A legal system rigorously enforced

Traditional Arab values

Ancient concepts of honour

The 18th-century traveller, Lady Montagu, noted that Arab women were more at liberty to follow their own will than their European counterparts and that the *abeyya* (what she describes as the 'black disguise') made it easier for women to take a lover.

THE BEDU – SURVIVAL OF THE MOST GENEROUS

Meaning 'nomadic', the name Bedu is today a bit of a misnomer. Though thought to number several hundred thousand, very few Bedu are still truly nomadic, though a few hang on to the old ways. After pitching their distinct black, goat-hair tents – the *beit ash-sha'ar* (literally 'house of hair') – they graze their goats, sheep or camels in an area for several months. When the sparse desert fodder runs out, it's time to move on again, allowing the land to regenerate naturally.

The hospitality of the Bedu is legendary, even in a region known for its generosity. Part of the ancient and sacrosanct Bedouin creed is that no traveller in need of rest or food should be turned away. Likewise, a traveller assumes the assured protection of his hosts for a period of three days, and is guaranteed a safe passage through tribal territory. Even today the Bedu escort travellers safely across the desert in Yemen (though now you pay for the service).

The philosophy is simple: you scratch my back, I'll scratch yours – only in the desert it's a matter of survival. Such a code of conduct ensures the survival of all in a difficult environment with scant resources. It allows the maintenance of a nomadic lifestyle and the continuation of trade. It's a kind of survival, in other words, of the most generous.

TEA & TALK

A *diwaniya* (gathering), usually conducted at someone's home – in a tent or on cushions just outside it, to be precise – is an important aspect of Gulf life, and any visitor who has the chance to partake in one will find it the best opportunity to observe Arab social life firsthand. The object of the gathering, which has its origin in Bedouin traditions of hospitality, is to drink endless cups of hot, sweet tea – oh, and to chew the political cud, of course. It is usually a 'man thing'. As one Kuwaiti woman explained, the women of the house are usually too busy living life to waste time discussing it.

Many Western people assume that men force women to cover up. In fact, this is generally not the case except in some extreme societies in Arabia. Women often opt for such coverings in order to pass more comfortably through male company. Nor is it a stated part of Islam. Indeed, Bedu women maintain that the custom, which protects the skin and hair from the harsh penalties of sun and sand, predates Islam.

Arabian Youth

They wear baseball caps with the peak reversed, they've got the latest iPads and smartphones, they stay out late with friends and are rude to their elders. A few drink, fewer take drugs. They watch unsavoury things on satellite TV and they communicate 'inappropriately' via the internet. They sleep a lot and aren't interested in learning. In this regard, Arab youth are no different from any other youth. The difference in Arab countries is that really wanton behaviour is rare and the period of abandonment relatively short.

Religious Zeal

Only a tiny minority of people on the Peninsula are involved in religious fundamentalism, and most of those channel their zeal into peaceful attempts to reconcile the liberties of modern life with the traditional values of Islam. Those who resort to violence to accomplish largely political aims are mistrusted by their own communities and considered misguided by most religious leaders. It is unfortunate that this small minority gain maximum media coverage and are the people upon whom the entire culture of the mostly peaceful, amiable, adaptable and tolerant Arabian Peninsula is judged.

Arts

If you chose one feature that distinguishes art in the Arabian Peninsula (and in the Arab world in general) from that of Western tradition, it would have to be the close integration of function with form. In other words, most Arab art has evolved with a purpose. That purpose could be as practical as embellishing the prow of a boat with a cowrie shell to ward off 'evil eye', or as nebulous as creating intricate and beautiful patterns to intimate the presence of God and invite spiritual contemplation. Purpose is an element that threads through all Peninsula art – craft, music, architecture and poetry.

Poetry

Nothing touches the heart of a Peninsula Arab quite like poetry. Traditionally dominating Arab literature, all the best-known figures of classical Arabic and Persian literature are poets, including the famed Omar Khayyam, the 11th-century composer of *rub'ai* (quatrains), and the 8th-century Baghdadi poet, Abu Nuwas. All great Arab poets were regarded

Hajj Statistics

Annual Number of pilgrims to Mecca for Hajj: 2.5 million

Quota of Muslims per country permitted to travel: 1000 per million inhabitants

The Bedu are known for their sense of humour which they list – alongside courage, alertness and religious faith – as one of the four secrets of life, encouraging tolerance and humility.

ORAL TRADITION

For the nomadic Bedu of Arabia, life is lived on the move. Permanence is virtually unknown – even the footsteps that mark their passing shift with the sands. The artistic expression of their culture has evolved to be similarly portable – weaving that can be rolled up and stowed on a camel, beadwork that can be tucked in a pocket, stories unfurled round the campfire at night.

Bedu tales, and their endless digressions, serve not just as entertainment. Allegories and parables are used to clarify a situation, to offer tactful advice to a friend, or to alert someone diplomatically to trouble or wrongdoing. More often, they lampoon corrupt leaders and offer a satirical commentary on current affairs – particularly those of the mistrusted 'townspeople'. They can be very funny, highly bawdy and verging on the libellous, depending on the persuasions of the teller.

On the Peninsula, there is said to be a tale for every situation. Travellers may be surprised at how often the Bedu resort to proverbs, maxims or stories during the course of normal conversation. It is said that the first proverb of all is: 'While a man may tell fibs, he may never tell false proverbs'!

Sadly, the modern world has encroached on the oral tradition. The advent of TV and other forms of entertainment has meant that the role that storytelling plays in Bedouin life has diminished. Now this valuable oral patrimony is in danger of disappearing forever.

as possessing knowledge forbidden to ordinary people and, as such, they served the purpose of bridging the human and spirit worlds.

To this day, poetry recitals play an important part in all national celebrations, and even the TV-watching young are captivated by a skilfully intoned piece of verse.

Poetry is part and parcel of the great oral tradition of storytelling that informs the literature of all Peninsula countries, the roots of which lie with the Bedu. Stories told by nomadic elders to the wide-eyed wonder of the young serve not just as after-dinner entertainment, but as a way of binding generations together in a collective oral history. As such, storytelling disseminates the principles of Islam and of tribal and national identity. It extols the virtues of allegiance, valour, endurance and hospitality – virtues that make life in a harsh environment tolerable.

Music

Like the oral tradition of storytelling, Arabian song and dance have also evolved for a purpose. Generally, music was employed to distract from hardship – like the songs of the seafarers marooned on stagnant Gulf waters, or the chanting of fishermen hauling in their nets. There are also harvest songs and love ballads, all of which are either sung unaccompanied or to syncopated clapping or drum beats. East African rhythms, introduced into Arab music from Arab colonies, lend much Peninsula music a highly hypnotic quality, and songs can last for over an hour.

While the austere Wahhabi and Ibadi sects discourage singing and dancing, no wedding or national celebration in the Peninsula would be the same without them. Men dance in circles, flexing their swords or ceremonial daggers while jumping or swaying. If they get really carried away, volleys of gunfire are exchanged above the heads of the crowd. Women have a tradition of dancing for the bride at weddings. Unobserved by men, they wear magnificent costumes (or modern ball gowns) and gyrate suggestively as if encouraging the bride towards the marital bed.

It shouldn't be supposed that just because traditional music plays a big part in contemporary Arab life, it's the only form of music. Pop music,

ARABIAN SAYINGS

The Son of a Duck is a Floater, by Arnander and Skipworth, is a fun collection of Arab sayings with English equivalents. It's worth buying just to see how wisdom is universal – not to mention the thoroughly enjoyable illustrations.

especially of the Amr Diab type, is ubiquitous and nightclubs are popular. There's even a classical orchestra in Oman and there are bagpipe bands.

Crafts

If there's one area in which function and form are most noticeably linked, it's in the craft traditions of the Peninsula – in the jewellery, silversmithing, weaving, embroidery and basket-making crafts that form the rich craft heritage of the Peninsula. Take jewellery, for example – the heavy silver jewellery, so distinctively worn by Bedouin women, was designed not just as a personal adornment but as a form of portable wealth. Silver amulets, containing rolled pieces of parchment or paper, bear protective inscriptions from the Quran, to guarantee the safety of the wearer. At the end of the life of a piece of jewellery, it is traditionally melted down to form new pieces as an ultimate gesture of practicality.

The sad fact of practical craft is that once the need for it has passed, there is little incentive to maintain the skills. Where's the point of potters in Al-Hofuf, Saudi Arabia and Bahla, Oman making clay ewers when everyone drinks water from branded plastic bottles? Aware of this fact, many governments throughout the region have encouraged the setting up of local craft associations in the hope of keeping alive such an important part of their heritage. Some of the best supported ventures in the region are the Bedouin weaving project at Sadu House in Kuwait City and the women's centres in Manama and Abu Dhabi.

The Omani Heritage Documentation Project is another worthy enterprise. Launched in 1996 to document Oman's great craft heritage and envisage ways to ensure its survival, it resulted after eight years of study in a two-volume book, *The Craft Heritage of Oman*, which has become the definitive guide to Oman's cottage industries. It is an inspiration to anyone with an interest in the arts and crafts of Oman and an invitation to other Peninsula countries to follow suit.

Ultimately, however, when a craft is hollowed of its function, when it provides a mere curiosity of the past or is redefined to provide souvenirs for tourists, it becomes only a shadow of itself.

Architecture

Styles across the region vary so considerably, it's hard to talk about Peninsula architecture under one umbrella – there's the multistorey mud edifices of Yemen and Southern Saudi; the round mud huts more akin to sub-Saharan architecture on the Tihama; the *barasti* (palm leaf) dwellings of eastern Arabia; the coral buildings of Jeddah; and the gypsum decoration of Gulf design.

THE CULTURE ARTS

Books: Arabian Arts

Contemporary Architecture in the Arab States (Udo Kultermann)

Islamic Arts (Jonathan Bloom & Sheila Blair)

Craft Heritage of Oman (Richardson & Dorr)

The Thousand and One Nights, translated by Richard Burton, is a collection of tales (including Ali Baba and Aladdin) that originate from Arabia, India and Persia. They are told, night by night, by the beautiful, beguiling narrator, Sheherazade to save herself from beheading by a vengeful king.

THE ART OF AIR CONTROL

Called *barjeel* in Arabic, wind towers are the Gulf States' own unique form of non-electrical air-conditioning. In most of the region's cities a handful still exist, sometimes attached to private homes, and sometimes carefully preserved or reconstructed at museums. In Sharjah (UAE) a set of massive wind towers is used to cool the modern Central Market building.

Traditional wind towers rise 5m or 6m above a house. They are usually built of wood or stone but can also be made from canvas. The tower is open on all four sides and so can catch even the breathiest of breezes. These mere zephyrs are channelled down a central shaft and into the room below. In the process, the air speeds up and is cooled. The cooler air already in the tower shaft pulls in and subsequently cools the hotter air outside through a simple process of convection.

Sitting beneath a wind tower on a hot and humid day, the temperature is noticeably cooler with a consistent breeze even when the air outside feels heavy and still.

GENUINE BEDOUIN – MADE IN INDIA?

One of the highlights of the Peninsula is undoubtedly a trip to the covered souqs and bazaars, some of which (especially in Jeddah, Kuwait, Doha, Muscat and Sana'a) have occupied the same chaotic labyrinthine quarters for hundreds of years. In these forerunners of the shopping mall, merchants sit behind piles of dates and olives, gold, frankincense and myrrh, in small shops often no bigger than a broom cupboard. Passing in between them are the water-sellers, itinerant cloth vendors, carters (complete with wheelbarrow in Kuwait) and carriers.

The scene (of haggling and gossiping, pushing and shoving, laughing and teasing) may not have changed much in centuries, but many of the goods have. Mostly practical items are on offer – aluminium pans, plastic trays, imports from China – but if you look hard, you can usually find items of traditional craft, even in the most modern of souqs.

There are *kilims* (rugs) and carpets; cotton clothing including *gutras* (white head cloth), *thobes* or *dishdashas* (man's shirt dresses) and embroidered dresses; Bedouin woven bags; decorative daggers and swords; copperware and brassware; olive and cedar woodcarvings; kohl (black eyeliner); old trunks and boxes; water pipes; embroidered tablecloths and cushion covers; leather and suede. But, the question is, is it real?

All tourists have seen them: the Roman coins from Syria, the Aladdin lamps from Cairo, the Bedouin jewellery torn from the brow of a virgin bride – the stories attempt to make up for the shameless lack of authentic provenance on the part of the item. While the region is home to some magnificent craft, only relatively few pieces make their way to places like Souq Waqif in Qatar, Mutrah Souq in Oman or Bab al-Bahrain in Bahrain. The vast majority of items on sale to tourists is imported from India, Pakistan and Iran and either sold as such, or more frequently passed off as 'genuine Bedouin' by less-scrupulous shopkeepers.

In common with other arts, Peninsula architecture is traditionally steered by purpose. The local climate plays an important role in this. The wind towers of the Gulf, for example, not only look attractive, they function as channels of cooler air; the gaily painted window frames of Yemeni and Asir dwellings in Saudi help waterproof the adobe. Security is another issue: the positioning of forts around and on top of rocky outcrops in the Hajar Mountains gives a foundation more solid than anything bricks and mortar might produce. And then there's the question of space: in the mountain areas of Saudi, Yemen and Oman, whole villages appear to be suspended in air, perched on top of inaccessible promontories, storeys piled high to save from building on precious arable land.

The one 'art form' that a visitor to the Peninsula can hardly miss is the modern tower block. In many Gulf cities, cranes almost outnumber buildings in the race to build the most extravagant confection of glass and steel. In the process, Peninsula architecture has become diverted from the traditional principle of functionality. Take the magnificent Emirates Palace in Abu Dhabi, for example, where you need to pack your trainers to get from bed to breakfast.

Increasingly, architects are expected to refer, in an almost talismanical way, to the visual vocabulary of Arab art: hence the pointed windows, false balconies, wooden screens and tent motifs of modern buildings across the Peninsula. Perhaps this is because many traditional buildings, with their economy of style and design, achieve something that modern buildings often do not – they blend in harmoniously with their environment.

Islamic Art

There can be no greater example of function at the heart of art than Islamic art. For a Muslim, Islamic art remains first and foremost an ex-

Fine Examples of Islamic Calligraphy

Beit al-Quran, Manama

Tareq Rajab Museum, Kuwait City

Museum of Islamic Art, Doha

Sharjah Museum of Islamic Civilisation, Shajah

pression of faith, and to this day people are cautious of 'art for art's sake', or art as an expression of the self without reference to community. Ask Arab students to draw a picture, and they'll often draw something with a message or a meaning rather than just a pretty picture.

A good example of instructive or inspirational visual art is calligraphy. Arabic is not just a language for Arabs – for Muslims throughout the world it is the language of the Quran, so it's a cohesive and unifying factor, imbued with a reverence that is hard for non-Muslims to understand. Islamic calligraphy, the copying of God's own words, is seen by many as a pious act and remains to this day the highest aesthetic practised in the Arab world. All over Arabia one can see magnificent examples of this highly refined art with its repetition of forms and symmetry of design.

The most visible expression of Islamic art, however, is surely the mosque. It too is built on mostly functional principles. In fact, the first mosques were modelled on the Prophet Mohammed's house. To this day the basic plan in providing a safe, cool and peaceful haven for worship has changed little – there's the open *sahn* (courtyard), the arcaded *riwaq* (portico), and the covered, often domed, prayer hall. A vaulted niche in the wall is called the mihrab; this serves to indicate the qibla, or direction of Mecca, towards which Muslims must face when they pray. The *minbar* (pulpit) is traditionally reached by three steps. The Prophet is said to have preached his sermons from the third step. Abu Bakr, his successor, chose to preach from the second step, and this is where most imams (prayer leaders) stand or sit today when preaching the Friday sermon.

The first minarets appeared long after Mohammed's death. Prior to that time, the muezzin (prayer caller) often stood on a rooftop or some other elevation so that he could be heard by as many townsfolk as possible.

Traditionally, mosques had an ablution fountain at the centre of the courtyard, often fashioned from marble. Today most modern mosques have a more practical row of taps and drains alongside.

The mosque serves the community in many ways. Groups of children receive Quranic lessons or run freely across the carpet; people sit in quiet contemplation of carved wood panels, tiled walls and marbled pillars; others simply enjoy a peaceful nap in the cool. As such, there is no greater expression of the way that art remains at the service of people – something that surprises secular, Western onlookers. By the same token, it will be interesting to see what Muslims make of the decorative art of Europe: work began on the Jean Nouvel–designed 'Louvre of the Desert' in Abu Dhabi in 2013, which will eventually showcase work from the Louvre in Paris. The decadence of the project, never mind the work on display, is bound to ruffle conservative feathers and challenge Peninsula people to reconsider what else could be meant by the term 'art'.

Sport

The people of the Arabian Peninsula love sport, and some Gulf countries, especially Qatar, are trying to promote themselves as venues for international events. This is no new phenomenon. For centuries, Arab men have been getting together in flat patches of desert to demonstrate their prowess in agility, speed and courage. Most of these traditional games, which involve barefoot running, ball games, wrestling and even rifle throwing, are hard for a visitor to fathom, but since 2007, the Gulf Cooperation Council (GCC) countries have been trying to encourage greater participation in these kinds of sports and they may well receive more popular promotion in future.

Best Places to See Traditional Wind Towers

Muharraq Island, Bahrain

Al Fahidi Historical Neighbourhood, Dubai

Al-Sharq Village & Spa, Qatar

Central Market, Sharjah

Yaum Al-Bahhar Village, Kuwait City

Olympic Medals won at London 2012

Qatar (two bronze: men's skeet, men's high jump)

Saudi Arabia (one bronze: equestrian)

Bahrain (one bronze: women's 1500m athletics)

Kuwait (one bronze: shooting)

East–West Football Connections

Wigan (Omani Ali Al-Habsi: goal-keeper)

Manchester City (Owned by Abu Dhabi and Etihad, football's biggest-ever sponsorship deal)

Barcelona (€150 million shirts from Qatar Foundation)

Many traditional sports involve skill in handling animals with camel and horse racing topping the bill and falconry being the fabled sport of kings. A curiosity of the east coast of Arabia (in the UAE and Oman) is bull butting – the pitching of one Brahman bull against another in a contest of strength. Much effort is taken to ensure the animals are not harmed but occasional injuries occur to ears or necks. Bull butting takes place in a dusty arena where the animals are nudged into a head-down position, and push and shove from one side of the arena to the other. The bulls are precious to their owners and much beloved so the minute the going gets tough, thankfully the tough get going. As such, it isn't exactly the most spectacular sport to watch, though it always draws a huge crowd of locals. The best places to see bull butting are near Muscat in Oman and at Fujairah in the UAE.

Camel Racing

Camel racing is a grumbling affair of camels (who'd really rather not run) and owners (who make sure they do). The rider, traditionally, is almost immaterial. Racing usually involves a long, straight track (camels are not very good at cornering) with very wide turns. Camel fanciers race alongside in their 4WDs to give their favourite camel encouragement.

Camel racing can be seen throughout the region from October to May. Authorities, sensitive about the bad press associated with the traditional recruitment of young jockeys, have mostly insisted on replacing child riders with lightweight adults or even with something more imaginative (see the boxed text). Visitors can see races in Al-Shahaniya in Qatar and Al-Marmoum Camel Racecourse en route to Al-Ain from Dubai.

During the flying season, October to February, 10,000 birds are tended at Doha's Falcon Hospital – a measure of how popular the sport remains. Top falcons can cost up to US$1 million.

Horse Racing

The breeding of horses, shipped from ports like Sur in Oman, has been a source of income in Arabia for centuries. Now, partly thanks to the efforts of Lady Anne Blunt, a 19th-century British horse breeder, the fleet-footed, agile Arab horse is raced all over the world.

Horse racing is a major spectator event for Peninsula people and the event is at its most expensive and glamorous in the Dubai Cup. Heads of states, royalty, celebrities and top international jockeys gather for the occasion. Like Ascot in the UK it's *the* place to be seen. The Meydan Racecourse in Dubai holds regular events.

Falconry

The ancient art of falconry is still practised across the Peninsula. It dates back at least to the 7th century BC when tradition has it that a Persian ruler caught a falcon to learn from its speed, tactics and focus. Modern

CAMEL ON COMMAND

Traditionally, camels were raced by child jockeys, who were often 'bought' from impoverished families in Pakistan and Bangladesh, trained in miserable conditions, kept deliberately underweight and then exposed to the dangers of regular racing. The plight of these young boys has attracted international condemnation over the years. Qatar and the UAE, among other Gulf States, banned the use of child jockeys but were then left with the problem of finding something similarly lightweight to replace them. Their novel solution could best be described as 'robo-rider'. These robotic jockeys are remote-controlled, look vaguely humanoid and can crack an electronic whip. The camels appear to respond just as well (or just as badly) to their new mounts, and future versions of this gadget will sport bug-eyes from which the corpulent owner can pretend he's thin again as he takes virtual strides at 60km/h around the racetrack.

BENDING IT LIKE AL-BECKHAM

One sure-fire entrée into conversation across the region is to talk about Beckham – or rather Al-Beckham – and football (soccer) in general. Peninsula men are obsessed with the game. But what distinguishes the sport in Arabia is not so much the players or the fans, but the extraordinary places where it's played.

There are pitches between fast lanes in Bahrain; motorway intersection pitches in Kuwait and shifting pitches, like the one in the UAE sand dunes, which has usually blown away before kick-off.

It's in Oman, however, that pitches are taken to new heights – like the one on the top of Jebel Shams, with goals strung out between two locally woven rugs, redefining the term 'mile-high club'. Omanis specialise in wet pitches, like the one near Bandar Khayran where the goalkeeper's job is to keep out the incoming tide, or the one cradled in the mouth of Wadi Tiwi and cropped by donkeys. Football even stops traffic in Oman. Best in the road-stopping category is the pitch bisected by the road from Hat to Wadi Bani Awf. When a game is on, all traffic on the only road that links both sides of the Hajar Mountains has to stop until half-time – a full 40 minutes of holding up one goat and a Lonely Planet author!

owners continue to admire their birds and lavish love and respect upon them.

Many raptors are bred for falconry on the Asir escarpment in Saudi but the easiest place to see a peregrine up close is in the Falcon Souq in Doha. The magical spectacle of birds being flown can be seen in Dubai and at most festivals, such as the Jenadriyah National Festival in Riyadh.

Modern Sports

A range of modern sports are popular in the region, including rally-driving, quad-biking, volleyball and even ice-skating. At Ski Dubai, there are even five ski runs boasting snow.

You can't possibly talk about sports in the area, however, and not mention football. At 4pm on a Friday, the men of just about every village in Arabia trickle onto the local waste-ground to play, all hopeful of joining international European clubs one day like some of their compatriots. Football is usually a shoeless business, on a desert pitch, played in *wizza* (cotton underskirt) and nylon strip but it is taken just as seriously as if it were played in a million-dollar stadium.

Betting is against Islamic principles, but at camel races, vast sums of money change hands in terms of prize money, sponsorship and ownership. A prize-racing camel can fetch over US$100,000.

Hajj: the Ultimate Traveller's Tale

Anyone who counts themselves as a traveller can't fail to be fascinated by hajj – the single largest annual travel event in the world. In the airports of the Middle East, the sense of anticipation among the Islamic pilgrims, dressed uniformly in simple white robes, is tangible as people congregate to perform this once-in-a-lifetime journey.

Hajj in History

Above Pilgrims at Mecca

Although only Muslims are permitted to participate in hajj, non-Muslims travelling in the region at the time of the annual pilgrimage can't help but be swept into the same sense of expectation and excitement as car horns and gun fire crackle the air, signalling the passage of the faithful. It immediately becomes apparent that this is no ordinary journey – it is a journey of extreme significance, anticipated from childhood, a source of inspiration in adulthood and a comfort in old age.

This is the story of hajj – the ultimate traveller's tale.

In the Beginning

Unlike most travellers' tales that are ad hoc by nature, hajj is a highly ritualised journey governed by tradition. Many aspects of the pilgrimage observable today have easily discernible roots in the history of hajj. That history can be traced to the story of Ibrahim (Abraham of the Old Testament), considered today as the founding father of the hajj tradition. The story goes like this.

The Search for Water

During his lifetime, Ibrahim's faith was tested many times. One trial involved taking his wife, Hajjar, and infant son, Ismail (Ishmael), to Arabia. Obeying Allah's command to leave them in Allah's hands, Ibrahim left Hajjar and Ismail in a dry valley with little food. Soon supplies ran out, and Hajjar began roaming the valley in a frantic search for sustenance. Eventually, failing to find anything, she fell to the ground in despair.

Pilgrims today commemorate that search for water by performing the *sa'ee*, walking seven times between the two hills of Safa and Marwah in Mecca.

Founding of Mecca

Ismail was now crying from hunger and thirst, so Hajjar prayed to Allah for help. As Ismail wailed, he stamped his foot upon the ground and suddenly up gushed a spring of water.

They named the spring Zamzam and in time, caravans and nomads began to water their camels there. Soon a desert settlement formed around the well. That settlement was Mecca, and Zamzam is the only natural source of water in the city to this day.

Rejecting Temptation

Ibrahim's greatest trial was still to come. Allah commanded him to take his son to the mountains and there slay him. Determined to demonstrate the strength of his faith, Ibrahim obeyed the commandment but on the way to the mountains, Shaitan (the Devil) intervened, harrying, cajoling, taunting and mocking Ibrahim to give up his mission. On the point of despair, Ibrahim overcame his temptation by throwing stones at Shaitan.

This act is commemorated today by the stoning of the *jamrah* (pillars) in Mina today.

Sacrifice

When Ibrahim arrived at the appointed place with knife drawn against his son's neck, he was commanded by Allah to allow Ismail to live, and to sacrifice a ram in his place.

This is remembered during Eid al-Adha (Festival of Sacrifice), when Muslims all over the world perform a ritual sacrifice, usually of a cow, sheep or goat, which is then prepared for family feasting.

Commitment to Pilgrimage

Ibrahim continued to visit Mecca. One day, Allah commanded him to build a house of worship and called on all believers to make the pilgrimage to Mecca. Ibrahim and Ismail constructed the Kaaba, a cube-shaped building, for worship.

Books: Firsthand Accounts of Hajj

One Thousand Roads to Mecca: Ten Centuries of Travelers Writing About the Muslim Pilgrimage, Michael Wolfe, 1999

The Hajj, FE Peters, 1995

HAJJ: THE ULTIMATE TRAVELLER'S TALE HAJJ IN HISTORY

Hajj pilgrims

This is the building which, to this day, Muslims are enjoined to circle while performing the *tawaf* (circumnavigation of the Kaaba).

Hajj & the Founding of Islam

Islam is the only religion that stipulates pilgrimage: 'Pilgrimage to the House is a duty to God for all those who can make the journey' (sura 3:98).

'Our Lord! Send amongst them a messenger of their own, who shall recite unto them your *aayaat* (verses) and instruct them in the book and the Wisdom and sanctify them.' (sura Al-Baqarah 2:129)

Despite the early religious origins of hajj, the pilgrimage to Mecca over time became corrupted by idolatry as the Kaaba became the focus of pagan worship. After the death of his father, Ismail tried to defend the spirit of hajj in an annual visit to Mecca. He recognised, however, that it would take more than his example to recharge people's faith and died with a prayer on his lips appealing for Allah's help.

Muslims believe that many prophets were sent through the ages to reveal the will of Allah but it was in AD 570, with the birth of a Meccan called Mohammed ibn Abdullah, that Ismail's prayer was most significantly answered. For 23 years, Prophet Mohammed spread a message of obedience to Allah and a law of peace and order in Arabia – a message that was to form the foundation of Islam, one of the most significant moments in world history.

Initially, the Meccans (many of them powerful merchants) objected to the rise of Islam, as the new religion jeopardised profits and revenues collected from visiting pagans. In 622, they forced Mohammed into exile in the town of Medina where he established a model Islamic community. Six years later, Mohammed returned to Mecca with thousands of followers. Destroying idols, he purified the Kaaba and rededicated the House for the worship of Allah alone.

Thousands of followers travelled from miles around to hear his sermon, expounding the concept of a united Muslim community. Hajj, focused on pilgrimage to a re-sanctified Kaaba and a celebration of the unshakeable faith shown by Ibrahim, became a cornerstone of the religion of Islam.

A Millennium of Pilgrimage

A Once-in-a-lifetime Journey

For most of the history of hajj, pilgrimage to Mecca was considered a journey made only once in a lifetime. This was largely due to the expense involved in undertaking the journey. Early pilgrims had novel ways of funding their pilgrimage. Some brought goods to sell from their countries of origin; some brought slaves, selling one or two along the way to finance the next leg of the journey. Camel and donkey caravans provided transportation for wealthier pilgrims: those with less funds had to walk, taking up to two years to arrive in Mecca from the fringes of the Islamic world.

Hajj remains a costly commitment that many can only afford to finance once, and there remains no obligation on the impoverished to fulfil this pillar of Islam. Most families, however, see it as a point of honour to ensure elders reach the holy cities, pooling their resources to make the trip possible. Novel methods of raising funds are still in evidence and something of the spirit of enterprise shown by the merchants of old can still be seen in Jeddah, for example, where pilgrims bring unwrapped home-grown products – coffee from Yemen, saffron and pistachios from Iran, spices from India – fresh from their suitcases.

Richard Burton's *Personal Narrative of a Pilgrimage to Al-Madinah and Meccah* (1874) offers a rare Western insight into the holy cities which he entered as an imposter under disguise.

HAJJ: THE ULTIMATE TRAVELLER'S TALE HAJJ IN HISTORY

Mecca-Medina Area

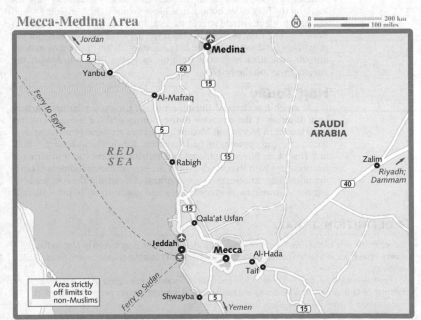

A Journey Beset with Hardship

Hajj over the centuries earned a reputation as a dangerous and difficult enterprise from which there was no guarantee of safe return. Indeed, hardship was considered part and parcel of the journey. Before setting off, pilgrims would draw up wills and appoint executors in the expectation of failing to make it back home. Bandits, highwaymen, robbers, warring tribes, kidnappers and disease were just some of the hazards pilgrims could expect during their attempt to reach the holy cities.

Despite the improved transportation, the provision of healthcare and security on arrival, and the promise of safe passage on return, there is a continuing expectation of hardship. Once in 30 years or so, hajj falls in the hottest summer months on earth. Ask pilgrims how they will cope as hajj once again approaches that testing time of soaring daytime temperatures and most will say they welcome the added challenge – they welcome the chance to demonstrate their faith in extremis.

The 12th-century hajji from Arab Spain, Ibn Jubayr, stayed in Mecca for eight months. *Travel of Ibn Jubayr* recounts that experience and is considered the first traveller's diary in Arabic.

Defenders of the Faithful

Security of hajj pilgrims as they travelled between countries of the crescent, en route to Mecca, was a traditional benchmark of a monarch's fitness to rule. The safety of the annual caravans that gathered in Cairo, Damascus and Baghdad perplexed caliphs and sultans alike, each eager to illustrate their strength, benevolence and religious rectitude in ensuring safe passage.

Leaders across the Muslim world still take their responsibility to their pilgrims seriously, spending large sums of money to ensure that infrastructure is in place to facilitate the pilgrims' journeys. As protectors of Mecca and Medina, each successive monarch since King Abdul Aziz, the founder of modern-day Saudi Arabia, has similarly sought to leave his mark on the holy cities, hoping to achieve favour in heaven, some would say, and to demonstrate strong leadership of the global community of Muslims. The King of Saudi Arabia takes personal responsibility for the pilgrimage, and every year the king, along with his entire government, uproots lock, stock and barrel from the capital in Riyadh to Jeddah, the 'hajj gateway' on the Red Sea.

Hajj Today

While much has changed since the time of the early pilgrims (particularly in terms of the character of the journey and the levels of comfort experienced in Mecca and Medina), what has remained consistent over the ages is the opportunity hajj represent for profound change – both in terms of an internal spiritual and religious journey and in terms of relationships with the outside world. An express commandment of faith, the pilgrimage to Mecca is seen as a way of cleansing the soul, eschewing the distractions of everyday life and reaffirming 'Islam' – literally

A DEFINITION OF HAJJ

Comprising one of the Five Pillars of Islam, 'hajj' describes the pilgrimage to Mecca that every able-bodied Muslim must perform at least once in their lives, finance and health allowing.

For the individual, hajj is a profoundly spiritual experience, cleansing of sin and reaffirming of faith. Pilgrims who complete hajj return to respect in their home countries, in recognition of the rite of passage that it represents.

Hajj is key to the cohesion of Islam as a global religion, drawing together Muslims from around the world in a single expression of faith.

Top Pilgrims help the elderly circle the Kaaba **Bottom** A campsite at Mina during hajj

Mecca

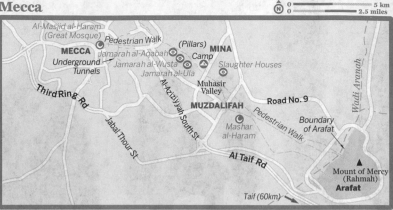

'submission' to Allah. By the end of the hajj journey Muslims are considered 'reborn' in the eyes of God.

Performing Hajj

Performed at the Great Mosque of Mecca and its immediate surrounds – Mina, Muzdalifah and the Mount of Mercy at Arafat – hajj takes place annually at a predetermined date, which advances annually by 10 days according to the lunar calendar on which the Islamic year is based.

Although the term is often taken to mean the entire journey from home, hajj is also used to refer to a very specific set of traditional rites that are carried out over the course of several days. Some of the most important of these rites are briefly described below.

The First Day (8th Dhul Hijja)

The rituals begin with the Day of Deliberation or Reflection, known as *yawm al-tarwiyah* in Arabic. On this day, pilgrims leave behind their distinguishing garb and with it all identification of status, wealth and nationality, and dress in *ihram*, two seamless, unsewn sheets that symbolise a state of consecration. This ritual is performed outside Mecca, and is accompanied by recitation of *an-niyyah* (the stating of intent).

On reaching the holy city of Mecca, pilgrims perform *tawaf al-qudum*, circling the Kaaba seven times, shoulder to shoulder with fellow pilgrims in the same state of reverence and reflection. After praying between the Black Stone and the door of the Kaaba, pilgrims then move to the Station of Ibrahim for further prayers.

Pilgrims drink the holy water of Zamzam before proceeding to the *sa'ee*, where they must run or walk seven times back and forth between the two hills of Safa and Marwah.

Thereafter, pilgrims enter the Great Mosque for the performance of further holy rites, before leaving for Mina to spend the night until summoned for dawn prayers.

The Second Day (9th Dhul Hijja)

Named the *yawm al-wuquf* (the Day of Standing), or *yawm 'Arafat* (the day of Arafat), pilgrims head for Arafat after the dawn prayer at Mina. Forming a key component of hajj, the *wuquf* (standing) involves pilgrims passing part of the day and night there.

Books:
About Hajj
& Its
Rituals

Hajj:Reflection on Its Rituals, Ali Shariati, 2005

Hajj:Journey to the Heart of Islam, Venetia Porter, 2012

'Mecca' is often used in English to mean any place drawing large crowds. As Mecca is the holiest city of Islam, some Muslims find this use of the term offensive.

Pilgrims climb the Mount of Mercy at Arafat

Most pilgrims stay from noon until after sunset, during which time they are expected to pray and recite frequently the *talbiyah* (the main, ritual recitation of hajj, and the words attributed to Ibrahim when he first summoned pilgrims to Mecca). Traditionally, this is a day of solemnity, reflection and the examination of conscience by pilgrims.

Some choose to climb the Mount of Mercy (Rahmah) at Arafat (though the crowds often prevent most from doing so). During the evening, pilgrims leave for Muzdalifah as part of the *nafrah* (rush) or *ifadah* (overflowing). There, pilgrims pray together and pass the night in each other's company.

The Third Day (10th Dhul Hijja)

During the Day of Sacrifice, or *yawm al-nahr* in Arabic, pilgrims begin the day in dawn prayers at Muzdalifah and then return to Mina. They collect small pebbles about the size of a chickpea – 49 pebbles if their stay in Mina lasts two days, 70 pebbles if they are able to stay for three days.

At Mina, pilgrims throw seven stones at the *jamrah* – 'pillars' (now replaced with walls) symbolising the temptation of Ibrahim by the devil.

Sacrifice follows, although pilgrims have one or two days to arrange for the slaughtering of an animal. A camel is considered the worthiest sacrifice, but an ox or ram are also acceptable.

It is at this point that a pilgrim's hair is clipped. Although only a lock of hair is required to be cut, many men choose to have their whole heads shaved. The shaving is a symbol of rebirth – showing that the sins of the pilgrim have been cleansed through the successful completion of hajj.

In 2004, due to the many injuries to pilgrims inflicted by the fervour of the stone throwing, Saudi hajj authorities replaced the pillars with long walls and stone basins designed to catch any ricocheting rocks.

On this day or the following, pilgrims head for the Masjid al-Haram in Mecca to carry out *tawaf al-ifadah* (or *tawaf az-ziyarah*), a second circling of the Kaaba.

The Final Days (11th, 12th & 13th Dhul Hijja)

Pilgrims spend their remaining days – known as *ayyam at-tashriq* (the Days of Drying Meat) – at Mina, each day casting seven stones at the three symbolic stone 'pillars' (now replaced with walls) between sunrise and sunset.

Before leaving Mecca, pilgrims usually perform *tawaf al-wada* (the circling of farewell).

Abstinence

During hajj, pilgrims enter a state of *ihram* that, in greatly simplified terms, requires abstinence from three main things: disturbing or harming other living things; indulging in sexual behaviour; and beautifying or adorning oneself. As part of *ihram*, men are forbidden to wear sewn clothes, or to cover the whole foot or head. Women are forbidden to cover their faces. This tangible illustration of the equality of all in the eyes of Allah is a defining feature of Muslim pilgrimage as monarchs and merchants, men and women, pray shoulder to shoulder during all the rites of hajj.

The Scale of Modern Hajj

Pilgrim Numbers

For an indication of the health of Islam in the modern world, one perhaps need look no further than the numbers of people attending hajj each year. Around 50 years ago no more than 10,000 pilgrims made the journey to Mecca whereas in 2012, for example, 3.1 million pilgrims officially performed hajj. Around 1.4 million pilgrims were from Saudi Arabia, but the remaining 1.7 million people arrived in Saudi Arabia from all parts of the world.

Further millions around the world also watch hajj live on TV and via the internet. Since 2004, Saudi radio has transmitted round-the-clock coverage of hajj in more than 12 languages.

Gaining a Visa for Hajj

In an attempt to keep the numbers of pilgrims manageable, only one hajj visa is issued per 1000 Muslim inhabitants of a country's population. Restrictions on pilgrims from Saudi Arabia are in place in order to allow more Muslims from other countries to visit and Saudis can perform hajj no more than once every five years.

Encouraging piety and charity, Islamic banks in Mecca facilitate official sacrifice by vouching to slaughter an animal on behalf of a pilgrim on an appointed day and sending the meat to developing-world countries.

Pilgrims who successfully complete hajj prefix their names with 'Al-Haj'. This appellation invites respect though hajj is performed as a mark of religious commitment, not to attain higher social status.

HAJJ CALENDAR

The table below shows the dates of hajj. *Yawm 'Arafat* (the main hajj day) is actually on the 9th of the month, but most pilgrims are already in Mecca by *yawm al-tarwiyah*, the 8th of the month.

ISLAMIC CALENDAR	ESTIMATED EQUIVALENT IN WESTERN CALENDAR
8–12 Dhul Hijja 1434H	13-16 October 2013
8–12 Dhul Hijja 1435H	2-5 October 2014
8–12 Dhul Hijja 1436H	21-24 September 2015
8–12 Dhul Hijja 1437H	9-12 September 2016

Al-Masjid Al-Haram

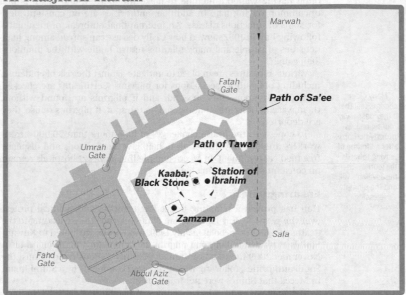

The wait for a hajj visa varies from country to country, with some pilgrims claiming to have waited 20 years or more for permission to travel and others claiming to have been charged exorbitant sums from profiteering agencies. On the whole, however, the system works well and politicians understand the importance of ensuring that the citizens of their own countries are well represented at the largest gathering of peoples in the world.

Hosting Hajj

General Logistics

For Saudi Arabia, the logistical challenges of hosting the annual hajj – the equivalent of 25 World Cups, or 30 simultaneous Super Bowls – are legion. To cater for an event of this magnitude, with this volume of people, an entire government department – the Ministry of Hajj – dedicates itself solely to the annual organisation of the pilgrimage.

Considerations include maintenance of the holy sites, such as replenishing the water of the Zamzam well, and ensuring adequate accommodation, drinking water, guidance and sanitation. Special pilgrim flights are scheduled by Saudi Arabian airlines, and at the height of hajj, planes arrive at Jeddah airport every minute. Boarding passes are issued two months in advance, and multilingual cabin crews are trained to assist pilgrims (many who haven't flown before) on flights.

As soon as one hajj ends, preparations for the next hajj begin.

Protecting Health

One of the biggest challenges Saudi authorities face during hajj is the control of health risks. Many pilgrims tend to be seriously ill or elderly,

In 2010, pilgrims arrived from 181 countries stretching from Mali to Indonesia. An estimated 25,000 pilgrims came from the UK; 13,000 from the US.

Entry to Mecca and Medina is prohibited to non-Muslims – although non-Muslims can view the Great Mosque of Medina from Le Meridien Hotel.

often having waited a lifetime to make the journey, and death is not uncommon during hajj. In addition, authorities are on constant alert for signs of infectious disease. An international outbreak of meningitis following hajj in 1987 showed how easily disease can spread among high densities of people and many pilgrims return home with the infamous 'hajj cough'.

Various measures are in place to mitigate against the risk of epidemic, including obligatory vaccinations for pilgrims. Certificates are checked meticulously upon entry to Saudi and if pilgrims are found without them, vaccinations are administered on the spot. If pilgrims refuse, they are deported.

To cope with the health challenges of hajj, more than 20,000 health workers are annually drafted in to help give vaccinations and dispense free medical treatment. In Mecca and Medina alone, 21 hospitals remain on constant standby during hajj.

> Many older pilgrims feel that if they pass away during hajj, especially perhaps after a lifetime of saving towards the journey, then this is Allah's will and the ultimate blessing.

Ensuring Safety

Hajj has proved a tempting target for terrorists and political protest over the years. In July 1987, Iranian Shiite pilgrims rioted, leading to the deaths of over 400 people; in July 1989, two bombs attributed to Kuwaiti Shiites exploded, killing one pilgrim and wounding 16 others; and in November 2009 thousands of Iranian pilgrims demonstrated against the Saudi authorities, following widely reported comments by a Sunni Imam in Mecca that Shiites were not true Muslims.

The management of large volumes of people in relatively confined spaces leads to its own troubles. In July 1990, 1426 pilgrims were trampled to death in a tunnel during a stampede en route to the plains of Arafat. Fatal incidents have also occurred during stone throwing at the pillars in Mina Valley. Road accidents and fire (in July 1997, 343 pilgrims were killed and 1500 injured when tents caught alight) have proved equally challenging to authorities.

> An estimated 9% to 20% of all pilgrims fail to return home annually, implying an increase in the Saudi population of a quarter of a million people every four years.

In order to manage the risks as well as possible, 63,000 armed security men patrol Mecca and Medina and 22,000 are employed in civil defence, showing the extent to which pilgrim safety is taken seriously.

The Future of Hajj

Usually travel is all about the journey rather than the arrival. When it comes to hajj, however, that is not the case. Throughout the ages, even when the holy cities were marked by little more than a dusty conglomeration of desert encampments, the first sighting of the Kaaba was a moment of wonder – an achievement of spiritual quest.

Over a millennium of pilgrimage, the infrastructure in Mecca and Medina has grown beyond imagination. Today the Great Mosque in Mecca alone boasts a total area of 356,000 sq metres, with a capacity for 773,000 people (and up to one million people during hajj season). As a point of comparison, the UK's Wembley Stadium holds 90,000 people, and the

UMRAH – THE LITTLE HAJJ

Many Muslims who have the time and funds choose to perform *umrah* (the 'lesser pilgrimage' or 'visitation'). This is a shortened version of hajj where rituals can be carried out over the course of hours rather than days.

Umrah can be performed at any time of year (except during hajj itself), at any time of day and night. Pilgrims are also allowed to perform *umrah* on behalf of someone else.

Many pilgrims say *umrah* is a quiet, peaceful and contemplative experience and worth experiencing in addition to hajj for this reason.

Top Keralan women perform hajj
Bottom Pilgrims on the Mount of Mercy

HAJJ GLOSSARY

hajj annual Muslim pilgrimage to Mecca and Medina

hajji pilgrim who has completed hajj

ihram holy state of consecration

Kaaba (literally 'cube') consecrated cuboid building covered in black cloth, containing ancient black stone, in the centre of the Grand Mosque in Mecca

PBUH 'Peace Be Upon Him' – follows every mention of Prophet Mohammed's name

sa'ee ritual walk

talbiyah the main, ritual recitation of hajj

tawaf circumnavigation of the Kaaba

umrah shortened pilgrimage to the holy cities outside hajj

Abraj al-Bait, a new 485-metre clocktower in Mecca, is visible from 40 kilometres away and comprises luxury hotels, malls and apartments for 15,000. A US$3bn project, it dwarfs the holy sites.

Dolphin Stadium in Miami holds 74,512 people, giving some indication of the scale and size of the holy sites. The buildings are designed to impress, with soaring minarets, polished marble, and prayer halls of immense proportions, and many pilgrims are overawed by their first sight of the cities. Much of the US$10 billion Saudi earns from the annual hajj is invested in enhancing this legacy.

But leaving a far more lasting impression, it is the congregation of the faithful, the sheer scale of the numbers who perform hajj, that many Muslims comment upon as the most uplifting part of the experience. Judging by the ever-growing number of pilgrims each year, anticipated by some sources to rise to 17 million by 2025, it is fair to say that Ibrahim's legacy has proved a spectacularly enduring one.

Islam

It is hard for most people in Western countries, where church and state are rigorously separated, to understand that for Muslims, there's little distinction between politics, culture and religion: each flows seamlessly through the other. Recognising the religious integrity of Peninsula people makes sense of certain customs and manners. In turn, it guides the traveller in appropriate conduct and minimises the chance of giving offence. Indeed, if you take the time to understand Islam, it will pay dividends when you interact with Arab people.

History

The Birth of Islam

Islam was founded in the early 7th century by the Prophet Mohammed. Born around AD 570 in the city of Mecca, Mohammed began receiving revelations at the age of 40 that continued for the rest of his life. Muslims believe these revelations, some received in Mecca, others in Medina, came directly from Allah through the angel Gabriel.

As Mohammed came from an oral tradition, he memorised the revelations, rather than writing them down, and then repeated them to friends and family. His contemporaries recognised the revelations as divine and they formed the basis of the Quran (meaning 'recitation' in Arabic). In turn, the Quran, as well as a series of suras (verses), became the basis of the new religion of Islam.

The Prophet Mohammed

Very little is known about the early years of Mohammed, other than that he was born around AD 570. His biography was written a century after his death and is more adulatory than factual.

Mohammed's early life doesn't appear to have been easy. His father died before he was born, and his mother died when Mohammed was six years old. Adopted by his grandfather, who also died shortly after, he was eventually sent to live with his uncle. With few means, the boy was obliged to start work early as a caravan trader. Mohammed's honesty, integrity and efficiency, however, didn't escape the eye of a much older, wealthy widow called Khadijah, who soon took him on as her agent. Eventually the couple married and had four

HISTORICAL ORIGINS OF ISLAM

AD 570
Prophet Mohammed, founder of the Islamic religion, is born in Mecca in today's Saudi Arabia.

610
Mohammed receives his first revelation. Considered by Muslims as the word of God, the revelations in the Quran subsequently lay the foundations of a new, monotheistic religion.

622
Mohammed and his followers flee Mecca for Medina, marking the beginning of the first Islamic state. The new religion spreads across the Peninsula.

632
Mohammed dies. The Muslim capital moves to Damascus, heading an empire stretching from Spain to India. Mecca and Medina grow as the spiritual homes of Islam.

656
Ali bin Abi Taleb, Mohammed's cousin and son-in-law, becomes caliph as the fourth of Mohammed's successors. His followers are known as Shiites ('partisans' of Ali).

661
Ali is assassinated by troops loyal to a distant relative of Mohammed. The Muslim community separates into two competing factions, Sunnis and Shiites.

680
Ali's son Hussein is murdered at Karbala (in today's southern Iraq). This further widens the gap between the two sects that exists to this day.

daughters. After Khadijah's death, Mohammed married several other wives (polygamy was acceptable) for political and altruistic reasons. In addition he had at least two concubines.

Sunnis & Shiites

Islam split into different sects soon after its foundation, based not so much on theological interpretation but on historical event.

When the Prophet died in 632, he left no instructions as to who should be his successor, or the manner in which future Islamic leaders (known as caliphs) should be chosen. The community initially chose Abu Bakr, the Prophet's closest companion and father-in-law, as the new leader of the Muslim faith, but not everyone was happy with this decision. Some supported the claim of Ali bin Abi Taleb, Mohammed's cousin and son-in-law. These supporters became known as Shiites ('partisans' of Ali). Ali eventually became caliph, the fourth of Mohammed's successors, in 656, but just five years later he was assassinated by troops loyal to the governor of Syria, Mu'awiyah bin Abu Sufyan (a distant relative of the Prophet), and Mu'awiyah became caliph.

From that point on the Muslim community separated into two competing factions. The Sunnis on the one hand favoured the Umayyads, the dynasty which was established by Mu'awiyah. According to Sunni doctrine, the caliph was both the spiritual leader of the Muslim community and the temporal ruler of the state. So long as a Muslim ruled with justice and according to the Sharia'a (Islamic law), he deserved the support of the Muslim community as a whole. Shiites, on the other hand, believed that only a descendant of the Prophet through Ali's line should lead the Muslims. Because Shiites have rarely held temporal power, their doctrine came to emphasise the spiritual position of their leaders, the imams.

In 680, Ali's son Hussein was murdered in brutal circumstances at Karbala (in today's southern Iraq), an event that further widened the gap between the two factions. The division and hostility between the two sects continues to this day.

As with any religion approaching one billion adherents, Islam has produced many sects, movements and offshoots within the traditional Sunni–Shiite division.

Teachings

Despite modern connotations with fundamentalism and the violent beginnings of Islam in the Peninsula itself, Islam is an inherently peace-

Over the centuries Sunnism has developed into the 'orthodox' strain of Islam and today comprises about 90% of the world's more than 1100 million Muslims. There are large Shiite minorities, however, spread across the Middle East – including in Bahrain.

....
DISTRIBUTION OF SUNNIS & SHIITES
....

This table shows the approximate distribution of Sunni and Shiite Muslims across the Arabian Peninsula. For updates of this information, consult www.populstat.info.

COUNTRY	SUNNI MUSLIMS	SHIITE MUSLIMS	OTHER RELIGIONS
Bahrain	25%	57%	18%
Kuwait	45%	30%	25%
Kuwait	45%	30%	25%
Oman	74% (Ibadi)	14%	12%
Qatar	92%	0%	8%
Saudi Arabia	93%	4%	3%
UAE	80%	16%	4%
Yemen	53%	47%	0%

AND YOUR RELIGION IS...?

After exchanging pleasantries with acquaintances on the Peninsula, the conversation inevitably tends towards three subjects that most Western people shy away from: sex, politics and religion. The level of frankness involved in some of these discussions can come as a surprise. Forewarned is forearmed, however, and there's no better way of getting under the skin of a nation than talking about the things that matter most in life.

While all three subjects may seem like potential minefields (don't talk about sex with the opposite gender, especially if you're male; if you're talking politics, avoid saying 'you' when you mean 'your government'), religion is the one topic of conversation that takes a bit of practice.

For most Muslims, however, tolerating Christians, Jews (both 'People of the Book'), Buddhists or Hindus is easy – knowing what to do with a heretic is the problem. Stating you don't believe in God is as good as saying you doubt the very foundation of a Muslim's life. So how do you say you're an atheist without causing offence? Try saying 'I'm not religious'. This will likely lead to understanding nods and then, on subsequent meetings, a very earnest attempt at conversion. Words like 'You'll find God soon, God willing' should be seen as a measure of someone's like for you and not as a rejection of your 'position'; a reasonable response would be *shukran* (thank you).

ful creed. The word 'Islam' means 'submission', or 'self-surrender'. It also means 'peace'. Taken as a whole, Islam is the attainment of peace – with self, society and the environment – through conscious submission to the will of God. To submit to the will of God does not just entail paying lip service to God through ceremony, but through all daily thoughts and deeds.

The principal teaching of Islam is that there is only one true God, creator of the universe. Muslims believe that the God of Islam is the same God of Christians and Jews, but that he has no son or partner and he needs no intermediary (such as priests). Muslims believe that the prophets, starting with Adam, including Abraham and Jesus, and ending with Mohammed, were sent to reveal God's word but that none of them were divine.

Historically, this creed obviously had great appeal to the scattered people of the Peninsula who were given access to a rich spiritual life without having to submit to incomprehensible rituals administered by hierarchical intermediaries. Believers needed only to observe the transportable Five Pillars of Islam in order to fulfil their religious duty. This is true to this day and is perhaps one of the reasons why Islam is one of the world's fastest growing religions.

The Five Pillars of Islam

Shahada

This is the profession of faith that Muslims publicly declare in every mosque, five times a day across the land: 'There is no God but Allah and Mohammed is his Prophet'. To convert to Islam, one needs only to state this with conviction three times.

Salat

Muslims are expected to pray five times a day: at sunrise, noon, midafternoon, sunset and night (usually 90 minutes after sunset). It's acceptable to pray at home or at the office, except for Friday noon prayers, which are performed preferably at a mosque. Prayer involves prostration in the direction of the Kaaba in Mecca (arrows in aircraft and in hotel

Websites on Islam

Al-Bab (www.al-bab.com) Comprehensive site providing links to information on and discussions of Islam.

Islamicity (www.islamicity.com) Good reference for non-Muslims interested in Islam.

rooms indicate the right direction) and the ritual recital of passages of the Quran. Before praying, a Muslim must perform 'ablution' (washing arms, hands, head and feet with water or sand) to indicate a willingness to be purified in spirit.

Zakat

This is the duty of alms giving. Muslims must give a portion of their salary (one-fortieth of a believer's annual income to be exact) to those in greater need than oneself.

Ramadan

Some people are excused the rigours of Ramadan, including young children and those whose health will not permit fasting. Travellers on a journey are also excused, although they are expected to fast on alternative days instead.

It was during the month of Ramadan that Mohammed received his first revelation in AD 610. Muslims mark this special event each year by fasting from sunrise until sunset throughout this holy month. During this time, Muslims must abstain from taking anything into their bodies, whether related to eating, drinking, having sex or smoking. The idea behind the fast is to bring people closer to Allah via spiritual and physical purity.

Hajj

Every Muslim capable of doing so (whether physically or financially) is expected to perform the hajj pilgrimage to Mecca, the holiest of cities, at least once in their lifetime. For a pilgrimage to qualify as a 'true' hajj, it can only be performed during a few specific days of the Muslim year. Visiting Mecca at any other time of the year is known as *umrah* (the 'lesser pilgrimage' or 'visitation'). Performing hajj is richly rewarded: all past sins are forgiven. Additionally, pilgrims are entitled to prefix their names with *Al-Haj* and doing so still evokes much respect in the community.

The Quran

Muslims believe that the Quran is the literal word of God, unlike the Bible or Torah which they believe were inspired by God but were recorded subject to human interpretation. For Muslims, the Quran is therefore not just the principal source of doctrine in Islam, but also a source of spiritual rapture in its own right. It is recited often with emotional elation, as a blessing to the reciter and the listener. The use of the 'sacred' language of Arabic, with its unique rhythms, gives the recitation a sacramental quality that eludes translation, and many Muslims around the world still learn large portions of the Quran in its original form to feel closer to God's words.

Sharia'a

Given the belief in the Quran's physical sacredness, Islamic law forbids the touching or reciting of an Arabic Quran without special ablution. Travellers should be aware of this when visiting mosques and refrain from touching the holy book.

As there is no distinction between life and religion in Islam, it follows that a set of principles or 'laws' based on Islamic teaching should shape the general conduct of life. The 'legal' implications of those principles is referred to as Sharia'a, although it is not 'law' in a Western sense and is widely open to differences of interpretation.

In matters of dispute, or where someone breaks the moral code of Islam, Muslim scholars turn either to the Quran or to the Sunnah, a body of works recording the sayings and doings of the Prophet (and some of his companions) for guidance. However, there are many Sunnah authorities, and their reliability is in turn determined by different schools of Islamic jurisprudence.

Sharia'a law has come to be associated with extreme forms of punishment meted out to transgressors in some Arab countries: amputation of limbs for repeat-offending thieves, flogging of those caught committing adultery, public beheading for murderers. These punishments, associated mostly with the austere Hanbali school of jurisprudence in Saudi Arabia, are intended as a deterrent first and foremost and are only rarely enforced.

In some instances the Sharia'a is quite specific, such as in the areas of inheritance law and the punishments for certain offences. In many other cases it provides only guidelines.

Jihad

If there is one term that is more misunderstood than Sharia'a by people in the West, it is the term 'jihad'. This has come to be seen as the rallying cry-to-arms of so-called Muslim fundamentalists against Western regimes and is assumed to apologise for acts of terrorism. It is true that for some fundamentalists jihad represents a violent struggle to preserve the Islamic faith from the encroachment of a different set of moral values (or, as they would see it, a lack of moral values). For these people, it also represents a struggle against what they consider to be the bullying of countries whose political and economic dominance impinges upon the rights and freedoms of Islamic peoples – in Palestine and Iraq in particular.

The interpretation of jihad as being solely about waging war on alternative ways of governance and of living, however, is a very narrow definition that most Islamic people wholeheartedly reject. Indeed, violent behaviour runs counter to Islamic teaching regarding justice, tolerance and peace. In fact, the word jihad means 'striving' or 'struggle' and has much broader connotations than the translation usually ascribed to it by the Western media. Far from 'holy war', it more often means 'striving in the way of the faith' – struggling against one's own bad intentions, or rooting out evil, 'indecency' or oppression in society. Islam dictates that this struggle should occur through peaceful, just means so that wisdom prevails, not through anger and aggression.

Jihad in a political context, as the 'struggle to defend the faith', has been the subject of intense debate among Muslim scholars for the last 1400 years. In as much as it refers to the right of a nation to defend itself against oppression, there isn't a nation on earth that wouldn't claim the same right. Nevertheless, for most scholars (both past and present) jihad refers primarily to a spiritual rather than nationalistic, political or military concept.

A scholar or judge learned in Sharia'a law has to determine the proper 'Islamic' position or approach to a problem using his own discretion. This partly explains the wide divergence in Muslim opinion on some issues – such as with regard to jihad today.

Customs & Ceremonies

You don't have to stay in the Arabian Peninsula for long to notice the presence of a 'third party' in all human interaction. Every official occasion begins with a reading from the Holy Quran. A task at work begins with an entreaty for God's help. The words *al-hamdu lillah* (thanks be to God) frequently lace sentences in which good things are related. Equally, the words *insha'allah* (God willing) mark all sentences that anticipate the future. These expressions are not merely linguistic decoration, they evidence a deep connection between society and faith.

For most Muslims, in other words, Islam is not just a religion, it's a way of life. It suggests what a Muslim should wear and what a Muslim should eat. It directs how income should be spent, who should inherit, and what amount. It guides behaviour and suggests punishment for transgression. Few other religions are as all-encompassing. Sometimes it is hard for Western observers to understand the part played by religion – in marriage and the role of women in particular – but looked at from an Arab perspective it is hard to see why some of the traditional Peninsula practices win such opprobrium from non-Islamic commentators, especially when placed in a historical context.

Turkey is the only Muslim country that has formally separated the religious sphere from the secular sphere.

Marriage

It is true that a Muslim man is permitted by Islam to have up to four wives (but a woman may have only one husband). As with many things within Islam, however, this came about through consideration of a particular historical context where women were left without a provider through war, natural disasters or divorce. Uniquely, it allows a 'certain latitude of nature' on behalf of men within the framework of the law, but holds men responsible for their actions.

Both the man and the woman must enter the marriage freely or else it is invalid.

Role of Women

Islam regards women, whether single or married, as individuals in their own right, with the right to own property and earnings without anyone dictating how they dispose of that income. A marriage dowry is given by the groom to the bride for the woman's personal use and she keeps her own name in marriage.

Mothers are highly honoured in Islam and far from being excluded from the mosque, as is sometimes believed by non-Muslims, they are exempted the duty to make it easier to fulfil their function as carer of children. Most mosques have separate prayer halls where women can worship without feeling uncomfortable because of the presence of men. Men are never permitted to enter the women's prayer hall but in some of the Grand Mosques, women are permitted, except during prayer times, to enter the men's prayer hall. In Mecca, all Muslims, male and female, stand shoulder to shoulder in the sacred places and pray together.

Although Islam permits a man to have four wives, each wife must be treated equally: 'if ye fear that ye shall not be able to deal justly, then only one' (The Quran, sura 4:3). Modern Muslim interpretation emphasises the impossibility of loving two wives equally.

Dress

Islam prescribes modest dress in public places for both men and women, which involves covering the legs, arms and head for men, and the hair and neck for women. It does not, however, mention the use of a veil. The origin of the custom of covering the body is unclear; it certainly predates Islam and to a large degree makes excellent sense in the ravaging heat of the Arabian Peninsula where exposure to the midday sun is dangerous to health.

Diet

Meat must be halal (permitted). In other words, slaughtered in the prescribed manner, with minimal cruelty and with consideration of the animal.

Muslims are forbidden to eat or drink anything containing pork or alcohol. Nor are they permitted to consume the blood or the meat of any animal that has died of natural causes. These strictures traditionally made good sense in the Arabian Peninsula where tapeworm was a common problem with pork meat and where the effect of alcohol is exaggerated by the extreme climate. These are still good guidelines today.

Islam & the West

In his introduction to the *Concise Encyclopaedia of Islam*, Professor Huston Smith quotes a *Newsweek* journalist commenting on the 1979 US–Iran crisis: 'We are heading into an expansion,' ran the article, 'of the American relationship with that complex of religion, culture and geography known as Islam...no part of the world is more hopelessly and systematically and stubbornly misunderstood by us.'

These are strong words and they reflect 1000 years of misinformation, mistrust and misrepresentation of the Muslim world by the West and vice versa. But to what extent can the same comment be made today when each country in the West has a sizable Muslim community, large proportions of Gulf students attend Western colleges, and expatriate workers from Peninsula countries return with a different story? The ordinary person in the street is better informed about alternative cultures than ever before in the history of East–West relations. So why does the myth-making persist?

Muslims and Christians confronted each other during the Inquisition, the Crusades and in numerous encounters throughout history. Religious propaganda was used as a way of helping each side achieve its purpose and the prejudices created persist to this day. Add to this the behaviour of a small minority who call themselves Muslim but who are not good ambassadors for the faith, and it would appear that the religion is doomed to be 'hopelessly and systematically and stubbornly misunderstood' for millennia to come.

On the other hand, if there is one positive outcome of the tensions between Islam and the West since September 11 it is surely the high-profile dialogue between ordinary people on what constitutes Islam and how it relates to Western culture. In newspapers and TV programs in every country of the West, the lexicon of Islam is becoming less alien and needs less definition. Debates about wearing the hijab (veil) that continue to dominate many media stories, for example, start with the premise that people are no longer ignorant of the custom.

Of course the dialogue hasn't always been a comfortable one as the publication of derogatory cartoons in Denmark and videos in USA show, nor has the outcome always made good sense, as with censoring Christian expression in case it causes offence to Muslims. Nonetheless, slowly but surely, each 'side' is lurching towards a better understanding of the limits of tolerance expected by the other, and the threatening aspect of the encounter is receding in the process.

This may not be entirely welcome to the governments on either side of the equation. There's an element of political convenience involved in old religious rivalries. After all, how does a government persuade its people to intervene in foreign affairs without drawing on old animosities? The origin of those old animosities is the subject of the following sections.

Shared Foundations of Monotheism

When in 2003 US General William Boykin, referring to a Muslim soldier, said 'I knew that my God was real, and his was an idol', it offended the Muslim world not so much because of the implied hierarchy of deities but because of the heretical nature of the comment. For all Muslims there is no God but God, and this uniqueness of God is the defining principle of all three major monotheistic religions: Islam, Christianity and Judaism.

The three religions have much in common as they all revere Jerusalem (the third holiest city after Mecca and Medina for Muslims) and they share the same prophets, including Abraham, Moses and Jesus. Crucially, however, Islam denies the divinity of any of these figures and teaches that Mohammed was the last prophet who will come before the day of judgement.

Foray into Europe

The monotheistic faiths became powerful cultural and political entities in the world because they broke the geographic confines of their origins. Islam is no exception and it soon spread across neighbouring countries, shifting capitals from Mecca to Damascus and then peacefully to Jerusalem. From here traders from Eastern Europe, the Mediterranean and North Africa were exposed to the new religion and recognised in it a practical, portable faith which they voluntarily took home with them.

The first major impact that Islam made on the West was through the campaigns of the Muslim armies who spread into Spain from North

Muslim Arabs introduced the concept of zero into European mathematics – without which there would be no computer age – not to mention other civilising influences such as coffee, paper-making and chess.

Islam, Muslims believe, is not a new religion but the refinement and ultimate manifestation of the monotheistic religions. As such, Muslims are respectful of Christianity and Judaism and their adherents (known as 'People of the Book'), and acknowledge the debt to the revelations of the Bible and Torah, predating the Quran.

Africa in 711 and settled in Andalusia. During their occupation of this part of Spain, they built the great citadels and mosques of Granada and Cordoba and entered into a creative and largely peaceful dynamic with Christendom that lasted for seven centuries.

The Crusades

Not everyone was pleased with the Muslim legacy, however, and pockets of resistance to the spread of Islam finally took a militant shape in the form of the Crusades which took place between 1096 and 1272. In the ominous name of a 'just war', Christian zealots wrested the Holy Land from the Muslims in 1099 in a battle to regain Jerusalem. Unfortunately, the nine Crusades attracted not only the pious but also every kind of adventurer and miscreant out looking for a fight, and victory was marked by wanton bloodletting. In 1204, for example, the sacking of Constantinople by Crusaders led by the Venetians involved widespread slaughter and looting – as evidenced by the bronze horses plucked from the hippodrome in Constantinople that now grace St Mark's Basilica in Venice.

Atrocities abounded on both sides, such as the slaughter of 2,700 Muslim men, women and children by Richard I of England and Philip II of France on 20th August 1191. Reprisals came swiftly in the form of the torture and slaying of Christian prisoners throughout Saladin's empire. Despite such animosity between the two sides, later travellers to the Holy Land were surprised to find Christians and Muslims settled into comfortable cohabitation. Indeed Christians throughout the succeeding centuries imitated many of the customs and manners of Muslims, particularly in terms of dress and eating.

Ottoman Expansion

The second great Islamic excursion into Europe came with the Ottoman Turks. They've come to be seen as an oppressive people, not least by TE Lawrence whose censure of the Turks in *Seven Pillars of Wisdom* finds resonance in Western history books throughout the 20th century. The tendency has been to emphasise Turkish military invasion rather than their cultural influence and in particularly the taking of Christian Constantinople in 1453 is traditionally seen as a traumatic event, impacting on Eu-

The early Islamic encounter with Europe resulted in cultural cross-pollination. The scholars of Muslim Spain translated classical works of medicine, astronomy, chemistry, philosophy and architecture from Greek and Roman sources, lost to the Europe of the Dark Ages. This helped bring about the Renaissance – upon which modern Europe is built.

FAMOUS EARLY MUSLIMS

Muslims contributed widely to the world's body of knowledge at a time when Europe was lost in the Dark Ages, but few of their names are recognised by people in the West today. Here is an introduction to four of the many intellectuals, travellers, medics and thinkers who deserve a better billing in Western history books:

Al-Khwarizmi (AD 780–850) Known as the 'Father of Algebra', Al-Khwarizmi combined Indian and Greek mathematical traditions and introduced Arabic numerals to Europe. He also built on Ptolemy's work to produce the first map of the world.

Ibn Sina (AD 980–1037) A great medical scholar, Ibn Sina wrote the *Book of Healing* and the *Canon of Medicine* – a medical encyclopaedia which was used throughout the West for over 600 years. Many modern clinics in Arabia are named after him.

Ibn Khaldun (AD 1332–95) Author of *The Book of Examples and Collections from Early and Later Information Concerning the Days of Arabs, Non-Arabs and Berbers*, Ibn Khaldun was the first historian to write on the philosophy of history and civilisation.

Ibn Battuta (AD 1304–69) A world-famous traveller, Ibn Battuta's pilgrimage to Mecca became a journey of 120,000km across North Africa, the Middle East and Asia. His travels in Saudi and Oman are commemorated in plaques at sites such as Bibi Miriam's Tomb (Qalhat).

ropean identity. This is a view, however, that is now being challenged by modern historians who point out that during the height of their reign in the 16th and 17th centuries, in an empire that stretched from Hungary to Libya, the Turks were welcomed by many as bringing culture and prosperity to countries under their control where they treated Christians and Jews with the respect accorded to monotheistic faith by the Quran.

Meanwhile in Arabia's arid Najd region, a new spirit of 'fundamentalism', or a return to pure Islamic principles, was taking shape in the form of Abd al-Wahhab (1703–1792). This ultra-conservative Sunni from Basra (present-day Iraq) was embraced by the Saud family who liked his teachings, and he became a significant influence on the expression of faith in Saudi. His followers, known as Wahhabis, launched various bids for political power and religious dominance over the succeeding centuries, including an audacious attack on the Shia city of Karbala in 1802, prefiguring movements such as the Brotherhood of Islam two centuries later.

Colonialism

When Napoleon's armies took aim at the Sphinx in the early 19th century, it marked a turning point in the relationship between the West and the Muslim world. The great powers of Europe, with large overseas colonies built on the industrial revolution, began to make incursions into Arab territory that were more to do with strategic influence than with faith.

There were also positive interactions during the era of colonialism. European explorers came to Arabia with a genuine interest in a culture that seemed less tainted by the effeteness of Western society. By the mid-20th century, the desire for learning drifted in the opposite direction, with many wealthy Muslims studying in Europe. They returned to their own countries bearing Western ideas, including democracy and individualism.

Pan-Arabism

European control of the Middle East diminished with the Suez Crisis of 1956 – the era in which Gamal Abdel Nasser became president of Egypt, bringing with him the notion of pan-Arabism. First appearing in 1915, pan-Arabism was a movement for unification among the Arab nations of the Middle East. It was a secular and mostly socialist movement with nationalist overtones that opposed any kind of Western influence or intervention in Arab affairs. Unity based on race only fulfilled half the equation and soon unity based on Islam became a more suggestive prospect.

Movements such as the Muslim Brotherhood in Egypt, led by the radical Sayyid Qutb, pursued a universal Islamic society through whatever means necessary, including violence and martyrdom. With this movement, a different dynamic towards the West came into being. The revolution in Iran in 1979, in which the monarchy was replaced by Muslim clerics, was a further indicator of a new expression of the old alliance of faith and the sword.

Recent Tensions

From a Muslim perspective, the politics of oil has dominated relations between the West and the Arab world since the 1970s. The wealth that has come from oil has been equally divisive within the Arab world, giving rise to fundamentalist Islamic elements who perceive the relationship between the West and the Arab world as a threat to traditional Islamic and Arabic values.

Many Muslims believe that the politics of oil was the prime motivator behind the 2003 invasion of Iraq. When on 16 September 2001, at Camp David, George W Bush used the term 'crusade' to describe the early days of the so-called War on Terror, many Arabs came to perceive the war in the region as the continuation of a legacy characterised by the bullying of the weak by the powerful.

ISLAM ISLAM & THE WEST

With about one billion people professing the faith, Islam is the world's second-largest religion after Christianity; around 50 countries have Muslim majorities and another 35 have significant minorities. Six million Muslims live in the USA – around 2% of the population.

Books: Islam & the West

Infidels (Andrew Wheatcroft; 2004)

The Crisis of Islam – Holy War and Unholy Terror (Bernard Lewis; 2004)

OTHER RELIGIONS ON THE PENINSULA

All the indigenous people of the Peninsula today are Muslim. One or two Muslim converts to Christianity wander in a state of miserable purgatory on the periphery of society, barred from all social interaction with family and friends by a decision that most Muslims would consider not just heretical but also a rejection of common sense, history and culture.

This is not the case with expatriate Christians whose religion is respected and provision for worship catered for in church services across the region. There are also Hindu and Buddhist temples tucked away in small suburbs of the region's big cities and travelling missions visit expat camps in rural areas to bring comfort to those separated from the familiar props of their home communities. Small enclaves of Jewish people who have lived on the Peninsula for centuries are given private latitude in Yemen as part of the Muslim culture of religious tolerance.

Saudi, as keeper of Islam's holiest shrines, is the exception: no religious observance is permitted other than Islam. That said, a blind eye is turned towards pockets of private worship among Christians.

The other feature that has characterised recent tensions between the West and the Arab world is the perceived Western bias towards Israel in the ongoing Arab-Israeli conflict. Until a solution to the relentless problem of cohabitation between Jews and Arabs in Israel is reached, the entire region will remain in a state of flux.

The key word regarding non-Islamic religious observance in the Arabian Peninsula today is discretion: whatever worship happens behind closed doors and which doesn't interfere with the beliefs of Muslims is considered a matter between the individual and their own conscience.

Keeping the Faith Today

Modern life requires compromises with religion, but then it always has. As such, there's not much that separates a Peninsula life from a Western one, except perhaps in the degrees of temptation and opportunity. That's changing as access to Western culture becomes more prevalent in the region.

Except in Saudi and Kuwait, alcohol is widely available and has become a source of curiosity and experimentation for many youngsters and a way of life for some Arabs who have studied and worked abroad. Drugs, largely smuggled in from across the Gulf, have led to addiction (together with the familiar misery, shame in the community and family disruption) in a small but growing number of Arabian youths who seek to emulate the kind of rock-star lifestyles they see celebrated on satellite TV.

All of these temptations and opportunities are causing a new generation, educated to think and research the truth for themselves, to question the knowledge handed down from their elders. The uprisings of the Arab Spring of 2011 were partly symptomatic of the pull in two directions between a traditional life, governed by Islamic principles and concern for society, and the realities of a modern life where the individual and his or her own personal needs and satisfactions take priority.

Covering Islam – How the Media and the Experts Determine How We See the Rest of the World (1997), by the late Edward W Said, examines the way in which the media portrays the Islamic world.

Despite the trend towards greater liberalism in most countries of the Arabian Peninsula, it's probably fair to say there is no less faith involved. The mosques are still full on a Friday; students still interrupt their studies to pray; kindly friends still attempt conversion to 'the one true faith' among their non-Islamic acquaintances, and driving continues to deteriorate in Ramadan as the overwhelming majority observe dawn to dusk fasting with the resultant lack of concentration on the roads. In modern Peninsula cities throughout the region, men still keep company in one place, the women in another, enjoying public company but coming together for family, intimacy and private time. This is the age-old pattern of Arab communities, indulging human passions but reining them in with the unconscious guidance of religion and culture and looking forward to the spiritual renewal represented by the once-in-a-lifetime pilgrimage to Mecca.

Flavours of Arabia

Anyone who has read of the lovers' feast prepared by Porphyro in Keats' 'Eve of St Agnes' may be lusting after 'lucent syrups, tinct with cinnamon' and 'spiced dainties' from 'silken Samarkand to cedared Lebanon'. The Arabic Orient has long been fabled for extravagant feasting and eating is indeed a central part of Peninsula life. The staple dishes may not immediately appeal to Western palates, but with knowledge of the customs informing their preparation, they assume a whole new flavour.

Staples & Specialities
Arabian

Breakfast
For most Arab people on the Peninsula, breakfast means eggs in some shape or form and locally produced salty white cheese with a glass of buttermilk or labneh (thin yoghurt) and tahini sweetened with date syrup. It might come with *fuul madamas*, a bean dish lubricated with olive oil, garnished on high days and holidays with pickles and eased along with olives. There may be lentils, heavily laced with garlic, to the chagrin of co-workers, and, of course, bread.

Known generically as *khobz*, bread (in up to 40 different varieties) is eaten in copious quantities with every meal. Most often it's unleavened and comes in flat discs about the size of a dinner plate (not unlike an Indian chapatti). It's traditionally torn into pieces, in lieu of knives and forks, and used to pinch up a morsel of meat, a scoop of dip and a nip of garnish.

Lunch
Lunch means one word only, and that is rice. Rice is often flavoured with a few whole cardamom pods (one of which always lurks beguilingly in the last mouthful) and at feasts with saffron and sultanas. Buried in or sitting on top of the rice will be some kind of delicious spiced stew, with okra or grilled and seasoned chicken, lamb, goat or even camel – but of course never pork, which is haram (forbidden) for Muslims. Popular seasoning includes some or even all of the following: cardamom, coriander, cumin, cinnamon, nutmeg, chilli, ginger, pepper and the all-important, health-giving and almost fla-

SEASONAL TREATS

January–February
Start atop Oman's Green Mountain for citrus delights such as oranges, sweet lemons and limes. Descend to the Dhofar coast for the sea's annual harvest of abalone and conches.

March–April
Head for the coastal plains to sample corn, tomatoes, capsicums and chillies. Cut across to the Al-Hasa region and sink your teeth into Saudi's first dates.

May–June
Search the plantations for papayas and green mangoes, salted and pickled, and eaten with lamb stew. Ascend the Asir Mountains in time for the *mishmish* (apricot) season.

July–August
Select a Ramadan tent for *iftar* specialities at a Gulf hotel. Spend *eid* in the desert towns of the interior where killing the fatted calf is more than just a metaphor.

September–October
Watch offloaded watermelons burst like fireworks on roads that follow ancient caravan routes. Taste honey-dipped sweetmeats with returning pilgrims following the same routes.

November–December
Venture into the hornbill-frequented wadis of Yemen for pomegranates, almonds and walnuts. Enjoy Western foods such as turkey and chestnuts, imported in time for Christmas.

vourless turmeric. In Yemen no one can escape the bitter, livid green froth of fenugreek used to put a punch in a minimal broth or bean dish.

Not surprisingly for a Peninsula with such a rich coastline, fish (fresh or dried) is an equally important lunchtime staple. Hamour (a species of grouper), beya (mullet), kingfish, Sultan Ibrahim and tuna are grilled, fried or barbecued and served with rice and chopped raw cabbage with the essential half lime or lemon. Sardines, piles of which spangle the shore in season and are raked into malodorous heaps between houses, are seldom eaten: they're usually dried for animal fodder.

Dinner

The evening meal is a ragged affair of competing interests – children clamouring for hot dogs or burgers, maids slipping them 'keep-quiet food', mothers going for a sandwich in Starbucks and grandmothers making sweetmeats and aubergine dips, nibbling on dates and trying to persuade fathers to enjoy the company of the family instead of going out for a kebab.

City people in the Peninsula enjoy going out and they are as likely to dine on Mongolian lamb chops, crab rangoon or spaghetti bolognaise as any other city dweller. More often than not, however, they'll opt for Lebanese food with its copious selection of hot and cold appetisers known as mezze. The peeled carrots, buffed radishes, whole lettuces and bunches of peppery spinach leaves, provided complimentary, are a meal in themselves.

Locals invariably entertain guests at home and go out to eat something different. For travellers to the region, it can therefore be difficult finding indigenous food. Ask locally where to sample indigenous food and you may find you're taken home for supper.

Snacks & Sweets

Western fast food has caught on among Peninsula people with the consumption of burger and fries verging on epidemic proportions. The concept has translated easily from traditional practices of visiting small eateries that sell kebabs, felafel and other types of sandwiches. *Shwarma* (meat sliced off a spit and stuffed in a pocket of pita-type bread with chopped tomatoes and garnish), usually served with some form of salad, is the snack of choice across the whole region. Outings to the coffeeshops that sell these traditional fast foods are more about sharing time with friends than eating and men in particular may spend all night on the same plastic chair, puffing on *sheesha* tobacco and sipping tea.

Peninsula people are not big on 'puddings', preferring fruits after (or often before) the meal, and thick fruit juices. On high days and holidays, however, baklava (made of filo and honey) or puddings – including *mahallabiye* (milk based) and *umm ali* (bread based) – might put in an appearance after lunch or supper.

Drinks

Nonalcoholic Drinks

If you want to try camel's milk without the stomach ache, you can often find it in supermarkets – next to the labneh, a refreshing drink of yoghurt, water, salt and sometimes crushed mint.

One of the best culinary experiences of travelling in the region is sampling the fresh fruit juices of pomegranate, hibiscus, avocado, sugar cane, mango, melon or carrot – or a combination of all sorts – served at juice stalls known as *aseer*. Mint and lemon or fresh lime is a refreshing alternative to soda.

Pork is haram (forbidden) to Muslims but it's sometimes available in Gulf supermarkets. Pork sections are easy to spot: customers slink out with sausages as if they're top-shelf items.

Every town has a baklava or pastry shop selling syrupy sweets made from pastry, nuts, honey and sometimes rose water. Sweets are ordered by a minimum weight of 250g.

If as a traveller you try to opt out of the fifth spoonful of sugar in your tea or coffee, you will inevitably be assumed to have diabetes.

Tea, known as *shai* or *chi libton*, could be tea *min na'ana* (with mint, especially in Saudi and Yemen), tea with condensed milk (in the Gulf) or black tea (in Oman), but whatever the flavour, it will contain enough sugar to make a dentist's fortune. The teabag is left in the cup and water is poured from maximum height as proof of your host's tea-making skills.

Coffee, known locally as *qahwa,* is consumed in copious quantities on the Peninsula and is usually strong. Arabia has a distinguished connection with coffee. Though no longer involved in the coffee trade, Al-Makha in Yemen gave its name to the blend of chocolate and coffee popularly known as 'mocha'. The traditional Arabic or Bedouin coffee is heavily laced with cardamom and drunk in small cups. Turkish coffee, which floats on top of thick sediment, is popular in the Gulf region.

Nonalcoholic beer is widely available. Incidentally, travellers shouldn't think that cans of fizzy drink will suffice for hydration in the desert: they often induce more thirst than they satisfy.

Coffeehouses & Coffeeshops

Across the Arabian Peninsula, there are bastions of old-world Arab hospitality that go by the name of 'coffeehouses'. These relics of an era, when people had more time to sit and chat, are places of male camaraderie and tend often to be no more than a mere hole-in-the-wall, a bench up against a souq alleyway, or even a favourite perch under a tree. These coffeehouses dispense coffee from copper pots or *chi libton* (tea) in disposable paper cups while *sheibas* (old men) with beards dish out dates, advice and opinions in equal measure to anyone who'll listen. For a male visitor, they offer a unique engagement with Arab society. Women are politely tolerated but it is more sensitive to leave the men to their bonding.

'Coffeeshops', on the other hand, welcome all-comers. These ubiquitous cafes, with their plastic chairs and compulsory string of fairy lights, are dotted across Arabia. They are usually run by expatriates from the subcontinent and they form the social hub of many small villages, selling kebabs, roasted chickens or omelettes rolled up in flat Arabic bread. Most are simple shopfronts with seating on the pavement but the more upmarket coffeeshops stretch to a plate and a napkin and are scented with the regional passion for *sheesha* (waterpipe).

Alcoholic Drinks

Despite its reputation as a 'dry' region, alcohol is available in all Peninsula countries, except Saudi Arabia, Kuwait and some of the Emirates (where both possession and consumption for locals and foreigners is strictly forbidden).

In the more liberal countries (such as Bahrain and Qatar and some parts of the UAE), bars, cocktail bars and even pubs can be found; in others (such as Yemen and Oman) usually only certain hotels (often mid- or

The world's oldest cultivated fruit has been the staple of Arabs for centuries. Of the world's 90 million date palms, 64 million are in Arab countries.

FLAVOURS OF ARABIA STAPLES & SPECIAL TIES

SAUDI BUBBLES

Saudi 'champagne' is less exciting than it sounds: it's a mixture of apple juice and Perrier water.

COFFEE CARRY-ON

Throughout the Peninsula there is an old and elaborate ritual surrounding the serving of coffee. In homes, offices and even at some hotels, you may well be offered a cup. To refuse is to reject an important gesture of welcome and hospitality, and you risk offending your host. 'Arabic' or 'Bedouin' coffee as it's known, is usually poured from an ornate, long-spouted pot known as a *dalla*, into tiny cups without handles. You should accept the cup with your right hand.

It's considered polite to drink at least three cups (the third is traditionally considered to bestow a blessing). More may be impolite; the best advice is to follow your host's lead. To show you've had sufficient, swivel the cup slightly between fingers and thumb.

upper range) are permitted to serve alcohol. Wine is served in most licensed restaurants in Bahrain, Oman, Qatar and the UAE.

Officially, no Peninsula country produces its own alcoholic drinks, though rumours abound where grapes and dates ferment. Where alcohol is available it's imported from the West and the high prices are intended to keep consumption low – not very successfully. The legal age to be served alcohol is usually 18 years old. You can't buy alcohol to take off the premises unless you are a resident and are eligible for a monthly quota.

Asian

All across Arabia large populations of expatriate peoples have brought their own cuisine to the Peninsula with the result that it dominates the menus of the region. For many Asian expats – often men on 'bachelor' contracts – breakfast, lunch and dinner consists of the same thing: rice and dhal, or rice and meat or vegetable curry, separated into three round metal lunchboxes, stacked one on top of the other, and including a bag of rolled up chapatti (Indian flat bread).

Providing a cheap and cheerful alternative to 'the lunchbox', and serving samosas, biryani or spicy mutton curry, a whole string of Indian and Pakistani restaurants have sprung up across the region, catering for hungry workers who would normally be looked after by wives and daughters. Those who do have their families with them enjoy as varied a cuisine as their nationality and local supermarket allow. British teachers eat roast beef for Friday lunch, Filipino nurses make chicken *adobo,* Sri Lankan maids try to win over their adoptive families to furious fish curries. In many of the big cities, the traveller can sample all these delights too, often in world-class restaurants.

Bedouin

When round him mid the burning sands, he saw
Fruits of the North in icy freshness thaw
And cooled his thirsty lip, beneath the glow
Of Mecca's sun, with urns of Persian snow.

Thomas Moore

Thomas Moore's 19th-century description of Bedouin delicacies, elaborated with sherbets and dainties, sounds enticing but the reality is far more prosaic. TE Lawrence memorably describes a feast with the Arab

> In Lebanese restaurants the number of mezze can run to 50 or more dishes and include delicacies like chopped liver, devilled kidney, sheep brain and other offal.

> As an extravagant gesture in a Bedouin emir's tent, a camel is stuffed with a sheep, which is stuffed with a goat, which is stuffed with a chicken.

THE SHEESHA EXPERIENCE

In any city across the Peninsula, two sensations mark the hot and humid air of an Arabian summer's evening: the wreaths of scented peach-flavoured smoke that spiral above the corner coffeeshop and the low gurgle of water, like a grumbling camel, in the base of the water pipe. Periodically banned by governments concerned for public morality (the pipes are not narcotic – only time-wasting), and inevitably returned to the street corners by the will of the people, these *sheesha* establishments are an indispensable part of Arabian social life.

In the traditional coffeehouses of the region, *sheesha* is an entirely male affair: men sprawl on cushions in Yemen, or lounge on benches in the souqs of Doha; they indolently watch the football on TV, occasionally breaking off from the sucking and puffing to pass a word of lazy complaint to their neighbour, snack on pieces of kebab, or hail the waiter for hot coals to awaken the drowsy embers of the *sheesha* bottle.

In Dubai, Manama and Muscat, however, *sheesha* has long since spread to the more family-oriented coffeeshop. It has even become a fashionable occupation in Western style cafes. Here, women in black *abeyyas* (full-length black robes) and sparkling diamante cuffs drag demurely on velvet-clad mouthpieces, their smoking punctuating a far more animated dialogue as they actively define the new shape of society.

Sheikh Sherif Nasir of Medina, in which he dips his fingers into a mess of boiling hot lamb fat while ripping the meat from the carcass. This was probably *kebsa* – a whole lamb stuffed with rice and pine nuts. The most prized pieces of this dish are the sheep's eyeballs, which irreverent hosts delight to this day in waving towards horrified Western guests.

Mostly, Bedouin food consists of whatever is available at a particular time, and hunger and thirst are far more attendant on a day's travelling in the desert than sumptuous feasting. Camel's milk and goat's cheese are staple parts of the diet as are dried dates and, of course, water. Water takes on a particularly precious quality when it is rationed and the Bedouin are renowned for consuming very little, particularly during the day when only small sips are taken, mostly to rinse the mouth.

The legendary hospitality of the Bedu means that travellers in the Empty Quarter (in Saudi) or the Sharqiya Sands (Oman) who bump into a Bedouin camp are bound to be invited to share 'bread and salt'. At the least this will involve Arabic coffee, camel's milk and a thatch of dried meat, usually with a host of flies dancing in the bowl. The flies don't harm the Bedu and it's unlikely they'll bother the traveller much either, but the milk can upset a sensitive stomach.

Habits & Customs

The main meal for most Peninsula people is usually a home-cooked family affair involving rice but there the similarities end. There is huge diversity in terms of the kinds of food prepared and the habits practised across the region. Here are a few selected customs that may give insight into the important place that dining has within the Arab community as a whole.

Shopping

Catering for food is largely a man's job and brothers are often dispatched to Thursday wholesale markets to find fresh produce. Giant shopping malls, like Carrefour, have met with instant success among city locals, perhaps because they resemble an air-conditioned version of the wholesale market. For many, however, buying meat from the livestock market is a matter of male pride and the animal will be taken home live ready for dispatch under specific Islamic guidelines.

Cooking

Dining is essentially a communal affair and it's traditional at the weekends for many families who work in the city to travel long distances back to their villages to enjoy 'mum's cooking'. Women almost exclusively prepare food: grinding spices, peeling vegetables and plucking chickens is seen as an opportunity to chat with female relatives and catch up on the news.

Eating

In more traditional towns and villages, men and women will eat separately with the eldest son helping to serve the men first while the women await their turn in another room. It's considered good manners for men to reserve the best parts of the meal for the women. Arab people assert that eating is enjoyed best, even by city dwellers with Western-style furniture, on the floor from shared dishes using bread and the right hand as utensils. This makes eating very easily transferable to an outdoor setting and indeed picnics are the number-one regional pastime.

Relaxing

A dish of rosewater, the petals harvested from Arabian mountains, marks the traditional end of a meal; diners rinse their hands in the scented water. Sleep is generally enjoyed by all after the midday meal.

The venue of preference for 'that special meal' for many Peninsula families is a well-lit grassy verge on a highway with kebabs brought in by the kilo.

FLAVOURS OF ARABIA HABITS & CUSTOMS

For an exquisite tang on the palate, dates should be eaten half ripe, biting the fruit lengthwise and savouring the bitter zest with the mellow ripe part. Don't forget to discard the pip discreetly in a napkin: Sinbad spat his out and blinded a genie's son who claimed mischievous revenge.

Ramadan

The holy month is a time of great conviviality and perhaps somewhat surprisingly, given that the month is about fasting and abstinence, many Arab people put on weight at this time. The reason for this is the long Ramadan nights which are generally marked by bonhomie and socialising and the sharing of seasonal delicacies and sweetmeats. The fast (between dawn and dusk) is broken each day with a communal breakfast comprising something light (like dates and *laban* – an unsweetened yoghurt drink) before prayers. Then comes *iftar* at which enough food is usually consumed to compensate for the previous hours of abstinence with socialising that continues well into the early hours. The venue for this communal meal is often the wali's office (equivalent to a town hall) or a specially erected Ramadan tent. People then rise again before dawn to prepare a meal to support them throughout the day.

Where to Eat & Drink

One of the undoubted pleasures of the modern cities of the Peninsula is the variety and quality of the restaurants. In the Gulf in particular, there is world-class dining in magnificent surroundings. One way for a visitor to experience some of the best of these dining experiences is to skip breakfast on a Friday and visit the local five-star hotel for Friday brunch – a regional speciality much beloved by locals and expats alike. A spectacular array of local, Middle Eastern and international dishes will be on display, decorated with ice carvings and garnished extravagantly, for a relatively modest price. Similarly, many hotels arrange weekly seafood nights, often with belly dancing or local entertainment. Again, this is often a more economic way of sampling the region's famous oysters, lobsters and prawns than reserving a table at an exclusive seafood restaurant.

Lebanese and Indian restaurants are the most prevalent throughout the region, followed by Chinese and Thai in the bigger towns. Food from all over the world is available in the Gulf cities. The hardest food to find in a restaurant is local, traditional fare but chains like Bin Ateeq in Muscat, and Souq Waqif in Doha, try to redress that imbalance.

On the whole, restaurants are open (mostly for expats) during lunch; they're closed in the afternoon and open from about 6pm to the early hours of the morning to cater for the late-night eating habits of most people across the region. In Saudi Arabia restaurants must comply with certain strict regulations (regarding segregation of men and women and the observation of prayer hours, for example).

In very local restaurants, seating is sometimes on the floor on mats. Shoes should be left outside the perimeters of the mats. Food is served from a communal plate placed on a tray.

Traditional snacks (such as *shwarma*) are quick, cheap and usually safe to eat, as the food is prepared and cooked in front of you.

There's also a good range of well-stocked supermarkets (selling many international foods) in the large cities and, increasingly, food halls are found in the malls.

During Ramadan, most hotels set up elaborate buffets of Ramadan specialities which non-Muslims are free to join. Alcohol is not available in Ramadan except as room service at hotels.

Vegetarians & Vegans

While Arab people are traditionally thought of as full-blooded, red-meat eaters, the reality is that for many of modest income across the region meat is a treat for high days and holidays. This fact, coupled with the influence of southern Indian cuisine introduced by large expat commu-

---

Books: Arabian Recipes

The Arab Table: Recipes & Culinary Traditions (May Bsisu)

Medieval Arab Cookery (Maxime Rodinson)

There are over 600 species of date. The best come from Al-Hasa in Saudi Arabia where a variety called *khlas* is presold to regular customers before it's even harvested.

Vegetarians beware! Some Peninsula chefs may regard vegetarianism as an incomprehensible Western indulgence or a kind of culinary apostasy. To avoid uncomfortable conversations about soup ingredients, stick to Indian restaurants.

EATING ETIQUETTE

Sharing a meal with Arab friends is a great way of cementing a newly formed friendship. But Peninsula eating etiquette is refined and complex. Here are a few tips. Note that food is traditionally shared by all from the same serving dishes, spread on a cloth on the floor, without the use of cutlery.

Pre-Meal

➡ If you're eating in someone's house, bring a small gift of flowers, chocolates or pastries, fruit or honey.

➡ Carry out your ablutions – it's polite to be seen to wash your hands before a meal.

➡ Don't sit with your legs stretched out – it's considered rude during a meal.

During the Meal

➡ Use only your right hand for eating or accepting food; the left is reserved for ablutions.

➡ Don't take the best part of the meal – such as the meat – until offered; it is usually saved until last.

➡ Mind your manners – your host will often lay the tastiest morsels in front of you; it's polite to accept them.

➡ Don't put food back on the plate, discard it in a napkin.

Post-Meal

➡ It's traditional to lavish food upon a guest; if you're full, pat your stomach contentedly.

➡ Leave a little food on your plate: traditionally, a clean plate was thought to invite famine.

➡ Feel free to pick your teeth after a meal – it is quite acceptable and toothpicks are often provided.

➡ Stay for coffee – it's polite to accept a cup of coffee after a meal and impolite to leave before it's served.

➡ Know when to go – the chatting is usually done before the meal, so once the meal is over it's time to leave – but don't go before the chief guest.

nities of vegetarian Hindus, means that vegetable dishes appear more often than might be expected on a restaurant menu.

Vegetarian staples include many bean and pulse dishes such as soup, *fuul* (fava bean paste) and dhal, or lentil stews. Chickpeas, either fried into felafel or ground into a paste with oil and garlic (hummus), are a common supplement. Aubergines and okra are used in many delicious stews, and salad vegetables are usually locally grown and organic.

Eating with Kids

Eating out as a family is becoming an increasingly popular pastime in the Peninsula for Arabs and expats: whole minibuses of relatives arrive to the outdoor, seaboard city venues, particularly in the winter months when huddling round a mobile stove is part of the fun. Equally, many parents join their children for a halal 'MacArabia' chicken roll-up or a beef pepperoni pizza in the spreading rash of Western fast-food outlets.

Children are welcome in restaurants across the Peninsula, except in the more exclusive, chic establishments of the Gulf, and many midrange restaurants provide children's menus. High chairs are not commonly available.

Fresh or powdered milk is widely available except in remote areas. Labneh and yoghurt are generally considered safe for children.

In most Peninsula countries, mixed dining is common in more expensive or modern city restaurants. In smaller establishments, men eat on the ground floor, while women and families eat upstairs in a section reserved for them.

Food Glossary

Note that because of the imprecise nature of transliterating Arabic into English, spellings will vary; for example, what we give as *kibbeh* may appear variously as *kibba, kibby* or even *gibeh*.

MIDDLE EASTERN MEZZE

baba ghanooj	smokey-flavoured dip of baked, mashed aubergine (eggplant), typically mixed with tomato and onion and sometimes pomegranate
batata hara	hot, diced potatoes fried with coriander, garlic and capsicum
börek	pastry pockets stuffed with salty white cheese or spicy minced meat with pine nuts; also known as sambousek
fatayer	small pastry triangles filled with spinach
fattoosha	fresh salad of onions, tomatoes, cucumber, lettuce and shards of crispy, thin, deep-fried bread
fuul	paste made from beans, tomatoes, onions, and chilli; also spelt foul, fool
hummus	chickpeas ground into a paste and mixed with tahini, garlic and lemon
kibbeh	minced lamb, bulgur wheat and pine nuts shaped into a lemon-shaped patty and deep fried
kibbeh nayye	minced lamb and cracked wheat served raw
kibda	liver, often chicken liver (*kibda firekh* or *kibda farouj*), usually sautéed in lemon or garlic
labneh	yoghurt paste, heavily flavoured with garlic or mint
lahma bi-ajeen	small lamb pies
loubieh	French bean salad with tomatoes, onions and garlic
mashi	baked vegetables, such as courgettes (zucchini), vine leaves, capsicums, or aubergines, stuffed with minced meat, rice, onions, parsley and herbs
mujadarreh	traditional 'poor person's' dish of lentils and rice garnished with caramelised onions
muttabal	similar to *baba ghanooj*, but the blended aubergine is mixed with tahini, yoghurt and olive oil to achieve a creamier consistency
shanklish	salad of small pieces of crumbled, tangy, eye-wateringly strong cheese mixed with chopped onion and tomato
soojuk	fried, spicy lamb sausage
tabbouleh	bulgur wheat, parsley and tomato–based salad, with a sprinkling of sesame seeds, lemon and garlic; also spelt tabouli
tahini	thin sesame seed paste
waraq aynab	vine leaves stuffed with rice and meat

MIDDLE EASTERN & ARABIAN MAIN COURSES

bamiya	okra-based stew
fasoolyeh	green-bean stew

felafel	deep-fried balls of mashed chickpeas, often rolled in Arabic bread with salad and hummus
hareis	slow-cooked wheat and lamb
kabbza	lamb or chicken cooked with onion, tomato, cucumber, grated carrot and other fruit
kebab	skewered, flame-grilled chunks of meat, usually lamb, but also chicken, goat, camel, fish or squid; also known as *sheesh* or *shish kebab*
kebab mashwi	meat paste moulded onto flat skewers and grilled
kebsa	whole stuffed lamb served on a bed of spiced rice and pine nuts; also known as *khuzi*
kofta	ground meat peppered with spices, shaped into small sausages, skewered and grilled
makbus	casserole of meat or fish with rice
mashboos	grilled meat (usually chicken or lamb) and spiced rice
mashkul	rice served with onions
mihammar	lamb cooked in yoghurt sauce and stuffed with nuts, raisins and other dried fruit
muaddas	rice served with lentils
mushkak game	seasoned camel meat grilled on a skewer – usually tough as old boots!
samak mashwi	fish barbecued over hot coals after basting in a date purée
shish tawooq	kebab with pieces of marinated, spiced chicken
shuwa	lamb cooked slowly in an underground oven
shwarma	Middle Eastern equivalent of Greek gyros or Turkish *doner kebap*; strips are sliced from a vertical spit of compressed lamb or chicken, sizzled on a hot plate with chopped tomatoes and garnish, and then stuffed or rolled in Arabic bread
ta'amiyya	see *felafel*

MIDDLE EASTERN PASTRIES & DESSERTS

asabeeh	rolled filo pastry filled with pistachio, pine and cashew nuts and honey; otherwise known as 'ladies' fingers'
baklava	a generic term for any kind of layered flaky pastry with nuts, drenched in honey
barazak	flat, circular cookies sprinkled with sesame seeds
isfinjiyya	coconut slice
kunafa	shredded wheat over a creamy, sweet cheese base baked in syrup
labneh makbus	sweet yoghurt cheese balls, sometimes made into a frittata-like creation or rolled in paprika; sometimes eaten for breakfast
mahallabiye	milk-based pudding
mushabbak	lacework shaped pastry drenched in syrup
umm ali	bread-based pudding made with sultanas and nuts, flavoured with nutmeg
zalabiyya	pastries dipped in rose water

The Natural Environment

For anyone who has travelled in Arabia, or had the privilege of being in the region after rains, it is immediately apparent that the Peninsula is far from a barren wasteland of undulating sands. On the contrary, the diverse desert landscapes support uniquely adapted plants and animals, particularly in the region's wadis (valleys) and oases. This extraordinary environment forms the backdrop for dramas of survival and endurance by the hardiest of inhabitants and is a revelation and a joy to visitors.

The Al-Hasa Oasis, near the town of Al-Hofuf in eastern Saudi Arabia, is the largest oasis in the world. Covering 2500 sq km, it's home to over three million palm trees.

The Land

Geology

The Arabian Peninsula is a treasure trove for geologists. Though not particularly rich in minerals or gems (except the copper that is found in northern Oman), the Peninsula reveals the earth's earliest history, supporting theories of plate tectonics and continental drift. Indeed, geologists believe that the Peninsula originally formed part of the larger landmass of Africa. A split in this continent created both Africa's Great Rift Valley (which extends from Mozambique up through Djibouti, into western Yemen, Saudi Arabia and Jordan) and the Red Sea.

As Arabia slipped away from Africa, the Peninsula began to 'tilt', with the western side rising and the eastern edge dropping, a process that led to the formation of the Gulf.

Extensive flooding millions of years ago led to the remains of marine life being deposited in layers of sediment across the tilted landmass – as the rich fossil remains found across Arabia indicate. When sufficient dead organic matter is laid down and trapped under the surface where a lack of oxygen prevents it from decaying to water and carbon dioxide, the raw material of hydrocarbons is produced – the origin, in other words, of oil and gas. The conversion from dead organic matter to hydrocarbon is subject to many other conditions such as depth and temperature. Arabia's geology is uniquely supportive of these conditions, and 'nodding donkeys' (drilling apparatus, capable of boring holes up to 5km deep) can be seen throughout the interior.

Governments across the region speculate endlessly on the quantity of reserves remaining. Given that the economies of all the Peninsula countries rely to a lesser or greater extent on oil and gas, this is one issue that can't be left to *insha'allah* (God's will). As such, Peninsula countries are busy diversifying their economic interests in case their reserves run out sooner rather than later.

Geography

Stand on top of Kuwait Towers and the eye roams unhindered along flat country. The low-lying coastal plains and salt flats stretch all along the limp waters of the northern Gulf until the Mussandam Peninsula brings the plain to an abrupt close. This is the environment of mudhoppers, wading birds and long stretches of dazzling-white sands.

Much of the interior is flat too but some major mountain ranges, like the Hajar Mountains of Oman and the Haraz Mountains of Yemen, bring an entirely different climate and way of life to the high ground.

There are no permanent river systems in the Peninsula. Water-laden clouds from the sea break across the mountains, causing rainfall to slide along wadis with dramatic speed. Smaller tributaries of water collect in the wadis from natural springs and create oases in the desert. In much of the Peninsula, the water table is close enough to the surface to hand-dig a well – a fact not wasted on the Bedu who survive on a system of wells and springs discovered or made by their ancestors. Irrigation, in the form of elaborate ducts and pipes (called *aflaj* in Oman), helps channel water through plantations, allowing more extensive farming in the region than might be supposed.

Ecosystems

Desert

The harsh lands of Arabia have for centuries attracted travellers from the Western world. According to Richard Burton, they were curious to see 'a haggard land infested with wild beasts, and wilder men...What could be more exciting? What more sublime?' Indeed, there is such awe in the words 'Arabian desert', it has been described by so many famous writers and travellers, and it is bound up so inseparably in Western fantasies of escape that it is hard to begin a description of it. The very words 'Empty Quarter' (a sea of dunes that lies at the heart of the Peninsula, straddling Saudi, Yemen, Oman and UAE) invite imaginative speculation, exploration and discovery.

To this day, people come to the desert expecting 'sand, sand, sand, still sand, and only sand and sand again'. The traveller who wrote those words (Alexander William Kinglake) curiously had only passed through gravel plains at that point (in 1834), but so strong is the connection between the words 'desert' and 'sand', he felt obliged to comment on what he thought he should see rather than on what was there.

In fact, the sand dunes of the Empty Quarter, or Rub al-Khali as it is known locally, may be the most famous geographical feature but they are not the only desert of interest. Much of the Peninsula is made up of flat, gravel plains dotted with outcrops of weather-eroded sandstone in the shape of pillars, mushrooms and ledges. Fine examples of these desert forms can be seen in Saudi Arabia, near Al-Ula, Bir Zekreet in Qatar and Duqm and the Huqf Escarpment in Oman.

There are many other kinds of desert too, including flat coastal plains and the infamous volcanic black Harra of northern Arabia.

Nowadays, camels (few of which are wild) and feral donkeys dominate the landscape of thorny acacia (low, funnel-shaped bushes) and life-supporting *ghaf* trees. Sheltering under these trees, sustained by the dew from the leaflets in the morning, are gazelle, protected colonies of oryx, and a host of smaller mammals – hares, foxes and hedgehogs – that provide a food source for the land's many raptors. Easier to spot are lizards, snakes and insects that provide the building blocks of the desert ecosystem.

Mountains

They may not be the mightiest mountains in the world but the ranges of the Peninsula are nonetheless spectacular. This is partly because they rise without preamble from flat coastal plains.

Geologists speak of the Peninsula in terms of the Arabian shield and Arabian shelf. The shield, which consists of volcanic sedimentary rock, comprises the western third of the landmass. The shelf comprises the lower-lying areas that slope away from the shield from central Arabia to the waters of the Gulf.

Ostriches once roamed the savannah-like plains of Arabia and crocodiles inhabited the rivers, but changing climate and human encroachment resulted in a change of resident wildlife.

The Peninsula has two main mountain ranges. The Hejaz range runs the length of Saudi Arabia's west coast, generally increasing in height as it tends southwards. The term 'mountain' may seem a misnomer for much of the range. Saudi's landmass looks like a series of half-toppled books, with flat plains ending in dramatic escarpments that give way to the next plain. The last escarpment drops spectacularly to the sea. If you follow the baboons over the escarpment rim, from the cool, misty, green reaches of Abha to Jizan on the humid, baking plains of the Tihama, the effect of this range is immediately felt. The settlers of the fertile mountains in their stone dwellings live such a different life to the goat herders in their mud houses on the plains, they may as well belong to different countries – and indeed the Tihama shares much in common with Eritrea and Ethiopia's Tigré region on the opposite side of the Red Sea.

The Haraz Mountains of Yemen give rise to Jabal an-Nabi Shu'ayb (3660m), the highest peak on the Peninsula. Forming part of the Great Rift Valley, the landmass of Yemen is predominantly mountainous, commonly rising 2000m or more and making farming a challenge. To compensate, Yemeni farmers cut elaborate terraces up the hillside to keep soil from washing away. These are shored up by stones and the maintenance of the terrace walls is a concern now that younger generations head to town in search of easier work than farming.

Arabia's other principal mountain range is found in the east of the Peninsula. Here, Oman's Hajar Mountains protect the communities around the Gulf of Oman from the encroachment of deserts from the interior. Terracing similar to that of Yemen can be seen on Jebel Akhdar and on pocket-handkerchief scraps of land in the Mussandam. The southern mountains of Oman, in the hills of Dhofar, catch the edge of the monsoon from India bringing light rains that cause the arid hills to burst into life during the summer when most of the rest of the Peninsula is desiccated by the heat.

The hills of southern Arabia are home to the elusive leopard, one of Arabia's most magnificent animals. It is the largest but not the only predatory mammal of the Peninsula: caracals, wolves, striped hyenas and sand cats are all resident (though in small and diminishing numbers) in the mountains and wadis of Oman in particular, where they prey on snakes and the plentiful rodents.

The stoic early 20th-century traveller, Charles Doughty, described the Harra as 'iron desolation...uncouth blackness... lifeless cumber of volcanic matter!' Even camels have trouble crossing the Harra as the small rocks heat in the sun and catch in their feet.

Gulf Landscapes, by Elizabeth Collas and Andrew Taylor, is a beautifully illustrated book that shows there's much more to the Gulf than its high-profile cities.

DESERT YES – DESERTED NO

Visiting any wilderness area carries a responsibility and no more so than a desert, where the slightest interference with the environment can wreak havoc with fragile ecosystems. The rocky plains of the interior may seem like an expanse of nothing, but that is not the case. Red markers along a road, improbable as they may seem on a cloudless summer day, indicate the height of water possible during a flash flood. A month or so later, a flush of tapering grasses marks the spot, temporary home to wasp oil beetles, elevated stalkers and myriad other life forms.

Car tracks scar a rock desert forever, crushing plants and insects not immediately apparent from the driver's seat. Rubbish doesn't biodegrade as it would in a tropical or temperate climate. The flower unwittingly picked in its moment of glory may miss its first and only opportunity for propagation in seven years of drought.

With a bit of common sense, however, and by taking care to stick to existing tracks, it's possible to enjoy the desert without damaging the unseen communities it harbours. It also pays to turn off the engine and just sit. At dusk, dramas unfold: a fennec fox chases a hedgehog, a wild dog trots out of the wadi without seeing the snake slithering in the other direction, tightly closed leaves relax in the brief respite of evening and a dung beetle rolls its reward homewards.

The mountains are the best (though far from the only) place to see wildflowers. After rains they bloom in abundance. In the wadis there is an abundance of pink-flowering oleander and tall stands of Sodom's apples; on the mountainsides juniper trees, wild olives, lavenders and many plants with medicinal properties flourish.

Seas

The Peninsula is bordered by three distinct seas, each of which has its own character.

The Red Sea, with its world-renowned underwater landscape and great diversity of tropical fish, is mostly calm, and its shores flat and sandy. Grouper, wrasse, parrotfish and snapper inhabit the colourful gardens of coral, sea cucumbers and sponge, while shark and barracuda swim beyond the shallows, only venturing into the reefs to feed or breed.

The Arabian Sea, home to dolphins and whales and five species of turtle, many of which nest along the eastern Arabian shore, has a split personality. Calm for much of the year, it becomes violently rough in the *khareef* (summer monsoon), casting up shells on some of the most magnificent, pristine, uninterrupted beaches in the world. Rimmed by cliffs for much of its length, this sea is punctuated with fishing villages that continue a way of life little changed in centuries, supported by seas rich in sardine and tuna.

The Gulf has a completely different character to the other two seas. Flat, calm, so smooth that at times it looks solid like a piece of shiny coal, it tends to be shallow for up to a kilometre from the shore. With lagoons edged with valuable mangroves, this is an important habitat for birds. It is also conducive to human development: much of the rim of the Gulf has been paved over or 'reclaimed' for the improbable new cities at its edge.

National Parks & Protected Areas

The idea of setting aside areas for wildlife runs contrary to the nature of traditional life on the Peninsula which was, and to some extent still is, all about maintaining a balance with nature, rather than walling it off. The Bedu flew their hunting falcons only between certain times of the year and moved their camels on to allow pasture to regrow. Fishermen selected only what they wanted from a seasonal catch, and threw the rest back. Goat and sheep herders of the mountains moved up and down the hillside at certain times of the year to allow for regrowth. Farmers let lands lie fallow so as not to exhaust the soil.

Modern practices, including settlement of nomadic tribes, sport hunting, trawler fishing and the use of pesticides in modern farming, have had such an impact on the natural environment over the past 50 years, however, that all governments in the region have recognised the need actively to protect the fragile ecosystems of their countries. This has resulted in the creation of protected areas (10% of the regional landmass) but, with tourism on the increase, there is a strong incentive to do more.

Most countries have established conservation schemes, with the UAE leading the way. Five per cent of the Emirate of Dubai is a protected area, thanks to the example set by the late Sheikh Zayed, posthumously named 'Champion of the Earth' by the UN Environment Programme (UNEP) in 2005. Sir Bani Yas Island has an important and growing collection of Arabian wildlife and Al Ain Zoo has been transformed into a sustainable wildlife centre. Arabia's Asir National Park is the largest on the Peninsula, comprising 450,000 hectares of Red Sea coast, escarpment and desert. In addition, Saudi authorities have designated 13 wildlife reserves (which amount to over 500,000 hectares) as part of a plan for more than 100 protected areas. Socotra in Yemen is a Unesco biosphere reserve and

Books: Seashells

Collectable Eastern Arabian Seashells (Donald Bosch)

Seashells of Eastern Arabia (Donald Bosch et al)

Books: Arabian Plants

Handbook of Arabian Medicinal Plants (SA Ghazanfar)

Vegetation of the Arabian Peninsula (SA Ghazanfar)

there are plans to designate the forests around Hawf and the Bura'a Forest in the Tihama into national parks. The Hawar Islands, home to epic colonies of cormorants and other migrant birds, are protected by the Bahrain government.

Although it has no national parks as such, Oman has an enviable record with regard to protection of the environment – a subject in which the sultan has a passionate interest. His efforts have repeatedly been acknowledged by the International Union for the Conservation of Nature. Sanctuaries for oryx, the internationally important turtle nesting grounds of Ras al-Jinz, tahr (a mountain-dwelling, goat-like mammal) and leopard sanctuaries provide protection for these endangered species.

Environmental Issues

Water

The major concern for all Peninsula countries, particularly those of the Gulf, is water – or rather the lack of it. Sustained periods of drought and increased water consumption over the past decade have led to a depleted water table. Saudi Arabia will run out of groundwater long before it runs out of oil.

Bahrain's freshwater underground springs have already dried up, leaving the country reliant on expensive desalinated water. Yemen's groundwater levels have in recent years dropped dramatically, due to the use of pumps for irrigation. Higher demand for residential use is another factor forcing countries to rethink ways of managing water. Modernisation of irrigation systems appears to be the way forward although public awareness has a role to play too. At present, it would be unthinkable to impose a hose-pipe ban (such as that which marks most summers in rainy Britain) on municipal and private gardens as flowering borders are considered the ultimate symbol of a modern, civilised lifestyle.

That said, mostly gone are the days when you could cross parts of Saudi and see great green circular fields dotted across the desert. There was much to regret in the attempt to make the desert bloom: while Saudi became an exporter of grain, it used up precious mineral deposits and lowered the water table, and to no great useful purpose – the country can easily afford to import grain at the moment; there may be times to come when it cannot, and many experts are of the opinion it's better to retain precious resources for an emergency.

Pollution & Rubbish

In a region where oil is the major industry, there is always a concern about spillage and leakage, and the illegal dumping of oil from offshore tankers is a constant irritation to the countries of the Gulf. The oil spillage, following the deliberate release of oil by the Iraqis during the Gulf War (p109), resulted in an environmental catastrophe which, though not quite as bad as initially predicted, caused significant damage that is still being addressed today.

The oil industry isn't the only sector responsible for environmental degradation. As one of the Peninsula's fastest-growing industries, tourism is becoming a major environmental issue – as seen at the turtle beaches of Ras al-Jinz, where many tourists show a dismal lack of respect for both the turtles and their environment. The irresponsible use of 4WD vehicles in 'dune bashing' is another lamentable problem.

By far the biggest concern created by larger numbers of visitors to the desert is the discarding of rubbish: indeed, for several decades the Arabian Peninsula has been afflicted by the scourge of plastic bags and tin cans. These are unceremoniously dumped out of car windows or discarded at picnic sites and can be seen drifting across the desert, tangled

Breeding Centre for Endangered Arabian Wildlife at www.breedingcentresharjah.com is a site dedicated to programs preserving the endangered species of the Peninsula.

Arabian Wildlife at www.arabian-wildlife.com is the online version of the Arabian Wildlife Magazine and covers 'all facets of wildlife and conservation in Arabia'.

Described by one critic as a 'big book, big bore', *Travels in Arabia Deserta*, by CM Doughty (1926) eccentrically describes the author's laborious travels. It nonetheless has a long list of devotees, including TE Lawrence.

GO LIGHT ON LITTER

There's a wonderful tale in *The Thousand and One Nights* that describes the inadvertent chain of devastation caused by a merchant spitting out his date pip and unknowingly blinding the son of a genie. It may not be immediately apparent to a visitor watching pink and blue plastic bags sailing in the breeze that Peninsula authorities are making concerted efforts to clean up the countryside. And they have a stiff task: according to some estimates, the average person uses 300 plastic bags a year, prompting Friends of the Earth Middle East to run a 'Say No to Plastic Bags' campaign. It's immensely difficult to avoid adding to the rubbish, especially when local attitude still maintains that every soft-drink can thrown on the ground represents one more job for the needy. Attitudes are beginning to change, however, thanks in part to educational schemes that target children and the adoption of environment days in Oman, UAE and Bahrain. 'Bag it' and 'out it' is a pretty good maxim as, hardy as it seems, the desert has a surprisingly fragile ecosystem that once damaged is as difficult to mend as the eye of a genie's son.

in trees or floating in the sea. Expatriates and many Peninsula Arabs don't feel it is their responsibility to 'bag it and bin it' – that would be stealing the job, so the argument goes, of the road cleaner. You can see these individuals on a scooter or even walking in the middle of summer with a dust pan and brush and a black bin liner, 100km from the nearest village. The idea that Arabs have inherited the throwaway culture from the Bedu and can't distinguish between organic and non-biodegradable is often cited but lacks credibility. The Bedu know very well that an orange peel, let alone a Coke can, does not decompose in a hurry in the dry heat of the Peninsula.

The Arab response to litter, like the Arab response to conservation in general, probably has more to do with a lack of interest in the great outdoors for its own sake. But times are changing, and school trips to wild places may just be the answer. In UAE, recycling was made mandatory in 2010 and Masdar City in Abu Dhabi is taking the lead on carbon-neutral living.

The sand cat, sand fox and desert hare have large ears, giving a large surface area from which to release heat, and tufts of hair on their paws that enable them to walk on blistering desert floors.

Survival Guide

Safe Travel

The Arabian Peninsula has a historical reputation for being a dangerous place, whether for political turmoil, the emergence of Islamic fundamentalism, the threat of terrorism, particularly in Yemen, and the recent democratic uprisings. However, the trouble spots are usually well defined, and as long as you stay away from these and keep track of political developments, you are unlikely to come to any harm.

Politics aside, the Peninsula is a very safe place compared with much of the West, boasting one of the lowest average crime rates in the world. That doesn't mean to say you should take unnecessary risks, but it does mean you don't have to worry unduly about theft, mugging and scams.

Visitors should be aware that most of the Arabian Peninsula comprises desert and this extreme environment can bring its own hazards, especially in temperatures that exceed 50°C in summer. With common sense and a few precautions, however, encountering this unique environment is one of the highlights of a Peninsula visit.

COUNTRY BY COUNTRY SAFETY STATUS

Safety is a subjective topic. As far as security in the Peninsula is concerned, most peoples' perceptions are shaped by media stories of Islamic fundamentalism. It's a picture that bears little relation to reality. Interestingly, Arabs travelling to the US share similar concerns, bearing in mind *Al-Jazeera* reports of violent gun crime, car-jacking and theft that appear to plague many of the cities of the West. Needless to say, day-to-day life in the Peninsula revolves around violence about as often as it does in Wyoming or Kent.

Fortunately, the people of the Middle East are ready and willing to distinguish between governments and their policies, and foreign travellers. You might receive the occasional question about politics, but you'll never be held personally accountable. Keep abreast of current events, visit your embassy for travel advice if you're feeling cautious, but otherwise (with the current exception of Bahrain and Yemen), just go.

Bahrain

At the time of writing (early 2013), political tensions following the Arab Spring uprisings in Bahrain of 2011 and 2012 were still running high. A ban on public demonstrations is in place and there are no-go areas around some towns outside the capital. Sporadic violent outbursts, fuelled by frustration from opposition groups in what they regard as a lack of government reform, remain commonplace.

Before booking a visit, check with your consulate. While there, take local advice from the concierge at your hotel, avoid large gatherings of people, and restrict your visit to the main areas of tourist interest.

PRE-TRIP ADVICE

The following government websites offer travel advisories and information on current hot spots.

➡ Australian Department of Foreign Affairs & Trade (www.smarttraveller.gov.au)

➡ British Foreign & Commonwealth Office (www.fco.gov.uk)

➡ Canadian Department of Foreign Affairs & International Trade (www.dfait-maeci.gc.ca)

➡ US State Department (www.travel.state.gov)

Kuwait

Since the Arab Spring of 2011, large gatherings of nationals protesting for more political freedom have alarmed authorities with the result that bans and curfews are periodically enforced. That said, this has little impact on the visitor and the areas of tourist interest in Kuwait remain safe to visit. As a precaution, however, it is worth keeping an eye on international news for any further unrest and checking with your consulate before booking a visit. While in Kuwait, avoid large gatherings of people.

Although the country has now been cleared of mines after the Gulf War, unfamiliar objects in the desert should not be touched and you should stick to established tracks.

Oman

This is one of the safest countries in the entire Middle East to visit and although there were minor skirmishes during the Arab Spring of 2011, the unrest was localised. Flashpoints have tended to be focused on Sultan Qaboos University in Muscat and around the town of Sohar.

The main danger in Oman is from the weather: flash floods, particularly in the mountains, often catch visitors unaware. As such, wadis should be avoided during and immediately after rain.

Qatar

The speed and volume of traffic is about the only thing to concern a traveller in Qatar and even women walking in Doha at night alone are unlikely to feel threatened. In the desert, getting stuck in soft sand near Khor al-Adaid is an inconvenience more than a life-threatening concern.

Saudi Arabia

Despite the pivotal role Saudi Arabia has played in terms of engendering Al-Qaeda, the government in Riyadh has made a concerted effort over the past few years to stamp out terrorism in the Kingdom. This has resulted in much improved relations with the West.

Tourism (almost exclusively in groups as independent travel remains virtually impossible) has increased in recent years and the security of these visitors is taken very seriously as the authorities seek to grow this nascent industry. Visitors need only to worry about road safety as the country has one of the worst accident records in the world.

UAE

The UAE is a very safe country to visit with little other to worry about than the high incidence of fatality on the roads (nearly 10 times that of the UK). Visitors also underestimate the strength of

AVOIDING TROUBLE

Some dos...

⇒ Be vigilant in the cities, keeping clear of large public gatherings.

⇒ Cooperate politely with security checks in hotel foyers and at road checkpoints.

⇒ Keep abreast of the news in English-language newspapers published locally.

⇒ Check the latest travel warnings online through your country's state department or ministry.

⇒ Consult your embassy/consulate in the region for specific concerns.

⇒ Register with your embassy/consulate on arrival if there has been recent issues around public order.

⇒ Trust the police, military and security services. They are overwhelmingly friendly, honest and hospitable, in common with their compatriots.

Some don'ts...

⇒ Don't be paranoid – the chances of running into trouble are no greater than at home.

⇒ Don't get involved if you witness political protests or civil unrest.

⇒ Don't strike up conversations of a stridently political nature with casual acquaintances.

⇒ Don't forget to carry some form of identification with you at all times including some or all of the following: passport; labour card; residence card; driving license; and travel permit (Saudi). It's helpful to carry something with the contact details of your next of kin and your blood type.

⇒ Don't touch any unidentified objects in the wilds – ordnance from earlier conflicts is still an occasional issue in Dhofar in Oman, Yemen and Kuwait.

IF YOU HAVE A CAR ACCIDENT...

➡ Don't move the car until the police arrive.

➡ Don't sign anything you don't understand in the accident report (as you may be accepting responsibility for an accident that wasn't your fault).

➡ Call your insurance or car-hire company immediately.

➡ Try at all costs to remain calm: aggression may be held against you and will only worsen the situation.

➡ The traffic police are generally helpful and friendly, and it's customary for men to shake hands with policemen before commencing discussions.

the current in the Gulf off the UAE coast; local guidelines should be observed.

Yemen

The determined and fierce crack-down on terrorism over the past few years in Saudi Arabia led to many Al-Qaeda militants finding a safe haven in Yemen, a country that has been teetering on the brink of failed-nation status for two decades or more. With a separatist insurgency in the south, a Shiite rebellion in the north, wide unemployment, an agricultural crisis and almost the entire adult male population addicted to qat (a mildly narcotic plant), the government is struggling to cope with the added pressure from Al-Qaeda. In addition, the uprising during the Arab Spring of 2011, resulting in the ousting of President Ali Abdullah Saleh, has given another challenge to the weakened authorities.

As the much publicised home of Osama bin Laden's father, and as the place from which the War on Terror was launched after the suicide bombing of the USS Cole in the port of Aden in 2000, Yemen has become what some commentators have called a 'spiritual homeland' for released Guantanamo detainees and other Islamic extremists. At the time of writing, the chief of security

in the US Embassy in Yemen had just been assassinated (October 2012) and a bounty placed on the head of the US Ambassador by Al-Qaeda (December 2012). In response US drone attacks, supported by the Saudi government, have continued into 2013.

Small groups of tourists and individual travellers are beginning to return to Sana'a, either oblivious or unmindful of the threats to their safety, but given the political instabilities, travellers who have no reason to go to Yemen must ask themselves if now is the best time for a visit. Travellers should understand, furthermore, that they run a very real risk of being kidnapped. Western hostages are considered useful currency as bargaining power for the release of political prisoners by extremists as well as for extortion by local bandits. Lonely Planet did not conduct on-the-ground research in Yemen for this guidebook due to security concerns.

DANGERS & ANNOYANCES

Road Accidents

Some cities across the region suffer from congestion, with rush-hour traffic in Muscat, Doha and Dubai rivalling that of Western cities. With the

increase in traffic, traffic accidents have become a major issue (particularly in Kuwait, Saudi Arabia and the UAE, which have some of the highest number of accidents per capita in the world) and are a cause for concern for visitors and residents alike.

The standard of driving on the Peninsula is poor, largely because driving tests are less exacting or are illegally dodged. Bad driving includes tailgating, queue-jumping, pushing-in, lack of indication, not using mirrors, jumping red lights and turning right across the traffic when sitting in the left lane. Car horns, used at the slightest provocation, take the place of caution and courtesy and no one likes to give way, slow down or wait. During Ramadan, drivers are often tired, thirsty, hungry and irritable (due to the day's fasting), and everyone is in that much more of a hurry – generally to get home for a nap.

The one good news story of the region is Oman, where (on the whole) drivers stick to the speed limits, let people into their lane and thank others for the same courtesy. Use of the horn is forbidden except in an emergency and you can be fined for having a dirty car.

Hazards to look out for while driving in the region include:

➡ animals on the road (particularly camels).

➡ dust storms that loom out of nowhere and obscure the road ahead.

➡ cars travelling without any lights.

➡ heavy rain washing out sections of road.

➡ sudden flash floods that sweep away vehicles that cross their path.

➡ wash-board surfaces (like a rumble strip) on graded roads that damage tyres.

➡ batteries that run out of juice without warning as they

are quickly exhausted in high temperatures.

Extreme Temperatures

The major hazard of the region is undoubtedly the weather. At any time of year, the high temperatures of midday, combined with high humidity, can quickly lead to heat exhaustion, sun stroke and serious burns. If you are travelling in the summer, breaking down on an empty road without water can literally be life-threatening. You should bear this in mind when planning a trip outside urban areas and think twice about travelling alone unless you are highly resourceful.

Avoiding problems is largely a matter of common sense: always carry more water than you think you'll need; cover your head and neck; wear sunglasses; cover up, especially between 11am and 3pm; and avoid too much activity in the summer months – in other words, do as the locals do!

Hazards at Sea

The waters of the Red Sea and the northern part of the Arabian Sea are usually calm and safe for swimming but it's worth avoiding the following hazards:

Strong Currents During the summer in eastern and southern Oman (July to September) and on the northern coast of Yemen, huge swells occur making swimming very dangerous. Every year there are casualties associated with the strong tides and powerful undercurrents. On some stretches of the normally quieter Gulf and Red Sea coasts, lifeguards using internationally recognised flags patrol the beach at weekends. Make sure you obey the red flag directives: in Dubai there are frequent casualties with tourists being swept out to sea in unexpected currents.

Pollution Litter affects many public beaches, despite the best efforts of local authorities, and tar can be a nuisance on a few wild beaches, released from irresponsible tankers. The practice is illegal but hard to police. Occasionally, raw sewage is illegally dumped in the sea to avoid queues and fees at sanitation depots.

Dangerous Marine Life Common hazards of the sea include stonefish (with a highly venomous sting), stingrays, jellyfish (which deliver a fairly innocuous but persistent sting), highly toxic sea snakes, some cones (with beautiful shells the handling of which can causes paralysis) and sharp coral (inflicting cuts that easily lead to infection in the climate). These problems can be avoided by wearing shoes and a t-shirt when swimming (also useful against sunburn). Sharks are common but only very rare incidents of aggressive behaviour have been reported and generally in predictable circumstances (such as in waters where fishermen are gutting fish).

Red Tide This bloom of blood-coloured algae can affect the waters of the Gulf and Arabian Sea for months at a time making swimming unappetising. It is not fully understood if these tides are harmful.

Hazards on Land

Most of the hazards of the desert are related to over-exposure to the sun and the danger of getting caught in a flash flood. This is when a wall of water rolls quickly across land too hard baked to absorb it, sweeping away everything that gets in its path. The key strategy to staying safe is to avoid camping in wadis, don't approach the mountains during rains, don't travel alone, and never cross roads where the water is flowing over the red marker signs.

IF BITTEN BY A SNAKE...

Snakes are some of the most remarkable creatures of the desert and deserve considerable respect for their survival skills. Most are non-venomous or only mildly toxic but a few are a bit more challenging. The only time you're likely to encounter them is camping in the sands or walking up wadis where they will make every attempt to avoid you – and you should do the same. If you are unlikely enough to get bitten follow this advice:

➡ Don't panic: half of those bitten by venomous snakes are not actually injected with poison (envenomed).

➡ Immobilise the bitten limb with a splint (eg a stick).

➡ Apply a bandage over the site, with firm pressure, similar to bandaging a sprain.

➡ Do not apply a tourniquet, or cut or suck the bite.

➡ Get the victim to medical help as soon as possible so that antivenin can be given if necessary.

➡ If you have the presence of mind, take a photo of the snake for identification to aid doctors in giving the appropriate antivenin.

KEEPING WOULD-BE SUITORS AT BAY

Engaging with locals is always a highlight of travel in the Middle East and it's easy for women to strike up conversation if they're travelling alone. The key, when interacting with local men, is to realise that initiating conversation can be misinterpreted. Here are some tips to deter would-be suitors:

➡ Master the art of detachment – remaining aloof in a conversation rather than animated – local women are masters at this.

➡ Keep the eye contact to a minimum – unless delivering the killer cold stare if someone oversteps the mark.

➡ Approach a woman for help first (for directions and so forth) rather than a man.

➡ Ask to be seated in the 'family' section if dining alone.

➡ Avoid sitting in the front seat of taxis and the back seat of buses.

➡ Invent or borrow a husband if the situation feels alarming but beware this may lead to uncomfortable questions about abandoning the home and kids.

➡ Retain your self-confidence and keep a sense of humour in compromising situations: this is far more effective than losing your temper or showing vulnerability.

➡ Insist on being told the family name of pestering individuals and their place of work – the threat of shame is often enough to dampen their ardour.

There are a few other land hazards to watch out for such as poisonous plants (eg pink oleander in the wadis, the Sodom's apples that strew the desert floor), camel spiders, scorpions that deliver a nasty but not fatal bite, large ants with painful bites, and annoying clusters of mosquitoes and wasps at certain times of the year. Snakes are also common in the region. Most problems can be avoided by wearing shoes and resisting the temptation to prod holes and overturn rocks.

WOMEN TRAVELLERS

Many women imagine that travel on the Peninsula is a lot more difficult and traumatic than it actually is. Unaccompanied women will certainly attract curious stares and glances, and occasionally comments, too, but they will receive hospitable treatment almost universally. It is essential to dress modestly in loose clothing in order to avoid giving offence and attracting trouble (see p40 for advice on what to wear).

Gender Segregation

It's important to be aware that there are 'men areas' and 'women areas' and that this is something that is enforced mainly by women, not by men. As such, it can be quite uncomfortable for both sexes if a woman sits in a male area; in some instances, it could compromise a woman's safety.

Traditional coffeehouses, cheaper restaurants, budget hotels, the front seat of taxis and the back seats of buses all tend to be men-only areas and it's culturally sensitive to avoid them – at some budget Gulf hotels, unaccompanied women may be refused a room. Women areas include family rooms in better restaurants, public beaches on certain days of the week and the front rows of buses.

Harrassment

Sometimes women may be followed (particularly on beaches) or find unwanted visitors in a hotel but this is far less prevalent than in other parts of the Middle East where there is more exposure to tourists. Sexual harassment in some Peninsula countries is considered a serious crime and the incidence of rape on the Peninsula is extremely low (far lower than in the West). Verbal harassment and sexual innuendo are more common.

Directory A–Z

Accommodation

Accommodation options throughout this book are listed in this order: budget, midrange and top end, and according to author preference within each category.

During local holiday periods (particularly over eid, the Islamic feast) and popular festivals (such as the shopping festivals in Dubai and Kuwait), as well as Western holidays (Christmas and New Year) and major fixtures (like the Dubai Rugby Sevens), travellers should book well in advance. Discounts in the summer (except in Salalah in Oman) are common.

Outside the big cities, accommodation is scarce and choice limited. Rooms in all categories generally have air-conditioning, hot water, telephone, fridge and TV (usually with satellite channels, including BBC and CNN).

Customs Regulations

Customs regulations vary from country to country, but in most cases they don't differ significantly from those in the West. All luggage is X-rayed and sometimes opened too. That said, with greater numbers of tourists arriving and in the drive to appear more tourist-friendly, many of the old customs nightmares (like long queues while officials check the contents of your soap box) are things of the past.

Alcohol It is strictly forbidden to take alcohol into dry or semi-dry regions (Kuwait, Qatar, Sharjah, Abu Dhabi and Saudi Arabia). Alcohol can only be taken into Oman by air. If you're caught attempting to smuggle in even small quantities of alcohol, punishments range from deportation and fines to imprisonment. In most other countries, foreigners (but not Muslims) are permitted a small duty-free allowance.

Drugs Those caught in possession of drugs (including ecstasy, amphetamines, cannabis and cocaine) can face the death penalty, which in Saudi Arabia, with its policy of zero tolerance, means what it says. Note that syringes and needles, and some medicinal drugs are also banned (such as tranquillisers and even some antidepressants and sleeping pills), unless you have a doctor's prescription to prove that you need them.

Israel & 'Incendiary' Material Books critical of Islam, Peninsula governments or their countries, or pro-Israeli books may be confiscated (though the days of removing labels from M&S underwear are thankfully now gone).

Money There are no restrictions on the import and export of money (in any currency) in and out of Peninsula countries.

Pork products Some countries make allowances for foreigners but it's better not to get stopped with a pork chop in your pocket.

Pornography Officials may construe images in style magazines, or women in swimwear as pornographic and remove the offending page from the magazine.

Video cassettes and DVDs Censors may well want to examine these and then allow you to collect them after a few days.

Discount Cards

Student, youth and senior-citizens cards are of little use anywhere on the Peninsula.

Electricity

All countries in the region have an electrical supply of 220 to 240V except Saudi Arabia which also has 110V.

240V/50Hz

240V/50Hz

Embassies & Consulates

Embassies are a fairly good, if somewhat cautious and at times alarmist, source of information on current hotspots and dangers. Many embassies advise travellers to register with them upon arrival, especially if you're staying in the country for an extended period: if you should disappear, have a serious accident, or suddenly need to be evacuated from the country, you will at least be in a better position to receive help. If you break the law, you're on your own! See the Directory sections of each individual destination chapter for lists of embassies and consulates.

Gay & Lesbian Travellers

Homosexual practices are illegal in all of the Peninsula countries. Under Sharia'a (Islamic) law, in some countries homosexuality incurs the death penalty (though punishment usually ranges from flogging to imprisonment or deportation). In other countries infractions solicit fines and/or imprisonment.

Westerners are unlikely to encounter outright prejudice or harassment so long as they remain discreet. However, this may well change if you become involved with a local. Room sharing is generally not a problem (it will be assumed that you're economising). Condoms are fairly widely available, though may be limited in selection. You're advised to bring your own supply.

Useful Resources

Gay Middle East (www.gaymiddleeast.com) Summary of legal and social issues regarding homosexuality in the region.

Global Gayz (www.globalgayz.com/middle-east) Country-by-country guide to gay and lesbian activity.

Insurance

Travel insurance covering accidents and medical problems is strongly advised, particularly as road traffic accidents are a major hazard of the region and problems can easily occur if visiting the desert (particularly on off-road excursions). Although some regional hospitals do not charge for emergency treatment, you cannot rely on this. If you need complicated surgery (for a fracture, for example), it can cost as much as it would to have private treatment in a Western country.

A policy that pays doctors or hospitals directly rather than you having to pay on the spot and claim later is a better option for the region. If you have to claim later make sure you keep all documentation.

Note that some policies specifically exclude 'dangerous activities', which can include activities you may want to engage in on the Peninsula, such as scuba diving, rock climbing, motorcycling and even trekking.

Internet Access

Staying connected in the Peninsula is easy. All countries have International Direct Dialling (IDD) facilities via satellite links. Mobile phones are easy to buy and local SIM cards are widely available in all cities and most airports across the region. Roaming charges apply for non-local SIM cards and it is worth checking the rates before travelling. Internet access is generally offered free in most midrange hotels and free wi-fi is becoming the norm in many coffeeshops and hotels. Unless you are off-road in the desert or camping in the mountains, use of all connectivity devices (iPhone, iPad and so forth) is virtually guaranteed.

Legal Matters

Although the law varies in specifics from country to country (see p33), it does share certain similarities. The legal system in all Peninsula countries is based wholly or partly on Sharia'a law, derived mainly from the Quran.

In the West, Sharia'a law is perceived as notoriously harsh and inflexible, but in reality there are basic tenets shared with Western legal values (such as the presumption of innocence until proven guilty). The severest punishment for a crime is in practice rarely exacted (even in Saudi Arabia).

Visitors should remember that they are subject to the laws of the country they find themselves in, and that ignorance of the law does *not* constitute a defence. In Saudi Arabia, in particular, it is vital that travellers (particularly women) acquaint themselves with the local laws.

If you are arrested and detained, call your embassy or consulate and wait until they arrive before you sign anything. In a car accident you mustn't move the car, even if you're causing a traffic jam, until the police arrive.

Money

The best way to carry money in the Peninsula is to take a supply of US dollars, pounds sterling or euros and rely on ATMs to withdraw additional funds.

The Peninsula used to be world famous as a low-tax area. Nowadays, however, a mixture of taxes, often reaching 17%, is added on top of hotel and restaurant prices.

ATMs

With the exception of Yemen where ATMs are confined to larger urban areas, virtually all banks in the region, from big cities to small villages, have ATMs from which you can withdraw funds from an overseas bank or gain a cash advance with a credit card. ATMs are also widespread in shopping malls and petrol stations.

ACCOMMODATION IN THE ARABIAN PENINSULA

ACCOMMODATION TYPE	REGIONAL NOTES
Camping	• Key areas for desert camping include Asir National Park in Saudi, Khor al-Adaid in Qatar, Sharqiya Sands and Jebel Shams in Oman. • With a 4WD and your own equipment, wild camping (without any facilities) is a highlight of the region. • Avoid camping in wadis, Bedouin areas and turtle beaches (ones with large pits at the top of the tide line) and remove all rubbish.
Budget Hotels	• The cheapest rooms are not suitable for women; in the Gulf, very cheap hotels may double as brothels. • There's no established network of backpacker hotels in the region and prices are much higher than international norms. • Yemen has the cheapest accommodation. • Dormitory-style hostels (men-only) are only available in UAE and Qatar.
Midrange Hotels	• Generally offer good value for money and are often family-run.
Top End Hotels	• Ranked as some of the best in the world with spas, personal fitness and shopping services, infinity pools, fine dining, world-class architecture and palatial interior design. • Often the only venue in town with a license to serve alcohol in countries where alcohol is permitted, so they tend to double as entertainment venues to non-residents.
Resorts	• Growing concept across the region offering retreats from the city but often in isolated locations with few surrounding amenities. • Range from basic Robinson Crusoe–style compounds (Al-Khawkha on Yemen's Red Sea) to sumptuous palace-hotels with underwater restaurants (Burj al-Arab in Dubai).

ACTIVITIES

The Peninsula offers many opportunities for engaging with the sea and with the desert interior although many of these activities require resourcefulness (such as survival and map-reading skills) or the help of a specialist agency (especially for rock climbing, caving and desert safaris). The Arabian and Red Seas offer some of the best diving and snorkelling in the world.

WHAT	WHERE	HOW	NOTES
Camel Treks	• Sharqiya Sands • Khor al-Adaid • Socotra	Arrange through local desert camps	Choose a mounted rather than a walking guide for a more authentic experience.
Diving & Snorkelling	• Jeddah • Muscat • Salalah • Musandam • Socotra	Contact Extra Divers (www.extradivers.com)	The Red Sea is one of the world's top diving destinations; the Arabian Sea offers easier access but has less coral. Both are wows in the water but low-key experiences on land.
Dhow Rides & Dolphin Spotting	• Manama • Doha • Musandam • Dubai • Muscat	See country directories for details	Go early in the morning for the best chance to see pods of dolphins in action. In Dubai you can swim with them.
Fishing	• Manama • Doha • Dubai • Muscat	Negotiate an hourly rate with local fishermen or book through the local marina	Common catches include yellowfin tuna (weighing between 25kg and 60kg), sail fish, barracuda and shark. Fishing licences are not needed on the Peninsula.
Golf	• Manama • Doha • Dubai • Muscat	See country directories for details	Designer golf courses with grass are becoming a signature feature of modern Gulf cities.
Hiking	• Oman • Yemen • Saudi Arabia	Book through local tour agencies	Oman has an established network of walking paths but signposts are limited. Most hiking in the Peninsula is ad hoc passing through small villages. Allow 1L of water per person per hour, wear light-coloured clothing and stay out of wadis during and after rain.
Off-Road Driving	• UAE • Oman	Pick up a locally-published off-road guidebook for routes and their challenges	Beware flash floods, soft sand and salt flats and stay on tracks to protect the fragile desert ecology.
Turkish Baths	• UAE • Saudi Arabia • Yemen	Ask at your hotel for a local recommendation	A great antidote for aching muscles, the hammam is otherwise known as a Turkish bath. Women should call ahead for a female assistant.
Water Sports	• All seaboard cities in the region	Organise through any of the region's seaboard five-star hotels and resorts	Water sports on offer include jet skiing, kite surfing, windsurfing, sailing and kayaking. Avoid southern Arabia during the summer when currents are ferocious.

Bargaining

Bargaining over prices is still very much a way of life on the Peninsula, although to a lesser extent than in some other Middle Eastern countries. Yemen and Oman are perhaps the exceptions, where aggressive bargaining can offend.

Prices rarely come down much below half the original quote, and 25% to 30% discount is more or less the norm.

Cash

Cash in US dollars, pounds sterling or euros is easily exchanged anywhere in the region.

In small businesses, including cheap restaurants, bus stations and budget hotels, and in rural areas, you will need cash for most transactions.

Credit Cards

Credit cards are widely accepted on the Peninsula (except Yemen) and almost everything can be paid for by plastic, right down to your morning coffee.

Visa and MasterCard are the most popular credit cards; Amex is less widely accepted. It's possible to get cash advances on credit cards.

Moneychangers

Moneychangers are easy to find in all Peninsula cities but the rates do not differ much from banks.

Tipping

Tips are not generally expected in the Gulf and the concept of *baksheesh,* well known throughout the rest of the Middle East, is little known on the Peninsula. That said, those who have contact with tourists (such as guides or hotel porters) have grown to expect tips.

Note that the service charge added to most hotel and restaurant bills is not an automatic gratuity that goes to the waiters. It usu-ally goes into the till and is often the restaurant's way of making the prices on the menu look 10% to 15% cheaper than they really are. Waiters in the Gulf tend to be paid derisory wages, so a small tip discreetly left on the table, while not required, is greatly appreciated if the service is good. The practice of automatic lavish tip-giving, however, can backfire as many establishments simply reduce the wages of their employees if they know that tips are expected.

Travellers Cheques

Travellers cheques (particularly from Amex and Thomas Cook) are exchangeable in big cities but seldom encountered and are becoming increasingly redundant in the region. With low levels of theft, it is hard to find a good reason to recommend using them in the Peninsula.

Opening Hours

Regional & Seasonal Variations Business hours vary from country to country and sometimes from region to region within a country (depending on climatic differences, such as those in highland/lowland Yemen). They also vary from institution to institution and from season to season (especially during Ramadan). Above all, Arabs are not known for blind obedience to rules, and business hours are often taken with a pinch of salt.

Weekend In Bahrain, Kuwait, Oman, Qatar and the UAE, the weekend is Friday and Saturday; elsewhere it is Thursday and Friday. Shops stay open for six days a week in all countries and many open for a limited period on Friday evening too. Major tourist sights usually open during the weekend – at last.

Banking Hours Bank opening hours vary throughout the region, but usually operate from 8am or 9am to noon or 1pm, either five or six days a week. Some reopen for a couple of hours in the afternoon. Foreign exchange facilities usually keep longer hours.

Ramadan Hours Government offices work shorter hours during Ramadan and businesses tend to open much later and close earlier, or else not open at all during the day but remain open for much of the night. Note that many restaurants close during the day throughout Ramadan or even remain closed for the month.

Tourist Attractions You can't rely on tourist sites opening as prescribed. If you're determined to see a particular museum or other attraction and haven't time to waste, it's worth calling ahead to make sure it's open as stated. That, alas, is still no guarantee!

OPEN SESAME

Where possible throughout this book we have given the opening times of places of interest. The information is usually taken from notices posted at the sites. However, often the reality on the ground is that sites open pretty much when the gate-guard feels like it. On a good day he'll be there an hour early, on a bad day he won't turn up at all. Who can blame him when in little-touristed sites, like some of those in Yemen or Oman, he may not see a visitor for days? All opening hours must be prefaced, therefore, with a hopeful *insha'allah* (God willing)!

Photography

Restrictions Do not photograph anything vaguely military in nature (including the police) or anything construed as 'strategic' (including airports, bridges and ports). In general terms, Bahrain and the UAE are the most relaxed countries on the Peninsula when it comes to photography, while Kuwait, Oman and Yemen seem to have the broadest definitions of what constitutes a 'strategic' site. In Saudi Arabia it often seems that the authorities just don't like cameras.

Photographing People Do not photograph anyone without their permission, especially women. In the more conservative countries, such as Saudi Arabia, Kuwait and some parts of Yemen, you can cause real offence in this way and may risk having stones thrown at you.

Photographing Poverty People on the Peninsula are often offended when you take photographs of run-down houses or anything that resembles poverty, as the tendency is to emphasise what the country has achieved in the last few decades.

Religious Sites Photography is usually allowed inside religious and archaeological sites (when entry is permitted), unless there are signs indicating otherwise. Avoid taking photos of religious observance.

Public Holidays

All Peninsula countries observe the main Islamic holidays listed below. Some of the Peninsula countries also observe the Gregorian New Year (1 January). Every state has its own national days and other public holidays.

Islamic New Year Also known as Ras as-Sana, it literally means 'the head of the year'.

Ashura The anniversary of the martyrdom of Hussein, the third *imam* (religious teacher) of the Shiites.

Prophet's Birthday Known as Moulid an-Nabi, it's 'the feast of the Prophet'.

Ramadan The ninth month of the Muslim calendar, this is when Muslims fast during daylight hours. How strictly the fast is observed depends on the country, but most Muslims conform to some extent. Foreigners are not expected to follow suit, but visitors should not smoke, drink or eat (including gum-chewing) in public during Ramadan. Hotels make provision for guests by erecting screens for discreet dining. Business hours tend to become more erratic and usually shorter and many restaurants close for the whole period. Alcohol is not available in Ramadan except as room service. As the sun sets each day, the fast is broken with something light (like dates and *laban*) before prayers. Then comes *iftar* (breakfast), at which enough food is usually consumed to compensate for the previous hours of abstinence. People then rise again before dawn to prepare a meal to support them throughout the day.

Eid al-Fitr The festivities mark the end of Ramadan fasting; the celebrations last for three days and are a time of family feasting and visiting.

Eid al-Adha This feast marks the time that Muslims make the pilgrimage to Mecca.

Islamic Calendar

Although most secular activities and day-to-day life are planned in the Peninsula according to the Gregorian calendar (the Western system), all Islamic holidays are calculated according to the Muslim calendar. For

ISLAMIC HOLIDAYS 2013–2018

Dates of Islamic holidays are dependent on moon sightings and consequently may occur a day later, but not generally earlier, than listed. Not all countries spot the moon on the same day (cloud cover doesn't count), so regional differences between countries occur each year. In fact, speculation regarding whether or not tomorrow will bring *eid* is the subject of great public debate and private expat exasperation. The following is therefore to be treated as a guide only!

YEAR HEJIRA	NEW YEAR	ASHURA	PROPHET'S BIRTHDAY	RAMADAN BEGINS	EID AL-FITR	EID AL-ADHA
1435	4 Nov 2013	13 Nov 2013	13 Jan 2014	28 Jun 2014	28 Jul 2014	4 Oct 2014
1436	25 Oct 2014	3 Nov 2014	3 Jan 2015	17 Jun 2015	18 Jul 2015	23 Sep 2015
1437	15 Oct 2015	24 Oct 2015	24 Dec 2015	6 Jun 2016	7 Jul 2016	12 Sep 2016
1438	3 Oct 2016	12 Oct 2016	12 Dec 2016	26 May 2017	26 Jun 2017	1 Sep 2017
1439	22 Sep 2017	1 Oct 2017	1 Dec 2017	15 May 2018	16 Jun 2018	21 Aug 2018

BARGAINING & BARTERING

Arabs are committed shoppers and they make an art form out it, promenading the main street and popping into a shop to vex the owner without any intention of buying. Buying, meanwhile, is a whole separate entertainment, focused on the business of bartering and bargaining.

Bartering implies that items do not have a value *per se*: their value is governed by what you are willing to pay balanced against the sum the vendor is happy to sell for. This subtle exchange, often viewed with suspicion by those from a fixed-price culture, is dependent on many factors, such as how many other sales the vendor has made that day, whether the buyer looks like a person who can afford an extra rial or two, and even whether the vendor is in a good mood or not.

As with all social interaction, there's an unwritten code of conduct that keeps negotiations sweet:

➡ Bartering is your chance to decide what you are willing to pay for an item so use your interpersonal skills to see if you can persuade the vendor to match it

➡ Haggling is a sociable activity, often conducted over refreshments, so avoid causing offence by refusing hospitality.

➡ Don't pay the first price quoted: this is often considered arrogant.

➡ Start below the price you wish to buy at, as you have room to compromise – but don't quote too low or the vendor may be insulted.

➡ If negotiations aren't going to plan, simply smile and say goodbye – you'll be surprised how often the word *ma'a salaama* (goodbye) brings the price down.

➡ Resist comparing prices with other travellers; if they were happy with what they paid, they certainly won't be if you tell them you bought the same thing for less.

---

visitors this can cause confusion (such as when trying to decipher official documents, including the date of expiry of travel permits and visa). Calendars showing parallel systems are available.

The Muslim year is based on the lunar cycle and is divided into 12 lunar months, each with 29 or 30 days. Consequently, the Muslim year is 10 or 11 days shorter than the Christian solar year, and the Muslim festivals gradually move around our year, completing the cycle in roughly 33 years.

Year zero in the Muslim calendar was when Mohammed and his followers fled from Mecca to Medina (AD 622 in the Christian calendar). This Hejira, or migration, is taken to mark the start of the new Muslim era, much as Christ's birth marks year zero in the Christian calendar. Just as BC denotes 'Before Christ', so AH denotes 'After Hejira'.

Smoking

Unlike in other parts of the Middle East, smoking is not particularly prevalent in the Arabian Peninsula. This has something to do with the strict interpretation of Islam and the discouragement of dependency on stimulants of any kind; partly to do with the general lack of advertising in most of the region; and partly to do with government drives to dissuade the young from starting the habit.

That doesn't mean to say you won't encounter smoking. The expat communities from India tend to smoke quite heavily and everyone across the region (even fashionably dressed young Arab women in city areas) enjoys a *sheesha* (water pipe filled with scented or fruit-flavoured tobacco) from time to time.

A government ban on smoking in public places, including restaurants, is in place in UAE and Oman. All top-end hotels offer nonsmoking rooms and there are always nonsmoking sections in more expensive restaurants.

Solo Travellers

Travel for Arabic people and Asian expats entails large convoys of family groups and great gatherings at the airport. As such, solo male travellers are often regarded either with sympathy or with suspicion, as it is inconceivable to most Arabian Peninsula people that someone might choose to travel alone.

A woman travelling on her own is an even hotter topic of discussion. Women will want to adopt you, men will either ignore you (out of respect) or treat you as a token man. Either way, you will inevitably be showered with well-meaning solicitations for your safe-keeping, extra help on public transport and even offers of accommodation.

Without Arabic, travelling in the Arabian Peninsula can be lonely at times: the roads are long and the deserts wide. Without an established network of tourism facilities, you may spend days without seeing another Westerner.

Single rooms are available in most hotels, though they're often just a few dollars cheaper than double rooms. Walking around alone seldom presents a safety problem.

One word of caution: if you travel away from urban areas in your own vehicle alone, you need to be quite resourceful. Many roads see very little traffic and you could wait hours before help arrives. It is not recommended that you go off-road alone.

Telephone

All the Peninsula countries have good networks and International Direct Dialling (IDD) facilities via satellite links.

Most cities and large towns have public telephone offices (either part of the post office, or privately run) from where you can make international calls and send faxes.

International calls cost up to US$2 per minute for most destinations. Rates don't usually vary during the day or night, but in some countries there are reductions at weekends. Public phones accept coins, phonecards and, in some countries, credit cards.

Mobile Phones

The use of mobile phones is widespread throughout the Peninsula and every country has its own (state-owned) national network. Some of these run on the GSM system (as in Europe), so if your phone works on GSM and your account allows you to roam, you'll be able to use your mobile on the Peninsula.

In other places you'll have to buy prepaid SIM cards. Beware though: the cost of using a mobile in some countries is higher than calls made on a landline.

Time

Saudi Arabia, Kuwait, Bahrain, Qatar and Yemen are three hours ahead of GMT/UTC. The UAE and Oman are four hours ahead of GMT/UTC. Daylight-saving time is not observed in any of the Gulf countries (in other words, the time remains constant throughout the year).

Toilets

Outside the midrange and top-end hotels and restaurants of the Peninsula (where Western-style toilets are found), visitors will encounter the Arab-style squat toilet (which, interestingly according to physiologists, encourages a far more natural position than the Western-style invention!).

It's a good idea to carry a roll of toilet paper with you on your travels: most toilets only provide water and the use of paper is considered barbaric.

Beyond the towns you're unlikely to find public toilets, except poorly maintained ones at filling stations.

Tourist Information

Despite the fact that tourism is a growing industry in the Peninsula, there are surprisingly few tourist offices. Staff training and office facilities are equally minimal. Sometimes the most you'll find is a free map (often very outdated) or an aged brochure.

There are two good, unofficial sources of information on the Peninsula: your hotel and the local travel agents (many of whom generously offer information without always expecting you to engage their services in return).

Travellers with Disabilities

Generally speaking, scant regard is paid to the needs of disabled travellers in the Peninsula. Steps, high kerbs and other assorted obstacles are everywhere. Roads are made virtually uncrossable by heavy traffic, while some doorways are narrow and many buildings have steep staircases and no lifts.

In the top-end hotels facilities are usually better (with lifts, ramps and more accommodating bathrooms) but still leave much to be desired. Trips have to be planned carefully, and may be restricted to luxury-level hotels and private, hired transport. There is an agency in **Oman** (☑99 329030; www.oad-oman.org), one of the more enlightened countries in this regard, specialising in making arrangements for disabled travellers.

Elderly people with physical difficulties will find that every effort will be made to welcome them. Arab people are highly respectful of the elderly.

Useful Resources

Before setting off for the Middle East, disabled travellers can get in touch with their national support organisation (preferably with the travel officer, if there is one). In the UK try www.disabledtravelers.com or contact the following:

SECURITY

On the whole, theft is rare in the region. Scams involving ATMs sometimes occur so beware of any unusual-looking key pads or signs of tampering.

RADAR (☎020-7250 3222; www.radar.org.uk; 250 City Rd, London EC1V 8AS)

Holiday Care Service
(☎0845 1249971; www.tourismforall.org.uk)

Women Travellers

Women travelling in the Arabian Peninsula will find they encounter far less harassment than in other Middle Eastern countries although inappropriate stares remain an issue. It is imperative to dress modestly (see p40) both to avoid unwanted attention and to avoid causing offence. For more on travelling in the region as a woman, see p480.

Visas

All countries except Saudi Arabia and Yemen issue tourist visas on arrival for most nationalities. This changes frequently, however, and it's imperative to check with the relevant embassy or consulate for the latest information.

Currently those with a UAE tourist visa may visit Oman overland without paying for an Omani visa.

The flow of foreigners in, out and around the Peninsula is carefully monitored and strictly controlled. As a result the visa application process ranges from fairly simple and straightforward (Oman) to nightmarishly complicated (Saudi Arabia). It also means that if you plan to travel from one country to another, where it involves passing through Saudi, you need to plan ahead.

An Israeli passport, or an Israeli stamp in your passport, can be a problem. If you have either of these, it's unwise to leave it to chance as to whether an official will notice it or not.

Passports need to be valid for at least six months beyond your expected departure date from the region.

Note also that most Peninsula countries require you to carry your passport with you at all times. Spot checks occasionally occur.

Collecting Visas

If you've arranged your visa in advance of arrival, make sure you have some proof of it with you before setting off (a fax or email with the visa number), or you may not be allowed to board your plane let alone enter the country of your destination.

Transit Visas

Saudi Arabia issues transit visas for people travelling overland between Jordan and Bahrain, Kuwait, Oman, Qatar, the UAE or Yemen. These transit visas can be sought from Saudi Arabian embassies in any of these countries with proof of onward connections beyond Saudi borders. They are not easy to obtain, however, as you often have to show you can't reach your destination by other means.

Travel Permits

Travel permits are necessary for travelling in Yemen and Saudi Arabia, and are obtainable in the countries themselves. They're also necessary for Omani

residents driving to the UAE although this regulation is not uniformly enforced.

Visa Sponsorship

If you cannot obtain a visa to the Peninsula on arrival or through an embassy, you can try to obtain one through a sponsor. This can be the hotel where you're planning to stay or a tour company.

In theory, a sponsor is a national of the country you are visiting, who is willing to vouch for your good behaviour and take responsibility for your departure when you're due to leave. You'll need to send details of your passport and itinerary a couple of weeks in advance to your sponsor. Make sure you obtain confirmation *in writing* (a fax is suitable) that your visa will be awaiting your arrival at the relevant airport before you leave.

The sponsorship process varies greatly from country to country (and is also liable to change – check current regulations with the local embassy). The documentation required also varies with each country, and processing can take anything from a few days to a few weeks.

Transport in the Arabian Peninsula

GETTING THERE & AWAY

Flights, tours and rail tickets can be booked online at www.lonelyplanet.com/bookings.

Entering the Country

➡ **By Air** Easy as the cities of the Gulf have developed into major international hubs.

➡ **By Sea** Some cruise ships call at Salalah, Muscat, Dubai and Doha and these ports offer passengers the opportunity to go ashore.

➡ **By Land** Moving between Oman and UAE is relatively easy and between Saudi and some of its neighbours is theoretically feasible for Saudi expats. Other than this, entering one country through another by land is not currently possible.

➡ **Visas** Available on arrival for many nationalities except in Saudi Arabia and Yemen. Check with embassies ahead of time as this information changes frequently in the region. See the Visa section under Directory for more details. Note that getting a visa for Saudi is highly challenging for independent travellers, including the elusive transit visa. See p489 for details.

➡ **Passports** Those with an Israeli passport or an Israeli stamp in their passport may be refused access.

Air

Airports & Airlines

The Peninsula, and the Gulf in particular, has some of the world's best airlines and most modern airports.

All major European, Asian and Middle Eastern airlines (with the obvious exception of El Al, the Israeli airline) serve the principal cities of the Arabian Peninsula and routes to the Americas and Australasia are increasing.

The national carriers of each Peninsula country links one country to another with regular flights at reasonable prices.

Tickets

Dubai, Abu Dhabi, Bahrain and Doha are the major transport hubs in the region. Dubai, the main link between Europe, Southeast Asia and Australasia, is the destination that offers the best hope of picking up cheaper fares. As such, it may be worthwhile to fly into Dubai and arrange onward travel from there.

Dubai grew as a city by attracting and entertaining stop over travellers between Europe and Asia and as such it has made an art out of the stopover market. Airlines support this continuing trend by offering 'stop over packages' which include hotel accommodation, airport

CLIMATE CHANGE & TRAVEL

Every form of transport that relies on carbon-based fuel generates CO_2, the main cause of human-induced climate change. Modern travel is dependent on aeroplanes, which might use less fuel per kilometre per person than most cars but travel much greater distances. The altitude at which aircraft emit gases (including CO_2) and particles also contributes to their climate change impact. Many websites offer 'carbon calculators' that allow people to estimate the carbon emissions generated by their journey and, for those who wish to do so, to offset the impact of the greenhouse gases emitted with contributions to portfolios of climate-friendly initiatives throughout the world. Lonely Planet offsets the carbon footprint of all staff and author travel.

transfers and a short tour, all for a very reasonable price.

Land

Border Crossings

Border crossings between Oman, Yemen and Saudi are closed. The most usable crossings are between Oman and UAE. These may take anything from 30 minutes to more than two hours. Showing patience, politeness and good humour is likely to speed up the process and it also helps to have a pen!

If you are travelling independently overland to the Middle East, you can only approach the region from Jordan into Saudi Arabia – but gaining a Saudi visa is a major hurdle.

Bus

The only bus routes entering the region are from Jordan through the Al-Umari border crossing, south of Azraq, Ad-Durra, south of Aqaba, and Al-Mudawwara, east of Aqaba. Services link Riyadh, Jeddah and Dammam with Aqaba and Amman.

Jordan Express Tourist Transport (JETT; ✆00962 6585 4679; www.jett.com. jo) The Jordanian national bus company has a reliable website and runs air-conditioned, modern coaches.

Car & Motorcycle

The following documents are required if you are hoping to enter the region with your own transport:

Green Card Issued by insurers. Insurance for some countries is only obtainable at the border.

International Driving Permit (IDP) Compulsory for foreign drivers and motorcyclists in Bahrain and Saudi Arabia. Most foreign licences are acceptable in the other Peninsula countries, but even in these places an IDP is recommended.

Vehicle Registration Documents Check with

your insurer whether you're covered for the countries you intend to visit and whether third-party cover is included.

AAA (www.aaauae.com) The Arabian Automobile Association can provide advice on documentation.

Sea

Cargo boats call erratically at Aden, Muscat and Jeddah on their way to Europe and Asia. Getting aboard is mostly a question of luck and being in the right place at the right time. Your passage may well be dependent upon the whim of the captain. Ask at the port of departure to see what boats are headed where.

Some offer comfortable passenger cabins (intended for crew family); for others you may need to come equipped with food, drink and bedding.

Cruise ships dock in a number of ports in the Peninsula, including Dubai, Muscat and Salalah.

Several ferry services operate to/from the Peninsula but they are not geared up for tourists. If you're in for an adventure then bear the following in mind:

➡ In summer, conditions may be impossibly hot, especially in deck class.

➡ Many passengers prefer to take their own food rather than rely on that served on board.

➡ Vehicles can be shipped on ferry services, but advance arrangements should be made.

➡ Ferry destinations and their timetables change frequently but most ferry companies have good websites where you can check current fares, routes and contact details.

EGYPT

The Alexandria-based Misr Edco Shipping Company and four Saudi companies sail between Jeddah and Suez.

The journey takes about 36 hours direct, about 72 hours via Aqaba. Misr Edco also sails about twice weekly between Port Safaga (Egypt) and Jeddah.

IRAN

If you're travelling to/from the east and want to avoid Iraq and Saudi Arabia, you can cross the Gulf Sea from Iran into Kuwait and Bahrain.

Ferries only have 1st-class (cabin) accommodation, but are much cheaper than the equivalent airfare, and most are overnight journeys. They are operated by **Valfajr-8 Shipping Company** (www. irantravellingcenter.com) in Tehran, which has a good online booking service.

Tours

Tours to the Peninsula are beginning to gain in popularity, and some offer two-country destinations between the UAE and Oman.

In the Peninsula itself there is a host of reputable tour agencies offering good tours at competitive prices. Check in the individual countries for details. Additionally, most regional airlines usually offer short tours of Peninsula cities for a reasonable supplement to an airfare.

Note that for Saudi Arabia, tours are often the only way of visiting the country. Restrictions in Yemen allow visitors to travel to most areas outside the capital only with a tour.

The tour agencies listed here are recommended:

Addicted to Travel (www. addictedtotravel.com) Based in the US; offers holidays to the region.

Adventure World (✆1300 363 055; www.adventureworld. com.au) Has branches in Adelaide, Brisbane, Melbourne and Perth (Australia) and is the agent for the UK's Explore Worldwide.

Kuoni (www.kuoni.co.uk) Offers comprehensive tours

of the UAE and Oman; UK-based.

Original World (www.originalworld.com) Offers multi-destination tours of the UAE, Oman and Yemen.

Passport Travel (☎03 9500 0444; www.travelcentre.com.au) Middle East specialist in Australia, assisting in tailor-made itineraries for individuals and groups.

Reiseservice Graw (www.firstclasstravel.de) Germany-based, and offering comprehensive tours to the Peninsula. Its website is in English and the service is available across Europe.

GETTING AROUND

As fuel is cheap throughout the region and vehicles are relatively inexpensive to buy, road transportation is the most popular means of travel within the Peninsula. Car hire (with or without driver) is inexpensive and travel by taxis and bus are cheap. A train service operates in Dubai, the only passenger service in the region.

The only complication of land travel is obtaining a transit visa for Saudi Arabia, which hampers transport from one Gulf country to another. As such, it's often easier for the traveller to move from country to country by air and there's a good air network linking all major Peninsula cities.

If you do decide to try your luck overland, bear in mind the following general advice:

➡ Although restrictions in some Gulf countries are beginning to relax, the rules regarding visas and land crossings in the region are subject to contradiction, misinformation and frequent change even between the UAE and Oman.

➡ You are strongly advised to check the latest information with relevant embassies before travelling.

➡ You need to have insurance for all countries you're passing through if driving.

➡ Many car-hire companies insist you return cars to country of original hire.

➡ Stories are legion of individuals who obtain visas in their country of origin only to find them invalid at the Saudi border: double-check with your local Saudi embassy and, if possible, with the authorities in Saudi Arabia.

➡ Check the book Directory and the Directory of each of the country chapters for detailed information about visas.

➡ Check the individual country transport chapters for information on border crossings.

Air

Reputable travel agencies in all major Peninsula cities can advise you about the best intercity deals and it's better to use their services than go directly to the airlines. Note that prices fluctuate considerably according to the season or if there's a public holiday (such as *eid*).

Airlines in the Arabian Peninsula

The Peninsula boasts some world-class airlines with good safety records, modern aircraft and well-trained crew. Dubai offers a famously slick international airport with superb facilities, including hotels, business centres and extensive duty-free sections. Some other key information:

➡ For detailed information on safety records visit www.airsafe.com.

➡ Award-winning Gulf Air, Emirates, Qatar Airways, Etihad and Oman Air are increasing their direct flight networks regularly.

➡ Yemenia (the national airline of Yemen) can be unreliable but still offers good service.

➡ Saudi Arabia, Oman, the UAE and Yemen have domestic flight networks, which are reasonably priced.

➡ Smaller regional airports are adequate, and many are in the process of being modernised and expanded.

➡ Arrival procedures are straightforward, quick and efficient. Note, however, the import prohibition on various items, particularly in Saudi Arabia.

Budget Airlines

The arrival of budget airlines in the region has recently revolutionised intercity transport on the Peninsula. As in Europe, the airlines tend to use less-frequented cities as their hubs to avoid the high taxes of major airports. This minor inconvenience is worth considering for the cheap travel they offer.

Air Arabia (☎06-508 8888; www.airarabia.com)

Al-Jazeera Airways (www.jazeeraairways.com; Kuwait)

Bahrain Air (☎17 463 330; www.bahrainair.net)

Bicycle

The Peninsula offers good cycling opportunities, cyclists are made welcome (the annual Tour of Oman attracts international cyclists including celebrities like 2012 Tour de France winner Bradley Wiggins) and police are helpful and friendly to all road users. Repair shops are easy to come by, and local expats are able 'bush mechanics'. Post any queries on the Thorn Tree on lonelyplanet.com under the Activities branch. Some difficulties to consider are as follows:

➡ In most cities, especially in the Gulf, it is very hazardous to cycle as car drivers are not used to anticipating cyclists.

➡ Most bicycles in the Peninsula are simple machines: spare parts for mountain or touring bikes are only available in major cities.

➡ The heat is a major challenge and cycling is not recommended from June to August or during midday at other times of the year.

Cyclists Touring Club (CTC; www.ctc.org.uk) UK-based organisation offering good tips and helpful website. Useful information sheets on cycling in different parts of the world.

Bus

Car ownership levels are so high across the Peninsula that little demand for public bus services exists. Where they do exist, they are often primarily intended for expat workers getting to and from their place of work. It's not too difficult to get between the main towns in Saudi Arabia, Oman and Yemen by bus, but Qatar, Bahrain, Kuwait and the UAE have fewer (if any) domestic services that meet the needs of tourists.

Of the major regional routes, there are four prin-

TRAVELLING BY LAND IN THE ARABIAN PENINSULA

Travelling between the countries of the Arabian Peninsula is challenging but not impossible. Check the following table for an overview of border crossing and visa information.

TO/FROM	FROM/TO	BORDER CROSSING NOTES	VISA OBTAINABLE AT BORDER?
Oman	Saudi Arabia	There was no border crossing open between Oman and Saudi At the time of writing	n/a
Oman (mainland)	UAE	The Wajaja border crossing is the most commonly used	yes
Oman (Musandam)	UAE The Al-Darah	Tibat border crossing was the only one open at the time of research	yes
Oman	Yemen	The Sarfait border crossing was closed to tourists at the time of writing	n/a
Saudi Arabia	Bahrain	The border crossing is on King Fahd Causeway	to Saudi: no to Bahrain: yes
Saudi Arabia	Kuwait	The border crossing is at Al-Khafji and is usually only used by those on public transport	to Saudi: no to Kuwait: yes
Saudi Arabia	Qatar	The border crossing is at Salwah and is usually only used by those on public transport	to Saudi: no to Qatar: yes
Saudi Arabia	UAE	The border crossing is at Sila	to Saudi: no to UAE: yes
Saudi Arabia	Yemen	This border crossing remains closed due to insurgency in the area	
Bahrain Qatar Kuwait UAE	Bahrain Qatar Kuwait UAE	A Saudi transit visa must be obtained before travelling overland between any of these countries. Saudi Transit Visa Details: • Application forms can be downloaded from www.saudiembassy.net. • Travellers must have a ticket with confirmed reservations and/or a visa for the country of final destination. • Transit times cannot exceed 72 hours. • Women can only apply for a transit visa if accompanied by a male relative: proof of kinship is required (ie marriage certificate etc). • Children need a copy of birth certificate. • If travelling by your own vehicle you are required to register your carnet at the embassy.	to Saudi: no to others: no (you need to show your visa for your final destination at the Saudi border to transit through the country)

cipal ones currently open to foreigners:

➡ Saudi Arabia to Bahrain

➡ Saudi Arabia and Bahrain to Kuwait

➡ Saudi Arabia and Bahrain to the UAE via Qatar

➡ UAE to Oman

Bus travel is usually comfortable, cheap and on schedule, roads are good, and air-conditioned buses are the norm, except in Yemen. Yemen's services vary according to the company; for example, Yemitco is fast, reliable and comfortable. Loud music or videos as well as heavy smoking can be unpleasant for many on some services.

In many countries women accompanied by men can sit anywhere, but women travelling alone are expected to sit in the front seats.

Reservations

It's always advisable to book bus seats in advance at bus stations, and it's a must over the Muslim weekend (Friday), as well as during public holidays such as eid.

Car & Motorcycle

Car ownership is virtually a must for expats in most Peninsula countries where cities cover large distances and there's little public transport. Motorcycles are also popular for getting around town. Spare parts are easier to find for Japanese models. The summer months are not conducive to motorcycling.

Bring Your Own Vehicle

Unless you're coming to live on the Peninsula for an extended duration, bringing your own vehicle may prove more trouble than it's worth. Obtaining a carnet de passage is expensive and progressing through the Peninsula (due to visa regulations and paperwork) can be challenging. For most short-term visitors, it makes more sense

to hire a car locally. For long-term residents it is cheaper and more straightforward to buy a car in-country and sell it before leaving.

Driving Licence

Travellers from the West can use their own national driving licences for a limited period in some Peninsula countries (including Oman and Saudi Arabia).

For longer stays an International Driving Permit (IDP), obtainable from your own country, is recommended (and required) by some countries.

To obtain a local licence you'll need to have a residency visa, plus the following documents:

➡ a valid foreigner's licence (and sometimes an IDP)

➡ a no-objection certificate (NOC) from your employer

➡ your accommodation rental contract

➡ photocopies of your passport

➡ passport-sized photos

➡ sometimes a certificate confirming your blood group

➡ some countries (such as Saudi Arabia) insist on Arabic translations of foreign documents

➡ for some expats a driving test may be required

Car Hire

Availability & Cost Car hire is possible in all Peninsula countries with international as well as local companies represented at international airports and five-star hotels. Costs are about average compared to international rates. Reservations are necessary in some countries during the peak tourism times, particularly during hajj, or major national or religious holidays.

Vehicle Type For desert or off-road driving, you will need a 4WD, available from all hire companies. Don't cut costs by hiring a sedan for off-road driving – for one

thing, your insurance will be null and void as soon as you leave the sealed road and secondly, you won't know whether the previous person who hired your car similarly abused the vehicle. If you break down, the hire company won't help you. Bike or motorcycle hire is near unheard of.

Documentation To hire a vehicle you'll need your driving licence and, for some Peninsula countries, an IDP and copies of both your passport and visa. The minimum age varies between 21 to 25. Invariably, credit cards are now a prerequisite.

Insurance

Insurance is compulsory. Given the large number of road traffic accidents, fully comprehensive insurance (as opposed to third-party) is strongly advised. This covers the ancient law of paying blood money in the event of the injury or death of a person (and sometimes animal). Car-hire companies automatically supply insurance, but check carefully the cover and conditions.

Make certain that you're covered for off-piste travel, as well as travel between Peninsula countries (if you're planning cross-border excursions). If you are taking the car outside Gulf Cooperation Council (GCC) borders, you'll need separate insurance.

In the event of an accident, don't move the vehicle until the police arrive and make sure you submit the accident report as soon as possible to the insurance company or, if hiring, the car-hire company.

Road Conditions & Driving Amenities

Road Quality With the exception of parts of Yemen, the Peninsula's road system is one of the best in the world with high-quality two- or four-lane highways. Few roads are unsealed (except in Yemen and Oman) and

DESET DRIVING

The following tips may help if going off-road, but there's no substitute for experience.

Pre-departure Planning

➡ Travel with another vehicle if you're heading for sandy areas so that you can pull each other out if you get stuck.

➡ Don't travel alone unless you can change a tyre (very heavy on 4WD vehicles).

➡ Use a local guide if planning an extended dune trip: navigation is not easy.

➡ Take a map and compass. A GPS and fully charged GSM phone are also useful but remember that GPS is only useful for knowing exactly where you're lost (and not how to find the way out) and phones don't work in some mountainous or remote areas.

➡ Bring a first-aid kit, at least 5L of water per passenger per day and enough food to last several days. Dried dates keep well in high temperatures.

➡ Check oil, tyre condition and tyre pressure before leaving.

➡ Bring a tool kit with a tow rope, shovel, sand ladders, spanner, jack, wooden platform (on which to stand the jack), tyre inflator (and a gauge) and jump leads.

➡ Tell someone (and in some countries the local authorities, too) where you're going.

Driving Tips

➡ In all desert areas follow prior tracks for the sanity of locals and for your own safety.

➡ Keep the acceleration up through areas of soft sand and do not stop!

➡ When approaching sandy inclines, engage low gear and increase acceleration.

➡ Never camp at the bottom of a wadi, even on a clear day. Be wary of wadis when rain threatens. Flash flooding rips through the narrow channels of a wadi with huge force. Each year many people lose their lives in this way.

➡ Engage low gear on extended mountain descents even if it slows your progress to walking speed; many people run into trouble by burning out their brakes.

Getting Stuck in Sand

➡ In sand, the minute you feel the wheels are digging in, stop driving. The more you accelerate, the deeper you'll sink.

➡ If your wheels are deeply entrenched, don't dig: the car will just sink deeper.

➡ Partially deflate the tyres (for greater traction), clearing the sand away from the wheel in the direction you want to go (ie behind if you're going to try to reverse out).

➡ Collect brushwood (you'll wish you brought the sand ladders!) and anything else available, and pack under the tyres, creating as firm a 'launch pad' as possible.

➡ Plan your escape route or you'll flip out of the sand only to land in the next dune. In most dune areas, there are compacted platforms of sand. Try to find one of these on foot so that you have somewhere safe to aim for.

➡ Engage low ratio and remember that going backwards can be as effective as going forwards, especially if you stalled going uphill: gravity is a great help.

➡ Remember that using low ratio consumes a lot of petrol. Make sure you top up when you can and reinflate your tyres before rejoining a sealed road.

What to Do if You're Lost

➡ Stay with your vehicle, where there's shade and water. The Bedu or local villagers will find you before you find them. It's easier for a search party to spot a vehicle than people wandering in the desert.

➡ Use mirrors, horns or fires to attract attention, and construct a large sign on the ground that can easily be seen from the air.

CARNETS

A *carnet de passage* is a booklet that is stamped on arrival and at departure to ensure that the vehicle leaves the country and has not been misappropriated. It's usually issued by a motoring organisation in the country where the vehicle is registered. Contact your local automobile association for details about required documentation at least three months in advance and bear the following in mind:

➡ You have to lodge a deposit to secure a carnet.

➡ If you default (ie you don't have an import and export stamp that match) then the country in question can claim your deposit, which can be up to 300% of the new value of the vehicle.

➡ Bank guarantees or carnet insurance are available.

➡ If your vehicle is irretrievably damaged or stolen, you may be suspected by customs officials of having sold the vehicle so insist on police reports.

➡ The carnet may need to specify any expensive spare parts, such as a gearbox, you bring with you. This is designed to prevent spare-part importation rackets.

4WDs are on the whole only necessary for driving off-road in the desert.

Off-road Routes The term 'off-road' refers to unsealed roads that have been graded, or levelled, with a roller, or tracks that have simply been made by cars driving along old camel or donkey tracks. To drive on any of these roads you need a 4WD. Responsible drivers stick to prior tracks and never cut new routes.

Fuel Petrol stations are widespread along major roadsides and in cities. On the desert roads they can be few and far between. Away from the main towns it's advisable to fill up whenever you get the chance as remote stations sometimes run out of fuel. Fuel is extremely cheap throughout the region. Most cars (except in Yemen) run on unleaded petrol.

Garages Found even in the smallest towns and villages in most countries, but are less common in Yemen. Spare parts (and servicing) are available for the most popular car models (Toyota and Land Rover especially).

Signposting Good throughout the region (bar only Yemen) and uses international symbols. English spelling of place names, however, is erratic and seldom matches the maps.

Parking A challenge in the cities. Traffic inspectors and parking meters are now more prevalent.

Hazards See the Safe Travel chapter (p478).

Road Rules

Non-compliance for the following common Peninsula road rules can lead to a hefty fine – although that may be of surprise considering the generally poor standard of driving.

➡ Driving is on the right side of the road in all Peninsula countries.

➡ Speed limits range between 100km/h and 120km/h on highways and 45km/h and 60km/h in towns and built-up areas. Speed cameras are in operation in most city areas and on highways.

➡ Seatbelt wearing is a legal requirement.

➡ The use of hand-held mobile phones while driving is an offence.

➡ The use of the horn is discouraged except in an emergency.

➡ You should keep your licence with you at all times and carrying a first-aid kit, fire extinguisher and warning triangle is required in some Peninsula countries.

➡ Driving under the influence of either alcohol (of any quantity) or drugs is not only considered a grave offence on the Peninsula, but also automatically invalidates your insurance and makes you liable for any costs in the event of an accident regardless of fault.

➡ Women are not permitted to drive in Saudi Arabia.

Hitching

Hitching is never entirely safe in any country and can't be recommended. Travellers who still decide to hitch should understand that they are taking a small but potentially serious risk. This is particularly the case in the Peninsula, where distances are great between towns and you can be marooned in isolated places with literally life-threatening consequences (for example, if you run out of water in summer). You may also find you end up spending days at someone's remote desert settlement because your driver wanted you to meet the family. Beware: the novelty of communal living quickly wears off! Women travelling alone should not hitch.

Nevertheless, hitching is not illegal in any Middle Eastern country and in many places it is common practice among locals. It's considered not so much an alternative to the public transport system as an extension of it. Throughout the Peninsula a raised thumb is a vaguely obscene gesture – instead, extend your right hand, palm down and wag it up and down briskly.

While it's normal for locals and Asian expats to hitch, it isn't something Westerners are expected to do. It can lead to suspicion from local police and is disappointing to come: in rural areas there's an expectation that tourism will bring income, but watching you hitch along with the locals isn't returning anticipated dividends.

Hitching isn't free. The going rate is usually the equivalent of the bus or shared taxi fare, but may be more if a driver takes you to an address or place off their route. Negotiate a fare *before* you get into the vehicle.

As a driver you'll often be flagged down for a ride: you might need to think what this might entail before offering one. Women drivers should never give a lift to a man.

Local Transport

As cars are relatively cheap to buy and run, public transport (particularly buses and minibuses in towns) tends to be used by less affluent members of the population.

Minibus & Bus

In most cities and towns, a minibus or bus service operates. Fares are cheap, regular and run on fixed routes. However, unless you're familiar with the town, they can be difficult to use (not all display their destination) and they're often crowded.

In some Peninsula countries, minibus or local bus services tend to connect residential or commercial areas, rather than providing a comprehensive network across the whole city.

Few countries have public minibuses to/from the airport, but top-end hotels and travel agents (if you're taking a tour) can usually provide a complementary minibus with advance notice. Some hotels provide bus services to city centres too.

Taxi

In the West, taxis are usually an avoidable luxury; in the Arabian Peninsula they are often the best way for travellers to get about town. Many cities have no other form of urban public transport, while there are also many rural routes that are only feasible in a taxi or private vehicle.

The way in which taxis operate varies widely from country to country, and often even from place to place within a country. So does the price.

REGULAR TAXI

The regular taxi (also known as 'contract', 'agency', 'telephone', 'private', 'engaged' or 'special taxi') is found in all the main Peninsula towns or cities, co-existing alongside less-expensive means of transport (such as shared taxis or minibuses).

Its main purpose is for transportation within a town or on a short rural trip. It is also often the only way of reaching airports or seaports and is generally considered safe for women travellers.

SHARED TAXI

Known also as 'collect', 'collective' or 'service taxi' in English, and *servees* in Arabic, most shared taxis can take up to four or five passengers, but some seat up to 12 and are indistinguishable from minibuses.

Shared taxis are far cheaper than private taxis and, once you get the hang of them, can be just as convenient. They're usually a little dearer than buses, but run more frequently and are usually faster (they don't stop as

---

TAXI TIPS

On the whole, taxi drivers in the Peninsula are helpful, honest and humorous – they're not, however, so scrupulous when it comes to the tariff. New arrivals are particularly tempting bait and a target for a bit of overcharging. Here are a few tips:

➡ Be aware that not all taxi drivers speak English. Generally, in cities used to international travellers they speak enough to get by, but not otherwise.

➡ *Always* negotiate a fare (or insist that the meter is used if it works) before jumping in. Town taxis sometimes have meters, most of which work only intermittently.

➡ Don't rely on street names (there are often several versions). If you're not going to a well-known place, find out if it's close to a local landmark. Alternatively, ask someone to write it down in Arabic.

➡ Check you'll be able to find a cab for the return journey: in many places it's safest to ask the taxi driver to wait.

➡ Avoid using unlicensed cab drivers at airports.

often or as long). They also tend to operate for longer hours than buses. Shared taxis function as urban, inter-city and rural transport.

Fixed-route taxis wait at the point of departure until full or nearly full. Usually they pick up or drop off passengers anywhere en route, but in some places they have fixed stops or stations. Generally a flat fare applies for each route, but sometimes it's possible to pay a partial fare.

On 'routeless' taxis, fares depend largely on time and distance and the number of passengers on board.

Beware of boarding an empty shared taxi. The driver may assume you want to hire the vehicle as a 'regular taxi' and charge accordingly. You may also have to wait a long time (sometimes several hours) for it to leave, particularly if it's destined for a remote place.

Passengers are expected to know where they are getting off. *Shukran* is thank you in Arabic and the usual cue for the driver to stop. Make it clear to the driver or other passengers if you want to be told when you reach your destination.

Train

The only train services in the region are in Saudi Arabia, which connects the capital with the east of the King-dom (running from Riyadh to Dammam, via Hofuf and Dhahran among other places), and a new metro service in Dubai. Plans are afoot to build a track along the Bati-nah coast of Oman.

Health

While prevention is better than cure, medical facilities in most Peninsula countries are of a high standard (though emergency and specialised treatment may not be so readily or extensively available).

Problems particular to the Peninsula include respiratory complaints (due to the arid climate and high levels of dust), sunburn and sunstroke, eye problems, and injuries resulting from the exceptionally high incidence of road accidents: it pays to be extra vigilant on the roads.

BEFORE YOU GO

Pre-Trip Registration

Travellers can register with the **International Association for Medical Advice to Travellers** (IMAT; www.iamat.org). The association's website can help travellers find recommended doctors in the region.

For travellers about to set off to very remote areas of the Peninsula, first-aid courses are offered by the Red Cross and St John Ambulance, and a remote-medicine first-aid course is offered by the Royal Geographical Society.

Insurance

You are strongly advised to have insurance (see p482) before travelling to the region. Check it covers the following:

➡ direct payments to health providers (or reimbursement later)

➡ emergency dental treatment

➡ evacuation or repatriation, or access to better medical facilities elsewhere

Recommended Vaccinations

The World Health Organization (WHO) recommends that all travellers, regardless of the region they are travelling in, should be covered for diphtheria, tetanus, measles, mumps, rubella, polio and hepatitis B.

Many vaccines take four to eight weeks to provide immunity. Ask your doctor for an International Certificate of Vaccination, listing all the vaccinations you've received.

MEDICAL CHECKLIST

Consider packing the following items:

☐ acetaminophen/paracetamol or aspirin
☐ antibacterial ointment for cuts and abrasions
☐ antibiotics (if travelling off the beaten track)
☐ antidiarrhoeal drugs
☐ antihistamines (for allergic reactions)
☐ anti-inflammatory drugs
☐ bandages, gauze and gauze rolls
☐ DEET-containing insect repellent for the skin
☐ iodine tablets (for water purification if hiking or staying in remote areas)
☐ oral rehydration salts
☐ permethrin-containing insect spray for clothing, tents, and bed nets
☐ steroid cream or cortisone (for allergic rashes)
☐ sun block

TRAVEL HEALTH WEBSITES

Lonely Planet (www.lonelyplanet.com) A good place to start.

Centers for Disease Control & Prevention (www.cdc.gov) Useful guide to health issues related to specific regions.

MD Travel Health (www.mdtravelhealth.com) Complete travel-health recommendations for every Peninsula country. It's updated daily and is free.

World Health Organization (www.who.int/ith/) Publishes a free, online book, *International Travel and Health*, revised annually.

It's a good idea to consult your government's travel health website before departure:

Australia (www.smartraveller.gov.au/tips/travel well)

UK (www.doh.gov.uk)

US (www.cdc.gov/travel)

Peninsula countries require proof of yellow-fever vaccination upon entry for travellers who have recently visited a country where yellow fever is found.

Travelling with Medication

Bring medications in their original, clearly labelled containers with a signed and dated letter from your physician describing your medical condition and the medications (including generic names).

If carrying syringes or needles, carry a physician's letter documenting their medical necessity.

Further Reading

➡ *Travel with Children* (Lonely Planet)

➡ *Traveller's Health* (Dr Richard Dawood)

➡ *International Travel Health Guide* (Stuart R. Rose)

➡ *The Travellers' Good Health Guide* (Ted Lankester)

IN THE ARABIAN PENINSULA

Availability & Cost of Health Care

Though some Peninsula countries allow travellers access to free state medical treatment in emergencies, you should not rely on this and are strongly advised to have insurance cover. The availability of healthcare in Arabia can be summarised thus:

➡ High ratio of doctors to patients (bar Yemen).

➡ Modern, well-equipped hospitals with well-qualified, English-speaking staff in all cities and most of the larger towns throughout the Peninsula.

➡ Emergency units in most hospitals.

➡ Limited and less well-equipped clinics in rural areas.

➡ Pharmacies (signposted with green crosses) able to dispense advice by well-trained, English-speaking staff who may assist in place of doctors in very remote areas.

➡ High standards of dental care in the larger towns and cities (though patchy in Yemen).

Infectious Diseases

Dengue Fever

Also known as break-bone fever, dengue is spread through mosquito bites. It causes a feverish illness, with a headache and muscle pains, that's like a bad, prolonged attack of influenza. There may also be a rash. Take precautions to avoid being bitten by mosquitoes.

Diphtheria

Diphtheria is spread through close respiratory contact. It causes a high temperature and a severe sore throat. Sometimes a membrane forms across the throat, requiring a tracheostomy to prevent suffocation.

Vaccination is recommended for those likely to be in close contact with the local population in infected areas. The vaccine is given as an injection by itself, or with tetanus, and lasts 10 years.

Hepatitis A

Hepatitis A is spread through contaminated food (particularly shellfish) and water. It causes jaundice and, although it is rarely fatal, can cause prolonged lethargy and delayed recovery. Symptoms include dark urine, a yellow colour to the whites of the eyes, fever and abdominal pain.

Hepatitis A vaccine (Avaxim, VAQTA, Havrix) is given as an injection; a single dose will give protection for up to a year, while a booster 12 months later will provide protection for a subsequent period of 10 years. Hepatitis A and typhoid vaccines can also be given as a single dose vaccine in the form of Hepatyrix or Viatim.

Hepatitis B

Infected blood, contaminated needles and sexual intercourse can all transmit hepatitis B. It can cause jaundice and affects the liver, occasionally causing liver failure. All travellers should make this a routine vaccination – many countries now give hepatitis B vaccination as part of routine childhood vaccination.

The vaccine is given by itself, or at the same time as the hepatitis A vaccine. A course protects for at least five years, and can be given over four weeks or six months.

HIV

HIV is spread via infected blood and blood products, sexual intercourse with an infected partner, and from an infected mother to her newborn child. It can also be spread through 'blood-to-blood' contacts such as contaminated instruments used during medical, dental, acupuncture and other body-piercing procedures, as well as from sharing intravenous needles.

All countries in the Peninsula require a negative HIV test as a requirement for some categories of visas except Bahrain and Yemen.

Malaria

The prevalence of malaria varies throughout the Peninsula. The risk is considered minimal in most cities, but may be more substantial in rural areas. Check with your doctor or local travel-health clinic for the latest information. Antimalarial tablets are essential if the risk is significant, and you should also be aware of the disease's symptoms.

Malaria almost always starts with marked shivering, fever and sweating. Muscle pains, headache and vomiting are also common. Symptoms may occur any time from a few days up to three weeks or more after being bitten by an infected mosquito, and you may still show symptoms even though you are taking preventative tablets.

Meningitis

Meningococcal infection is spread through close respiratory contact.

A meningococcal vaccination certificate covering the A and W135 strains is required as a condition of entry if embarking on a hajj pilgrimage to Mecca and Medina in Saudi Arabia, and for all travellers arriving from the meningitis belt of sub-Saharan Africa. Visas for pilgrimages are not issued unless proof of vaccination is submitted with the visa application.

Rabies

Spread through bites or licks (on broken skin) from any warm-blooded, furry animal, rabies can be fatal. The skin should be immediately and thoroughly cleaned. If there is any possibility that the animal is infected with rabies, immediate medical assistance should be sought. Animal handlers should be vaccinated, as should those travelling to remote areas where a reliable source of postbite vaccine is not available within 24 hours.

Three injections are needed over a month to vaccinate against rabies. If you have been bitten and have not been vaccinated, you will need a course of five injections starting within 24 hours or as soon as possible after the injury. Vaccination does not provide you with immunity; it merely buys you more time to seek appropriate medical help.

Tuberculosis

Tuberculosis (TB) is spread through close respiratory contact, and occasionally through infected milk or milk products.

TB can be asymptomatic, although symptoms can include a cough, weight loss or fever, months or even years after exposure. An X-ray is the best way of establishing if you have TB.

BCG vaccine is recommended for those likely to be mixing closely with the local population. BCG gives a moderate degree of protection against TB. It's usually only given in specialised chest clinics, and is not available in all countries. As it's a live vaccine, it should not be given to pregnant women or immunocompromised individuals.

Typhoid

Typhoid is spread through food or water that has been contaminated by infected human faeces.

The first symptom is usually fever or a pink rash on the abdomen. Septicaemia (blood poisoning) may also occur. Typhoid vaccine (Typhim Vi,

AIDS ON THE PENINSULA

Though it's strictly illegal for AIDS or HIV sufferers either to visit or to live on the Peninsula (and detection of the disease usually results in instant deportation), the region is not the AIDS-free place you might imagine. In recent years, prostitutes have flowed into the area under the guise of tourists. Locals have also returned infected after sexual adventures abroad. Additionally, there is something of a cultural taboo about condom use among many Arab men. Travellers who form new relationships should also note that fornication, adultery and homosexuality are considered grave crimes in some Peninsula states.

CALL ME A CAB!

If you find you suddenly require urgent medical treatment on the Peninsula, don't call an ambulance, call a cab. The ambulance services – where they exist – are usually reserved for road accidents when the victim is unconscious or immobile. It's common (and much quicker) to take a taxi.

Typherix) will give protection for three years. In some countries, the oral vaccine Vivotif is also available.

Yellow Fever

Yellow-fever vaccination is not required for any areas of the Peninsula, but any traveller coming from a country where yellow fever is found will need to show a vaccination certificate at immigration.

The yellow-fever vaccination must be given at an approved clinic, and is valid for 10 years. It is a live vaccine and must not be given to immunocompromised or pregnant travellers.

Environmental Hazards

Travellers' Diarrhoea
Prevention

➡ Avoid tap water

➡ Eat fresh fruit or vegetables you have peeled yourself or eat cooked produce

➡ Avoid dairy products that might contain unpasteurised milk or have been refrozen after defrosting.

Treatment

➡ Drink plenty of fluids

➡ Take an oral rehydration solution containing salt and sugar

➡ If you start having more than four or five loose stools a day, take an antibiotic (usually containing quinolone) and an antidiarrhoeal agent (such as loperamide)

➡ Seek medical attention if the diarrhoea is bloody, persists for more than 72 hours, or is accompanied by fever, shaking, chills or severe abdominal pain.

Heat Illness

Heat exhaustion occurs following heavy sweating and excessive fluid loss. In the summer months, temperatures can reach 50°C and in such conditions even a round of golf can be dangerous.

Symptoms include headache, dizziness and tiredness. Aim to drink sufficient water so that you produce pale, diluted urine. To treat heat exhaustion, drink lots of water, cool down in an air-conditioned room and add a little more table salt to foods than usual.

Heatstroke is a much more serious condition, and occurs when the body's heat-regulating mechanism breaks down. An excessive rise in body temperature leads to the cessation of sweating, irrational and hyperactive behaviour, and eventually loss of consciousness and death.

Rapid cooling of the body by spraying with water or fanning is an effective treatment. Emergency fluid and electrolyte replacement (by intravenous drip) is also usually required.

Insect Bites & Stings

Using DEET-based insect repellents will help prevent mosquito bites.

Bed bugs and sometimes scabies are occasionally found in hostels and cheap hotels. They cause very itchy lumpy bites – spray the mattress or find new lodgings!

Scorpions are common in the desert. Although their bite can be painful, it's rarely life threatening.

Avoid walking on sand dunes in bare feet, and don't prod holes in wadis, to avoid snake encounters.

Travelling With Children

Travelling with children in the Arabian Peninsula poses no specific health problems for children between the months of November and March. For the rest of the year, however, the extreme temperatures, often combined with high humidity, pose high threats of dehydration and heat exhaustion making a summer visit best avoided. Extra care should be taken to avoid prolonged exposure to the sun at all times of the year. For more information, see p37.

TAP WATER

Tap water is safe to drink in Gulf cities and in Oman (but not in Yemen or Saudi, nor in rural areas where water is delivered by tanker), but it doesn't agree with everyone. It's easier to stick to bottled water (found everywhere), boil water for 10 minutes, or use water-purification tablets or a filter. Never drink water from wadis (valleys or riverbeds) or streams as animals are usually watered in them.

Women's Health

Some health considerations for women travelling in the region:

➡ Condoms should be checked before use as they crack in the hot climate.

➡ The **International Planned Parent Federation** (www.ippf.org) can advise about the availability of contraception in each Peninsula country.

➡ Tampons are not always available outside the major cities in the Peninsula;

sanitary towels are more widespread.

➡ High standards of obstetric and antenatal facilities are offered throughout the Peninsula (though less so in Yemen), particularly in the larger cities.

Language

Arabic is the official language on the Arabian Peninsula, but English is widely understood. Note that there are significant differences between the MSA (Modern Standard Arabic) – the official lingua franca of the Arab world, used in schools, administration and the media – and the colloquial language, ie the everyday spoken version. The Arabic variety spoken throughout the Arabian Peninsula (and provided in this chapter) is known as Gulf Arabic.

Read our coloured pronunciation guides as if they were English and you'll be understood. Note that a is pronounced as in 'act', aa as the 'a' in 'father', ai as in 'aisle', aw as in 'law', ay as in 'say', ee as in 'see', i as in 'hit', oo as in 'zoo', u as in 'put', gh is a throaty sound (like the Parisian French 'r'), r is rolled, dh is pronounced as the 'th' in 'that', th as in 'thin', ch as in 'cheat' and kh as the 'ch' in the Scottish *loch*. The apostrophe (') indicates the glottal stop (like the pause in the middle of 'uh-oh'). The stressed syllables are indicated with italics and (m) and (f) refer to the masculine and feminine word forms respectively.

BASICS

Hello.	اهلا و سهلا.	ah·lan was ah·lan
Goodbye.	مع السلامة.	ma' sa·laa·ma
Yes.	نعم.	na·'am
No.	لا.	la
Please.	من فضلك.	min fad·lak (m)
	من فضلك.	min fad·lik (f)

WANT MORE?

For in-depth language information and handy phrases, check out Lonely Planet's *Middle East Phrasebook*. You'll find it at **shop.lonelyplanet.com**, or you can buy Lonely Planet's iPhone phrasebooks at the Apple App Store.

Thank you.	شكران.	shuk·ran
Excuse me.	اسمح.	is·mah (m)
	اسمحي لي.	is·mah·ee lee (f)
Sorry.	مع الاسف.	ma' al·as·af

How are you?
كيف حالك/حالك؟ kayf haa·lak/haa·lik (m/f)

Fine, thanks. And you?
بخير الحمد الله. bi·khayr il·ham·du·li·laa
و انت/و انتِ؟ win·ta/win·ti (m/f)

What's your name?
اش اسمَك/اسمِك؟ aash is·mak/is·mik (m/f)

My name is ...
اسمي ... is·mee ...

Do you speak English?
تتكلم انجليزية؟ tit·kal·am in·glee·zee·ya (m)
تتكلمي انجليزية؟ tit·ka·la·mee in·glee·zee·ya (f)

I don't understand.
مو فاهم. moo faa·him

Can I take a photo?
ممكن اتصور؟ mum·kin at·saw·ar

ACCOMMODATION

Where's a ...?	وين ...؟	wayn ...
campsite	مخيم	moo·khay·am
hotel	فندق	fun·dug

Do you have a ... room?	عندك/عندك غرفة ...؟	'and·ak/'and·ik ghur·fa ... (m/f)
single	لشخص واحد	li·shakhs waa·hid
double	لشخصين	li·shakh·sayn
twin	مع سريرين	ma' sa·ree·rayn

How much is it per ...?	بكم كل ...؟	bi·kam kul ...
night	ليلة	lay·la
person	شخص	shakhs

Signs	
Entrance	مدخل
Exit	خروج
Open	مفتوح
Closed	مقفول
Toilets	المرحاض
Men	رجال
Women	نساء

Can I get another (blanket)?
احتاج الى (برنوس) ah·taaj i·la (bar·noos)
الثاني من فضلك؟ i·thaa·nee min fad·lak

The (air conditioning) doesn't work.
(الكنديشان) (il·kan·day·shan)
ما يشتغل. ma yish·ta·ghil

DIRECTIONS

Where's the ...? ... من وين min wayn ...
bank البنك il·bank
market السوق i·soog
post office مكتب البريد mak·tab il·ba·reed

Can you show me (on the map)?
لو سمحت وريني law sa·maht wa·ree·nee
(علخريطة)؟ ('al·kha·ree·ta)

What's the address?
ما العنوان؟ ma il·'un·waan

Could you please write it down?
لو سمحت اكتبه لي؟ law sa·maht ik·ti·boo lee (m)
لو سمحت اكتبه لي؟ law sa·maht ik·ti·bee lee (f)

How far is it?
كم بعيد؟ kam ba·'eed

How do i get there?
كيف ممكن اوصل kayf mum·kin aw·sil
هناك؟ hoo·naak

EATING & DRINKING

Can you recommend a ...? ممكن تنصح/ mum·kin tan·sah/
تنصحي ...؟ tan·sa·hee ... (m/f)
cafe قهوة gah·wa
restaurant مطعم ma·ta'm

I'd like a/the ..., please. اريد... a·reed ...
من فضلك. min fad·lak
nonsmoking section المكان il·ma·kaan
ممنوع mam·noo·a'
تدخين tad·kheen
table for (four) طاولة (اربعة) taa·wi·lat (ar·ba')
اشخاص ash·khaas

What would you recommend?
اش تنصح؟ aash tan·sah (m)
اش تنصحي؟ aash tan·sa·hee (f)

What's the local speciality?
اش الطبق المحلي؟ aash i·ta·bak il·ma·ha·lee

Do you have vegetarian food?
عندك طعم نباتي؟ 'an·dak ta·'am na·baa·tee

I'd like (the) ..., please. عطني/ 'a·ti·nee/
عطيني الـ ... 'a·tee·nee il ...
من فضلك. min fad·lak (m/f)
bill قائمة kaa·'i·ma
drink list قائمة kaa·'i·mat
المشروبات il·mash·roo·baat
menu قائمة الطعام kaa·'i·mat i·ta·'aam
that dish الطبق i·tab·ak
هاذاك haa·dhaa·ka

Could you prepare a meal without ...? ممكن mum·kin
تطبخها/ tat·bakh·ha/
تطبخيها tat·bakh·ee·ha
بدون ...؟ bi·doon ... (m/f)
butter زبدة zib·da
eggs بيض bayd
meat stock مرق لهم ma·rak la ham

I'm allergic to ... عندي 'an·dee
حساسية لـ ... ha·saa·see·ya li ...
dairy produce الألبان il·al·baan
gluten قمح ka·mah
nuts كرزات ka·ra·zaat
seafood السمك و i·sa·mak wa
المحارات al·ma·haa·raat

coffee ... نقهوة ... kah·wa ...
tea ... شاي ... shay ...
with milk بالحليب bil·ha·leeb
without sugar بدون شكر bi·doon shi·ker

bottle of beer بوتل بيرة boo·til bee·ra
glass of beer قلاس بيرة glaas bee·ra
(orange) juice عصير 'a·seer
(برتقال) (bor·too·gaal)
(mineral) water ماي may
(معدني) (ma'a·da·nee)

... wine ... خمر ... kha·mar
red احمر ah·mer
sparkling فوار fa·waar
white ابيض ab·yad

EMERGENCIES

Help! مساعد! moo·saa·'id (m)
مساعدة! moo·saa·'id·a (f)

Go away! ابعد! ib·ad (m)
ابعدي! ib·ad·ee (f)

I'm lost. انا ضعت. a·na duht

Call ...! تصل على ... ! ti·sil 'a·la ... (m)
تصلي على ... ! ti·si·lee 'a·la ... (f)

a doctor طبيب ta·beeb
the police الشرطة i·shur·ta

Where are the toilets?
وين المرحاض؟ wayn il·mir·haad

I'm sick.
انا مريض. a·na ma·reed (m)
انا مريضة. a·na ma·ree·da (f)

SHOPPING & SERVICES

Where's a ...? من وين ...؟ min wayn ...

department محل ضخم ma·hal dukh·um
store
grocery محل ma·hal
store ابقالية ib·gaa·lee·ya
newsagency محل ma·hal
يبيع جرائد yi·bee·a' ja·raa·id
souvenir محل سياحي ma·hal say·aa·hee
shop
supermarket سوبرمركت soo·ber·mar·ket

I'm looking for ...
مدور على ... moo·daw·ir 'a·la ... (m)
مدورة على ... moo·daw·i·ra 'a·la ... (f)

Can I look at it?
ممكن اشوف؟ mum·kin a·shoof

Do you have any others?
عندك اخرين؟ 'and·ak ukh·reen (m)
عندك اخرين؟ 'and·ik ukh·reen (f)

It's faulty.
فيه خلل. fee kha·lal

How much is it?
بكم؟ bi·kam

Can you write down the price?
ممكن تكتبلي/ mum·kin tik·tib·lee/
تكتبيلي السعر؟ tik·tib·ee·lee i·si'r (m/f)

That's too expensive.
غالي جدا. ghaa·lee jid·an

What's your lowest price?
اش السعر الاخر؟ aash i·si'r il·aa·khir

There's a mistake in the bill.
فيه غلط في الفطورة. fee gha·lat fil fa·too·ra

Where's ...? من وين ...؟ min wayn ...

a foreign صراف si·raaf
exchange office
an ATM مكينة صرف ma·kee·nat sarf

What's the exchange rate?
ما هو السعر؟ maa hoo·wa i·sa'r

Where's the local internet cafe?
من وين انترنيت كفي؟ min wayn in·ter·net ka·fay

How much is it per hour?
بكم كل ساعة؟ bi·kam kul saa·a'

Where's the nearest public phone?
وين اقرب تلفون wayn ak·rab til·foon
عمومي؟ 'u·moo·mee

I'd like to buy a phonecard.
اريد اشري كرت a·reed ish·ree kart
لتلفون. li·til·foon

TIME & DATES

What time is it?
الساعة كم؟ i·saa·a' kam

It's (two) o'clock.
الساعة (ثنتين). i·saa·a' (thin·tayn)

Half past (two).
الساعة (ثنتين) و نس. i·saa·a' (thin·tayn) wa nus

At what time ...?
الساعة كم ...؟ i·saa·a' kam ...

At ...
الساعة ... i·saa·a'...

yesterday ... البارح ... il·baa·rih ...
tomorrow ... باكر ... baa·chir ...
morning صباح sa·baah
afternoon بعد الظهر ba'd a·thuhr
evening مساء mi·saa

Monday يوم الاثنين yawm al·ith·nayn
Tuesday يوم الثلاثة yawm a·tha·laa·tha
Wednesday يوم الاربعة yawm al·ar·ba'
Thursday يوم الخميس yawm al·kha·mees
Friday يوم الجمعة yawm al·jum·a'
Saturday يوم السبت yawm a·sibt
Sunday يوم الاحد yawm al·aa·had

Question Words		
When?	متى؟	ma·ta
Where?	وين؟	wayn
Who?	من؟	man
Why?	لاش؟	laysh

TRANSPORT

Is this the ... (to Riyadh)?	هذا ال ... يروح (لرياض)؟	haa·dha al ... yi·roh (li·ree·yaad)
boat	سفينة	sa·fee·na
bus	باص	baas
plane	طيارة	tay·aa·ra
train	قطار	gi·taar
What time's the ... bus?	الساعة كم الباص ...؟	a·saa·a' kam il·baas ...
first	الاول	il·aw·al
last	الاخر	il·aa·khir
next	القادم	il·gaa·dim
One ... ticket (to Doha), please.	تذكرة ... (الدوحة) س فضلك.	tadh·ka·ra ... (a·do·ha) min fad·lak
one-way	ذهاب بص	dhee·haab bas
return	ذهاب و اياب	dhee·haab wa ai·yaab

How long does the trip take?
كم الرحلة تستغرق؟   kam i·rah·la tis·tagh·rik

Is It a direct route?
الرحلة متواصلة؟   i·rah·la moo·ta·waa·si·la

What station/stop is this?
ما هي المحطة هاذي؟   maa hee·ya il·ma·ha·ta haa·dhee

Please tell me when we get to (Al-Ain).
لو سمحت   law sa·maht
خبرني/خبريني   kha·bir·nee/kha·bir·ee·nee
وقت ما نوصل الى (العين).   wokt ma noo·sil i·la (al·'ain) (m/f)

How much is it to (Sharjah)?
بكم الى (شارقة)؟   bi·kam i·la (shaa·ri·ka)

Please take me to (this address).
من فضلك خذني (علعنوان هاذا).   min fad·lak khudh·nee ('al·'un·waan haa·dha)

Turn left/right.
لف يسار/يمين.   lif yee·saar/yee·meen (m)
لفي يسار/يمين.   li·fee yee·saar/yee·meen (f)

Please stop here.
لو سمحت وقف هنا.   law sa·maht wa·gif hi·na

Please wait here.
لو سمحت استنا هنا.   law sa·maht is·ta·na hi·na

I'd like to hire a ...	اريد استأجر ...	a·reed ist·'aj·ir ...
4WD	سيارة فيها دبل	say·aa·ra fee·ha da·bal

Numbers

1	١	واحد	waa·hid
2	٢	اثنين	ith·nayn
3	٣	ثلاثة	tha·laa·tha
4	٤	اربع	ar·ba'
5	٥	خمسة	kham·sa
6	٦	ستة	si·ta
7	٧	سبعة	sa·ba'
8	٨	ثمانية	tha·maan·ya
9	٩	تسعة	tis·a'
10	١٠	عشرة	'ash·ar·a
20	٢٠	عشرين	'ash·reen
30	٣٠	ثلاثين	tha·la·theen
40	٤٠	اربعين	ar·ba'·een
50	٥٠	خمسين	kham·seen
60	٦٠	ستين	sit·een
70	٧٠	سبعين	sa·ba'·een
80	٨٠	ثمانين	tha·ma·neen
90	٩٠	تسعين	ti·sa'·een
100	١٠٠	مية	mee·ya
1000	١٠٠٠	الف	alf

Note that Arabic numerals (in the second column), unlike letters, are read from left to right.

car	سيارة	say·aa·ra
with ...	مع ...	ma' ...
a driver	دريول	dray·wil
air conditioning	كنديشان	kan·day·shan
How much for ... hire?	كم الإيجار ...؟	kam il·ee·jaar ...
daily	كل يوم	kul yawm
weekly	كل اسبوع	kul us·boo·a'

Is this the road to (Abu Dhabi)?
هذا الطريق الى (ابو ظبي)؟   haa·dha i·ta·reeg i·la (a·boo da·bee)

I need a mechanic.
احتاج ميكانيك.   ah·taaj mee·kaa·neek

I've run out of petrol.
ينضب البنزين.   yan·dab al·ban·zeen

I have a flat tyre.
عندي بنشار.   'and·ee ban·shar

ARABIC ALPHABET

Arabic is written from right to left. The form of each letter changes depending on wheth-er it's at the start, in the middle or at the end of a word or whether it stands alone.

Word-Final	Word-Medial	Word-Initial	Alone	Letter
ـا	ـا	ا	ا	alef'
ـب	ـب	بـ	ب	'ba
ـت	ـتـ	تـ	ت	'ta
ـث	ـثـ	ثـ	ث	'tha
ـج	ـجـ	جـ	ج	jeem
ـح	ـحـ	حـ	ح	'ha
ـخ	ـخـ	خـ	خ	'kha
ـد	ـد	د	د	daal
ـذ	ـذ	ذ	ذ	dhaal
ـر	ـر	ر	ر	'ra
ـز	ـز	ز	ز	'za
ـس	ـسـ	سـ	س	seen
ـش	ـشـ	شـ	ش	sheen
ـص	ـصـ	صـ	ص	saad
ـض	ـضـ	ضـ	ض	daad
ـط	ـط	ط	ط	'ta
ـظ	ـظ	ظ	ظ	'dha
ـع	ـعـ	عـ	ع	ain'
ـغ	ـغـ	غـ	غ	ghain
ـف	ـفـ	فـ	ف	'fa
ـق	ـقـ	قـ	ق	kuf
ـك	ـكـ	كـ	ك	kaf
ـل	ـلـ	لـ	ل	lam
ـم	ـمـ	مـ	م	mim
ـن	ـنـ	نـ	ن	nun
ـه	ـهـ	هـ	ه	'ha
ـو	ـو	و	و	waw
ـي	ـيـ	يـ	ي	'ya
	ء			hamza
ـأ	ـأ	أ	أ	a
ـأ	ـأ	أ	أ	u
ـإ	ـإ	إ	إ	i
ـأ	ـأ	أ	أ	' (glottal stop)
ـآ	ـآ	آ	آ	aa
ـو	ـؤ	أو	أو	oo
ـي	ـيـ	إني	إني	ee
ـؤ	ـؤ	أؤ	أؤ	aw
ـي	ـيـ	أني	أني	ay

GLOSSARY

Following is a list of some unfamiliar words you might meet in the text. For a list of common foods you may encounter, see p466.

abeyya – woman's full-length black robe; also *abaya*

abra – water taxi

agal – black head-rope used to hold a *gutra* in place; also *igal*

ardha – traditional Bedouin dance

attar – rosewater

badghir – wind tower

barasti – palm-frond material used in building the traditional coastal houses of the Gulf region, especially along the coast of Oman

barjeel – wind tower

Bedouin – (pl Bedu) a nomadic desert dweller

beit ash-sha'ar – Bedouin goat-hair tent

bijou – service taxi

bukhnoq – girl's head covering

burda – traditional Qatari cloak

burj – tower

burka – see hijab

compound – residential area of expats, usually with high security (Gulf States)

corniche – seaside road

dalla – traditional copper coffeepot

dhow – traditional Arab boat rigged with a *lateen* (triangular) sail; also *sambuq* or *sambuk*

dishdasha – man's floor-length shirt-dress, usually of white cotton cloth, worn in Oman

diwan – Muslim meeting room or reception room

diwaniya – gatherings, usually at someone's home

eid – Islamic feast

Eid al-Adha – Feast of Sacrifice marking the pilgrimage to Mecca

Eid al-Fitr – Festival of Breaking the Fast, celebrated at the end of Ramadan

emir – literally 'prince'; Islamic ruler, military commander or governor

falaj – traditional irrigation channel

GCC – Gulf Cooperation Council; members are Saudi Arabia, Kuwait, Bahrain, Qatar, Oman and the UAE

gutra – white head-cloth worn by men in Saudi Arabia and the Gulf States; also *shemaag*

hajj – annual Muslim pilgrimage to Mecca; one of the Five Pillars of Islam

halal – literally 'permitted'; describes food permitted to Muslims including animals slaughtered according to the prescribed Islamic customs; also *halaal*

hammam – bathhouse

haram – literally 'forbidden'; anything forbidden by Islamic law; also prayer hall

hijab – woman's head scarf or veil, worn for modesty

Hejira – Islamic calendar; Mohammed's flight from Mecca to Medina in AD 622

iftar – the breaking of the day's fast during Ramadan

imam – preacher or prayer leader; Muslim cleric

insha'allah – 'If Allah wills it'; 'God willing'

iqama – residence permit and identity document (Saudi Arabia)

jambiya – tribesman's ceremonial dagger (Yemen and southern Saudi Arabia)

jamrah – pillars

jebel – hill, mountain; also *jabal*, *gebel*

jihad – literally 'striving in the way of the faith'; holy war

jizari – people of the Gulf

Kaaba – the rectangular structure at the centre of the Grand Mosque in Mecca (containing the Black Stone) around which hajj pilgrims circumambulate; also *Kabaa* and *Qaaba*

khanjar – tribal curved dagger; also *khanja* (Oman and southern Saudi Arabia)

khareef – southeast monsoon, from mid-June to mid-August in Oman

khor – rocky inlet or creek

kilim – flat, woven mat

kohl – eyeliner

Kufic – type of highly stylised old Arabic script

kuma – Omani cap

madrassa – Muslim theological seminary; also modern Arabic word for school

mafraj – (pl mafarej) 'room with a view'; top room of a tower house (Yemen)

majlis – formal meeting room; also parliament

mandoos – Omani wooden chest

manzar – attic; room on top of a tower house (Yemen)

mashrabiyya – ornate carved wooden panel or screen; feature of Islamic architecture

masjid – mosque

medina – city, town, especially the old quarter

midan – city or town square

mihrab – niche in a mosque indicating the direction of Mecca

mina – port

minaret – mosque tower

minbar – pulpit used for sermons in a mosque

misbah – prayer beads

muezzin – cantor who sings the call to prayer

mutawwa – religious police charged with upholding Islamic orthodoxy (Saudi Arabia)

Nabataeans – ancient trading civilisation based around Petra in Jordan

qat – mildly narcotic plant, the leaves of which are chewed

Ramadan – Muslim month of fasting; one of the Five Pillars of Islam

ras – cape or headland; also head

sabkha – soft sand with a salty crust

sadu – Bedouin-style weaving

salat – prayer; one of the Five Pillars of Islam

sambuq – see *dhow*; also *sambuk*

shahada – the profession of faith that Muslims publicly declare in every mosque, five times a day; one of the Five Pillars of Islam

shai – tea

sharia – street

Sharia'a – Islamic law

sheesha – water pipe used to smoke tobacco; also *nargileh* or hubble-bubble

sheikh – head of a tribe; religious leader; also *shaikh*

Shiite – one of the two main branches of Islam

souq – market

stele – (pl stelae) stone or wooden commemorative slab or column decorated with inscriptions or figures

sultan – absolute ruler of a Muslim state

Sunni – one of the two main branches of Islam

suras – chapters of the Quran

tawaf – circling required during the pilgrimage to Mecca

thobe – men's floor-length shirt-dress similar to a *dishdasha*, but more fitting, worn in the Gulf; also *thawb*

umrah – Islamic ritual performed outside of hajj; literally 'little pilgrimage'

wadi – valley or river bed, often dry except after heavy rainfall

Wahhabi – conservative and literalist 18th-century Sunni orthodoxy prevailing throughout Saudi Arabia and Qatar

wali – regional head in Oman, similar to mayor

wusta – influence gained by way of connections in high places

yashmak – veil

zakat – the giving of alms; one of the Five Pillars of Islam

Behind the Scenes

SEND US YOUR FEEDBACK

We love to hear from travellers – your comments keep us on our toes and help make our books better. Our well-travelled team reads every word on what you loved or loathed about this book. Although we cannot reply individually to postal submissions, we always guarantee that your feedback goes straight to the appropriate authors, in time for the next edition. Each person who sends us information is thanked in the next edition – the most useful submissions are rewarded with a selection of digital PDF chapters.

Visit **lonelyplanet.com/contact** to submit your updates and suggestions or to ask for help. Our award-winning website also features inspirational travel stories, news and discussions.

Note: We may edit, reproduce and incorporate your comments in Lonely Planet products such as guidebooks, websites and digital products, so let us know if you don't want your comments reproduced or your name acknowledged. For a copy of our privacy policy visit lonelyplanet.com/privacy.

OUR READERS

Many thanks to the travellers who used the last edition and wrote to us with helpful hints, useful advice and interesting anecdotes:
Sergio Boccia, Vicky Challacombe, Laurent Duffault, Jonathan Foreman, Mario Giaquinto, Pj Henry, Maarten Jan Oskam, Julian Lloyd, Barney Smith, John Soar, Jeremy Vera and Peter Voelger.

AUTHOR THANKS

Jenny Walker

I am grateful to Her Excellency, Maitha Al-Mahrouqi, Undersecretary, Ministry of Tourism, Oman, for sharing her valuable time, to Mr Peter Keage, Advisor to HE at MoT, and Mr Hussain Ahmed Al-Farsi, Campus Manager at CCE for their kind facilitation. Guidebooks are team efforts: thanks to fellow authors Andrea, Stuart and Anthony, and LP HQ staff, especially super-supportive CE, Ilaria Walker. To my husband, travelling companion, research guru and most beloved Sam Owen, thanks simply don't sum it up. Suffice to say, without him, my part in this edition would not have materialised.

Stuart Butler

I'm indebted to many people for their advice, help and encouragement with my Yemen chapter. The current security issues in Yemen sadly meant I was unable to visit Yemen for this edition. Therefore, extra big thanks must go to my friend in Sana'a Shakib Al Khayyat of Marib Travel & Tourism who helped me remotely update Sana'a and some surrounding areas. Big thanks to Jenny Walker and Ilaria Walker for patience and, finally, as always, thanks to my wife Heather, young son Jake and the new baby who (unlike Jake) waited until after hand-in day to be born!

Anthony Ham

Thanks to Ilaria Walker for putting her trust in me and to Jenny Walker for sound advice. Thanks also to a number of people within Saudi Arabia who helped me gather information – they have asked to remain anonymous.

Andrea Schulte-Peevers

Big thanks to the many wonderful people who plied me with tips, insights and ideas and/or opened doors, including Wendy Mervis, Katie Foster, Tammy Gan, Sara Gacem, Katie King, Sarah Hameister, Nina Rezec, Bassam Kundakci, Yasmin Hussein and Kiran Kor. Heartfelt thanks to David for his patience and support and for braving the mad Dubai traffic, the world's fastest roller coaster and various other challenges.

ACKNOWLEDGMENTS

Climate map data adapted from Peel MC, Finlayson BL & McMahon TA (2007) 'Updated World Map of the Köppen-Geiger Climate Classification', Hydrology and Earth System Sciences, 11, 1633¬44.

Cover photograph: Guide relaxing on dune. Sharqiya (Wahiba) Sands, Ash Sharqiyah, Oman, Middle East, John Elk/Gettyimages ©

THIS BOOK

This 4th edition of Lonely Planet's *Oman, UAE and Arabian Peninsula* guidebook was researched and written by Jenny Walker, Stuart Butler, Anthony Ham and Andrea Schulte-Peevers. The previous edition was written by Jenny Walker, Andrea Schulte-Peevers, Stuart Butler and Iain Shearer.

This guidebook was commissioned in Lonely Planet's Melbourne office, and produced by the following:

Commissioning Editor
Ilaria Walker

Coordinating Editor
Luna Soo

Coordinating Cartographers Anthony Phelan, Andrew Smith

Coordinating Layout Designer Joseph Spanti

Managing Editors Annelies Mertens, Angela Tinson

Managing Cartographers Alison Lyall, Adrian Persoglia

Managing Layout Designer Chris Girdler

Assisting Editors Anne Mason, Kate Morgan, Alan Murphy, Charlotte Orr, Monique Perrin

Cover Research
Naomi Parker

Internal Image Research
Kylie McLaughlin

Assisting Cartographers
Laura Matthewman, Xavier di Toro

Language Content
Branislava Vladisavljević

Thanks to Shahara Ahmed, Brigitte Ellemor, Ryan Evans, Larissa Frost, Jane Hart, Genesys India, Jouve India, Andi Jones, Indra Kilfoyle, Trent Paton, Dianne Schallmeiner, Kerrianne Southway, John Taufa, Gerard Walker, Juan Winata

Index

NOTES

Map Legend

Sights
- Beach
- Bird Sanctuary
- Buddhist
- Castle/Palace
- Christian
- Confucian
- Hindu
- Islamic
- Jain
- Jewish
- Monument
- Museum/Gallery/Historic Building
- Ruin
- Sento Hot Baths/Onsen
- Shinto
- Sikh
- Taoist
- Winery/Vineyard
- Zoo/Wildlife Sanctuary
- Other Sight

Activities, Courses & Tours
- Bodysurfing
- Diving/Snorkelling
- Canoeing/Kayaking
- Course/Tour
- Skiing
- Snorkelling
- Surfing
- Swimming/Pool
- Walking
- Windsurfing
- Other Activity

Sleeping
- Sleeping
- Camping

Eating
- Eating

Drinking & Nightlife
- Drinking & Nightlife
- Cafe

Entertainment
- Entertainment

Shopping
- Shopping

Information
- Bank
- Embassy/Consulate
- Hospital/Medical
- Internet
- Police
- Post Office
- Telephone
- Toilet
- Tourist Information
- Other Information

Geographic
- Beach
- Hut/Shelter
- Lighthouse
- Lookout
- Mountain/Volcano
- Oasis
- Park
- Pass
- Picnic Area
- Waterfall

Population
- Capital (National)
- Capital (State/Province)
- City/Large Town
- Town/Village

Transport
- Airport
- Border crossing
- Bus
- Cable car/Funicular
- Cycling
- Ferry
- Metro station
- Monorail
- Parking
- Petrol station
- Subway station
- Taxi
- Train station/Railway
- Tram
- Underground station
- Other Transport

Note: Not all symbols displayed above appear on the maps in this book

Routes
- Tollway
- Freeway
- Primary
- Secondary
- Tertiary
- Lane
- Unsealed road
- Road under construction
- Plaza/Mall
- Steps
- Tunnel
- Pedestrian overpass
- Walking Tour
- Walking Tour detour
- Path/Walking Trail

Boundaries
- International
- State/Province
- Disputed
- Regional/Suburb
- Marine Park
- Cliff
- Wall

Hydrography
- River, Creek
- Intermittent River
- Canal
- Water
- Dry/Salt/Intermittent Lake
- Reef

Areas
- Airport/Runway
- Beach/Desert
- Cemetery (Christian)
- Cemetery (Other)
- Glacier
- Mudflat
- Park/Forest
- Sight (Building)
- Sportsground
- Swamp/Mangrove

Andrea Schulte-Peevers
United Arab Emirates Born and raised in Germany and educated in London and at UCLA, Andrea Schulte-Peevers has travelled the distance to the moon and back in her visits to dozens of countries, including several in the Arab world. She's authored or contributed to some 60 Lonely Planet titles, including the previous editions of this guide and the *Dubai* city guide. After years of living in Los Angeles, Andrea now makes her home in Berlin.

OUR STORY

A beat-up old car, a few dollars in the pocket and a sense of adventure. In 1972 that's all Tony and Maureen Wheeler needed for the trip of a lifetime – across Europe and Asia overland to Australia. It took several months, and at the end – broke but inspired – they sat at their kitchen table writing and stapling together their first travel guide, *Across Asia on the Cheap*. Within a week they'd sold 1500 copies. Lonely Planet was born.

Today, Lonely Planet has offices in Melbourne, London and Oakland, with more than 600 staff and writers. We share Tony's belief that 'a great guidebook should do three things: inform, educate and amuse'.

OUR WRITERS

Jenny Walker

Coordinating Author; Bahrain, Kuwait, Oman, Qatar Jenny Walker's first involvement with Arabia was as a student, collecting butterflies for her father's book on entomology in Saudi Arabia. Subsequent academic studies – in the perception of the Arabic Orient in English literature – resulted in an undergraduate dissertation (Stirling University), postgraduate thesis (Oxford University) and ongoing PhD studies (Nottingham Trent University). Resident in Oman for 15 years, where she is an Associate Dean at the Caledonian University College of Engineering, Jenny has written extensively on the Middle East for Lonely Planet and other publications, and co-authored *Off-Road in the Sultanate of Oman* with her husband, Sam Owen. Her travels in over 100 countries extend from Uruguay to Mongolia. Jenny also wrote the Plan Your Trip, Understand and Survival sections.

Stuart Butler

Yemen Englishman Stuart Butler first visited Yemen nearly 20 years ago. Since that first captivating trip he has returned many times and contributed many Yemeni-based articles and photographs to magazines. In 2004 he became one of the lucky few to surf the wild south coast of Yemen. His travels for Lonely Planet have taken him across the Middle East and beyond, from the desert beaches of Pakistan to the coastal jungles of Colombia. Stuart now lives on the beautiful beaches of southwest France with his wife and young children. His website is www.stuartbutlerjournalist.com.

Read more about Stuart at
lonelyplanet.com/members/stuartbutler

Anthony Ham

Saudi Arabia Anthony Ham has been writing for Lonely Planet for over a decade, and although he was first hired to go to Saudi Arabia, it was not until four years later that he finally obtained a visa. He later wrote the Lonely Planet guide to Saudi Arabia. He also has a Masters Degree in Middle Eastern politics. He has travelled extensively throughout the Middle East and has coordinated Lonely Planet's *Middle East* guide among others. A freelance writer and photographer, Anthony divides his time between Melbourne and Madrid.

Read more about Anthony at
lonelyplanet.com/members/anthony_ham

OVER PAGE MORE WRITERS

Published by Lonely Planet Publications Pty Ltd
ABN 36 005 607 983
4th edition – Sep 2013
ISBN 978 1 74220 009 5
© Lonely Planet 2013   Photographs © as indicated 2013
10 9 8 7 6 5 4 3 2 1
Printed in China

Although the authors and Lonely Planet have taken all reasonable care in preparing this book, we make no warranty about the accuracy or completeness of its content and, to the maximum extent permitted, disclaim all liability arising from its use.